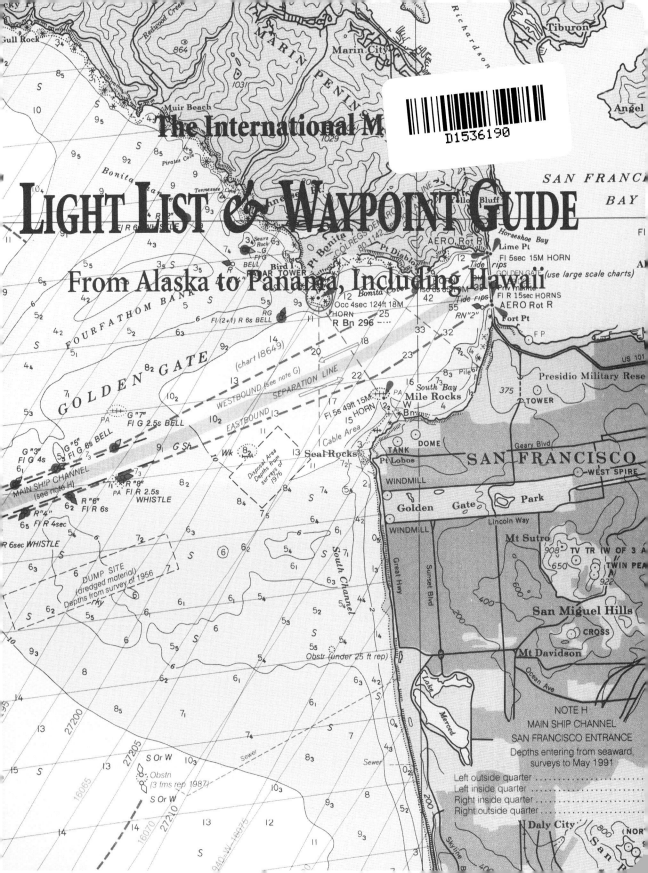

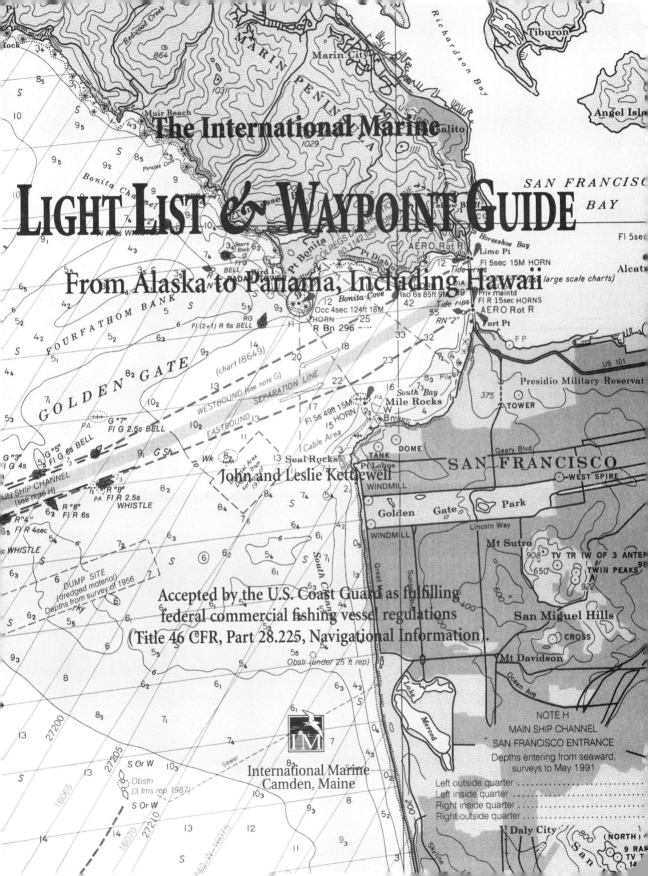

The International Marine
LIGHT LIST & WAYPOINT GUIDE

From Alaska to Panama, Including Hawaii

John and Leslie Kettlewell

Accepted by the U.S. Coast Guard as fulfilling
federal commercial fishing vessel regulations
(Title 46 CFR, Part 28.225, Navigational Information).

International Marine
Camden, Maine

International Marine/
Ragged Mountain Press
A Division of The **McGraw-Hill** Companies

10   9   8   7   6   5   4   3   2   1

Library of Congress Cataloging-in-Publication Data
The International Marine light list & waypoint guide : from Alaska to Panama, including Hawaii / John and Leslie Kettlewell [editors].
     p.   cm.
    ISBN 0-07-034390-X (alk. paper)
    1. Aids to navigation—Pacific Coast (North America)—Lists. 2. Aids to navigation—Hawaii—Lists. I. Kettlewell, John. II. Kettlewell, Leslie. III. International Marine.
VK1243. I54   1997
387. 1'55'097—dc21

                     97-37390
                       CIP

Questions regarding the content of this book should be addressed to:
    International Marine
    P.O. Box 220
    Camden, ME 04843

Questions regarding the ordering of this book should be addressed to:
    The McGraw-Hill Companies
    Customer Service Department
    P.O. Box 547
    Blacklick, OH 43004
    Retail customers: 1-800-262-4729
    Bookstores: 1-800-722-4726

The International Marine Light List & Waypoint Guide is printed on 60-pound Renew Opaque Vellum, an acid-free paper that contains 50 percent recycled waste paper (preconsumer) and 10 percent postconsumer waste paper. ♲

This book was typeset in Adobe Utopia and Adobe Univers
Printed by R.R. Donnelley
Design by Tim Seymour
Production and page layout by Janet Robbins and Mary Ann Hensel

The prudent mariner will not rely solely on any single aid to navigation, including GPS or loran units utilizing latitude/longitude readings taken from this book. All positions should be checked carefully against the latest chart of the area, and courses should be plotted to ensure they don't cross dangerous waters. All information in this book, including light and buoy characteristics and positions, is subject to change at any time.

The data in this book was obtained from official government sources and updated using the National Imagery and Mapping Agency's *Notice to Mariners*. Prudent mariners will continue to so update the data.

Major revisions have been made recently to the government aids to navigation listings for Mexico. Mariners should review *Notice to Mariners* carefully for further changes, and should expect to see similar revisions made to listings in other Central American countries.

Neither the authors nor the publisher makes any guarantee of the accuracy or completeness of this data, or of its suitability for any purpose. Neither the authors nor the publisher shall have any liability for errors or omissions or for any results obtained from the use of this information. Readers use this publication at their sole risk and discretion.

PREFACE

GPS has revolutionized the world of navigation. I can remember groping my way through the fog, straining every sensory nerve for any elusive clue to my position, with maybe an occasional input from an unreliable flasher-type depthsounder. We would steer strict compass courses between buoys, using the classic time/speed/distance equations, scribbling on a soggy notepad in the cockpit.

Finding a buoy, then identifying it, allowed a brief moment of relief; then it was off on the new heading, time noted, compass course repeated, eyes straining, sounds playing tricks on us. And then loran arrived. At first I didn't trust it. Those electronic numerals looked so precise, but I knew about signal skip, poor crossing angles, baseline extension problems. And sometimes the readout just didn't make sense.

But gradually I learned my way around those problems and began to trust that mysterious black box, after I nearly ran down a few waypoints in the fog. Then GPS became available, but at first only world cruisers were willing to pay a couple of thousand dollars for the latest and the greatest. I watched in awe as a GPS salesman plotted our position down to the very pier we were standing on at a boat show. He told me confidently prices would never drop below $1,500.

GPS units now cost less than $200, cheaper than many depthsounders. Every boat has one, or should. I've been using one for several years now, and I hate to admit it, but I rely on it, as many boaters do. Of course I still keep track of my dead reckoning, and I do check my position by watching the depthsounder, or taking a bearing. But that electronic black box is the one I use the most, the one that gets me home in the fog.

Even so, I've learned never to trust any one instrument totally—especially the GPS. One summer my unit began to give readings that were maybe a half mile off. Not terrible, but enough to sink someone not double-checking. There were no warning messages, no blinking displays—nothing to indicate the box was leading me into danger. (Fortunately I don't interface my GPS with an autopilot.)

The manual said this was not possible, but the manufacturer replaced my unit with no questions asked. The Coast Guard's Notice to Mariners comes to mind:

". . . prudent mariners will not rely solely on any single aid to navigation. . . . "

Be a prudent mariner, and use this book only as one of many "aids to navigation," and always question what your black boxes are telling you.

—JOHN KETTLEWELL

Sources of Information

The information in this book on lights, buoys, fog signals, and daymarks was obtained from the following publications:

- *Light List Volume VI: Pacific Coast and Pacific Islands,* Department of Transportation, U.S. Coast Guard, U.S. Government Printing Office, 1996.
- *Pub. 111, List of Lights, Radio Aids, and Fog Signals, The West Coasts of North and South America (Excluding Continental U.S.A. and Hawaii), Australia, Tasmania, New Zealand, and the Islands of the North and South Pacific Oceans,* National Imagery and Mapping Agency, 1996.

To purchase these books, contact a National Ocean Service chart agent, or order direct from NOAA Distribution Division, N/ACC3, Riverdale, MD 20737; 800-638-8972, 301-436-6990.

The information in this book was updated through *Notice to Mariners,* No. 10, 1997, National Imagery and Mapping Agency, which is prepared jointly with the National Ocean Service and the U.S. Coast Guard. Users of this book should continue to update the information using *Notice to Mariners* or a *Local Notice to Mariners* for their region. Contact your local Coast Guard District Commander to obtain the local notices:

- Eleventh District (California, Arizona, and Nevada), Building 50-6, Coast Guard Island, Alameda, CA 94501; 510-437-2984.
- Thirteenth District (Oregon, Washington, Idaho, and Montana), Federal Building, 915 Second Avenue, Seattle, WA 98174; 206-220-7280.
- Fourteenth District (Hawaii, American Samoa, Marshall Islands, Mariana Islands, and Caroline Islands), Prince Kalanianaole Federal Building, 9th Floor, Room 9139, 300 Ala Moana Boulevard, Honolulu, HI 96850; 808-541-2317.
- Seventeenth District (Alaska), P.O. Box 25517, Juneau, AK 99802; 907-463-2262.

Aids to Navigation Included

We have not included every aid to navigation appearing on the nearly 600 pages of the government light lists; we have included those we believe are most useful to the mariner. Most of them feature a plotted latitude/longitude position in the government books; they include most, if not all, of the major sea buoys, approach buoys, fixed lights, and lighthouses for most areas. Readers may find that an occasional major aid to navigation is omitted because either its position is frequently moved, or its location is not provided in the light list.

Aids to navigation are not listed for areas where mariners are unlikely to use loran or GPS: inland rivers, bays, lakes, and areas where the Coast Guard frequently shifts markers to reflect changes in the channel. Freshwater areas such as the Sacramento River, Lake Tahoe, and the Columbia River above Portland and Vancouver are not included. Scientific research buoys, and deep-ocean buoys are not included unless they might be used frequently by coastal cruisers.

How to Use This Book

Arrangement

The book is divided into 14 chapters covering the West Coast from Alaska to Panama, including the Hawaiian Islands. Within each chapter the aids to navigation are listed in alphabetical order, except when they fall under a secondary heading. For instance, San Diego Harbor's many geographic subdivisions—such as Glorietta Bay, the Sweetwater Channel, and the Coronado Cays Channel—are listed geographically. Aids to navigation for Glorietta Bay and the Sweetwater Channel are grouped geographically under those subheadings, so that mariners will be able to follow the channel in a logical sequence—for example, many channels begin with buoy #1 and proceed to #2, #3, #4, etc.

Many major aids are also cross-referenced under other names or headings where they might logically be expected to appear. For example, Ballast Point Light B appears both under the *B*s, and under the San Diego subheading "Approaches." Another example would be Point Wilson Light (Washington), which appears with the *P*s and under the heading "Admiralty Inlet," because it is a useful light in the approach to Puget Sound.

The mariner is also directed to the appropriate listing when the sequence or arrangement of the aids is not completely obvious. For instance, many aids in Puget Sound are grouped under the name of the bay, channel, or passage where they are located, so to find aids to navigation for Seattle, mariners are referred to Shilshole Bay and Boat Basin, Elliott Bay, and Georgetown Reach Range. A note is placed after the heading Seattle: "*See* Shilshole Bay and Boat Basin, Elliott Bay, and Georgetown Reach Range." "*See*" references are also used when an aid to navigation has more than one name, or is known by a local name different from its official name. And "*Also see*" notes direct users to closely related aids.

Occasionally an aid to navigation is not listed within the state where it is located if most mariners would not look for it there. For instance, aids for the Columbia River may be located in either Oregon or Washington. Readers of the Washington and Oregon chapters are referred to the Columbia River chapter for those listings.

Aids are listed in more than one chapter when they may be useful to boaters in more than one state or province, or when the exact sailing jurisdiction may not be clear to the mariner. Several lights and buoys in the Strait of Juan De Fuca fall into this category (Washington and British Columbia), as does Lizard Point Light (British Columbia and Alaska).

Our standard format closely follows the one used in the government light lists.

Name of the aid to navigation appears on the first line of each listing. Whenever possible the name is the same as that used in the government light list or on the chart of the area. We have occasionally changed the name to one more commonly used by mariners and have cross-referenced the official name. And we have corrected the rare errors in the government listings. The first line may also include parenthetical notes defining the location of the aid. Standard abbreviations for *north* (N), *south* (S), *east* (E), *west* (W), and for combinations of these directions (NE, NW, SE, SW, etc.) are used.

Buoys or lights that have no name in the government list always have at least a number or letter designation. To some of these listings we have added the names of local geographic features associated with the aid. In most cases unnamed aids are listed under subheadings familiar to mariners: Morro Bay Channel, Shilshole Bay, Swinomish Channel, etc.

Position of the aid is the first entry in the body of the listing. These latitude/longitude positions are taken directly from the government publications and have been updated from *Notice to Mariners* as described previously under Sources of Information. The first numbers are latitudes (N for north), the second numbers are longitudes (W for west). These positions are given in degrees, minutes, and tenths of minutes. (Some listings do not include tenths of minutes. These positions should be assumed to be accurate only to the nearest minute.) *Caution: Do not confuse tenths of minutes with seconds. Your loran or GPS should be adjusted to display tenths of minutes.*

The positions of some aids, such as the rear half of a range, may refer to other geographic features or aids to navigation. For example, the rear range light in Shilshole Bay in Washington is described as being 250 yards, 146° from the front light. In areas outside the U.S., these distances may be given in metric units (1 meter = 3.28 feet; 1 kilometer = .54 nautical mile).

Characteristics of the aid follow its latitude/longitude, beginning with the type of light if it's a lighted aid. The following standard abbreviations may be used throughout:

Al - alternating

B - black

bl - blast

Bu - blue

C - Canadian

Dir - directional

E - east

ec - eclipsed

ELB - exposed location buoy

ev - every

F - fixed

fl - flash

Fl - flashing

FS - fog signal

ft. - feet

Fl (2) - group flashing

G - green

horiz - horizontal

intens - intensified

I - interrupted

IQ - interrupted quick flashing

Iso - isophase (equal interval)

IVQ - interrupted very quick flashing

kHz - kilohertz

km - kilometer

LFl - long flash

lt - lighted

LNB - large navigational buoy

MHz - megahertz

mi. - mile or miles

min. - minute

Mo - Morse code

N - north

obsc - obscured

Oc - occulting

ODAS - Ocean Data Acquisition System (anchored oceanographic buoy)

Or - orange

Q - quick flashing

R - red

Ra ref - radar reflector

RBN - radiobeacon

S - south

s - seconds

si. - silent

SPM - single point mooring buoy

UQ - ultra quick flashing

unintens - unintensified

vert - vertical

Vi - violet

vis - visible

VQ - very quick flashing

W - west (when the abbreviation clearly could not mean
white)

W - white (when the abbreviation clearly could not mean
west)

Y - yellow

See Appendix A, "Characteristics of Lights," for more information on the flashing sequences of these lights.

Height above mean high water from the focal plane of the
fixed light is given in feet (to convert to meters, divide by 3.28).

Range of lighted aids to navigation in nautical miles is next
(1 nautical mile = 6,076.1 feet, or 1.15 statute miles). For lights
of alternating colors, the ranges are shown for each color.
Radiobeacon range is also listed in nautical miles. If the range
is not listed, it was not available from the government publication. See Appendix C, the "Geographic Range Table," and
Appendix D, the "Luminous Range Diagram," for more information on range.

Dayboard is next, including the type of structure (if any). This information includes descriptions of fixed lighthouses, types of structures (piling, dolphin, skeleton tower, etc.), colors of floating aids, and references to the location of the structure. Dayboards are designated by the following abbreviations:

1. First Letter—shape or purpose:

   S   Square. Marks the port (left) side of channels when the mariner is proceeding from seaward.

   T   Triangle. Marks the starboard (right) side of channels when the mariner is proceeding from seaward.

   J   Junction (square or triangle). Marks channel junctions or bifurcations in the preferred channel, or wrecks or obstructions which may be passed on either side. The color of the top band has lateral significance for the preferred channel.

   M   Safe water (octagon). Marks the fairway or middle of the channel.

   K   Range (rectangle). When both the front and rear range dayboards are aligned on the same bearing, the observer is on the azimuth of the range; usually marks the center of the channel.

   N   No lateral significance (diamond or rectangle). Used for special purpose, warning, distance, or location markers.

2. Second Letter—key color:

   B - black

   G - green

   R - red

   W - white

   Y - yellow

3. Third Letter—color of center stripe on range dayboards only

4. Additional Information after a hyphen:

   -I   Intracoastal Waterway—a yellow reflective horizontal strip on a dayboard. Indicates the aid to navigation marks the Intracoastal Waterway.

-SY   Intracoastal Waterway—a yellow reflective square on a dayboard. Indicates the aid to navigation is a port hand mark for vessels traversing the Intracoastal Waterway. This symbol may appear on a triangular daymark where the Intracoastal Waterway coincides with a waterway having the opposite orientation of buoyage.

-TY   Intracoastal Waterway—a yellow reflective triangle on a dayboard. Indicates the aid to navigation is a starboard hand mark for vessels traversing the Intracoastal Waterway. This symbol may appear on a square daymark where the Intracoastal Waterway coincides with a waterway having the opposite orientation of buoyage. See Appendix B, "Dayboard Abbreviations," for a complete list of these combinations.

Remarks follow all other entries. They include notes about fog horns, bells, racon characteristics, arcs of visibility for lighthouses, radar reflectors, and passing lights. If the aid is maintained by private interests or government agencies other than the Coast Guard, that fact is noted.

Special Navigation Aids

Lighthouses are placed on shore or on marine sites and usually do not show lateral markings. They assist the mariner in determining his position or a safe course, or warn of obstructions and dangers to navigation. Lighthouses with no lateral significance usually exhibit a white light.

Occasionally lighthouses use sectored lights to mark shoals or warn mariners of other dangers. Lights so equipped show one color from most directions and a different color, or colors, over definite arcs of the horizon as indicated in this book and on the appropriate nautical chart. These sectors provide approximate bearing information, and the observer should note a change of color as the boundary between the sectors is crossed. Since sector bearings are not precise, they should be considered as a warning only, and used in conjunction with a nautical chart.

Large navigational buoys (LNBs) were developed to replace lightships and are placed at points where it is impractical to build lighthouses. The unmanned LNBs are 40 feet in diameter with light towers approximately 40 feet above the water. LNBs are equipped with lights, sound signals, radiobeacons, and racons. They often have passing lights and emergency lights. The traditional red color of LNBs has no lateral significance, but is intended to improve visibility.

Seasonal aids to navigation are placed into service or changed at specific times of the year. The dates of these changes are usually noted here, but, in general, seasonal aids are on station during the pleasure-boating season.

Ranges are nonlateral aids to navigation systems employing dual structures—when the two structures are viewed in alignment, they assist the mariner in maintaining a safe course. When ranges are used, the appropriate nautical chart must be consulted to determine whether the range marks the centerline of the navigable channel. The chart will also indicate what portion of the range may be safely navigated. Ranges display rectangular dayboards of various colors and are generally but not always lighted. When lighted, ranges may display lights of any color.

Sound signal is a generic term used to describe aids to navigation that produce an audible signal to assist the mariner in fog or other periods of reduced visibility. These aids can be activated manually, remotely, or by fog detector. With a fog detector, there may be a delay in the automatic activation of the signal. Additionally, fog detectors may not be capable of detecting patchy fog. Sound signals are distinguished by their tone and phase characteristics.

Tones are determined by the devices producing the sound: diaphones, diaphragm horns, sirens, whistles, bells, or gongs.

Phase characteristics are defined by the signal's sound pattern: the number and duration of blasts and silent periods per minute. Sound signals sounded from fixed structures generally produce a specific number of blasts and silent periods each minute when operating. Buoy sound signals are irregular since they are generally activated by the motion of the sea. Buoys commonly produce no sound signal when seas are calm. Mariners are reminded that buoy positions are not always reliable.

The characteristic of a sound signal is located near the end of the listing. Unless it is specifically stated that a sound signal "operates continuously" or that the signal is a bell, gong, or whistle on a buoy, the reader may assume that the sound signal operates only during times of fog, reduced visibility, or adverse weather.

An emergency signal is sounded at some locations when the main and standby signals are inoperative.

Caution: Mariners should not rely on sound signals to determine their position. Distance cannot be accurately determined by sound intensity. Occasionally, sound signals may not be heard in areas close to their location, and signals may not sound at all where fog exists close to, but not at, the location of the sound signal.

Racon is an acronym for *RAdar beaCON*. Racons, when triggered by pulses from a vessel's radar, will transmit a coded reply to that radar. This reply identifies the racon station with a series of dots and dashes that appear on the radar display emanating radially from the racon. This display represents the approximate range and bearing to the racon. Although racons may be used on both laterally significant and nonlaterally significant aids to navigation, the racon signal itself is for identification purposes only, and therefore carries no lateral significance. Racons are also used on bridges to indicate the point of best passage.

All racons operate in the marine radar X-band from 9,300 to 9,500 MHz. Some frequency-agile racons also operate in the 2,900- to 3,000-MHz marine radar S-band.

Racons have a typical output of 100 to 300 milliwatts and are considered short-range aids to navigation. Reception varies from a nominal range of 6 to 8 nautical miles for a buoy-mounted racon to as much as 17 nautical miles for a racon with a directional antenna mounted 50 feet high on a fixed structure. It must be understood that these are nominal ranges, dependent upon many factors.

The racon presentation begins about 50 yards beyond the racon position and persists for a number of revolutions of the radar antenna (depending on its rotation rate). Distance to the racon can be measured to the point at which the racon flash begins, but the figure obtained will be greater than the ship's distance from the racon because of the slight response delay in the racon apparatus.

Radar operators may notice some broadening or spoking of the racon presentation when their vessel nears the source of the racon. This effect can be minimized by adjustment of the IF gain or sweep gain control of the radar. If desired, the racon presentation can be virtually eliminated by operation of the FTC (fast time constant) controls of the radar.

Radar reflectors are incorporated as special fixtures on many aids to navigation. They make the aid easier to locate by enhancing the reflected radar signal. They do not, however, positively identify a radar target as an aid to navigation.

Radiobeacons were the first electronic aids to navigation that provided offshore coverage and position-fixing capability in any weather. However, as the system has been gradually superseded by more accurate and more precise systems like Loran-C and GPS, it is now being phased out. The Coast Guard continues to operate about 20 radiobeacons in the United States, and mariners will find others outside the U.S. The latter may be aerobeacons, engineered for use by aircraft, but they can prove useful for marine navigation due to their great range. *Note: This publication does not include every radiobeacon available.*

In order to use this system, the mariner needs a radio direction finder, which is a specifically designed radio receiver with a directional antenna. This antenna is used to determine the direction of the signal being emitted by the shore station, relative to the vessel.

When the distance to a radiobeacon is greater than 50 miles, a correction is usually applied to the bearing before it's plotted on a Mercator chart. These corrections, as well as other information on the system, are contained in the National Imagery and Mapping Agency's *Pub. 117 Radio Navigational Aids.*

Loran-C is an electronic aid-to-navigation system consisting of shore-based radio transmitters. *Loran* is an acronym for *LOng RAnge Navigation.* The loran system enables users equipped with the proper receiver to determine their position quickly and accurately, day or night, in practically any weather.

A Loran-C chain consists of three to five transmitting stations separated by several hundred miles. Within a chain, one station is designated as master, the others as secondaries (sometimes called *slaves*). Each secondary station is identified as either Whiskey (W), X-ray (X), Yankee (Y), or Zulu (Z).

The master station is always the first station to transmit a series of nine pulses. The secondary stations then follow in turn, transmitting eight pulses each, at precisely timed intervals. The cycle repeats itself endlessly. The length of the cycle is measured in microseconds and is called a *group repetition interval* (GRI).

Loran-C chains are designated by the four most significant digits of their GRI. For example, a chain with a GRI of 99,400 microseconds is referred to as 9940. A different GRI is used for each chain because all Loran-C stations broadcast in the same 90- to 110-kHz frequency band.

The Loran-C system can be used in either a hyperbolic or range mode. In the widely used hyperbolic mode (commonly used by pleasure craft), a Loran-C line of position is determined by measuring the time difference between synchronized pulses received from two separate transmitting stations. In the range mode, a line of position is determined by measuring the time required for Loran-C pulses to travel from a transmitting station to the user's receiver.

A user's position is determined by locating the intersection of two lines of position on a Loran-C chart. Most receivers have built-in coordinate converters that will automatically display the receiver's latitude and longitude, so that a chart without Loran-C overprint may be used.

Caution: Since the latitude/longitude computation in some receivers (particularly older models) is based on an all-seawater propagation path, positioning errors may occur if the Loran-C signals from the various stations must travel overland (which most do). Manufacturers have reduced these errors by applying additional secondary phase factors, or ASF corrections. Most users will leave ASF turned on most of the time, but when using readouts obtained from others, should determine whether *they* used ASF. Differences in position can be significant.

There are two types of Loran-C accuracy: absolute and repeatable. Absolute accuracy is a measure of the receiver's ability to precisely determine latitude and longitude from the time differences measured. Repeatable accuracy is a measure of the receiver's ability to return to a position where readings have been taken previously.

The absolute accuracy of Loran-C is reported by the Coast Guard to be about 0.25 nautical miles, 95 percent of the time, with standard Loran-C charts. However, mariners have reported much greater absolute accuracy in practical use. Mariners should periodically determine the absolute accuracy in a particular area by comparing their receiver's readouts with a known charted location.

Repeatable accuracy depends on many factors, so measurements must be taken to determine the level achievable in a particular area. Coast Guard surveys have found repeatable accuracies between 30 and 170 meters in most areas. Loran-C position determination on or near the baseline extensions is subject to significant errors, and should be avoided whenever possible. The use of sky waves is not recommended when the mariner is within 250 miles of a station, and corrections for these areas are not usually tabulated.

If the timing or pulse shape of a master-secondary pair deviates from specified tolerances, the first two pulses of the secondary station's pulse train will blink on and off. The Loran-C receiver sees this blinking signal and warns the user. This warning will continue until the signals are once again in tolerance. A blinking signal is not exhibited during off-air periods, when a separate receiver alarm indicates any loss of signal. Never use a blinking secondary signal for navigation.

With the introduction of GPS in recent years, Loran-C is due to be phased out; at this time, however, it appears the system will be fully operational until at least the year 2000.

GPS

The Global Positioning System (GPS) is a satellite-based radionavigation system with worldwide coverage, providing continuous navigation, position, and timing information to air, marine, and land users. The GPS system is operated and controlled by the U.S. Air Force and the Department of Defense (DOD), and has reached full operating capability (FOC).

Although GPS was originally intended for military use only, federal radionavigation policy has now established that it will be available for civilian use, with some restrictions. Whenever advance notice is possible, the DOD will inform the Coast Guard before imposing such restrictions on the civilian use of GPS satellites.

The Department of Commerce transmits recorded time information on stations WWV/WWVH (5, 10, 15, and 20 MHz); and during the 40-second interval between time ticks, atmospheric and navigation information is announced by voice. Listen at minutes 14 and 15 on WWV, and minutes 43 and 44 on WWVH, for GPS status information.

Accuracy is the big question with GPS. Unlike Loran-C, GPS has only one type of accuracy at this time. The DOD has turned on a system called *selective availability* (SA), which essentially makes GPS nonrepeatable. Selective availability is designed to throw in a random position error, thereby preventing enemy warheads from finding our hardened silos in time of war. Plots of GPS positions taken over time from a fixed point indicate the highly random nature of the signals, with the potential for position jumps of up to 200 meters within a few seconds. In practical terms, SA limits civilian GPS accuracy to within 100 meters, 95 percent of the time. (If SA were turned off, civilian users could expect accuracy within 10 to 30 meters, 95 percent of the time.) Tests by experienced mariners indicate that most readings will be much more accurate than the 100-meter figure, with the occasional 5 percent falling outside a 100-meter circle.

This random inaccuracy means mariners must change the habits they developed using Loran-C, and stop recording on-site waypoints when an accurate position is available from either the chart or a government light list. We must emphasize this important point—GPS readings are *not* highly repeatable at this time (if SA were turned off, they would become much more repeatable). Coast Guard tests have determined that repeatable accuracy falls to 141 meters, 95 percent of the time. There is always the possibility the mariner will push the "Save" button at the very instant the random signal has wandered to its maximum.

What this means is that the mariner is better off, in terms of accuracy, taking a latitude/longitude position from one of the Coast Guard light lists, the largest-scale chart of an area, or this book, and using it as a waypoint. Of course, not every charted aid to navigation has a latitude/longitude position listed here, and mariners will continue to collect their own. But on-site readings must be used with greater caution, and readings from other boaters should always be regarded as even less reliable.

Datum issues can affect the accuracy of your GPS. Mariners within the United States will probably be using charts based upon the latest datum, NAD-83 (very similar to WGS-84, which is used by most GPS units), but many foreign charts use the older NAD-27 datum, or one of dozens of other datums. Check your GPS unit's handling of this problem before relying on positions outside the U.S. Users will have to adjust their receivers for positions taken from NAD-27 charts. In addition, charts in many parts of the Pacific still rely on old 19th-century, and earlier, surveys. Latitude/longitude readings from these charts may not correspond closely with the readouts from your GPS, whichever datum you are using.

System accuracy displays, satellite status, and signal strength are available on most receivers. The accuracy indicator is a misleading display and should probably be read in relative terms. In other words, if the display says your position should be accurate to within 30 meters, it is probably not correct because SA limits the absolute accuracy to about 100 meters. However, you will soon develop a sense of the normal range of these readings—if 30 meters or so is usually displayed, you know something is up when 100 meters is suddenly displayed.

Once you have that familiarity with the normal readings, the satellite status and signal strength indicators can be useful.

Some units offer a graphic device showing the relative signal strengths of the various satellites. This can be useful for determining at a glance how good your reception is. Occasionally a satellite is removed from service temporarily, and this readout can let you know that, but your unit will automatically search out the active satellites to continue providing positioning data. Some receivers may be adversely affected by being placed under a hard cabintop, or too close to the back side of a cabin. When mounting a GPS antenna, try out several positions before settling on the one with the best reception, but be careful if you are doing this ashore. Large buildings and metal structures can block GPS signals.

Differential GPS (DGPS) has been implemented by the Coast Guard to retrieve the accuracy lost to SA. In fact, the Coast Guard believes DGPS will provide close to 2-meter accuracy up to 100 miles offshore. DGPS is a system of shore-based radiobeacons (often on the site of an old radiobeacon station) that constantly measure the inaccuracy of the SA signal. The DGPS station then broadcasts a correction factor, which can be received by boats equipped with DGPS units. Receivers are now available that incorporate DGPS units, but many older receivers can be interfaced with a separate DGPS module.

The Federal Aviation Administration is also very interested in improving the accuracy of civilian GPS and is now developing a Wide Area Augmentation System (WAAS) to provide corrections similar to DGPS corrections. Moreover, the WAAS system will have much broader coverage than DGPS, and may provide even greater accuracy. Marine receivers will probably be developed to take advantage of these correction factors.

Much of this quest for accuracy may become redundant if the DOD decides to turn off SA. At this time it appears the intention is to make the full accuracy of the civilian GPS signal available within three to five years, but there is no definite schedule.

Other Functions

Speed is a commonly used function, but it can lead to inaccuracy if it is not used properly. Because of the jumpiness of the SA signal, latitude/longitude readings are constantly shifting, even if your boat isn't. The receiver calculates speed by comparing the shifting position readings over a certain time span.

Most receivers allow the user to adjust the averaging period for "fast" (shorter time span) or "slow" (longer time span) averaging. Increasing the span with the "slow" setting will usually improve the accuracy of the speed readout because the jumpiness of the signal gets averaged out. But this also reduces the frequency of speed updates, meaning small changes in speed won't show up. This might upset some sailors trying to use the GPS to trim sails for maximum power, or the powerboater who wants to see what a change in rpm does to his speed. A knot log or speedometer is better for those functions, but the GPS speed readout is good for finding average speed over the course of several minutes or several hours.

Course over ground is also affected by the averaging mode selected. Again, small course changes won't show up in the "slow" mode, but the overall course accuracy will improve. Accuracy of this function is probably as good as the ability of the average person to steer an accurate compass course—within a degree or two. Many receivers can report course headings as either "true" or "magnetic" readings. Magnetic readings incorporate local magnetic variation, which many receivers automatically add in for you. Just be sure you understand what your unit is telling you.

Course to steer to a waypoint is a valuable function used by almost every GPS navigator. Read the section above on accuracy before inputting your waypoints, and remember that the best waypoints, at this time, are the ones that come right from the government light lists (like the ones in this book). Be careful to input your waypoints using the same units as published—in this book, degrees, minutes, and tenths of minutes. Many receivers can be programmed to accept seconds instead of tenths of minutes, but you shouldn't use that mode unless you are really good at converting one to the other (divide seconds by 60 to get tenths of a minute).

The course to steer will be very accurate if you are at least a few miles from the waypoint—in fact the farther away you are, the more accurate the course. Unfortunately, the accuracy of the reading declines as you get closer because of the jumpiness of the SA signal. But if you have DGPS, the accuracy should remain excellent. One trick is to check the course carefully about 1 mile from the waypoint. Keep steering the last suggested course toward the waypoint even if the readout changes as you get closer. Unless you are in a strong current, or are being blown off course, the course to steer from 1 mile out should bring you close to the waypoint. Don't try to steer the course indicated by the receiver within a few hundred yards of a waypoint, as the course reading will be jumping all over the place.

Some units offer a graphic display of the course to steer—the user simply keeps a pointer between two lines, and the boat stays on course to the selected waypoint. However, the graphic display may lead the boater nearing a waypoint to steer erratically, chasing the ever-moving SA signal around the buoy or light. So this type of display should be used with caution, and the actual course should be checked periodically.

A point to keep in mind is that the GPS course is a great-circle course, which can be useful to the offshore navigator. A great-circle route is the shortest distance between two points on our globe-shaped earth, although it may not be the same as a course plotted on a Mercator chart over long distances. The difference between the two courses is not significant in normal coastal piloting. Offshore navigators should remember the GPS unit may be inputting local magnetic variation automatically, and the great-circle course will be a magnetic one.

Distance to go is a very useful feature. The reading will be in nautical miles, but some units can also be set to read in statute miles, which might come in handy for boating on inland waters. This is another reading affected by the averaging time selected, and tends to be more accurate the farther away you are from the waypoint. Don't depend on this reading to be more accurate than the 100-meter accuracy of the system.

Cross-track error tells you how far you've wandered from a course between two waypoints. This can be a useful feature in cross currents or winds. Many units have an optional graphic display of the boat's relationship to the ideal straight-line course between the waypoints. Mariners must be careful not to simply steer a course back to the ideal course line, but to review this new heading on an appropriate chart of the area. Read the section above concerning graphic course-steering displays. And remember that this function becomes less useful as you near the waypoint because of SA inaccuracies.

Time may also be displayed by your GPS, but the readout is not identical to Greenwich Mean Time (now known as *Coordinated Universal Time,* or *UTC*). GPS time may vary by up to a few seconds. Users should compare GPS time to the time signals available on WWV and WWVH.

For more information on GPS and navigation in general we highly recommend Captain Bill Brogdon's book, *Boat Navigation for the Rest of Us* (International Marine, 1995).

The Navigation Information Service (NIS) was established by the Coast Guard to provide 24-hour-a-day data on the GPS, DGPS, Loran-C, and Omega electronic navigation systems. The information provided includes present or future satellite outages and constellation changes, user instructions and tutorials, lists of service and receiver providers/users, and other useful material. Contact the NIS as follows:

Commanding Officer
U.S. Coast Guard
NAVCEN
7323 Telegraph Road
Alexandria, VA 22310-3998
Phone: 703-313-5900
Fax: 703-313-5920
Fax on demand: 703-313-5931/32
BBS: 703-313-5910
Internet: http:/www.navcen.uscg.mil

Oil well structures exist along the Beaufort Seacoast between 147° and 149° west longitude.

A

Aaron Island Light 2
58 26.3N, 134 49.6W, Fl R 2.5s, 20 ft., 4 mi., TR on skeleton tower.

ADAK ISLAND

Kuluk Shoal Lighted Bell Buoy 2
51 54.7N, 176 30.6W, Fl R 6s, 4 mi., red.

Finger Shoal Lighted Bell Buoy 3
51 51.7N, 176 34.2W, Fl G 2.5s, 4 mi., green.

Gannet Rocks Light 4
51 52.0N, 176 36.5W, Fl R 4s, 45 ft., 4 mi., TR on skeleton tower, obscured from 102° to 214°.

Gannet Rocks Buoy 4A
51 51.9N, 176 36.6W, red nun.

Sweeper Cove

Entrance Light 5
51 51.5N, 176 35.5W, Fl G 6s, 55 ft., 5 mi., SG on skeleton tower.

Jetty Light 6
51 51.6N, 176 37.8W, Fl R 6s, 28 ft., 3 mi., TR on spindle.

Light 7
51 51.3N, 176 37.7W, Fl G 4s, 75 ft., 3 mi., SG on skeleton tower.

Range Front Light
51 51.2N, 176 39.3W, F G, 31 ft., KRW on pile structure, lighted throughout 24 hours.

Range Rear Light
475 yards, 253° from front light, F G, 91 ft., KRW on pile, lighted throughout 24 hours.

Aiaktalik Island Light 5
56 43.9N, 154 03.1W, Fl G 6s, 57 ft., 5 mi., SG on square frame.
Also see Geese Channel.

Aikens Rock Daybeacon 3
55 54.0N, 133 15.7W, SG on skeleton tower.

Ajax Reef Light 3
55 00.1N, 131 27.7W, Fl G 4s, 31 ft., 4 mi., SG on skeleton tower.

Akhiok
See Moser Bay.

Akun Strait Light
54 07.9N, 165 39.6W, Fl W 4s, 46 ft., 5 mi., on skeleton tower.

Akutan Point Light 2
54 07.7N, 165 43.7W, Fl R 6s, 163 ft., 5 mi., TR on skeleton tower.

Aleutski Channel
See Alidale Channel.

ALIDALE CHANNEL

Also see Sitka Sound, Eastern Channel, Western Channel, *and* Sitka Harbor.

Turning Island Light 11
57 02.6N, 135 20.2W, Fl G 2.5s, 16 ft., 5 mi., SG on skeleton tower, obscured sector from 062° to 153°.

Crescent Boat Harbor Daybeacon 1
57 02.9N, 135 19.9W, 22 ft., SG on pile.

Sheldon Jackson Fish Pen Lights (2)
57 02.9N, 135 19.5W, Fl W 4s, on fish pen, private aids.

Crescent Harbor East Breakwater Light 4
57 04.0N, 135 19.8W, Fl R 2.5s, 19 ft., 4 mi., TR on square frame.

Crescent Harbor West Breakwater Light 3
57 02.9N, 135 19.8W, Fl G 2.5s, 20 ft., 4 mi., SG on square frame structure.

Aleutski Channel Daybeacon 2
57 02.8N, 135 20.4W, TR on pile.

Aleutski Channel Daybeacon 4
57 02.8N, 135 20.6W, TR on pile.

Japonski Harbor Entrance Daybeacon 5
57 02.8N, 135 20.8W, SG on pile.

Japonski Harbor Entrance Light 6
57 02.8N, 135 20.8W, Fl R 6s, 12 ft., 4 mi., TR on pile.

Japonski Harbor Daybeacon 7
57 02.9N, 135 20.9W, SG on pile.

Alligator Island Light
58 28.5N, 152 47.3W, Fl W 6s, 72 ft., 7 mi., NR on skeleton tower.

Althorp Rock Light 3
58 10.0N, 136 21.6W, Fl G 2.5s, 18 ft., 3 mi., SG on square frame.

Amelius Island Shoal Lighted Buoy 5
56 10.2N, 133 49.7W, Fl G 2.5s, 4 mi., green.

Amook Island Rock Buoy 1
57 25.6N, 153 50.8W, green can.

Anchor Point Light
59 46.1N, 151 52.0W, Fl W 5s, 41 ft., 15 mi., NR on skeleton tower, obscured from 174° to 346.5°.

Anchorage
See Knik Arm Shoal Buoys, Point Woronzof Range, *and* Point Mackenzie Light 11.

Ancon Rock Buoy 2
58 22.4N, 135 55.9W, red nun.

Andronica Island Light
55 20.7N, 160 03.7W, Fl W 4s, 115 ft., 7 mi., on square frame, obscured from 275° to 291.5° and from 317° to 078°.

Angle Point Light
55 14.3N, 131 25.6W, Fl W 6s, 24 ft., 6 mi., NR on skeleton tower, obscured from 132° to 288°, high-intensity beam toward 119°.

Applegate Shoals Light
60 21.3N, 147 23.6W, Fl W 2.5s, 24 ft., 6 mi., NR on skeleton tower.
Also see Prince William Sound.

Arch Point Light 2
55 12.3N, 161 54.3W, Fl R 4s,
78 ft., 5 mi., TR on skeleton tower,
obscured from 105° to 213°.

AUKE BAY

Boat Harbor Daybeacon 1
58 23.0N, 134 39.3W, SG on
steel pile.

Boat Harbor Light 2
58 22.9N, 134 39.2W, Fl R 2.5s,
17 ft., 3 mi., TR on post.

Breakwater Lights (4)
58 23.0N, 134 39.0W, Fl Y 4s,
10 ft., NY on post, private aids.

B

Bailey Ledge Light
53 51.6N, 166 33.6W, Fl W 4s,
20 ft., 5 mi., NR on spindle,
radar reflector.
Also see Unalaska Island.

Bailey Rock Daybeacon 2
55 15.4N, 131 36.1W, TR on
spindle.

Balandra Shoal Buoy 3
55 28.5N, 133 13.8W, green can.
Also see San Alberto Bay.

**Ballena Island Shoal Lighted
Buoy 2**
55 28.2N, 133 13.2W, Fl R 4s,
3 mi., red.
Also see San Alberto Bay.

Bar Harbor, Ketchikan
See Tongass Narrows.

Baralof Bay Light
55 14.4N, 160 32.0W, Fl W 4s,
60 ft., 5 mi., NR on skeleton tower,
obscured from 089° to 222°.

Barren Island Light
54 44.6N, 131 21.0W, Fl W 4s,
85 ft., 7 mi., NR on skeleton tower.

Barrier Island Lighted Bell Buoy 4
56 12.6N, 133 42.1W, Fl R 6s,
4 mi., red.

Bartlett Cove
See Glacier Bay.

Battery Island Light 6
57 03.6N, 135 22.9W, Fl R 6s,
16 ft., 4 mi., TR on small house,
obscured from 263° to 061°.
Also see Western Channel.

Battery Point Light
59 12.6N, 135 21.9W, Fl W 4s,
60 ft., 6 mi., NR on skeleton tower,
obscured from 325° to 157°.
Also see Haines and Skagway.

Bay Point Daybeacon BP
56 20.2N, 133 09.8W, 20 ft., SG
on pile.

Beacon Point Daybeacon BP
56 56.4N, 132 59.7W, SG on skeleton tower.

Bear Cape Light 2
60 23.3N, 146 43.8W, Fl R 6s,
39 ft., 6 mi., TR on skeleton tower,
obscured from 209° to 011°.
Also see Prince William Sound.

Beauclerc Island Light
56 15.4N, 133 51.3W, Fl W 2.5s,
30 ft., 6 mi., NR on skeleton tower,
obscured from 049° to 186°.

BECHEVIN BAY

**Channel should be navigated
with caution due to shifting
shoals.**

Entrance Buoy BB
55 06.2N, 163 29.5W, red and
white stripes.

Buoy 1
55 05.7N, 163 28.7W, green can.

Buoy 2
55 05.6N, 163 29.0W, red nun.

Buoys 3–6
Green cans and red nuns.

Cape Krenitzin Light 7
55 03.8N, 163 25.5W, Fl G 6s,
30 ft., 5 mi., SG on skeleton
tower, radar reflector.

Buoy 8
55 03.1N, 163 25.4W, red nun.

Buoy 10
55 02.5N, 163 25.1W, red nun.

Chunak Point Daybeacon 2CP
55 02.3N, 163 28.1W, TR on skeleton tower.

Buoys 11–16
Green cans and red nuns.

Rocky Point Light 6
54 58.3N, 163 26.6W, Fl R 6s,
5 mi., TR on skeleton tower.

Buoys 17–19
Green cans and red nuns.

St. Catherine Cove Daybeacon 4
54 59.8N, 163 29.4W, TR on
square frame, use only with
local knowledge.

Buoys 20–30
Red nuns and green cans.

Beck Island Light
56 02.9N, 132 51.8W, Fl W 4s,
27 ft., 5 mi., NR on skeleton tower,
obscured from 340° to 061°.

Beecher Pass Daybeacon 2
56 35.6N, 133 01.2W, TR on
spindle.
Also see Duncan Canal.

Beecher Pass Light 4
56 34.8N, 133 04.5W, Fl R 4s,
15 ft., 3 mi., TR on skeleton tower,
obscured from 270° to 005°.

Bend Light
See The Bend Light.

Big Gavanski Island Light 3
57 08.4N, 135 25.0W, Fl G 2.5s,
22 ft., 4 mi., SG on skeleton tower,
obscured from 010° to 154°.
Also see Sitka Sound.

Big Rose Island Light 21
57 27.4N, 135 32.4W, Fl G 4s,
17 ft., 4 mi., SG on skeleton tower,
obscured from 004° to 150°.
Also see Rose Island Rock Light 19
and Rose Channel Rock
Daybeacon.

Bill Point Light
57 15.1N, 133 32.6W, Fl W 4s,
12 ft., 6 mi., NR on pile, obscured
from 264° to 338°.

Billings Head Light
54 17.8N, 165 31.4W, Fl W 4s,
210 ft., 6 mi., NR on small house,
obscured from 256.5° to 090.5°.

Bird Rock Light 2
57 12.5N, 133 35.4W, Fl R 2.5s,
30 ft., 5 mi., TR on skeleton tower.

Black Bay Rocks Daybeacon 4
57 42.3N, 136 09.3W, TR on pile.

Black River Entrance Light
62 20.9N, 165 21.2W, Fl W 4s,
20 ft., 7 mi., NR on skeleton
tower, maintained from July 1
to Nov. 1.

Black Rock Light
55 01.4N, 131 03.6W, Fl W 6s, 55 ft.,
6 mi., NR on cylindrical house on
pyramidal skeleton tower.

BLAKE CHANNEL

Also see Eastern Passage.

Light 1
56 12.6N, 131 55.4W, Fl G 4s,
28 ft., 4 mi., SG on skeleton
tower, higher intensity beam
up channel.

Light 2
56 20.8N, 132 00.4W, Fl R 4s,
15 ft., 5 mi., TR on skeleton
tower, higher intensity beam
down channel, obscured from
133° to 233°.

Light 4
56 22.6N, 132 05.2W, Fl R 2.5s,
12 ft., 4 mi., TR on spindle.

Blank Island Light
55 16.0N, 131 38.4W, Fl W 2.5s,
37 ft., 6 mi., NR on skeleton tower,
obscured from 042° to 197.5°.

Bligh Reef Light
60 50.3N, 146 53.0W, Fl W 4s,
59 ft., 9 mi., NR on pile structure.
Also see Prince William Sound.

Bluff Point (Behm Canal) Light
55 53.0N, 131 44.8W, Fl W 6s,
12 ft., 6 mi., NR on skeleton tower.

**Bluff Point Shoal (Shumagin
Islands) Lighted Gong Buoy 1**
55 11.4N, 161 52.5W, Fl G 2.5s,
4 mi., green.

Boat Rock Light
54 46.8N, 130 48.0W, Fl W 2.5s,
46 ft., 6 mi., NR on skeleton tower,
obscured from 049° to 210°.

Brad Rock Daybeacon
57 22.4N, 135 41.5W, 15 ft., SG
on spindle.

Broad Island Light
57 35.1N, 135 23.6W, Q W, 14 ft.,
6 mi., NR on skeleton tower,
obscured from 152° to 297°.

**Brownson Island Rocks
Daybeacon BI**
55 56.0N, 132 06.8W, SG on
spindle.

**Burnett Inlet Buoy 2 (marks
entrance to Burnett Inlet and
1 1/2-fathom shoal)**
56 03.9N, 132 28.3W, red nun.

BURNT ISLAND CHANNEL

Daybeacon 2
56 56.7N, 133 56.2W, 8 ft., TR on
pile.

Daybeacon 3
56 56.8N, 133 55.5W, 7 ft., SG on
pile.

Daybeacon 4
56 56.7N, 133 55.3W, 8 ft., TR on
pile.

Burnt Island Light 5
55 58.4N, 133 17.8W, Fl G 4s,
15 ft., 4 mi., SG on skeleton tower,
obscured from 004° to 157.5°.
Also see El Capitan Passage.

Busby Island Light
60 53.7N, 146 49.0W, Fl W 6s
(R sector), 48 ft., white 9 mi.,
red 6 mi., NR on skeleton tower,
obscured from 245° to 003°,
red from 003° to 044°.
Also see Prince William Sound.

Bush Point Light 2
57 13.1N, 153 13.0W, Fl R 4s,
17 ft., 5 mi., TR on steel skeleton
tower.

Bushy Island Light
56 16.6N, 132 57.6W, Fl W 4s,
22 ft., 6 mi., NR on skeleton
tower on brown cylindrical base,
obscured from 358° to 111°.

Bushy Point Light
55 43.9N, 131 43.9W, Fl W 4s,
18 ft., 6 mi., NR on skeleton tower.

Butterworth Island Light 2
56 32.2N, 133 04.5W, Fl R 2.5s,
21 ft., 4 mi., TR on frame structure.
Also see Duncan Canal.

Button Island Shoal Buoy 5
56 12.1N, 132 14.9W, green can.
Also see Zimovia Strait.

C

Caamano Point Light
55 29.9N, 131 59.0W, Fl W 6s,
41 ft., 6 mi., NR on steel post,
obscured from 124° to 276°.

Caines Head Light
59 59.0N, 149 23.3W, Fl W 4s,
35 ft., 5 mi., NR on pile, obscured
from 043° to 214°.

Calder Rocks Lighted Buoy 6
56 15.6N, 133 43.4W, Fl R 4s,
4 mi., red.

California Rock Lighted Buoy 3
55 18.9N, 131 36.2W, Fl G 4s,
4 mi., green.
Also see Tongass Narrows.

Cape Alitak Light
56 50.6N, 154 18.4W, Fl W 6s,
63 ft., 7 mi., NR on small house,
obscured from 190° to 263°.

Cape Bartolome Light
55 13.8N, 133 36.9W, Fl W 6s,
158 ft., 7 mi., NR on skeleton
tower, obscured from 148° to 263°.

Cape Chacon Light
54 41.4N, 132 01.0W, Fl W 2.5s,
50 ft., 6 mi., NR on frame,
obscured from 112° to 226.5°.

Cape Chiniak Light
57 37.7N, 152 09.2W, Fl W 6s,
120 ft., 8 mi., NR on skeleton
tower, obscured from 001° to 052°
and from 257° to 260°.

Cape Deceit Light
66 06.0N, 162 45.2W, Fl W 6s,
200 ft., 7 mi., NR on skeleton
tower, maintained from July 1
to Nov. 1.

Cape Decision Light
56 00.1N, 134 08.2W, Fl W 5s,
96 ft., 18 mi., white square concrete building with square tower
rising from center, obscured from
134° to 245°.

Cape Edgecumbe Light
56 59.9N, 135 51.4W, Fl W 4s,
100 ft., 7 mi., NR on square frame,
obscured from 149.5° to 321°.
Also see Sitka Sound.

Cape Elizabeth Light
59 08.8N, 151 52.6W, Fl W 6s,
48 ft., 9 mi., NR on square tower.

Cape Espenberg Light
66 33.4N, 163 36.5W, Fl W 2.5s,
28 ft., 6 mi., NR on skeleton tower,
maintained from July 1 to Nov. 1.

Cape Etolin Light
60 26.3N, 166 10.0W, Fl W 6s,
40 ft., 6 mi., on skeleton tower,
maintained from July 1 to Nov. 1.

Cape Fanshaw Light
57 11.1N, 133 34.4W, Fl W 4s,
33 ft., 7 mi., NR on skeleton tower,
obscured from 210° to 299°.

Cape Flores Lighted Buoy 2
55 21.4N, 133 17.7W, Fl R 4s,
3 mi., red.

Cape Greig Light
57 44.5N, 157 42.8W, Fl W 6s,
350 ft., 6 mi., NR on skeleton
tower.

Cape Hichinbrook Light
60 14.3N, 146 38.8W, Fl W 15s,
235 ft., 25 mi., white square tower
on corner of building, obscured
from 134° to 135° and 138° to
283°.

Cape Hichinbrook Radiobeacon
60 14.3N, 146 38.8W, W (·--),
150 ft., 292 kHz, antenna at
Cape Hichinbrook Light.

Cape Krenitzin Light 7
55 03.8N, 163 25.5W, Fl G 6s,
30 ft., 5 mi., SG on skeleton
tower, radar reflector.
Also see Bechevin Bay.

Cape Lynch Light
55 46.9N, 133 42.1W, Fl W 6s,
50 ft., 6 mi., NR on small house,
obscured from 196° to 315°.

Cape Mohican Light
60 12.7N, 167 27.5W, Fl W 6s,
285 ft., 7 mi., NR on skeleton
tower, maintained from July 1
to Nov. 1.

Cape Muzon Light
54 39.8N, 132 41.5W, Fl W 6s,
80 ft., 7 mi., NR on skeleton tower,
obscured from 089° to 297°.

Cape Ommaney Light
56 09.6N, 134 39.7W, Fl W 6s,
168 ft., 8 mi., on post, obscured
from 117° to 251°.

Cape Pankof Light
54 39.5N, 163 03.7W, Fl W 6s,
82 ft., 6 mi., NR on square frame,
obscured from 101° to 217°.

Cape Prince of Wales Light
65 38.0N, 168 07.2W, Fl W 6s,
20 ft., 7 mi., NR on skeleton tower,
maintained from July 1 to Nov. 1.

Cape Rodney Light
64 38.5N, 166 23.8W, Fl W 4s,
24 ft., 7 mi., NR on skeleton tower,
maintained from July 1 to Nov. 1.

Cape Sarichef Light
54 35.9N, 164 55.8W, Fl W 2.5s,
170 ft., 8 mi., NR on skeleton
tower, obscured from 223.5° to
018.5°.

Cape Seniavin Light
56 24.0N, 160 08.8W, Fl W 6s,
175 ft., 7 mi., NR on small house.

Cape Spencer Light
58 11.9N, 136 38.4W, Fl W 10s,
105 ft., 24 mi., white square concrete tower on rectangular
concrete building.

Cape St. Elias Bell Buoy 2
59 44.8N, 144 38.1W, red.

Cape St. Elias Light
59 47.9N, 144 35.9W, Fl W 10s,
85 ft., 15 mi., white square tower
at corner of rectangular building,
obscured from 160° to 287° and
from 018.5° to 027°.

Cape Stephens Light
63 32.4N, 162 18.8W, Fl W 4s,
200 ft., 7 mi., NR on skeleton
tower, maintained from July 1
to Nov. 1.

Cape Strait Light
56 59.9N, 133 05.5W, Fl W 6s,
30 ft., 6 mi., NR on skeleton tower,
obscured from 314.5° to 120°.

Cape Ulitka Light
56 33.7N, 133 43.7W, Fl W 6s,
115 ft., 6 mi., NR on skeleton
tower, obscured from 310° to 053°.

Caton Shoal Buoy 6
55 19.8N, 160 31.6W, red nun.

Center Island Reef Daybeacon 3
54 48.1N, 132 23.0W, SG on pile.

Channel Island Light 14
55 23.7N, 131 45.9W, Fl R 4s,
24 ft., 5 mi., TR on skeleton tower
on concrete base, obscured from
238° to 268°.
Also see Tongass Narrows.

**Channel Island Rock Lighted
Buoy 7**
60 36.5N, 145 48.8W, Fl G 2.5s,
4 mi., green.
Also see Prince William Sound.

Chapin Island Range
See Karheen Passage.

Chatham Strait Light 20
58 02.8N, 134 48.6W, Fl R 4s,
35 ft., 4 mi., TR on skeleton tower,
obscured from 175° to 353°.

Chignik Spit Light
56 18.6N, 158 23.0W, Fl W 4s,
35 ft., 7 mi., NR on skeleton
tower, obscured west of 238°.

Chilkoot Inlet East Light
59 01.0N, 135 11.8W, Fl W 2.5s,
25 ft., 5 mi., NR on skeleton tower,
obscured from 166° to 337°.
Also see Haines and Skagway.

Chisik Island Light
60 05.8N, 152 33.7W, Fl W 4s,
215 ft., 8 mi., NR on square frame.

Chugach Passage Lighted Buoy 2
59 09.0N, 151 45.4W, Fl R 2.5s,
4 mi., red.

Chugach Passage Lighted Buoy 3
59 10.9N, 151 47.6W, Fl G 4s,
4 mi., green.

CLARK BAY

Jarvis Island Light 1
55 30.4N, 132 33.6W, Fl G 4s,
12 ft., 4 mi., SG on spindle.

Clark Bay Light 2
55 29.9N, 132 35.1W, Fl R 2.5s,
8 ft., 4 mi., TR on spindle,
obscured from 042° to 155°.

**Hollis Ferry Terminal East
Dolphin Light**
55 29.4N, 132 37.1W, Fl R 6s,
32 ft., on dolphin, private aid.

**Hollis Ferry Terminal West
Dolphin Light**
55 29.4N, 132 37.3W, F R, 34 ft.,
on dolphin, private aid.

Lighted Buoy 3
55 29.2N, 132 36.7W, Fl G 2.5s,
3 mi., green.

Daybeacon 5
55 29.3N, 132 37.1W, SG on pile.

Clover Passage Daybeacon CP
55 28.6N, 131 48.0W, TR on pile.

Clover Passage Entrance Light
55 28.7N, 131 48.8W, Fl W 6s,
20 ft., 5 mi., NR on skeleton tower,
obscured from 102° to 230°.

Coghlan Island Daybeacon
58 21.8N, 134 42.0W, SG on pile.

Cohen Island Rock Light
59 33.0N, 151 28.0W, Fl W 4s,
79 ft., 8 mi., NR on skeleton
tower, higher intensity beam
from 060° to 120°.
Also see Kachemak Bay.

Cohen Reef Daybeacon CR
58 25.9N, 134 48.3W, JG on
spindle.

COLD BAY

Channel Lighted Buoy 1
55 05.5N, 162 31.9W, Fl G 4s,
3 mi., green.

Kaslokan Point Light 2
55 06.2N, 162 31.5W, Fl R 4s,
15 ft., 5 mi., TR on steel square
frame, obscured from 193° to
336°.

Channel Lighted Buoy 3
55 06.7N, 162 32.0W, Fl G 2.5s,
4 mi., green.

Channel Buoy 4
55 07.1N, 162 31.7W, red nun.

Delta Point Light
55 11.5N, 162 38.7W, Fl W 4s,
48 ft., 6 mi., NR on skeleton tower.

Aero Dock Lights (2)
55 12.5N, 162 41.6W, Fl R 6s,
17 ft., on dolphins, private aids.

Colt Island Light
58 17.0N, 133 44.4W, Fl W 4s,
24 ft., 5 mi., NR on pile.

Columbine Rock Daybeacon 19
57 15.8N, 135 35.0W, SG on
square frame.
Also see Neva Strait.

Cominco Red Dog Racon Light
67 34.7N, 164 03.2W, Fl (2) W 10s,
112 ft., 10 mi., on tower, racon: K
(-·-), maintained from June 1 to
Nov. 1, private aid.

Cone Island Daybeacon 2
55 26.8N, 133 36.3W, TR on pile.
Also see Pigeon Island
Daybeacon 3.

Controller Bay
See Martin Islands Light.

COOK INLET

**Oil well structures exist in Cook
Inlet from Kalgin Island to the
mouth of the Beluga River.
Some buoys may be located outside of the wire dragged area.**

*Also see individual lights, buoys,
harbors, and bays for aids to
navigation.*

**Lower Cook Inlet Junction
Lighted Bell Buoy CI**
60 04.7N, 152 09.8W, Fl (2+1) G
6s, 4 mi., green and red bands,
maintained from May 1 to Nov. 1.

Lighted Bell Buoy 5
61 08.2N, 150 20.3W, Fl G 4s,
4 mi., green, maintained from
May 1 to Nov. 1.
Also see Fire Island Light 6.

COPPER RIVER DELTA

**Caution: Only mariners with a
thorough knowledge of area
should attempt passage into the
Delta unless during emergency
situations.**

Softuk Bar Channel Light S
60 13.6N, 144 57.8W, Oc W 4s,
12 ft., 6 mi., NR on skeleton tower,
maintained from May 1 to Oct. 1.

Kokenhenic Bar Channel Light K
60 13.4N, 145 09.0W, Fl W 4s,
12 ft., 5 mi., NR on skeleton tower,
maintained from May 1 to Oct. 1.

Grass Island Bar Channel Light G
60 15.0N, 145 17.4W, Fl W 6s,
12 ft., 6 mi., NR on skeleton tower,
maintained from May 1 to Oct. 1.

Peter Dahl Bar Channel Light P
60 16.0N, 145 22.1W, Fl W 2.5s,
12 ft., 5 mi., NR on skeleton tower,
maintained from May 1 to Oct. 1.

Egg Island Light E
60 22.2N, 145 45.0W, Fl W 6s,
33 ft., 9 mi., NR on skeleton tower.

**Egg Island Lighted Whistle
Buoy EI**
60 17.4N, 145 43.2W, Mo (A) W,
6 mi., red and white stripes.

Point Bentinck

Point Bentinck Light
60 23.7N, 146 05.2W, Fl W 4s,
47 ft., 6 mi., NR on skeleton tower.

**Point Bentinck Bar Lighted Bell
Buoy 1**
60 19.3N, 145 59.8W, Fl G 4s,
4 mi., green.

Buoy S
60 11.8N, 144 56.4W, red and
white nun.

Buoy K
60 11.5N, 145 09.4W, red and
white nun.

Buoy G
60 13.2N, 145 18.7W, red and
white nun.

Buoy P
60 16.0N, 145 34.7W, red and
white nun.

Mummy Island Light
60 27.7N, 145 59.4W, Fl W 4s,
21 ft., 5 mi., NR on skeleton tower.
Also see Prince William Sound.

Cordova
See Prince William Sound.

Cornwallis Point Light
56 55.9N, 134 16.4W, Fl W 4s,
34 ft., 6 mi., NR on small house,
obscured from 140° to 315°.

Cozian Reef Lighted Bell Buoy 3
57 34.0N, 135 25.6W, Fl G 6s,
4 mi., green.

Crafton Island Light
60 30.7N, 147 56.1W, Fl W 4s,
70 ft., 6 mi., NR on skeleton tower,
obscured from 328° to 146°.
Also see Prince William Sound.

CRAIG HARBOR

Fish Egg Reef Lighted Buoy 3
55 28.4N, 133 09.6W, Fl G 2.5s,
3 mi., green.

Craig Buoy 4
55 28.8N, 133 09.4W, red nun.

Saltery Point Shoal Daybeacon 6
55 28.8N, 133 08.7W, TR on pile.

Craig Breakwater Lights (3)
55 28.9N, 133 08.7W, Fl R 4s,
13 ft., on breakwater, private aids.

Craig Shoal Lighted Buoy 7
55 29.2N, 133 08.8W, Fl G 4s,
4 mi., green.

Craig Point Light
56 27.4N, 132 43.0W, Fl W 6s,
11 ft., 7 mi., NR on square frame,
obscured from 301° to 096°.

Crescent Harbor, Sitka
See Alidale Channel.

Crowley Lighted Mooring Buoy
58 43.0N, 157 03.8W, Q W, white
cylinder, maintained from April
15 to Sept. 15, private aid.

Crowley Mooring Buoy
59 01.9N, 158 27.1W, white cylinder, maintained from April 15
to Sept. 15., private aid.

Culross Island Light
60 44.8N, 148 06.8W, Fl W 4s,
40 ft., 6 mi., NR on skeleton tower,
obscured from 334° to 128°.
Also see Prince William Sound.

Curacao Reef Buoy 8
55 39.3N, 133 28.4W, red nun.

Cutter Rocks Light CR
55 17.3N, 131 31.5W, Fl (2+1) R 6s,
11 ft., 3 mi., JR on skeleton tower.

D

Danger Point Light
57 30.9N, 134 36.4W, Fl W 6s,
30 ft., 7 mi., NR on skeleton
tower on concrete pier.

Davidson Inlet
See Surf Point Light.

December Point Light DP
56 32.9N, 132 57.7W, Fl R 6s,
15 ft., 4 mi., TR on pile.
Also see Wrangell Narrows.

Decision Point Light
60 48.4N, 146 27.3W, Fl W 4s,
35 ft., 5 mi., NR on skeleton tower,
obscured from 315° to 105°.
Also see Prince William Sound.

Deep Bay Entrance Daybeacon 1
57 26.0N, 135 35.6W, SG on post.

Deepwater Point Light
57 10.3N, 134 14.2W, Fl W 4s,
17 ft., 5 mi., NR on skeleton tower,
obscured from 180° to 288°.

Deer Harbor Bell Buoy 1
57 56.2N, 136 34.6W, green,
maintained from May 15 to
Sept. 30.

Delta Point Light
55 11.5N, 162 38.7W, Fl W 4s,
48 ft., 6 mi., NR on skeleton tower.
Also see Cold Bay.

Desconocida Reef Buoy 10
55 41.3N, 133 31.5W, red nun.

Dippy Island Rock Daybeacon 3
57 41.4N, 136 07.7W, SG on
spindle on pier.

Diver Islands Light
55 10.7N, 133 15.9W, Fl W 4s,
130 ft., 7 mi., NR on post,
obscured from 186° to 007°.

Double Rock Daybeacon 8
56 12.2N, 132 15.5W, 16 ft., TR
on pile.
Also see Zimovia Strait.

Douglas Boat Harbor Light 1D
58 16.6N, 134 23.2W, Fl G 4s,
17 ft., 4 mi., SG on skeleton tower.
Also see Juneau and Gastineau
Channel.

Driest Point Light 4
55 10.6N, 131 36.4W, Fl R 6s,
29 ft., 4 mi., TR on spindle,
obscured from 177° to 328°.

Drift River Terminal Lights (2)
60 33.2N, 152 08.2W, F R, 50 ft.,
on mooring dolphins, horn: 1
blast every 20s, private aids.

DRY PASS

Daybeacon 2
56 09.5N, 133 22.8W, TR on post.

Daybeacons 3–26
SGs and TRs on piles, posts, or
spindles.

Daybeacon 28
56 09.2N, 133 27.7W, TR on spindle.

Dry Spruce Bay Entrance Light
57 57.3N, 153 06.2W, Fl W 6s,
76 ft., 6 mi., NR on skeleton tower.

Dry Spruce Island Rock Light 7
57 57.9N, 153 04.2W, Fl G 4s,
30 ft., 4 mi., SG on post.

DRY STRAIT

Light 1
56 35.0N, 132 32.6W, Fl G 4s,
29 ft., 4 mi., SG on skeleton tower.

Daybeacon 3
56 36.5N, 132 33.1W, 24 ft., SG on
skeleton tower.

Light 5
56 38.2N, 132 36.7W, Fl G 6s,
17 ft., 4 mi., SG on square frame.

Duck Creek Light
58 57.3N, 157 01.9W, Fl W 6s,
48 ft., 5 mi., NR on skeleton tower.

Duck Point Light
57 12.7N, 133 31.0W, Fl W 6s,
17 ft., 6 mi., NR on skeleton tower,
obscured from 140° to 257°.

DUNCAN CANAL

Foremost Rock Daybeacon
56 30.1N, 133 00.3W, 20 ft., NR
on post.

Butterworth Island Light 2
56 32.2N, 133 04.5W, Fl R 2.5s,
21 ft., 4 mi., TR on frame structure.

Daybeacon 3
56 32.5N, 133 05.4W, 21 ft., SG
on frame structure.

Beecher Pass Daybeacon 2
56 35.6N, 133 01.2W, TR on spindle.

Beecher Pass Light 4
56 34.8N, 133 04.5W, Fl R 4s,
15 ft., 3 mi., TR on skeleton tower,
obscured from 270° to 005°.

Daybeacon
56 38.6N, 133 06.1W, NR on
spindle.

E

East Amatuli Island Light
58 54.9N, 151 57.1W, Fl W 6s,
120 ft., 8 mi., NR on skeleton
tower, obscured from 076° to 147°.

East Channel Daybeacon 2
55 09.3N, 131 36.4W, TR on spindle.

East Chugach Light
59 06.4N, 151 26.6W, Fl W 6s,
325 ft., 7 mi., NR on skeleton
tower, obscured from 118° to 227°.

East Clump Light 7
55 20.7N, 131 41.3W, Fl G 6s,
15 ft., 5 mi., SG on square frame.
Also see Tongass Narrows.

East Foreland Buoy 2
60 42.4N, 151 30.6W, red nun,
maintained from May 1 to Nov. 1.

East Foreland Light
60 43.2N, 151 24.4W, Fl W 6s,
294 ft., 9 mi., NR on skeleton
tower, obscured from 208° to 010°.

East Island Light
54 52.2N, 131 11.8W, Fl W 2.5s,
43 ft., 7 mi., NR on skeleton tower,
obscured from 014° to 184°.

East Pinta Rocks Buoy 1
57 05.5N, 133 58.5W, green can.
Also see West Pinta Rocks Light.

Easterly Island Light
55 53.8N, 132 05.5W, Fl W 4s,
28 ft., 6 mi., NR on skeleton tower.

EASTERN CHANNEL

Also see Sitka Sound, Alidale
Channel, Western Channel, *and*
Sitka Harbor.

The Eckholms Light
57 00.6N, 135 21.5W, Fl W 6s,
33 ft., 6 mi., NR on skeleton tower.

**Simpson Rock Lighted Bell
Buoy 5**
57 01.2N, 135 20.7W, Fl G 4s,
4 mi., green.

Tsaritsa Rock Lighted Buoy 7
57 01.2N, 135 19.5W, Fl G 2.5s,
3 mi., green.

Rocky Patch Lighted Buoy RP
57 01.7N, 135 18.4W, Fl (2+1) R 6s,
4 mi., red and green bands.

Rocky Patch Buoy 9A
57 01.8N, 135 17.7W, green can.

Entry Point Light 1
57 02.0N, 135 15.0W, Fl G 6s,
22 ft., 4 mi., SG on square frame,
obscured from 086° to 248°.

The Twins Light 9
57 02.1N, 135 18.8W, Fl G 4s,
14 ft., 4 mi., SG on skeleton tower,
obscured from 030° to 146°.

Rockwell Light
57 02.2N, 135 20.0W, F R, 50 ft.,
white octagonal tower with
dwelling attached, private aid.

Mitchell Rock Daybeacon
57 02.3N, 135 20.4W, NR on pile.

Surf Rock Light
57 01.9N, 135 22.6W, Fl W 4s,
15 ft., 5 mi., NR on spindle.

EASTERN PASSAGE

Also see Blake Channel.

The Narrows Light 5
56 21.8N, 132 06.7W, Fl G 2.5s,
12 ft., 2 mi., SG on pile.

Light 7
56 22.1N, 132 10.3W, Fl G 4s,
12 ft., 4 mi., SG on skeleton
tower, higher intensity beam
up channel.

Airport Runway Rock Light
56 29.1N, 132 21.3W, Fl W 6s,
15 ft., 4 mi., NR on spindle.

Light
56 29.6N, 132 22.2W, Fl W 2.5s,
13 ft., 6 mi., NR on skeleton tower.

Eckholms Light
See The Eckholms Light.

EDNA BAY

Entrance Light
55 56.3N, 133 37.0W, Fl W 6s,
23 ft., 6 mi., NR on skeleton tower,
obscured from 104° to 240°.

Buoy 2
55 56.5N, 133 39.0W, red nun.

Light 3
55 56.5N, 133 39.5W, Fl G 4s,
20 ft., 4 mi., SG on small house.

Shoal Buoys (about 10)
55 57.8N, 133 37.4W, white cans
with orange bands and orange
diamond worded SHOAL, private
aids.

North Daybeacon E
55 57.8N, 133 37.4W, TR on pile.

**East Edna Bay Log Breakwater
Lights (3)**
55 57.8N, 133 37.5W, Fl Y 6s, 4 ft.,
on log breakwater, private aids.

Eek Point Light
55 08.3N, 132 40.0W, Fl W 2.5s,
19 ft., 6 mi., NR on square frame,
obscured from 103° to 237°.

Egegik Entrance Buoy 1
58 15.5N, 157 42.1W, green can,
maintained from May 1 to
Sept. 30.

Egg Island Light
63 36.7N, 161 44.6W, Fl W 6s,
90 ft., 7 mi., NR on skeleton tower,
maintained from July 1 to Nov. 1.

Egg Island Light E
60 22.2N, 145 45.0W, Fl W 6s,
33 ft., 9 mi., NR on skeleton tower.
Also see Copper River Delta.

**Egg Islands Lighted Whistle
Buoy EI**
60 17.4N, 145 43.2W, Mo (A) W,
6 mi., red and white stripes.

Ekuk Range Front Light
58 47.9N, 158 33.2W, Q W, 20 ft.,
KRW on skeleton tower, visible all
around, higher intensity on
rangeline.

Ekuk Range Rear Light
1,000 feet, 341° from front light,
Iso W 6s, 42 ft., KRW on skeleton
tower, visible all around, higher
intensity on rangeline.

El Capitan Passage

Daybeacon 1
55 55.7N, 133 18.3W, SG on pile.

Hub Rock Daybeacon 3
55 56.5N, 133 17.9W, SG on pile.

North Island Daybeacon
55 57.9N, 133 19.5W, NR on spindle.

Burnt Island Light 5
55 58.4N, 133 17.8W, Fl G 4s, 15 ft., 4 mi., SG on skeleton tower, obscured from 004° to 157.5°.

Eldred Rock Light
58 58.3N, 135 13.2W, Fl W 6s, 91 ft., 8 mi., white octagonal tower on building, higher intensity beam up Chilkoot Inlet, higher intensity beam down Lynn Canal.

Elfin Cove

Entrance Light 2
58 11.7N, 136 21.1W, Fl R 4s, 48 ft., 3 mi., TR on small house, obscured from 292° to 096°.

Outer Light
58 11.8N, 136 21.1W, Fl W 4s, 20 ft., 6 mi., NR on square frame.

Daybeacon 3
58 11.7N, 136 21.0W, SG on pile.

Daybeacon 5
58 11.7N, 136 20.9W, SG on pile.

Daybeacon 6
58 11.6N, 136 20.9W, TR on pile.

Daybeacon 7
58 11.6N, 136 20.7W, SG on pile.

Elovoi Island (Peril Strait) Light 26
57 33.9N, 135 28.1W, Fl R 6s, 18 ft., 4 mi., TR on skeleton tower, obscured from 308° to 037°.

Elovoi Rock Daybeacon 1
56 49.3N, 135 22.8W, SG on pile.
Also see Sitka Sound.

Elrington Passage
See Prince William Sound.

Emerald Island Buoy 9
55 44.5N, 133 40.2W, green can.

Entrance Island Light 24
57 17.5N, 135 36.3W, Fl R 6s, 30 ft., 5 mi., TR on skeleton tower, obscured from 154° to 345°.
Also see Neva Strait.

Entrance Point Shoal (Marmot Bay) Lighted Buoy 5
57 54.8N, 152 31.7W, Fl G 2.5s, 3 mi., green.

Entry Point Light 1
57 02.0N, 135 15.0W, Fl G 6s, 22 ft., 4 mi., SG on square frame, obscured from 086° to 248°.
Also see Eastern Channel.

Eureka Channel Daybeacon 1
54 46.9N, 132 23.3W, SG on pile.

Evans Island Light
59 59.1N, 148 07.5W, Fl W 2.5s, 20 ft., 6 mi., NR on skeleton tower, obscured from 084° to 249°.
Also see Prince William Sound.

Eye Opener Light
See The Eye Opener Light.

Fairway Island Light 32
57 26.6N, 134 52.3W, Fl R 6s, 55 ft., 4 mi., TR on abandoned dwelling, obscured from 297° to 098°.

False Point Pybus Daybeacon
57 21.1N, 133 52.5W, NR on skeleton tower.

False Point Retreat Light 4
58 22.2N, 134 58.2W, Fl R 6s, 25 ft., 3 mi., TR on skeleton tower.
Also see Point Retreat Light.

Faust Rock Lighted Bell Buoy FR
58 25.1N, 134 55.7W, Fl (2+1) R 6s, 4 mi., red and green bands.

Favorite Reef Light 2
58 22.8N, 134 51.7W, Fl R 4s, 33 ft., 5 mi., TR on pile.

Fern Reef Lighted Buoy 3A
55 29.1N, 133 15.9W, Fl G 4s, 4 mi., green.
Also see San Alberto Bay.

Fire Island

Also see Race Point.

Fire Island Light 6
61 07.6N, 150 16.9W, Fl R 6s, 30 ft., 7 mi., TR on skeleton tower, racon: N (-·).
Also see Cook Inlet, Lighted Bell Buoy 5.

Range Front Light
61 10.3N, 150 12.0W, Q W, 125 ft., KRB on pile structure, visible 4° each side of rangeline.

Range Rear Light
433 yards, 242° from front light, Iso W 6s, 166 ft., KRB on pile structure, visible 4° each side of rangeline.

Fish Egg Reef Lighted Buoy 3
55 28.4N, 133 09.6W, Fl G 2.5s, 3 mi., green.
Also see Craig Harbor.

Fishermans Harbor Daybeacon 1
55 58.4N, 133 47.9W, SG on spindle.

Fishermans Harbor Light
55 58.0N, 133 47.7W, Fl W 4s (R sector), 17 ft., 4 mi., NR on skeleton tower, red sector from 153° to 200°.

Five Fathom Shoal Lighted Buoy F
56 21.8N, 133 14.1W, Fl (2+1) R 6s, 4 mi., red and green bands.

Five Finger Light
57 16.2N, 133 37.9W, Fl W 10s, 81 ft., 17 mi., white concrete tower rising from center of building.

Five Mile Island Light
56 28.2N, 132 30.7W, Fl W 4s, 34 ft., 5 mi., NR on pile, obscured from 329° to 100°.

Flat Island Light
59 19.9N, 151 59.7W, Fl W 4s, 70 ft., 8 mi., NR on skeleton tower.

Foggy Point Light
54 55.5N, 130 58.6W, Fl W 4s, 17 ft., 6 mi., NR on skeleton tower.

Foremost Rock Daybeacon
56 30.1N, 133 00.3W, 20 ft., NR on post.
Also see Duncan Canal.

Found Island Light
56 06.2N, 132 04.8W, Fl W 6s,
34 ft., 7 mi., NR on skeleton tower.

Found Island Rock Daybeacon
56 06.8N, 132 04.3W, NR on spindle on concrete pier.
Also see Zimovia Strait.

**Fourth of July South Breakwater
Light**
60 05.1N, 149 21.6W, Fl R 4s, 9 ft.,
on pedestal, private aid.
Also see Seward.

Fox Island Light
54 57.3N, 162 26.0W, Fl W 6s,
40 ft., 6 mi., NR on steel square
frame, obscured from 280° to
021°.

Freshwater Bay Daybeacon 5
57 54.3N, 135 08.1W, SG on
spindle.

Funter Bay Buoy 3
58 14.5N, 134 54.4W, green can.

Funter Bay Entrance Light 1
58 14.6N, 134 55.0W, Fl G 2.5s,
16 ft., 4 mi., SG on pedestal on
house, obscured from 114° to 248°.

G

Gambier Bay Entrance Light 2
57 27.9N, 133 55.2W, Fl R 6s,
16 ft., 4 mi., TR on skeleton tower.

Gannet Rocks Light 4
51 52.0N, 176 36.5W, Fl R 4s,
45 ft., 4 mi., TR on skeleton tower,
obscured from 102° to 214°.
Also see Adak Island.

Gastineau Channel
See Juneau and Gastineau Channel.

GEESE CHANNEL

Lighted Gong Buoy 1
56 44.8N, 153 53.1W, Fl G 2.5s,
4 mi., green.

Buoy 3
56 43.5N, 153 58.5W, green can.

Lighted Bell Buoy 4
56 43.7N, 153 59.1W, Fl R 4s,
3 mi., red.

Aiaktalik Island Light 5
56 43.9N, 154 03.1W, Fl G 6s,
57 ft., 5 mi., SG on square frame.

George Island Light 2
58 12.7N, 136 22.9W, Fl R 6s,
48 ft., 4 mi., TR on skeleton tower,
obscured from 019° to 048°.

George Rock Light
58 18.9N, 134 42.0W, Fl W 6s,
17 ft., 6 mi., NR on skeleton tower.

Gibby Rock Light 2
58 19.6N, 134 41.3W, Fl R 6s,
30 ft., 4 mi., TR on post.

GLACIER BAY

**National Park Aircraft Safety
Zone Marker Buoys (4 buoys, NE
of main dock airplane float)**
White with two orange bands
and orange circle worded AIR-
CRAFT SAFETY ZONE, main-
tained from May 15 to Oct. 1,
private aids.

Rush Point Shoal Buoy 1
58 28.1N, 136 03.4W, green can,
maintained from May 1 to Oct. 1.

Glacier Island Light
60 52.3N, 147 05.5W, Fl W 6s,
38 ft., 9 mi., NR on skeleton tower,
obscured from 040° to 225°.
Also see Prince William Sound.

Gnat Cove Log Boom Markers (2)
55 22.9N, 131 19.7W, NW on log
boom worded DANGER LOG
BOOM, private aids.

Goat Island Light
55 10.1N, 132 53.6W, Fl W 4s,
21 ft., 5 mi., NR on skeleton tower,
obscured from 093° to 261°.
Also see Sukkwan Strait.

Goloi Sandspit Light 3
55 06.6N, 161 55.5W, Fl G 4s,
17 ft., 5 mi., SG on steel skeleton
tower, obscured from 229° to
328°.

Goose Island Light
60 42.8N, 146 43.6W, Fl W 6s,
38 ft., 6 mi., NR on skeleton tower,
obscured from 151° to 313°.
Also see Prince William Sound.

Grand Island Light
58 06.0N, 134 06.5W, Fl W 6s,
47 ft., 6 mi., NR on skeleton tower,
obscured from 335° to 116°.

Grand Point Light
57 05.5N, 133 11.2W, Fl W 4s,
16 ft., 7 mi., NR on pile, obscured
from 189° to 305°.

Grant Island Light
55 33.3N, 131 43.7W, Fl W 6s,
18 ft., 7 mi., NR on skeleton tower.

Grantley Harbor Daybeacon 2
65 16.4N, 166 21.4W, TR on tower,
maintained from July 1 to Nov. 1.

Grantley Harbor Light
65 16.7N, 166 20.9W, Fl W 4s,
15 ft., 7 mi., NG on skeleton tower,
maintained from July 1 to Nov. 1.

Grass Island Bar Channel Light G
60 15.0N, 145 17.4W, Fl W 6s,
12 ft., 6 mi., NR on skeleton tower,
maintained from May 1 to Oct. 1.
Also see Copper River Delta.

Grave Island Light
57 16.0N, 134 05.0W, Fl W 4s,
18 ft., 6 mi., NR on spindle,
obscured from 031° to 167°.

Grave Point Light
58 03.7N, 134 03.1W, Fl W 2.5s,
45 ft., 6 mi., NR on skeleton tower,
obscured from 156° to 280°.

Graves Harbor Daybeacon 2
58 17.1N, 136 41.7W, TR on pile.

Graveyard Point Light
58 52.1N, 157 00.8W, Fl W 4s,
40 ft., 6 mi., NR on skeleton tower.

Gravina Point Light 3
60 37.4N, 146 15.2W, Fl G 6s,
27 ft., 5 mi., SG on skeleton tower,
obscured from 120° to 264°.
Also see Prince William Sound.

Greentop Island Light
57 51.3N, 136 29.1W, Fl W 6s,
79 ft., 6 mi., NR on post,
obscured from 143° to 318°.

Guard Islands Light
55 26.8N, 131 52.9W, Fl W 10s,
74 ft., 17 mi., white square tower
on rectangular building.
Also see Tongass Narrows.

Guide Rocks Daybeacon 4
54 49.6N, 132 21.5W, TR on pile.

Gull Island Light GI
55 08.3N, 131 36.4W, Fl (2+1) R 6s,
20 ft., 5 mi., JR on spindle.

Gustavus Lighted Buoy 1
58 23.2N, 135 44.7W, Fl G 4s,
3 mi., green.

H

Hague Channel
See Herendeen Bay.

Hague Rock Light
54 33.1N, 162 24.1W, Fl W 4s,
60 ft., 6 mi., NR on square frame.

HAINES AND SKAGWAY

Katzehin River Flats Lighted Bell Buoy 4
59 11.7N, 135 20.1W, Fl R 6s,
3 mi., red.

Battery Point Light
59 12.6N, 135 21.9W, Fl W 4s,
60 ft., 6 mi., NR on skeleton tower,
obscured from 325° to 157°.

Haines Small Boat Harbor Light 2
59 13.9N, 135 26.3W, Fl R 2.5s,
26 ft., 3 mi., TR on skeleton tower.

Nukdik Point Daybeacon 1
59 14.7N, 135 25.3W, 30 ft., SG
on post.

Indian Rock Light
59 16.4N, 135 24.0W, Fl W 6s,
15 ft., 7 mi., NR on pile structure,
higher intensity beam down
Chilkoot Inlet.

Skagway Terminal 2 Dock Light
59 26.9N, 135 19.6W, F R, 30 ft.,
on mooring dolphin, private aid.

Skagway Breakwater Light 2
59 26.9N, 135 19.4W, Fl R 4s, 19 ft.,
4 mi., TR on skeleton tower.

Skagway Terminal Dock Light
59 27.0N, 135 19.7W, Fl R 4s, on
dolphin, private aid.

Light
59 26.8N, 135 21.7W, Fl W 2.5s,
20 ft., 5 mi., NR on skeleton tower.

Hamilton Island Daybeacon
56 06.9N, 133 34.2W, 16 ft., NR on
square frame.

Hanin Rock Light
57 50.1N, 152 18.9W, Q W, 43 ft.,
6 mi., white cylindrical house.
Also see Kodiak.

Hanks Island Rock Lighted Bell Buoy 5
60 36.0N, 145 59.5W, Fl G 4s,
4 mi., green.
Also see Prince William Sound.

Hanus Reef Light
58 07.8N, 135 00.0W, Fl W 2.5s,
25 ft., 6 mi., NR on skeleton
tower on concrete pier.

Harriet Point Light
60 23.8N, 152 14.2W, Fl W 6s,
95 ft., 8 mi., NR on square frame,
higher intensity beam up and
down channel.

Harris Island Light 2
55 00.2N, 131 32.1W, Fl R 6s,
16 ft., 4 mi., TR on skeleton tower,
obscured from 294° to 083°.

Harvester Island Spit Light 2
57 38.2N, 153 59.7W, Fl R 4s,
22 ft., 3 mi., TR on square frame
on dolphin.

Hat Island Light
56 22.5N, 132 25.6W, Fl W 4s,
23 ft., 6 mi., NR on skeleton tower,
obscured from 091° to 234°.
Also see Zimovia Strait.

Hattie Island (W side of island, Canada)
55 17.2N, 129 58.4W, Fl W 6s, 21 ft.,
5 mi., orange circular slatwork
daymark on pole, visible 171° to
336°.

HAWK INLET

Buoy 2
58 04.7N, 134 47.8W, red nun.

Daybeacon 3
58 05.5N, 134 47.1W, SG on pile.

Buoy 4
58 05.2N, 134 46.9W, red nun.

Light 5
58 05.6N, 134 46.7W, Fl G 4s,
33 ft., 4 mi., SG on pile.

Range Front Light
58 05.1N, 134 46.5W, Q W, 19 ft.,
KRW on single pile.

Range Rear Light
58 04.9N, 134 46.5W, Iso W 6s,
23 ft., KRW on single pile.

Light 6
58 05.9N, 134 46.4W, Fl R 4s,
33 ft., 4 mi., TR on pile.

East Shoal Light 8
58 06.2N, 134 46.4W, Fl R 2.5s,
20 ft., 4 mi., TR on dolphin.

Entrance Light
58 06.5N, 134 46.5W, Fl W 4s,
13 ft., 4 mi., NR on skeleton tower,
obscured from 006° to 264°.

Helm Bay Light
55 34.8N, 131 55.7W, Fl W 4s, 14 ft.,
7 mi., NR on skeleton tower.

Helm Point Light
55 49.6N, 134 16.2W, Fl W 6s,
140 ft., 6 mi., NR on skeleton
tower, obscured from 067° to 188°.

Helm Rock Lighted Buoy 8
56 22.2N, 133 38.6W, Fl R 4s, 4 mi.,
red.

HERENDEEN BAY

Herendeen Bay
Aids maintained from May 15 to
Dec. 10.
Also see Port Moller.

Buoy 4
55 58.1N, 160 39.2W, red nun.

Buoy 5
55 57.9N, 160 38.6W, green can.

Buoys 6–9
Red nuns and green cans.

Hermanos Islands
See San Christoval Channel.

Hetta Inlet Log Boom Buoys (9)
55 15.8N, 132 39.2W, white and
orange buoys marked DANGER
LOG BOOM, private aids.

Hid Reef Lighted Whistle Buoy 2
55 04.1N, 131 40.5W, Fl R 4s,
4 mi., red.

High Island Light
55 24.1N, 132 09.9W, Fl W 6s,
40 ft., 6 mi., NR on skeleton tower,
obscured from 330° to 132°.

Highwater Island Shoal Lighted Buoy 23
57 16.9N, 135 36.1W, Fl G 4s,
3 mi., green.
Also see Neva Strait.

Hill Island Light
57 43.7N, 136 16.6W, Fl W 4s,
60 ft., 6 mi., NR on square frame,
obscured from 111° to 264°.

Hobart Bay Light 2
57 23.9N, 133 27.9W, Fl R 4s,
30 ft., 4 mi., TR on steel post.

Hog Island Light
58 00.1N, 152 41.2W, Fl W 4s (2 R
sectors), 40 ft., white 6 mi., red
4 mi., NR on skeleton tower, red
sector from 024° to 088° and from
188° to 242°, obscured from 088°
to 188°.

Hog Rocks Light
55 10.7N, 131 17.0W, Fl W 4s,
23 ft., 7 mi., NR on truncated
multi-pile structure.

Hoggatt Bay Light
56 45.9N, 134 39.3W, Fl W 2.5s,
40 ft., 5 mi., NR on skeleton tower,
obscured from 134° to 307°.

**Hoggatt Reef (Peril Strait) Light
25**
57 32.8N, 135 30.9W, Fl G 6s,
25 ft., 4 mi., SG on pile.

HOLKHAM BAY

Range Front Light
57 46.0N, 133 38.6W, Q W, KRW
on skeleton tower, light maintained from May 1 to Oct. 1.

Range Rear Light
48 yards, 215° from front light,
Oc W 4s, KRW on skeleton tower,
light maintained from May 1 to
Oct. 1.

Buoy 1
57 46.9N, 133 38.0W, green can,
maintained from May 1 to Oct. 1.

Buoy 2
57 46.8N, 133 37.5W, red nun,
maintained from May 1 to Oct. 1.

Hollis Ferry Terminal
See Clark Bay.

Homer
See Kachemak Bay.

Hood Bay Buoy 1
57 25.5N, 134 33.0W, green can.

**Hood Bay Entrance Lighted
Buoy 2**
57 25.1N, 134 33.4W, Fl R 6s,
4 mi., red.

Hoonah Breakwater Light 2
58 06.5N, 135 27.0W, Fl R 4s,
38 ft., 3 mi., TR on post.

Hoonah Breakwater Light 3
58 06.4N, 135 26.9W, Fl G 2.5s,
38 ft., 3 mi., SG on post.

Hooper Bay Buoy 1
Green oil drum, maintained from
June 1 to Aug. 1, private aid.

**Hooper Bay Channel Stakes
(about 12)**
Maintained from June 1 to Aug.
1, private aids.

Horse Shoal Light 1
58 15.2N, 134 42.3W, Fl G 6s,
15 ft., 4 mi., SG on pile.

**Humboldt Harbor Breakwater
Light 2**
55 19.9N, 160 30.2W, Fl R 2.5s,
24 ft., 3 mi., TR on pile.

**Humboldt Harbor Breakwater
Light 3**
55 19.9N, 160 30.1W, Fl G 2.5s,
24 ft., 3 mi., SG on pile.

Hump Island Daybeacon
55 31.1N, 131 45.3W, NR on
skeleton tower.

**Humpback Rock Lighted Whistle
Buoy 1**
57 42.8N, 152 14.2W, Fl G 4s,
4 mi., green.

**Hutchinson Reef Lighted Whistle
Buoy 4**
57 50.0N, 152 17.4W, Fl R 4s,
4 mi., red.
Also see Kodiak.

Hydaburg
See Sukkwan Strait.

Hyder Harbor Entrance Buoy 1
55 54.3N, 130 00.6W, green can.

Icy Passage Light 2
58 23.2N, 135 37.8W, Fl R 6s,
22 ft., 4 mi., TR on skeleton tower.

Idaho Rock Lighted Buoy 4
55 19.0N, 131 36.1W, Fl R 4s, 4 mi.,
red.
Also see Tongass Narrows.

Ikatan Bay Light 3
54 46.9N, 163 21.9W, Fl G 4s,
78 ft., 5 mi., SG on skeleton tower.

Ikatan Bay Light 1
54 46.5N, 163 11.1W, Fl G 6s,
81 ft., 6 mi., SG on skeleton tower.

Iliasik Islands Light
55 02.2N, 161 56.4W, Fl W 6s,
95 ft., 7 mi., NR on square frame,
obscured from 120.5° to 254°.

Iliasik Passage Buoy 6
55 02.0N, 161 56.1W, red nun.

Iliasik Passage Lighted Buoy 5
55 01.7N, 161 55.3W, Fl G 2.5s,
4 mi., green.

Iliuliuk Bay and Harbor
See Unalaska Island.

Ilkognak Rock Light 1
57 54.8N, 152 47.0W, Fl G 4s,
18 ft., 4 mi., SG on skeleton
tower, higher intensity beam
toward 078°.

Indian Rock Light
59 16.4N, 135 24.0W, Fl W 6s,
15 ft., 7 mi., NR on pile structure,
higher intensity beam down
Chilkoot Inlet.
Also see Haines and Skagway.

**Indian Rock (Felice Strait)
Lighted Buoy 6**
55 01.8N, 131 20.8W, Fl R 4s,
3 mi., red.

Inner Point Daybeacon
58 13.9N, 134 35.4W, NR on
skeleton tower.

ISANOTSKI STRAIT

Light 8
54 51.4N, 163 23.5W, Fl R 6s,
21 ft., 5 mi., TR on skeleton tower.

Light 5
54 49.5N, 163 22.5W, Fl G 6s,
14 ft., 4 mi., SG on skeleton tower.

Light 4
54 48.9N, 163 21.7W, Fl R 4s,
4 mi., TR on square frame,
obscured from 000° to 135°.

J

Japonski Harbor
See Alidale Channel.

Jarvis Island Light 1
55 30.4N, 132 33.6W, Fl G 4s,
12 ft., 4 mi., SG on spindle.
Also see Clark Bay.

Johnstone Point Light
60 29.0N, 146 36.8W, Fl W 5s,
57 ft., 14 mi., NR on skeleton
tower, obscured from 256° to 052°.
Also see Prince William Sound.

Junction Island Light J
57 59.9N, 136 19.0W, Q W, 20 ft.,
4 mi., NR on skeleton tower,
obscured from 042° to 171°.
Also see Lisianski Inlet.

JUNEAU AND GASTINEAU CHANNEL

Also see Mendenhall Bar
Channel.

Marmion Island Light
58 11.9N, 134 15.4W, Fl W 6s,
50 ft., 6 mi., NR on skeleton tower,
obscured from 022° to 147°.

Sheep Creek Light 2
58 15.5N, 134 19.8W, Fl R 4s, 12 ft.,
5 mi., TR on small house on
square pile structure, higher
intensity beam down channel.

**Sheep Creek Salmon Pen Lights
(2)**
58 15.8N, 134 20.3W, Fl Y 2.5s,
5 mi., battery boxes, private aids.

Juneau Isle Light
58 16.6N, 134 23.1W, Fl W 2.5s,
15 ft., 6 mi., NR on skeleton tower.

Douglas Boat Harbor Light 1D
58 16.6N, 134 23.2W, Fl G 4s,
17 ft., 4 mi., SG on skeleton tower.

Rock Dump Lighted Buoy 2A
58 17.1N, 134 23.8W, Q R, 3 mi.,
red.

Lawson Creek Bar Light 3
58 17.3N, 134 24.4W, Fl G 2.5s,
22 ft., 4 mi., SG on dolphin, higher intensity beam down channel.

Light 4
58 17.8N, 134 25.4W, Fl R 2.5s,
15 ft., 3 mi., , TR on dolphin.

Harris Harbor Light 1H
58 18.1N, 134 25.8W, Fl G 4s,
15 ft., 4 mi., SG on dolphin.

Aurora Basin Light 1A
58 18.3N, 134 26.0W, Fl G 2.5s,
25 ft., 3 mi., SG on breakwater.

Aurora Basin Light 1B
58 18.4N, 134 25.4W, Fl G 4s,
31 ft., 4 mi., SG on skeleton tower.

Norway Point Mooring Buoys (2)
58 18.5N, 134 26.5W, white spherical, private aids.

K

KACHEMAK BAY

Tutka Bay Entrance Buoy 2
59 29.5N, 151 33.2W, red nun.

Cohen Island Rock Light
59 33.0N, 151 28.0W, Fl W 4s,
79 ft., 8 mi., NR on skeleton
tower, higher intensity beam
from 060° to 120°.

Archimandritof Shoals Lighted Buoy 3
59 35.5N, 151 26.2W, Fl G 2.5s,
3 mi., green.

Homer Spit Light
59 36.0N, 151 24.6W, Fl G 6s, 34 ft.,
5 mi., on tower on top of hotel
roof, obscured from 040° to 060°.

Homer Main Dock Lights (2)
59 36.2N, 151 24.6W, F R, on pier,
private aids.

Homer Breakwater Light 2
59 36.2N, 151 24.9W, Q R, 20 ft.,
4 mi., TR on skeleton tower.

Homer Chevron Fuel Float Lights (2)
59 36.2N, 151 25.1W, F R, 2 ft.,
on float, private aids.

Homer Fuel Dock Lights (2)
59 36.3N, 151 25.0W, Q G, 30 ft.,
on dock, private aids.

Homer Spit

South Lighted Mooring Buoy
59 36.2N, 151 24.8W, Fl W 6s,
white with blue band, private aid.

Deepwater South Dolphin Light
59 36.3N, 151 24.8W, Fl R 6s,
12 ft., on dolphin, private aid.

Deepwater South Dock Lights (2)
59 36.3N, 151 24.9W, F R, 30 ft.,
on pier, private aids.

Deepwater North Dock Lights (2)
59 36.4N, 151 24.9W, F R, 30 ft.,
on pier, private aids.

Deepwater Dolphin Light
59 36.4N, 151 24.9W, Fl R 4s, on
dolphin, private aid.

North Lighted Mooring Buoy
59 36.5N, 151 24.9W, Fl W 6s,
white with blue band, private aid.

Gull Island Light 2
59 35.1N, 151 19.8W, Fl R 4s,
94 ft., 4 mi., TR on skeleton tower.

Halibut Cove Light 2
59 36.0N, 151 12.9W, Fl R 6s,
70 ft., 4 mi., TR on small house,
obscured from 024° to 119°.

Halibut Cove Daybeacon 4
59 35.8N, 151 12.7W, TR on pipe
on rock.

Kake
See Keku Strait.

Kakuktahuk Pass Entrance Light
63 09.2N, 163 35.6W, Fl W 2.5s,
18 ft., 8 mi., NR on skeleton
tower, radar reflector, maintained
from July 1 to Nov. 1.

Kakul Narrows Light 4
57 22.4N, 135 41.0W, Fl R 2.5s,
27 ft., 4 mi., TR on skeleton tower.

Kakul Rock Lighted Buoy 2
57 21.7N, 135 41.9W, Fl R 6s,
4 mi., red.

KALGIN ISLAND

Kalgin Island South Light
60 20.7N, 152 05.1W, Fl W 2.5s,
65 ft., 6 mi., NR on square frame.

**Kalgin Island West Channel
Lighted Bell Buoy 2**
60 26.9N, 152 06.6W, Fl R 2.5s,
4 mi., red, maintained from
May 1 to Nov. 1.

Kalgin Island Light
60 29.0N, 151 50.6W, Fl W 4s,
140 ft., 7 mi., NR on square
frame, obscured from 028°
to 142°.

Kane Islands Light 25
57 19.4N, 135 39.8W, Fl G 2.5s,
40 ft., 4 mi., SG on square frame,
obscured from 342° to 103°.
Also see Neva Strait.

KARHEEN PASSAGE

Tonowek Narrows Daybeacon 2T
55 45.3N, 133 20.5W, TR on pile.

Daybeacon 1
55 46.3N, 133 19.4W, SG on skeleton tower.

Point Swift Shoal Buoy 2
55 46.3N, 133 18.9W, red nun.

Buoy 3
55 46.5N, 133 18.0W, green can.

Buoy 4
55 46.9N, 133 17.0W, red nun.

Buoy 5
55 47.2N, 133 17.4W, green can.

Chapin Island Range Front Daybeacon
55 47.8N, 133 18.7W, KRW on skeleton tower.

Chapin Island Range Rear Daybeacon
60 yards, 306° from front daybeacon, KRW on skeleton tower.

Daybeacon 6
55 47.8N, 133 18.4W, TR on spindle.

Buoy 8
55 48.4N, 133 19.0W, red nun.

Peep Rock Light
55 49.1N, 133 19.9W, Fl W 4s,
17 ft., 7 mi., NR on skeleton tower.

Kasaan Light
55 32.1N, 132 23.8W, Fl W 4s,
12 ft., 6 mi., NR on small house,
obscured from 120.5° to 302.5°.

Kasaan Log Boom Buoys (3)
55 29.5N, 132 21.6W, white and
orange buoys worded DANGER
LOG BOOM, private aids.

Kashevarof Passage Daybeacon 2
56 12.9N, 133 01.3W, 25 ft., TR on
pile.

Kashevarof Passage Light
56 10.8N, 133 01.3W, Fl W 6s,
27 ft., 6 mi., NR on skeleton tower.

Kasiana Island Shoal Daybeacon 1
57 05.4N, 135 24.4W, SG on pile.
Also see Sitka Sound.

KASILOF

Entrance Channel Lighted Buoy 1
60 23.4N, 151 23.6W, Fl G 2.5s,
4 mi., green, maintained from
May 1 to Nov. 1.

Kasilof River Channel Light
60 23.2N, 151 18.9W, Iso W 6s,
12 ft., 6 mi., NR on skeleton tower,
maintained from May 1 to Nov. 1.

**Entrance Channel Buoys (9,
marks channel into Kasilof River)**
Red nuns and green cans, maintained from May 1 to Nov. 1.

Kaslokan Point Light 2
55 06.2N, 162 31.5W, Fl R 4s,
15 ft., 5 mi., TR on steel square
frame, obscured from 193° to
336°.
Also see Cold Bay.

Katzehin River Flats Lighted Bell Buoy 4
59 11.7N, 135 20.1W, Fl R 6s,
3 mi., red.
Also see Haines and Skagway.

KEKU STRAIT

Entrance Light (southern portion)
56 31.6N, 133 43.8W, Fl W 6s,
20 ft., 4 mi., NR on pile.

Daybeacon 2
56 33.9N, 133 43.4W, TR on pile.

Daybeacon 4
56 34.8N, 133 42.8W, TR on pile.

Daybeacon 4A
56 35.0N, 133 42.5W, TR on pile.

Daybeacons 6–43
TRs and SGs on piles.

Keku Strait Entrance Island Light
56 48.6N, 133 47.9W, Fl W 2.5s,
4 mi., NR on skeleton tower.

Salt Point Light
56 50.7N, 133 52.0W, Fl W 6s,
17 ft., 3 mi., NR on pile, obscured
from 168° to 259°.

Kake Entrance Light 2
56 59.1N, 134 01.2W, Fl R 2.5s,
27 ft., 5 mi., TR on spindle.

Kake Cannery Flats Buoy 5
56 58.2N, 133 57.3W, green can.

Kake Harbor Light 7
56 58.3N, 133 56.9W, Fl G 2.5s,
25 ft., 4 mi., SG on spindle.

Kake Channel Lighted Buoy 3
56 59.3N, 133 59.5W, Fl G 4s,
3 mi., green.

Kake Harbor Daybeacon 1
56 58.4N, 133 56.8W, SG on post.

Kake Cannery Flats Buoy 9
56 57.9N, 133 56.2W, green can.

Kake Salmon Pen Light
56 58.0N, 133 55.7W, Fl W 2.5s,
10 ft., on small house, maintained from May 1 to Sept. 30,
private aid.

Kake Harbor Light
56 57.6N, 133 57.2W, Fl W 4s,
16 ft., 5 mi., NR on square frame,
obscured from 285° to 097°.

Kake Ferry Terminal North Light
56 57.7N, 133 55.3W, Fl R 6s,
32 ft., on dolphin, private aid.

Kake Ferry Terminal Middle Light
56 57.7N, 133 55.3W, F R, 32 ft.,
on dolphin, private aid.

Kake Ferry Terminal South Light
56 57.6N, 133 55.3W, F R, 32 ft.,
on dolphin, private aid.

**Sealaska Timber Company
Mooring Buoys (3)**
White cans, private aids.

Portage Pass Light 10
56 57.4N, 133 55.4W, Fl R 4s,
15 ft., 4 mi., TR on pile.

Portage Pass Daybeacon 11
56 57.0N, 133 54.4W, SG on pile.

Portage Pass Light 13
56 56.8N, 133 54.0W, Fl G 2.5s,
15 ft., 3 mi., SG on spindle.
Also see Burnt Island Channel.

Kelp Rocks Buoy 1
55 09.5N, 131 37.9W, green can.

KENAI

Kenai Entrance Channel Lighted Buoy 1KE
60 31.3N, 151 20.6W, Fl G 4s, 4 mi., green, maintained from May 1 to Nov. 1.

Kenai River Light 3
60 33.0N, 151 15.7W, Fl G 2.5s, 40 ft., 4 mi., TR on pile.

Collier Pier Lights (2)
60 40.4N, 151 23.5W, Q R, 22 ft., on dolphins, private aids.

Philips LNG Dock Lights (2)
60 40.7N, 151 23.8W, Q R, 40 ft., on pier, private aids.

Kenai Pipeline Company Dock Lights (2)
60 40.9N, 151 23.8W, F R, 35 ft., on dolphins, private aids.

Kenasnow Rock Lighted Buoy 2
57 30.0N, 134 36.3W, Fl R 2.5s, 4 mi., red.

Ketchikan
See Tongass Narrows.

Key Reef Light
56 09.6N, 132 49.9W, Fl W 6s, 43 ft., 6 mi., NR on pile on truncated concrete pyramid.

Khantaak Island Light
59 33.6N, 139 47.0W, Fl W 4s, 28 ft., 6 mi., NR on skeleton tower, obscured from 149° to 311°. *Also see* Yakutat Bay.

Khaz Breaker Lighted Whistle Buoy 2
57 31.2N, 136 07.7W, Fl R 6s, 4 mi., red.

KILLISNOO HARBOR

Entrance Lighted Buoy 2
57 27.7N, 134 34.5W, Fl R 2.5s, 4 mi., red.

Light 3
57 28.0N, 134 34.0W, Fl G 6s, 23 ft., 4 mi., SG on spindle.

Lone Rock Daybeacon 4
57 27.9N, 134 33.5W, TR on pile.

Lighted Buoy 6
57 28.3N, 134 33.8W, Fl R 4s, 3 mi., red.

Angoon Ferry Terminal Light
57 28.3N, 134 33.9W, Fl R 6s, 32 ft., on dolphin, private aid.

Light 7
57 28.3N, 134 34.1W, Fl G 4s, 16 ft., 4 mi., SG on small house on skeleton structure on concrete pier.

Killisnoo Island Reef Buoy 2
57 28.7N, 134 36.0W, red nun.

KING COVE

Deepwater South Dolphin Light
55 03.3N, 162 19.4W, Fl R 6s, 21 ft., 3 mi., on dolphin, private aid.

Deepwater North Dolphin Light
55 03.4N, 162 19.4W, Fl R 6s, 21 ft., 3 mi., on dolphin, private aid.

Harbor Entrance Light 1
55 03.5N, 162 19.4W, Fl G 2.5s, 25 ft., 3 mi., SG on pile.

Harbor Entrance Light 2
55 03.5N, 162 19.4W, Fl R 6s, 23 ft., 4 mi., TR on pile.

Kingsmill Point Light
56 50.6N, 134 25.2W, Fl W 6s, 25 ft., 6 mi., NR on small house, obscured from 207° to 005°.

KLAG BAY

Entrance Daybeacon 1
57 36.7N, 136 06.1W, SG on post.

The Gate Daybeacon A
57 36.8N, 136 06.1W, NG on post on concrete.

Klag Island Daybeacon B
57 37.1N, 136 06.0W, 30 ft., NR on pile.

KLAWOCK INLET

Klawock Reef Lighted Buoy 1
55 30.6N, 133 11.2W, Fl G 4s, 4 mi., green.

Klawock Reef Buoy 2
55 30.4N, 133 11.2W, red nun.

Klawock Junction Lighted Buoy KL
55 30.4N, 133 10.6W, Fl (2+1) R 6s, 4 mi., red and green bands.

Klawock Reef Buoy 3
55 30.5N, 133 10.5W, green can.

Klawock Tow Channel Entrance Light 2TC
55 29.9N, 133 11.6W, Fl R 6s, 21 ft., 4 mi., TR on spindle.

Klawock Tow Channel Daybeacon 3TC
55 30.2N, 133 10.9W, SG on pile.

Klawock Tow Channel Daybeacon 4TC
55 30.3N, 133 10.4W, TR on pile.

Buoy 6
55 30.3N, 133 09.6W, red nun.

Shoal Lighted Buoy 8
55 32.6N, 133 07.1W, Fl R 2.5s, 4 mi., red.

Wadleigh Island Buoy 9
55 33.6N, 133 06.9W, green can.

Klawock Logging Dock Lights (2)
55 33.2N, 133 06.6W, Fl R 10s, 18 ft., on dock, private aids.

Highwater Rock Daybeacon 1
55 33.6N, 133 06.3W, SG on pile.

Klawock Harbor Entrance Light 2
55 33.4N, 133 06.3W, Fl R 4s, 20 ft., 4 mi., TR on small house on skeleton tower on concrete pier.

Klawock Ledge Daybeacon 3
55 33.4N, 133 06.2W, SG on pile.

Klawock Control Daybeacons (3)
NW on pile worded SLOW 5 MPH, one located on Klawock Ledge Daybeacon 3 and one on each corner of dock, private aids.

Klokachef Island Light
57 24.2N, 135 54.4W, Fl W 6s, 85 ft., 7 mi., NR on square frame, obscured from 155.5° to 291°.

Knight Island Passage
See Prince William Sound.

Knik Arm Shoal Lighted Buoy 7
61 12.2N, 150 05.4W, Q G, 4 mi., green, maintained from May 1 to Nov. 1.

Knik Arm Shoal North Side Buoy 2KA
61 12.4N, 150 05.6W, red nun, maintaincd from May 1 to Nov. 1.

Knudson Cove Daybeacon
55 28.4N, 131 47.8W, NR on pile.

Knudson Cove Floating Dock Daybeacon
55 28.4N, 131 47.8W, SG on breakwater, private aid.

KODIAK

North Entrance

Williams Reef Lighted Whistle Buoy 1
57 50.3N, 152 09.5W, Fl G 4s, 4 mi., green.

Channel Lighted Whistle Buoy 3
57 50.9N, 152 13.7W, Fl G 6s, 4 mi., green.

Hutchinson Reef Lighted Whistle Buoy 4
57 50.0N, 152 17.4W, Fl R 4s, 4 mi., red.

Hanin Rock Light
57 50.1N, 152 18.9W, Q W, 43 ft., 6 mi., white cylindrical house.

Channel Lighted Whistle Buoy 5
57 49.3N, 152 18.0W, Fl G 2.5s, 4 mi., green.

Channel Lighted Whistle Buoy 7
57 48.9N, 152 18.7W, Fl G 4s, 4 mi., green.

Channel Lighted Buoy 8
57 48.7N, 152 19.5W, Fl R 2.5s, 4 mi., red.

Spruce Cape Light
57 49.3N, 152 19.5W, FlW 10s, 40 ft., 18 mi., NR on skeleton tower.

Channel Lighted Buoy 10
57 48.2N, 152 20.8W, Fl R 6s, 4 mi., red.

Woody Island Light
57 47.8N, 152 20.3W, Fl W 6s, 50 ft., 5 mi., NR on square frame, obscured from 228° to 040°. *Also see* Woody Island.

Channel Buoy 11
57 47.7N, 152 20.9W, green can.

Channel Lighted Bell Buoy KH
57 47.7N, 152 21.5W, Fl (2+1) R 6s, 4 mi., red and green bands.

Channel Buoy 13
57 47.4N, 152 22.1W, green can.

Cyane Rock Lighted Bell Buoy 15
57 47.4N, 152 23.2W, Q G, 4 mi., green.

Kodiak Harbor

Ferry Dock Lights (2)
57 47.2N, 152 24.1W, F R, 18 ft., pedestal, private aids.

Harbor Daybeacon 2
57 47.1N, 152 24.5W, TR on pile.

Boat Harbor Light 1
57 47.1N, 152 24.6W, Fl G 4s, 18 ft., 5 mi., SG on skeleton tower.

Saint Herman Bay and Harbor

North Entrance Daybeacon 1
57 47.0N, 152 24.5W, SG on pile.

North Entrance Light 2
57 46.9N, 152 24.6W, Fl R 6s, 17 ft., 4 mi., TR on skeleton tower.

South Entrance Light 8
57 46.7N, 152 25.0W, Fl R 2.5s, 8 ft., 4 mi., TR on multi-pile structure.

South Approach Buoy 1
57 46.5N, 152 25.3W, green can.

St. Herman Harbor South Entrance Light 3
57 46.5N, 152 25.1W, Fl G 4s, 4 mi., SG on spindle.

St. Herman Harbor South Entrance Light 4
57 46.4N, 152 25.1W, Fl R 6s, 4 mi., TR on spindle.

South Entrance Daybeacon 7
57 46.7N, 152 25.0W, SG on pile.

St. Paul Harbor

Entrance Midchannel Lighted Whistle Buoy SP
57 44.1N, 152 24.3W, Mo (A) W, 5 mi., red and white stripes with red spherical topmark.

Entrance Light
57 44.3N, 152 25.8W, Fl W 6s, 38 ft., 10 mi., NR on skeleton tower.

Entrance Channel Lighted Bell Buoy 2
57 44.5N, 152 25.2W, Fl R 4s, 4 mi., rcd.

Entrance Channel Lighted Whistle Buoy 3
57 44.4N, 152 25.5W, Fl G 2.5s, 3 mi., green.

Entrance Channel Buoy 5
57 44.5N, 152 26.1W, green can.

Entrance Channel Lighted Bell Buoy 6
57 45.1N, 152 26.9W, Q R, 3 mi., red.

Entrance Channel Lighted Buoy 7
57 45.3N, 152 27.0W, Fl G 2.5s, 3 mi., green.

Gull Island Rocks Lighted Buoy 8
57 46.6N, 152 25.9W, Fl R 6s, 4 mi., red.

Gull Island Lighted Buoy GI
57 46.7N, 152 26.0W, Fl (2+1) G 6s, 3 mi., green with red band.

Container Terminal Pier 3 Lights (6)
57 46.9N, 152 26.1W, F R, 17 ft., on pier, private aids.

Kodiak City Dock Pier 2 Lights (2)
57 47.1N, 152 25.5W, F R, 16 ft., on pedestal, private aids.

Gull Island Lighted Buoy 10
57 46.9N, 152 25.2W, Fl R 2.5s, 3 mi., red.

Entrance Channel Buoy 11
57 47.0N, 152 24.7W, green can.

Womens Bay

Front Range Light
57 43.4N, 152 28.8W, Q W, 43 ft., KRB on skeleton tower.

Rear Range Light
630 yards, 211.1° from front light, Oc W 4s, 90 ft., KRB on skeleton tower.

Entrance Channel Buoy 2
57 44.4N, 152 27.9W, red nun.

Entrance Channel Lighted Bell Buoy 3
57 44.3N, 152 27.7W, Fl G 2.5s, 4 mi., green.

Entrance Channel Buoy 5
57 44.0N, 152 28.1W, green can.

Entrance Channel Lighted Buoy 6
57 43.8N, 152 28.5W, Fl R 2.5s,
4 mi., red.

Entrance Channel Lighted Bell Buoy 7
57 43.8N, 152 28.4W, Fl G 4s,
4 mi., green.

Entrance Channel Lighted Buoy 8
57 43.7N, 152 28.7W, Fl R 4s,
3 mi., red.

Entrance Channel Buoy 9
57 43.5N, 152 28.7W, green can.

Entrance Channel Lighted Buoy 11
57 43.4N, 152 29.4W, Fl G 6s,
4 mi., green.

Entrance Channel Buoy 12
57 43.4N, 152 30.0W, red nun.

Entrance Channel Lighted Buoy 13
57 43.2N, 152 30.2W, Q G, 3 mi.,
green.

Entrance Channel Lighted Buoy 14
57 42.9N, 152 30.7W, Q R, 3 mi.,
red.

Lighted Buoy 16
57 43.0N, 152 31.7W, Fl R 4s,
3 mi., red.

Buoy 18
57 43.6N, 152 31.2W, red nun.

Middle Shoal Buoy 19
57 43.8N, 152 31.1W, green can.

Koka Island Passage Daybeacon 1
56 54.8N, 135 23.7W, SG on pile.
Also see Sitka Sound.

Kokenhenic Bar Channel Light K
60 13.4N, 145 09.0W, Fl W 4s,
12 ft., 5 mi., NR on skeleton tower,
maintained from May 1 to Oct. 1.
Also see Copper River Delta.

Koniuji Island Light 5
57 55.8N, 152 50.3W, Fl G 2.5s,
70 ft., 4 mi., SG on skeleton
tower, higher intensity beam
toward 296.5°.

KOOTZNAHOO INLET

Light 2
57 30.3N, 134 35.0W, Fl R 4s,
14 ft., 5 mi., TR on post.

Daybeacon 4
57 30.0N, 134 34.7W, TR on steel
post.

Daybeacon 6
57 29.9N, 134 34.2W, TR on pile.

Kotzebue Buoys (about 8, mark entrance to Kotzebue)
Red nuns or green cans, maintained from July 1 to Sept. 20.

Koyuk River Entrance Buoys (about 12, mark sides of channel across flats, outer buoy about 9 miles from mouth of river)
Red or green oil drums, maintained from July 1 to Oct. 1.

Kupreanof Strait Buoy K
57 59.6N, 153 10.8W, green and red bands, can.

KUSKOKWIM BAY

Buoys maintained from June 1 to Oct. 1.

Buoy 2
59 18.7N, 162 18.5W, red nun.

Buoy 3
59 27.0N, 162 18.8W, green can.

Buoys 4–12
Red nuns and green cans.

Kuskokwim River Buoys (about 30, mark from Kuskokwim River Entrance to Johnson River)
Red or green oil drums, maintained from June 1 to Oct. 1.

Kwiguk Pass Entrance Light
62 48.1N, 164 53.1W, Fl W 2.5s,
18 ft., 8 mi., NR on skeleton
tower, radar reflector.

Kwigillingol River Entrance Buoys (about 12, mark channel into river)
Red or green oil drums, maintained from May 15 to Oct. 15.

LARSEN BAY

Entrance Rock Lighted Buoy 1
57 32.7N, 153 58.6W, Fl G 2.5s,
4 mi., green.

Buoy 2
57 32.5N, 153 59.1W, red nun.

Buoy 3
57 32.5N, 153 59.1W, green can.

Range Front Light
57 32.7N, 154 00.2W, Q W, 35 ft.,
KRG on skeleton tower.

Range Rear Light
140 yards, 291.5° from front light,
Iso W 6s, 45 ft., KRG on skeleton
tower.

Larzatita Island Reef Light
55 35.0N, 133 19.7W, Fl W 4s,
22 ft., 6 mi., NR on caisson.
Also see San Christoval Channel.

Last Timber Point Light 6
57 58.7N, 152 59.0W, Fl R 4s,
35 ft., 4 mi., TR on small house.

Latax Rocks Light
58 41.4N, 152 29.0W, Fl W 4s,
40 ft., 8 mi., NR on post.

Lazy Bay Light 2
56 53.5N, 154 13.0W, Fl R 4s,
25 ft., 6 mi., TR on skeleton tower.

Lemesurier Island Light
58 19.1N, 136 02.5W, Fl W 6s,
42 ft., 6 mi., NR on small house,
obscured from 280° to 086°.

Lemon Point Rock Light
56 04.4N, 134 06.7W, Fl W 6s,
26 ft., 5 mi., NR on multiple pile
structure.

Letnikof Cove Light 2
59 10.4N, 135 24.0W, Fl R 4s,
25 ft., 4 mi., TR on small house,
obscured from 256° to 358°.

Level Island Lighted Buoy 11
56 27.1N, 133 02.5W, Fl G 4s,
4 mi., green.

Lewis Reef Light 11
55 22.5N, 131 44.3W, Fl G 2.5s,
15 ft., 5 mi., SG on concrete
pyramid.
Also see Tongass Narrows.

Libby Island Light
58 16.4N, 136 46.4W, Fl W 4s,
53 ft., 6 mi., NR on pile, obscured
from 089° to 206°.

Liesnoi Shoal Lighted Buoy 11
57 24.2N, 135 36.6W, Fl G 2.5s,
4 mi., green.

Lighthouse Point Light
58 28.9N, 152 39.2W, Fl W 4s,
60 ft., 5 mi., NR on small house,
obscured from 285° to 073.5°.

Lincoln Rock West Light
56 03.4N, 132 41.8W, Fl W 6s,
58 ft., 8 mi., NR on skeleton
tower on concrete base.

LISIANSKI INLET

Light
58 05.9N, 136 28.0W, Fl W 6s,
65 ft., 5 mi., NR on small house,
obscured from 333° to 133°.

Column Point Buoy 1
58 07.0N, 136 27.6W, green can.

Light 2
58 04.2N, 136 25.9W, Fl R 4s,
55 ft., 4 mi., TR on small house,
obscured from 316° to 147°.

Daybeacon 4
58 02.1N, 136 22.0W, TR on
spindle.

Light 5
58 01.7N, 136 20.0W, Fl G 6s,
50 ft., 4 mi., SG on small house,
obscured from 149° to 320°.

Junction Island Light J
57 59.9N, 136 19.0W, Q W, 20 ft.,
4 mi., NR on skeleton tower,
obscured from 042° to 171°.

Pelican Entrance Light
57 57.3N, 136 13.8W, Fl W 4s,
17 ft., 5 mi., NR on post.

Lisianski Point Light 4
57 09.0N, 135 24.5W, Fl R 4s,
41 ft., 4 mi., TR on skeleton tower,
obscured from 158° to 318°.
Also see Sitka Sound.

LISIANSKI STRAIT

Light 2
57 50.7N, 136 26.1W, Fl R 4s,
53 ft., 4 mi., TR on skeleton tower,
obscured from 024° to 210°.

Light 4
57 56.1N, 136 21.7W, Fl R 6s,
25 ft., 5 mi., TR on skeleton
tower, obscured from 165° to
330°, high-intensity beam toward
southeast entrance to strait.

Daybeacon 5
57 59.1N, 136 22.7W, SG on pile.

Light 6
57 59.4N, 136 22.2W, Fl R 2.5s,
25 ft., 4 mi., TR on steel skeleton
tower.

Light 8
58 00.2N, 136 21.2W, Fl R 4s,
15 ft., 4 mi., TR on pile, obscured
from 275° to 036°.

Little Branch Bay Light
56 18.2N, 134 50.7W, Fl W 4s,
109 ft., 5 mi., NR on skeleton
tower, obscured from 111.5°
to 338°.

Little Island Light
58 32.4N, 135 02.8W, Fl W 4s,
50 ft., 7 mi., NR on skeleton tower.

**Lituya Bay Entrance Channel
Range Front Light**
58 37.6N, 137 39.5W, Q W, 22 ft.,
KRW on skeleton tower, obscured
from 048° to 348°, higher intensity on rangeline.

**Lituya Bay Entrance Channel
Range Rear Light**
475 yards, 007.5° from front
light, Iso W 6s, 37 ft., KRW on
skeleton tower, obscured from
170° to 222°, higher intensity
on rangeline.

Lively Islands Light
55 13.7N, 133 05.1W, Fl W 6s,
20 ft., 6 mi., NR on skeleton tower,
obscured from 158° to 333°.

Lively Rock Lighted Buoy 9
55 09.4N, 131 35.2W, Fl G 4s,
4 mi., green.

**Lizard Point (on extremity,
Canada)**
54 50.0N, 130 16.5W, Fl W 6s,
24 ft., white cylindrical tower.

Lonetree Point Light
59 58.9N, 148 12.0W, Fl W 4s,
30 ft., 6 mi., NR on skeleton tower,
obscured from 280° to 063°.
Also see Prince William Sound.

Lord Rock Light
54 43.5N, 130 49.2W, Fl W 4s,
38 ft., 7 mi., NR on skeleton tower.

Low Island Reef Buoy 7
57 55.0N, 152 32.9W, green can.

Low Point Daybeacon
56 27.5N, 132 55.5W, 12 ft., NR
on square frame.

**Lower Cook Inlet Junction
Lighted Bell Buoy CI**
60 04.7N, 152 09.8W, Fl (2+1) G 6s,
4 mi., green and red bands,
maintained from May 1 to Nov. 1.

Lowrie Island Light
54 51.6N, 133 31.9W, Fl W 6s,
52 ft., 9 mi., NR on skeleton tower.

**Lyman Anchorage Log Boom
Buoys (7)**
White and orange buoys worded
DANGER LOG BOOM, private
aids.

Lynn Canal Southwest Light
58 20.0N, 135 03.0W, Fl W 4s,
33 ft., 5 mi., NR on skeleton tower,
obscured from 358° to 168°.

M

**Makhnati Rock Lighted Whistle
Buoy 2**
57 02.2N, 135 23.8W, Fl R 2.5s,
4 mi., red.
Also see Western Channel.

Malina Point Light
58 02.3N, 153 22.0W, Fl W 2.5s,
80 ft., 6 mi., NR on small house,
higher intensity beam toward
110°.

**Marguerite Bay Log Rafting Boom
Markers (3)**
55 42.1N, 131 38.5W, NW on log
boom worded DANGER LOG
BOOM, private aids.

**Marguerite Bay Log Storage
Markers (2)**
55 42.1N, 131 38.1W, NW on log
boom worded DANGER LOG
BOOM, private aids.

Marmion Island Light
58 11.9N, 134 15.4W, Fl W 6s,
50 ft., 6 mi., NR on skeleton tower,
obscured from 022° to 147°.
Also see Juneau and Gastineau
Channel.

Martin Islands Light
60 09.9N, 144 36.4W, Fl W 6s,
150 ft., 6 mi., NR on skeleton
tower, obscured from 174° to 225°.

Mary Island Light
55 05.9N, 131 11.0W, Fl W 6s,
76 ft., 6 mi., on white square
tower on white building,
obscured from 341° to 150°.

Mastic Rock Daybeacon
55 15.5N, 131 24.1W, NR on pile.

McArthur Pass Light
59 27.8N, 150 20.2W, Fl W 4s,
45 ft., 6 mi., NR on skeleton tower,
obscured from 074° to 256°.

**McArthur Reef Lighted Bell
Buoy MR**
56 23.6N, 133 10.6W, Fl (2+1) G 6s,
4 mi., green and red bands.

McClellan Rock Light
57 27.2N, 135 01.6W, Fl W 6s,
17 ft., 7 mi., NR on cylindrical pier.

McDonald Rock Lighted Buoy MR
57 25.1N, 133 37.8W, Fl (2+1) R 6s,
4 mi., red and green bands.

**McHenry Ledge Lighted Bell
Buoy 2**
55 46.8N, 132 18.3W, Fl R 2.5s,
4 mi., red.

McLean Point Light
54 47.5N, 131 57.4W, Fl W 4s,
58 ft., 5 mi., NR on skeleton tower,
obscured from 012° to 165.5°.

Meares Island Light
55 16.3N, 133 10.6W, Fl W 6s,
13 ft., 5 mi., NR on skeleton tower,
obscured from 290° to 105°.

**Mekoryuk Breakwater Day-
beacon 2**
60 23.3N, 166 11.0W, TR on skeleton tower.

Mellen Rock Light
55 01.6N, 132 40.0W, Fl W 4s,
32 ft., 6 mi., NR on post.

MENDENHALL BAR CHANNEL

Also see Juneau and Gastineau
Channel.

Light 5
58 19.1N, 134 27.4W, Fl G 6s,
15 ft., 4 mi., SG on dolphin, tide
gauge shows depth over bar.

Buoy 7
58 19.4N, 134 27.9W, green can.

**Buoys (about 14, mark sides of
channel from Salmon Creek to
Daybeacon 14)**
Red nuns and green cans, maintained from April 1 to Nov. 1.

Daybeacon 14
58 20.8N, 134 32.3W, TR on pile.

Daybeacon 15
58 20.7N, 134 32.6W, SG on
dolphin.

Daybeacon 17
58 20.6N, 134 34.2W, SG on
dolphin.

Daybeacon 18
58 20.7N, 134 35.2W, TR on
dolphin.

Daybeacon 19
58 20.4N, 134 35.7W, SG on
dolphin.

Daybeacon 19A
58 20.2N, 134 36.7W, SG on
dolphin.

Light 21
58 19.9N, 134 36.9W, Fl G 4s,
15 ft., 4 mi., SG on dolphin, tide
gauge shows depth over bar.

METLAKATLA

Boat Harbor Light 2
55 07.9N, 131 35.1W, Fl R 2.5s,
20 ft., 4 mi., TR on spindle.

Inner Harbor Daybeacon 3
55 07.8N, 131 35.1W, SG on pile.

Inner Harbor Daybeacon 5
55 07.8N, 131 35.2W, SG on pile.

Inner Harbor Daybeacon 7
55 07.8N, 131 35.1W, SG on pile.

Village Point Light 4
55 07.9N, 131 34.6W, Fl R 4s,
40 ft., 3 mi., TR on skeleton tower.

Breakwater Light 1
55 07.7N, 131 34.2W, Fl G 4s,
10 ft., 4 mi., SG on skeleton
tower, concrete base.

**Middle Ground Shoal Lighted Bell
Buoy 2**
60 32.5N, 146 22.1W, Fl R 6s,
4 mi., red.
Also see Prince William Sound.

**Middle Point (Stephens Passage)
Light**
58 14.9N, 134 37.7W, Fl W 4s,
20 ft., 5 mi., NR on skeleton
tower on rock.

**Middle Point (Peril Strait)
Light 14**
57 26.3N, 135 34.5W, Fl R 4s,
23 ft., 4 mi., TR on skeleton tower.

Midway Islands Light
57 50.2N, 133 48.8W, Fl W 4s,
83 ft., 5 mi., NR on skeleton tower,
obscured from 162° to 210°.

Midway Rock Light MR
56 31.8N, 132 57.9W, Fl (2+1) R 6s,
16 ft., 4 mi., JR on skeleton
tower.
Also see Wrangell Narrows.

Minnie Reef Daybeacon 5
57 43.2N, 136 10.3W, SG on
spindle on concrete foundation.

Misery Island Daybeacon 1
55 44.6N, 132 16.6W, 15 ft., SG
on post.
Also see Myers Chuck.

Mitchell Point Lighted Buoy 9
56 25.4N, 133 10.8W, Fl G 6s,
4 mi., green.

Mitchell Rock Daybeacon
57 02.3N, 135 20.4W, NR on pile.
Also see Eastern Channel.

Moira Rock Light
55 05.0N, 131 59.9W, Fl W 4s,
40 ft., 5 mi., NR on skeleton tower.

Moose Point Light
60 57.3N, 150 41.2W, Fl W 4s,
15 ft., 9 mi., NR on skeleton
tower.

Moose Point Lighted Buoy MP
60 59.2N, 150 54.2W, Fl (2+1) R 6s,
4 mi., red and green bands,
maintained from May 1 to Nov. 1.

Morgan Point Light
55 02.4N, 162 20.2W, Fl W 4s,
120 ft., 6 mi., NR on steel square
frame, obscured from 039°
to 206°.

Morris Reef Lighted Bell Buoy 35
57 27.8N, 134 48.5W, Fl G 4s,
4 mi., green.

Morskoi Rock Buoy 2
57 20.6N, 135 53.7W, red nun,
maintained from May 15 to
Sept. 30.

MOSER BAY

Akhiok Reef Buoy 1
56 54.8N, 154 07.9W, green can.

Moser Bay Light 2
56 58.3N, 154 06.4W, Fl R 6s,
22 ft., 5 mi., TR on skeleton tower.

Moser Bay Buoy 3
56 58.4N, 154 06.8W, green can.

Moser Bay Buoy 4
56 58.9N, 154 08.0W, red nun.

Moss Cape Lighted Buoy 4
55 07.1N, 161 56.3W, Fl R 6s,
4 mi., red.

Mountain Point Daybeacon 2
55 17.6N, 131 32.5W, TR on pile.

Mountain Point Light
55 17.6N, 131 32.9W, Fl W 6s,
29 ft., 6 mi., NR on skeleton tower,
obscured from 117° to 282°.

Mummy Island Light
60 27.7N, 145 59.4W, Fl W 4s,
21 ft., 5 mi., NR on skeleton tower.
Also see Copper River Delta.

MYERS CHUCK

Misery Island Daybeacon 1
55 44.6N, 132 16.6W, 15 ft., SG
on post.

Daybeacon 3
55 44.6N, 132 15.8W, SG on tower.

Light 4
55 44.5N, 132 15.8W, Fl R 4s,
19 ft., 5 mi., TR on skeleton
tower, obscured from 318° to 041°
for vessels transiting Myers
Chuck Inner Harbor, obscured
from 106° to 041° for vessels transiting Clarence Strait, higher
intensity beam on 264°.

N

Naked Island (Prince William Sound)
See Prince William Sound.

Naked Island Light
58 15.3N, 134 56.7W, Fl W 6s,
44 ft., 7 mi., NR on square tower.

Naknek Entrance Daybeacon 1
58 43.3N, 157 02.9W, SG on small
house.

Naknek, South, City Dock Lights (2)
58 43.0N, 157 00.0W, Fl R 6s,
30 ft., on dock, private aids.

Narrow Point Light
55 47.5N, 132 28.6W, Fl W 6s,
35 ft., 6 mi., NR on skeleton tower,
obscured from 337° to 152°.

Nelson Lagoon Light
56 00.9N, 161 06.2W, Fl W 2.5s,
15 ft., 6 mi., NR on skeleton tower.

Nesbitt Reef Light
56 13.2N, 132 51.8W, Fl W 2.5s,
27 ft., 5 mi., NR on skeleton
tower on concrete pier.

NEVA STRAIT

Also see Olga Strait *for southern
portion of channel.*

Neva Point Reef Light 12
57 14.1N, 135 33.1W, Fl R 6s,
17 ft., 5 mi., TR on pile, obscured
from 147° to 217°.

Whitestone Narrows

Rock Lighted Buoy 13
57 14.5N, 135 33.8W, Fl G 4s,
4 mi., green.

Whitestone Point Light 14
57 14.7N, 135 33.7W, Fl R 2.5s,
11 ft., 4 mi., TR on steel structure,
obscured from 170° to 347°.

Channel Buoy 15
57 14.8N, 135 34.0W, green can.

Channel Lighted Buoy 17
57 14.9N, 135 34.0W, Q G, 3 mi.,
green.

Whitestone Sandspit Buoy 18
57 15.1N, 135 34.0W, red nun.

Channel Range Front Light
57 15.2N, 135 34.2W, Q W, 24 ft.,
KRW on pile.

Channel Range Rear Light
135 yards, 345° from front light, F
W, 32 ft., KRW on skeleton tower.

Columbine Rock Daybeacon 19
57 15.8N, 135 35.0W, SG on
square frame.

Lighted Buoy 20
57 15.8N, 135 34.9W, Fl R 4s,
3 mi., red.

Wyville Reef Lighted Buoy 22
57 16.3N, 135 35.5W, Fl R 2.5s,
4 mi., red.

Highwater Island Shoal Lighted Buoy 23
57 16.9N, 135 36.1W, Fl G 4s,
3 mi., green.

Entrance Island Light 24
57 17.5N, 135 36.3W, Fl R 6s,
30 ft., 5 mi., TR on skeleton tower,
obscured from 154° to 345°.

Kane Islands Light 25
57 19.4N, 135 39.8W, Fl G 2.5s,
40 ft., 4 mi., SG on square frame,
obscured from 342° to 103°.

New Year Islands Light
60 18.7W, 147 55.1W, Fl W 6s,
23 ft., 6 mi., NR on skeleton tower,
obscured from 193° to 316°.
Also see Prince William Sound.

Niblack Point Daybeacon
55 33.0N, 132 07.2W, NR on post.

Nichols Bay Entrance Daybeacon
54 42.1N, 132 05.4W, NR on
spindle.

Ninefoot Shoal Buoy 4
57 34.8N, 136 05.8W, red nun.

NINILCHIK

Channel Entrance Light
60 03.3N, 151 39.9W, Fl W 4s,
15 ft., 5 mi., NR on spindle, use
only with local knowledge.

Ninilchik Rock Sill North Daybeacon
60 03.3N, 151 39.9W, NW on post
worded DANGER SUBMERGED
ROCK SILL.

Ninilchik Rock Sill South Daybeacon
60 03.3N, 151 39.9W, NW on post
worded DANGER SUBMERGED
ROCK SILL 66 YARDS.

NOAA Data Buoys

NOAA Data Lighted Buoy 46001
56 17.3N, 128 10.8W, Fl (4) Y 20s,
yellow boat-shaped hull.

NOAA Data Lighted Buoy 46003
51 51.8N, 155 55.0W, Fl (4) Y 20s,
yellow boat-shaped hull.

NOAA Data Lighted Buoy 46061
60 13.1N, 146 50.0W, Fl (4) Y 20s,
yellow boat-shaped weather
buoy.

NOAA Data Lighted Buoy 46035
56 57.7N, 177 44.0W, Fl (4) Y 20s,
yellow disc-shaped hull.

Noisy Islands Light
57 55.9N, 153 33.8W, Fl W 6s,
80 ft., 7 mi., NR on skeleton tower,
obscured from 223° to 339°.

Nome

East Jetty Light
64 29.8N, 165 24.9W, Fl R 4s,
15 ft., 3 mi., on post, maintained
from July 1 to Nov. 1.

West Jetty Light
64 29.8N, 165 24.9W, Fl G 4s,
15 ft., 3 mi., on post, maintained
from July 1 to Nov. 1.

Range Front Light
64 29.9N, 165 24.9W, Q W, 15 ft.,
KRW on skeleton tower, maintained from July 1 to Nov. 1.

Range Rear Light
52 yards, 009° from front light,
Iso W 6s, 26 ft., KRW on wooden
tower, maintained from July 1 to
Nov. 1.

Nome Terminal Light
64 29.6N, 165 26.3W, Fl G 2.5s,
34 ft., post on box, maintained
from July 15 to Nov. 15, private aid.

Nome Terminal Bridge West Light
64 30.0N, 165 26.2W, F R, 26 ft.,
post on box, obscured from 197°
to 017°, maintained from July 15
to Nov. 15, private aid.

Nome Terminal Bridge East Light
64 30.0N, 165 26.1W, F R, 26 ft.,
post on box, obscured from 017°
to 197°, maintained from July 15
to Nov. 15, private aid.

North Foreland Dock Lights (2)
61 02.5N, 151 09.9W, Fl W 2.5s,
13 ft., 4 mi., on pier, private aids.

North Head Light
54 13.3N, 165 58.8W, Fl W 6s,
60 ft., 6 mi., NR on small house,
obscured from 257° to 054°.

North Inian Pass Light
58 16.3N, 136 24.1W, Fl W 4s,
64 ft., 5 mi., NR on skeleton tower,
obscured from 260° to 051°.

Northeast Arm Light 1
57 47.1N, 153 27.2W, Fl G 6s,
58 ft., 5 mi., SG on skeleton tower,
obscured from 139° to 282.5°.

Northwest Corner Light
66 34.8N, 164 24.4W, Fl W 6s,
75 ft., 7 mi., NR on skeleton tower,
maintained from July 1 to Nov. 1.

Nukdik Point Daybeacon 1
59 14.7N, 135 25.3W, 30 ft., SG on
post.
Also see Haines and Skagway.

Nushagak Bay Entrance Buoy 2
58 33.7N, 158 24.3W, red nun,
maintained from May 1 to
Sept. 30.

Nut Island Light N
57 12.2N, 153 09.6W, Fl (2+1) R 6s,
40 ft., 3 mi., JR on steel square
frame.

O

Ocean Cape Light
59 32.1N, 139 51.3W, Fl W 6s,
130 ft., 9 mi., NR on skeleton
tower, obscured from 134° to 309°.
Also see Yakutat Bay.

Ohio Rock Lighted Buoy OR
55 23.8N, 131 46.3W, Fl (2+1) R 6s,
4 mi., red and green bands.
Also see Tongass Narrows.

Okwega Pass Light OP
63 02.5N, 163 39.6W, Fl (2+1) G 6s,
18 ft., 3 mi., JG on skeleton
tower.

Old Harbor

Daybeacon 2
57 12.5N, 153 17.9W, 15 ft., TR
on pile.

Daybeacon 3
57 12.5N, 153 18.0W, 15 ft., SG
on pile.

Daybeacon 4
57 12.5N, 153 18.0W, 15 ft., TR
on pile.

Old Sitka Rocks Light 2
57 06.9N, 135 24.7W, Fl R 6s,
30 ft., 4 mi., TR on skeleton tower.
Also see Sitka Sound.

Olga Strait

Light 5
57 11.3N, 135 28.0W, Fl G 6s,
15 ft., 5 mi., SG on dolphin.

Daybeacon 7
57 12.4N, 135 29.5W, SG on
dolphin.

Lighted Buoy 9
57 12.6N, 135 29.7W, Fl G 4s,
4 mi., green.

Light 11
57 13.7N, 135 32.2W, Fl G 4s,
15 ft., 3 mi., SG on skeleton tower.
Also see Neva Strait *for continuation of channel.*

Orca Bay and Inlet
See Prince William Sound.

Otstoia Island Light
57 33.7N, 135 27.0W, Fl W 4s,
17 ft., 6 mi., NR on skeleton tower,
obscured from 110° to 247°.

Otstoia Island Lighted Buoy 2
57 33.6N, 135 26.9W, Fl R 4s,
3 mi., red.

Ouzinkie Narrows Daybeacon 4
57 54.7N, 152 30.8W, TR on
spindle.

P

Pankof Breaker Buoy 1
54 42.8N, 162 59.9W, green can.

Parida Island South Reef Buoy 5
55 30.0N, 133 13.8W, green can.
Also see San Alberto Bay.

Passage Canal
See Prince William Sound.

Patterson Point Light
56 32.4N, 134 38.3W, Fl W 2.5s,
50 ft., 6 mi., NR on spindle.

**Pearse Canal, Island Light
(Canada)**
54 47.1N, 130 36.5W, Fl W 4s,
18 ft., white square daymarks on
E, S, and W sides of square skeleton tower.

Peep Rock Light
55 49.1N, 133 19.9W, Fl W 4s,
17 ft., 7 mi., NR on skeleton tower.
Also see Karheen Passage.

Pelican Entrance Light
57 57.3N, 136 13.8W, Fl W 4s,
17 ft., 5 mi., NR on post.
Also see Lisianski Inlet.

Peninsula Point Reef Buoy 2
55 23.1N, 131 44.5W, red nun.
Also see Tongass Narrows.

**Pennock Island Reef Lighted
Buoy PR**
55 20.3N, 131 40.1W, Fl (2+1) G 6s,
3 mi., green and red bands.
Also see Tongass Narrows.

Peril Strait Light 22
57 29.5N, 135 32.5W, Fl R 2.5s,
13 ft., 4 mi., TR on skeleton tower,
obscured from 159° to 340°.

Perl Island Light 1
59 07.1N, 151 38.4W, Fl G 2.5s,
80 ft., 5 mi., SG on skeleton tower,
obscured from 311° to 117°.

Perl Rock Light
59 05.4N, 151 41.7W, Fl W 4s,
66 ft., 8 mi., NR on square tower.

Perry Island Light
60 39.3N, 147 56.0W, Fl W 6s,
35 ft., 6 mi., NR on skeleton tower,
obscured from 126° to 266°.
Also see Prince William Sound.

Peschani Point Light
57 32.2N, 135 19.3W, Fl W 2.5s,
15 ft., 6 mi., NR on skeleton tower.

Peter Dahl Bar Channel Light P
60 16.0N, 145 22.1W, Fl W 2.5s,
12 ft., 5 mi., NR on skeleton tower,
maintained from May 1 to Oct. 1.
Also see Copper River Delta.

Petersburg
See Wrangell Narrows.

Piedras Island Reef Buoy 9
55 33.7N, 133 18.0W, green can.
Also see San Christoval Channel.

Pigeon Island Daybeacon 3
55 25.8N, 133 34.0W, SG on
spindle.
Also see Cone Island Daybeacon 2.

Pigeon Island Daybeacon 4
55 25.8N, 133 34.1W, TR on
steel pile.

Pigeon Pass Daybeacon 5
55 25.7N, 133 33.8W, SG on
spindle.

Pilot Rock Light
59 44.5N, 149 28.2W, Fl W 4s,
100 ft., 6 mi., NR on skeleton
tower.

Pinta Rock Lighted Bell Buoy 2
58 10.0N, 135 27.2W, Fl R 4s,
4 mi., red.

**Pleasant Island Lighted Bell
Buoy 11**
58 18.4N, 135 39.3W, Fl G 2.5s,
4 mi., green.

Pleiades Light
60 14.4N, 148 00.6W, Fl W 4s,
30 ft., 6 mi., NR on skeleton tower,
obscured from 343° to 131°.
Also see Prince William Sound.

Point Adolphus Light
58 17.2N, 135 47.0W, Fl W 4s,
20 ft., 6 mi., NR on small house,
obscured from 305° to 122°.

Point Alexander Light
56 30.5N, 132 57.0W, Fl W 4s,
17 ft., 7 mi., NR on skeleton tower,
obscured from 162° to 293°.
Also see Wrangell Narrows.

Point Ancon Light
56 24.3N, 132 33.3W, Fl W 6s,
20 ft., 6 mi., NR on square frame,
obscured from 214° to 014°.

Point Arboleda Light
55 19.2N, 133 28.4W, Fl W 4s,
33 ft., 6 mi., NR on spindle.

Point Arden Light
58 09.6N, 134 10.7W, Fl W 4s,
50 ft., 6 mi., NR on skeleton
tower, obscured from 332° to
118°.

Point Armargura Ledge Buoy 1
55 26.6N, 133 21.7W, green.

Point Augusta Light
58 02.4N, 134 57.1W, Fl W 4s,
48 ft., 6 mi., NR on skeleton tower,
obscured from 290° to 135°.

**Point Baker Anchorage
Daybeacon**
56 21.3N, 133 37.1W, 22 ft., NR
on small house.

Point Baker Light
56 21.5N, 133 37.1W, Fl W 6s,
20 ft., 6 mi., NR on skeleton tower.

Point Benham Light
57 29.0N, 135 11.9W, Fl W 4s,
19 ft., 6 mi., NR on square frame,
obscured from 310° 117°.

**Point Bentinck Bar Lighted Bell
Buoy 1**
60 19.3N, 145 59.8W, Fl G 4s,
4 mi., green.

Point Bentinck Light
60 23.7N, 146 05.2W, Fl W 4s,
47 ft., 6 mi., NR on skeleton tower.
Also see Copper River Delta.

Point Colpoys Light
56 20.2N, 133 11.9W, Fl W 6s,
19 ft., 6 mi., NR on skeleton tower,
obscured from 302° to 102°.

Point Cornwallis Light
54 42.2N, 132 52.4W, Fl W 4s,
193 ft., 7 mi., NR on skeleton
tower.

Point Craven Light
57 27.8N, 134 52.0W, Fl W 2.5s,
35 ft., 5 mi., NR on skeleton tower,
obscured from 078° to 157°.

Point Crowley Light
56 07.2N, 134 15.5W, Fl W 4s,
45 ft., 6 mi., NR on skeleton tower,
obscured from 174° to 330°.

Point Davidson Light
54 59.7N, 131 36.9W, Fl W 6s,
33 ft., 6 mi., NR on skeleton tower,
obscured from 138° to 250°.

Point Eleanor Light
60 34.8N, 147 33.8W, Fl W 6s,
45 ft., 6 mi., NR on skeleton tower,
obscured from 301° to 091°.
Also see Prince William Sound.

Point Ellis Light
56 34.0N, 134 20.0W, Fl W 4s,
30 ft., 7 mi., NR on spindle.

Point Elrington Light
59 56.2N, 148 15.0W, Fl W 6s,
30 ft., 7 mi., NR on skeleton tower,
obscured from 198° to 354°.
Also see Prince William Sound.

Point Esther Light
60 47.1N, 148 06.0W, Fl W 6s,
31 ft., 6 mi., NR on skeleton tower,
obscured from 108° to 276°.
Also see Prince William Sound.

Point Francis Light
55 39.8N, 131 49.5W, Fl W 2.5s,
32 ft., 7 mi., NR on skeleton tower.

Point Gambier Light
57 26.1N, 133 50.4W, Fl W 4s,
38 ft., 6 mi., NR on skeleton tower,
obscured from 083° to 217°.

Point Gardner Light
57 00.6N, 134 36.9W, Fl W 4s,
65 ft., 7 mi., NR on skeleton tower.

Point Harrington Buoy 4
56 10.7N, 132 44.4W, red nun.

Point Harris Light
56 17.4N, 134 18.0W, Fl W 6s,
32 ft., 7 mi., NR on skeleton tower,
obscured from 180° to 313°.

Point Helen Light
60 09.2N, 147 46.0W, Fl W 6s,
35 ft., 6 mi., NR on skeleton tower,
obscured from 083° to 228°.
Also see Prince William Sound.

Point Highfield Reef Daybeacon
56 29.0N, 132 23.8W, 18 ft., NR
on pile.
Also see Wrangell Harbor.

Point Hilda Light
58 13.0N, 134 30.4W, Fl W 6s,
20 ft., 5 mi., NR on square frame
structure, obscured from 080° to
274°.

Point Hugh Light
57 37.2N, 133 48.4W, Fl W 6s,
34 ft., 6 mi., NR on skeleton
tower, obscured from 351.5° to
173°.

Point Incarnation Light
55 33.3N, 133 37.4W, Fl W 2.5s,
19 ft., 6 mi., NR on small house,
obscured from 292° to 070°.

Point Lavinia Light
58 13.3N, 136 21.3W, Fl W 6s,
60 ft., 6 mi., NR on skeleton tower,
obscured from 278° to 073°.

Point Lockwood Light PL
56 33.4N, 132 57.9W, Fl G 4s,
15 ft., 4 mi., SG on skeleton tower,
obscured from 027° to 166°.
Also see Wrangell Narrows.

Point Lull Light
57 18.6N, 134 48.4W, Fl W 4s,
50 ft., 6 mi., NR on skeleton tower.

Point Macartney Light
57 01.5N, 134 03.5W, Fl W 6s,
20 ft., 6 mi., NR on pile, obscured
from 200° to 329°.

Point Mackenzie Light 11
61 14.3N, 149 59.2W, Fl G 6s,
80 ft., 5 mi., SG on square frame,
obscured from 106° to 255° and
from 258° to 281°.

Point Marsh Light
54 42.7N, 132 17.7W, Fl W 4s,
74 ft., 6 mi., NR on skeleton tower,
obscured from 127° to 265°.

Point McCartey Buoy 3
55 06.7N, 131 41.8W, green can.
Also see West Channel Lighted
Bell Buoy 4.

Point McCartey Light
55 06.8N, 131 42.4W, Fl W 6s,
44 ft., 5 mi., NR on skeleton
tower, obscured from 080° to
090°, and from 113° to 197°.

Point Pigot Light
60 48.1N, 148 21.4W, Fl W 6s,
25 ft., 6 mi., NR on skeleton tower,
obscured from 100° to 247°.
Also see Prince William Sound.

Point Pogibshi Light
59 25.5N, 151 53.1W, Fl W 2.5s,
94 ft., 6 mi., NR on skeleton tower.
Also see Port Graham.

Point Possession Light
61 02.0N, 150 24.3W, Fl W 6s,
60 ft., 9 mi., NR on skeleton tower,
obscured from 221° to 051°.

Point Retreat Light
58 24.7N, 134 57.3W, Fl W 6s,
63 ft., 9 mi., white square concrete tower on building.
Also see False Point Retreat
Light 4.

Point Romanof Light
63 12.0N, 162 50.0W, Fl W 6s,
25 ft., 7 mi., NR on skeleton tower,
maintained from July 1 to Nov. 1.

Point Sherman Light
58 51.3N, 135 09.1W, Fl W 4s,
47 ft., 6 mi., NR on spindle.

Point Siroi Island Light 12
57 25.2N, 135 35.4W, Fl R 2.5s,
15 ft., 4 mi., TR on skeleton tower,
obscured from 272° to 025°.

Point Spencer Light
65 16.6N, 166 50.9W, Fl W 6s,
22 ft., 7 mi., NR on skeleton tower,
maintained from July 1 to Nov. 1.

**Point St. Albans Reef Lighted Bell
Buoy 3**
56 05.2N, 133 54.6W, Fl G 4s,
4 mi., green.

Point Stanhope Buoy 2
56 00.2N, 132 37.0W, red nun.

Point Stephens Rock Buoy 2
58 25.3N, 134 46.2W, red nun.

Point Woronzof Range Front Light
61 12.1N, 150 01.3W, F G, 55 ft.,
KRW on skeleton tower, visible 4°
each side of rangeline.

Point Woronzof Range Rear Light
275 yards, 079.0° from front light,
F G, 145 ft., KRW on skeleton
tower, visible 4° each side of
rangeline.

Pond Reef Light 16
55 26.2N, 131 48.9W, Fl R 2.5s,
13 ft., 4 mi., TR on skeleton tower.
Also see Tongass Narrows.

Popof Reef Lighted Gong Buoy 5
55 20.2N, 160 31.0W, Fl G 2.5s,
3 mi., green.

Popof Strait Entrance Light 1
55 21.3N, 160 30.3W, Fl G 4s,
50 ft., 5 mi., SG on skeleton tower.

Popof Strait Lighted Buoy 3
55 20.7N, 160 31.1W, Fl G 6s,
4 mi., green.

PORT ALEXANDER

Light
56 14.4N, 134 39.0W, Fl W 4s (R
sector), 68 ft., 5 mi., NR on skeleton tower, red sectors from 225°
to 252° and 330° to 347°,
obscured from 347° to 061°.

Entrance Buoy
56 14.4N, 134 38.9W, red nun.

Range Front Light
56 14.7N, 134 39.1W, Q G, 14 ft.,
KRW on skeleton tower on concrete pier, visible all around.

Range Rear Light
65 yards, 334° from front light, Iso G 6s, 29 ft., KRW on skeleton tower on concrete pier, visible all around.

Port Althorp
See Elfin Cove, Althorp Rock Light 3, *and* Three Hill Island Light.

Port Chatham Entrance Light
59 12.5N, 151 46.6W, Fl W 2.5s, 40 ft., 6 mi., NR on skeleton tower.

Port Chatham Shoal Buoy PC
59 12.8N, 151 46.6W, green and red bands, can.

Port Frederick Light 3
58 07.9N, 135 27.9W, Fl G 6s, 26 ft., 4 mi., SG on skeleton tower, obscured from 245° to 357°, higher intensity beam toward 042°.

Port Graham

Entrance Shoal Buoy 1
59 22.7N, 151 54.3W, green can.

Entrance Light
59 22.3N, 151 54.1W, Fl W 4s, 50 ft., 5 mi., NR on small house, obscured from 313° to 070°.

Buoy 3
59 22.4N, 151 52.6W, green can.

Passage Island Spit Buoy 4
59 22.1N, 151 52.4W, red nun.

North Spit Buoy 5
59 21.8N, 151 51.6W, green can.

South Spit Buoy 6
59 21.4n, 151 50.2W, red nun.

Point Pogibshi Light
59 25.5N, 151 53.1W, Fl W 2.5s, 94 ft., 6 mi., NR on skeleton tower.

Port Moller

Also see Herendeen Bay.

Entrance Buoy 2
56 00.0N, 160 39.2W, red nun, maintained from May 15 to Dec. 10.

Entrance Buoy 3
55 59.3N, 160 36.8W, green can, maintained from May 15 to Dec. 10.

Light 5
55 58.7N, 160 34.8W, Fl G 2.5s, 18 ft., 4 mi., SG on steel tower.

Harbor Spit Daybeacon
55 54.8N, 160 34.8W, NR on skeleton tower.

Port Nellie Juan
See Prince William Sound.

Port Protection Daybeacon
56 20.2N, 133 38.1W, 18 ft., NR on single steel pile.

Port Protection Light
56 19.6N, 133 36.8W, Fl W 6s, 19 ft., 6 mi., NR on pile, obscured from 290° to 095°.

Port Wakefield Lighted Buoy 2
57 51.5N, 152 51.6W, Fl R 4s, 4 mi., red.

Port Walter Light
56 23.2N, 134 38.2W, Fl W 4s, 20 ft., 8 mi., NR on skeleton tower, obscured from 308° to 037°.

Portage Bay Daybeacon 2
57 00.5N, 133 19.7W, TR on skeleton tower.

Portage Bay Light 3
57 00.3N, 133 19.5W, Fl G 4s, 16 ft., 5 mi., SG on skeleton tower, obscured from 201° to 329°.

Portage Pass
See Keku Strait.

Portland Island Light
58 21.1N, 134 45.5W, Fl W 2.5s, 20 ft., 6 mi., NR on pile, obscured from 328° to 338°.

Potato Point Light 11
61 03.4N, 146 41.8W, Oc G 4s, 38 ft., 5 mi., SG on skeleton tower, higher intensity beam towards 050° and 213°, obscured from 031° to 220°.
Also see Prince William Sound.

Potter Rock Lighted Bell Buoy
55 18.1N, 131 34.7W, Fl (2+1) R 6s, 4 mi., red and green bands.

Poundstone Rock Lighted Bell Buoy PR
58 31.7N, 134 56.0W, Fl (2+1) R 6s, 4 mi., red and green bands.

Povorotni Island Light
57 30.9N, 135 33.3W, Q W, 20 ft., 5 mi., NR on small house, obscured from 314° to 032°.
Also see Peril Strait Light 22.

Prince William Sound

Seal Rocks Light
60 09.8N, 146 50.3W, Fl W 6s, 48 ft., 8 mi., NR on skeleton tower, racon: K (-·-).

Seal Rocks Shoal Lighted Whistle Buoy 1
60 10.0N, 146 44.9W, Fl G 4s, 4 mi., green.

Schooner Rock Light 1
60 18.4N, 146 54.5W, Fl G 6s, 65 ft., 6 mi., SG on skeleton tower, obscured from 358° to 129°.

Bear Cape Light 2
60 23.3N, 146 43.8W, Fl R 6s, 39 ft., 6 mi., TR on skeleton tower, obscured from 209° to 011°.

Johnstone Point Light
60 29.0N, 146 36.8W, Fl W 5s, 57 ft., 14 mi., NR on skeleton tower, obscured from 256° to 052°.

Middle Ground Shoal Lighted Bell Buoy 2
60 32.5N, 146 22.1W, Fl R 6s, 4 mi., red.

Orca Bay

Gravina Point Light 3
60 37.4N, 146 15.2W, Fl G 6s, 27 ft., 5 mi., SG on skeleton tower, obscured from 120° to 264°.

Hanks Island Rock Lighted Bell Buoy 5
60 36.0N, 145 59.5W, Fl G 4s, 4 mi., green.

Channel Island Rock Lighted Buoy 7
60 36.5N, 145 48.8W, Fl G 2.5s, 4 mi., green.

The Narrows Light 8
60 36.2N, 145 47.5W, Fl R 6s, 12 ft., 5 mi., TR on skeleton tower, higher intensity beam toward Orca Bay.

Light 9
60 37.9N, 145 45.1W, Fl G 6s,
12 ft., 5 mi., SG on skeleton
tower, higher intensity beam
down western channel.

North Island Rock Light 10
60 37.7N, 145 42.7W, Fl R 6s,
14 ft., 3 mi., TR on concrete pile.

Orca Inlet

Channel Lighted Buoy 12
60 37.5N, 145 41.6W, Fl R 4s,
3 mi., red.

Channel Buoy 14
60 36.8N, 145 41.9W, red nun.

Channel Lighted Buoy 15
60 36.8N, 145 41.6W, Fl G 4s,
3 mi., green.

Channel Lighted Buoy 16
60 35.9N, 145 42.6W, Fl R 2.5s, red.

Light 18
60 34.5N, 145 44.7W, Fl R 4s,
10 ft., 4 mi., TR on steel pile.

**Channel Junction Lighted Bell
Buoy OI**
60 34.0N, 145 45.6W, Fl (2+1) R 6s,
4 mi., red and green bands.

**North Containment Dock
Lights (2)**
60 33.1N, 145 45.9W, Fl R 4s,
25 ft., on pier, private aids.

Spike Island Light
60 33.0N, 145 46.2W, Fl W 6s,
35 ft., 7 mi., NR on skeleton tower.

Cordova Boat Harbor Light 2
60 32.8N, 145 46.1W, Fl R 4s,
16 ft., 3 mi., TR on skeleton tower.

South Channel Buoys (about 16)
Red nuns and green cans, maintained from May 15 to Nov. 1,
marks channel from Mummy
Island northeastward, route
requires local knowledge,
extreme caution advised due to
shifting shoals.
Also see Copper River Delta.

Odiak Slough Buoys (2)
60 32.3N, 145 45.8W, red spherical, dry at MLLW, private aids.

Odiak Pharos Light
60 32.2N, 145 45.8W, F W, 26 ft.,
white octagonal tower, private
aid.

West Channel

Light 2
60 36.9N, 145 45.7W, Fl R 4s,
30 ft., 4 mi., TR on skeleton tower.

Lighted Buoy 3
60 35.0N, 145 45.1W, Fl G 2.5s,
3 mi., green.

Lighted Buoy 4
60 34.6N, 145 45.6W, Fl R 2.5s,
4 mi., red.

Main Channel

**Knowles Head Shoal Lighted Bell
Buoy 4**
60 40.5N, 146 44.1W, Fl R 4s,
4 mi., red.

NOAA Data Lighted Buoy 46060
60 35.0N, 146 50.0W, Fl (4) Y 20s,
yellow disc-shaped hull.

Red Head Light
60 40.3N, 146 30.2W, Fl W 4s,
38 ft., 6 mi., NR on skeleton tower,
obscured from 134° to 308°.

Goose Island Light
60 42.8N, 146 43.6W, Fl W 6s,
38 ft., 6 mi., NR on skeleton
tower, obscured from 151° to
313°.

Bligh Reef Lighted Bell Buoy 6
60 50.5N, 146 54.4W, Fl R 4s,
4 mi., red.

Bligh Reef Light
60 50.3N, 146 53.0W, Fl W 4s,
59 ft., 9 mi., NR on pile structure.

Glacier Island Light
60 52.3N, 147 05.5W, Fl W 6s,
38 ft., 9 mi., NR on skeleton tower,
obscured from 040° to 225°.

Busby Island Light
60 53.7N, 146 49.0W, Fl W 6s (R
sector), 48 ft., white 9 mi., red
6 mi., NR on skeleton tower,
obscured from 245° to 003°, red
from 003° to 044°.

Tatitlek Narrows

Daybeacon 1
60 51.2N, 146 41.3W, 12 ft., SG
on spindle.

Daybeacon 2
60 51.8N, 146 41.7W, 12 ft., TR
on spindle.

Daybeacon 4
60 52.1N, 146 42.4W, TR on pile.

Daybeacon 6
60 52.4N, 146 42.7W, 12 ft., TR
on spindle.

Daybeacon 8
60 53.6N, 146 43.2W, 10 ft., TR
on spindle.

Valdez Arm

Lighted Bell Buoy 9
60 57.2N, 146 52.5W, Fl G 4s,
4 mi., green.

Rocky Point Light 10
60 57.0N, 146 47.1W, Fl R 4s,
38 ft., 5 mi., TR on skeleton tower,
obscured from 211° to 335°.

Potato Point Light 11
61 03.4N, 146 41.8W, Oc G 4s,
38 ft., 5 mi., SG on skeleton
tower, higher intensity beam
towards 050° and 213°, obscured
from 031° to 220°.

Valdez Narrows Buoy 11A
61 03.3N, 146 41.6W, green can.

Entrance Point Light 12
61 03.8N, 146 39.7W, Fl (2) R 5s,
38 ft., 5 mi., TR on skeleton tower,
obscured from 210° to 000°.

Middle Rock Light 13
61 04.9N, 146 39.2W, Q G, 30 ft.,
7 mi., SG on concrete pier, higher
intensity beam down Valdez Arm.

Port Valdez

Entrance Island Light 14
61 05.1N, 146 36.8W, Fl R 2.5s,
38 ft., 5 mi., TR on skeleton tower,
obscured from 266° to 063°.

Light 15
61 07.3N, 146 34.0W, Fl G 4s,
12 ft., 5 mi., SG on skeleton tower,
obscured from 071° to 269°.

Mooring Buoy BM
61 05.3N, 146 24.7W, white can
with blue bands, private aid.

Saw Island Mooring Buoys (4)
61 05.3N, 146 24.7W, blue and
white bands, private aids.

**Valdez Marine Terminal Lighted
Mooring Buoys (about 7)**
Fl Y 6s, 1 mi., yellow with white
reflector, mooring for oil containment boom, private aids.

Berth 5 Lights (2)
61 05.4N, 146 24.6W, Q W, 35 ft.,
on mooring dolphins, private
aids.

Berth 4 Lights (2)
61 05.3N, 146 24.0W, Q R, 35 ft.,
on mooring dolphins, private
aids.

Breakwater Light
61 05.2N, 146 23.6W, Q G, 24 ft.,
private aid.

Berth 3 Lights (2)
61 05.3N, 146 23.2W, Q W, 35 ft.,
on mooring dolphins, private
aids.

Berth 1 Lights (3)
61 05.4N, 146 22.4W, Q R, 35 ft.,
on mooring dolphins, private
aids.

**Solomon Gulch Lighted Mooring
Buoys (7)**
Fl Y 2.5s, yellow, mooring for oil
containment boom, private aids.

Valdez Boat Harbor Light 2
61 07.4N, 146 21.2W, Fl R 4s,
22 ft., 5 mi., TR on skeleton tower.

Valdez Boat Harbor Light 3
61 07.4N, 146 21.3W, Fl G 4s,
33 ft., 4 mi., SG on skeleton tower.

**Valdez Container Terminal
Lights (2)**
61 07.3N, 146 18.5W, F G, 16 ft.,
private aids.

Naked Island

Lighted Mooring Buoy A
60 40.3N, 147 21.1W, Fl W 2.5s,
white with blue band, private aid.

C-LAB-1 Lighted Research Buoy
60 36.2N, 147 12.7W, Q Y, yellow,
private aid.

Lighted Mooring Buoy C
60 38.6N, 147 27.8W, Fl W 2.5s,
white with blue band, private aid.

Western Sound

Smith Island Lighted Bell Buoy 1
60 32.0N, 147 17.3W, Fl G 2.5s,
4 mi., green.

Pennsylvania Rock Buoy 2
60 26.7N, 147 24.1W, red nun.

Seal Island Light
60 25.8N, 147 24.9W, Fl W 4s,
45 ft., 6 mi., NR on skeleton tower,
obscured from 273° to 032°.

Applegate Shoals Light
60 21.3N, 147 23.6W, Fl W 2.5s,
24 ft., 6 mi., NR on skeleton tower.

Point Eleanor Light
60 34.8N, 147 33.8W, Fl W 6s,
45 ft., 6 mi., NR on skeleton tower,
obscured from 301° to 091°.

**Lone Island Shoal Lighted Bell
Buoy 2**
60 38.2N, 147 47.3W, Fl R 4s,
4 mi., red.

Perry Island Light
60 39.3N, 147 56.0W, Fl W 6s,
35 ft., 6 mi., NR on skeleton tower,
obscured from 126° to 266°.

Culross Island Light
60 44.8N, 148 06.8W, Fl W 4s,
40 ft., 6 mi., NR on skeleton tower,
obscured from 334° to 128°.

**Lake Bay Lighted Mooring Buoys
(4)**
Fl Y 2.5s, yellow, mooring for oil
containment boom, private aids.

Point Esther Light
60 47.1N, 148 06.0W, Fl W 6s,
31 ft., 6 mi., NR on skeleton tower,
obscured from 108° to 276°.

Passage Canal

Point Pigot Light
60 48.1N, 148 21.4W, Fl W 6s,
25 ft., 6 mi., NR on skeleton tower,
obscured from 100° to 247°.

Decision Point Light
60 48.4N, 146 27.3W, Fl W 4s,
35 ft., 5 mi., NR on skeleton tower,
obscured from 315° to 105°.

Trinity Point Light
60 48.4N, 148 34.1W, Fl W 6s,
39 ft., 6 mi., NR on skeleton tower,
obscured from 262° to 079°.

Delong Pier Lights (3)
60 46.7N, 148 40.0W, F R, 12 ft.,
on bullrail, maintained by U.S.
Army.

**Whittier Passenger Dock
Lights (2)**
60 46.7N, 148 41.7W, Fl R 6s, 3 ft.,
on dock, private aids.

Marginal Wharf Light
60 46.6N, 148 40.5W, F R, 12 ft.,
on post, private aid.

Whittier Breakwater Light 1
60 46.7N, 148 41.6W, Fl G 4s, 8 ft.,
3 mi., SG on skeleton tower,
obscured from 233° to 078°.

Port Nellie Juan

Light
60 35.9N, 148 06.1W, Fl W 2.5s,
23 ft., 5 mi., NR on skeleton tower,
obscured from 281° to 070°.

**Main Bay Lighted Mooring
Buoys (6)**
Fl Y 2.5s, yellow, mooring for oil
containment boom, private aid.

Knight Island Passage

Crafton Island Light
60 30.7N, 147 56.1W, Fl W 4s,
70 ft., 6 mi., NR on skeleton tower,
obscured from 328° to 146°.

New Year Islands Light
60 18.7N, 147 55.1W, Fl W 6s,
23 ft., 6 mi., NR on skeleton tower,
obscured from 193° to 316°.

Pleiades Light
60 14.4N, 148 00.6W, Fl W 4s,
30 ft., 6 mi., NR on skeleton tower,
obscured from 343° to 131°.

Point Helen Light
60 09.2N, 147 46.0W, Fl W 6s,
35 ft., 6 mi., NR on skeleton tower,
obscured from 083° to 228°.

Sawmill Bay

Buoy 1
60 03.2N, 148 01.3W, green can.

Crab Bay Daybeacon 2
60 04.0N, 148 00.5W, 6 ft., TR on
steel pile, tide gauge, private aid.

**Sawmill Bay Lighted Mooring
Buoys (13)**
Fl Y 2.5s, yellow, mooring for oil
containment boom, private aids.

Light 3
60 03.2N, 148 02.2W, Fl G 4s,
14 ft., 5 mi., SG on skeleton tower,
obscured from 293° to 062°.

Buoy 5
60 03.0N, 148 03.2W, green can.

Buoy 6
60 03.0N, 148 03.7W, red nun.

Elrington Passage

Light
60 02.8N, 148 00.7W, Fl W 6s,
25 ft., 6 mi., NR on skeleton tower,
obscured from 061° to 270°.

Evans Island Light
59 59.1N, 148 07.5W, Fl W 2.5s,
20 ft., 6 mi., NR on skeleton tower,
obscured from 084° to 249°.

Lonetree Point Light
59 58.9N, 148 12.0W, Fl W 4s,
30 ft., 6 mi., NR on skeleton tower,
obscured from 280° to 063°.

Point Elrington Light
59 56.2N, 148 15.0W, Fl W 6s,
30 ft., 7 mi., NR on skeleton tower,
obscured from 198° to 354°.

Prokoda Island Light 2
57 54.6N, 152 30.4W, Fl R 4s,
40 ft., 4 mi., TR on small house,
higher intensity beam toward
120°, obscured from 148° to 274°.

**Prudhoe Bay Waterflood
Daybeacons (2)**
70 24.8N, 148 31.5W, 10 ft., NW
on pile worded DANGER SUB-
MERGED PIPELINE, maintained
during ice-free season, private
aids.
Note: Oil well structures exist
along the Beaufort Seacoast
between 147° and 149° west
longitude.

**Prudhoe Bay Waterflood Intake
Safety Zone Daybeacons (2)**
70 24.6N, 148 31.7W, 10 ft.,
NW on pile worded DANGER
RESTRICTED AREA, maintained
during ice-free season, private
aids.

RACE POINT

Range Front Light
61 09.9N, 150 13.6W, Iso W 6s,
176 ft., KRW on multi-pile
structure, visible 4° each side
of rangeline.

Range Rear Light
1,100 yards, 058° from front light,
F W, 252 ft., KRW on multi-pile
structure, visible 4° each side of
rangeline.

Race Point Light
61 10.1N, 150 13.5W, Fl W 2.5s
(R sector), 170 ft., white 7 mi., red
5 mi., NR on skeleton tower,
red sector from 068° to 235°,
obscured from 235° to 038°.

**Ramsden Point (on extremity,
Canada)**
54 59.0N, 130 06.2W, Fl (3) W 12s,
27 ft., orange ball daymark on
pole, obscured from 117.5° to
260°.

Raspberry Strait Light
58 09.6N, 153 13.4W, Fl W 6s,
50 ft., 6 mi., NR on small house.

Ratz Harbor Entrance Light
55 53.3N, 132 35.9W, Fl W 4s,
20 ft., 5 mi., NR on skeleton tower.

Red Bluff Daybeacon
58 14.1N, 157 29.1W, NR on
skeleton tower.

Red Head Light
60 40.3N, 146 30.2W, Fl W 4s,
38 ft., 6 mi., NR on skeleton tower,
obscured from 134° to 308°.
Also see Prince William Sound.

Reef Island Light
55 04.7N, 130 12.2W, Fl W 4s,
19 ft., 6 mi., NR on spindle, higher intensity beam up Portland
Canal, higher intensity beam
down Pearse Canal, obscured
from 020.5° to 197.5°.

Refuge Cove
See Tongass Narrows.

Riley Channel Entrance Light
66 47.0N, 161 52.5W, Fl W 6s,
17 ft., 7 mi., NR on skeleton tower,
maintained from July 1 to Nov. 1.

Rockwell Light
57 02.2N, 135 20.0W, F R, 50 ft.,
white octagonal tower with
dwelling attached, private aid.
Also see Eastern Channel.

Rocky Island Light 13
58 10.6N, 135 03.1W, Fl G 4s,
43 ft., 4 mi., SG on square frame.

Rocky Patch Buoy 9A
57 01.8N, 135 17.7W, green can.
Also see Eastern Channel.

Rocky Patch Lighted Buoy RP
57 01.7N, 135 18.4W, Fl (2+1) R 6s,
4 mi., red and green bands.

Rocky Point (Golovnin Bay) Light
64 23.9N, 163 09.0W, Fl W 2.5s,
175 ft., 7 mi., NR on skeleton
tower, maintained from July 1 to
Nov. 1.

**Rocky Point (Bechevin Bay)
Light 6**
54 58.3N, 163 26.6W, Fl R 6s,
5 mi., TR on skeleton tower.
Also see Bechevin Bay.

**Rocky Point Light (Valdez Arm)
10**
60 57.0N, 146 47.1W, Fl R 4s,
38 ft., 5 mi., TR on skeleton tower,
obscured from 211° to 335°.
Also see Prince William Sound.

Rodman Rock Buoy 1
57 29.8N, 135 14.4W, green can.

Rookery Island Light
56 18.9N, 133 06.4W, Fl W 4s,
40 ft., 6 mi., NR on skeleton tower,
obscured from 353° to 097°.

Rosa Reef Light 15
55 24.8N, 131 48.2W, Fl G 6s,
24 ft., 6 mi., SG on caisson.
Also see Tongass Narrows.

Rose Channel Rock Daybeacon
57 27.7N, 135 33.0W, NR on
skeleton tower.
Also see Rose Island Rock Light
19, Big Rose Island Light 21, *and*
Peril Strait Light 22.

Rose Island Rock Light 19
57 27.3N, 135 32.4W, Q G, 17 ft.,
4 mi., SG on skeleton tower,
obscured from 080° to 190°.
Also see Big Rose Island Light 21,
Rose Channel Rock Daybeacon,
and Peril Strait Light 22.

Round Islands Light
54 46.7N, 132 30.4W, Fl W 2.5s (R
sector), 56 ft., 6 mi., NR on skeleton tower, red from 327° to 346°,
obscured from 149.5° to 327°.

Round Point Light
56 16.7N, 132 39.5W, Fl W 6s,
24 ft., 5 mi., NR on spindle,
obscured from 006.5° to 201.5°.

Round Rock Light
57 15.6N, 133 56.2W, Fl W 6s,
49 ft., 6 mi., NR on skeleton tower.

Rugged Island Light
59 50.3N, 149 22.4W, Fl W 6s,
438 ft., 7 mi., NR on square
frame, obscured from 059° to
111° and from 114° to 221°.

Rush Point Shoal Buoy 1
58 28.1N, 136 03.4W, green can,
maintained from May 1 to Oct. 1.
Also see Glacier Bay.

S

Saint Herman Bay
See Kodiak.

Salmon River Shoal Buoy 3
55 54.4N, 130 00.3W, green can.

Salt Point Light
56 50.7N, 133 52.0W, Fl W 6s,
17 ft., 3 mi., NR on pile, obscured
from 168° to 259°.
Also see Keku Strait.

SAN ALBERTO BAY

Also see San Christoval Channel.

**Ballena Island Shoal Lighted
Buoy 2**
55 28.2N, 133 13.2W, Fl R 4s,
3 mi., red.

Balandra Shoal Buoy 3
55 28.5N, 133 13.8W, green can.

Fern Reef Lighted Buoy 3A
55 29.1N, 133 15.9W, Fl G 4s,
4 mi., green.

Parida Island South Reef Buoy 5
55 30.0N, 133 13.8W, green can.

Lighted Buoy 7
55 32.3N, 133 15.1W, Fl G 6s,
4 mi., green.

SAN CHRISTOVAL CHANNEL

Also see San Alberto Bay.

**Hermanos Islands Reef Lighted
Bell Buoy 8**
55 33.7N, 133 17.8W, Fl R 4s,
4 mi., red.

Piedras Island Reef Buoy 9
55 33.7N, 133 18.0W, green can.

**Hermanos Island Range Front
Daybeacon**
55 34.2N, 133 17.9W, KRW on
spindle.

**Hermanos Island Range Rear
Daybeacon**
210 yards, 104° from front daybeacon, KRW on spindle.

**San Christoval Three Fathom
Buoy SC**
55 34.5N, 133 19.1W, green and
red bands, can.

Larzatita Island Reef Light
55 35.0N, 133 19.7W, Fl W 4s,
22 ft., 6 mi., NR on caisson.

**Sand Point Airport Warning
Buoys (4)**
55 19.4N, 160 31.6W, white with
orange bands and diamond
worded DANGER LOW FLYING
AIRCRAFT, can, private aids.

Sand Point Dock Light
55 19.9N, 160 30.2W, Fl R 10s,
10 ft., private aid.

Sawmill Bay
See Prince William Sound.

Saxman Breakwater Light
55 18.9N, 131 35.8W, F R, 15 ft.,
on post, private aid.
Also see Tongass Narrows.

Schooner Rock Light 1
60 18.4N, 146 54.5W, Fl G 6s,
65 ft., 6 mi., SG on skeleton tower,
obscured from 358° to 129°.
Also see Prince William Sound.

Scotch Cap Light
54 23.7N, 164 44.7W, Fl W 6s,
110 ft., 9 mi., NR on skeleton
tower, obscured from 104° to 276°.

Scrub Island Buoy 7
55 08.5N, 131 34.9W, green can.

Scrub Island Lighted Buoy 5
55 08.2N, 131 34.5W, Fl G 6s,
4 mi., green.

Seal Cape Light
55 21.9N, 161 15.3W, Fl W 4s,
75 ft., 6 mi., NR on skeleton tower,
obscured from 172° to 235°.

Seal Island Light
60 25.8N, 147 24.9W, Fl W 4s,
45 ft., 6 mi., NR on skeleton tower,
obscured from 273° to 032°.
Also see Prince William Sound.

Seal Rocks Light
59 31.2N, 149 37.8W, Fl W 6s,
285 ft., 8 mi., NR on small house.

**Seal Rocks (Prince William
Sound) Light**
60 09.8N, 146 50.3W, Fl W 6s,
48 ft., 8 mi., NR on skeleton
tower, racon: K (-·-).

**Seal Rocks Shoal (Prince William
Sound) Lighted Whistle Buoy 1**
60 10.0N, 146 44.9W, Fl G 4s,
4 mi., green.

Sealion Rocks Light
55 27.9N, 163 12.2W, Fl W 6s,
94 ft., 7 mi., on skeleton tower.

Security Bay Light 1
56 52.4N, 134 22.4W, Fl G 4s,
32 ft., 4 mi., SG on skeleton tower,
obscured from 235° to 323°.

SELDOVIA BAY

Entrance Light
59 27.1N, 151 43.3W, Fl W 6s,
64 ft., 7 mi., NR on small house,
obscured from 205° to 084° and
from 091° to 101°.

Lighted Buoy 1
59 26.9N, 151 43.4W, Fl G 2.5s,
4 mi., green.

Lighted Buoy 2
59 26.8N, 151 43.5W, Fl R 4s,
4 mi., red.

Light 3
59 26.5N, 151 43.3W, Fl G 4s,
45 ft., 3 mi., SG on small house.

Seldovia Dock Lights (2)
59 26.5N, 151 43.2W, F R, 15 ft.,
pole, private aids.

Buoy 4
59 26.4N, 151 43.5W, red nun.

Seldovia Breakwater Light 5
59 26.3N, 151 43.1W, Fl G 2.5s,
22 ft., 3 mi., SG on skeleton tower.

Sentinel Island Light
58 32.8N, 134 55.4W, Fl W 10s,
86 ft., 16mi., white square tower
on fog signal building, obscured
from 152° to 296°.

Sergius Narrows Buoy 8
57 24.4N, 135 37.9W, red nun.

Sergius Narrows Light 9
57 24.5N, 135 37.9W, Fl G 4s,
17 ft., 4 mi., SG on skeleton tower,
obscured from 080° to 243°.

Settler Cove Breakwater Light 2
57 52.3N, 152 51.8W, Fl R 2.5s,
24 ft., 4 mi., TR on single pile.

Settler Cove Daybeacon 1
57 52.2N, 152 51.5W, SG on pile.

SEWARD

Fourth of July South Breakwater Light
60 05.1N, 149 21.6W, Fl R 4s, 9 ft.,
on pedestal, private aid.

Seward Forest Products Dock Mooring Lights (2)
60 05.8N, 149 21.5W, Fl R 2.5s,
20 ft., on dolphins, private aids.

Seward Marine Dock Light
60 05.9N, 149 26.5W, F R, on end
of dock, private aid.

Boat Harbor Light 1
60 06.8N, 149 26.1W, Fl G 2.5s,
12 ft., 4 mi., SG on pile.

East Breakwater Light 2
60 06.9N, 149 26.1W, Fl R 4s,
16 ft., 5 mi., TR on skeleton tower.

West Breakwater Light 3
60 06.9N, 149 26.2W, Fl G 4s,
16 ft., 5 mi., SG on skeleton tower.

Railroad Pier Buoy 2
60 06.9N, 149 25.5W, red nun.

Seward Coal Dock Lighted Buoy
60 06.8N, 149 25.8W, Q W, white
with orange bands, private aid.

Seward Coal Dock Mooring Buoy
60 06.8N, 149 25.8W, white with
blue band, private aid.

Seward Coal Dolphin Light
60 06.8N, 149 25.8W, Fl G 6s,
10 ft., on pile dolphin, private aid.

Seward Cargo Dock Mooring Dolphin Light
60 07.0N, 149 25.7W, Fl R 6s,
24 ft., on dolphin, private aid.

Alaska Railroad Dock West Light
60 07.1N, 149 25.7W, F R, 31 ft.,
on post on dock, private aid.

Alaska Railroad Dock East Light
60 07.1N, 149 25.6W, F R, 31 ft.,
on post on dock, private aid.

Seward Sediment Control Groin Markers (3)
60 07.0N, 149 25.0W, 25 ft., NW
on pile, private aids.

Shakan Bay Light
56 08.9N, 133 37.5W, Fl W 4s,
25 ft., 6 mi., NR on skeleton
tower on small house, obscured
from 314° to 048°.

Shakan Strait Daybeacon
56 07.8N, 133 30.3W, 20 ft., NR
on square frame.

Shakmanof Point Light
57 55.5N, 152 35.3W, Fl W 6s, 60 ft.,
6 mi., NR on skeleton tower.

Shaktoolik River Entrance Light
64 22.8N, 161 14.1W, Fl W 4s, 14 ft.,
7 mi., NR on skeleton tower.

Sheep Creek Light 2
58 15.5N, 134 19.8W, Fl R 4s,
12 ft., 5 mi., TR on small house
on square pile structure, higher
intensity beam down channel.
Also see Juneau and Gastineau
Channel.

Sheep Creek Salmon Pen Lights (2)
58 15.8N, 134 20.3W, Fl Y 2.5s,
5 mi., battery boxes, private aids.

Sheep Island Lighted Buoy 3
57 12.8N, 153 15.0W, Fl G 2.5s,
3 mi., green.

Sheldon Point Light
62 32.2N, 165 01. 3W, Fl W 2.5s,
18 ft., 6 mi., NR on skeleton
tower, maintained from July 1 to
Nov. 1.

SHELTER COVE

Breakwater Light 2
55 28.4N, 133 08.6W, Fl R 4s,
30 ft., 4 mi., TR on steel pile.

Entrance Range Front Daybeacon
55 28.5N, 133 08.5W, KRW on
skeleton tower.

Entrance Range Rear Daybeacon
37 yards, 048° from front daybeacon, KRW on skeleton tower.

Herring Cove Log Boom Markers (3)
NW on log boom worded DAN-
GER LOG BOOM, private aids.

Shelter Cove Log Boom Markers (3)
55 32.1N, 131 20.6W, white and
orange markers worded DANGER
LOG BOOM, private aids.

Shelter Island Light
58 22.5N, 134 48.5W, Fl W 4s,
19 ft., 7 mi., NR on skeleton tower,
obscured from 020° to 158°.

Ship Island Light
55 35.9N, 132 12.2W, Fl W 4s,
40 ft., 7 mi., NR on skeleton
tower, partially obscured by trees
between island and main shore
from 180° to 305°.

Shishmaref Light
66 15.5N, 166 02.4W, Fl W 4s,
18 ft., NR on skeleton tower.

Shoe Island Light
54 57.1N, 132 44.7W, Fl W 6s,
20 ft., 5 mi., NR on skeleton tower,
obscured from 313° to 088°.

Shoe Island Shoal Buoy 2
54 57.3N, 132 45.6W, red nun.

Shoemaker Bay Smallboat Harbor Light 1
56 25.0N, 132 21.2W, Fl G 4s,
20 ft., 3 mi., SG on pile.
Also see Wrangell Harbor *and*
Zimovia Strait.

Shoemaker Bay Smallboat Harbor Light 2
56 25.0N, 132 21.1W, Fl R 2.5s,
20 ft., 3 mi., TR on pile.

Signal Island Light 4
57 02.8N, 135 23.6W, Fl R 4s,
48 ft., 4 mi., TR on skeleton tower,
obscured from 217° to 005°.
Also see Western Channel.

Simpson Rock Lighted Bell Buoy 5
57 01.2N, 135 20.7W, Fl G 4s,
4 mi., green.
Also see Eastern Channel.

Sisters Light
See The Sisters Light.

SITKA HARBOR

Also see Sitka Sound, Eastern
Channel, Alidale Channel, *and*
Western Channel.

Sitka Breakwater Light 8
57 03.7N, 135 22.0W, Fl R 2.5s,
19 ft., 4 mi., TR on pile.

Sitka Breakwater Light 7
57 03.8N, 135 21.9W, Fl G 4s,
19 ft., 3 mi., SG on pile.

Japonski Island Daybeacon 2
57 03.4N, 135 22.5W, 24 ft., TR
on spindle.

Sitka Southwest Harbor Entrance Daybeacon 4
57 03.5N, 135 22.0W, TR on
spindle.

Sitka Harbor Channel Lighted Buoy 9
57 03.2N, 135 21.0W, Q G, 3 mi.,
green.

Harbor Rock Daybeacon
57 03.2N, 135 20.9W, NR on single-pile tower.

Sitka Harbor Channel Lighted Buoy 11 (marks eastern limits of dredged channel south of Horseshoe Rocks)
57 03.2N, 135 20.9W, Fl G 4s,
3 mi., green.

SITKA SOUND

Also see Eastern Channel, Alidale Channel, Western Channel, *and* Sitka Harbor.

South

Elovoi Rock Daybeacon 1
56 49.3N, 135 22.8W, SG on pile.

Koka Island Passage Daybeacon 1
56 54.8N, 135 23.7W, SG on pile.

Cape Edgecumbe Light
56 59.9N, 135 51.4W, Fl W 4s,
100 ft., 7 mi., NR on square frame,
obscured from 149.5° to 321°.

Vitskari Island Light
57 00.0N, 135 32.7W, Fl W 6s,
50 ft., 9 mi., NR on skeleton
tower, racon: O (---).

Kulichkof Rock Lighted Buoy 2
56 59.9N, 135 27.0W, Fl R 4s,
4 mi., red.

North

Kasiana Island Shoal Daybeacon 1
57 05.4N, 135 24.4W, SG on pile.

Old Sitka Rocks Light 2
57 06.9N, 135 24.7W, Fl R 6s,
30 ft., 4 mi., TR on skeleton tower.

Big Gavanski Island Light 3
57 08.4N, 135 25.0W, Fl G 2.5s,
22 ft., 4 mi., SG on skeleton tower,
obscured from 010° to 154°.

Lisianski Point Light 4
57 09.0N, 135 24.5W, Fl R 4s,
41 ft., 4 mi., TR on skeleton tower,
obscured from 158° to 318°.

Sitkalidak Passage Light 4
57 12.6N, 153 16.6W, Fl R 6s,
30 ft., 4 mi., TR on skeleton tower.

Skagway
See Haines and Skagway.

Skin Island Light
55 18.1N, 132 04.4W, Fl W 4s,
33 ft., 6 mi., NR on skeleton tower,
obscured from 006° to 152°.

Skipwith Reefs Buoy 2
58 00.7N, 152 39.3W, red nun.

Skowl Point Light
55 25.7N, 132 16.2W, Fl W 4s,
15 ft., 5 mi., NR on skeleton tower.

Slate Islands Light
55 05.3N, 131 03.2W, Fl W 4s,
33 ft., 5 mi., NR on spindle,
obscured from 121° to 247°.

Sledge Island Light
64 29.8N, 166 11.9W, Fl W 6s,
32 ft., 7 mi., NR on skeleton tower,
obscured from 326° to 080°,
maintained from July 1 to Nov. 1.

Smoky Point Light
57 37.5N, 157 41.5W, Fl W 4s,
40 ft., 6 mi., NR on skeleton tower.

Snipe Island (Felice Strait) Light 5
55 00.2N, 131 23.3W, Fl G 6s, 20 ft.,
4 mi., SG on skeleton tower.

Snipe Point (Behm Canal) Light
55 55.5N, 131 36.9W, Fl W 2.5s,
18 ft., 5 mi., NR on skeleton
tower, higher intensity down
Behm Canal and Hassler Pass.

Snipe Rock (Ogden Passage) Daybeacon 1
57 38.2N, 136 10.7W, SG on
spindle.

Snow Passage Lighted Buoy 4
56 16.1N, 132 56.6W, Fl R 6s,
4 mi., red.

Snow Passage Lighted Buoy SP
56 19.2N, 133 05.3W, Fl (2+1) R 6s,
4 mi., red and green bands.

Softuk Bar Channel Light S
60 13.6N, 144 57.8W, Oc W 4s,
12 ft., 6 mi., NR on skeleton tower,
maintained from May 1 to Oct. 1.
Also see Copper River Delta.

Sola Rock Daybeacon SR
55 25.5N, 133 28.9W, JR on
spindle.

South Craig Point Light
56 23.4N, 132 37.4W, Fl W 2.5s,
24 ft., 5 mi., NR on pile, obscured
from 006° to 178°.

South Inian Pass Lighted Bell Buoy 6
58 13.8N, 136 15.5W, Fl R 4s,
4 mi., red.

South Naknek City Dock Lights (2)
58 43.0N, 157 00.0W, Fl R 6s,
30 ft., on dock, private aids.
Also see Naknek Entrance
Daybeacon 1.

South Niblack Islands Light
56 00.4N, 132 05.4W, Fl W 2.5s,
24 ft., 5 mi., NR on square frame,
higher intensity up and down
channel.

South Passage Light
58 15.3N, 136 06.9W, Fl W 2.5s,
5 mi., NR on skeleton tower,
obscured from 121° to 280°.

South Passage Light 8
58 14.8N, 135 54.4W, Fl R 4s,
5 mi., TR on skeleton tower,
obscured from 230° to 049°.

Spanish Islands Light
55 59.2N, 134 06.3W, Fl W 6s,
38 ft., 7 mi., NR on skeleton tower,
obscured from 263° to 061°.

Spasski Island Light 12
58 08.0N, 135 16.3W, Fl R 6s,
30 ft., 5 mi., TR on small house,
obscured from 315° to 088°.

Spike Island Light
60 33.0N, 145 46.2W, Fl W 6s,
35 ft., 7 mi., NR on skeleton tower.
Also see Prince William Sound.

Spire Island Reef Light SI
55 16.1N, 131 30.0W, Fl G 4s,
30 ft., 4 mi., SG on square truncated concrete pyramid.

Spithead Light
53 53.8N, 166 30.9W, Fl W 4s, 38 ft., 5 mi., NR on skeleton tower, obscured in Unalaska Bay when less than 215.5°.
Also see Unalaska Island.

Spruce Cape Light
57 49.3N, 152 19.5W, Fl W 10s, 40 ft., 18 mi., NR on skeleton tower.
Also see Kodiak.

St. Catherine Cove Daybeacon 4
54 59.8N, 163 29.4W, TR on square frame, use only with local knowledge.
Also see Bechevin Bay.

St. George Harbor

Range Front Light
56 34.2N, 169 40.1W, Q W, 36 ft., KRW on tower.

Range Rear Light
311 yards, 076° from front light, Iso W 6s, 76 ft., KRW on tower.

Entrance Daybeacon
56 34.0N, 169 40.2W, NG on tower.

Daybeacon 2
56 34.2N, 169 39.9W, TR on spindle.

St. Herman Bay
See Kodiak.

St. Ignace Rock Light
55 25.7N, 133 23.7W, Fl W 6s, 20 ft., 6 mi., NR on skeleton tower.

St. Paul Harbor, Kodiak Island.
See Kodiak.

St. Paul Harbor, Pribilof Islands

Jetty Light 2
57 07.8N, 170 17.2W, Fl R 4s, 40 ft., 4 mi., TR on spindle.

Jetty Light 3
57 07.7N, 170 17.1W, Fl G 4s, 30 ft., 4 mi., SG on spindle.

Outfall Range Daybeacons (2)
57 07.2N, 170 16.1W, NW on post worded OUTFALL NO ANCHORING, private aids.

Stag Point Light
54 59.1N, 162 18.1W, Fl W 4s, 23 ft., 6 mi., NR on skeleton tower.

Star Rock Bell Buoy
57 49.8N, 136 28.1W, green and red bands, maintained from May 15 to Sept. 30.

Starr Point Light 3
57 45.3N, 153 22.1W, Fl G 4s, 30 ft., 4 mi., SG on skeleton tower.

Station Island Light
56 29.7N, 132 45.8W, Fl W 2.5s, 19 ft., 5 mi., NR on square frame structure.

Steamer Point Light
56 13.4N, 132 42.8W, Fl W 4s, 30 ft., 5 mi., NR on skeleton tower, obscured from 213° to 017°.

Stewart Dolphin West (Canada)
55 54.8N, 130 00.1W, Fl (3) G 12s, 23 ft., 8-pile dolphin.

Stewart Light (Canada)
55 54.7N, 129 59.4W, Fl (3) W 12s, 12 ft., square skeleton tower.

Strait Island Lighted Bell Buoy 7
56 22.4N, 133 42.0W, Fl G 6s, 4 mi., green.

Strauss Rock Buoy SR
58 21.6N, 134 48.5W, green and red bands, can.

Sugarloaf Island Shoal Lighted Whistle Buoy 2
58 17.4N, 136 53.4W, Fl R 6s, 4 mi., red.

Sukkwan Strait

Hydaburg Buoy 2
55 11.7N, 132 49.1W, red nun.

Buoy SS
55 12.0N, 132 49.8W, green can with red band.

Hydaburg Buoy 4
55 12.1N, 132 49.6W, red nun.

Sukkwan Narrows Buoy 6
55 12.1N, 132 50.3W, red nun.

Sukkwan Narrows Buoy 7
55 12.3N, 132 50.3W, green can.

Hydaburg Daybeacon 8
55 12.4N, 132 50.0W, TR on pile.

Hydaburg Daybeacon
55 12.9N, 132 50.2W, NR on spindle.

Hydaburg Boat Basin Daybeacon 2
55 12.6N, 132 49.8W, TR on pile.

Hydaburg Boat Basin Daybeacon 3
55 12.7N, 132 49.8W, SG on spindle.

Sukkwan Narrows Light
55 12.1N, 132 50.5W, Fl W 4s, 16 ft., 5 mi., NR on skeleton tower, obscured from 252° to 019°.

Sukkwan Narrows Buoy 4
55 11.6N, 132 51.3W, red nun.

Sukkwan Narrows Buoy 2
55 11.3N, 132 51.6W, red nun.

Goat Island Light
55 10.1N, 132 53.6W, Fl W 4s, 21 ft., 5 mi., NR on skeleton tower, obscured from 093° to 261°.

Turn Rock Daybeacon
55 10.0N, 132 55.0W, NR on spindle.

Sukoi Islets Light
56 53.7N, 132 56.6W, Fl W 4s, 18 ft., 6 mi., NR on skeleton tower on concrete pier, obscured from 177° to 329°.

Sullivan Island Daybeacon 2 (marks rock)
58 57.9N, 135 21.3W, 30 ft., TR on spindle.

Sullivan Island Light
58 53.9N, 135 18.2W, Fl W 4s, 24 ft., 7 mi., NR on skeleton tower on rock, higher intensity beam down channel, obscured from 090° to 190°.

Suloia Point Light 5
57 23.4N, 135 39.0W, Fl G 2.5s, 22 ft., 4 mi., SG on steel skeleton tower, obscured from 021° to 190°.

Surf Point Light
55 50.0N, 133 38.0W, Fl W 4s, 29 ft., 6 mi., NR on skeleton tower, obscured from 290° to 060°.

Surf Rock Light
57 01.9N, 135 22.6W, Fl W 4s,
15 ft., 5 mi., NR on spindle.
Also see Eastern Channel.

Surge Bay Entrance Light
57 58.6N, 136 33.7W, Fl W 4s,
65 ft., 6 mi., NR on post,
obscured from 176° to 016°.

Susitna Flats Light
61 15.2N, 150 29.3W, Fl W 4s,
9 mi., NR on skeleton tower,
racon: K (-·-).

**Swanson Harbor Channel Stakes
(about 10)**
58 13.1N, 135 07.1W, 8 ft., pilings,
tide gauges show least depth,
private aids.

Swanson Harbor Entrance Light 2
58 11.6N, 135 04.7W, Fl R 6s,
21 ft., 4 mi., TR on skeleton tower,
obscured from 144° to 299°.

Sweeper Cove
See Adak Island.

T

Table Island Light
57 11.4N, 152 55.2W, Fl W 4s,
106 ft., 7 mi., NR on small house.

Taiya Inlet
See Haines and Skagway.

Talsani Island Light
59 04.7N, 135 16.4W, Fl W 6s,
16 ft., 6 mi., NR on skeleton tower,
obscured from 325° to 133°.

Tamgas Harbor Buoy 1
55 02.0N, 131 31.3W, green can.

Tamgas Harbor Entrance Light
55 01.3N, 131 30.8W, Fl W 4s,
30 ft., 4 mi., NR on small house
on skeleton tower.

Tatitlek Narrows
See Prince William Sound.

Tatoosh Islands Light
55 32.2N, 131 49.9W, Fl W 2.5s,
30 ft., 7 mi., NR on skeleton tower.

Tebenkof Bay Daybeacon 3
56 25.6N, 134 06.5W, SG on post
on pyramidal concrete pier.

Tebenkof Bay Light 1
56 27.0N, 134 08.3W, Fl G 4s,
14 ft., 4 mi., SG on small house,
obscured from 142° to 339°.

Tee Harbor Control Buoy
58 24.8N, 134 45.6W, white nun
with two orange bands and
orange circle worded SLOW
NO WAKE, private aid.

Tee Harbor Light
58 25.7N, 134 46.0W, Fl W 6s,
33 ft., 6 mi., NR on skeleton tower,
obscured from 150° to 325°.

TENAKEE INLET

Entrance Light 1
57 46.3N, 134 56.1W, Fl G 4s,
33 ft., 5 mi., SG on spindle.

Daybeacon 2
57 46.5N, 135 08.4W, TR on
spindle.

Daybeacon T
57 50.7N, 135 24.9W, JR on
spindle.

Light 4
57 46.5N, 135 11.9W, Fl R 6s,
30 ft., 4 mi., TR on small house.

**Tenakee Boat Harbor Entrance
Light 1**
57 46.7N, 135 09.3W, Fl G 4s,
15 ft., 3 mi., SG on pile.

Tenakee Reef Light
57 46.2N, 135 13.7W, Fl W 4s,
23 ft., 5 mi., NR on small house
on skeleton tower.

Tenakee Reef Daybeacon
57 46.6N, 135 14.1W, NR on pile.

The Bend Light
58 50.0N, 156 59.9W, Fl W 6s,
25 ft., 5 mi., NR on skeleton tower.

The Eckholms Light
57 00.6N, 135 21.5W, Fl W 6s,
33 ft., 6 mi., NR on skeleton tower.
Also see Eastern Channel.

The Eye Opener Light
56 23.2N, 133 16.6W, Fl W 2.5s,
28 ft., 7 mi., NR on skeleton
tower on brown cylindrical base.

The Sisters Light
58 10.3N, 135 15.5W, Fl W 4s,
69 ft., 7 mi., on FAA building.

The Twins Light 9
57 02.1N, 135 18.8W, Fl G 4s,
14 ft., 4 mi., SG on skeleton tower,
obscured from 030° to 146°.
Also see Eastern Channel.

**Thin Point Lighted Whistle
Buoy 2**
54 54.9N, 162 32.4W, Fl R 6s,
4 mi., red.

Thomas Basin Entrance Light 2
55 20.3N, 131 38.6W, Fl R 2.5s,
28 ft., 3 mi., TR on steel tower.
Also see Tongass Narrows.

THOMAS BAY

Entrance Buoy 1
56 59.3N, 132 58.3W, green can.

Entrance Lighted Bell Buoy 2
56 59.1N, 132 57.9W, Fl R 6s, 4
mi., red.

Buoy 4
56 59.9N, 132 57.7W, red nun.

THORNE BAY

Entrance Light 2
55 40.8N, 132 27.5W, Fl R 6s,
16 ft., 5 mi., TR on skeleton tower,
obscured from 135° to 243°.

Channel Light 3
55 40.7N, 132 27.9W, Fl G 2.5s,
15 ft., 4 mi., SG on pile, obscured
from 305° to 055°.

Channel Light 5
55 40.3N, 132 28.6W, Fl G 4s,
15 ft., 4 mi., SG on pile.

South Arm Light
55 39.6N, 132 30.1W, Fl W 4s,
22 ft., 4 mi., NR on pile.

Daybeacon 7
55 40.6N, 132 31.7W, SG on pile.

Three Brothers Light 8
57 55.4N, 152 33.2W, Fl R 4s,
32 ft., 3 mi., TR on skeleton tower
on concrete pier.

Three Brothers Reef Buoy 6
57 55.1N, 152 32.7W, red nun.

Three Hill Island Light
58 09.2N, 136 23.0W, Fl W 4s,
80 ft., 7 mi., NR on skeleton tower,
obscured from 094° to 289°.

Thumb Cove Fish Pen Marker
60 00.3N, 149 21.0W, 2 ft., private
aid.

Thumb Cove Light
60 00.4N, 149 20.0W, Fl W 6s,
42 ft., 6 mi., NR on pile, obscured
from 113° to 249°.

Tlevak Narrows Light 2
55 15.8N, 133 07.0W, Fl R 4s, 22 ft.,
4 mi., TR on skeleton tower,
obscured from 152° to 279°.

Tlevak Narrows Buoy 4
55 16.0N, 133 08.2W, red nun.

Tokeen Harbor Entrance Light
55 56.2N, 133 19.9W, Fl W 6s,
35 ft., 6 mi., NR on skeleton tower,
obscured from 128° to 255°.

TONGASS NARROWS

West Channel Lighted Buoy 2
55 18.0N, 131 36.4W, Fl R 2.5s,
3 mi., red.

West Channel Light 4
55 19.1N, 131 38.6W, Fl R 4s,
18 ft., 5 mi., TR on skeleton tower,
obscured from 126° to 315°.

West Channel Lighted Buoy 5
55 19.2N, 131 38.9W, Fl G 4s,
3 mi., green.

East Channel Entrance Buoy 2
55 18.6N, 131 35.3W, red nun.

Saxman Breakwater Light
55 18.9N, 131 35.8W, F R, 15 ft.,
on post, private aid.

California Rock Lighted Buoy 3
55 18.9N, 131 36.2W, Fl G 4s,
4 mi., green.

Idaho Rock Lighted Buoy 4
55 19.0N, 131 36.1W, Fl R 4s,
4 mi., red.

**Standard Oil Company Pier
Lights (2)**
55 20.1N, 131 37.7W, F R, private
aids.

Thomas Basin Entrance Light 2
55 20.3N, 131 38.6W, Fl R 2.5s,
28 ft., 3 mi., TR on steel tower.

**East Channel Lighted Buoy 4A
(marks 4-fathom shoal)**
55 20.4N, 131 39.0W, Fl R 4s,
4 mi., red.

**Pennock Island Reef Lighted
Buoy PR**
55 20.3N, 131 40.1W, Fl (2+1) G
6s, 3 mi., green and red bands.

**Wreck Lighted Buoy WR6 (marks
sunken barge)**
55 20.7N, 131 40.4W, Q R, 3 mi.,
red.

Bar Harbor

South Entrance Light 2S
55 20.9N, 131 40.7W, Fl R 4s,
11 ft., 4 mi., TR on skeleton tower
on concrete base.

South Entrance Daybeacon 3S
55 20.9N, 131 40.7W, SG on skeleton tower on concrete base.

Entrance Light 2
55 20.9N, 131 41.1W, Fl R 2.5s,
8 ft., 4 mi., TR on skeleton tower.

Entrance Daybeacon 3
55 21.0N, 131 41.1W, SG on skeleton tower.

North Entrance Light 2N
55 21.1N, 131 41.4W, Fl R 6s, 8 ft.,
4 mi., TR on caisson.

Tongass Narrows cont'd

East Clump Light 7
55 20.7N, 131 41.3W, Fl G 6s,
15 ft., 5 mi., SG on square frame.

Buoy 9
55 21.8N, 131 43.2W, green can.

Marine Highway Wharf Lights (2)
55 21.4N, 131 42.0W, Fl R 4s,
13 ft., 3 mi., on boxes on concrete
wharf, private aids.

Lighted Buoy 10
55 22.4N, 131 43.6W, Fl R 2.5s,
4 mi., red.

Lewis Reef Light 11
55 22.5N, 131 44.3W, Fl G 2.5s,
15 ft., 5 mi., SG on concrete
pyramid.

Peninsula Point Reef Buoy 2
55 23.1N, 131 44.5W, red nun.

Channel Island Light 14
55 23.7N, 131 45.9W, Fl R 4s,
24 ft., 5 mi., TR on skeleton tower
on concrete base, obscured from
238° to 268°.

Ohio Rock Lighted Buoy OR
55 23.8N, 131 46.3W, Fl (2+1) R
6s, 4 mi., red and green bands.

Refuge Cove

Entrance Light 2
55 24.0N, 131 45.0W, Fl R 6s,
15 ft., 4 mi., TR on skeleton tower.

Daybeacon 3
55 24.1N, 131 45.0W, SG on skeleton tower.

Daybeacon 5
55 24.2N, 131 44.8W, SG on
spindle

Rosa Reef Light 15
55 24.8N, 131 48.2W, Fl G 6s,
24 ft., 6 mi., SG on caisson.

Pond Reef Light 16
55 26.2N, 131 48.9W, Fl R 2.5s,
13 ft., 4 mi., TR on skeleton tower.

Vallenar Point Buoy 17
55 25.8N, 131 50.5W, green can.

Vallenar Rock Light
55 25.9N, 131 51.8W, Fl W 2.5s,
18 ft., 6 mi., NR on spindle.

Guard Islands Light
55 26.8N, 131 52.9W, Fl W 10s,
74 ft., 17 mi., white square tower
on rectangular building.

Tongass Reef Daybeacon
54 47.2N, 130 44.7W, NR on
skeleton tower.

Tonki Cape Light
58 21.1N, 151 59.2W, Fl W 4s,
75 ft., 8 mi., NR on skeleton tower.

Tonowek Narrows Daybeacon 2T
55 45.3N, 133 20.5W, TR on pile.
Also see Karheen Passage.

Tow Channel
See Wrangell Narrows.

Tracy Arm Light
57 49.3N, 133 34.5W, Fl W 4s,
6 mi., NR on skeleton tower, light
maintained from May 1 to Oct. 1.

Trap Rock Buoy 3
56 11.3N, 132 13.4W, green can.
Also see Zimovia Strait.

Tree Point Light
54 48.2N, 130 56.0W, Fl W 6s,
86 ft., 9 mi., white square tower
on building, obscured from 158°
to 318°.

Trinity Point Light
60 48.4N, 148 34.1W, Fl W 6s,
39 ft., 6 mi., NR on skeleton tower,
obscured from 262° to 079°.
Also see Prince William Sound.

Tsaritsa Rock Lighted Buoy 7
57 01.2N, 135 19.5W, Fl G 2.5s,
3 mi., green.
Also see Eastern Channel.

Turn Rock Daybeacon
55 10.0N, 132 55.0W, NR on spindle.
Also see Sukkwan Strait.

Turnabout Island Light
57 07.9N, 133 59.3W, Fl W 4s,
23 ft., 6 mi., NR on spindle,
obscured from 270° to 048°.

Turning Island Light 11
57 02.6N, 135 20.2W, Fl G 2.5s,
16 ft., 5 mi., SG on skeleton
tower, obscured sector from 062°
to 153°.
Also see Alidale Channel.

Twin Islands Light TI
55 08.6N, 131 13.0W, Fl G 6s,
19 ft., 5 mi., SG on skeleton tower,
obscured from 324° to 081°.

Twins Light 9
See The Twins Light 9.

Two Tree Island Light
56 29.7N, 132 38.1W, Fl W 6s,
22 ft., 6 mi., NR on pile.

U

Ugamak Island Light
54 13.7N, 164 47.9W, Fl W 4s,
98 ft., 8 mi., NR on skeleton tower.

Ugashik River Entrance Buoy 1
57 37.5N, 157 52.2W, green can,
maintained from May 1 to
Sept. 30.

Ukolnoi Island Light
55 14.7N, 161 39.6W, Fl W 6s,
35 ft., 6 mi., NR on steel square
frame, obscured from 238°
to 052°.

**Unalakleet River Buoys (about 6,
mark channel into Unalakleet)**
Red nuns or green cans, maintained from June 1 to Nov. 1.

Unalakleet River South Spit Light
63 52.1N, 160 47.3W, Fl W 4s,
15 ft., 7 mi., NR on skeleton tower.

UNALASKA ISLAND

Ulakta Head Light
53 55.5N, 166 30.5W, Fl W 4s,
61 ft., 5 mi., NR on skeleton tower,
obscured from 331° to 122°.

**Iliuliuk Bay Entrance Lighted Bell
Buoy 2**
53 54.5N, 166 29.7W, Fl R 4s,
4 mi., red.

Spithead Light
53 53.8N, 166 30.9W, Fl W 4s,
38 ft., 5 mi., NR on skeleton
tower, obscured in Unalaska Bay
when less than 215.5°.

**Rocky Point Shoal Lighted Buoy
RP**
53 53.4N, 166 31.3W, Fl (2+1) G 6s,
3 mi., green and red bands.

Iliuliuk Bay Lighted Buoy 4
53 53.1N, 166 31.5W, Fl R 6s,
4 mi., red.

APL Dolphin Lights (2)
Fl R 2.5s, 12 ft., on pile dolphins,
private aids.

APL Shoal Lighted Buoys (2)
Q W, white with orange bands
and diamond, private aids.

Unalaska Channel Lighted Buoy 5
53 52.6N, 166 32.1W, Fl G 2.5s,
4 mi., green.

Iliuliuk Reef Lighted Buoy 6
53 52.6N, 166 32.0W, Fl R 4s,
4 mi., red.

Iliuliuk Harbor Entrance Buoy 8
53 52.7N, 166 32.2W, red nun.

**Iliuliuk Harbor South Channel
Buoy 10**
53 52.6N, 166 32.8W, red nun.

**Iliuliuk Harbor South Channel
Buoy 11**
53 52.5N, 166 32.8W, green can.

**Iliuliuk Harbor South Channel
Buoy 12**
53 52.5N, 166 32.9W, red nun.

**Iliuliuk Harbor South Channel
Buoy 13**
53 52.5N, 166 33.0W, green can.

Unalaska Bay

Hog Island Lighted Buoy HI
53 55.2N, 166 34.2W, Fl G (2+1) 6s,
4 mi., green and red bands.

Hog Island Lighted Buoy 3
53 53.5N, 166 34.9W, Fl G 4s,
4 mi., green.

Captains Bay

South Amaknak Rocks Buoy 5
53 51.8N, 166 33.3W, green can.

Bailey Ledge Light
53 51.6N, 166 33.6W, Fl W 4s,
20 ft., 5 mi., NR on spindle, radar
reflector.

Swallow Reef Buoy 6
53 50.6N, 166 35.6W, red nun.

Unga Reef Lighted Buoy 4
55 20.3N, 160 31.3W, Fl R 4s,
3 mi., red.

Unga Spit Light
55 24.4N, 160 43.5W, Fl W 6s,
40 ft., 6 mi., NR on skeleton tower,
obscured from 280.5° to 060°

Usher Rock Shoal Lighted Buoy 5
57 03.1N, 135 23.8W, Fl G 4s,
3 mi., green.
Also see Western Channel.

V

Valdez
See Prince William Sound.

Vallenar Point Buoy 17
55 25.8N, 131 50.5W, green can.
Also see Tongass Narrows.

Vallenar Rock Light
55 25.9N, 131 51.8W, Fl W 2.5s,
18 ft., 6 mi., NR on spindle.

Vanderbilt Reef Light
58 35.5N, 135 01.1W, Fl W 2.5s,
36 ft., 6 mi., NR on skeleton
tower on concrete pier, higher
intensity beam up channel.

Vank Island Light
56 26.9N, 132 36.0W, Fl W 4s,
24 ft., 7 mi., NR on pile, obscured
from 110° to 264°.

Vichnefski Rock Light
56 26.3N, 133 00.9W, Fl W 4s,
33 ft., 6 mi., NR on skeleton
tower, 1¼-fathom rock,
630 yards, 214° from light.

View Cove Entrance Light
55 03.2N, 132 57.9W, Fl W 4s,
35 ft., 6 mi., NR on skeleton tower.

Village Rock (Tuxekan Passage) Daybeacon VR
55 53.3N, 133 15.4W, JR on pile.

Village Rock (Zimovia Strait) Daybeacon 12
56 12.9N, 132 17.6W, 22 ft., TR on single steel pile.
Also see Zimovia Strait.

Village Islands Light 13
56 12.8N, 132 18.1W, Fl G 4s, 17 ft., 4 mi., SG on pile.

Village Islands Rock Daybeacon 15
56 13.1N, 132 19.1W, 22 ft., SG on post on concrete pier.

Vitskari Island Light
57 00.0N, 135 32.7W, Fl W 6s, 50 ft., 9 mi., NR on skeleton tower, racon: O (---).
Also see Sitka Sound.

W

Walden Rock Light 6
55 16.3N, 131 36.7W, Fl R 6s, 20 ft., 4 mi., TR on pile.

Wallace Rock Buoy 2
54 51.1N, 132 27.0W, red nun.

Walrus Island Light
56 01.3N, 160 49.0W, Fl W 4s, 24 ft., 7 mi., NR on skeleton tower.

Warburton Island Light
55 07.9N, 131 38.0W, Fl W 4s, 35 ft., 5 mi., NR on skeleton tower, obscured from 063° to 189°.

Warm Spring Bay Light
57 04.8N, 134 46.5W, Fl W 4s, 27 ft., 7 mi., NR on skeleton tower, obscured from 308° to 101°.

Washington Bay Light
56 43.1N, 134 23.7W, Fl W 4s, 33 ft., 6 mi., NR on spindle.

Wayanda Ledge Buoy 10
57 24.4N, 135 37.7W, red nun.

Wessels Reef Buoy 1
59 47.7N, 146 05.5W, green can.

West Cape Shoal Buoy 1
54 55.5N, 162 27.9W, green can.

West Channel Lighted Bell Buoy 4
55 08.8N, 131 39.7W, Fl R 2.5s, 4 mi., red.
Also see Point McCartey Buoy 3 *and* Point McCartey Light.

West Francis Rock Lighted Buoy 6
57 24.3N, 135 38.4W, Fl R 2.5s, 4 mi., red.

West Pinta Rocks Light
57 05.2N, 134 00.7W, Fl W 2.5s, 30 ft., 6 mi., NR on pile.
Also see East Pinta Rocks Buoy 1.

West Rock Light
56 21.2N, 133 38.2W, Fl W 2.5s, 20 ft., 6 mi., NR on skeleton tower.

Western Channel

Also see Sitka Sound, Eastern Channel, Alidale Channel, *and* Sitka Harbor.

Makhnati Rock Lighted Whistle Buoy 2
57 02.2N, 135 23.8W, Fl R 2.5s, 4 mi., red.

Signal Island Light 4
57 02.8N, 135 23.6W, Fl R 4s, 48 ft., 4 mi., TR on skeleton tower, obscured from 217° to 005°.

Usher Rock Shoal Lighted Buoy 5
57 03.1N, 135 23.8W, Fl G 4s, 3 mi., green.

Battery Island Light 6
57 03.6N, 135 22.9W, Fl R 6s, 16 ft., 4 mi., TR on small house, obscured from 263° to 061°.

Whale Island Light
63 29.5N, 161 59.8W, Fl W 4s, 53 ft., 7 mi., NR on skeleton tower.

Whale Pass Resort Dock Lights (2)
56 06.2N, 133 06.8W, F R, private aids.

Whale Passage Daybeacon 1
56 08.2N, 133 03.2W, SG on pile, passage marked with SGs and TRs on piles.

Whale Passage (Kodiak Island) Daybeacon 4
57 55.4N, 152 48.0W, TR on post.

Whirlpool Point Light
56 37.0N, 154 05.6W, Fl W 2.5s, 51 ft., 8 mi., NR on small house on skeleton tower.

White Cliff Lighted Bell Buoy 12
55 43.9N, 133 39.7W, Fl R 4s, 4 mi., red.

Whitestone Narrows
See Neva Strait.

Whittier
See Prince William Sound.

Williams Reef Lighted Whistle Buoy 1
57 50.3N, 152 09.5W, Fl G 4s, 4 mi., green.
Also see Kodiak.

Windham Bay Entrance Light
57 33.7N, 133 32.6W, Fl W 6s, 35 ft., 6 mi., NR on small house.

Wolcott Reef Buoy
57 40.1N, 154 12.2W, red and green bands, nun.

Womens Bay
See Kodiak.

Wood Spit Light
57 44.3N, 133 34.5W, Fl W 2.5s, 27 ft., 5 mi., NR on tower on concrete base.

Woody Island

Also see Kodiak.

Woody Island Light
57 47.8N, 152 20.3W, Fl W 6s, 50 ft., 5 mi., NR on square frame, obscured from 228° to 040°.

Channel Lighted Buoy 2
57 47.1N, 152 21.7W, Fl R 2.5s, 3 mi., red.

Channel Buoy 3
57 46.8N, 152 21.8W, green can.

Channel Buoy 4
57 46.6N, 152 22.3W, red nun.

Channel Lighted Buoy 5
57 45.6N, 152 22.4W, Fl G 6s, 4 mi., green.

Channel Buoy 6
57 45.1N, 152 24.0W, red nun.

Woronkofski Point Daybeacon
56 26.3N, 132 28.8W, 18 ft., NR on skeleton tower.

Wrangell Harbor

Also see Shoemaker Bay *and* Zimovia Strait.

Breakwater Light 2
56 28.0N, 132 23.1W, Fl R 4s,
21 ft., 5 mi., TR on skeleton tower.

Dock Lights (4)
56 28.3N, 132 23.4W, F G, 12 ft.,
on dock and dolphins, private
aids.

Daybeacons 4–8
TRs and SGs on piles.

Point Highfield Reef Daybeacon
56 29.0N, 132 23.8W, 18 ft., NR
on pile.

WRANGELL NARROWS

Point Alexander Light
56 30.5N, 132 57.0W, Fl W 4s,
17 ft., 7 mi., NR on skeleton tower,
obscured from 162° to 293°.

Midway Rock Light MR
56 31.8N, 132 57.9W, Fl (2+1) R 6s,
16 ft., 4 mi., JR on skeleton
tower.

December Point Light DP
56 32.9N, 132 57.7W, Fl R 6s,
15 ft., 4 mi., TR on pile.

Point Lockwood Light PL
56 33.4N, 132 57.9W, Fl G 4s,
15 ft., 4 mi., SG on skeleton tower,
obscured from 027° to 166°.

Channel Light 1
56 34.0N, 132 58.1W, Fl G 2.5s,
22 ft., 3 mi., SG on concrete pier.

Channel Light 2
56 34.1N, 132 58.2W, Fl R 2.5s,
22 ft., 3 mi., TR on steel pile
structure.

Channel Lighted Buoy 2A
Fl R 2.5s, 3 mi., red.

Channel Lighted Buoy 3
56 34.2N, 132 58.5W, Fl G 2.5s,
3 mi., green.

Channel Lighted Buoy 3A
56 34.6N, 132 58.6W, Fl G 4s,
4 mi., green.

Channel Light 4
56 34.5N, 132 58.5W, Fl R 2.5s,
3 mi., TR on cylindrical base.

Tow Channel Buoy 1TC
56 34.2N, 132 58.1W, green can.

Tow Channel Buoy 3TC
56 34.4N, 132 58.2W, green can.

Tow Channel Buoy 4TC
56 34.7N, 132 58.4W, red nun.

Channel Light 5
56 34.9N, 132 58.6W, Fl G 2.5s,
16 ft., 3 mi., SG on skeleton tower.

Channel Light 8
56 35.6N, 132 58.5W, Fl R 2.5s,
9 ft., 3 mi., TR on dolphin.

Burnt Island Range Front Light
56 36.4N, 132 58.6W, F Y, 10 ft.,
KRW on multi-pile steel structure, visible 4° each side of
rangeline.

Burnt Island Range Rear Light
390 yards, 356.5° from front light,
F Y, 26 ft., KRW on dolphin, visible 4° each side of rangeline.

Channel Lighted Buoy 9
56 35.9N, 132 58.6W, Fl G 4s,
4 mi., green.

Channel Light 10
56 36.1N, 132 58.5W, Q R, 15 ft.,
3 mi., TR on steel pile structure.

Daybeacon 10A
56 36.3N, 132 58.5W, TR on steel
pile.

Channel Light 11
56 36.4N, 132 58.5W, Fl G 2.5s,
15 ft., 3 mi., SG on pyramid.

Channel Buoy 13
56 36.6N, 132 58.4W, green can.

Channel Buoy 13A
56 36.7N, 132 58.4W, green can.

Channel Light 14
56 36.7N, 132 58.3W, Fl R 2.5s,
15 ft., 3 mi., TR on steel pile
structure.

**Bush Top Island Range Front
Light**
56 37.9N, 132 57.1W, F W, 15 ft.,
KRW on steel pile structure, visible 4° each side of rangeline.

Bush Top Island Range Rear Light
460 yards, 029° from front light,
F W, 28 ft., KRW on skeleton tower,
visible 4° each side of rangeline.

Channel Light 15
56 37.4N, 132 57.7W, Fl G 2.5s,
15 ft., 3 mi., SG on steel pile
structure.

Channel Light 16
56 37.4N, 132 57.5W, Fl R 2.5s,
15 ft., 3 mi., TR on steel pile
structure.

Channel Light 17
56 37.7N, 132 57.3W, Fl G 2.5s,
15 ft., 3 mi., SG on steel pile
structure.

Channel Light 18
56 37.8N, 132 56.9W, Fl R 2.5s,
19 ft., 3 mi., TR on white truncated concrete structure.

Channel Light 19
56 38.0N, 132 56.8W, Fl G 2.5s,
20 ft., 3 mi., SG on steel structure,
on cylindrical concrete pier.

Channel Light 21
56 38.3N, 132 56.0W, Q G, 15 ft.,
3 mi., SG on steel pile structure.

Blind Point Range Front Light 24
56 38.6N, 132 55.4W, Q W, 17 ft.,
4 mi., KRW on steel pile structure, TR oriented up channel, visible all around, constant intensity all around.

Blind Point Range Rear Light
268 yards, 050.3° from front light,
F W, 31 ft., KRW on steel pile
structure.

Channel Light 25
56 38.8N, 132 55.4W, Fl G 2.5s,
15 ft., 3 mi., SG on pile structure.

Channel Lighted Buoy 26
56 38.8N, 132 55.2W, Fl R 4s,
3 mi., red.

Channel Light 27
56 38.9N, 132 55.3W, Fl G 2.5s,
15 ft., 3 mi., SG on dolphin.

Channel Lighted Buoy 28
56 39.0N, 132 55.2W, Fl R 4s,
3 mi., red.

Channel Lighted Buoy 29
56 39.1N, 132 55.3W, Fl G 2.5s,
3 mi., green.

Tow Channel Buoy 5TC
56 38.8N, 132 55.6W, green can,
used by tows with a draft of 9 ft.
or less.

Tow Channel Buoy 7TC
56 39.2N, 132 55.4W, green can,
used by tows with a draft of 9 ft.
or less.

Channel Light 31
56 39.3N, 132 55.5W, Q G, 13 ft.,
3 mi., SG on pile on concrete
pier.

Channel Light 32
56 39.4N, 132 55.5W, Q R, 15 ft.,
3 mi., TR on steel pile structure.

Channel Light 32A
56 39.5N, 132 55.6W, Fl R 4s,
15 ft., 3 mi., TR on steel pile
structure.

Channel Lighted Buoy 33
56 39.5N, 132 55.7W, Fl G 4s,
4 mi., green.

Channel Light 34
56 39.7N, 132 55.7W, Fl R 2.5s,
15 ft., 3 mi., TR on dolphin.

Channel Lighted Buoy 36
56 39.9N, 132 55.8W, Fl R 4s,
3 mi., red.

Channel Light 37
56 40.0N, 132 55.9W, Q G, 21 ft.,
3 mi., SG on skeleton tower on
concrete pier.

Channel Light 38
56 40.1N, 132 55.9W, Fl R 2.5s,
15 ft., 3 mi., TR on dolphin.

Channel Daybeacon 39
56 40.1N, 132 56.1W, SG on spindle on pyramid.

Channel Light 40
56 40.3N, 132 56.1W, Fl R 2.5s,
21 ft., 3 mi., TR on skeleton tower
on concrete pier.

Channel Lighted Buoy 42
56 40.4N, 132 56.2W, Fl R 4s,
3 mi., red.

Channel Light 43
56 41.0N, 132 56.7W, Q G, 13 ft.,
3 mi., SG on dolphin.

Channel Light 44
56 41.1N, 132 56.6W, Fl R 2.5s,
15 ft., 3 mi., TR on steel pile
structure.

Channel Lighted Buoy 46
56 41.5N, 132 57.0W, Fl R 2.5s,
3 mi., red.

Channel Light 47
56 41.5N, 132 57.1W, Fl G 2.5s,
15 ft., 3 mi., SG on steel pile
structure.

Channel Light 48
56 41.7N, 132 57.0W, Fl R 2.5s,
15 ft., 3 mi., TR on dolphin.

Channel Light 49
56 42.1N, 132 57.0W, Q G, 12 ft.,
4 mi., SG on dolphin.

Channel Light 50
56 42.3N, 132 56.9W, Fl R 2.5s,
15 ft., 4 mi., TR on steel pile
structure.

Channel Light 51
56 44.3N, 132 57.5W, Fl G 6s,
43 ft., 5 mi., SG on skeleton tower,
obscured from 349° to 148°.

Beckhams Beach Daybeacon 51A
56 46.2N, 132 58.7W, SG on pile.

Channel Light 52
56 46.9N, 132 58.9W, Fl R 4s,
13 ft., 4 mi., TR on pile structure,
higher intensity beam down
channel.

Reid Landing Dock Light
56 46.9N, 132 58.8W, F R, 14 ft.,
on post, private aid.

Channel Lighted Buoy 53
56 48.0N, 132 59.2W, Fl G 4s,
4 mi., green.

**Petersburg Creek Range Front
Light**
56 48.5N, 132 59.3W, F W, 10 ft.,
KRW on dolphin, visible 4° each
side of rangeline.

**Petersburg Creek Range Rear
Light**
341 yards, 353.2° from front light,
F W, 24 ft., KRW on dolphin, visible 4° each side of rangeline.

Channel Light 54
56 48.2N, 132 59.1W, Fl R 2.5s,
15 ft., 3 mi., TR on steel pile
structure.

Channel Light 56
56 48.4N, 132 59.1W, Q R, 15 ft.,
3 mi., TR on pile structure.

Channel Light 58
56 48.5N, 132 58.9W, Fl R 2.5s,
15 ft., 3 mi., TR on steel pile
structure.

Petersburg Bar Range Front Light
56 48.4N, 132 59.4W, F W, 13 ft.,
KRW on steel pile structure, visible 4° each side of rangeline.

Petersburg Bar Range Rear Light
519 yards, 235.5° from front light,
F W, 30 ft., KRW on pile structure,
visible 4° each side of rangeline.

**Marine Highway Terminal
Lights (2)**
56 48.5N, 132 58.7W, F R, 15 ft.,
on pier, private aids.

Petro Marine Fuel Dock Lights (2)
56 48.6N, 132 58.3W, F R, 13 ft.,
on pier, private aids.

**Chatham Strait Seafood Pier
Lights (2)**
56 48.8N, 132 57.9W, F R, 18 ft.,
on building, private aids.

Channel Lighted Buoy 59
56 48.9N, 132 58.0W, Fl G 2.5s,
3 mi., green.

**Petersburg Fisheries
Incorporated (PFI) Dock Lights (2)**
56 48.9N, 132 57.6W, F R, 14 ft.,
on building, private aid.

**Petersburg Fisheries
Incorporated (PFI) Dolphin Light**
56 48.9N, 132 57.5W, F R, 15 ft.,
on dolphin, private aid.

Channel Lighted Buoy 60
56 49.0N, 132 57.5W, Fl R 2.5s,
4 mi., red.

Channel Daybeacon 61
56 49.5N, 132 56.7W, SG on post.

Channel Lighted Buoy 62
56 49.6N, 132 56.1W, Fl R 4s,
4 mi., red.

**North Entrance Lighted Bell Buoy
WN**
56 49.8N, 132 55.8W, Mo (A) W,
5 mi., red and white stripes with
red spherical topmark.

Wyville Reef Lighted Buoy 22
57 16.3N, 135 35.5W, Fl R 2.5s,
4 mi., red.
Also see Neva Strait.

Y

YAKUTAT BAY

Ocean Cape Light
59 32.1N, 139 51.3W, Fl W 6s,
130 ft., 9 mi., NR on skeleton
tower, obscured from 134° to 309°.

Entrance Lighted Whistle Buoy 2
59 32.0N, 139 57.2W, Fl R 2.5s,
4 mi., red.

Lighted Whistle Buoy 4
59 35.6N, 139 51.1W, Fl R 4s,
4 mi., red.

Buoy 6
59 42.6N, 139 41.9W, red nun.

Buoy 8
59 41.4N, 139 38.7W, red nun.

Khantaak Island Light
59 33.6N, 139 47.0W, Fl W 4s,
28 ft., 6 mi., NR on skeleton tower,
obscured from 149° to 311°.

Yakutat Roads Light 1
59 33.5N, 139 45.9W, Fl G 2.5s,
15 ft., 3 mi., SG on post.

Yakutat Roads Light 2
59 34.1N, 139 44.8W, Fl R 4s,
12 ft., 3 mi., TR on tower,
obscured from 292° to 021°.

Yasha Island Shoal Lighted Buoy 2
56 58.9N, 134 34.6W, Fl R 6s,
4 mi., red.

Yellow Point Light 16
57 26.9N, 135 33.7W, Q R, 17 ft.,
3 mi., TR on square frame,
obscured from 265° to 034°.

Yellow Point Rock Daybeacon 18
57 26.9N, 135 33.2W, TR on concrete pier.

YUKON RIVER

Lights are maintained from July 1
to Nov. 1.

North Entrance Light
63 02.5N, 163 23.1W, Fl W 6s,
19 ft., 8 mi., NR on skeleton
tower, obscured from 286° to
161°, radar reflector.

Middle Entrance Light
63 04.6N, 164 37.7W, Fl W 4s,
18 ft., 8 mi., NR on skeleton
tower, obscured from 176° to
266°, radar reflector.

South Entrance Light
62 35.4N, 164 59.6W, Fl W 6s,
20 ft., 8 mi., NR on skeleton
tower, radar reflector.

Yuzhni Point Buoy 2
57 55.2N, 152 47.0W, red nun.

Z

ZIMOVIA STRAIT

Found Island Rock Daybeacon
56 06.8N, 132 04.3W, NR on spindle on concrete pier.

Light 2
56 11.0N, 132 12.8W, Fl R 2.5s,
23 ft., 4 mi., TR on pile.

Trap Rock Buoy 3
56 11.3N, 132 13.4W, green can.

Button Island Shoal Buoy 5
56 12.1N, 132 14.9W, green can.

Light 6
56 12.2N, 132 15.2W, Fl R 2.5s,
24 ft., 4 mi., TR on pile.

Double Rock Daybeacon 8
56 12.2N, 132 15.5W, 16 ft., TR
on pile.

Buoy 9
56 11.9N, 132 15.6W, green can.

Buoy 10
56 11.9N, 132 15.6W, red nun.

Midchannel Rock Daybeacon
56 12.2N, 132 16.3W, JR on single
steel pile.

Village Rock Daybeacon 12
56 12.9N, 132 17.6W, 22 ft., TR on
single steel pile.

Village Islands Light 13
56 12.8N, 132 18.1W, Fl G 4s,
17 ft., 4 mi., SG on pile.

**Village Islands Rock Daybeacon
15**
56 13.1N, 132 19.1W, 22 ft., SG on
post on concrete pier.

Daybeacon
56 21.2N, 132 22.0W, NR on
spindle.

Hat Island Light
56 22.5N, 132 25.6W, Fl W 4s,
23 ft., 6 mi., NR on skeleton tower,
obscured from 091° to 234°.

Alaska

Some latitude/longitude positions are only reported in whole minutes in the government light lists (rather than to the nearest tenth of a minute). These positions should be assumed to be less accurate than those reported with greater precision.

A

Abrams Island
52 32.2N, 128 49.8W, Fl (3) W 12s, 22 ft., 5 mi., square skeleton tower, visible 357° to 204°.

ACTIVE PASS

Georgina Point (N extremity of Mayne Island)
48 52.4N, 123 17.4W, F Fl W 10s, 57 ft., 12 mi., white cylindrical tower, visible 055° to 090° and 180° to 253°, high-intensity flash superimposed every 10s, radiobeacon, diaphone: 1 blast every 30s, horn points 025°.

Active Pass Radiobeacon
48 52.4N, 123 17.4W, AP (·- ·-·-), 50 mi., 378 kHz, A2A, carrier signal, a bearing error could result from coastal refraction.

Mary Anne Point, Galiano Island
48 51.7N, 123 18.7W, Q W, 25 ft., white cylindrical tower, green band at top, radar reflector.

Galiano Island (E end, S side)
48 51.7N, 123 20.9W, Q G, 21 ft., white cylindrical tower, green band at top, radar reflector.

Helen Point
48 51.5N, 123 20.6W, Q W, 23 ft., white cylindrical tower, red band at top.

Addenbroke Island (W end)
51 36.2N, 127 51.8W, Fl W 5s, 95 ft., 15 mi., on structure, horn: (two tone) 1 blast every 30s.

Agnew Passage
49 46N, 123 59W, Q G, 25 ft., white tower, green band at top.

Aguilar Point
48 50.4N, 125 08.4W, Q W R, 16 ft., white cylindrical tower, red band at top, white 055.5° to 058°.

Ahlstrom Point
49 47N, 124 09W, Fl G 4s, 21 ft., white cylindrical tower, green band at top.

Alarm Rock (SE end)
48 57.5N, 123 40.4W, Fl (2) W 6s, 19 ft., 5 mi., white cylindrical tower, radar reflector.

Alberni (W side of channel, at entrance to Somass River)
49 14.3N, 124 49.3W, Fl G 4s, 17 ft., pile beacon with black, white, and green square daymark.
Also see Somass River.

Albert Head
48 23.2N, 123 28.6W, Fl W 5s, 90 ft., 19 mi., white cylindrical tower.

Albert Head Calibration Radiobeacon
48 23.2N, 123 28.6W, T (-), 300 kHz, A2A, transmits upon request through Victoria Marine Radio (VAK).

Alert Bay Radiobeacon
50 35.2N, 126 55.5W, YAL (-·-- ·- ·-··), 25 mi., 335 kHz, A2A, carrier signal.

Algerine Passage
See Rebecca Rock.

Alice Arm (S of Hans Point)
55 25.6N, 129 40.1W, Fl R 4s, 19 ft., 5 mi., square skeleton tower.

Alice Arm (wharf)
55 28.2N, 129 29.7W, Fl G 4s, 14 ft., skeleton tower, two black, white, and green square daymarks.

Allen Point (S bank of Gardner Canal)
53 27N, 128 24W, Fl W 6s, 16 ft., 5 mi., skeleton tower.

Alliford Bay (SW of Kwuna Point)
53 12.8N, 131 59.5W, Fl W 4s, 15 ft., square tower.

Amos Island, Nicolaye Channel
50 01N, 127 21W, Fl W 4s, 27 ft., white cylindrical tower.

Amphitrite Point (N side of entrance to channel)
48 55.3N, 125 32.4W, Fl W 12s, 58 ft., 13 mi., white rectangular tower, horn: 1 blast every 20s.

Arachne Reef Light
48 41.1N, 123 17.6W, Fl (2+1) G 6s, 22 ft., white cylindrical tower with green band at top.
Also see Haro Strait.

Archibald Islands (on northernmost rocky islet)
54 12.9N, 130 49.9W, Fl W 4s, 28 ft., square skeleton tower.

Ashdown Island (W extremity)
53 03.7N, 129 13.7W, Fl (3) W 12s, 26 ft., 5 mi., square skeleton tower.
Also see Levy Point.

Assits Island (W extremity)
48 56.3N, 125 01.9W, Q R, 14 ft., white cylindrical tower, red band at top.

Atrevida Point
49 39N, 126 26W, Q G, 24 ft., white cylindrical tower, green band at top.

B

Baeria Rock (on highest rock of group)
48 57.0N, 125 09.2W, Fl W 4s, 40 ft., white cylindrical mast.

Baker Inlet
53 49N, 129 57W, Fl R 6s, 15 ft., square skeleton tower.

Baker Point (on extremity)
52 48.2N, 129 12.8W, Fl W 6s, 17 ft., 5 mi., square skeleton tower.

Balaklava Island
See Scarlett Point.

Ballenas Island (N point of island)
49 21.0N, 124 09.5W, F Fl W 10s,
70 ft., 17 mi., white tower, visible
040° to 307°, horn: 1 blast every
60s, high-intensity flash superimposed every 10s.

Bamber Point, Viscount Island
50 42N, 126 14W, Fl W 4s, 22 ft.,
white cylindrical tower, red band
at top.

**Bare Point, Chemainus Bay
(extremity of pt.)**
48 55.8N, 123 42.3W, Fl G 4s,
41 ft., white cylindrical tower,
green band at top.
Also see Chemainus Bay.

Bark Island (Gunboat Passage)
52 10.0N, 128 02.9W, Fl W 6s,
10 ft., square skeleton tower.

Barrett Rock (off shore on reef)
54 14.6N, 130 20.5W, Fl R 6s,
17 ft., 5 mi., white cylindrical
tower, red band at top, horn:
2 blasts every 20s.
Also see Prince Rupert Harbor.

Baynes Channel North
48 27N, 123 16W, Q G, 21 ft.,
white cylindrical tower, green
band at top.

Bear Point
50 21.9N, 125 40.3W, Fl W 4s,
21 ft., white cylindrical tower.

**Beaumont Island (N end of
island)**
52 17.7N, 127 56.6W, Fl W 6s,
23 ft., square skeleton tower,
visible 063° to 324°.

Beaver Cove
See Lewis Point.

Beaver Passage
See Hankin Rock.

Beaver Point (N tip)
48 46N, 123 22W, Fl G 4s, 28 ft.,
white cylindrical tower, green
band at top.

Bedwell Harbor
See Hay Point.

Bedwell Island
50 28.6N, 127 53.7W, Fl G 4s,
29 ft., white cylindrical tower,
green band at top.

Ben Mohr Rock Lighted Buoy UK
48 51.6N, 123 23.4W, Fl (2+1) R 6s,
red and green bands.

Benson Island
48 53.2N, 125 22.6W, Q G, 26 ft.,
white cylindrical tower, green
band at top.

**Berens Island (SE extremity of
island, W side of harbor entrance)**
48 25.5N, 123 23.5W, Q G, 20 ft.,
6 mi., white cylindrical tower,
green band at top, radar reflector.
Also see Victoria.

Berry Point (N extremity)
49 17.7N, 122 59.2W, Fl R 4s,
15 ft., 10 mi., white cylindrical
tower, red band at top.
Also see Vancouver.

Berryman Point (NW of point)
49 09.4N, 125 40.6W, Fl W 4s,
16 ft., 5 mi., white cylindrical
mast, red and white triangular
daymark.

Bilton Point
49 00.7N, 124 52.3W, Fl W 4s,
22 ft., 5 mi., white cylindrical
tower, green band at top.

Bird Islet
49 21.7N, 123 17.4W, Fl R 4s,
16 ft., white cylindrical tower, red
band at top, radar reflector.

**Birnie Island (on rock S of Knox
Point)**
54 35.4N, 130 27.7W, Fl W 4s,
28 ft., white mast.

Blackrock Point
53 12.5N, 129 20.5W, Fl (3) R 12s,
27 ft., 5 mi., skeleton tower.

Blinkhorn Peninsula (N side)
50 33N, 126 47W, Fl (3) W 12s,
42 ft., 8 mi., white cylindrical
tower, green band at top.

Block Head, Farrant Island
53 18N, 129 20W, Fl W 6s, 20 ft.,
aluminum mast.

Block Islands
53 09.0N, 129 43.9W, Fl W 6s,
23 ft., square skeleton tower.

Blow Reef
52 11N, 128 04W, Fl W 6s, 16 ft.,
tower.

Blue Heron Bay and Basin
See Tsehum.

Boat Bay
50 31N, 126 35W, Q R, 35 ft.,
white cylindrical tower, red band
at top, obscured N of 102°.

Boat Bluff, Sarah Island
52 38.6N, 128 31.4W, Oc W R 3.5s,
39 ft., square skeleton tower,
white 291° to 336°, red 336° to
093°, white 093° to 134°, horn:
1 blast every 20s.
Also see Sarah Island.

Boat Islet
48 48.7N, 123 19.3W, Fl (2) R 6s,
23 ft., white cylindrical tower, red
band at top.

Bodega (NE of island)
49 44N, 126 37W, Fl R 4s, 17 ft.,
white cylindrical mast.

Bonilla Island (W side)
53 29.6N, 130 38.1W, Fl W R 5s,
121 ft., white cylindrical tower,
red 334° to 360°, white 360°
to 168°, red 168° to 198°,
obscured elsewhere, horn:
1 blast every 30s.

Bonilla Point Fisheries
48 35.7N, 124 43.0W, Fl W R 4s,
56 ft., 9 mi., skeleton tripod
tower, fluorescent orange triangular slatwork daymark, Fl R to E
of line between Bonilla Point and
Tatoosh Island, Fl W to W of
Fisheries light from June 1 to
Dec. 7.

Borde Island (N point)
53 05.1N, 129 07.2W, Fl W 4s,
23 ft., 5 mi., white skeleton tower.

Bordelais Islets
48 49.1N, 125 13.8W, Fl W 4s,
90 ft., white cylindrical tower,
green band at top.

Bosquet Point
See Penrose Island.

Boston Point
49 39.7N, 126 36.7W, Fl G 4s,
25 ft., white cylindrical tower,
green band at top.

BOUNDARY PASS

Also see Washington chapter.

Gowlland Point Light
48 44.1N, 123 11.0W, Fl W 4s,
35 ft., white cylindrical tower,
green band at top.

Skipjack Island Light (U.S.)
48 44.0N, 123 02.4W, Fl W 4s,
55 ft., 5 mi., NB on steel tower,
obscured from 261° to 347°.

Saturna Island Light
48 47.0N, 123 02.7W, Fl W 15s,
121 ft., white, 17 mi., F R, 102 ft.,
red, 16 mi., on red skeleton
tower, white light visible from
149° to 060°, red light visible from
156° to 211.5°.

**Shoal Isolated Danger Lighted
Bell Buoy DB (U.S.)**
48 45.9N, 123 00.9W, Fl (2) W 5s,
6 mi., black with red horizontal
stripes.

Rosenfeld Rock Lighted Buoy U59
48 48.2N, 123 01.6W, Fl G, green,
racon: U (··-).

Patos Island Light (U.S.)
48 47.3N, 122 58.3W, Fl W 6s (2 R
sectors), 52 ft., white 9 mi., red
6 mi., white square tower on fog
signal house, red from 011.5° to
059.5°, covers six-fathom shoal,
red from 097° to 114°, covers
Rosenfeld Rock, horn: 1 blast
every 30s, operates continuously.

Breakwater Island
49 08N, 123 41W, Fl R 4s, 20 ft.,
white cylindrical tower.

**Broad Cove (S of Haddington
Island)**
50 35.0N, 127 01.4W, F W R G,
21 ft., white cylindrical tower,
green 155° to 158.5°, white 158.5°
to 163°, red 163° to 166.5°, radar
reflector.

Brockton Island (NW end)
50 29.3N, 127 46.3W, Fl R 4s,
18 ft., white cylindrical tower, red
band at top.

**Brockton Point (W side of
Vancouver Harbor)**
49 18N, 123 07W, Q W R, 40 ft.,
11 mi., white square tower, red
band, marked "Speed Limit 5 KTS.
Coal Harbor," red 289° to 313°
over Burnaby Shoal, white elsewhere, horn: 3 blasts every 60s.
Also see Vancouver.

Broken Islands (SW extremity)
50 30.7N, 126 17.9W, Fl W 4s,
32 ft., 8 mi., white cylindrical
tower.

Brooke Shoal
55 22.9N, 129 42.9W, Fl (3) W 12s,
13 ft., fluorescent orange tower.

Brooks Bay
See Donald Islets.

Brotchie Ledge Light
48 24.4N, 123 23.2W, F Fl G 10s,
20 ft., white cylindrical tower,
green band at top, F G with high-
intensity green flash every 10s,
horn: 1 blast every 20s, horn
points southward, radar reflector.
Also see Victoria.

Brown Bay
50 10.0N, 125 22.0W, Fl G 4s,
20 ft., 10 mi., white cylindrical
tower, green band at top,
obscured from 326° to 333.5°.

Brown Passage
See Triple Islands.

Browning Entrance
53 38.1N, 130 33.8W, Fl W 6s,
41 ft., 5 mi., lattice tower, visible
020° to 264°.

**Brunswick Point (E side of
Montagu Channel)**
49 32N, 123 16W, Fl R 4s, 33 ft.,
white cylindrical tower, red band
at top.

Buckley Bay Ferry Landing
49 32N, 124 51W, F Y, 25 ft., on
dolphin, horn: 1 blast every 30s,
private light.
Also see Denman Island.

Bull Harbor (entrance)
50 55N, 127 56W, Fl W 4s, 13 ft.,
5 mi., lantern on 9-pile dolphin.

Bully Island (W side)
53 47.9N, 130 19.5W, Fl W 6s,
22 ft., 5 mi., white cylindrical
tower.

Burial Island (NE side)
48 46N, 123 34W, Q R, 28 ft.,
white cylindrical tower, red band
at top.

Burnaby Shoal
49 18N, 123 07W, Q R, 31 ft.,
6 mi., white cylindrical tower, red
band at top, radar reflector, bell:
2 strokes in quick succession
every 5s.
Also see Vancouver.

**Bush Rock, Skincuttle Inlet
(N end)**
52 18.3N, 131 16.6W, Fl W 6s,
30 ft., 5 mi., skeleton tower,
obscured 310°–352°.
Also see Copper Island.

Butterworth Rocks
54 14.1N, 130 58.5W, Fl W 6s,
53 ft., 8 mi., white tripod tower,
racon: X (-··-).

C

Calamity Point
49 19N, 123 08W, Fl W 4s, 19 ft.,
8 mi., white cylindrical tower,
green band at top, on 16-pile
dolphin, horn: 1 blast every 30s.
Also see Vancouver.

Calvert Island
See Clark Point.

Calvert Point
See Pitt Point.

Camp Point
50 23.1N, 125 49.6W, Q G, 20 ft.,
white cylindrical tower, green
band at top.

**Campbell River (head of break-
water)**
50 01.5N, 125 14.2W, Fl G 4s,
16 ft., cylindrical mast.

Campbell River (N breakwater)
50 01.7N, 125 14.4W, Fl W 4s,
20 ft., 5 mi., center pile of 5-pile
dolphin, black and white square
daymark.

Canal Island (W side)
49 41.3N, 126 35.1W, Fl R 4s,
18 ft., white cylindrical tower, red
band at top.

Canoe Pass Lighted Bell Buoy T14
49 02.3N, 123 15.3W, Fl R, red
buoy, radar reflector, bell.

Canoe Rock, Moresby Passage
48 44N, 123 20W, Fl (3) W 12s,
19 ft., 5 mi., white cylindrical
tower, red band at top.

Cape Beale (SE pt. of entrance to Barkley Sound)
48 47.2N, 125 12.9W, Fl W 5s (R sector), 170 ft., 15 mi., red square skeleton tower, white slatwork daymarks on 3 sides, visible 311° to 182°, white 311° to 097°, red 097° to 182°, radiobeacon, diaphone: 1 blast every 60s, there is foul ground in Barkley Sound north of 109°, enter only with local knowledge or a pilot.

Cape Beale Radiobeacon
48 47.2N, 125 12.9W, CB (-·-· -···), 20 mi., 312 kHz, A2A, carrier signal.

Cape Caution
51 09.8N, 127 47.1W, Fl W 6s, 71 ft., 6 mi., square skeleton tower.

Cape Cockburn
49 40N, 124 12W, Fl (3) W 12s, 50 ft., 5 mi., white cylindrical tower, red band at top.

Cape Farewell
53 21.5N, 129 13.6W, Fl (3) W 12s, 25 ft., 7 mi., skeleton tower.

Cape Lazo (N part)
49 42N, 124 52W, Iso W 2s, 150 ft., 11 mi., red skeleton tower.

Cape Lazo Aviation Light
49 43N, 124 53W, Fl W 10s, steel tower.

Cape Mark
52 09.0N, 128 32.3W, Fl W 4s, 50 ft., square skeleton tower, visible 330° to 194°.

Cape Mudge
49 59.9N, 125 11.7W, F W R, Fl W R 5s, 58 ft., 17 mi., white octagonal tower, white 316° to 134°, red 134° to 149.5°, white 149.5° to 151°, high-intensity white and red flash superimposed every 5s, horn (2): 1 blast every 30s, horns point 148° and 312°, horns sound in unison.

Cape Roger Curtis (W extremity)
49 20.4N, 123 25.9W, Fl (3) W 12s, 36 ft., 5 mi., white cylindrical tower.

Cape Scott
50 46.9N, 128 25.5W, Fl W 10s, 229 ft., 21 mi., white square skeleton tower, visible 344° to 246°, radiobeacon, horn: 3 blasts every 60s, horn points 290°.

Cape Scott Radiobeacon
50 47.0N, 128 25.5W, ZES (--·· ····), 125 mi., 354 kHz, A2A, carrier signal.

Cape St. James (on island)
51 56.2N, 131 00.9W, Fl W 5s, 315 ft., 17 mi., white octagonal tower, white dwelling, visible 207°–122°.

Captain Island
49 47N, 124 00W, Fl W 4s, 25 ft., 5 mi., white cylindrical tower.

Carmanah Light
48 36.7N, 124 45.0W, Fl W 5s, 175 ft., 19 mi., white octagonal concrete tower, diaphone: 3 blasts every 60s.

Carmanah Radiobeacon
48 36.7N, 124 45.0W, D (-··), 40 mi., 329 kHz.

Carne Rock, Reid Passage
52 18N, 128 22W, Fl W 6s, 14 ft., 5 mi., skeleton tower.

Carterer Point (E side of Hardwicke Island)
50 27.5N, 125 45.8W, Q W, 20 ft., white cylindrical tower, green band at top.

Casey Point (on edge of shoal off the point)
54 16.5N, 130 21.6W, Q R, 20 ft., white 7-pile dolphin.
Also see Prince Rupert Harbor.

Centre Island
49 51N, 126 56W, Fl R 4s, 24 ft., white cylindrical tower, red band on top.

Chaatl Island
See Tcenakun Point.

Channel Islands (on N end of Northern Channel Island)
48 48.1N, 123 22.8W, Fl W 4s, 29 ft., 5 mi., white cylindrical tower.

Channel Rock (Uganda Channel)
50 05.6N, 125 02.2W, Q R, 20 ft., white cylindrical tower, red band at top.

Chatham Point
50 20.0N, 125 26.4W, F W, Fl G 5s, 20 ft., 12 mi., white cylindrical tower, green band at top, high-intensity green flash superimposed every 5s, radar reflector, horn(2): 1 blast every 20s, horns point 113° to 293°.

Chearnley Passage
54 01.6N, 130 41.2W, Q W, 19 ft., skeleton tower.

CHEMAINUS BAY

Bare Point (extremity of pt.)
48 55.8N, 123 42.3W, Fl G 4s, 43 ft., white cylindrical tower, green band at top.

Chemainus Range Front Light (N end of wharf)
48 55.5N, 123 42.7W, F G, 27 ft., white cylindrical mast, fluorescent red slatwork daymark.

Chemainus Range Rear Light
226 meters, 198.8° from front light, F G, 45 ft., white cylindrical mast, red daymark, white stripe.

Cholberg Point
50 55N, 127 44W, Q W, 40 ft., white cylindrical tower.

Chrome Island Range Front Light (SE entrance to Baynes Sound)
49 28.3N, 124 41.0W, F Y, 46 ft., white mast, red daymark, white stripe, visible on rangeline only.

Chrome Island Range Rear Light
93.3 meters, 097.8° from front light, Fl Y 5s, Fl W 5s, 72 ft., white cylindrical tower, yellow light visible on rangeline only, horn: 2 blasts every 60s, horn points E.

Chrow Island (NW extremity)
48 54.6N, 125 28.2W, Fl W 4s, 132 ft., 5 mi., white cylindrical tower.

Chup Point (E side)
48 57.3N, 125 01.7W, Fl G 4s, 14 ft., white cylindrical tower, green band at top.

Cinque Island
50 17.7N, 125 23.9W, Fl R 4s, 22 ft., white cylindrical mast, red and white triangular daymark.

Clark Point, Calvert Island
51 25.8N, 127 53.2W, Q W, 36 ft., white cylindrical tower.

Clarke Rock
49 14N, 123 56W, Fl G 4s, 22 ft., white cylindrical tower, green band at top.

Clerke Peninsula (S end)
49 36.2N, 126 32.2W, Fl W 4s, 41 ft., 5 mi., white cylindrical tower.

Cliffe Point
50 27.9N, 127 56.2W, Fl W 4s, 35 ft., 6 mi., white cylindrical tower, red band at top.

Clio Island (W end)
49 23.6N, 126 11.0W, Fl W 4s, 56 ft., 5 mi., white cylindrical mast, red and white triangular daymark, orange triangle in center.

Clio Point
53 54N, 128 43W, Fl W 6s, 23 ft., skeleton tower.

Clive Island (on rock SE of Piers Island)
48 42.1N, 123 24.2W, Q G, 17 ft., white cylindrical tower, green band at top.

Clo-oose Approach Lighted Whistle Buoy YJ
48 38.8N, 124 49.8W, Mo (A) W, red and white stripes.

Coal Harbor
49 17.6N, 123 07.5W, Fl R 4s, 22 ft., white cylindrical tower, red band at top, on 9-pile dolphin. *Also see* Vancouver.

Coal Island (NW point)
48 41.5N, 123 23.2W, Fl G 4s, 26 ft., white tower, green band at top.

Coaster Channel
48 53.0N, 125 19.1W, Fl W 4s, 24 ft., white cylindrical tower.

Coffin Island (N side of entrance to Ladysmith Harbor)
48 59N, 123 45W, Fl W 4s, 19 ft., 5 mi., white cylindrical tower, green band at top, radar reflector.

Colburne Passage South
48 42N, 123 25W, Fl G 4s, 15 ft., white cylindrical tower, green band at top.

COMOX

Also see Goose Spit *and* Courtenay River.

Comox Radiobeacon
49 45.0N, 124 57.0W, QQ (--·- ---·-), 400 kHz, aero.

Comox Bar Bell Buoy P54
49 40N, 124 52W, Fl R, red buoy marked P54, radar reflector, bell.

Bar Range Front Light (W side of Baynes Sound)
49 37.4N, 124 54.5W, Iso Y 1.5s, 37 ft., square skeleton tower, white daymark, red stripe.

Bar Range Rear Light
284 meters, 222.0° from front light, Iso Y 2s, 76 ft., square skeleton tower, white daymark, red stripe.

Government Wharf (head of breakwater)
49 40N, 124 56W, Fl R 4s, 12 ft., white cylindrical mast.

East Breakwater
49 40.1N, 124 55.6W, Fl G 4s, 11 ft., mast.

Conconi Reef
48 49.4N, 123 17.4W, Q W, 20 ft., 5 mi., white cylindrical tower, red band at top.

Cone Island
See Legge Point *and* Freeman Point.

Connis Islet
53 45.5N, 130 19.0W, Q W, 15 ft., white cylindrical tower.

Cook Point (edge of shoal)
53 48.4N, 132 12.1W, Fl W 4s, 13 ft., square skeleton tower.

Coolidge Point, Cousins Inlet
52 21N, 127 43W, Fl (3) W 12s, 19 ft., white cylindrical tower. *Also see* Wearing Point *and* Cousins Inlet.

Copper Island, Skincuttle Inlet (E point of E island)
52 21N, 131 10W, Fl (3) W 12s, 50 ft., 5 mi., white cylindrical tower, visible 163°–039° *Also see* Bush Rock.

Cormorant Island
See Yellow Bluff.

Cornwall Point
53 30N, 128 22W, Q W, 16 ft., white square mast, white slatwork daymark.

Cortes Bay
50 08.8N, 124 55.4W, Q R, 20 ft., white cylindrical tower, red band at top.

Cortes Island
See Lewis Channel.

COURTENAY RIVER

Also see Comox *and* Goose Spit.

Courtenay River Light
49 40N, 124 57W, Fl W 4s, 14 ft., 5 mi., black, white, and green square daymark on 5-pile dolphin.

Range Front Light (on river bank)
49 40.6N, 124 57.5W, Q Y, 14 ft., red daymark, white stripe, on 4-pile dolphin.

Range Rear Light
61 meters, 321° from front light, Q Y, 21 ft., red daymark, white stripe, on 5-pile dolphin.

Cousins Inlet
52 19.7N, 127 44.9W, Fl W 6s, 10 ft., 5 mi., square skeleton tower. *Also see* Wearing Point *and* Coolidge Point.

Cracroft Point
50 33.0N, 126 40.7W, Fl R 4s, 24 ft., white cylindrical structure.

Crane Islands (on summit of Westerly Island)
50 51N, 127 31W, Fl W 4s, 50 ft., 5 mi., white cylindrical tower, green bands at top.

Crescent Beach
49 01N, 122 56W, Fl R 4s, 22 ft., 7-pile dolphin, red and white triangular daymark.

Crescent Channel
49 03N, 122 54W, Q R, 15 ft., 5-pile dolphin, red and white triangular daymark.

Crofton, Osborn Bay (N side)
48 52.8N, 123 37.7W, Fl W 4s, 19 ft., 5 mi., white cylindrical tower, whistle: 1 blast every 30s, on end of Crofton government wharf.

Croker Point
48 46N, 123 12W, Fl R 4s, 15 ft., white cylindrical mast, red and white triangular daymark.

Current Passage Directional Light
50 24.5N, 125 48.6W, Dir F W R G, 15 ft., 11 mi., white cylindrical tower, red 326° to 330°, white 330° to 336°, green 336° to 340°, white sector indicates preferred channel.

Currie Islet
See Gosling Rocks.

Cyril Rock (off Grilse Point)
49 48N, 124 36W, Q G, 24 ft., white cylindrical tower, green band at top.

D

Danger Reef (N end of eastern-most rock)
49 03.3N, 123 42.8W, Q W, 22 ft., 5 mi., white cylindrical tower, 0.5 mi. berth should be given when passing southward.

D'Arcy Island Light (SW of island)
48 34.0N, 123 17.0W, Fl R 4s, 23 ft., white cylindrical tower with red band at top.
Also see Haro Strait.

Darrell Bay
49 40.1N, 123 10.1W, F Y (3), radar reflector, marks ferry landing, private aid.

Darwin Point (NW of point)
52 34.5N, 131 37.7W, Fl W 6s, 39 ft., 5 mi., square skeleton tower.

Davison Point (N side of entrance to Tasu Sound)
52 44.5N, 132 06.7W, Fl W 6s, 130 ft., 7 mi., white cylindrical tower.
Also see Tasu Narrows *and* Tasu Sound.

Dawson Islands (on easternmost island)
53 43.0N, 132 20.2W, Fl W 4s, 31 ft., 5 mi., square skeleton tower, visible 129° to 092°.

De Horsey Island (E side of island)
54 07.9N, 130 07.3W, Fl W 4s, 19 ft., 5 mi., skeleton tower, white daymark.

Dead Tree Point Radiobeacon
53 21.0N, 131 56.4W, Z (--··), 25 mi., 248 kHz, A2A, aero.

Dead Tree Point Whistle Buoy C19
53 21N, 131 54W, Fl G, black buoy, radar reflector, whistle.

Deadman Island (S of island)
49 17.5N, 123 07.4W, Q R, 17 ft., 4-pile dolphin.
Also see Vancouver.

Deadman Islands (W side of S islet)
49 09.7N, 125 12.5W, Fl R 4s, 18 ft., white cylindrical mast.

Dean Point, W Redonda Islands
50 17N, 124 47W, Q G, 20 ft., white cylindrical tower, green band at top.
Also see Pryce Channel *and* Waddington Channel.

Dearth Island
See Glaholm Island.

Deas Point
52 23.1N, 127 12.9W, Fl W 6s, 15 ft., 5 mi., skeleton tower.

Deep Bay
See Mapleguard Point.

DENMAN ISLAND

Also see Hornby Island Ferry Landing.

Denman Island Light
49 32N, 124 50W, Fl W 4s, 20 ft., 5 mi., white cylindrical tower, red band at top.

West Ferry Landing
49 32N, 124 49W, F Y, 25 ft., on dolphin, horn: 1 blast every 30s, private light.

Buckley Bay Ferry Landing
49 32N, 124 51W, F Y, 25 ft., on dolphin, horn: 1 blast every 30s, private light.

East Ferry Landing
49 30N, 124 42W, F Y, 25 ft., on dolphin, horn: 1 blast every 30s when required, private light.

Dent Island (W extremity)
50 25N, 125 13W, Q R, 26 ft., white cylindrical tower, red band at top.

Descanso Bay (W side)
49 11N, 123 52W, Fl W 4s, 20 ft., 5 mi., white cylindrical tower.

Devestation Island (N side of island)
54 19.4N, 130 29.1W, Fl R 4s, 17 ft., white cylindrical tower, red band at top.

Dibuxante Point
49 08N, 123 43W, Q R, 21 ft., white cylindrical tower, red band at top.
Also see Gabriola Passage East.

Dillon Rock, Shushartie Bay
50 51N, 127 51W, Q G (60 fl. per min.), 21 ft., white cylindrical tower, green band at top, radar reflector.

Discovery Island Light (E extremity)
48 25.5N, 123 13.5W, Fl W 5s, 93 ft., white cylindrical tower, light obscured from 050.5° to 146°, horn: 1 blast every 60s.
Also see Haro Strait.

Dock Island (NE Islet of Little Group)
48 40N, 123 21W, Q G, 37 ft., white cylindrical tower, green band at top.
Also see Little Group Rock.

Dodd Narrows
See Joan Point.

Dodge Cove Range Front Light
54 17.4N, 130 22.9W, F Y, 18 ft., 3-pile dolphin, orange and black daymark.
Also see Prince Rupert Harbor.

Dodge Cove Range Rear Light
115.2 meters, 253.2° from front light, F Y, 20 ft., 3-pile dolphin, orange and black daymark, visible 239° to 266°.

Donald Islets, Brooks Bay
50 13.9N, 127 48.4W, Fl (2) W 6s, 90 ft., 6 mi., white mast, red and white triangular daymark.

Donald Point
52 17.6N, 128 05.9W, Fl W 6s, 15 ft., 5 mi., square skeleton tower, visible 055° to 240°.

Dorothy Island (N end)
53 40N, 128 51W, Fl W 6s, 19 ft., white square mast.

Double Island (N side of inlet)
49 50.7N, 126 59.8W, Fl W 10s, 39 ft., 14 mi., white cylindrical tower, green band on top.

Double Islets
54 57.7N, 129 56.8W, Fl (3) W 12s, 26 ft., square skeleton tower, orange stripes.

Doyle Island (SE extremity)
50 48.3N, 127 27.5W, Fl W 5s, 46 ft., 15 mi., white cylindrical tower, green band at top.

Drew Harbor (N extremity of Rebecca Spit)
50 06.5N, 125 11.6W, Fl G 4s, 18 ft., white cylindrical tower, green band at top.

Driver Point (entrance to Stewardson Inlet)
49 26.8N, 126 16.0W, Q W, 23 ft., white cylindrical tower.

Dryad Point
52 11N, 128 07W, Oc W R 5s, 38 ft., white square tower, white 142.5° to 206.5°, red 206.5° to 339°, white 339° to 039.5°, horn (2): 1 blast every 20s, horns point N and S.

Du Vernet Point
54 18.8N, 130 23.9W, Q R, 11 ft., white tower, red band at top.

Duckers Island South (easternmost island)
52 55.0N, 129 11.5W, Fl W 4s, 27 ft., 5 mi., mast.

Duff Islet (entrance Fife Sound)
50 45.4N, 126 43.3W, Fl (3) W 12s, 29 ft., white cylindrical tower.

Dugout Rocks
51 22.0N, 127 48.4W, Fl (3) W 12s, 68 ft., square skeleton tower.

Dundas Island
54 27.6N, 130 56.8W, Fl W 6s, 34 ft., square skeleton tower.

Dunsmuir Point
49 09.2N, 124 48.5W, Fl W 4s, 22 ft., 5 mi., white cylindrical tower, green band at top.

Dupont Island
52 56.5N, 129 26.2W, Fl W 6s, 27 ft., 5 mi., white skeleton tower.

Earl Ledge
50 24.7N, 125 55.2W, Fl R 4s, 16 ft., white cylindrical tower, red band at top, intensified on 276°.

Earls Cove
49 45.2N, 124 00.5W, F G, on gantry, ferry terminal, radar reflector, horn: 1 blast every 30s.

East Cracroft Island Range Front Light (N side)
50 34.8N, 126 14.5W, Q Y, 20 ft., white cylindrical mast, red daymark, white stripe.

East Cracroft Island Range Rear Light
29 meters, 271° from front light, Q Y, 49 ft., white cylindrical mast, red daymark, white stripe, visible on rangeline only.

East Kinahan Island (NE extremity)
54 12.8N, 130 23.6W, Fl W 6s, 24 ft., 5 mi., white cylindrical tower.

Ecstall Island (northern extrem-ity)
54 10N, 129 57W, Fl W 6s, 17 ft., mast with white slatted daymark, visible 053° to 270°.

Edward Point
52 26.4N, 127 16.3W, Fl W 6s, 24 ft., skeleton tower.

Edye Passage, Useless Point
54 02.4N, 130 33.7W, Fl W 6s, 20 ft., 5 mi., white cylindrical tower.

Egg Island (on summit)
51 15N, 127 50W, Fl W 5s, 290 ft., 16 mi., lattice tower, radiobeacon, horn: 1 blast every 60s, horn points 270°.

Egg Island Radiobeacon
51 14.9N, 127 49.9W, UEM (··· · --), 25 mi., 207 kHz, A2A.

Ehatisaht (on point)
49 53N, 126 49W, Fl W 4s, 29 ft., white cylindrical mast.

Ekins Point (on Gambier Island)
49 32N, 123 23W, Fl (3) W 12s, 21 ft., white cylindrical tower.

Emilia Island
53 45.5N, 128 58.4W, Fl W 6s, 11 ft., 5 mi., square skeleton tower, visible 231° to 064°.

English Bay
See Vancouver.

Enterprise Reef (W rock of reef)
48 51N, 123 21W, Q R, 21 ft., F W R W, 12 ft., white cylindrical tower, red band at top, radar reflector, white 107.5° to 110°, red 110° to 121°, white 121° to 123.5°.

Entrance Island (N approach to Nanaimo)
49 12.6N, 123 48.4W, F Fl W 5s, 61 ft., 15 mi., white cylindrical tower, horn: 2 blasts every 60s, high-intensity flash superimposed every 5s.
Also see Nanaimo Harbor.

Epsom Point (on extremity)
49 30N, 124 01W, Fl W 4s, 21 ft., 5 mi., white cylindrical tower.

ESQUIMALT

Scroggs Rocks (W side)
48 25.6N, 123 26.3W, Fl R 4s, 24 ft., white cylindrical tower, red band at top.

Fisgard Light (W side of entrance to Esquimalt Harbor)
48 25.8N, 123 26.8W, Iso W 2s (R sector), 71 ft., 14 mi., white cylindrical tower with red brick dwelling attached, tower illuminated below balcony by floodlights, red sector from 195° to 332°, to clear Scrogg Rocks light must show white in approach from eastward.

Inskip Islands Range Front Light
48 27N, 123 26W, F Y, 18 ft., white cylindrical mast, white daymark, fluorescent red stripe.

Inskip Islands Range Rear Light
F Y, 33 ft., tripod skeleton tower, white daymark, fluorescent red stripe.

Estevan Point (SW extremity)
49 23.0N, 126 32.5W, Fl (2) W 15s,
125 ft., 17 mi., white octagonal
tower, radiobeacon, diaphone:
1 blast every 60s, horn points 210°.

Estevan Point Radiobeacon
49 23.0N, 126 32.5W, EP (· ·--·),
125 mi., 374 kHz, A2A.

Europa Point
53 25.8N, 128 32.6W, Fl W 4s,
16 ft., square skeleton tower.

Fair Harbor (E side of)
50 04.1N, 127 08.5W, Fl W 4s,
35 ft., white cylindrical tower.

Fair Harbor Approach (on rock)
50 04.5N, 127 09.3W, Fl G 4s,
18 ft., white cylindrical tower,
green band at top.

False Bay, Lasqueti Island (inner pt., S side of entrance)
49 29N, 124 22W, Fl W 4s, 18 ft.,
white cylindrical tower.

False Creek
See Vancouver.

Fane Island
48 48N, 123 16W, Fl G 4s, 23 ft.,
white cylindrical tower, green
band at top.

Fanny Island
50 27.2N, 125 59.6W, Fl (3) W 12s,
21 ft., 5 mi., white cylindrical
mast.

Farewell Point (E side of point)
52 08N, 127 53W, Fl W 6s, 16 ft.,
5 mi., square skeleton tower.

Farrant Island
See Block Head.

Fegan Islets
49 32N, 124 23W, Fl W 4s, 26 ft.,
5 mi., white cylindrical tower.

Fernie Island (SE extremity)
48 40.7N, 123 23.4W, Fl G 4s,
26 ft., 5 mi., white cylindrical
tower, green band at top.

Fiddle Reef
48 26N, 123 17W, Q R, 23 ft.,
7 mi., white cylindrical tower,
red 013.3° to 062°, white 062° to
170.5°, red 170.5° to 216°, white
216° to 013.3°.

Fife Sound
See Duff Islet.

Fin Rock
53 14.0N, 129 21.6W, Fl (3) G 12s,
23 ft., skeleton tower.

Finisterre Island (N extremity)
49 25N, 123 18W, Q W, 44 ft.,
5 mi., white cylindrical tower.

Fir Cone Point
See Coal Island.

First Narrows
See Vancouver.

Fisgard Light (W side of entrance to Esquimalt Harbor)
48 25.8N, 123 26.8W, Iso W 2s
(R sector), 71 ft., 14 mi., white
cylindrical tower with red brick
dwelling attached, tower illuminated below balcony by floodlights, red sector from 195° to
332°; to clear Scrogg Rocks, light
must show white in approach
from eastward.
Also see Esquimalt.

Fishermans Cove (Robson)
49 21N, 123 17W, Fl R 4s, 19 ft.,
white cylindrical tower, red band
at top.

Flagpole Point
52 20.9N, 126 55.6W, Fl (3) W 12s,
17 ft., square skeleton mast.

Flatrock Island (near highest point)
52 06.5N, 131 10.0W, Fl W 6s,
77 ft., 5 mi., square mast.

Flora Inlet (N side off St. Johns Point)
49 31N, 124 35W, Fl W 4s, 68 ft.,
7 mi., white skeleton tower.

Flowery Islet (highest point of islet)
53 13.3N, 132 00.3W, Q W, 32 ft.,
square skeleton tower.

Fog Rocks (on largest rock)
51 58.3N, 127 55.0W, Fl W 4s,
23 ft., 5 mi., tower.

Folger Island
48 49.8N, 125 15.0W, Fl (3) R 12s,
132 ft., 5 mi., white cylindrical
tower, visible 345° to 233°.

Forbes Island (S side)
48 57N, 125 25W, Q R, 42 ft.,
white cylindrical tower, red band
at top.

Forrest Island
48 39.2N, 123 19.3W, Fl R 4s,
36 ft., white cylindrical tower,
red band at top.

Fort Point
54 59.1N, 129 54.9W, Fl W 4s,
19 ft., square skeleton tower,
orange stripes.

Francis Island
48 55.3N, 125 31.3W, Fl (3) W 12s,
30 ft., 5 mi., white cylindrical
mast, higher intensity on 058°.

Francis Point
49 36N, 124 03W, Fl (3) W 12s,
34 ft., white cylindrical tower.

Franklin River
49 06.2N, 124 49.3W, Q R, 24 ft.,
white cylindrical tower, red band
at top, on 9-pile dolphin.

Frederick Island
53 56.3N, 133 11.8W, Fl W 6s,
55 ft., 5 mi., square mast, visible
000° to 215°.

Frederick Point (at edge of bar)
54 15.5N, 130 21.5W, Fl G 4s,
21 ft., white cylindrical tower,
green band at top.
Also see Prince Rupert Harbor.

Freeman Passage (on island)
53 49.8N, 130 37.6W, Fl (3) W 12s,
16 ft., 5 mi., square skeleton
tower, visible 242° to 217°.

Freeman Point (S extremity of Cone Island)
52 33.2N, 128 29.3W, Fl W 4s,
20 ft., 5 mi., square skeleton tower.

French Creek (outer end of breakwater)
49 21N, 124 21W, Q R, 20 ft.,
white cylindrical mast.

Frigon Islets (SW point of west-ernmost island)
50 25.1N, 127 29.6W, Fl W 4s, 16 ft.,
5 mi., white cylindrical mast.

Fulford Harbor
48 46N, 123 27W, Fl W 4s, 20 ft.,
on dolphin, horn: 1 blast every
20s, on ferry terminal close SE,
private aid.
Also see Jackson Rock.

G

Gabriola Passage East
49 07N, 123 41W, Fl G 4s, 17 ft.,
white cylindrical tower, green
band at top.
Also see Dibuxante Point.

Gabriola Reefs, on Thrasher Rock
49 09.0N, 123 38.4W, Fl (3) W 12s,
34 ft., white cylindrical tower,
green band at top, radar reflector,
racon: W (·--).

Gabriola Reefs Lighted Buoy UM
49 07.7N, 123 39.3W, Fl (2+1) G
6s, green and red bands.

Galiano Light (E end, S side)
48 51.7N, 123 20.9W, Q G, 21 ft.,
white cylindrical tower, green
band at top, radar reflector.
Also see Active Pass.

**Gallows Point (S end of
Protection Island)**
49 10.2N, 123 55.0W, Al R W 10s,
26 ft., white cylindrical tower,
red band at top, horn: 1 blast
every 20s.
Also see Nanaimo Harbor.

Gambier Island
See Ekins Point.

**Ganges Harbor (on Second Sister
Island)**
48 50.2N, 123 27.2W, Fl R 4s,
27 ft., white cylindrical tower,
red band at top.

**Ganges Harbor, Grace Islet (SE
extremity)**
48 51.1N, 123 29.5W, Fl G 4s,
29 ft., white cylindrical tower,
green band at top.

Garcin Rocks (middle rock)
52 12.5N, 130 57.9W, Fl W 6s,
64 ft., square skeleton tower.

Gayward Rock
50 01.3N, 127 23.4W, Q W, 27 ft.,
white cylindrical tower.

**Genn Island (on NW extremity of
island)**
54 05.9N, 130 17.5W, Fl R 6s,
30 ft., white cylindrical tower,
red band at top.

George Point
54 02.5N, 132 34.0W, Q G, 15 ft.,
skeleton tower, black, white, and
green square daymark.

**Georgina Point (N extremity of
Mayne Island)**
48 52N, 123 17W, F W, Fl W 10s,
57 ft., 12 mi., white cylindrical
tower, visible 055° to 253°, high-
intensity flash superimposed
every 10s, radiobeacon.
Also see Active Pass.

Gertrude Point
53 38N, 129 14W, Fl W 4s, 18 ft.,
5 mi., square skeleton tower.

Gibson Island
See Watson Rock.

GIBSONS LANDING

Gibsons Landing Rock
49 24N, 123 30W, Fl G 4s, 23 ft.,
white cylindrical tower, green
band at top.

Outer End of Breakwater
49 24N, 123 30W, Fl R 4s, 16 ft.,
white cylindrical mast, red and
white triangular daymark.

South Breakwater
Fl G 4s, 20 ft., white cylindrical
mast, black, white, and green
daymark.

Gillard Island
50 24N, 125 09W, Q G, 20 ft.,
white cylindrical tower, green
band at top.

Gillat Island (W side)
53 14.7N, 131 53.9W, Fl (3) W 12s,
22 ft., square skeleton tower.

**Glaholm Island (off NW end of
Dearth Island)**
52 15.8N, 128 12.7W, Fl W 6s,
13 ft., square skeleton tower.

Godkin Point
50 54N, 127 56W, Fl R 4s, 48 ft.,
5 mi., white cylindrical tower, red
band at top, radar reflector.

Goose Spit (W end)
49 39.6N, 124 55.4W, Q R, 18 ft.,
white cylindrical tower, red band
at top, radar reflector, 2 F G,
2 mi., shown in Courtenay River.
Also see Comox *and* Courtenay
River.

Gore Island
49 39N, 126 23W, Fl R 4s, 21 ft.,
white cylindrical tower, red band
at top.

Gore Island West
49 39N, 126 26W, Q R, 26 ft.,
white cylindrical tower, red band
at top.

Gosling Rocks, Currie Islet
51 51N, 128 27W, Fl W 6s, 56 ft.,
7 mi., square tower.

**Gossip Shoals Lighted Bell Buoy
U47**
Fl G, green.

Goudge Island
48 41N, 123 24W, Fl W 4s, 19 ft.,
white cylindrical tower.

Governor Rock Lighted Buoy U45
48 54.8N, 123 29.8W, Fl G, green.

Gowgaia Point
52 24N, 131 35W, Fl W 6s, 98 ft.,
square skeleton tower.

**Gowlland Point Light, South
Pender Island**
48 44.1N, 123 11.0W, Fl W 4s,
35 ft., white cylindrical tower,
green band at top.
Also see Boundary Pass.

Grace Islands (SW extremity)
49 26N, 123 27W, Fl W 4s, 20 ft.,
white cylindrical tower.

Grace Islet
See Ganges Harbor.

Grant Island
See Wilbraham Point.

Grant Reef Buoy QM
49 52N, 124 46W, Fl (2+1) G, red
and green bands, marked QM,
radar reflector.

Grappler Rock
48 56.4N, 123 36.1W, Fl R 4s,
20 ft., white cylindrical tower, red
band at top.

Grave Point
48 51N, 123 35W, Fl G 4s, 17 ft.,
white cylindrical mast.

Grebe Islets
49 20.5N, 123 16.5W, Fl (3) R 12s,
23 ft., white cylindrical tower, red
band at top, radar reflector.

Green Island (SW point of island)
54 34.1N, 130 42.4W, Fl W 5s,
63 ft., 13 mi., white tower, diaphone: 1 blast every 30s, horn
points 239°.

Greentop Islet
54 10.7N, 130 24.6W, Fl W 6s,
43 ft., 5 mi., white cylindrical
tower.

Greenwood Point
50 30.6N, 128 01.6W, Q G, 22 ft.,
white cylindrical tower, green
band at top.

Grenville Channel (opposite Saunders Creek)
53 36.3N, 129 41.6W, Fl W 4s,
14 ft., square skeleton tower.

Grief Point (on W extremity)
49 48.3N, 124 31.5W, Fl (2) W 6s,
35 ft., 9 mi., white cylindrical
tower, red band at top.

Grief Point East (on end of S breakwater)
49 48N, 124 31W, Fl R 4s, 14 ft.,
white cylindrical mast.

Griffin Point
53 04N, 128 33W, Fl W 6s, 20 ft.,
5 mi., white cylindrical mast.

Griffiths Islet
50 27N, 125 30W, Q R, 22 ft.,
white cylindrical tower, red band
at top.

Grilse Point
See Cyril Rock.

Grindstone Island (on rock N of Grindstone Pt.)
54 18.6N, 130 23.1W, Fl R 4s, 13 ft.,
white tower, red band at top.

Gull Rocks (highest of group)
54 08N, 130 31W, Fl R 6s, 26 ft.,
rectangular skeleton tower.

Gunboat Passage
See Bark Island.

Haans Islet
53 02.3N, 131 41.2W, Fl (3) W 12s,
16 ft., square skeleton tower.

Haddington Island (on drying rock)
50 36N, 127 01W, Q G, 20 ft.,
6 mi., white cylindrical tower,
green band at top, radar reflector.

Haddington Island (S side)
50 35.9N, 127 01.5W, Q W, 15 ft.,
white cylindrical tower.
Also see Broad Cove.

Haddington Reefs (pier)
50 36.5N, 127 00.6W, Fl R 2s,
30 ft., 8 mi., white cylindrical
tower, red band at top, horn (2):
1 blast every 20s, horns point
SE and NW.

Haig Rock
52 36.4N, 128 55.3W, Fl W 6s, 28 ft.,
5 mi., square skeleton tower.

Hakai Passage
See Odlum Point.

Hand Island (E side)
48 57.2N, 125 18.4W, Fl W 4s,
13 ft., white cylindrical mast, visible 108° to 005°, obscured 005° to
011°, visible 011° to 040°.

Hand Island Passage
48 56.7N, 125 19.6W, Q W, 27 ft.,
5 mi., white cylindrical tower.

Hankin Rock (SW entrance to Beaver Passage)
53 42N, 130 25W, Fl W 4s, 33 ft.,
5 mi., square skeleton tower,
radar reflector.

Hanmer Island (N extremity)
54 03.8N, 130 14.6W, Q W, 23 ft.,
square skeleton tower.

Hanmer Island (S extremity)
54 03N, 130 15W, Fl R , 14 ft.,
white cylindrical tower, red band
at top, visible 282° to 127°.

Hanmer Rocks
54 19.5N, 130 49.3W, Fl (3) W 12s,
28 ft., white tower, racon: M (--).

Hanson Island (E side)
50 34.0N, 126 41.6W, Q W R,
18 ft., white cylindrical mast, red
127° to 160°, white 160° to 345°.

Harbor Rock, Stewart Narrows
53 23.3N, 129 16.5W, Fl G 4s,
15 ft., square skeleton tower.

Harbormaster Point
52 04N, 128 03W, Fl W 6s, 14 ft.,
5 mi., square skeleton tower.

Harbott Point
50 22N, 125 08W, Fl R 4s, 28 ft.,
white cylindrical tower.

Hardwicke Island
See Carterer Point.

HARDY BAY

Hardy Bay (N of wharf)
50 44N, 127 29W, Fl R 4s, 22 ft.,
white cylindrical tower, red band
at top.

Beacon (SE of government wharf)
50 43N, 127 29W, Q R, 15 ft.,
white cylindrical mast, red and
white triangular daymark.

Boat Basin (N light)
50 42.9N, 127 29.3W, Fl R 4s,
21 ft., white cylindrical mast.

Boat Basin (S light)
50 42.8N, 127 29.3W, Fl G 4s,
21 ft., white cylindrical mast.

HARO STRAIT

Also see Washington chapter.

Discovery Island Light
48 25.5N, 123 13.5W, Fl W 5s,
93 ft., white cylindrical tower,
light obscured from 050.5° to
146°, horn: 1 blast every 60s.

Lighted Buoy VD
48 27.1N, 123 10.8W, Fl (2+1)
W 6s, red and green bands.

Lime Kiln Light (U.S.)
48 31.0N, 123 09.2W, Fl W 10s,
55 ft., 17 mi., octagonal tower
attached to fog signal building,
two dwellings about 150 yards
southeast, horn: 1 blast every
30s, operates continuously.

Zero Rock Light
48 31.4N, 123 17.4W, Fl W 4s,
28 ft., white cylindrical tower,
green band on top, radar reflector.

Little Zero Rock Lighted Buoy V30
48 31.9N, 123 19.7W, Q R, red.

Kelp Reefs Light
48 32.9N, 123 14.1W, Q W, 35 ft.,
octagonal tower attached to
building.

D'Arcy Island Light (SW of island)
48 34.0N, 123 17.0W, Fl R 4s,
23 ft., white cylindrical tower
with red band at top.

Mosquito Pass Buoy 1 (U.S.)
48 34.8N, 123 10.9W, green can.

Kellett Bluff Light (U.S.)
48 35.3N, 123 12.1W, Fl W 4s,
80 ft., 7 mi., NB on house.

Mandarte Island
48 38.3N, 123 17.8W, Fl G 4s,
15 ft., white cylindrical tower,
green band at top.

**Danger Shoal Lighted Horn Buoy
(SW of shoal, U.S.)**
Fl (2+1) G 6s, 6 mi., green and red
bands, horn: 1 blast every 30s.

Tom Point Light
48 39.8N, 123 16.3W, Fl W 4s,
21 ft., white cylindrical tower
with green band at top.

Arachne Reef Light
48 41.1N, 123 17.6W, Fl (2+1)
G 6s, 22 ft., white cylindrical
tower with green band at top.

Turn Point Light (U.S.)
48 41.3N, 123 14.2W, Fl W 2.5s,
44 ft., 8 mi., white concrete tower,
light obscured from 260.5° to
357°, horn: 2 blasts every 30s,
operates continuously.

Point Fairfax Light
48 42.0N, 123 17.8W, Fl (3) W 12s,
33 ft., on white tower, 4 lights.

Harris Island
51 00N, 127 34W, Fl W 4s, 43 ft.,
white cylindrical mast.

Harris Rock
54 13.0N, 130 45.9W, Fl W 6s,
16 ft., square skeleton tower.

Hartley Bay (breakwater)
53 25.4N, 129 14.9W, Q R 1s,
26 ft., square skeleton tower.

**Haswell Island, Selwyn Inlet
(S side)**
52 51.7N, 131 41.1W, Fl (3) W 12s,
27 ft., 5 mi., square skeleton
tower.
Also see Selwyn Point.

Hattie Island (W side of island)
55 17.2N, 129 58.4W, Fl W 6s,
21 ft., 5 mi., orange circular slatwork daymark on pole, visible
171° to 336°.

**Havannah Islets (on southern-
most rock)**
50 32.2N, 126 15.0W, Q G, 22 ft.,
white cylindrical tower, green
band at top.

Havelock Rock
54 06N, 130 29W, Fl W 4s, 15 ft.,
skeleton tower.

Hawkesbury Island
53 37.1N, 129 10.8W, Fl W 6s,
21 ft., square skeleton tower.

Hay Point, Bedwell Harbor
48 44.7N, 123 13.7W, Q R, 23 ft.,
white cylindrical tower, red band
at top.

**Hayden Passage (on rock in mid-
dle of pass)**
49 24N, 126 06W, Fl R 4s, 17 ft.,
white cylindrical tower, red band
at top.

Hecate Strait, Browning Entrance
See Browning Entrance.

Helen Point
48 51.5N, 123 20.6W, Q W, 23 ft.,
white cylindrical tower, red band
at top.
Also see Active Pass.

HELMCKEN ISLAND

Helmcken Island (S side of island)
50 23.6N, 125 52.2W, Q W R,
30 ft., white cylindrical tower, red
274° to 280.5°, white 280.5° to
114.3°, green 114.3° to 122.3°,
white sector indicates preferred
channel.

Range Beacon, Directional Light
50 23.9N, 125 51.4W, Dir F W R G,
16 ft., 11 mi., white cylindrical
tower, red 284° to 293°, white
293° to 296.5°, green 296.5° to
302°, white sector indicates preferred channel.

Helmcken Island (N side)
50 24.4N, 125 52.5W, Q G, 23 ft.,
white cylindrical tower, green
band at top.

Herbert Reefs (near N end of reef)
54 01N, 130 14W, Fl (3) W 12s,
20 ft., 5 mi., white square skeleton tower.

Hernando Island
See Spilsbury Point.

Hewitt Island
52 52.4N, 128 29.8W, Fl W 4s,
12 ft., square skeleton tower.

Hickey Point
50 27.0N, 126 05.1W, Fl W 4s,
29 ft., 6 mi., square skeleton
tower.

Hiekish Narrows
52 50N, 128 27W, Fl W 6s, 16 ft.,
skeleton tower.

Hilton Point
53 48.9N, 128 52.2W, Fl W 4s,
20 ft., 5 mi., square skeleton tower.

Hippa Island
53 32.7N, 133 00.6W, Fl W 4s,
100 ft., 5 mi., white mast, visible
325° to 170°.

Hocking Point
49 05.3N, 124 49.9W, Fl G 4s,
29 ft., white cylindrical mast,
green band at top.

**Hodgson Reefs Lighted Whistle
Buoy D84 (W of reefs)**
54 23N, 130 32W, Fl R, red buoy
marked D84, radar reflector,
whistle.

Hohm Island
49 13.7N, 124 49.5W, Fl W 4s,
27 ft., white cylindrical tower.

Hole in the Wall
See Maurelle Island.

Holland Rock
54 10.4N, 130 21.6W, Fl (3) W 12s,
24 ft., square skeleton tower.

Holliday Island (N end)
54 37.4N, 130 45.5W, Fl W 6s,
30 ft., 5 mi., white slatwork daymark, visible 109° to 354°.

Hope Island
See Nahwitti Point.

Hope Point
49 26N, 123 22W, Fl (3) W 12s,
23 ft., 5 mi., white cylindrical
tower.

Horn Island (N end)
52 46.2N, 132 03.4W, Fl W 10s,
16 ft., 5 mi., square skeleton tower.

Hornby Island Ferry Landing
49 31N, 124 42W, F Y, 25 ft., on dolphin, horn: 1 blast every 30s when required.
Also see Denman Island.

Hornby Point
52 09N, 131 06W, Fl W 6s, 18 ft., 5 mi., white rectangular skeleton tower.

Horseshoe Bay
See Tyee Point.

Hoskyn Inlet
See Whiterock Island.

Hudson Island North
48 58N, 123 40W, Fl R 4s, 17 ft., white cylindrical tower, red band at top.
Also see Preedy Harbor.

Hudson Rocks (summit of SW islet)
49 13.4N, 123 55.6W, Fl W 4s, 29 ft., white cylindrical tower, red band at top.

Hyde Rock (E side of Liddle Channel)
55 23.7N, 129 41.1W, Fl W 6s, 16 ft., skeleton mast.

Hyndman Reefs (on reef)
52 15.8N, 128 14.6W, Fl G 6s, 21 ft., square skeleton tower.

I

Idol Point (on extremity)
52 14N, 128 17W, Fl W 6s, 24 ft., 5 mi., white cylindrical tower, visible 093° to 304°.

Ildstad Islands (SE extremity of E island)
50 30.9N, 127 41.8W, Fl W 4s, 33 ft., 5 mi., white cylindrical mast.

Indian Arm
See Vancouver.

INTERNATIONAL BOUNDARY

Boundary Ranges A, B, and C (front and rear) are maintained by the International Boundary Commission, United States and Canada.

Range A Front Light
49 00.1N, 123 05.4W, F W, 180 ft., rectangular-shaped, orange daymark on gray skeleton tower, visible on rangeline only, the front range has an oscillating red and white light south of the boundary, and a green and white light north of the boundary, lighted throughout 24 hours.

Range A Rear Light
49 00.1N, 123 04.0W, F W, 258 ft., rectangular-shaped, orange daymark on gray pile, on same structure as International Boundary Range B Rear Light, visible westward, F R aircraft warning light on top of tower, lighted throughout 24 hours.

Obstruction Light
49 00.1N, 123 01.2W, Fl Y 4s, 36 ft., on rectangular block.

Range B Front Light
49 00.1N, 123 02.1W, F G, 65 ft., rectangular-shaped, orange daymark on gray skeleton tower, visible on rangeline only.

Range B Rear Light
49 00.1N, 123 04.0W, F G, 258 ft., rectangular-shaped, orange daymark on gray pile, on same structure as International Boundary Range A Rear Light, visible eastward, F R aircraft warning light on top of tower.

Range C Front Light
49 00.1N, 122 46.9W, Q G, 37 ft., rectangular-shaped, orange daymark on gray skeleton tower.
Also see Semiahmoo Bay, Washington.

Range C Rear Light
49 00.1N, 122 45.4W, F G, 80 ft., rectangular-shaped, orange daymark on gray tower, visible on rangeline only.

Inverness Passage (mouth of Skenna River Point)
54 11.9N, 130 15.7W, Fl W 4s, 12 ft., white skeleton tower.

Iphigenia Point (SW extremity of Langara Island)
54 11.4N, 133 00.5W, Fl W 6s, 40 ft., 5 mi., white mast, visible 309.7° to 126°.

Isabella Island, Satellite Channel (SE end)
48 44N, 123 26W, Q W, 28 ft., white cylindrical tower, green band at top.

Ivory Island, Robb Point
52 16.2N, 128 24.3W, Fl W 5s, 73 ft., 18 mi., red skeleton tower, visible 281° to 165.5°, diaphone: 1 blast every 30s.
Also see Perrin Anchorage.

J

Jacinto Island South (SE end of island)
52 56.5N, 129 36.7W, Fl W 4s, 79 ft., 5 mi., square skeleton tower.

Jacinto Point Light
54 34.8N, 131 04.5W, Fl W 6s, 35 ft., 5 mi., skeleton tower.

Jack Point
49 10N, 123 54W, Fl G 4s, 17 ft., white cylindrical tower, green band at top.
Also see Nanaimo Harbor.

Jackscrew Island
48 57.0N, 123 35.1W, Fl W 4s, 19 ft., 5 mi., white cylindrical tower, red band at top.

Jackson Rock
48 45N, 123 26W, Q R, 19 ft., white cylindrical tower, red band at top.
Also see Fulford Harbor.

James Island (NW extremity)
48 37.1N, 123 22.7W, Fl W 4s, 22 ft., white square mast on 5-pile dolphin.

James Point (W side of entrance)
50 50N, 126 59W, Fl W 4s, 30 ft., 5 mi., white cylindrical tower.

Jeannette Island (S, on largest island)
50 55.3N, 127 24.8W, Fl W 4s, 32 ft., 8 mi., white cylindrical tower, red band at top.

British Columbia

Jesse Island (E extremity)
49 12N, 123 57W, Q R, 24 ft.,
white cylindrical tower, red band
at top.

Jewitt Cove
49 42.0N, 126 36.0W, Fl W 4s,
21 ft., 5 mi., white cylindrical
mast.

Joan Point (W side of Dodd Narrows)
49 08.1N, 123 49.1W, Q W, 29 ft.,
5 mi., white cylindrical tower,
green band at top.

Jorkins Point, Swindle Island
52 26.4N, 128 29.1W, Fl W 6s,
28 ft., 5 mi., square skeleton tower.

Junction Point
See Lewis Channel.

Kains Island
See Quatsino Island Light *and*
Quatsino Radiobeacon.

Kanaka Bluff (W end)
48 43.6N, 123 23.1W, Fl W 4s,
26 ft., 6 mi., white cylindrical
tower, red band at top.

Karouk Island (W side of island)
50 05N, 127 10W, Fl W 4s, 27 ft.,
5 mi., white cylindrical tower.

Kelp Reefs Light
48 32.9N, 123 14.1W, Q W, 35 ft.,
octagonal tower attached to
building.
Also see Haro Strait.

Kelpie Point
51 44.0N, 127 59.7W, Fl W 4s,
21 ft., on structure.

Kendrick Inlet
49 43N, 126 38W, Fl W 4s, 19 ft.,
white cylindrical mast, radar
reflector

Kennedy Island
See Marked Tree Bluff.

Kersey Point
53 47N, 128 52W, Fl (3) W 12s,
21 ft., mast, white square slatwork daymark.

Keswar Point (S side)
53 37.6N, 130 21.0W, Fl W 6s,
27 ft., 5 mi., skeleton tower,
visible 315° to 126°.

Kindakun Point
53 19N, 132 46W, Fl W 4s, 67 ft.,
skeleton tower.

Kingcome Point (N extremity)
53 18.0N, 128 54.4W, Q W, 20 ft.,
5 mi., skeleton tower, visible
107° to 312°.

Kingui Island (SW extremity, N side of entrance to Cumshewa Inlet)
53 01.5N, 131 37.9W, Fl W 6s,
26 ft., square skeleton tower,
visible 285°–157°.

Kiwash Island (S end of island)
51 51.7N, 127 53.5W, Fl W 4s,
16 ft., skeleton tower.

Klewnuggit, Morning Reef (NW rock)
53 40.7N, 129 46.0W, Q W, 13 ft.,
5 mi., square skeleton tower.

Knight Inlet
See Wedge Island.

Koskimo Island
50 28.6N, 127 51.3W, Q R, 14 ft.,
white cylindrical tower, red band
at top.

Kuhushan Point
49 53N, 125 07W, Fl (2) W 6s,
58 ft., 11 mi., white skeleton tower.

Kunakun Point
53 28N, 132 54W, Fl W 6s, 70 ft.,
skeleton tower.

Kunechin Islets
49 37.2N, 123 48.2W, Fl (2) W 6s,
20 ft., white cylindrical mast.

Kwakume Point (on SW end of island)
51 41.5N, 127 53.3W, Fl (3) W 12s,
23 ft., square skeleton tower.

Kwuna Point (on end of government wharf)
53 12.9N, 131 59.4W, Fl W 6s,
15 ft., square skeleton tower.

Ladysmith Harbor
See Coffin Island.

Langara Point (NW point)
54 15.4N, 133 03.5W, Fl W 5s,
160 ft., 19 mi., white hexagonal
tower, visible 055° to 265°,

radiobeacon, horn: 1 blast every
60s, horn points 329°, white
dwelling 135 yards E of light.
Also see Iphigenia Point.

Langara Island Radiobeacon
54 15.4N, 133 03.5W, H (····),
150 mi., 314 kHz, A2A.

Larsen Harbor
53 38N, 130 32W, Q R, 16 ft.,
skeleton tower.

Lasqueti Island
See False Bay.

Laurel Point (NW extremity)
48 25.5N, 123 22.5W, Q R, 21 ft.,
6 mi., white cylindrical tower, red
band at top, radar reflector.
Also see Victoria.

Law Island (N end)
52 16.1N, 128 10.3W, Fl W 4s,
20 ft., 5 mi., square skeleton
tower, visible 090° to 270°.

Lawn Point Range Front Light
53 25.5N, 131 54.8W, F W, 38 ft.,
square skeleton tower, fluorescent orange slatwork daymark,
black stripe, racon: L (·−··).

Lawn Point Range Rear Light
157.5 meters, 270° from front
light, F W, 73 ft., square skeleton
tower, fluorescent orange slatwork daymark, black stripe.

Lawyer Islands (summit of north-ernmost island)
54 06.8N, 130 20.6W, Fl W 5s,
126 ft., 15 mi., skeleton tower,
obscured from 321° to 322° and
from 324° to 326°.

Leading Point
54 58.8N, 129 50.9W, Fl W 6s,
19 ft., square skeleton tower,
orange stripes.

Learmonth Island (on rock N of island)
53 40.7N, 132 27.2W, Fl W 6s, 21 ft.,
5 mi., square skeleton tower.

Leeson Point (near S extremity of reef, off point)
50 32.1N, 127 37.6W, Q G, 16 ft.,
white cylindrical tower, green
band at top.

Legace Point
52 28N, 128 25W, Fl W 4s, 32 ft.,
5 mi., skeleton tower.

Legge Point, Cone Island
52 36N, 128 31W, Fl W 6s, 10 ft.,
square skeleton tower.

Lennard Island (SW point)
49 06.6N, 125 55.3W, Fl W 10s,
115 ft., 21 mi., white cylindrical
tower, red band at top, diaphone:
2 blasts every 60s, horns point
180° and 270°, fog signal 100
yards SE of light.

Levy Point (NE end of Ashdown Island)
53 04.7N, 129 12.1W, Fl R 6s,
16 ft., square skeleton tower.
Also see Ashdown Island.

Lewis Channel Junction Point (E side of Cortes Island)
50 08.4N, 124 53.6W, Fl G 4s,
29 ft., white cylindrical tower,
green band at top.

Lewis Point (W side of entrance to Beaver Cove)
50 33.1N, 126 51.3W, Fl G 4s,
32 ft., white cylindrical tower,
green band at top.

Lewis Reef
48 25.6N, 123 16.8W, Q R, 22 ft.,
5 mi., white cylindrical tower, red
band at top, radar reflector.

Limestone Islet
48 58.9N, 124 58.3W, Q W, 28 ft.,
5 mi., white cylindrical tower.

Lions Gate Bridge (S)
49 18.9N, 123 08.3W, F W R G,
194 ft., on bridge structure, green
303° to 304°, white 304° to 306°,
red 306° to 307°, white sector
indicates preferred channel.
Also see Vancouver.

Lions Gate Bridge (N)
49 19.0N, 123 08.2W, F W R G,
190 ft., on bridge structure, green
303° to 304°, white 304° to 306°,
red 306° to 307°, white sector
indicates preferred channel.

Little Group Rock
48 41N, 123 22W, Fl W 4s, 16 ft.,
5 mi., white cylindrical tower.
Also see Dock Island.

Little Zero Rock Lighted Buoy V30
48 31.9N, 123 19.7W, Q R, red.
Also see Haro Strait.

Lizard Point (on extremity)
54 50.0N, 130 16.5W, Fl W 6s,
24 ft., white cylindrical tower.

Lizard Point (NE side of Malcolm Island)
50 40.3N, 126 53.6W, Fl W 4s,
18 ft., 6 mi., white cylindrical
tower, green band at top.
Also see Pulteney Point.

Logan Rock
53 02.2N, 129 28.6W, Fl W 4s,
42 ft., square skeleton tower.

Lombard Point
52 29N, 128 57W, Fl W 4s, 46 ft.,
5 mi., white cylindrical tower.

Lone Tree Point (E side of Stamp Narrows)
49 11N, 124 49W, Q R, 25 ft.,
white cylindrical tower, red band
at top.
Also see Stamp Narrows.

Long Harbor (on rock)
48 51.1N, 123 26.5W, Q R, 19 ft.,
white cylindrical tower, red band
at top.

Lookout Island (E end of Brown Channel)
49 59.9N, 127 26.8W, F Fl G 5s,
50 ft., 16 mi., white cylindrical
tower, green band at top on
white rectangular building,
horn: 1 blast every 20s, high-
intensity green flash superimposed every 5s.

Lookout Point
49 23N, 123 17W, Q R, 26 ft.,
white cylindrical tower, red band
at top.

Lorte Island (S end)
50 27N, 125 27W, Fl W 4s, 18 ft.,
white cylindrical tower, red band
at top.

Low Island (on NW end of the northern islet)
52 55N, 131 32W, Fl W 6s, 56 ft.,
5 mi., square skeleton tower,
obscured from 311° to 339°.

Lucy Island, Parry Passage
See Parry Passage.

Lucy Island (NE extremity of E island)
54 17.7N, 130 36.4W, Fl R 5s,
71 ft., 14 mi., white tower, visible
094.5° to 351.5°, horn: 2 blasts
every 60s, horn points 050°.

Lucy Islands North
54 18.1N, 130 37.2W, Q W, 23 ft.,
white cylindrical tower.

Lund (E end of S Copeland Island)
49 59.8N, 124 47.6W, Fl W 4s, 21 ft.,
5 mi., white cylindrical tower.
Also see Major Islet.

Lyall Island (SW end)
50 27N, 125 36W, Fl (3) W 12s,
20 ft., white cylindrical tower.

Lyall Point
48 58.2N, 125 19.3W, Q R, 30 ft.,
white cylindrical tower, red band
at top.

M

Macktush Creek
49 06.6N, 124 49.3W, Q G, 24 ft.,
white cylindrical tower, green
band at top, on 9-pile dolphin.

Maitland Island
53 42.2N, 129 04.5W, Fl W 4s, 14 ft.,
5 mi., square skeleton tower.

Major Brown Rock (entrance to Rivers Inlet)
51 25.5N, 127 42.0W, Fl W 6s,
43 ft., square skeleton tower.

Major Islet
49 59.3N, 124 48.9W, Fl (3) W 12s,
102 ft., 5 mi., white cylindrical
tower, red band at top.
Also see Lund.

Makwazniht Island (NW end)
50 33.4N, 127 33.3W, Q W, 10 ft.,
5 mi., white cylindrical mast.

Malaspina Strait
See Nelson Rock.

Malcolm Island
See Lizard Point *and* Pulteney
Point.

Malibu Rapids
50 10N, 123 51W, Q G, 18 ft.,
white cylindrical tower, green
band at top.

Man Island
53 07.7N, 129 46.3W, Fl (3) W 12s, 40 ft., square skeleton tower.

Mandarte Island
48 38.3N, 123 17.8W, Fl G 4s, 15 ft., white cylindrical tower, green band at top.
Also see Haro Strait.

Mapleguard Point (Deep Bay, SW end of point)
49 28N, 124 44W, Fl W 4s, 30 ft., 7 mi., white cylindrical tower, green band at top.

Marble Island (W extremity)
53 12.1N, 132 40.0W, Fl W 6s, 110 ft., 5 mi., white mast, visible 330° to 148°.

Marked Tree Bluff (on N end of W Kennedy Island)
54 04.1N, 130 09.8W, Fl W 6s, 28 ft., 5 mi., square skeleton tower.

Marktosis
49 16.7N, 126 03.7W, Fl W 4s, 15 ft., 5 mi., white cylindrical tower.

Mary Anne Point, Galiano Island
48 51.7N, 123 18.7W, Q W, 25 ft., white cylindrical tower, green band at top, radar reflector.
Also see Active Pass.

Mary Point, Verney Passage
53 33.0N, 128 58.0W, Q W, 16 ft., skeleton tower, white square slat-work daymark.

Mary Tod Island (SW extremity of breakwater)
48 25.5N, 123 17.9W, Fl R 4s, 20 ft., white cylindrical mast.

Masset Inlet Harbor Entrance Range Front Light
54 02N, 132 12W, F Y, 22 ft., square skeleton tower, fluorescent orange slatwork daymark, black stripe.

Masset Inlet Harbor Entrance Range Rear Light
1534 meters, 165.7° from front light, F Y, 45 ft., square skeleton tower, fluorescent orange slatwork daymark, black stripe.

Masterman Islands (NE extremity of NE island)
50 45.5N, 127 25.3W, Fl (3) W 12s, 32 ft., 7 mi., white cylindrical tower, green band at top.

Mate Island (E end)
49 21.0N, 126 15.9W, Q W, 33 ft., white cylindrical tower, green band at top, radar reflector.

Matilda Inlet (outer edge of reef, W side of entrance)
49 18.2N, 126 04.4W, Fl W 4s, 17 ft., 5 mi., white cylindrical tower, red band at top.

Maud Island (on rock on W side of island)
50 07.8N, 125 20.9W, Q R, 28 ft., white cylindrical tower, red band at top.

Maud Island South
50 07.7N, 125 20.5W, Fl R 4s, 22 ft., white cylindrical structure, red band at top.

Maude Island (near E end of island)
49 16N, 124 05W, Fl W 4s, 32 ft., 5 mi., white cylindrical tower, red band at top.
Also see Nanoose Harbor.

Maurelle Island, Hole in the Wall (W entrance)
50 18N, 125 12W, Q R, 24 ft., white cylindrical tower, red band at top.

Maurus Channel (on rock E side of channel)
49 12.2N, 125 55.8W, Fl R 4s, 19 ft., white cylindrical tower, red band.

McCoy Cove (E side)
53 02.1N, 131 39.2W, F W R G, 16 ft., platform on tree stump, G 082°–090°, W 090°–092°, R 092°–101°, white sector indicates preferred channel.

McCreight Point, Pitt Island
53 12N, 129 30W, Fl W 6s, 25 ft., 5 mi., square skeleton tower.

McEwan Rock
51 03.5N, 127 37.8W, Fl (3) W 12s, 62 ft., 5 mi., white cylindrical mast.

McInnes Island (on bluff S side of island)
52 16N, 128 43W, Fl W 5s, 105 ft., white rectangular tower, visible 292.5° to 115°, radiobeacon, horn: 2 blasts every 60s, horn points 206°.

McInnes Island Radiobeacon
52 15.7N, 128 43.3, MS (-- ···), 100 mi., 380 kHz, A2A, carrier signal.

McKay Island
49 18.7N, 126 03.5W, Fl R 4s, 31 ft., white cylindrical tower, red band at top.

McKay Reach
See Trivett Point.

McMullen Point
50 14.8N, 125 23.7W, Fl W 4s, 28 ft., 5 mi., white cylindrical tower, green band at top.

McNiffe Rock
50 31.3N, 127 36.7W, Fl W 4s, 15 ft., 5 mi., cylindrical tower, green band at top.

Merry Island (SE extremity)
49 28N, 123 55W, F Fl W 15s, 60 ft., 16 mi., white square tower, diaphone: 3 blasts every 60s, horn points S, high-intensity flash superimposed every 15s.

Metlakatla Harbor
See Shrub Island.

Metlakatla Passage (N tip of small island)
54 20.2N, 130 25.3W, F W R G, 9 ft., square skeleton mast, orange daymark, black vertical stripe, red 073° to 077°, white 077° to 080°, green 080° to 085°., white sector marks channel.

Mill Bay
54 59.7N, 129 53.3W, Q W, 19 ft., square skeleton tower, orange stripes.

Mist Rock
50 25.8N, 127 30.1W, Fl (2+1) G 6s, 21 ft., white cylindrical tower, green band at top.

Money Point
53 22.9N, 129 09.8W, Fl (3) W 12s, 21 ft., skeleton tower.

Monks Islet (N side of W entrance to Calmus Passage)
49 13.9N, 126 00.9W, Fl (3) W 12s, 46 ft., 5 mi., white cylindrical mast.

Montagu Channel
See Brunswick Point.

Moore Island (NW point)
53 47.4N, 130 31.2W, Fl W 6s,
17 ft., skeleton tower, visible 008°
to 250°.

Morfee Island (S end), Calmus Passage
49 13N, 125 57W, Q W, 40 ft.,
white cylindrical tower, green
band at top.

Morning Reef
See Klewnuggit.

Mouat Point
48 46N, 123 19W, Fl R 4s, 22 ft.,
5 mi., white cylindrical tower, red
band at top, radar reflector.

MUCHALAT INLET

North Shore
49 39N, 126 21W, Q G, 22 ft.,
white cylindrical tower, green
band at top.

East, North Shore
49 39N, 126 16W, Fl G 4s, 21 ft.,
white cylindrical tower, green
band at top.

South Shore
49 39N, 126 13W, Fl R 4s, 21 ft.,
white cylindrical tower, red band
at top.

Mystery Reef Bell Buoy Q25
49 55N, 124 43W, Fl G, black buoy
marked Q25, radar reflector, bell.

N

Nahwitti Point (SW side of Hope Island)
50 54.3N, 127 59.0W, Fl W 2s,
50 ft., 13 mi., white cylindrical
tower, radar reflector, horn:
1 blast every 30s.

NANAIMO HARBOR

Entrance Island (N approach to Nanaimo)
49 12.6N, 123 48.4W, F Fl W 5s,
61 ft., 15 mi., white cylindrical
tower, horn: 2 blasts every 60s,
high-intensity flash superimposed every 5s.

Gallows Point (S end of Protection Island)
49 10.2N, 123 55.0W, Al R W 10s,
26 ft., white cylindrical tower,
red band at top, horn: 1 blast
every 20s.

Jack Point
49 10N, 123 54W, Fl G 4s, 17 ft.,
white cylindrical tower, green
band at top.

South Side of Entrance to Harbor
49 10.0N, 123 54.9W, Q G, 24 ft.,
white cylindrical tower on 3-pile
dolphin.

Entrance Groin (E of Assembly Wharf)
49 09.8N, 123 55.2W, Fl G 4s, 24 ft.,
white cylindrical tower, green
band at top, on 3-pile dolphin.

Collier Range Front Light
49 09.9N, 123 55.7W, Iso G 1.5s,
48 ft., triangular skeleton tower,
red daymark, white stripe.

Collier Range Rear Light
254.1° from front light, Iso G 2s,
78 ft., triangular skeleton tower,
red daymark, white stripe.

Ferry Terminal
49 10.0N, 123 55.9W, Q W R G,
20 ft., red 250° to 257°, white 257°
to 270.5°, green 270.5° to 278°,
white sector is preferred channel.

NANOOSE HARBOR

Maude Island (near E end of island)
49 16N, 124 05W, Fl W 4s, 32 ft.,
5 mi., white cylindrical tower,
red band at top.

Richard Point (N side of entrance to harbor)
49 16N, 124 07W, Fl R 4s, 26 ft.,
white cylindrical tower, red band
at top.

Breakwater
49 15.9N, 124 08.2W, Q Y.

Ranch Point Pier (E end)
49 15.9N, 124 08.9W, Fl Y.

Ranch Point Pier (W end)
49 16.0N, 124 09.0W, Fl Y.

Napier Point
52 08N, 128 08W, Q W, 16 ft.,
square skeleton tower.

Nelson Rock, Malaspina Strait
49 39N, 124 07W, Fl W 4s, 17 ft.,
5 mi., white cylindrical tower, red
band at top.

Nimpkish Bank Light
50 34.7N, 126 56.9W, Q W, 26 ft.,
5 mi., white cylindrical mast on
6-pile dolphin, radar reflector.

Noble Islets (W point of W islet of group)
50 49.3N, 127 35.5W, Q R, 34 ft.,
white cylindrical tower, red band
at top.

Nootka (summit of San Rafael Island)
49 35.6N, 126 36.8W, F Fl W 12s,
102 ft., 15 mi., red square skeleton tower with white daymark,
visible 192° to 069°, high-intensity flash superimposed every 12s,
horn: 2 blasts every 60s, horn
points SE.

North Arm Breakwater
49 15.3N, 123 16.0W, Fl G 4s,
9 mi., cylindrical mast, white
and green square daymark.

North Arm Entrance Westerly (near NW extremity of North Arm Jetty)
49 15.5N, 123 16.7W, Fl (3) W 12s,
26 ft., 7 mi., white cylindrical
tower.

North Rachael Island
54 12.8N, 130 33.4W, Fl W 6s,
20 ft., white cylindrical tower,
visible 095° to 285°.
Also see South Rachael Island.

North Reef (E side of Stuart Channel)
48 54.8N, 123 37.5W, Fl (3) W 12s,
22 ft., white cylindrical tower.

Northeast Point, Texada Island
48 43N, 124 21W, Fl W 4s, 31 ft.,
7 mi., white cylindrical tower,
green band at top.

Northwest Rocks (on largest rock)
53 33N, 130 38W, Fl (3) W 12s,
53 ft., mast.

Norway Island (NW end)
48 58.9N, 123 37.6W, Fl Y, 10 ft., mast, private aid, maintained from April 30 to Oct. 1.

Nose Point
48 50.6N, 123 25.1W, Q W, 28 ft., white cylindrical tower.

Nuchatilitz (NW extremity of unnamed island)
49 49N, 126 59W, Fl W 4s, 38 ft., white cylindrical tower.

Numas Island
50 45.9N, 127 04.3W, Fl W 4s, 21 ft., 7 mi., white cylindrical structure.

O

Observatory Inlet (on small islet)
55 09.9N, 129 54.0W, Fl W 6s, 13 ft., 5 mi., tower.

Octopus Point
48 48N, 123 34W, Fl G 4s, 20 ft., white cylindrical mast.

Odlum Point (W side of Hakai Passage)
51 41.6N, 128 07.1W, Fl W 6s, 70 ft., 5 mi., on structure.

Ogden Point Breakwater Light
48 24.8N, 123 23.6W, Q R, 40 ft., white square tower, red band around bottom, horn: 1 blast every 30s, horn points 205°.
Also see Victoria.

Ohlsen Point
50 32.1N, 127 34.2W, Q G, 15 ft., 5 mi., cylindrical tower, green band at top.

Oldfield Breakwater (on floating breakwater)
54 18N, 130 21W, Q R, 7 ft., white triangular daymark.
Also see Prince Rupert Harbor.

Oldfield Terminal (on barge)
54 17.4N, 130 21.5W, F R, 18 ft., cylindrical mast, private light.

One Tree Islet (on N side)
54 33.8N, 130 26.3W, Fl R 4s, 17 ft., square tower.

Ormiston Point (E shore of Pitt Island)
53 34N, 129 39W, Fl W 6s, 15 ft., white cylindrical tower.
Also see Pitt Island.

Osborn Bay
See Crofton.

Osborne Island
54 17.2N, 130 51.1W, Fl R 6s, 33 ft., white cylindrical tower.

P

Pachena Point (near extremity)
48 43.4N, 125 05.8W, Fl (2) W 7.5s, 185 ft., 17 mi., white octagonal tower, horn: 1 blast every 60s, horn points 150°, 200 yards SE of light.

Pam Rock
49 29N, 123 18W, Fl W 4s, 38 ft., 5 mi., white cylindrical tower.

Panther Point Lighted Buoy U44
Fl R, red.

Parizeau Point (on easternmost dolphin)
54 17.3N, 130 22.1W, Fl W 6s, 15 ft., three-pile dolphin.
Also see Prince Rupert Harbor.

Parry Passage (E extremity of Lucy Island)
54 10.9N, 132 58.3W, Fl W 4s, 26 ft., 5 mi., white skeleton tower.

Parson Island
50 34.5N, 126 41.0W, Fl W 4s, 20 ft., 7 mi., white cylindrical structure.

Patey Rock (entrance to Saanich Inlet)
48 42N, 123 31W, Fl (3) W 12s, 23 ft., 5 mi., white cylindrical tower, green band at top.

Patricia Bay Breakwater
48 39.2N, 123 27.0W, Fl R 4s, 17 ft., cylindrical mast, red and white triangular daymark.

Pearse Canal, Island Light
54 47.1N, 130 36.5W, Fl W 4s, 18 ft., white square daymarks on E, S, and W sides of square skeleton tower.

Pearson Point
55 27.4N, 129 30.1W, Fl W 6s, 17 ft., 5 mi., skeleton tower, visible 206°–045°.

Peile Point
48 51.0N, 123 24.2W, Fl W 4s, 25 ft., 5 mi., white cylindrical tower.

Pelly Island (S extremity)
48 25.5N, 123 23.0W, Fl G 4s, 21 ft., 6 mi., white cylindrical tower, green band at top, radar reflector.
Also see Victoria.

Pender Harbor (near N end of William Island)
49 38N, 124 04W, Q R, 15 ft., white cylindrical tower, red band at top.

Penrose Island (N extremity, Bosquet Point)
51 30.6N, 127 44.0W, Fl W 6s, 24 ft., square skeleton tower, obscured by Lone Island 073° to 087°.

Perrin Anchorage (E of Ivory Island)
52 16.5N, 128 23.4W, Fl W 4s, 17 ft., square skeleton tower, visible 139° to 029°.
Also see Ivory Island.

Peterson Islet (N end)
50 23.4N, 125 54.8W, Fl G 4s, 20 ft., white cylindrical tower, green band at top.

Phillimore Point, Galiano Island (on extremity)
48 52.3N, 123 23.4W, Q R, 24 ft., 5 mi., white cylindrical tower, red band at top.

Piers Island
See Clive Island.

Pill Point (SW end of Seddall Island)
48 57.9N, 125 04.8W, Fl R 4s, 36 ft., white cylindrical tower, red band at top.

Pine Island (SW point of island)
50 58.5N, 127 43.6W, F W, Fl R 10s, 86 ft., 19 mi., white square skeleton tower, high-intensity red flash superimposed every 10s, radiobeacon, horn (2): 2 blasts every 60s, horns point 146° and 240°, horns sound in unison.

Pine Island Radiobeacon
50 58.6W, 127 43.6W, P (·---·), 40 mi., 318 kHz, A2A.

Pitt Island (on W side of Grenville Channel)
53 42.3N, 129 49.0W, Fl W 6s, 16 ft., 5 mi., square skeleton tower.
Also see Ormiston Point *and* McCreight Point.

Pitt Point (SE of Calvert Point)
53 53.0N, 130 06.6W, Fl W 6s, 13 ft., 5 mi., square skeleton tower.

Plover Point
53 16.8N, 129 18.2W, Fl W 4s, 12 ft., square skeleton tower.

Pocahontas Point
48 59.0N, 124 55.1W, Q G, 20 ft., white cylindrical tower, green band at top.

Point Atkinson (N point of entrance)
49 19.8N, 123 15.8W, Fl (2) W 5s, 108 ft., 20 mi., white hexagonal tower with 6 buttresses, radiobeacon, diaphone: 3 blasts every 60s.
Also see Vancouver.

Point Atkinson Radiobeacon
49 19.8N, 123 15.8W, AE (·- ·), 30 mi., 320 kHz, A2A, carrier signal, calibration service is available upon request through Vancouver Radio (VAI), frequency used is 320 kHz, characteristic signal is T (-).

Point Cowan
49 20.1N, 123 21.6W, Q W, 67 ft., white cylindrical tower.

Point Cumming
53 18.7N, 129 07.2W, Fl W 6s, 20 ft., 6 mi., square skeleton tower.

Point Fairfax Light
48 42.0N, 123 17.8W, Fl (3) W 12s, 33 ft., on white tower, 4 lights.
Also see Haro Strait.

Point Grey Lighted Bell Buoy Q62
49 17.4N, 123 15.9W, Q R, red.

Point Roberts
See Washington chapter.

Point Upwood (SE extremity of Texada Island)
49 29.4N, 124 08.4W, Fl (3) W 12s, 36 ft., 5 mi., white cylindrical tower, red band at top.

Pointer Island (SE end)
52 04N, 127 57W, Oc W 6s, 39 ft., 8 mi., aluminum skeleton tower.

Pointer Rocks (on S rock)
54 36.3N, 130 32.2W, Fl W 6s, 21 ft., white cylindrical tower.

Polly Point
49 13.0N, 124 49.0W, Fl R 4s, 14 ft., 6 mi., white cylindrical tower, red band at top.

Popham Island (NW extremity)
49 21.8N, 123 29.4W, Fl R 4s, 38 ft., white cylindrical tower, red band at top.

PORLIER PASS

Lighted Bell Buoy U41
Fl G, green.

Race Point, Galiano Island, Range Front Light
49 00.7N, 123 35.1W, F Y, Q W, 21 ft., white square tower, visible 162.5° to 264.5°, horn: 1 blast every 30s.

Virago Point Range Rear Light
445.2 meters, 196.1° from front light, F Y, 32 ft., white square tower.

Virago Rock
49 00.8N, 123 35.5W, Q W R, 23 ft., 5 mi., white cylindrical structure, green band at top, red 024° to 229°, white elsewhere, radar reflector.

PORPOISE HARBOR

Porpoise Harbor (N side of entrance)
54 11.9N, 130 18.9W, Fl G 4s, 14 ft., white cylindrical tower, green band at top.

Range Front Light (on Flora Bank, W side of Lelu Island)
54 12.0N, 130 17.9W, F Y, 12 ft., mast, rectangular daymark, fluorescent orange and black stripes.

Range Rear Light
85 meters, 072.9° from front light, F Y, 27 ft., mast, rectangular daymark, fluorescent orange and black stripes.

No. 1 (off W end of Lelu Island, on drying rock)
54 12.1N, 130 18.2W, Fl R 4s, 18 ft., skeleton tower.

No. 2 (W side of channel)
54 12.5N, 130 17.8W, Q G, 15 ft., skeleton tower.

No. 3 (E side of channel on drying rock)
54 12.7N, 130 17.4W, Q R, 23 ft., square skeleton tower, fluorescent orange daymark, black stripe.

Port McNeill (breakwater)
50 36.6N, 127 05.3W, Fl W 4s, 13 ft., white cylindrical mast.

Port Moody
See Vancouver.

Port San Juan Lighted Whistle Buoy YK
48 32.1N, 124 29.0W, Mo (A) W, red and white stripes.
Also see San Juan Point Light.

Port Simpson (breakwater)
54 33.7N, 130 25.7W, Q R, 15 ft., square skeleton tower.

Portlock Point (E extremity of Prevost Island)
48 49.7N, 123 21.0W, Q W, 51 ft., 7 mi., white square tower, horn: 1 blast every 20s.

POWELL RIVER

Range Front Light
49 52.3N, 124 33.5W, F Y.

Range Rear Light
510 feet, 032.5° from front light, F Y.

Floating Breakwater Entrance, North
49 52N, 124 33W, Fl G 4s, on floating breakwater, private light.

Floating Breakwater Entrance, South
Fl R 4s, 23 ft., on floating breakwater, private light.

Preedy Harbor
48 58.1N, 123 41.0W, Q R, 17 ft., white cylindrical tower, red band at top, rock dries 9 feet, radar reflector.
Also see Hudson Island North.

Prideaux Island, Sechart Channel
48 56.6N, 125 16.2W, Fl G 4s, 21 ft., white cylindrical tower, green band at top, visible 096° to 289°.

PRINCE RUPERT HARBOR

Radiobeacon
54 15.8N, 130 25.3W, PR (·--· ·-·), 100 mi., 218 kHz, A2A.

Barrett Rock (off shore on reef)
54 14.6N, 130 20.5W, Fl R 6s, 17 ft., 5 mi., white cylindrical tower, red band at top, horn: 2 blasts every 20s.

Frederick Point (at edge of bar)
54 15.5N, 130 21.5W, Fl G 4s, 21 ft., white cylindrical tower, green band at top.

Casey Point (on edge of shoal off the point)
54 16.5N, 130 21.6W, Q R, 20 ft., white 7-pile dolphin.

Parizeau Point (on easternmost dolphin)
54 17.3N, 130 22.1W, Fl W 6s, 15 ft., three-pile dolphin.

Oldfield Terminal (on barge)
54 17.4N, 130 21.5W, F R, 18 ft., cylindrical mast, private light.

Oldfield Breakwater (on floating breakwater)
54 18N, 130 21W, Q R, 7 ft., white triangular daymark.

Dodge Cove Range Front Light
54 17.4N, 130 22.9W, F Y, 18 ft., 3-pile dolphin, orange and black daymark.

Dodge Cove Range Rear Light
115.2 meters, 253.2° from front light, F Y, 20 ft., 3-pile dolphin, orange and black daymark, visible 239° to 266°.

Seal Cove
54 20.2N, 130 16.6W, Q W, 16 ft., white cylindrical tower.

Princesa Channel (E entrance)
49 43N, 126 38W, Fl G 4s, 19 ft., white cylindrical tower, green band at top, radar reflector.

Princess Royal Island
See Quarry Point.

Principe Channel
53 23.6N, 129 54.3W, Fl W 6s, 20 ft., 5 mi., square skeleton tower.
Also see Keswar Point *and* Wheeler Island.

Prospect Point (under bluff at point)
49 19N, 123 08W, Iso R 2s, 35 ft., 6 mi., white square tower, red band at top, horn: 1 blast every 20s.
Also see Vancouver.

Pryce Channel, Redonda Islands
50 18N, 124 50W, Fl G 4s, 23 ft., white cylindrical tower, green band at top.
Also see Waddington Channel *and* Dean Point.

Pulteney Point, Malcolm Island
50 37.9N, 127 09.2W, Fl R 10s, 40 ft., visible 278° to 145°, 12 mi., F R 36 ft., visible 131° to 143°, white square tower, horns (2): 3 blasts every 60s, horns point 118° and 295°, sound in unison.
Also see Lizard Point.

Q

Quarry Point (E side of Princess Royal Island)
52 54N, 128 31W, Fl G 6s, 16 ft., square mast.

Quathiaski Cove
50 02.7N, 125 13.3W, Fl G 4s, 20 ft., white cylindrical tower, green band at top.

Quatsino Island Light (SE end, N side of entrance to Quatsino Sound)
50 26.5N, 128 01.9W, F Fl W 5s, 90 ft., 15 mi., white cylindrical tower, visible 224° to 104°, high-intensity flash superimposed every 5s, radiobeacon, horn: 1 blast every 30s, horn points 140°.

Quatsino Radiobeacon
50 26.5N, 128 01.8W, B (-···), 50 mi., 296 kHz, A2A.

R

Race Passage East
50 22.9N, 125 48.8W, Fl G 4s, 18 ft., white cylindrical tower, green band at top.

Race Point, Galiano Island
See Porlier Pass.

Race Point (on E extremity)
50 06.8N, 125 19.4W, Q G, 77 ft., white cylindrical tower, green band at top.

RACE ROCKS

Race Rocks Light (on Great Race Rock)
48 17.9N, 123 31.8W, Fl W 10s, 118 ft., 18 mi., alternate black and white bands on cylindrical stone tower, with dwelling attached, horn: 3 blasts every 60s, should not be approached within 1 mile to clear Rosedale Reef.

Race Rocks Radiobeacon
48 17.9N, 123 31.8W, J (·---), 309 kHz.

Race Rocks Calibration Radiobeacon
48 17.9N, 123 31.8W, T (-), 30 mi., 309 kHz, A2A, transmits upon request through Victoria Marine Radio (VAK), 24 hours prior notice is required.

South Cautionary Lighted Buoy VF
48 14.1N, 123 31.9W, Fl Y 4s, yellow.

Traffic Lane Separation Lighted Buoy PA
48 12.4N, 123 27.7W, Fl Y 4s, 6 mi., yellow.

East Cautionary Lighted Buoy VG
48 16.1N, 123 27.7W, Fl Y 4s, yellow.

Ramsbotham Island (SE extremity)
52 41.9N, 129 02.1W, Fl W 4s, 23 ft., square skeleton tower, visible 125° to 325°.

Ramsden Point (on extremity)
54 59.0N, 130 06.2W, Fl (3) W 12s, 27 ft., orange ball daymark on pole, obscured from 117.5° to 260°.

Ray Point Range Front Light
50 34.8N, 126 12.0W, Q Y, 20 ft., white cylindrical mast, red daymark, white stripe.

Ray Point Range Rear Light
31 meters, 087.8° from front light, Q Y, 36 ft., white cylindrical mast, red daymark, white stripe, visible on rangeline only.

Rebecca Rock, Algerine Passage
49 49N, 124 39W, Fl W 2s, 30 ft., 11 mi., white cylindrical tower, radar reflector.

Rebecca Spit
See Drew Harbor.

Reception Point
49 28N, 123 53W, Fl (3) W 12s, 24 ft., 5 mi., white cylindrical tower, red band at top, radar reflector.

Redcliff Point (N end of Graham Reach)
53 09N, 128 38W, Fl W 4s, 16 ft., white square mast.

Redonda Island, Lewis Channel (W side)
50 14.6N, 124 58.6W, Fl W 4s, 23 ft., 5 mi., white cylindrical tower, red band at top.

Redonda Islands
See Pryce Channel, Waddington Channel, *and* Dean Point.

Refuge Cove
50 07N, 124 51W, Fl R 4s, 21 ft., white cylindrical tower, red band at top.

Refuge Island Boat Harbor
54 07N, 132 19W, Dir F W R G, 16 ft., square skeleton tower, red 206° to 213°, white 213° to 216°, green 216° to 223°, white sector indicates preferred channel.

Regatta Rocks
52 13N, 128 08W, Fl R 4s, 19 ft., white cylindrical tower, red band at top.

Reid Passage
See Carne Rock.

Richard Point (N side of entrance to Nanoose Harbor)
49 16N, 124 07W, Fl R 4s, 26 ft., white cylindrical tower, red band at top.
Also see Nanoose Harbor.

Richard Rock
48 59.3N, 125 19.6W, Fl G 4s, 23 ft., white cylindrical tower, green band at top.

Richards Point (on extremity)
55 17.3N, 129 48.8W, Fl W 6s, 16 ft., 5 mi., tower.

Ripple Point
50 22N, 125 35W, Fl W 4s, 20 ft., 5 mi., white cylindrical tower, green band at top.

Rivers Inlet
See Major Brown Rock.

Rix Island (NE end)
53 31.5N, 128 44.2W, Fl W 6s, 13 ft., square skeleton tower.

Robb Point
See Ivory Island.

Roberson Point (W of point)
54 19.4N, 130 24.5W, F W R G, 9 ft., square skeleton mast, orange daymark, black vertical stripe, red 110.5° to 114°, white 114° to 118°, green 118° to 124°, white sector marks the channel.

Roberson Point Signal Station (NW of point)
54 19.4N, 130 24.9W, F W R G, 16 ft., square skeleton mast, orange daymark, black vertical stripe, red 138° to 142°, white 142° to 146°, green 146° to 151°, white sector marks channel.
Also see Metlakatla Passage.

Roberts Bank
49 05.2N, 123 18.6W, Fl W 5s, 37 ft., 16 mi., white cylindrical tower, red band at top, on piles, horn: 1 blast every 20s, racon: R (·-·).

Roberts Bank Lighted Buoy TA
49 04.4N, 123 22.8W, Fl W, yellow buoy, radar reflector, racon: L (·-··).

Robson
See Fishermans Cove.

Rock Point
50 20N, 125 30W, Q W G, 19 ft., white cylindrical tower, green band at top.

Rogers Reef
49 08N, 123 41W, Q W, 18 ft., 5 mi., white cylindrical tower.

Rolston Island
50 01.3N, 127 21.9W, Fl R 4s, 16 ft., mast with red, white, and orange triangular daymark.

Rooney Point
54 01N, 132 10W, Fl R 6s, 17 ft., 6-pile dolphin.

Rosenfeld Rock Lighted Buoy U59
48 48.2N, 123 01.6W, Fl G, green, racon: U (··-).
Also see Boundary Pass.

Round Island (N side)
50 44N, 127 22W, Fl W 4s, 39 ft., 5 mi., white cylindrical tower.

Rugged Islands (N pt. of N island)
50 19N, 127 55W, Fl W 4s, 33 ft., white cylindrical mast, obscured 318° to 050°.

Rugged Point (on end of N point)
49 58.2N, 127 15.0W, Fl W 4s, 51 ft., 5 mi., white square mast, red and white triangular daymark.

Ryan Point Reef
54 21.6N, 130 29.9W, Fl W 6s, 15 ft., skeleton tower, visible 023° to 177°.

S

Sabine Channel
See Texada Island.

Sainty Point (S entrance to Grenville Channel)
53 22N, 129 19W, Fl W 4s, 15 ft., white cylindrical tower.

Salter Point
49 41.0N, 126 35.1W, Q G, 21 ft., white cylindrical tower, green band at top.

Saltery Bay
49 46.9N, 124 10.5W, F G, on outer dolphin, ferry terminal, radar reflector, horn: 1 blast every 20s.

Saltspring Island, Single Station Range
48 55N, 123 33W, F W R G, 21 ft., white cylindrical tower, red 264° to 268°, white 268° to 272°, green 272° to 276°, white sector indicates preferred channel.

San Carlos Point
49 41.2N, 126 31.2W, Q W, 22 ft., 6 mi., white cylindrical tower.

San Jose Islets
48 54.1N, 125 03.4W, Fl W 4s, 24 ft., 5 mi., white cylindrical tower, red band at top.

San Juan Point Light
48 31.9N, 124 27.4W, Fl R 5s, 57 ft., 12 mi., white cylindrical tower, red band at top, on corner of white building, horn: 1 blast every 30s.
Also see Port San Juan Lighted Whistle Buoy YK.

SAND HEADS

Sand Heads Light (50 yards from outer end of Steveston Jetty)
49 06.4N, 123 18.1W, F W Fl R 5s, 43 ft., 12 mi., fluorescent orange, square tower on white rectangular building, high-intensity red flash superimposed every 5s on F W, horn: 1 blast every 30s, horn points 244°, radiobeacon.

Radiobeacon
49 06.4N, 123 18.1W, G (--·), 180s, 30 mi., 307 kHz, A2A, carrier signal.

Lighted Bell Buoy S1
49 06.2N, 123 18.5W, Fl G, green.

Sandspit Aviation Light
53 15N, 131 49W, Fl W 2s.

Sangster Island (SW point)
49 25.4N, 124 11.5W, Fl W R 4s, 54 ft., 5 mi., white cylindrical tower, red 267° to 300°.

Santiago
49 47.3N, 126 39.2W, Fl W 4s, 19 ft., white cylindrical mast, black, white, and green square daymark.

Sarah Island (N end)
52 53N, 128 31W, Fl (3) W 12s, 24 ft., 5 mi., skeleton tower.
Also see Boat Bluff.

Saturna Island Light (extremity of East Point)
48 47.0N, 123 02.7W, Fl W 15s, 121 ft., white, 17 mi., F R, 102 ft., red, 16 mi., on red skeleton tower, white light visible from 149° to 060°, red light visible from 156° to 211.5°.
Also see Boundary Pass.

Saunders Creek
See Grenville Channel.

Savary Island (on government wharf)
49 56.8N, 124 46.7W, Fl W 4s, 21 ft., 5 mi., lantern on top of shed.

Scarlett Point, Balaklava Island
50 51.6N, 127 36.7W, Fl W 5s, 83 ft., 18 mi., white cylindrical tower, horn: 1 blast every 30s, horn points 025.7°.

Schooner Cove (extremity of breakwater)
49 17N, 124 08W, Fl G 4s, 24 ft., white cylindrical mast, black, white, and green square daymark.

Schooner Reefs (W Georgia Strait)
49 17.6N, 124 07.7W, Fl (2+1) G 6s, 17 ft., white cylindrical mast, fluorescent orange, white, green, and black diamond daymark.

Scroggs Rocks Light (W side)
48 25.6N, 123 26.3W, Fl R 4s, 24 ft., white cylindrical tower, red band at top.
Also see Esquimalt.

Scudder Point
52 26.8N, 131 14.2W, Fl W 6s, 18 ft., square skeleton tower.

Sea Otter Cove
50 40N, 128 21W, Fl W 4s, 16 ft., white cylindrical tower.

Seabird Rocks
48 45.0N, 125 09.2W, Fl W 4s, 66 ft., 5 mi., white cylindrical tower, red band at top.

Seal Cove
54 20.2N, 130 16.6W, Q W, 16 ft., white cylindrical tower.
Also see Prince Rupert Harbor.

Seal Rocks (highest rock of group)
54 00.0N, 130 47.4W, Fl W 6s, 43 ft., 5 mi., white cylindrical tower, racon: S (···).

Sechelt Islets
49 44N, 123 54W, Q G, 23 ft., white cylindrical tower, green band at top.

Second Narrows
See Vancouver.

Second Sister Island
See Ganges Harbor.

Secret Cove Entrance
49 32N, 123 58W, Q R, 14 ft., white cylindrical mast, red and white triangular daymark.

Seddall Island
See Pill Point.

Selma Park (on outer end of breakwater)
49 28N, 123 45W, Fl R 4s, 27 ft., 5 mi., white cylindrical tower, red band at top.

Selwyn Inlet, Haswell Island (S side)
52 51.7N, 131 41.1W, Fl (3) W 12s, 27 ft., 5 mi., square skeleton tower.

Selwyn Point
52 51.7N, 131 50.7W, Fl W 6s, 17 ft., square skeleton tower.

Senanus Island (NW extremity)
48 36N, 123 29W, Fl W 4s, 28 ft., 5 mi., white cylindrical tower.

Separation Head
50 10.7N, 125 21.3W, Fl R 4s, 20 ft., white cylindrical structure, red upper portion.

Separation Point
48 44.6N, 123 34.1W, Fl W 4s, 20 ft., 5 mi., white cylindrical tower.

Serpent Point
52 05N, 128 00W, Q W, 17 ft., white cylindrical tower.

Seymour Island (S side)
50 28.7N, 125 52.1W, Fl W 4s, 16 ft., 5 mi., white cylindrical mast.

Shag Rock
54 09.5N, 132 39.0W, Fl (3) W 12s, 28 ft., square skeleton tower.

Sharp Point
49 20.9N, 126 15.5W, Fl W 10s, 60 ft., white cylindrical tower, horn: 1 blast every 30s.

Shears Island
49 00.0N, 125 19.4W, Fl R 4s, 22 ft., white cylindrical tower, red band at top.

Sheringham Point Light
48 22.6N, 123 55.2W, Fl G 15s, 72 ft., 14 mi., white hexagonal tower attached to rectangular dwelling.

Shkgeaum Bay Range Front Light
54 18.6N, 130 24.4W, F Y, 13 ft., cylindrical mast, white daymark, red stripe.

Shkgeaum Bay Range Rear Light
229 meters, 172° from front light, F Y, 28 ft., cylindrical mast, white daymark, red stripe.

Shoal Point (W of shoal)
48 25.4N, 123 23.5W, Q R, 19 ft., 6 mi., white cylindrical tower, red band at top, 19-pile dolphin, horn: 1 blast every 12s, horn points 213°.
Also see Victoria.

Shrub Island, Metlakatla Harbor (NW side of shoal)
54 19.8N, 130 27.6W, Q R, 18 ft., white cylindrical tower, red band at top.

Shushartie Bay
See Dillon Rock.

Shute Reef (on rock)
48 43N, 123 26W, Q R, 23 ft., white cylindrical tower.

SIDNEY

Also see Victoria/Sidney Island Radiobeacon.

Sidney Spit (NW extremity)
48 39N, 123 21W, Fl (3) R 12s, 20 ft., white cylindrical tower, red band at top.

Breakwater
48 39.2N, 123 23.4W, Fl R, 23 ft., 5 mi., cylindrical mast, two red and white rectangular daymarks.

Ferry Wharf Range Front Light
48 38.6N, 123 23.7W, F R, 38 ft., on ferry slip elevator, whistle: 2 blasts every 30s, private aid operated by ferry personnel when required for ferry movements only.

Ferry Wharf Range Rear Light
2.7 meters, 314° 42' from front, F R, 39 ft., on ferry slip elevator.

Silva Bay
49 09N, 123 41W, Fl G 4s, 16 ft., white round mast, black, white, and green square daymark.

Silva Bay, Rock (SE of Tugboat Island)
49 09N, 123 41W, Fl W 4s, 20 ft., white cylindrical tower.
Also see Tugboat Island Light.

Sisters Island (on E and largest rock)
49 29N, 124 26W, Fl (2) W 15s, 70 ft., 21 mi., white cylindrical tower, radiobeacon, diaphone: 3 blasts every 60s, horns point NW and E, horns sound in unison.

Sisters Island Radiobeacon
49 29.2N, 124 26.0W, M (--), 30 mi., 315 kHz, A2A, carrier signal.

Skenna River Point
See Inverness Passage.

Skincuttle Inlet, Bush Rock (N end)
52 18.3N, 131 16.6W, Fl W 6s, 30 ft., 5 mi., skeleton tower, obscured 310°–352°.

Skincuttle Inlet, Copper Island (E point of E island)
52 21N, 131 10W, Fl (3) W 12s, 50 ft., 5 mi., white cylindrical tower, visible 163°–039°

Skookum Island
49 44N, 123 53W, Fl W 4s, 23 ft., 5 mi., white cylindrical tower.

Skookumchuck Narrows
49 46N, 123 56W, Fl G 4s, 20 ft., white cylindrical tower, green band at top.

Slippery Rock
54 24.0N, 130 29.7W, Fl (3) W 12s, 22 ft., 9 mi., white cylindrical tower.

Sloop Islet
53 45.5N, 132 14.6W, Fl W 6s, 16 ft., 5 mi., tower.

Snake Island (N end)
49 13.1N, 123 53.4W, Fl W 4s, 33 ft., white cylindrical tower, green band at top, obscured from 350° to 011°.

Snug Cove
49 22.8N, 123 19.3W, Fl G 4s, 28 ft., white cylindrical tower, green band at top.

Snug Cove North
49 23N, 123 20W, Fl R 4s, 20 ft., white cylindrical tower, red band at top.

Sointula (breakwater)
50 38N, 127 02W, Fl W 4s, 29 ft., white cylindrical mast, red and white triangular daymark.

Solander Island
50 07N, 127 56W, Fl W 10s, 309 ft., white cylindrical tower.

Somass River
49 14.7N, 124 49.5W, Q G, 24 ft., white cylindrical tower, green band at top, white daymark on dolphin, red stripe on S side of tower.
Also see Alberni.

SOOKE HARBOR

Whiffin Spit Light (E end of spit, Sooke Inlet)
48 21.5N, 123 42.6W, Q W, 21 ft., 6 mi., white cylindrical tower with green band at top, horn: 1 blast every 30s, operated only on request to Vancouver Coast Guard Radio.

Outer Range Front Light
48 22N, 123 42W, F Y, 9 ft., 5-pile dolphin, white daymark, red stripe.

Outer Range Rear Light
101 meters, 049.7° from front light, F Y, 18 ft., 5-pile dolphin, white daymark, red stripe.

Inner Range Front Light
48 22N, 123 42W, F Y, 11 ft., 5-pile dolphin, white daymark, red stripe.

Inner Range Rear Light
35 meters, 007.6° from front light, F Y, 16 ft., 5-pile dolphin, white daymark, red stripe.

Harbor Range Front Light
48 12.9N, 123 43.7W, F Y, 10 ft., cylindrical mast, white daymark, red stripe, on dolphin, visible on rangeline only.

Harbor Range Rear Light
37 meters, 300° from front light, F Y, 15 ft., cylindrical mast, white daymark, red stripe, on dolphin, visible on rangeline only.

South Bay (W end of small island)
53 09.9N, 132 03.9W, Fl W 4s,
17 ft., skeleton tower.

South Rachael Island (S end of island)
54 11.8N, 130 33.3W, Fl R 4s,
26 ft., white cylindrical tower,
red band.
Also see North Rachael Island.

Southey Point (N extremity of Saltspring Island)
48 56.7N, 123 35.7W, Q W, 20 ft.,
5 mi., white cylindrical tower.

Spanish Bank
See Vancouver.

Spencer Creek
48 59.3N, 124 53.5W, Fl R 4s, 17 ft.,
skeleton mast, red and white
daymark on SW and NE faces.

Spider Channel (N end of Spider Island)
51 51.8N, 128 15.5W, Fl W 4s,
56 ft., square skeleton tower.

Spilsbury Point (N tip of Hernando Island)
50 00.2N, 124 56.6W, Q W, 20 ft.,
5 mi., white cylindrical tower.

Split Head (near S end of channel)
52 40.6N, 128 32.8W, Fl W 4s,
29 ft., skeleton tower.

Squamish

Approach (entrance to channel)
49 40.8N, 123 09.8W, Fl R 4s,
20 ft., center pile of 19-pile dolphin, red and white triangular
daymark.

Terminal No. 1
49 41.0N, 123 10.5W, Fl G 4s,
18 ft., mast on dolphin.

Terminal No. 2
49 40.9N, 123 10.3W, Fl W 4s,
17 ft., mast on dolphin.

St. Johns Point
See Flora Inlet.

Stamp Narrows
49 11.0N, 124 49.3W, Q G, 28 ft.,
white cylindrical tower, green
band at top, on 7-pile dolphin.
Also see Lone Tree Point.

Staniforth Point
53 34.2N, 128 48.9W, Fl (3) W 12s,
19 ft., square skeleton tower.

Star Point (S side, opposite Handy Creek)
48 58.6N, 124 56.7W, Fl W 4s,
17 ft., 5 mi., white cylindrical
tower, red band at top.

Starling Point
49 23.6N, 126 13.8W, Q W, 17 ft.,
white cylindrical tower.

Steamer Point
49 53N, 126 48W, Q W, 19 ft.,
white cylindrical tower.

Steep Island
50 04.8N, 125 15.2W, Q W, 21 ft.,
white cylindrical tower, red band
at top.

Stenhouse Shoal Whistle Buoy D59
54 20N, 130 56W, Fl G, port,
green, marked D59, whistle,
racon: C (-·-·).

Steveston Jetty
See Sand Heads.

Stewart Dolphin West
55 54.8N, 130 00.1W, Fl (3) G 12s,
23 ft., 8-pile dolphin.

Stewart Light
55 54.7N, 129 59.4W, Fl (3) W 12s,
12 ft., square skeleton tower.

Stewart Narrows
See Harbor Rock.

Stimpson Reef
50 29.7N, 126 12.1W, Fl R 4s,
17 ft., white cylindrical structure,
red band at top.

Stockham Island (off W end)
49 10.3N, 125 54.4W, Fl R 4s,
17 ft., white cylindrical tower, red
band at top.

Story Point
52 08.9N, 128 08.0W, Fl W 4s,
17 ft., square skeleton tower.

Straggling Islands (on W end of largest island)
50 35.7N, 127 42.1W, Fl W 4s,
19 ft., 5 mi., white cylindrical
tower, red band at top.

Striae Islands (E islet)
54 05.2N, 132 14.8W, Fl (3) W 12s,
20 ft., square skeleton tower.

Sunny Island (on rock off S point of island)
52 11.3N, 127 52.1W, Fl W 4s,
20 ft., skeleton tower.

Surgeon Islets (N extremity)
50 53.5N, 126 52.2W, Fl R 4s,
21 ft., white cylindrical tower,
red band at top.

Susan Rock
52 17.2N, 128 30.2W, Fl W 6s,
65 ft., 5 mi., white skeleton tower.

Sutil Point Bell Buoy Q20
50 00N, 125 00W, Fl R, red buoy
marked Q20, radar reflector, bell.

Sutlej Point
52 22.6N, 126 48.2W, Fl W 4s,
19 ft., skeleton tower.

Swale Rock (S side of E entrance to Sechart Channel)
48 55.6N, 125 13.2W, Fl (3) W 12s,
25 ft., white cylindrical tower.

Swindle Island
See Jorkins Point.

Tahsis Narrows

NE Side of Narrows
49 52N, 126 42W, Q W, 20 ft.,
white cylindrical tower, red band
at top.

South Side
49 52N, 126 41W, Fl (2) W 6s,
20 ft., white cylindrical tower,
green band at top.

N Side of E Entrance
49 52N, 126 40W, Fl W 4s, 16 ft.,
5 mi., white cylindrical tower.

Tasu Narrows
52 44.7N, 132 06.4W, Fl G 4s,
46 ft., square skeleton tower,
visible 195° to 033°.
Also see Davison Point.

Tasu Sound (S side of entrance)
52 45.0N, 132 05.7W, Fl (3) W 12s,
30 ft., mast, visible 032° to 052°.
Also see Davison Point.

Tattenham Ledge Buoy Q51
49 31N, 123 59W, Fl G, green
buoy marked Q51, radar reflector.

Tcenakun Point, Chaatl Island
53 09.1N, 132 35.0W, Fl W 4s,
87 ft., 5 mi., white mast.

Ten Mile Point
49 03.6N, 124 50.4W, Fl R 4s,
27 ft., white cylindrical tower,
red band at top.

Tenas Island (on NW side of island)
52 42.5N, 128 33.1W, Fl R 6s,
24 ft., square skeleton tower.

Texada Island (N side of Sabine Channel, on island)
49 32N, 124 14W, Fl R 4s, 27 ft.,
white cylindrical tower, red band
at top.
Also see Northeast Point *and*
Point Upwood.

Thrasher Rock, Gabriola Reefs
49 09.0N, 123 38.4W, Fl (3) W 12s,
34 ft., white cylindrical tower,
green band at top, radar reflector,
racon: W (·--).
Also see Gabriola Passage East.

Thulin Passage (N end)
50 01.8N, 124 49.5W, Fl G 4s,
28 ft., white cylindrical tower,
green band at top.

Thurlow Island
See Vansittart Point.

Tibbs Islet
49 13.8N, 126 06.5W, Fl W 4s, 36 ft.,
5 mi., white cylindrical mast.

TOFINO

Breakwater
49 09.3N, 125 54.0W, Fl W 4s,
22 ft., cylindrical tower, two red
and white rectangular daymarks,
red triangle in center.

East Breakwater
49 09.3N, 125 54.0W, Q R, 13 ft.,
white square mast, red triangular
daymark.

Tofino Radiobeacon
49 02.9N, 125 42.3W, YAZ
(-·-- ·- --··), 50 mi., 359 kHz, A2A,
carrier signal, a bearing error could
result from coastal refraction.

Tom Island
53 32.6N, 129 36.2W, Fl (3) W 12s,
18 ft., square skeleton tower.

Tom Point Light (on small islet E of point)
48 39.8N, 123 16.3W, Fl W 4s,
21 ft., white cylindrical tower
with green band at top.
Also see Haro Strait.

Tomkinson Point, Ursula Channel
53 25.8N, 128 54.2W, Fl W 6s,
14 ft., square skeleton tower.

Toquart Bay
49 00.7N, 125 20.3W, Q G, 18 ft.,
white cylindrical tower, green
band at top.

Tree Bluff Lighted Bell Buoy D86
54 25.8N, 130 30.8W, Fl R, red
buoy, marked D86, radar reflector, bell.

Trial Islands Light (Ripple Point, SE end of S island)
48 23.7N, 123 18.2W, F W, Fl G 5s,
93 ft., 15 mi., white cylindrical
tower, FW with high-intensity
green flash every 5s, horn:
2 blasts every 60s, horn points
181° from a white rectangular
building close southeastward
of lighthouse.

Tribune Rock
50 51N, 127 34W, Fl G 4s, 22 ft.,
white cylindrical tower, green
band at top.

Triple Islands (NW rock of group, S side of Brown Passage)
54 17.6N, 130 52.8W, Fl (2) W 8s,
82 ft., white tower, radiobeacon,
horn: 1 blast every 60s, horn
points 278°.

Triple Islands Radiobeacon
54 17.7N, 130 52.8W, O (---),
50 mi., 308 kHz, A2A.

Trivett Point, McKay Reach
53 18.5N, 129 02.1W, Fl W 4s, 17 ft.,
5 mi., square skeleton tower.

TSAWWASSEN

Ferry Breakwater (W end of S breakwater)
49 00.1N, 123 07.6W, Q R, 26 ft.,
white cylindrical tower, red band
at top, radar reflector.

Ferry South
49 00N, 123 08W, Oc W 10s, 18 ft.,
on dolphin, radar reflector, horn:
1 blast every 20s, horn points
270°, private light.

Light
49 00.5N, 123 08.5W, Fl Y 4s,
29 ft., on long center pile of
7-pile dolphin, radar reflector.

Range Front Light
49 00N, 123 08W, F G, 36 ft., ferry
slip gantry.

Range Rear Light
270 meters, 016.9° from front
light, F G, 59 ft., mast.

TSEHUM

Tsehum Harbor
48 40.3N, 123 24.1W, Fl R 4s,
15 ft., pile dolphin, red and white
triangular daymark, red triangle
in center.

Breakwater
48 40.3N, 123 24.2W, F G, private
aid.

Entrance
48 40.3N, 123 24.3W, Q R, 22 ft.,
white cylindrical mast with daymarks facing E and W.

Blue Heron Bay Entrance
48 40N, 123 25W, Fl W 4s, 16 ft.,
white pile dolphin, white, black,
and green daymark.

Blue Heron Basin
48 40N, 123 25W, Q G, 15 ft.,
white pile dolphin, white, black,
and green square daymark.

Tsowwin Narrows (E side, on spit)
49 46.6N, 126 38.5W, Q R, 16 ft.,
cylindrical mast on 9-pile dolphin, two red and white triangular daymarks, radar reflector.

Tsowwin Narrows West
49 46N, 126 39W, Q G, 21 ft.,
white cylindrical tower, green
band at top.

Tugboat Island Light
49 08.9N, 123 41.0W, Fl W 4s,
20 ft., white cylindrical mast,
black, white, and green square
daymark.
Also see Silva Bay.

**Tugwell Reef Lighted Bell
Buoy D61**
Fl G, green.

Tuna Point
50 28.5N, 126 00.1W, Fl R 4s,
30 ft., white cylindrical tower,
red band at top.

Turn Island
50 20.7N, 125 27.8W, Q R, 40 ft.,
white cylindrical mast, red and
white triangular daymark.

Tuzo Rock
48 26N, 123 22W, Q G, 21 ft.,
6 mi., white cylindrical tower,
green band at top, radar reflector.
Also see Victoria.

Twin Islands
49 21.1N, 122 53.4W, Fl R 4s,
30 ft., white cylindrical tower,
red band at top.
Also see Vancouver.

Tyee Point (Johnstone Strait)
50 23.1N, 125 47.0W, Q R, 25 ft.,
white cylindrical tower, red band
at top.

**Tyee Point (on rock W side of
entrance to Horseshoe Bay)**
49 23N, 123 16W, Q W, 17 ft.,
white cylindrical tower.

TYEE SPIT

Range Front Light
50 02.9N, 125 15.6W, Q Y, 15 ft.,
on 3-pile dolphin, white daymark, red stripe, visible on rangeline only.

Range Rear Light
50.9 meters, 205.7° from front
light, Q Y, 23 ft., on 3-pile dolphin, white daymark, red stripe,
visible on rangeline only.

North Breakwater
50 02.4N, 125 14.6W, Fl G 4s,
17 ft., on 7-pile dolphin.

South Breakwater
50 02.2N, 125 14.5W, Q G, 24 ft.,
tower with black, white, and
green square daymark.

U

Uganda Channel
See Channel Rock.

Ursula Channel
See Tomkinson Point.

Useless Point, Edye Passage
See Edye Passage.

V

VANCOUVER

Approaches

**Point Atkinson (N point of
entrance)**
49 19.8N, 123 15.8W, Fl (2) W 5s,
108 ft., 20 mi., white hexagonal
tower with 6 buttresses,
radiobeacon, diaphone: 3 blasts
every 60s.
Also see Vancouver.

Point Atkinson Radiobeacon
49 19.8N, 123 15.8W, AE (·- ·),
30 mi., 320 kHz, A2A, carrier
signal, calibration service is
available upon request through
Vancouver Radio (VAI), frequency used is 320 kHz, characteristic
signal is T (-).

**Vancouver Approach Lighted
Buoy QA**
49 16.6N, 123 19.2W, Fl Y, yellow,
racon: G (--·).

Spanish Bank and
English Bay

Spanish Bank Anchorage E
49 17.1N, 123 13.1W, Q Y, 21 ft.,
5 mi., cylindrical mast on 4-pile
dolphin, orange daymark, white
stripe, radar reflector.

Spanish Banks No. 1
49 16.7N, 123 15.6W, Fl R 4s,
23 ft., white cylindrical tower, red
band at top, on 9-pile dolphin,
radar reflector.

Spanish Banks No. 2
49 17.4N, 123 14.8W, Fl (2) R 6s,
24 ft., white cylindrical tower, red
band at top, on dolphins, radar
reflector.

Spanish Bank
49 17.3N, 123 13.5W, Fl W 4s,
23 ft., 6 mi., white cylindrical
tower, red band at top, on 9-pile
dolphin, radar reflector.

**English Bay Anchorage East (on
breakwater)**
49 17N, 123 11W, Q Y, 16 ft., 5 mi.,
lantern on railing.

First Narrows

Beacon (N side of Narrows)
49 19N, 123 09W, Fl G 5s, 23 ft.,
10 mi., white cylindrical tower,
green band at top, on 19-pile
dolphin.

**Prospect Point (under bluff at
point)**
49 19N, 123 08W, Iso R 2s, 35 ft.,
6 mi., white square tower, red
band at top, horn: 1 blast every
20s.

Lions Gate Bridge (S)
49 18.9N, 123 08.3W, F W R G,
194 ft., on bridge structure, green
303° to 304°, white 304° to 306°,
red 306° to 307°, white sector
indicates preferred channel.

Lions Gate Bridge (N)
49 19.0N, 123 08.2W, F W R G,
190 ft., on bridge structure, green
303° to 304°, white 304° to 306°,
red 306° to 307°, white sector
indicates preferred channel.

Calamity Point
49 19N, 123 08W, Fl W 4s, 19 ft.,
8 mi., white cylindrical tower,
green band at top, on 16-pile
dolphin, horn: 1 blast every 30s.

Brockton Point (W side of Vancouver Harbor)
49 18N, 123 07W, Q W R, 40 ft., 11 mi., white square tower, red band, marked "Speed Limit 5 KTS. Coal Harbor," red 289° to 313° over Burnaby Shoal, white elsewhere, horn: 3 blasts every 60s.

Burnaby Shoal
49 18N, 123 07W, Q R, 31 ft., 6 mi., white cylindrical tower, red band at top, radar reflector, bell: 2 strokes in quick succession every 5s.

Deadman Island (S of island)
49 17.5N, 123 07.4W, Q R, 17 ft., 4-pile dolphin.

Coal Harbor
49 17.6N, 123 07.5W, Fl R 4s, 22 ft., white cylindrical tower, red band at top, on 9-pile dolphin.

Terminal Dock East
49 18N, 123 03W, Fl R 4s, 11 ft., dolphin.

Second Narrows

Highway Bridge
49 17.7N, 123 01.6W, F W, 148 ft., W side of roadway.

Highway Bridge (lower)
49 18N, 123 01W, F G, 144 ft., marks center of navigation channel, visible from E and W approach.

Highway Bridge (upper)
F Y, 164 ft., marks center of navigation channel from W approach.

Light
49 17.8N, 123 00.5W, Fl W 4s, 22 ft., 5 mi., white cylindrical tower, green band at top, on dolphin, radar reflector.

Light (S edge of band about 1,296 meters E of bridge)
48 17.8N, 123 00.4W, Fl W 4s, 23 ft., white cylindrical tower, green band at top, on dolphin, radar reflector.

Light, East
49 17.9N, 122 59.8W, Fl G 4s, 16 ft., on center of 19-pile dolphin, radar reflector.

Berry Point (N extremity)
49 17.7N, 122 59.2W, Fl R 4s, 15 ft., 10 mi., white cylindrical tower, red band at top.

Indian Arm

Woodlands
49 20.5N, 122 55.2W, Fl G 4s, 16 ft., white cylindrical tower with green band at top, lights continue up Indian Arm.

Twin Islands
49 21.1N, 122 53.4W, Fl R 4s, 30 ft., white cylindrical tower, red band at top.

Croker Island South
49 25.8N, 122 51.8W, Fl (2) W 6s, 20 ft., 5 mi., white cylindrical tower.

Granite Falls
49 26.9N, 122 51.8W, Q R, 22 ft., white cylindrical tower, red band at top.

Port Moody

Gosse Point
49 17.6N, 122 55.5W, Fl R 4s, 28 ft., white cylindrical tower, red band at top.

Best Point
49 22.8N, 122 52.8W, Fl W 4s, 17 ft., white cylindrical tower.

Roche Point (S extremity)
49 18.0N, 122 57.4W, Fl W 4s, 18 ft., white cylindrical tower.

Burns Point (N side of entrance to Port Moody)
49 17.6N, 122 55.1W, Fl W 4s, 19 ft., white cylindrical tower, green band at top.

Carraholly Point
49 17.6N, 122 54.5W, Fl G 4s, 17 ft., white cylindrical tower, green band at top.

Reed Point
49 17.5N, 122 52.4W, Q R, 33 ft., white cylindrical tower, red band at top, on dolphin.

Range Front Light
49 17.6N, 122 51.3W, F Y, 77 ft., white cylindrical mast, triangular white daymark, red stripe.

Range Rear Light
96 meters, 090.5° from front light, F Y, 87 ft., white cylindrical mast, inverted triangular white day mark, red stripe.

False Creek

Directional Light
49 17N, 123 08W, Dir F W R G, 23 ft., white cylindrical mast, red 128° to 131°, white 131° to 132°, green 132° to 135°.

Vancouver Rock Lighted Whistle Buoy E54 (W of rock)
52 21N, 128 30W, Fl R, red buoy, marked E54, radar reflector, whistle.

Vansittart Point (S side of Thurlow Island)
50 22.6N, 125 44.6W, Fl R 4s, 32 ft., white cylindrical tower, red band at top.

Venn Passage (on drying rock)
54 18.7N, 130 23.5W, Q G, 15 ft., white cylindrical tower, green band at top.

Vernaci Island (off W side of island)
49 38.2N, 126 35.5W, Fl (3) W 12s, 26 ft., 5 mi., white cylindrical mast.

Verney Passage
See Mary Point.

Vesuvius Bay (extremity of wharf)
48 53N, 123 34W, nautophone: 2 blasts every 30s.

VICTORIA

Victoria/Sidney Island Radiobeacon
48 37.8N, 123 19.1W, YJ (-·-- ·---), 75 mi., 233 kHz, A2A, aero.

Victoria Harbor Fairway Lighted Whistle Buoy VH
48 22.5N, 123 23.5W, Mo (A) W, red and white stripes, racon: S (···).

Brotchie Ledge Light
48 24.4N, 123 23.2W, F Fl G 10s, 20 ft., white cylindrical tower, green band at top, F G with high-intensity green flash every 10s, horn: 1 blast every 20s, horn points southward, radar reflector.

Ogden Point Breakwater Light
48 24.8N, 123 23.6W, Q R, 40 ft., white square tower, red band acylindrical bottom, horn: 1 blast every 30s, horn points 205°.

Berens Island (SE extremity of island, W side of harbor entrance)
48 25.5N, 123 23.5W, Q G, 20 ft., 6 mi., white cylindrical tower, green band at top, radar reflector.

Shoal Point (W of shoal)
48 25.4N, 123 23.5W, Q R, 19 ft., 6 mi., white cylindrical tower, red band at top, 19-pile dolphin, horn: 1 blast every 12s, horn points 213°.

Pelly Island (S extremity)
48 25.5N, 123 23.0W, Fl G 4s, 21 ft., 6 mi., white cylindrical tower, green band at top, radar reflector.

Laurel Point (NW extremity)
48 25.5N, 123 22.5W, Q R, 21 ft., 6 mi., white cylindrical tower, red band at top, radar reflector.

Tuzo Rock
48 26N, 123 22W, Q G, 21 ft., 6 mi., white cylindrical tower, green band at top, radar reflector.

Victoria Shoal Lighted Buoy U43
48 55.2N, 123 30.9W, Fl G, green.

Virago Point and Rock
See Porlier Pass.

Viscount Island
See Bamber Point.

W

Waddington Channel, Redonda Islands
50 14N, 124 49W, Fl G 4s, 23 ft., white cylindrical tower, green band at top.
Also see Pryce Channel *and* Dean Point.

Wain Rock
48 41.3N, 123 29.3W, Fl G 4s, 23 ft., white cylindrical tower with green band at top.

Walkem Island (on rock)
50 21.5N, 125 31.4W, Fl R 4s, 18 ft., white cylindrical structure, red band at top.

Walker Island
52 06N, 128 07W, Fl W 6s, 26 ft., 5 mi., white cylindrical tower, visible 310.5° to 168.5°.

Walker Rock, Trincomali Channel
48 55.4N, 123 29.6W, Fl (3) W 12s, 23 ft., F W R G (sectors), 22 ft., 6 mi., white cylindrical tower, green from 082° to 088°, white from 088° to 092°, red from 092° to 099°, radar reflector.

Walsh Rock
52 38N, 128 57W, Q W, 23 ft., white cylindrical tower.

Watcher Island (W point)
51 16.3N, 127 43.0W, Fl W 4s, 39 ft., 5 mi., square skeleton tower, visible 357° to 250°

Watson Rock (SW of Gibson Island, NW entrance to Grenville Channel)
53 55.4N, 130 10.3W, Fl W 4s, 13 ft., square skeleton tower.

Wearing Point, Cousins Inlet
52 18.0N, 127 45.6W, Fl W 4s, 20 ft., 5 mi., square skeleton tower.
Also see Cousins Inlet *and* Coolidge Point.

Wedge Island (entrance to Knight Inlet)
50 38N, 126 43W, Q W, 34 ft., white cylindrical tower.

Welby Shoals Lighted Buoy P60
49 59N, 125 09W, Fl R, red buoy marked P60, radar reflector.

Westerly Island
See Crane Islands.

Westerly Jetty Light
49 15.5N, 123 16.7W, Fl (3) W 12s, 26 ft., white circular tower.

Westshore Terminals Jetty (elbow)
49 00.7N, 123 09.8W, Fl Y, private light.

Westshore Terminals Jetty (W head)
49 00.7N, 123 10.0W, Fl Y, private light.

Westview Fishing Harbor (head of S breakwater)
49 50N, 124 32W, Fl R 4s, 15 ft., white cylindrical tower, red band at top, Fl G on N breakwater head.

Westview Fishing Harbor, North Rock (breakwater)
49 50N, 124 32W, Fl W 4s, 25 ft., 5 mi., white cylindrical mast.

Whaletown Bay
50 06.4N, 125 03.4W, Fl G 4s, 19 ft., white cylindrical tower, green band at top.

Wheeler Island (SW corner)
53 33.0N, 130 08.6W, Fl W 4s, 29 ft., square skeleton tower.

Whiffin Spit Light (E end of spit, Sooke Inlet)
48 21.5N, 123 42.6W, Q W, 21 ft., 6 mi., white cylindrical tower with green band at top, horn: 1 blast every 30s, operated only on request to Vancouver Coast Guard Radio.
Also see Sooke Harbor.

White Islets
49 25.1N, 123 42.6W, Fl W 4s, 35 ft., white cylindrical tower, radar reflector.

White Point
52 04.5N, 127 57.9W, Fl R 6s, 29 ft., skeleton tower, red and white daymark.

White Rock Breakwater
49 01.0N, 122 48.4W, Fl W 4s, 15 ft., 4-pile dolphin.

Whiterock Island, Hoskyn Inlet
50 14.6N, 125 06.6W, Q W, 18 ft., white cylindrical tower.

Whitesand Island
54 30.8N, 130 44.8W, Fl W 4s, 22 ft., white skeleton tower.

Whittlestone Point
48 48.7N, 125 10.8W, Dir F W R G, 44 ft., 13 mi., white cylindrical tower, red 064.5° to 068.5°, white 068.5° to 076.5°, green 076.5° to 080.5°, white sector indicates preferred channel.

Wiah Point (end of reef NE of point)
54 07N, 132 18W, Fl W 6s, 30 ft., 5 mi., square skeleton tower.

Wilbraham (Gowlland) Point (SW end of Grant Island)
49 30.7N, 123 58.1W, Fl R 4s, 35 ft., white cylindrical tower, red band at top, radar reflector.

Wilf Rock
49 08.2N, 125 58.5W, Fl W 4s, 40 ft., 6 mi., white cylindrical tower, maintained from April 15 to Sept. 15.

Wilfred Point
50 07.8N, 125 21.5W, Q G, 22 ft., white cylindrical tower, green band at top.

William Head Light
48 20.6N, 123 31.6W, Fl (2) G, 0.5s fl. 1.0s ec., 0.5s fl. 4.0s ec., 36 ft., white tower, green band at top, whistle: 1 blast every 30s.

William Island
See Pender Harbor.

Wizard Islet
48 51.5N, 125 09.5W, Fl (2) W 6s, 16 ft., white cylindrical mast.

Woodlands
49 20.5N, 122 55.2W, Fl G 4s, 16 ft., white cylindrical tower with green band at top, lights continue up Indian Arm.
Also see Vancouver.

Work Island (W end)
53 10.7N, 128 41.5W, Fl W 6s, 18 ft., 5 mi., square skeleton tower.

Y

Yellow Bluff, Cormorant Island
50 35.2N, 126 57.1W, Fl W R 4s, 28 ft., 6 mi., white cylindrical tower, red band at top, red 289° to 302°, white 302° to 289°.

York Point (S extremity of peninsula)
53 05.5N, 129 10.4W, Q W, 34 ft., square skeleton tower.

Z

ZEBALLOS INLET

South
49 54N, 126 48W, Fl G 4s, 25 ft., white cylindrical tower, green band at top, visible 171° to 024°.

North Side
49 58N, 126 51W, Q R, 22 ft., white cylindrical tower, red band at top.

West (on islet)
49 57N, 126 49W, Q W, 52 ft., white cylindrical tower, green band at top.

Zero Rock Light
48 31.4N, 123 17.4W, Fl W 4s, 28 ft., white cylindrical tower, green band on top, radar reflector.
Also see Haro Strait.

Zuciarte Channel (E side of Bligh Island)
49 39N, 126 29W, Fl (3) W 12s, 22 ft., white cylindrical tower, green band at top.

Zuciarte Channel South
49 36N, 126 31W, Fl R 4s, 31 ft., white cylindrical tower, red band at top.

Washington

Aids to navigation for the Columbia River are listed in a separate chapter.

A

Aberdeen
See Grays Harbor.

ADMIRALTY INLET

Also see Puget Sound Traffic Lane.

Point Wilson Light
48 08.6N, 122 45.3W, Oc W & Fl R 20s, 51 ft., white 16 mi., red 15 mi., white octagonal tower on fog signal building, horn: 1 blast every 30s.

Keystone Harbor Entrance Light 1
48 09.4N, 122 40.3W, Q G, 12 ft., on piling, private aid.

Keystone Harbor Entrance Light 2
48 09.4N, 122 40.3W, Fl R 4s, 13 ft., 5 mi., TR on platform.

Point Hudson Light
48 07.0N, 122 45.0W, Iso R 6s, 25 ft., 7 mi., NB on skeleton tower, horn: 2 blasts every 20s.

Point Hudson Spit Lighted Bell Buoy 2
48 07.3N, 122 44.7W, Fl R 4s, 4 mi., red.

Marrowstone Point Light
48 06.1N, 122 41.3W, Oc W 4s, 28 ft., 9 mi., white square structure, light obscured from 040° to 090°, lighted throughout 24 hours, horn: 2 blasts every 30s.

Bush Point Light
48 01.8N, 122 36.4W, Fl W 2.5s, 25 ft., 11 mi., white pyramidal building.

Puget Sound Traffic Lane Separation Lighted Buoy SC
48 01.9N, 122 38.2W, Fl Y 4s, 4 mi., yellow.

Colvos Rocks Light
47 57.1N, 122 40.3W, Fl W 4s, 34 ft., 5 mi., NB on skeleton tower.

Double Bluff Light
47 58.1N, 122 32.8W, Oc G 4s, 60 ft., 8 mi., NG on skeleton tower.

Double Bluff Lighted Buoy 1
Fl G 4s, 4 mi., green.

Puget Sound Traffic Lane Separation Lighted Buoy SD
47 57.9N, 122 34.8W, Fl Y 4s, 6 mi., yellow.

Foulweather Bluff Lighted Bell Buoy 2
Fl R 4s, 4 mi., red.

Puget Sound Traffic Lane Separation Lighted Buoy SE
47 55.4N, 122 29.6W, Fl Y 4s, 6 mi., yellow, racon: T (-).

Skunk Bay Light
47 55.2N, 122 34.1W, F R, 210 ft., white octagonal tower, private aid.

AGATE PASSAGE

Agate Passage Light 2
47 43.4N, 122 33.4W, Fl R 4s, 20 ft., 5 mi., TR on dolphin.

Agate Point Buoy 2A
Red nun.

Lighted Buoy 4
47 42.5N, 122 34.2W, Fl R 4s, 4 mi., red.

Agate Pass Salmon Pen Light (marks floating salmon pen)
47 42.3N, 122 34.6W, Fl Y 6s, private aid.

Point Bolin Reef Light 6
47 41.8N, 122 34.6W, Fl R 2.5s, 15 ft., 4 mi., TR on dolphin, radar reflector.

Alaska Hydro-Train Lights
See Elliott Bay.

Albert Head Light (Canada)
48 23.2N, 123 28.6W, Fl W 5s, 90 ft., 19 mi., white circular tower.

ALDEN BANK

Lighted Gong Buoy A
Fl (2+1) R 6s, 5 mi., red and green bands.

Buoy 5
48 48.9N, 122 48.9W, green can.

Lighted Bell Buoy B
48 47.1N, 122 48.9W, Fl (2+1) R 6s, 5 mi., red and green bands.

Alki Point Light
47 34.6N, 122 25.2W, Fl W 5s, 39 ft., 15 mi., white octagonal tower attached to building, horn: 2 blasts every 30s, lighted throughout 24 hours.
Also see East Passage.

Allyn Dock Light
47 23.0N, 122 49.5W, F W, 14 ft., on float at end of dock, private aid.

ANACORTES HARBOR

Also see Guemes Channel

Cap Sante Waterway

Junction Lighted Buoy A
48 30.7N, 122 35.6W, Fl (2+1) R 6s, 4 mi., red and green bands.

Daybeacon 1 (15 ft. outside channel limit)
48 30.7N, 122 35.8W, SG on pile, radar reflector.

Light 2 (15 ft. outside channel limit)
Fl R 2.5s, 15 ft., 3 mi., TR on dolphin.

Daybeacon 3 (15 ft. outside channel limit)
SG on pile.

Daybeacon 4
TR on dolphin.

Light 5
48 30.7N, 122 36.3W, Fl G 4s, 14 ft., 5 mi., SG on dolphin.

Light 6
Fl R 4s, 14 ft., 5 mi., TR on dolphin.

Anacortes Channel and Fidalgo Bay

Fidalgo Bay Shoal Buoy 2
48 30.6N, 122 35.1W, red nun.

Junction Lighted Buoy A
48 30.7N, 122 35.6W, Fl (2+1) R 6s, 4 mi., red and green bands.

Anacortes Channel Buoy 3
Green can.

Anacortes Channel Light 4
48 30.5N, 122 36.0W, Fl R 4s, 13 ft., 4 mi., TR on pile structure.

Anacortes Marina Entrance Light
48 30.1N, 122 36.0W, Fl W 10s, 11 ft., on pile, private aid.

Fidalgo Marina Light 1
48 29.9N, 122 36.0W, F G, 6 ft., on breakwater, private aid.

Fidalgo Marina Light 2
48 29.9N, 122 36.0W, F R, 6 ft., on breakwater, private aid.

Fidalgo Marina Lights (2)
48 29.8N, 122 36.0W, F Y, 6 ft., on breakwater, private aids.

Texaco Oil Company Wharf Lights (2)
48 30.6N, 122 34.6W, F R, 25 ft., mooring platform, private aids.

Shell Oil Company Wharf Lights (2)
48 30.5N, 122 34.1W, F R, 18 ft., 16 ft., horn: 1 blast every 30s, private aids.

Anthonys Lighthouse
47 59.7N, 122 13.4W, Fl W 2.5s, 60 ft., 10 mi., red and white wooden building, private aid.
Also see Port Gardner and Snohomish River.

Apple Cove Point Light
47 48.9N, 122 28.9W, Fl W 4s, 18 ft., 5 mi., NB on pile structure.

Arachne Reef Light (Canada)
48 41.1N, 123 17.6W, Fl (2+1) G 6s, 22 ft., white circular tower with green band at top.
Also see Haro Strait.

Atlantic Richfield Light A
F R, 28 ft., on mooring dolphin, private aid.

Also see Intalco Lights, Tosco Northwest Lights, *and* Sandy Point Lights.

Atlantic Richfield Light B
F R, 28 ft., on mooring dolphin, private aid.

B

Bainbridge Reef Lighted Bell Buoy 4
47 34.1N, 122 31.1W, Fl R 4s, 4 mi., red.
Also see Rich Passage.

Baker Bay
See Columbia River chapter.

Balch Passage
See Eagle Island.

Bass Point Light
47 35.7N, 122 39.6W, F Y, 5 ft., on pile structure, private aid.

Battle Point Light
Fl W 4s, 17 ft., 5 mi., NB on pile structure.

Bay Center Channel
See Willapa Bay.

Beans Point Fish Pen Lights (2)
Fl Y 6s, 4 ft., on pedestal, private aids.
Also see Rich Passage.

Becks Pier Light
47 36.6N, 122 12.6W, F R, 6 ft., on dolphin, private aid.
Also see Lake Washington.

Belle Rock Sector Light
Fl W 2.5s (R sector), 22 ft. white 5 mi., 20 ft., red 9 mi., NB on black cylindrical base, red from 173° to 177°, covers 42-foot shoal, higher intensity white beam up and down channel, aid displays 2 separate lights, white over red.
Also see Rosario Strait.

Bellevue Marina Dock Lights (2)
47 36.6N, 122 12.5W, F R, 4 ft., private aids.

BELLINGHAM BAY

Also see Bellingham Channel

Post Point Lighted Bell Buoy 2
48 42.8N, 122 31.8W, Fl R 4s, 5 mi., red.

Ferry Pier Light
48 43.4N, 122 30.7W, F R, 12 ft., on dolphin, private aid.

Starr Rock Buoy 4 (35 yards W of rock)
Red nun.

Georgia Pacific Outfall Lighted Buoy
48 44.0N, 122 30.9W, Fl Y 10s, orange and white bands, private aid.

Whatcom Waterway Sector Light
48 44.6N, 122 29.8W, Fl W 6s (R sector), 16 ft., white 9 mi., red 7 mi., red from 306° to 035°, westerly edge covers Post Point Lighted Bell Buoy 2.

Whatcom Waterway Range Front Light
48 45.1N, 122 29.1W, Q G, 41 ft., KRB on platform on building, visible 1.25° each side of range-line.

Whatcom Waterway Range Rear Light
393 yards, 045.2° from front light, Iso G 6s, 70 ft., KRB on skeleton tower, visible 1.25° each side of rangeline.

I and J Waterway Light 1
48 44.9N, 122 30.2W, Fl G 2.5s, 15 ft., 5 mi., SG on pile.

I and J Waterway Buoy 2
48 45.0N, 122 30.0W, red nun.

I and J Waterway Light 3
Fl G 4s, 16 ft., 3 mi., SG on riprap.

Bellingham Breakwater Entrance Light 2
48 45.2N, 122 30.4W, Oc R 4s, 24 ft., 7 mi., TR on steel tower, horn: 1 blast every 15s.

Bellingham Breakwater Entrance Light 1
Fl G 4s, 17 ft., 6 mi., SG on pile.

Squalicum Creek Entrance Lighted Buoy 1
48 45.3N, 122 31.0W, Fl G 4s, green.

Squalicum Creek Entrance Light 2
48 45.4N, 122 30.9W, Fl R 4s, 16 ft., 5 mi., TR on post.

Bellingham Breakwater North Entrance Light 4
48 45.5N, 122 30.7W, Fl R 6s, 17 ft., 5 mi., TR on pile.

Squalicum Creek Waterway Range Front Light
48 45.6N, 122 30.6W, Q G, 28 ft., KRB on skeleton tower, private aid.

Squalicum Creek Waterway Range Rear Light
170 yards, 037° from front light, Iso G 6s, 37 ft., KRB on skeleton tower, private aid.

Rocks Junction Lighted Buoy (marks S edge of rocks)
48 40.4N, 122 35.5W, Fl (2+1) R 6s, 5 mi., red and green bands.
Also see Hale Passage.

BELLINGHAM CHANNEL

Also see Rosario Strait *and* Bellingham Bay.

Yellow Bluff Reef Obstruction Daybeacon
48 31.9N, 122 39.4W, NW on dolphin worded DANGER REEF, radar reflector.

Lighted Bell Buoy 4
48 32.2N, 122 40.2W, Fl R 4s, 5 mi., red.

Deepwater Bay South Fish Pen Lights (2)
48 33.2N, 122 41.0W, Fl Y 6s, on steel salmon pen, private aids.

Secret Harbor Fish Pen Lights (2)
48 33.5N, 122 41.0W, Fl Y 6s, on steel salmon pen, private aids.

Deepwater Bay North Fish Pen Lights (2)
48 33.7N, 122 40.7W, Fl Y 6s, on steel salmon pen, private aids.

Light 5
48 34.0N, 122 40.1W, Fl G 4s, 16 ft., 5 mi., SG, higher intensity beam up and down channel.

Lighted Buoy 6
48 35.5N, 122 39.1W, Fl R 4s, 3 mi., red.

Light 7
Fl G 4s, 32 ft., 5 mi., SG.

Buoy 8
48 36.3N, 122 37.8W, red nun.

Vendovi Cove Light
48 36.9N, 122 36.7W, Fl Y 4s, 15 ft., steel tower, private aid.

Viti Rocks Light
48 38.0N, 122 37.4W, Fl W 2.5s, 45 ft., 5 mi., NB on steel tower.

Viti Rocks Lighted Bell Buoy 9
48 37.8N, 122 37.1W, Q G, 3 mi., green.

Eliza Rock Junction Light
Fl (2+1) G 6s, 21 ft., 5 mi., JG on house.

Ben Ure Island Light 2
48 24.2N, 122 37.7W, Fl R 4s, 25 ft., 4 mi., TR on tower.
Also see Deception Pass.

Bird Rocks Light
48 35.9N, 123 00.9W, Fl W 4s, 15 ft., 5 mi., NB on white platform on pile structure.
Also see San Juan Channel.

Black Rock Light 9
48 32.8N, 122 45.9W, Fl G 4s, 10 ft., 4 mi., SG on skeleton tower.
Also see Rosario Strait.

Blaine
See Semiahmoo Bay.

Blair Waterway
See Tacoma Harbor.

BLAKE ISLAND

Also see East Passage *and* Colvos Passage.

Blakely Harbor Aquaculture Pen Light A
47 35.7N, 122 30.6W, Fl W 4s, private aid.

Light 1
Fl G 4s, 11 ft., SG on pile structure, private aid.

Daybeacon 30
TR on pile, private aid.

Daybeacons 2–6
TRs and SGs on piles, private aids.

East Light
47 32.5N, 122 28.8W, Fl W 4s, 18 ft., 5 mi., NB on skeleton tower.

Reef Buoy A
47 31.8N, 122 29.4W, white and orange bands, spherical buoy, private aid.

Blakely Island Light
48 31.9N, 122 48.5W, Fl R 6s, 12 ft., 5 mi., TR on pile.
Also see Rosario Strait.

Blakely Island Shoal Lighted Buoy DS
48 34.1N, 122 50.7W, Fl (2) W, 5 mi., black and red horizontal stripes.

Blakely Rock Light
47 35.7N, 122 28.8W, Fl W 4s, 16 ft., 5 mi., NB on skeleton tower.

Blind Bay Rock Daybeacon
48 35.0N, 122 55.9W, NW worded DANGER ROCK, private aid.

Boeing Creek Reef Buoy A
47 45.1N, 122 23.1W, white and orange bands, spherical buoy, private aid.

Boulder Reef Lighted Bell Buoy 2
Fl R 4s, 4 mi., red.
Also see Sinclair Island Lighted Bell Buoy 4 *and* Rosario Strait.

BOUNDARY PASS

Also see British Columbia chapter.

Gowlland Point Light (Canada)
48 44.1N, 123 11.0W, Fl W 4s, 35 ft., white circular tower, green band at top.

Skipjack Island Light
48 44.0N, 123 02.4W, Fl W 4s, 55 ft., 5 mi., NB on steel tower, obscured from 261° to 347°.

Saturna Island Light (Canada)
48 47.0N, 123 02.7W, Fl W 15s, 121 ft., white, 17 mi., F R, 102 ft., red, 16 mi., on red skeleton tower, white light visible from 149° to 060°, red light visible from 156° to 211.5°.

Shoal Isolated Danger Lighted Bell Buoy DB
48 45.9N, 123 00.9W, Fl (2) W 5s, 6 mi., black with red horizontal stripes.

Rosenfeld Rock Lighted Buoy U59 (Canada)
48 48.2N, 123 01.6W, Fl G, green, racon: U (··-).

Patos Island Light
48 47.3N, 122 58.3W, Fl W 6s (2 R sectors), 52 ft., white 9 mi., red 6 mi., white square tower on fog signal house, red from 011.5° to 059.5°, covers six-fathom shoal, red from 097° to 114°, covers Rosenfeld Rock, horn: 1 blast every 30s, operates continuously.

Brisco Point Light 8
Fl R 4s, 40 ft., 4 mi., TR on white house, light obscured from 105° to 242°.
Also see Dana Passage.

Brotchie Ledge Light (Canada)
48 24.4N, 123 23.2W, F Fl G 10s, 20 ft., white circular tower, green band at top, F G with high-intensity green flash every 10s, horn: 1 blast every 20s, horn points southward, radar reflector.

Browns Point Light
47 18.4N, 122 26.7W, Fl W 5s, 38 ft., 12 mi., white tower, horn: 2 blasts every 30s, light obscured from 217° to 002°.
Also see East Passage.

Buckeye Shoal Lighted Bell Buoy 14 (marks shoal W of Sinclair Island)
Fl R 6s, 5 mi., red.
Also see Rosario Strait.

Budd Inlet
See Olympia Harbor.

Burrows Bay Junction Buoy (marks submerged rock)
Red and green bands, nun.

Burrows Island Light
48 28.7N, 122 42.8W, Fl W 6s (R sector), 57 ft., white 10 mi., red 8 mi., white square tower on building, red from 311° to 009°, covers Allan Island and Dennis Shoal, horn: 2 blasts every 30s.
Also see Rosario Strait.

Bush Point Light
48 01.8N, 122 36.4W, Fl W 2.5s, 25 ft., 11 mi., white pyramidal building.
Also see Admiralty Inlet.

C

Camano Head Buoy 1 (marks submerged rocks)
48 03.0N, 122 21.3W, green can.
Also see Saratoga Passage.

Cap Sante Waterway
See Anacortes Harbor.

Cape Disappointment Light
46 16.5N, 124 03.1W, Al W R 30s, 220 ft., white 22 mi., red 18 mi., white conical tower with white band at top and bottom, black band in middle, light obscured northward of 137.5°.
Also see Columbia River chapter.

Cape Flattery Light
48 23.5N, 124 44.2W, Fl W 15s (R sector), 165 ft., white 18 mi., red 14 mi., white conical tower on white sandstone dwelling, red from 160° to 170°, covers Duncan and Duntze Rocks, light is obscured from 271° to 007.5°, horn: 2 blasts every 60s, operates continuously.
Also see Duntze Rock Lighted Whistle Buoy 2D.

Carlyon Beach Light
47 10.9N, 122 56.2W, Q W, 15 ft., private aid.
Also see Squaxin Passage.

Carmanah Light (Canada)
48 36.7N, 124 45.0W, Fl W 5s, 175 ft., 19 mi., white octagonal concrete tower, diaphone: 3 blasts every 60s.

CARR INLET

Wyckoff Shoal Buoy 1
47 14.5N, 122 42.9W, green can.

Wyckoff Shoal Buoy 3
47 14.4N, 122 43.0W, green can.
Also see Pitt Passage.

Kopachuck State Park Buoy (marks fish haven)
47 18.6N, 122 41.4W, orange and white bands, private aid.

Lighted Buoy B
F W, orange and white bands, shows quick blue light during test operations, U.S. Navy maintained.

Test Buoy G
47 14.8N, 122 39.0W, white can, maintained by U.S. Navy.

Test Buoy H
47 14.9N, 122 39.1W, white can, maintained by U.S. Navy.

Von Geldern Cove Light
47 16.3N, 122 45.4W, Fl Y 8s, 22 ft., on steel pile, private aid.

Case Shoal Daybeacon
47 51.6N, 122 40.5W, NW on pile worded DANGER SHOAL.
Also see Hood Canal.

Case Shoal Light 6
47 50.6N, 122 40.5W, Fl R 2.5s, 15 ft., 5 mi., TR on pile, radar reflector.

Cathlamet Channel
See Columbia River chapter.

Cattle Point Light
48 27.0N, 122 57.8W, Fl W 4s, 94 ft., 5 mi., white octagonal tower, horn: 1 blast every 15s, operates continuously from June 1 to Nov. 15.
Also see San Juan Channel.

Cedar River Flats Daybeacon 2
46 42.1N, 123 57.7W, 20 ft., TR on pile structure.
Also see Willapa Bay.

Center Island
See Lopez Sound.

Charley Creek Dike Daybeacon 2
46 57.4N, 123 50.7W, TR on dolphin.
Also see Grays Harbor.

Chehalis River
See Grays Harbor.

Church Point Light 6
Fl R 6s, 20 ft., 4 mi., TR on skeleton tower.
Also see Hammersley Inlet.

Clallam Reef Bell Buoy 1
48 16.1N, 124 15.5W, green can.

Clam Bay Fish Pen Lights (2)
Fl Y 6s, 8 ft., on pile, private aids.
Also see Rich Passage.

Clements Reef Buoy
48 45.8N, 122 52.1W, white with orange bands, can, orange diamond worded DANGER REEF.

Clements Reef Buoy 2
48 46.6N, 122 53.5W, red nun, marks reef.

Cliff Island Light 3
Fl G 6s, 15 ft., 5 mi., SG on square house.
Also see San Juan Channel.

Columbia River
See Columbia River chapter.

COLVOS PASSAGE

Also see Blake Island.

Point Vashon Light
47 30.8N, 122 28.3W, Fl W 4s, 17 ft., 7 mi., NB on pile structure.

Light 3
Fl G 6s, 15 ft., 4 mi., SG on pile.

Light 4
Fl R 6s, 15 ft., 5 mi., TR on tower.

Light 5
Fl G 4s, 17 ft., 5 mi., SG on house.

Light 6
47 22.6N, 122 32.9W, Fl R 4s, 15 ft., 4 mi., TR on pile structure, light obscured from 022° to 153°.

Colvos Rocks Light
47 57.1N, 122 40.3W, Fl W 4s, 34 ft., 5 mi., NB on skeleton tower.
Also see Admiralty Inlet *and* Hood Canal.

Commencement Bay
See Tacoma Harbor.

Cornet Bay
See Deception Pass.

Crescent Bay Bell Buoy 2
48 10.3N, 123 43.5W, red.

CULTUS BAY

Entrance Buoy 1
47 54.5N, 122 24.0W, green can, private aid.

Entrance Buoy 2
Red nun, private aid.

Daybeacons 3–24
Numbered piles, private aids.

Cypress Reef Daybeacon C
48 36.8N, 122 43.3W, JR on pile.
Also see Rosario Strait.

D

DABOB BAY

Tskutsko Point Light
47 41.6N, 122 50.0W, Fl W 4s, 15 ft., 5 mi., NB on pile, radar reflector.
Also see Hood Canal.

Dosewallips Flats Light 15
47 41.6N, 122 52.7W, Fl G 4s, 15 ft., 5 mi., SG on pile, radar reflector.

Seal Rock Daybeacon
47 42.9N, 122 53.1W, NW on pipe worded DANGER ROCKS.

Pulali Point Light
47 44.3N, 122 51.2W, Fl W 4s, 30 ft., 5 mi., NG on white house, radar reflector.

Navy Warning Lights (5)
Fl R 5s, Fl Y 5s; Fl R 5s lights will be displayed when the area is closed to navigation during naval operations; Fl Y 5s lights will be displayed when the area requires caution; when lights are not operational area is clear to transit; U.S. Navy maintained.

Quilcene Bay Light 2
47 46.7N, 122 51.2W, Fl R 4s, 26 ft., 5 mi., TR on pile, obscured from 170° to 260°, radar reflector.

Quilcene Bay Fish Pen Light A
47 47.3N, 122 51.0W, Fl Y 6s, 6 mi., on wooden fish pen, private aid.

Quilcene Bay Fish Pen Light B
47 47.3N, 122 51.0W, Fl Y 6s, 6 mi., on wooden fish pen, private aid.

Tabook Point Light 18
47 44.7N, 122 48.6W, Fl R 6s, 15 ft., 5 mi., TR on pile, radar reflector.

Damon Point Light
46 57.0N, 124 06.4W, Fl Y 4s, 20 ft., 5 mi., NB on pile structure, radar reflector.
Also see Grays Harbor.

DANA PASSAGE

Itsami Ledge Light 7
47 10.6N, 122 50.2W, Fl G 4s, 20 ft., 5 mi., SG on dolphin.

Hartsene Island Fish Pen Lights (6)
47 10.7N, 122 51.0W, Fl Y 6s, on aquaculture facility, private aid.

Brisco Point Light 8
Fl R 4s, 40 ft., 4 mi., TR on white house, light obscured from 105° to 242°.

Dofflemyer Point Light
47 08.5N, 122 54.5W, Iso W 6s, 30 ft., 9 mi., white pyramidal tower, horn: 1 blast every 15s.

Danger Shoal Lighted Horn Buoy (SW of shoal)
Fl (2+1) G 6s, 6 mi., green and red bands, horn: 1 blast every 30s.
Also see Haro Strait.

D'Arcy Island Light (Canada)
48 34.0N, 123 17.0W, Fl R 4s, 23 ft., white circular tower with red band at top.
Also see Haro Strait.

Davidson Rock Light 1
Fl G 4s, 15 ft., 6 mi., SG on platform, higher intensity beam toward Burrows Island Light.
Also see Rosario Strait.

Decatur Reef Lighted Buoy 2
47 34.9N, 122 28.6W, Fl R 6s, 4 mi., red, radar reflector.

DECEPTION PASS

Light 1
Fl G 4s, 60 ft., 6 mi., SG on white cylindrical house on skeleton tower.

Ben Ure Island Light 2
48 24.2N, 122 37.7W, Fl R 4s, 25 ft., 4 mi., TR on tower.

Cornet Bay Daybeacons 1–8
SWs with black or red numbers on piles, private aids.

Deepwater Bay

Also see Bellingham Channel.

Deepwater Bay South Fish Pen Lights (2)
48 33.2N, 122 41.0W, Fl Y 6s, on steel salmon pen, private aids.

Secret Harbor Fish Pen Lights (2)
48 33.5N, 122 41.0W, Fl Y 6s, on steel salmon pen, private aids.

Deepwater Bay North Fish Pen Lights (2)
48 33.7N, 122 40.7W, Fl Y 6s, on steel salmon pen, private aids.

Deer Harbor Pier Light
F R, 15 ft., on pile, private aid.
Also see San Juan Channel.

Dennis Shoal Buoy 6
48 27.5N, 122 43.0W, red nun.
Also see Rosario Strait.

Des Moines Marina

Also see East Passage.

Light 1A
47 24.1N, 122 19.9W, F G, 35 ft., on pier, private aid.

Light B
47 24.1N, 122 19.8W, F Y, 35 ft., on pier, private aid.

Light 4
47 24.1N, 122 19.9W, Q R, 13 ft., 4 mi., TR on breakwater, private aid.

Light C
47 24.1N, 122 19.8W, F Y, 35 ft., on pier, private aid.

Breakwater Obstruction Light
47 23.8N, 122 19.9W, Fl Y 6s, 13 ft., 5 mi., NY on breakwater, private aid.

Destruction Island Light
47 40.5N, 124 29.2W, Fl W 10s, 147 ft., 18 mi., white conical tower with black gallery, horn: 1 blast every 30s, operates continuously.

Devils Head Light 4
47 10.0N, 122 45.9W, Fl R 6s, 16 ft., 4 mi., TR on dolphin.
Also see Nisqually Reach.

Discovery Island Light (Canada)
48 25.5N, 123 13.5W, Fl W 5s, 93 ft., white circular tower, light obscured from 050.5° to 146°, horn: 1 blast every 60s.
Also see Haro Strait.

Dofflemyer Point Light
47 08.5N, 122 54.5W, Iso W 6s, 30 ft., 9 mi., white pyramidal tower, horn: 1 blast every 15s.
Also see Dana Passage.

Dosewallips Flats Light 15
47 41.6N, 122 52.7W, Fl G 4s, 15 ft., 5 mi., SG on pile, radar reflector.
Also see Hood Canal *and* Dabob Bay.

Double Bluff Light
47 58.1N, 122 32.8W, Oc G 4s, 60 ft., 8 mi., NG on skeleton tower.
Also see Admiralty Inlet.

Double Bluff Lighted Buoy 1
Fl G 4s, 4 mi., green.

Drayton Passage Light 2
47 10.7N, 122 44.6W, Fl R 4s, 20 ft., 4 mi., TR on dolphin.

Dtokoah Point Lighted Bell Buoy 1
48 22.6N, 124 35.3W, Fl G 4s, 4 mi., green.

Duntze Rock Lighted Whistle Buoy 2D
48 25.0N, 124 45.0W, Fl R 4s, 4 mi., red.
Also see Cape Flattery Light.

Duwamish Head Light
47 35.9N, 122 23.3W, Fl W 2.5s, 15 ft., 18 mi., NB on pile structure, obscured from 324° to 045°, horn: 2 blasts every 20s.
Also see Elliott Bay.

Duwamish Waterway
See Georgetown Reach Range.

Eagle Harbor

Creosote Light 1
Fl G 6s, 30 ft., 7 mi., SG on dolphin.

Light 3
Fl G 2.5s, 15 ft., 5 mi., SG on dolphin, bell: 1 stroke every 10s.

Light 4
47 37.3N, 122 29.8W, Fl R 4s, 15 ft., 4 mi., TR on dolphin, higher intensity beam down channel.

Sand Spit Lighted Buoy 5
47 37.2N, 122 30.2W, Fl G 4s, 4 mi., green.

Bainbridge Island Boat Yard East Light
47 37.0N, 122 30.5W, Fl Y 4s, 15 ft., on pile, private aid.

Bainbridge Island Boat Yard West Light
47 37.0N, 122 30.6W, Fl Y 4s, 15 ft., on pile, private aid.

Marina Lights (2)
F R, 4 mi., private aids.

Line Mooring System Lighted Buoys (5)
47 37.2N, 122 31.1W, Fl Y 2.5s, mooring cable 200 feet in length, five lighted yellow spar buoys connected with cable 2 feet above water's surface.

Eagle Island Reef Lighted Buoy 9
47 11.4N, 122 42.0W, Fl G 2.5s, 3 mi., green.

Eagle Island Sector Light
47 11.3N, 122 41.7W, Fl W 4s (R sector), 18 ft., 5 mi., NB on skeleton tower, red sector from 081° to 121°.

East Passage

Alki Point Light
47 34.6N, 122 25.2W, Fl W 5s, 39 ft., 15 mi., white octagonal tower attached to building, horn: 2 blasts every 30s, lighted throughout 24 hours.

Puget Sound Traffic Separation Lighted Buoy T
47 34.6N, 122 27.0W, Fl Y 4s, Fl Y 2.5s, 6 mi., yellow, Fl Y 2.5s high-intensity flash tube.

West Seattle Reef Buoy
47 33.4N, 122 24.4W, white with orange bands, spar, private aid.

Blake Island East Light
47 32.5N, 122 28.8W, Fl W 4s, 18 ft.,
5 mi., NB on skeleton tower.
Also see Blake Island.

Fauntleroy Cove Fog Signal
47 31.4N, 122 23.7W, siren: 1 blast
every 24s, private aid.

**Puget Sound Traffic Lane
Separation Lighted Buoy TA**
47 26.9N, 122 24.3W, Fl Y 4s,
6 mi., yellow.

Three Tree Point Light
47 27.0N, 122 23.0W, Fl W 2s,
25 ft., 11 mi., white skeleton
tower, horn: 1 blast every 15s.

Point Heyer Reef Buoy A
47 25.1N, 122 25.6W, white and
orange bands, spherical buoy,
private aid.

Des Moines Marina

Light 1A
47 24.1N, 122 19.9W, F G, 35 ft.,
on pier, private aid.

Light B
47 24.1N, 122 19.8W, F Y, 35 ft.,
on pier, private aid.

Light 4
47 24.1N, 122 19.9W, Q R, 13 ft.,
4 mi., TR on breakwater, private
aid.

Light C
47 24.1N, 122 19.8W, F Y, 35 ft.,
on pier, private aid.

Breakwater Obstruction Light
47 23.8N, 122 19.9W, Fl Y 6s,
13 ft., 5 mi., NY on breakwater,
private aid.

Robinson Point Light
47 23.3N, 122 22.5W, Fl (2) W 12s,
40 ft., 14 mi., white octagonal
tower, horn: 1 blast every 30s.

**Puget Sound Traffic Lane
Separation Lighted Buoy TB**
47 23.1N, 122 21.2W, Fl Y 4s, Fl Y
2.5s, 6 mi., yellow, Fl Y 2.5s high-
intensity flash tube.

**Three Tree Point Yacht Club
Racing Buoy J (buoys A, I, and L
in vicinity)**
47 22.9N, 122 22.8W, white spar
buoy, private aid.

**Saltwater State Park Buoy (marks
fish haven)**
47 22.4N, 122 19.6W, white with
orange bands, private aid.

**Puget Sound Traffic Lane
Separation Lighted Buoy TC**
47 19.5N, 122 27.4W, Fl Y 4s,
Fl Y 2.5s, 6 mi., yellow, Fl Y 2.5s
high-intensity flash tube.

Browns Point Light
47 18.4N, 122 26.7W, Fl W 5s,
38 ft., 12 mi., white tower, horn:
2 blasts every 30s, light obscured
from 217° to 002°.

East Point Light 3
Fl G 6s, 21 ft., 6 mi., SG on steel
tower.
Also see Saratoga Passage.

East Waterway
See Elliott Bay.

EDIZ HOOK

Also see Port Angeles.

Light
48 08.4N, 123 24.1W, Fl G (2) W 10s,
60 ft., white 17 mi., green 14 mi.,
on corner of white square building, horn: 1 blast every 30s.

Radiobeacon
48 08.4N, 123 24.1W, K (-·-),
317 kHz, antenna 600 yards,
094° from Ediz Hook Light.

Port Angeles Harbor Buoy 1
Green can.

Lighted Buoy 2
48 08.3N, 123 24.0W, Fl R 2.5s,
5 mi., red.

Coast Guard Mooring

Breakwater Obstruction Light
48 08.4N, 123 24.7W, Fl Y 4s,
12 ft., 4 mi., NY on concrete wall.

Basin Light 1
48 08.4N, 123 24.8W, Fl G 4s,
14 ft., 4 mi., SG on pier.

Basin Light 2
48 08.4N, 123 24.8W, Fl R 4s,
12 ft., 4 mi., TR on concrete wall.

Basin Light 3
48 08.4N, 123 24.9W, Fl G 2.5s,
14 ft., 3 mi., SG on multi-pile.

Basin Light 4
48 08.4N, 123 24.9W, Fl R 2.5s,
17 ft., 3 mi., TR on pier.

Salmon Pen Light A
48 08.3N, 123 25.1W, Fl Y 6s,
on aquaculture facility, private
aid.

Salmon Pen Light B
48 08.3N, 123 25.3W, Fl Y 6s, on
aquaculture facility, private aid.

EDMONDS

**Underwater Park Buoys (2)
(marks seaward corner of
Edmonds Underwater Park)**
47 48.9N, 122 23.1W, white with
orange bands near top and at
waterline worded WARNING
UNDERWATER PARK BOATS
KEEP CLEAR, private aids.

Dock Fog Signal
47 48.2N, 122 23.8W, on top of
building, horn: 2 blasts every 30s,
private aid.

Storm Sewer Outfall Daybeacon
47 48.4N, 122 23.7W, white daymark worded DANGER END
OF PIPE on pipe, private aid.

South Breakwater Light
47 48.4N, 122 23.6W, Fl Y 4s,
18 ft., on multi-pile structure,
private aid.

**Small Boat Harbor Entrance
Light 1**
47 48.6N, 122 23.4W, F G, 18 ft.,
SW on dolphin, private aid.

**Small Boat Harbor Entrance
Light 2**
47 48.5N, 122 23.4W, F R, 19 ft.,
TR on pedestal, private aid.

Fishing Reef Buoys (2)
47 48.7N, 122 23.3W, white cans
with orange band and diamond,
private aids.

Eliza Rock Junction Light
Fl (2+1) G 6s, 21 ft., 5 mi., JG on
house.
Also see Bellingham Channel
and Bellingham Bay.

ELLIOTT BAY

Also see Georgetown Reach Range, Duwamish Waterway.

Marina West Entrance Light 1
47 37.7N, 122 23.8W, Fl G 10s, private aid.

Marina West Entrance Light 2
47 37.7N, 122 23.8W, Fl R 10s, private aid.

Breakwater Light A
47 37.8N, 122 23.8W, Fl Y 10s, private aid.

Breakwater Light B
47 37.7N, 122 23.8W, Fl Y 10s, private aid.

Breakwater Light C
47 37.6N, 122 23.3W, Fl Y 10s, private aid.

Breakwater Light D
47 37.7N, 122 23.3W, F Y, private aid.

Marina East Entrance Light 1
47 37.6N, 122 23.2W, Fl G 10s, private aid.

Marina East Entrance Light 2
47 37.7N, 122 23.3W, Fl R 10s, private aid.

Smith Cove Buoy 1
47 37.7N, 122 23.1W, green can.

Smith Cove Buoy 3
Green can.

Fish Haven Buoy A
47 37.5N, 122 22.4W, white can with orange bands near top and waterline, orange diamond with center cross worded FISHING REEF, radar reflector, private aid.

Fish Haven Buoy B
47 37.5N, 122 22.3W, white can with orange bands near top and waterline, orange diamond with center cross worded FISHING REEF, radar reflector, private aid.

Shipmates Light
47 37.3N, 122 21.8W, Fl W 2.5s, 25 ft., on brown hexagonal structure, private aid.

Fish Pen Lights (2)
44 37.4N, 122 22.1W, Fl Y 6s, private aids.

Colman Ferry Terminal Lights (2)
47 36.2N, 122 20.4W, F R, 19 ft., on dolphin, horn: 2 blasts every 15s, fog light 36 feet above water, F W exhibited when fog signal is in operation, private aids.

East Waterway Pier Light
47 35.4N, 122 20.7W, Q R, 12 ft., private aid.

Alaska Hydro-Train Light A
47 35.0N, 122 22.3W, Fl Y 4s, 14 ft., on dolphin, private aid.

Alaska Hydro-Train Light B
47 35.1N, 122 22.2W, Fl R 4s, 8 ft., on dolphin, private aid.

Duwamish Head Light
47 35.9N, 122 23.3W, Fl W 2.5s, 15 ft., 18 mi., NB on pile structure, obscured from 324° to 045°, horn: 2 blasts every 20s.

Everett
See Port Gardner.

Evergreen Point Bridge North Fog Signal
On fender pontoon, horn (low tone): 1 blast every 30s, private aid.
Also see Lake Washington.

Evergreen Point Bridge South Fog Signal
On fender pontoon, horn (high tone): 2 blasts every 30s, private aid.

Ewing Island Reef Daybeacon
48 45.7N, 122 52.6W, NW on pile worded DANGER REEF, maintained from March 15 to Oct. 15.

F

Fauntleroy Cove Fog Signal
47 31.4N, 122 23.7W, siren: 1 blast every 24s, private aid.
Also see East Passage.

Fauntleroy Point Light
Fl W 4s, 37 ft., 7 mi., NB on skeleton tower.
Also see Rosario Strait.

Fidalgo Bay
See Anacortes Harbor.

Fisgard Light (Canada)
48 25.8N, 123 26.8W, Iso W 2s (R sector), 71 ft., 14 mi., white circular tower with red brick dwelling attached, tower illuminated below balcony by floodlights, red sector from 195° to 332°, to clear Scrogg Rocks light must show white in approach from eastward.

FISHERMAN BAY

Also see San Juan Channel.

Fisherman Bay Sector Light
48 31.5N, 122 55.2W, Fl W 4s (R sector), 15 ft., 5 mi., NR on pile structure, red from 172.5° to 069.5°.

Entrance Daybeacon 4
TR on pile.

Channel Daybeacon 5
SG on pile.

Channel Buoy 7
48 31.1N, 122 55.0W, green can.

Channel Buoy 8
48 30.9N, 122 54.9W, red nun.

Flat Point Light
48 33.2N, 122 55.3W, Fl R 2.5s, 15 ft., 5 mi., TR on pile.
Also see San Juan Channel.

Foulweather Bluff Light 1
47 55.9N, 122 37.3W, Fl G 4s, 21 ft., 6 mi., SG on skeleton tower, obscured from 202° to 335°, radar reflector.
Also see Hood Canal.

Foulweather Bluff Lighted Bell Buoy 2
Fl R 4s, 4 mi., red.
Also see Admiralty Inlet.

Fourmile Rock Light
Fl G 6s, 15 ft., 7 mi., SG on skeleton tower.

Fox Island, State Fisheries Salmon Pen Lights (2) (mark fish pens)
47 16.1N, 122 38.7W, Fl Y 5s, 5 mi., on corner of dock, private aids.

Fox Island Rock Buoy 1
47 16.5N, 122 38.7W, green can.

FRIDAY HARBOR

Also see San Juan Channel.

Minnesota Reef Daybeacon 1
48 32.2N, 122 59.3W, SG on pile,
radar reflector.

Brown Island Daybeacon 2
TR on multi-pile structure, radar
reflector.

Pier Lights (2)
48 32.7N, 123 00.6W, Fl R 5s,
6 mi., pile, private aids.

North Breakwater Light
48 32.4N, 123 00.9W, Fl G 4s, 8 ft.,
3 mi., SG on pedestal.

Marina Entrance Light 1
48 32.4N, 123 00.9W, Fl G 2.5s,
8 ft., 3 mi., SG on pile, displays
Q Y during seaplane operations.

Marina Entrance Light 2
48 32.4N, 123 00.9W, Fl R 2.5s,
8 ft., 3 mi., TR on pile, displays
Q Y during seaplane operations.

G

Gedney Island Buoy 1
48 00.3N, 122 17.7W, green can.
Also see Possession Sound.

**Gedney Island Fishing Reef
Buoy A**
47 59.8N, 122 18.6W, white and
orange bands, spherical buoy,
private aid.

**Georgetown Reach Range Front
Light (Duwamish Waterway)**
47 32.6N, 122 20.1W, Q R, KRB
on pile, visible 4° each side of
rangeline, private aid.

**Georgetown Reach Range Rear
Light**
230 yards, 160° from front light,
Iso R 6s, KRB on pile, visible 4°
each side of rangeline, private
aid.

Gibson Point Light 6
47 13.1N, 122 36.1W, Fl R 4s,
22 ft., 6 mi., TR on dolphin, light
visible from 222° to 055°.
Also see The Narrows.

Gig Harbor Light
47 19.7N, 122 34.4W, Fl R 4s,
13 ft., 3 mi., hexagonal concrete
building, private aid.
Also see The Narrows.

Glen Cove
See Port Townsend.

GRAYS HARBOR

Entrance

Grays Harbor Light
46 53.3N, 124 07.0W, Al W R 30s,
123 ft., white 19 mi., red 17 mi.,
white truncated octagonal pyramidal tower, horn: 1 blast every
15s, maintained from June 1 to
Oct. 1, fog signal is located 2,350
yards, 327.5° from light tower.

**Approach Lighted Whistle Buoy
GH**
46 51.9N, 124 14.3W, Mo (A) W,
6 mi., red and white stripes,
racon: G (--·).

Bar Range Front Light
46 55.8N, 124 09.6W, Q R, 18 ft.,
KRB on skeleton tower, visible 4°
each side of rangeline.

Bar Range Rear Light
500 yards, 039.3° from front light,
Iso R 6s, 61 ft., KRB on skeleton
tower, visible 4° each side of
rangeline.

Entrance Lighted Whistle Buoy 2
46 52.7N, 124 12.7W, Fl R 4s,
4 mi., red.

Entrance Lighted Whistle Buoy 3
46 55.0N, 124 14.8W, Fl G 4s,
4 mi., green.

Entrance Lighted Whistle Buoy 4
46 53.7N, 124 11.8W, Fl R 4s,
3 mi., red.

Entrance Lighted Gong Buoy 5
46 54.8N, 124 12.6W, Fl G 4s,
3 mi., green.

Entrance Lighted Whistle Buoy 6
46 54.3N, 124 11.2W, Fl R 2.5s,
3 mi., red.

Entrance Lighted Whistle Buoy 8
46 54.5N, 124 10.9W, Q R, 3 mi.,
red, Fl R 2.5s, high-intensity
flashtube.

Entrance Lighted Bell Buoy 9
46 54.7N, 124 10.1W, Fl G 4s,
3 mi., green.

Point Chehalis Range Front Light
46 54.5N, 124 07.4W, F R, 27 ft.,
KRB on pile structure, visible 1°
each side of rangeline, lighted
throughout 24 hours.

Point Chehalis Range Rear Light
330 yards, 093° from front light,
F R, 51 ft., KRB on skeleton tower,
visible 1° each side of rangeline,
lighted throughout 24 hours.

South Jetty Sound Signal
47 54.3N, 124 09.0W, horn: 1 blast
every 15s, maintained from June
1 to Oct. 1.

Main Channel

Channel Lighted Whistle Buoy 11
46 54.7N, 124 08.8W, Q G, 4 mi.,
green.

Channel Lighted Whistle Buoy 13
46 55.4N, 124 07.5W, Fl G 4s,
4 mi., green.

Junction Lighted Bell Buoy A
46 55.0N, 124 06.8W, Fl (2+1) R 6s,
4 mi., red and green bands.

South Bay Channel

Point Chehalis Lighted Buoy 2
46 54.8N, 124 07.2W, Q R, 5 mi.,
red.

**Grays Harbor Entrance Small
Boat Warning Sign**
46 54.8N, 124 06.9W, Q Y (2),
20 ft., NW worded ROUGH BAR,
light oriented upstream, lights
flashing when seas exceed four
feet in height, lights extinguished
for lesser bar conditions, but
with no guarantee that bar is
safe.

Point Chehalis Light 4
46 54.9N, 124 06.8W, Fl R 4s,
15 ft., 4 mi., TR on dolphin.

Point Chehalis Light 6
Fl R 4s, 15 ft., 4 mi., TR on
platform.

Westhaven

Light 7
46 54.8N, 124 06.5W, Fl G 4s,
17 ft., 4 mi., SG on multi-pile
structure.

Outer Breakwater North Light 8
46 54.6N, 124 06.5W, Fl R 4s, 15 ft., 4 mi., TR on pile, higher intensity beam up channel.

Outer Breakwater South Light 10
Q R, 15 ft., 4 mi., TR on pile, higher intensity beam down channel.

South Breakwater Light 11
Fl G 4s, 16 ft., 5 mi., SG on dolphin.

Cove Southeast Entrance Light 1
46 54.4N, 124 06.2W, Fl G 2.5s, 16 ft., 4 mi., SG on dolphin, light is obscured from 138.5° to 242.5°.

Cove Southeast Entrance Light 2
Fl R 2.5s, 16 ft., 3 mi., TR on dolphin.

South Reach

South Reach Range A Front Light
46 55.2N, 124 03.0W, Q R, 21 ft., KRB on pile structure, higher intensity beam on rangeline, obscured to northeast, radar reflector.

South Reach Range A Rear Light
600 yards, 092.3° from front light, Iso R 6s, 50 ft., KRB on skeleton tower on pile structure. visible 4° each side of rangeline.

South Reach Lighted Bell Buoy 14
46 55.3N, 124 06.3W, Q R, 4 mi., red.

South Reach Lighted Buoy 15
46 55.4N, 124 06.3W, Q G, 4 mi., green.

South Reach Lighted Buoy 15A
46 55.3N, 124 05.4W, Fl G 4s, 4 mi., green.

South Reach Light 16
46 55.1N, 124 05.0W, Fl R 4s, 15 ft., 4 mi., TR on dolphin, higher intensity beam up and down channel.

South Reach Lighted Buoy 17
46 55.3N, 124 04.2W, Fl G 4s, 4 mi., green.

South Reach Lighted Bell Buoy 18
46 55.2N, 124 04.2W, Fl R 4s, 4 mi., red.

South Reach Daybeacon 20
TR on pile structure.

South Reach Lighted Gong Buoy 21
46 55.3N, 124 03.4W, Q G, 4 mi., grccn.

South Reach Junction Buoy SC
46 55.3N, 124 02.8W, red and green bands, nun.

South Reach Range AA Front Light
46 55.1N, 124 03.7W, Q R, 21 ft., KRB on pile structure, visible 4° each side of rangeline, passing light is obscured from 030° to 150°, radar reflector.

South Reach Range AA Rear Light
242 yards, 246.7° from front light, Iso R 6s, 38 ft., KRB on skeleton tower on pile structure, visible 4° each side of rangeline.

South Reach Buoy 23
46 55.6N, 124 02.4W, green can.

South Reach Lighted Bell Buoy 24
46 55.6N, 124 01.9W, 4 mi., red.

North Channel

North Channel Range B Front Light
46 55.5N, 124 01.7W, Q W, 24 ft., KRB on skeleton tower on pile structure, visible all around, higher intensity on rangeline.

North Channel Range B Rear Light
617.6 yards, 222.3° from front light, Iso W 6s, 48 ft., KRB on pile structure, visible all around, higher intensity on rangeline.

North Channel Lighted Buoy 25
46 55.9N, 124 01.2W, Q G, 4 mi., green.

North Channel Lighted Bell Buoy 26
46 56.2N, 124 00.5W, Fl R 2.5s, 4 mi., red.

North Channel Lighted Buoy 27
46 56.5N, 124 00.4W, Fl G 2.5s, 4 mi., green.

North Channel Buoy 28
46 57.0N, 123 59.4W, red nun.

North Channel Range C Front Light
46 57.9N, 123 58.4W, Q W, 39 ft., KRB on pile structure, visible all around, higher intensity on rangeline, radar reflector.

North Channel Range C Rear Light
900 yards, 043° from front light, Iso W 6s, 70 ft., KRB on pile structure, visible 4° each side of rangeline, radar reflector.

North Channel Lighted Buoy 29
46 57.1N, 123 59.6W, Fl G 4s, 4 mi., green.

North Channel Lighted Buoy 30
46 57.5N, 123 58.9W, Q R, 4 mi., red.

North Channel Range D Front Light
46 57.6N, 123 59.2W, Q W, 22 ft., KRB on pile structure, visible 4° each side of rangeline.

North Channel Range D Rear Light
333 yards, 259.7° from front light, Iso W 6s, 47 ft., KRB on pile structure, visible 4° each side of rangeline.

North Channel Range E Front Light
46 58.2N, 123 55.1W, Q G, 20 ft., KRB on pile structure, visible 4° each side of rangeline.

North Channel Range E Rear Light
665 yards, 075° from front light, Iso G 6s, 56 ft., KRB on pile structure, visible 4° each side of rangeline.

North Channel Lighted Buoy 32
46 57.5N, 123 58.7W, Fl R 2.5s, red.

North Channel Lighted Buoy 34
46 57.7N, 123 58.0W, Fl R 4s, 4 mi., red.

North Channel Lighted Buoy 35
46 57.9N, 123 57.0W, Fl G 4s, 4 mi., green.

North Channel Lighted Buoy 36
46 57.9N, 123 56.4W, Fl R 2.5s, 3 mi., red.

North Channel Lighted Buoy 40
46 58.1N, 123 55.4W, Q R, 4 mi.,
red.

**North Channel Range F Front
Light**
46 58.2N, 123 55.7W, Q W, 27 ft.,
KRB on pile structure, visible all
around, higher intensity on
rangeline.

**North Channel Range F Rear
Light**
370 yards, 273.9° from front
light, Iso W 6s, 35 ft., KRB on
pile structure, visible 4° each
side of rangeline.

North Channel Lighted Buoy 44
46 58.0N, 123 54.2W, Fl R 2.5s,
4 mi., red.

North Channel Daybeacon 46
46 58.0N, 123 53.7W, TR on pile.

North Channel Daybeacon 46A
46 58.0N, 123 53.5W, TR on pile,
radar reflector.

Cow Point

Reach Range G Front Light
46 57.4N, 123 50.3W, Q W, 15 ft.,
KRB on pile structure, on same
structure as Aberdeen Range K
Front Light, visible all around,
higher intensity on rangeline.

Reach Range G Rear Light
600 yards, 120° from front light,
Iso W 6s, 27 ft., KRB on pile
structure, visible 4° each side
of rangeline.

**Aberdeen Terminal No. 1 Pier
Lights (2)**
46 57.9N, 123 51.3W, F R, 14 ft.,
private aids.

**Aberdeen Terminal No. 2 Pier
Lights (2)**
46 57.8N, 123 51.2W, F R, 19 ft.,
private aids.

Turning Basin Daybeacon 48
46 57.6N, 123 51.1W, TR on pile.

Turning Basin Daybeacon 50
46 57.5N, 123 51.0W, TR on pile.

**Grays Harbor North Channel
Light 51**
Fl G 4s, 15 ft., 5 mi., SG on
dolphin.

Pier Lights (2)
F R, 15 ft., private aids.

Reach Range H Front Light
46 57.6N, 123 49.4W, Q R, 15 ft.,
KRB on pile structure, visible 2°
each side of rangeline.

Reach Range H Rear Light
500 yards, 091° from front light,
Iso R 6s, 26 ft., KRB on pile
structure, visible 2° each side
of rangeline.

Reach Range J Front Light
46 57.6N, 123 49.5W, Q G, 16 ft.,
KRB on pile structure, visible all
around, higher intensity on
rangeline.

Reach Range J Rear Light
283 yards, 071.8° from front light,
Iso G 6s, 26 ft., KRB on skeleton
tower, visible 2° each side of
rangeline.

Aberdeen

Reach Range K Front Light
46 57.4N, 123 50.4W, Q W, 15 ft.,
KRB on pile, on same structure as
Cow Point Reach Range G Front
Light, visible all around, higher
intensity on rangeline.

Reach Range K Rear Light
1,000 yards, 232° from front
light, Iso W 6s, 30 ft., KRB on
pile structure, visible 4° each
side of rangeline.

**Grays Harbor North Channel
Light 55**
46 57.8N, 123 49.7W, Fl G 4s,
15 ft., 5 mi., SG on dolphin.

Harbor Light 1
46 58.4N, 123 48.4W, Q G, 20 ft.,
6 mi., SG on dolphin.

Reach Range L Front Light
46 58.5N, 123 48.3W, Q R, 21 ft.,
KRB on dolphin, visible 2° each
side of rangeline.

Reach Range L Rear Light
350 yards, 050° from front light,
Iso R 6s, 37 ft., KRB on skeleton
tower on pile structure, visible 2°
each side of rangeline.

Harbor Light 3
46 58.6N, 123 47.7W, Fl G 4s,
20 ft., 4 mi., SG on dolphin, higher intensity beam down river.

Chehalis River Light 4
46 57.4N, 123 46.1W, Fl R 4s,
15 ft., 4 mi., TR on skeleton
tower, higher intensity beam
up and down river.

North Bay

Lighted Buoy 1
46 55.9N, 124 06.5W, Fl G 4s,
4 mi., green.

Buoy 2
46 56.0N, 124 05.7W, red nun.

Buoy 4
46 56.5N, 124 06.0W, red nun.

Damon Point Light
46 57.0N, 124 06.4W, Fl Y 4s,
20 ft., 5 mi., NB on pile structure,
radar reflector.

South Channel

Light 6
Fl R 2.5s, 16 ft., 4 mi., TR on dolphin, visible all around, higher
intensity beam down channel.

Johns River Entrance Light 8
Fl R 4s, 15 ft., 7 mi., TR on dolphin, higher intensity beam up
and down channel.

Johns River Daybeacon 1
SG on pile.

Johns River Daybeacon 3
SG on pile.

Weyerhaeuser Outfall Lights (2)
46 57.4N, 123 50.9W, Fl Y 10s, on
dolphins at end of submerged
outfall pipe, private aids.

Charley Creek Dike Daybeacon 2
46 57.4N, 123 50.7W, TR on
dolphin.

Green Point Light
48 38.0N, 123 06.4W, Fl W 4s,
20 ft., 6 mi., NB on skeleton
tower.
Also see San Juan Channel.

GUEMES CHANNEL

Also see Cap Sante Waterway
and Anacortes Harbor.

Lighted Buoy 2
48 30.7N, 122 41.9W, Fl R 2.5s,
4 mi., red, radar reflector.

Shannon Point Light
48 30.6N, 122 41.0W, Fl W 4s,
15 ft., 6 mi., NB on dolphin, horn:
1 blast every 30s, operates continuously.

Anacortes Ferry Breakwater Light
48 31.2N, 122 37.4W, Fl R 4s,
14 ft., on breakwater, private aid.

Anacortes Ferry Terminal Light A
48 30.5N, 122 40.5W, Fl Y 10s,
12 ft., on dolphin, private aid.

Anacortes Ferry Terminal Light B
Fl Y 10s, 12 ft., on dolphin, private aid.

Lighted Buoy 3
48 31.3N, 122 39.4W, Fl G 2.5s,
4 mi., green.

Lighted Buoy 4
48 31.2N, 122 39.2W, Fl R 4s,
4 mi., red.

Lighted Buoy 5
48 31.4N, 122 38.5W, Fl G 4s,
4 mi., green.

Anacortes Dock Lights (2)
48 31.3N, 122 36.4W, F R, 10 ft.,
on dock, private aids.

HALE PASSAGE (NEAR BELLINGHAM)

**Rocks Junction Lighted Buoy
(marks S edge of rocks)**
48 40.4N, 122 35.5W, Fl (2+1) R 6s,
5 mi., red and green bands.
Also see Bellingham Bay.

Inati Bay Reef Buoy
48 40.5N, 122 37.2W, white with
orange bands worded DANGER
ROCK.

Lummi Island Light 3
48 41.5N, 122 38.7W, Fl G 4s,
16 ft., 6 mi., SG on tower.

**Lummi Island Ferry Landing
Light**
48 43.2N, 122 40.7W, Fl R 4s,
12 ft., private aid.

Point Francis Shoal Buoy 4
48 41.7N, 122 38.3W, red nun.

Lummi Point Lighted Buoy 5
48 44.1N, 122 41.2W, Fl G 4s,
5 mi., green.

Point Migley Lighted Buoy
48 45.3N, 122 43.5W, Fl (2+1) R 6s,
3 mi., red and green bands.

Hale Passage (near The Narrows)
See Fox Island.

HAMMERSLEY INLET

Hungerford Point Light 2
47 12.3N, 122 56.2W, Fl R 4s,
3 mi., TR on pile structure.

Libby Point Light 4
47 12.1N, 122 59.3W, Fl R 4s,
18 ft., 4 mi.

Church Point Light 6
Fl R 6s, 20 ft., 4 mi., TR on skeleton tower.

Harbor Rock Daybeacon
48 37.8N, 122 58.7W, NR on iron
spindle, rock bares 6 feet at
MLLW.

HARO STRAIT

Also see British Columbia
chapter.

Discovery Island Light (Canada)
48 25.5N, 123 13.5W, Fl W 5s,
93 ft., white circular tower, light
obscured from 050.5° to 146°,
horn: 1 blast every 60s.

Lighted Buoy VD (Canada)
48 27.1N, 123 10.8W, Fl (2+1) W 6s,
red and green bands.

Lime Kiln Light
48 31.0N, 123 09.2W, Fl W 10s,
55 ft., 17 mi., octagonal tower
attached to fog signal building,
two dwellings about 150 yards
southeast, horn: 1 blast every
30s, operates continuously.

Zero Rock Light (Canada)
48 31.4N, 123 17.4W, Fl W 4s, 28 ft.,
white cylindrical tower, green
band on top, radar reflector.

**Little Zero Rock Lighted Buoy
V30 (Canada)**
48 31.9N, 123 19.7W, Q R, red.

Kelp Reefs Light (Canada)
48 32.9N, 123 14.1W, Q W, 35 ft.,
octagonal tower attached to
building.

D'Arcy Island Light (Canada)
48 34.0N, 123 17.0W, Fl R 4s,
23 ft., white circular tower with
red band at top.

Mosquito Pass Buoy 1
48 34.8N, 123 10.9W, green can.
Also see Mosquito Pass.

Kellett Bluff Light
48 35.3N, 123 12.1W, Fl W 4s,
80 ft., 7 mi., NB on house.

**Danger Shoal Lighted Horn Buoy
(SW of shoal)**
Fl (2+1) G 6s, 6 mi., green and red
bands, horn: 1 blast every 30s.

Tom Point Light (Canada)
48 39.8N, 123 16.3W, Fl W 4s,
21 ft., white circular tower with
green band at top.

Arachne Reef Light (Canada)
48 41.1N, 123 17.6W, Fl (2+1) G 6s,
22 ft., white circular tower with
green band at top.

Turn Point Light
48 41.3N, 123 14.2W, Fl W 2.5s,
44 ft., 8 mi., white concrete tower,
light obscured from 260.5° to
357°, horn: 2 blasts every 30s,
operates continuously.

Point Fairfax Light (Canada)
48 42.0N, 123 17.8W, Fl (3) W 12s,
33 ft., on white tower, 4 lights.

**Hartsene Island Fish Pen
Lights (6)**
47 10.7N, 122 51.0W, Fl Y 6s, on
aquaculture facility, private aid.
Also see Dana Passage.

**Hat Island Marina Breakwater
Light 2**
48 01.2N, 122 19.2W, F R, 8 ft., on
pile structure, private aid.

Hat Island Marina Lighted Buoy A
48 01.3N, 122 19.2W, Q Y, on raft,
private aid.
Also see Possession Sound.

Hazel Point Light
47 41.6N, 122 46.2W, Fl W 4s,
15 ft., 5 mi., NB on pile, radar
reflector.
Also see Hood Canal.

Washington

Hein Bank Lighted Buoy 1
48 22.0N, 123 02.2W, Fl G 6s,
5 mi., green, racon: K (-·-).

Hein Bank Lighted Isolated Danger Buoy DH
48 21.1N, 123 02.8W, Fl (2) W 5s,
6 mi., black with red band.

Hiram M. Chittenden Locks
See Lake Washington Ship Canal.

HOLMES HARBOR

Also see Saratoga Passage.

Buoy 1
48 06.2N, 122 31.9W, green can.

Facility Raft Light
48 02.8N, 122 32.7W, Fl Y 6s, on
aquaculture raft, private aid.

South Mussel Raft Lights (2)
48 02.5N, 122 32.0W, Fl Y 6s, on
mussel raft, private aids.

North Mussel Raft Lights (2)
48 02.6N, 122 32.1W, Fl Y 6s, 4 ft.,
on mussel raft, private aids.

HOOD CANAL

Colvos Rocks Light
47 57.1N, 122 40.3W, Fl W 4s, 34 ft.,
5 mi., NB on skeleton tower.

Port Ludlow Buoy 2 (marks S limit of Colvos Rocks)
47 56.7N, 122 39.5W, red nun.
Also see Port Ludlow.

Tala Point Junction Light
47 55.9N, 122 39.5W, Fl (2+1) R 6s,
15 ft., 5 mi., JR on dolphin.

Foul Weather Bluff Light 1
47 55.9N, 122 37.3W, Fl G 4s,
21 ft., 6 mi., SG on skeleton
tower, obscured from 202° to
335°, radar reflector.

Point Hannon Light 2
47 53.3N, 122 36.6W, Fl R 2.5s,
15 ft., 4 mi., TR on skeleton tower.

Mariculture Lighted Buoys (2)
47 52.9N, 122 36.7W, Fl Y 6s,
orange and white spherical
buoys, private aids.

Port Gamble Range Front Light
47 52.8N, 122 34.7W, Q W, 26 ft.,
KRB on skeleton tower, visible all
around, higher intensity on
rangeline.

Port Gamble Range Rear Light
300 yards, 001° from front light,
Iso W 6s, 40 ft., KRB on skeleton
tower, visible 4° each side of
rangeline.

Port Gamble Light 1
47 51.8N, 122 34.7W, Fl G 4s,
15 ft., 4 mi., SG on dolphin.

Port Gamble Inner Light 3
Fl G 6s, 18 ft., 5 mi., SG on
dolphin.

Bridge West Channel Fog Signal
47 52.0N, 122 38.0W, horn: 1 blast
every 20s, private aid.

Bridge Main Channel Fog Signal
horn: 1 blast every 30s, private
aid.

Bridge East Channel Fog Signal
horn: 1 blast every 20s, private
aid.

Sisters Rock Light 4
47 51.5N, 122 38.5W, Fl R 4s,
15 ft., 5 mi., TR on wooden crib.

Case Shoal Daybeacon
47 51.6N, 122 40.5W, NW on pile
worded DANGER SHOAL.

Case Shoal Light 6
47 50.6N, 122 40.5W, Fl R 2.5s,
15 ft., 5 mi., TR on pile, radar
reflector.

Light 5
47 49.6N, 122 39.0W, Fl G 2.5s,
15 ft., 5 mi., SG on pile, radar
reflector.

Light 7
Fl G 4s, 15 ft., 5 mi., SG on pile
structure.

Light 8
47 49.0N, 122 41.2W, Fl R 4s,
15 ft., 6 mi., TR on dolphin, higher intensity beam down channel.

Bangor Explosive Anchorage Lighted Buoy A
47 45.8N, 122 43.4W, Fl Y 6s,
6 mi., yellow.

Light 10
Fl R 4s, 16 ft., 4 mi., TR on multi-
pile structure, high-intensity
beam up and down channel,
light obscured from 029° to 170°.

Trident Submarine Range Front Daybeacon
47 45.2N, 122 45.3W, KRW on
pile, private aid.

Trident Submarine Range Rear Daybeacon
250 yards, 233° from front daybeacon, KRW on pile, private aid.

Bangor Explosive Anchorage Lighted Buoy B
47 44.4N, 122 44.5W, Fl Y 6s,
6 mi., yellow.

Hazel Point Light
47 41.6N, 122 46.2W, Fl W 4s,
15 ft., 5 mi., NB on pile, radar
reflector.

Light 11
47 41.3N, 122 44.9W, Fl G 4s,
15 ft., 6 mi., SG on dolphin,
radar reflector.

Oak Head Light 12
47 40.9N, 122 48.7W, Fl R 4s,
15 ft., 5 mi., TR on pile, radar
reflector.

Light 11A
47 39.8N, 122 47.9W, Fl G 2.5s,
20 ft., 6 mi., SG on pile, radar
reflector.

Seabeck Marina Light
47 38.7N, 122 49.7W, Fl Y 2.5s,
4 ft., on pile, private aid.

Light 13
47 39.4N, 122 49.7W, Q G, 15 ft.,
5 mi., SG on dolphin, radar
reflector.

Misery Point Reef Buoy A
47 39.6N, 122 49.6W, white
with orange bands, sphere,
private aid.

Misery Point Mussel Pen Light C
47 39.3N, 122 50.2W, Fl Y 6s,
4 mi., on 40-foot floating pen,
private aid.

Tskutsko Point Light
47 41.6N, 122 50.0W, Fl W 4s,
15 ft., 5 mi., NB on pile, radar
reflector.
Also see Dabob Bay.

Dosewallips Flats Light 15
47 41.6N, 122 52.7W, Fl G 4s, 15 ft., 5 mi., SG on pile, radar reflector.

Hope Island

Also see Skagit Bay.

Light 14
Fl R 2.5s, 23 ft., 4 mi., TR on skeleton tower.
Also see Deception Pass.

Fish Pen Light A
48 24.4N, 122 33.6W, Fl Y 6s, 5 ft., on aquaculture facility, private aid.

Fish Pen Light C
48 24.4N, 122 33.7W, Fl Y 6s, 5 ft., on aquaculture facility, private aid.

Huckleberry Island Light 6
48 32.2N, 122 34.0W, Fl R 2.5s, 73 ft., 4 mi., TR on platform, radar reflector.
Also see Padilla Bay.

Hungerford Point Light 2
47 12.3N, 122 56.2W, Fl R 4s, 3 mi., TR on pile structure.
Also see Hammersley Inlet.

Hunter Bay
See Lopez Sound.

Hunter Point Light 1
47 10.4N, 122 55.2W, Fl G 4s, 15 ft., 7 mi., SG on tower.
Also see Squaxin Passage.

Hylebos Waterway
See Tacoma Harbor.

I

I and J Waterway
See Bellingham Bay.

Iceberg Point Light 2
48 25.3N, 122 53.7W, Fl R 4s, 35 ft., 7 mi., TR on white square concrete house, horn: 1 blast every 30s, operates continuously from June 1 to Nov. 15.
Also see San Juan Channel.

Ideal Cement Range Front Daybeacon
48 10.0N, 123 57.5W, KRW on piles, private aid.

Ideal Cement Range Rear Daybeacon
133 yards, 180° from front daybeacon, KRW on piles, private aid.

Ilwaco
See Columbia River chapter.

Inati Bay Reef Buoy
48 40.5N, 122 37.2W, white with orange bands worded DANGER ROCK.
Also see Hale Passage.

Intalco North and South Lights (2)
48 50.6N, 122 43.2W, F R, 24 ft., horn: 2 blasts every 15s, private aids.
Also see Sandy Point Lights, Tosco Northwest Lights, *and* Atlantic Richfield Lights.

International Boundary

Boundary Ranges A, B, and C (front and rear) are maintained by the International Boundary Commission, United States and Canada.

Range A Front Light
49 00.1N, 123 05.4W, F W, 180 ft., rectangular-shaped, orange daymark on gray skeleton tower, visible on rangeline only, the front range has an oscillating red and white light south of the boundary, and a green and white light north of the boundary, lighted throughout 24 hours.

Range A Rear Light
49 00.1N, 123 04.0W, F W, 258 ft., rectangular-shaped, orange daymark on gray pile, on same structure as International Boundary Range B Rear Light, visible westward, F R aircraft warning light on top of tower, lighted throughout 24 hours.

Obstruction Light
49 00.1N, 123 01.2W, Fl Y 4s, 36 ft., on rectangular block.

Range B Front Light
49 00.1N, 123 02.1W, F G, 65 ft., rectangular-shaped, orange daymark on gray skeleton tower, visible on rangeline only.

Range B Rear Light
49 00.1N, 123 04.0W, F G, 258 ft., rectangular-shaped, orange daymark on gray pile, on same structure as International Boundary Range A Rear Light, visible eastward, F R aircraft warning light on top of tower.

Range C Front Light
49 00.1N, 122 46.9W, Q G, 37 ft., rectangular-shaped, orange daymark on gray skeleton tower.
Also see Semiahmoo Bay.

Range C Rear Light
49 00.1N, 122 45.4W, F G, 80 ft., rectangular-shaped, orange daymark on gray tower, visible on rangeline only.

Itsami Ledge Light 7
47 10.6N, 122 50.2W, Fl G 4s, 20 ft., 5 mi., SG on dolphin.
Also see Dana Passage.

J

James Island Light
47 54.3N, 124 38.8W, Fl W 6s, 150 ft., 9 mi., white house, horn: 2 blasts every 30s, operates continuously, light is obscured from 068° to 101° and from 111° to 293°.
Also see Quillayute River.

John Wayne Marina
See Sequim Bay.

Johns River

Also see Grays Harbor.

Entrance Light 8
Fl R 4s, 15 ft., 7 mi., TR on dolphin, higher intensity beam up and down channel.

Daybeacon 1
SG on pile.

Daybeacon 3
SG on pile.

Johnson Point Light 5
47 10.7N, 122 48.9W, Fl G 6s,
22 ft., 7 mi., SG on pile.
Also see Nisqually Reach.

Jones Island Rock Daybeacon
48 37.2N, 123 02.6W, NW worded
DANGER ROCKS.

Juanita Bay Shoal Daybeacon
47 41.8N, 122 13.1W, NW on pile
worded DANGER SHOAL.
Also see Lake Washington.

K

Kala Point Light 2
48 03.5N, 122 46.0W, Fl R 4s, 25 ft.,
5 mi., TR on skeleton tower.
Also see Port Townsend.

Kalama
See Columbia River chapter.

Kamilche Sea Farm Lighted Buoy A
47 07.5N, 123 01.2W, Fl Y 5s,
yellow, private aid.

Kellett Bluff Light
48 35.3N, 123 12.1W, Fl W 4s,
80 ft., 7 mi., NB on house.
Also see Haro Strait.

Kellett Ledge Buoy 3
48 27.0N, 122 47.5W, green can.
Also see Rosario Strait.

Kelp Reefs Light (Canada)
48 32.9N, 123 14.1W, Q W, 35 ft.,
octagonal tower attached to
building.
Also see Haro Strait.

Kenmore Channel Lighted Buoy 2
47 45.1N, 122 15.8W, Fl R 2.5s,
3 mi., red.
Also see Lake Washington.

Kenmore Channel Lighted Buoy 4
47 45.2N, 122 15.7W, Fl R 4s,
3 mi., red.

Keystone Harbor Entrance Light 1
48 09.4N, 122 40.3W, Q G, 12 ft.,
on piling, private aid.
Also see Admiralty Inlet.

Keystone Harbor Entrance Light 2
48 09.4N, 122 40.3W, Fl R 4s,
13 ft., 5 mi., TR on platform.

KILISUT HARBOR

Buoy 2
48 04.8N, 122 44.6W, red nun.

Buoy 3
Green can.

Buoy 5
Green can.

Daybeacons 6–17
TRs and SGs on piles, radar
reflectors.

Kingston Small Boat Harbor Light 2
47 47.7N, 122 29.9W, Fl R 4s, 13 ft.,
5 mi., TR on skeleton tower.

Klas Rocks, Mats Mats Bay Entrance Lighted Bell Buoy 1
47 57.8N, 122 40.3W, Q G, 4 mi.,
green.
Also see Mats Mats Bay.

Klas Rocks Buoy 2
47 57.7N, 122 40.3W, red nun.

Kopachuck State Park Buoy (marks fish haven)
47 18.6N, 122 41.4W, orange and
white bands, private aid.
Also see Carr Inlet.

L

La Conner
See Swinomish Channel.

LAKE UNION

Also see Lake Washington Ship
Canal.

Test Area Lighted Buoy A
47 38.4N, 122 20.2W, Fl Y 2.5s,
yellow, marks rectangular test
area, private aid.

Test Area Lighted Buoy B
Fl Y 2.5s, yellow, marks rectangular test area, private aid.

Test Area Lighted Buoy C
Fl Y 2.5s, yellow, marks rectangular test area, private aid.

Test Area Lighted Buoy D
Fl Y 2.5s, yellow, marks rectangular test area, private aid.

Buoy 13
Green can.

Shoal Buoy 2
47 37.8N, 122 20.2W, red nun.

National Ocean Service Dolphin Light
47 38.2N, 122 19.8W, F R, 15 ft.,
dolphin, maintained by National
Ocean Service, Seattle.

Flo Villa Lights (2)
F R, 10 ft., dolphin, private aids.

Channel Buoy 16
47 39.2N, 122 19.4W, red nun.

Union Bay Channel Buoys 27, 28, 29, 30, and 31
Green cans and red nuns.
Also see Lake Washington.

LAKE WASHINGTON

Also see Lake Union.

Webster Point Light 33
47 38.9N, 122 16.6W, Fl G 4s,
19 ft., 6 mi., SG on white house
on pile structure, light obscured
from 121° to 199°.

Juanita Bay Shoal Daybeacon
47 41.8N, 122 13.1W, NW on pile
worded DANGER SHOAL.

NOAA Pier Clearance Lights (2)
47 41.3N, 122 15.5W, F R, 20 ft.,
on NW and NE corners of pier,
private aids.

Kenmore Channel Lighted Buoy 2
47 45.1N, 122 15.8W, Fl R 2.5s,
3 mi., red.

Kenmore Channel Lighted Buoy 4
47 45.2N, 122 15.7W, Fl R 4s,
3 mi., red.

Evergreen Point Bridge North Fog Signal
On fender pontoon, horn (low
tone): 1 blast every 30s, private
aid.

Evergreen Point Bridge South Fog Signal
On fender pontoon, horn
(high tone): 2 blasts every 30s,
private aid.

Bellevue Marina Dock Lights (2)
47 36.6N, 122 12.5W, F R, 4 ft.,
private aids.

Becks Pier Light
47 36.6N, 122 12.6W, F R, 6 ft., on dolphin, private aid.

Meydenbauer Bay Yacht Club Lights (6)
47 36.5N, 122 12.5W, F R, F G, 10 ft., red light on left end and green light on right end of each pier as seen from the bay, private aids.

South Leschi Breakwater Lights (6)
47 36.1N, 122 16.9W, F R, 10 ft., on dolphins, private aids.

North Leschi Breakwater Lights (4)
47 36.3N, 122 16.8W, F R, 10 ft., on dolphins, private aids.

Andrews Bay Daybeacon
NW on pile worded DANGER SUBMERGED ROCKS.

Mercer Island Pipeline Buoy
47 32.3N, 122 12.6W, white can with orange bands and diamond worded PIPE XING, private aid.

LAKE WASHINGTON SHIP CANAL
Also see Shilshole Bay and Boat Basin, *and* Lake Union.

Lower Guide Wall Light
47 40.1N, 122 24.3W, F R, 8 ft., 11 mi., pile structure, maintained by U.S. Army Corps of Engineers.

Canal Signals
F R (see remarks), F G, 10 ft., if neither light is shown vessels bound for large lock must stop at Stop sign (below small lock) until directed to proceed, red light must not be passed by vessels bound for large lock, green light indicates that they may proceed, vessels bound for small lock may disregard lights and proceed to Stop sign below that lock, maintained by U.S. Army Corps of Engineers.

Upper Guide Wall Light
F R, 14 ft., on pile structure, maintained by U.S. Army Corps of Engineers.

Lawson Reef Junction Lighted Bell Buoy
48 24.1N, 122 43.0W, Fl (2+1) R 6s, 5 mi., red and green bands.
Also see Rosario Strait.

Lawson Reef Lighted Bell Buoy 2
48 24.7N, 122 46.4W, Fl R 2.5s, 4 mi., red.

Lawson Rock Buoy 2 (near Blakeley Island)
48 31.8N, 122 47.1W, red nun.
Also see Rosario Strait.

Lawson Rock Danger Daybeacon (near Blakeley Island)
48 31.8N, 122 47.3W, NW on pile worded DANGER ROCK, radar reflector.

Leadbetter Point Buoy 1
46 38.4N, 124 07.3W, green can.
Also see Willapa Bay.

Leo Reef Light
Fl W 4s, 7 ft., 5 mi., NB on black pyramidal base.

Libby Point Light 4
47 12.1N, 122 59.3W, Fl R 4s, 18 ft., 4 mi.
Also see Hammersley Inlet.

Liberty Bay
See Port of Poulsbo.

Lime Kiln Light
48 31.0N, 123 09.2W, Fl W 10s, 55 ft., 17 mi., octagonal tower attached to fog signal building, two dwellings about 150 yards southeast, horn: 1 blast every 30s, operates continuously.
Also see Haro Strait.

Little Zero Rock Lighted Buoy V30 (Canada)
48 31.9N, 123 19.7W, Q R, red.
Also see Haro Strait.

Long Island Junction Light
46 32.3N, 123 58.7W, Fl (2+1) G 6s, 15 ft., 5 mi., JG on dolphin, higher intensity beam up and down channel.
Also see Willapa Bay.

Longview
See Columbia River chapter.

LOPEZ SOUND

Lopez Pass Light 2
Fl R 4s, 21 ft., 5 mi., TR on house.
Also see Rosario Strait.

Ram Island Rock Daybeacon 4
48 28.4N, 122 50.2W, TR on skeleton tower, radar reflector.

Hunter Bay Aquaculture Lighted Buoys (2)
48 28.1N, 122 51.3W, Fl Y 6s, yellow cans, private aids.

Mud Bay Daybeacon (on reef)
NR on spindle.

Center Island Reef Daybeacon
48 29.1N, 122 50.2W, NW on pile worded DANGER ROCK, radar reflector.

Center Island Reef Daybeacon 6
48 29.1N, 122 50.2W, TR on pile, radar reflector.

Undertakers Reef Daybeacon 8
48 31.3N, 122 49.6W, TR on spindle, radar reflector.

LUMMI ISLAND
Also see Hale Passage *and* Rosario Strait.

Lummi Island Light 3
48 41.5N, 122 38.7W, Fl G 4s, 16 ft., 6 mi., SG on tower.

Lummi Island Ferry Landing Light
48 43.2N, 122 40.7W, Fl R 4s, 12 ft.

Lummi Point Lighted Buoy 5
48 44.1N, 122 41.2W, Fl G 4s, 5 mi., green.

Village Point Light 18
Fl R 4s, 24 ft., 5 mi., TR on skeleton tower, higher intensity beam towards Rosario Strait and Boundary Bay, obscured from 180° to 264°.

Lummi Rocks Light 16A
48 40.2N, 122 40.1W, Fl R 6s, 20 ft., 6 mi., TR on skeleton tower.
Also see Rosario Strait.

Lydia Shoal Lighted Gong Buoy 13
48 36.0N, 122 46.7W, Q G, 3 mi.,
green.
Also see Rosario Strait.

Lyle Point Light 2
47 07.4N, 122 42.0W, Fl R 4s,
15 ft., 6 mi., TR on dolphin.
Also see Nisqually Reach.

Lynch Cove Dock Light 1
47 25.3N, 122 54.0W, F W, 14 ft.,
private aid.

Lynch Cove Dock Light 3
F W, 14 ft., private aid.

M

Marrowstone Point Light
48 06.1N, 122 41.3W, Oc W 4s,
28 ft., 9 mi., white square structure, light obscured from 040°
to 090°, lighted throughout 24
hours, horn: 2 blasts every 30s.
Also see Admiralty Inlet.

MATS MATS BAY

Entrance Lighted Bell Buoy 1
47 57.8N, 122 40.3W, Q G, 4 mi.,
green.

Klas Rocks Buoy 2
47 57.7N, 122 40.3W, red nun.

Channel Light 3
47 57.7N, 122 40.9W, Fl G 4s,
15 ft., 4 mi., SG on pile.

Channel Light 5
47 57.7N, 122 41.1W, Q G, 10 ft.,
4 mi., SG on steel tower.

Range Front Light
47 57.7N, 122 41.1W, Q R, 17 ft.,
KRB on tower.

Range Rear Light
63 yards, 261.3° from front light,
Iso R 6s, 28 ft., KRB on skeleton
tower.

Channel Light 7
47 57.4N, 122 41.2W, Fl G 4s, 25 ft.,
4 mi., SG on skeleton tower.

Buoy 8
47 57.4N, 122 41.2W, red nun.

McCurdy Point Buoy 4
48 08.7N, 122 50.7W, red nun.

Meadow Point Lighted Buoy 1
47 41.8N, 122 24.6W, Fl G 4s,
4 mi., green.

**Meydenbauer Bay Yacht Club
Lights (6)**
47 36.5N, 122 12.5W, F R, F G,
10 ft., red light on left end and
green light on right end of
each pier as seen from the bay,
private aids.
Also see Lake Washington.

Minor Island Light
48 19.5N, 122 49.2W, Fl W 4s,
24 ft., 5 mi., white cylindrical
house on white square house.

Misery Point Mussel Pen Light C
47 39.3N, 122 50.2W, Fl Y 6s,
4 mi., on 40-foot floating pen,
private aid.
Also see Hood Canal.

Misery Point Reef Buoy A
47 39.6N, 122 49.6W, white with
orange bands, sphere, private
aid.

MOSQUITO PASS

Also see Haro Strait.

Buoy 1
48 34.8N, 123 10.9W, green can.

Daybeacon 2
48 35.0N, 123 10.3W, TR on pile.

Buoy 3
Green can.

Daybeacon 4
TR on pile.

Buoy 6
Red nun.

Mud Bay
See Lopez Sound.

Mukilteo Light
47 56.9N, 122 18.3W, Fl W 5s,
33 ft., 14 mi., white octagonal
tower attached to building, horn:
1 blast every 30s.
Also see Possession Sound.

N

Nahcotta Channel
See Willapa Bay.

Narrows, The
See The Narrows.

NEAH BAY

Neah Bay Light
Fl R 6s, 46 ft., 7 mi., TR on
skeleton tower, light obscured
from 114° to 196°, horn: 1 blast
every 30s.

Inner Daybeacon 2
48 22.5N, 124 36.0W, TR on single
pile.

**Marina Breakwater Obstruction
Light A**
48 22.1N, 124 36.4W, Fl Y 6s, 6 ft.,
4 mi., NY on pole.

**Marina Breakwater Obstruction
Light B**
48 22.1N, 124 36.5W, Fl Y 4s, 6 ft.,
4 mi., NY on pole.

Marina Entrance Light 1
48 22.2N, 124 36.8W, Q G, 6 ft.,
4 mi., SG on pole.

**Nemah River Channel Entrance
Daybeacon 1**
46 34.6N, 123 56.9W, SG on
dolphin.
Also see Willapa Bay.

New Dungeness Light
48 10.9N, 123 06.6W, Fl W 5s, 67 ft.,
22 mi., white conical tower on
dwelling, horn: 1 blast every 30s.

**New Dungeness Sand Spit Lighted
Bell Buoy 2**
48 11.5N, 123 05.7W, Fl R 4s,
3 mi., red.

Nisqually Flats
See Nisqually Reach.

NISQUALLY REACH

**Tolmie Beach State Park Buoy
(marks fish haven)**
47 07.5N, 122 46.2W, orange and
white bands, private aid.

Oro Bay Lighted Buoy 2
47 08.3N, 122 42.1W, Fl R 2s, red,
private aid.

Oro Bay Lighted Buoy 3
47 08.3N, 122 42.2W, Fl G 2s,
green, private aid.

Oro Bay Lighted Buoy 4
47 08.3N, 122 41.7W, Fl R 2s, red, private aid.

Nisqually Flats Lighted Buoy 1
47 06.7N, 122 41.9W, Fl G 2.5s, 5 mi., green.

Lyle Point Light 2
47 07.4N, 122 42.0W, Fl R 4s, 15 ft., 6 mi., TR on dolphin.

Nisqually Flats Lighted Buoy 3
47 07.3N, 122 45.1W, Fl G 4s, 4 mi., green.

Devils Head Light 4
47 10.0N, 122 45.9W, Fl R 6s, 16 ft., 4 mi., TR on dolphin.

Johnson Point Light 5
47 10.7N, 122 48.9W, Fl G 6s, 22 ft., 7 mi., SG on pile.

North Head Light
46 17.9N, 124 04.7W, Fl (2) W 30s, 194 ft., 26 mi., white conical tower, light is obscured eastward of 181°.

Oak Bay Buoy 2
48 00.2N, 122 41.6W, red nun.

OAK HARBOR

Also see Saratoga Passage.

Lighted Buoy 2
48 15.5N, 122 37.5W, Fl R 4s, 3 mi., red.

Daybeacon 4
TR on pile.

Light 5
Fl G 4s, 15 ft., 5 mi., SG on dolphin.

Shoal Lighted Buoy 5A
Fl G 4s, green, marks shoal.

Buoy 7
48 16.3N, 122 38.9W, green can.

Lighted Buoy 8
Fl R 6s, 4 mi., red.

Daybeacon 10
TR on pile.

Light 11
Fl G 6s, 15 ft., 5 mi., SG on dolphin.

Light 12
Fl R 2.5s, 22 ft., 3 mi., TR on dolphin.

Daybeacon 14
TR on pile.

Marina

Breakwater Light 2
48 17.2N, 122 38.1W, Oc R 11s, 8 ft., on breakwater, private aid.

Breakwater Light
48 17.1N, 122 38.1W, Oc Y 11s, 8 ft., on breakwater, private aid.

South Entrance Light 1
48 17.0N, 122 38.1W, Oc G 11s, 8 ft., on breakwater, private aid.

South Entrance Light 2
48 17.0N, 122 38.1W, Oc R 11s, 8 ft., on pile, private aid.

North Entrance Light 1
48 17.2N, 122 38.1W, Oc G 11s, 17 ft., on pile, private aid.

North Entrance Light 2
48 17.2N, 122 38.1W, Oc R 11s, 17 ft., on pile, private aid.

Oak Head Light 12
47 40.9N, 122 48.7W, Fl R 4s, 15 ft., 5 mi., TR on pile, radar reflector.
Also see Hood Canal.

Obstruction Island
See Obstruction Pass Light *and* Peavine Pass Light 1.

Obstruction Pass Light
Fl W 4s, 23 ft., 5 mi., NR on white house.
Also see Rosario Strait

Ogden Point Breakwater Light (Canada)
48 24.8N, 123 23.6W, Q R, 40 ft., white square tower, red band around bottom, horn: 1 blast every 30s, horn points 205°.

OLYMPIA HARBOR

Approaches

Olympia Shoal Light
47 05.5N, 122 55.2W, Q W, 25 ft., 8 mi., NB on skeleton tower, horn: 1 blast every 30s.

West Olympia Shoal Light 1
47 05.5N, 122 55.5W, Fl G 4s, 21 ft., 5 mi., SG on dolphin.

Budd Inlet Light 2
47 05.5N, 122 55.8W, Fl R 4s, 15 ft., 4 mi., TR on dolphin.

Olympia Entrance Lighted Buoy 2A
47 05.1N, 122 55.8W, Fl R 2.5s, 3 mi., red.

Olympia Entrance Light 3
47 05.1N, 122 55.6W, Fl G 2.5s, 22 ft., 4 mi., SG on white platform on dolphin.

Range Front Light
47 03.9N, 122 54.4W, Q G, 15 ft., KRB on dolphin, visible all around, higher intensity on rangeline.

Range Rear Light
325 yards, 144.6° from front light, Iso G 6s, 40 ft., KRB on skeleton tower, visible 4° each side of rangeline.

Olympia Channel Lighted Buoy 4
47 04.4N, 122 55.0W, Fl R 6s, 3 mi., red.

Olympia Channel Light 5
Fl G 4s, 17 ft., 5 mi., SG on pile structure.

Olympia Channel Lighted Buoy 6
Fl R 2.5s, 3 mi., red.

Olympia Channel Lighted Buoy 8
47 03.9N, 122 54.5W, Fl R 4s, 3 mi., red.

Olympia Channel Buoy 10
Red nun.

Olympia Turning Basin Buoys 12, 14, 16, and 18
Red nuns.

East Bay

Junction Light (40 ft. outside channel limit)
47 04.0N, 122 54.5W, Fl (2+1) G 6s, 15 ft., 3 mi., JG on pile.

Light 1 (40 ft. outside channel limit)
47 03.7N, 122 53.9W, Fl G 2.5s, 28 ft., 3 mi., SG on pile.

Light 2 (40 ft. outside channel limit)
Fl R 2.5s, 28 ft., 3 mi., TR on pile.

Daybeacon 3 (40 ft. outside channel limit)
SG on pile.

Light 4
Fl R 4s, 9 ft., 3 mi., TR on platform.

Olympia Inner Range Front Light
47 04.1N, 122 54.5W, Q W, 14 ft., 6 mi., KRB on dolphin.

Olympia Inner Range Rear Light
235 yards, 354° from front light, Iso W 6s, 23 ft., KRB on dolphin.

Onamac Point Light 6
Fl R 6s, 15 ft., 5 mi., TR.
Also see Saratoga Passage.

Onamac Point Reef Buoy A
48 11.3N, 122 32.4W, white and orange bands, spherical buoy, private aid.

Orcas Island North Shore Buoy
48 42.9N, 122 53.4W, white with orange bands, can, orange diamond worded DANGER REEF.

Orcas Island North Shore Daybeacon
48 42.9N, 122 53.6W, NW on pile worded DANGER SUBMERGED ROCKS, maintained from March 15 to Oct. 15.
Also see Parker Reef Light.

Orchard Point Light
47 33.9N, 122 31.9W, Oc W 4s, 34 ft., 9 mi., white pyramidal concrete tower, horn: 2 blasts every 20s.
Also see Rich Passage.

ORCHARD ROCKS

Also see Rich Passage.

Lighted Buoy 6
Fl R 2.5s, 4 mi., red.

Fish Pen Lights (3)
47 34.6N, 122 31.7W, Fl Y 6s, on aquaculture facility, private aids.

Daybeacon
JR on pile.

ORO BAY

Also see Nisqually Reach.

Lighted Buoy 2
47 08.3N, 122 42.1W, Fl R 2s, red, private aid.

Lighted Buoy 3
47 08.3N, 122 42.2W, Fl G 2s, green, private aid.

Lighted Buoy 4
47 08.3N, 122 41.7W, Fl R 2s, red, private aid.

P

PADILLA BAY

Vendovi Island Light 2
48 36.5N, 122 35.9W, Fl R 6s, 13 ft., 5 mi., TR on platform, radar reflector.

William Point Light
48 35.0N, 122 33.6W, Fl W 4s, 13 ft., 5 mi., NB.

Lighted Bell Buoy 4
48 34.7N, 122 35.8W, Fl R 4s, 4 mi., red.

Lighted Gong Buoy 5
48 33.5N, 122 34.5W, Fl G 4s, 4 mi., green.

Huckleberry Island Light 6
48 32.2N, 122 34.0W, Fl R 2.5s, 73 ft., 4 mi., TR on platform, radar reflector.

Saddlebag Island Light 7
48 32.1N, 122 33.5W, Fl G 2.5s, 26 ft., 4 mi., SG on platform, radar reflector.

Palix River Light 15
46 37.9N, 123 56.6W, Fl G 4s, 5 mi., SG on dolphin.
Also see Willapa Bay.

Parker Reef Light
Fl W 4s, 15 ft., 5 mi., NR on pile structure, radar reflector.

Partridge Bank Buoy 1
48 15.5N, 122 50.2W, green can.

Partridge Bank Lighted Bell Buoy 3
48 14.8N, 122 50.0W, Fl G 6s, 6 mi., green.
Also see Point Partridge.

Patos Island Light
48 47.3N, 122 58.3W, Fl W 6s (2 R sectors), 52 ft., white 9 mi., red 6 mi., white square tower on fog signal house, red from 011.5° to 059.5°, covers six-fathom shoal, red from 097° to 114°, covers Rosenfeld Rock, horn: 1 blast every 30s, operates continuously.
Also see Boundary Pass.

Peale Passage Fish Pen Lights (2)
47 11.7N, 122 54.2W, Fl Y 6s, private aids.

Peapod Rocks Light 15
Fl G 4s, 35 ft., 5 mi., SG on white octagonal house.
Also see Rosario Strait.

PEARL ISLAND

Also see Roche Harbor.

Pearl Island Light 1
48 37.0N, 123 10.2W, Fl G 4s, 15 ft., 4 mi., SG on skeleton tower.

Pearl Island Pier Lights (2)
F R, 16 ft., on dolphins, private aids.

Pearl Island Dock Light
F R, 18 ft., on pile, private aid.

Peavine Pass Light 1
48 35.3N, 122 49.3W, Fl G 4s, 22 ft., 5 mi., SG on skeleton tower.

Peavine Pass Rocks Daybeacon
NR on spindle, radar reflector.

PENN COVE

Snatelum Point Buoy 1 (marks shoal off point)
48 13.7N, 122 37.3W, green can.
Also see Saratoga Passage.

Penn Cove Mussel Raft Lights (4)
48 13.2N, 122 42.1W, Fl Y 6s, on aquaculture facility, private aids.

West Coast Blue Mussel Lights (2)
48 13.1N, 122 42.6W, Fl Y 6s, on two wooden aquaculture rafts, private aids.

Rolling Hills Pier Light
48 14.2N, 122 42.5W, Fl Y 5s,
16 ft., on end of pier, private aid.

PITT PASSAGE

Also see Carr Inlet.

North Shoal Daybeacon 4.
47 13.5N, 122 42.8W, TR on pile.

Rocks Daybeacon
47 13.1N, 122 43.0W, NW on pile
worded DANGER SHOAL.

Buoy 6
47 13.0N, 122 43.0W, red nun.

Point Bolin Reef Light 6
47 41.8N, 122 34.6W, Fl R 2.5s,
15 ft., 4 mi., TR on dolphin, radar
reflector.
Also see Agate Passage.

**Point Defiance Ferry Dolphin
Light**
47 18.4N, 122 30.8W, Fl R 10s,
on dolphin, private aid.

Point Defiance Light
47 19.0N, 122 32.9W, Fl W 6s,
21 ft., 11 mi., NG on pile structure, horn: 1 blast every 15s.
Also see The Narrows.

Point Evans Light 4
Fl R 4s, 18 ft., 4 mi., TR on pile.
Also see The Narrows.

Point Fairfax Light (Canada)
48 42.0N, 123 17.8W, Fl (3) W 12s,
33 ft., on white tower, 4 lights.
Also see Haro Strait.

Point Glover Light 9
47 35.4N, 122 33.0W, Q G, 25 ft.,
6 mi., SG on platform, horn:
1 blast every 30s.
Also see Rich Passage.

Point Hannon Light 2
47 53.3N, 122 36.6W, Fl R 2.5s,
15 ft., 4 mi., TR on skeleton
tower.
Also see Hood Canal.

Point Herron Light 12
47 33.9N, 122 36.8W, Fl R 6s,
24 ft., 7 mi., TR on pile structure,
horn: 1 blast every 30s.
Also see Rich Passage.

Point Heyer Reef Buoy A
47 25.1N, 122 25.6W, white and
orange bands, spherical buoy,
private aid.
Also see East Passage.

POINT HUDSON

Also see Port Townsend *and*
Admiralty Inlet.

Point Hudson Light
48 07.0N, 122 45.0W, Iso R 6s,
25 ft., 7 mi., NB on skeleton
tower, horn: 2 blasts every 20s.

**Point Hudson Spit Lighted Bell
Buoy 2**
48 07.3N, 122 44.7W, Fl R 4s,
4 mi., red.

Point Hudson Marina Light
48 06.9N, 122 44.9W, F Y, 24 ft.,
on pile, private aid.

Point Migley Lighted Buoy
48 45.3N, 122 43.5W, Fl (2+1) R 6s,
3 mi., red and green bands.
Also see Hale Passage.

Point Monroe Light
47 42.5N, 122 30.7W, Iso W 6s,
30 ft., 6 mi., NG on skeleton
tower, obscured from 321°
to 089°.

Point No Point Light
47 54.7N, 122 31.6W, Fl (3) W 10s,
27 ft., 19 mi., white octagonal
tower on building, horn: 2 blasts
every 30s.

Point Partridge Light
48 13.5N, 122 46.2W, Fl W 5s,
105 ft., 18 mi., NB on skeleton
tower, horn: 1 blast every 30s,
lighted throughout 24 hours.

**Point Partridge Lighted Bell
Buoy 5**
48 13.2N, 122 47.0W, Fl G 4s,
4 mi., green.
Also see Partridge Bank buoys.

Point Polnell Light
48 16.4N, 122 33.6W, Fl W 6s,
100 ft., 6 mi., NB on steel tower,
higher intensity beam toward
Onamac Point.
Also see Saratoga Passage.

POINT ROBERTS

Also see International Boundary.

Point Roberts Light
48 58.3N, 123 05.0W, Fl (2) W 15s,
30 ft., 15 mi., NR on skeleton
tower.

Lighted Bell Buoy 4
48 57.1N, 122 59.2W, Fl R 4s,
5 mi., red.

The Basin Light 1
48 58.4N, 123 03.8W, Fl G 4s,
15 ft., on pile, private aid.

The Basin Light 2
48 58.4N, 123 03.8W, Fl R 4s,
20 ft., on southwest end of breakwater, private aid.

The Basin Breakwater Light
48 58.4N, 123 03.7W, Fl Y 10s,
20 ft., on northeast end of breakwater, private aid.

Point Vashon Light
47 30.8N, 122 28.3W, Fl W 4s, 17 ft.,
7 mi., NB on pile structure.
Also see Colvos Passage.

POINT WELLS

Range Front Light
47 47.1N, 122 23.8W, F R, 44 ft.,
KRB on skeleton tower, visible 4°
each side of rangeline.

Range Rear Light
337 yards, 149° from front light,
F R, 81 ft., KRB on skeleton tower,
visible 4° each side of rangeline.

Fog Signal
47 46.9N, 122 23.8W, on pole,
horn: 1 blast every 30s, private
aid.

Point White Light 10
47 35.4N, 122 34.0W, Fl R 4s,
15 ft., 5 mi., TR on dolphin, radar
reflector.
Also see Rich Passage.

Point Wilson Light
48 08.6N, 122 45.3W, Oc W &
Fl R 20s, 51 ft., white 16 mi., red
15 mi., white octagonal tower on
fog signal building, horn: 1 blast
every 30s.
Also see Admiralty Inlet.

Point Wilson Lighted Buoy 6
48 09.1N, 122 45.9W, Fl R 4s,
4 mi., red.

Pole Pass Light 2
48 36.1N, 122 59.4W, Fl R 4s, 15 ft.,
4 mi., TR on skeleton tower.
Also see San Juan Channel.

Polnell Point Light
See Point Polnell Light.

Port Angeles

Also see Ediz Hook.

Port Dock Light
48 07.6N, 123 26.2W, F Y, 17 ft., on
pile, private aid.

Boat Haven Lighted Buoy 3
48 07.7N, 123 26.9W, Fl G 4s,
4 mi., green.

Mooring Basin West Light
48 07.6N, 123 27.1W, F R, 17 ft.,
on dolphin, private aid.

Mooring Basin East Light
48 07.6N, 123 27.1W, F G, 17 ft.,
on breakwater, private aid.

Boat Haven Light
48 07.6N, 123 27.1W, Fl W 2.5s,
17 ft., on mast, private aid.

Port Gamble

Also see Hood Canal.

Range Front Light
47 52.8N, 122 34.7W, Q W, 26 ft.,
KRB on skeleton tower, visible all
around, higher intensity on
rangeline.

Range Rear Light
300 yards, 001° from front light,
Iso W 6s, 40 ft., KRB on skeleton
tower, visible 4° each side of
rangeline.

Light 1
47 51.8N, 122 34.7W, Fl G 4s,
15 ft., 4 mi., SG on dolphin.

Inner Light 3
Fl G 6s, 18 ft., 5 mi., SG on
dolphin.

Port Gardner and Snohomish River

Also see Possession Sound.

Steamboat Flats Light
48 00.9N, 122 16.2W, Fl W 2.5s,
29 ft., 5 mi., NB on pile structure,
radar reflector.

Lighted Bell Buoy 1
47 59.4N, 122 15.1W, Fl G 6s,
5 mi., green.

**Anchorage Obstruction Lighted
Buoy AO**
47 58.9N, 122 14.8W, Fl Y 4s,
5 mi., yellow.

NOAA Research Lighted Buoy PG
47 59.1N, 122 13.5W, Fl Y 4s, gray
and yellow, 10 feet above water's
surface.

Snohomish River

Entrance Range Front Light
47 59.5N, 122 13.4W, Q R, 33 ft.,
KRB on skeleton tower, visible 4°
each side of rangeline.

Entrance Range Rear Light
1063 yards, 037.4° from front
light, Iso R 6s, 100 ft., KRB on
skeleton tower, visible 4° each
side of rangeline.

Lighted Buoy 3
47 58.9N, 122 14.1W, Fl G 2.5s,
4 mi., green.

Light 5
47 59.3N, 122 13.8W, Fl G 4s,
16 ft., 5 mi., SG on multi-pile.

NAVSTA Pier Lights (2)
47 59.5N, 122 13.4W, F R, 9 ft., on
northwest and southwest corner
of pier, private aids.

Anthonys Lighthouse
47 59.7N, 122 13.4W, Fl W 2.5s,
60 ft., 10 mi., red and white
wooden building, private aid.

**Port of Everett Jetty Island
Lights (3)**
48 00.2N, 122 13.6W, Fl Y 4s, on
float, private aid.

Range Front Light
48 01.1N, 122 13.4W, Q G, 17 ft.,
KRB on skeleton tower, visible all
around, higher intensity on
rangeline.

Range Rear Light
339 yards, 002.5° from front light,
Iso G 6s, 40 ft., KRB on same
structure as Snohomish River
Range C Rear Daybeacon, visible
all around, higher intensity on
rangeline.

Range A Front Daybeacon
48 00.6N, 122 13.6W, KRB on
skeleton tower.

Range A Rear Daybeacon
79 yards, 213.7° from front daybeacon, KRB on skeleton tower.

Range B Front Daybeacon
48 00.9N, 122 13.5W, KRB on
skeleton tower.

Range B Rear Daybeacon
233 yards, 236.1° from front daybeacon, KRB on skeleton tower.

Range C Front Daybeacon
48 01.1N, 122 13.3W, KRB on
skeleton tower.

Range C Rear Daybeacon
267 yards, 255.1° from front daybeacon, KRB on skeleton tower,
on same structure as Snohomish
River Range Rear Light.

Buoy 5A
48 01.2N, 122 12.9W, green can.

Channel Light 6
Fl R 4s, 15 ft., 5 mi., TR on pile.

Port Ludlow

Also see Hood Canal.

**Buoy 2 (marks S limit of Colvos
Rocks)**
47 56.7N, 122 39.5W, red nun.

Light 4
47 55.3N, 122 40.9W, Q R, 15 ft.,
3 mi., TR on dolphin.

Port Ludlow Marina Buoy
47 55.3N, 122 41.0W, red nun,
private aid.

**Meydenbauer Yacht Club
Mooring Pier Light**
47 55.0N, 122 41.4W, F Y, 8 ft.,
private aid.

Port Madison

See Point Monroe Light, Treasure Island Shoal Daybeacon 2, *and* Agate Passage Light 2.

Port Orchard

Marina Entrance Light 1
Fl G 4s, 10 ft., on pile, private aid.

Marina Entrance Light 2
Fl R 4s, 5 ft., on pedestal, private aid.

Yacht Club Light A
47 32.4N, 122 38.8W, Fl Y 10s, 7 ft., on breakwater, private aid.

Yacht Club Light 2
47 32.4N, 122 38.8W, Fl R 10s, 7 ft., on breakwater, private aid.

Yacht Club Light 3
47 32.4N, 122 38.7W, Fl G 10s, 7 ft., on breakwater, private aid.

Yacht Club Light D
47 32.4N, 122 38.7W, Fl Y 10s, 7 ft., on breakwater, private aid.

Port of Poulsbo

Liberty Bay Daybeacon 2
47 42.5N, 122 37.6W, TR on pile.

Liberty Bay Marina Lights (2)
F R, 2 mi., on corner of marina, private aids.

Poulsbo Yacht Club Breakwater Lights (2)
47 43.6N, 122 38.5W, F Y, concrete breakwater, private aids.

South Breakwater Light B
Fl Y 10s, private aid.

Middle Breakwater Light C
Fl Y 5s, 16 ft., private aid.

North Breakwater Light D
Fl R 5s, 16 ft., on dolphin, private aid.

Port San Juan Lighted Whistle Buoy YK (Canada)
48 32.1N, 124 29.0W, Mo (A) W, red and white stripes.
Also see San Juan Point Light.

Port Townsend

Point Hudson Light
48 07.0N, 122 45.0W, Iso R 6s, 25 ft., 7 mi., NB on skeleton tower, horn: 2 blasts every 20s.

Point Hudson Spit Lighted Bell Buoy 2
48 07.3N, 122 44.7W, Fl R 4s, 4 mi., red.

Point Hudson Marina Light
48 06.9N, 122 44.9W, F Y, 24 ft., on pile, private aid.

Port of Port Townsend Dolphin Light A
48 06.9N, 122 45.1W, Fl Y 4s, 17 ft., dolphin, private aid.

Port of Port Townsend Dolphin Light B
48 06.9N, 122 45.2W, Fl Y 4s, 17 ft., dolphin, private aid.

Ferry Dock Lights (2)
48 06.5N, 122 45.9W, Fl Y 10s, private aids.

Breakwater Light 1
48 06.5N, 122 46.3W, Fl G 4s, 15 ft., 5 mi., SG on tower.

Breakwater Light 2
Fl R 4s, 15 ft., 4 mi., TR on steel tower.

Paper Dock Light A
48 05.6N, 122 47.5W, F R, 30 ft., on post on building, horn: 1 blast every 19s, visible from 168° to 348°, private aid.

Paper Dock Light B
48 05.6N, 122 47.5W, F G, 30 ft., on post on building, private aid.

Island Dock Light A
48 05.6N, 122 47.6W, F R, 25 ft., on post on dock corner, private aid.

Island Dock Light B
48 05.6N, 122 47.6W, F G, 25 ft., on post on dock corner, private aid.

Outfall Lighted Buoy
48 05.4N, 122 47.6W, Fl Y 8s, yellow, private aid.

Kala Point Light 2
48 03.5N, 122 46.0W, Fl R 4s, 25 ft., 5 mi., TR on skeleton tower.

Canal Light 4
Fl R 4s, 16 ft., 5 mi., TR on dolphin.

Canal Light 6
Fl R 4s, 13 ft., 5 mi., TR on steel tower.

Canal Daybeacon 7
SG on dolphin, radar reflector.

Possession Sound

Possession Point Lighted Bell Buoy 1
47 53.8N, 122 23.1W, Fl G 4s, 5 mi., green.

Mukilteo Light
47 56.9N, 122 18.3W, Fl W 5s, 33 ft., 14 mi., white octagonal tower attached to building, horn: 1 blast every 30s.

Washington State Ferry Dolphin Light
47 57.0N, 122 18.1W, Fl Y 10s, 16 ft., private aid.

Clinton Shoal Buoy
47 58.6N, 122 20.9W, white with orange bands, spherical, private aid.

Gedney Island Fishing Reef Buoy A
47 59.8N, 122 18.6W, white and orange bands, spherical buoy, private aid.

Gedney Island Buoy 1
48 00.3N, 122 17.7W, green can.

Hat Island Marina Lighted Buoy A
48 01.3N, 122 19.2W, Q Y, on raft, private aid.

Hat Island Marina Breakwater Light 2
48 01.2N, 122 19.2W, F R, 8 ft., on pile structure, private aid.

Poulsbo
See Port of Poulsbo.

Protection Island Southwest Spit Buoy 1
48 06.9N, 122 57.9W, green can.

Pt. Chehalis
See Grays Harbor.

Puffin Island Shoal Light 19
Fl G 4s, 20 ft., 5 mi., SG on house on cylindrical structure.
Also see Rosario Strait.

PUGET SOUND TRAFFIC LANE

Entrance Lighted Buoy S
48 12.4N, 123 06.6W, Fl Y 4s, 4 mi., yellow, racon: Z (--··).

Separation Lighted Buoy SA
48 11.5N, 122 49.8W, Fl Y 4s, 4 mi., yellow, racon: M (--).

Separation Lighted Buoy SC
48 01.9N, 122 38.2W, Fl Y 4s, 4 mi., yellow.
Also see Admiralty Inlet.

Separation Lighted Buoy SD
47 57.9N, 122 34.8W, Fl Y 4s, 6 mi., yellow.

Separation Lighted Buoy SE
47 55.4N, 122 29.6W, Fl Y 4s, 6 mi., yellow, racon: T (-).
Also see Admiralty Inlet.

Separation Lighted Buoy SF
47 45.9N, 122 26.3W, Fl Y 4s, 6 mi., yellow, racon: G (--··).

Separation Lighted Buoy SG
47 39.7N, 122 27.9W, Fl Y 4s, 6 mi., yellow, racon: N (-·).

Separation Lighted Buoy T
47 34.6N, 122 27.0W, Fl Y 4s, Fl Y 2.5s, 6 mi., yellow, Fl Y 2.5s high-intensity flash tube.
Also see East Passage.

Separation Lighted Buoy TA
47 26.9N, 122 24.3W, Fl Y 4s, 6 mi., yellow.

Separation Lighted Buoy TB
47 23.1N, 122 21.2W, Fl Y 4s, Fl Y 2.5s, 6 mi., yellow, Fl Y 2.5s high-intensity flash tube.

Separation Lighted Buoy TC
47 19.5N, 122 27.4W, Fl Y 4s, Fl Y 2.5s, 6 mi., yellow, Fl Y 2.5s high-intensity flash tube.
Also see East Passage.

Pulali Point Light
47 44.3N, 122 51.2W, Fl W 4s, 30 ft., 5 mi., NG on white house, radar reflector.
Also see Dabob Bay.

Puyallup Waterway
See Tacoma Harbor.

Q

Quartermaster Harbor Shoal Buoy 2
47 20.9N, 122 28.6W, red nun.

QUILCENE BAY

Also see Dabob Bay.

Quilcene Bay Light 2
47 46.7N, 122 51.2W, Fl R 4s, 26 ft., 5 mi., TR on pile, obscured from 170° to 260°, radar reflector.

Fish Pen Light A
47 47.3N, 122 51.0W, Fl Y 6s, 6 mi., on wooden fish pen, private aid.

Fish Pen Light B
47 47.3N, 122 51.0W, Fl Y 6s, 6 mi., on wooden fish pen, private aid.

QUILLAYUTE RIVER

Approach Lighted Whistle Buoy Q
47 53.1N, 124 40.5W, Mo (A) W, 5 mi., red and white stripes.

James Island Light
47 54.3N, 124 38.8W, Fl W 6s, 150 ft., 9 mi., white house, horn: 2 blasts every 30s, operates continuously, light is obscured from 068° to 101° and from 111° to 293°.

Entrance Buoy 2
47 53.7N, 124 38.8W, red nun.

Direction Light
47 54.5N, 124 38.7W, Iso W 6s (R & G sectors), 15 ft., on pile, on same structure as Quillayute River Entrance Light 3, white visible 1° each side of centerline of channel bearing 001°, red visible from 358.5° to 000°, green visible from 002° to 003.5°.

Entrance Light 3
47 54.5N, 124 38.7W, Fl G 4s, 15 ft., 4 mi., SG on pile, on same structure as Quillayute River Direction Light, obscured on rangeline.

Entrance Buoy 3A
47 54.5N, 124 38.6W, green can, maintained from May 1 to Oct. 1.

Buoy 5
Green can, position shifted with changing conditions, maintained from May 1 to Oct. 15.

Buoy 7
Green can, position shifted with changing conditions, maintained from May 1 to Oct. 15.

Entrance Small Boat Warning Sign
Q Y (2), 34 ft., NW worded ROUGH BAR, lights flashing when seas exceed four feet in height, lights extinguished for lesser sea conditions, but with no guarantee that bar is safe.

Boat Basin Light 1
47 54.6N, 124 38.3W, Fl G 4s, 17 ft., 3 mi., SG on dolphin.

Boat Basin Light 2
47 54.6N, 124 38.3W, Fl R 4s, 17 ft., 3 mi., TR on dolphin.

R

RACE ROCKS (CANADA)

Race Rocks Light
48 17.9N, 123 31.8W, Fl W 10s, 118 ft., 18 mi., alternate black and white bands on circular stone tower, with dwelling attached, horn: 3 blasts every 60s, should not be approached within 1 mile to clear Rosedale Reef.

Race Rocks Radiobeacon
48 17.9N, 123 31.8W, J (·---), 309 kHz.

South Cautionary Lighted Buoy VF
48 14.1N, 123 31.9W, Fl Y 4s, yellow.

Traffic Lane Separation Lighted Buoy PA
48 12.4N, 123 27.7W, Fl Y 4s, 6 mi., yellow.

East Cautionary Lighted Buoy VG
48 16.1N, 123 27.7W, Fl Y 4s, yellow.

Reef Point Junction Lighted Buoy
48 31.7N, 122 43.6W, Fl (2+1) R 6s,
5 mi., red and green bands.
Also see Rosario Strait *and*
Bellingham Channel.

Reid Rock Lighted Bell Buoy
48 32.9N, 122 59.4W, Fl (2+1) G 6s,
5 mi., green and red bands,
rock has depth of 2.5 fathoms
over it.
Also see San Juan Channel.

RICH PASSAGE

**Bainbridge Reef Lighted Bell
Buoy 4**
47 34.1N, 122 31.1W, Fl R 4s,
4 mi., red.

Orchard Point Light
47 33.9N, 122 31.9W, Oc W 4s,
34 ft., 9 mi., white pyramidal
concrete tower, horn: 2 blasts
every 20s.

Orchard Rocks Lighted Buoy 6
Fl R 2.5s, 4 mi., red.

Clam Bay Fish Pen Lights (2)
Fl Y 6s, 8 ft., on pile, private aids.

Rich Passage Fish Pen Lights (2)
47 34.5N, 122 31.6W, Fl Y 6s, on
aquaculture facility, private aids.

Orchard Rocks Fish Pen Lights (3)
47 34.6N, 122 31.7W, Fl Y 6s, on
aquaculture facility, private aids.

Orchard Rocks Daybeacon
JR on pile.

Beans Point Fish Pen Lights (2)
Fl Y 6s, 4 ft., on pedestal, private
aids.

Lighted Buoy 8
47 35.6N, 122 32.6W, Fl R 2.5s,
4 mi., red.

Point Glover Light 9
47 35.4N, 122 33.0W, Q G, 25 ft.,
6 mi., SG on platform, horn:
1 blast every 30s.

Point White Light 10
47 35.4N, 122 34.0W, Fl R 4s,
15 ft., 5 mi., TR on dolphin,
radar reflector.

Waterman Point Light 11
47 35.1N, 122 34.3W, Oc G 4s,
26 ft., 7 mi., SG on skeleton
tower, horn: 1 blast every 15s.
Also see Point Herron Light 12.

Richardson Daybeacon
48 26.9N, 122 54.6W, NR on white
box.
Also see Twin Rocks Daybeacon
and San Juan Channel.

Robinson Point Light
47 23.3N, 122 22.5W, Fl (2) W 12s,
40 ft., 14 mi., white octagonal
tower, horn: 1 blast every 30s.
Also see East Passage.

ROCHE HARBOR

Also see Mosquito Pass.

Pearl Island Light 1
48 37.0N, 123 10.2W, Fl G 4s, 15 ft.,
4 mi., SG on skeleton tower.

Pearl Island Pier Lights (2)
F R, 16 ft., on dolphins, private
aids.

Pearl Island Dock Light
F R, 18 ft., on pile, private aid.

North Roche Harbor Dock Light
F R, 10 ft., on pile, private aid.

Roche Harbor Junction Buoy
Red and green bands, nun, rock
is marked by kelp and has 2 fathoms over it.

Rolling Hills Pier Light
48 14.2N, 122 42.5W, Fl Y 5s,
16 ft., on end of pier, private aid.
Also see Penn Cove.

ROSARIO STRAIT

**Traffic Lane Entrance Lighted
Buoy R**
48 16.4N, 123 06.7W, Fl Y 4s,
6 mi., yellow, racon: T (-).

**Traffic Lane Separation Lighted
Buoy RA**
48 19.8N, 122 58.6W, Fl Y 6s,
7 mi., yellow, racon: N (-·).

**Lawson Reef Junction Lighted
Bell Buoy**
48 24.1N, 122 43.0W, Fl (2+1) R 6s,
5 mi., red and green bands.

Davidson Rock Light 1
Fl G 4s, 15 ft., 6 mi., SG on platform, higher intensity beam
toward Burrows Island Light.

Lawson Reef Lighted Bell Buoy 2
48 24.7N, 122 46.4W, Fl R 2.5s,
4 mi., red.

Kellett Ledge Buoy 3
48 27.0N, 122 47.5W, green can.

**Williamson Rocks Lighted Gong
Buoy 4**
48 26.8N, 122 42.4W, Fl R 4s,
5 mi., red.

Dennis Shoal Buoy 6
48 27.5N, 122 43.0W, red nun.

Burrows Island Light
48 28.7N, 122 42.8W, Fl W 6s (R
sector), 57 ft., white 10 mi., red
8 mi., white square tower on
building, red from 311° to 009°,
covers Allan Island and Dennis
Shoal, horn: 2 blasts every 30s.

Lopez Pass Light 2
Fl R 4s, 21 ft., 5 mi., TR on house.

Belle Rock Sector Light
Fl W 2.5s (R sector), 22 ft. white
5 mi., 20 ft., red 9 mi., NB on
black cylindrical base, red from
173° to 177°, covers 42-foot shoal,
higher intensity white beam up
and down channel, aid displays
2 separate lights, white over red.

Reef Point Junction Lighted Buoy
48 31.7N, 122 43.6W, Fl (2+1) R 6s,
5 mi., red and green bands.
Also see Bellingham Channel.

Fauntleroy Point Light
Fl W 4s, 37 ft., 7 mi., NB on skeleton tower.

**Lawson Rock Buoy 2 (near
Blakeley Island)**
48 31.8N, 122 47.1W, red nun.

**Lawson Rock Danger Daybeacon
(near Blakeley Island)**
48 31.8N, 122 47.3W, NW on pile
worded DANGER ROCK, radar
reflector.

Blakeley Island Light
48 31.9N, 122 48.5W, Fl R 6s,
12 ft., 5 mi., TR on pile.

Black Rock Light 9
48 32.8N, 122 45.9W, Fl G 4s,
10 ft., 4 mi., SG on skeleton
tower.

Tide Point Light 12
48 35.1N, 122 44.5W, Fl R 2.5s,
15 ft., 4 mi., TR on pile.

Obstruction Pass Light
Fl W 4s, 23 ft., 5 mi., NR on white house.

Lydia Shoal Lighted Gong Buoy 13
48 36.0N, 122 46.7W, Q G, 3 mi., green.

Cypress Reef Daybeacon C
48 36.8N, 122 43.3W, JR on pile.

Buckeye Shoal Lighted Bell Buoy 14 (marks shoal W of Sinclair Island)
Fl R 6s, 5 mi., red.

Peapod Rocks Light 15
Fl G 4s, 35 ft., 5 mi., SG on white octagonal house.

Lighted Bell Buoy 16
48 38.4N, 122 42.9W, Q R, 4 mi., red.

Boulder Reef Lighted Bell Buoy 2
Fl R 4s, 4 mi., red.

Sinclair Island Lighted Bell Buoy 4
48 38.3N, 122 40.1W, Fl R 2.5s, 5 mi., red.

Lummi Rocks Light 16A
48 40.2N, 122 40.1W, Fl R 6s, 20 ft., 6 mi., TR on skeleton tower.

The Sisters Light 17
48 41.7N, 122 45.4W, Fl G 2.5s, 40 ft., 4 mi., SG on structure.

Traffic Lane Lighted Buoy C
48 40.6N, 122 42.8W, Fl Y 4s, 6 mi., yellow, racon: N (-·).

Village Point Light 18
Fl R 4s, 24 ft., 5 mi., TR on skeleton tower, higher intensity beam towards Rosario Strait and Boundary Bay, obscured from 180° to 264°.

Puffin Island Shoal Light 19
Fl G 4s, 20 ft., 5 mi., SG on house on cylindrical structure.

Traffic Lane Separation Lighted Buoy CA
48 45.3N, 122 46.5W, Fl Y 4s, 6 mi., yellow, racon: M (--).

S

Saddlebag Island Light 7
48 32.1N, 122 33.5W, Fl G 2.5s 26 ft., 4 mi., SG on platform, radar reflector.
Also see Padilla Bay.

Salmon Bank Lighted Gong Buoy 3
48 25.6N, 122 58.6W, Fl G 4s, 4 mi., green.
Also see San Juan Channel.

SAN JUAN CHANNEL

Iceberg Point Light 2
48 25.3N, 122 53.7W, Fl R 4s, 35 ft., 7 mi., TR on white square concrete house, horn: 1 blast every 30s, operates continuously from June 1 to Nov. 15.

Salmon Bank Lighted Gong Buoy 3
48 25.6N, 122 58.6W, Fl G 4s, 4 mi., green.

Cattle Point Light
48 27.0N, 122 57.8W, Fl W 4s, 94 ft., 5 mi., white octagonal tower, horn: 1 blast every 15s, operates continuously from June 1 to Nov. 15.

Cape San Juan Community Moorage Lights (3)
Fl Y 10s, on floats, private aids.

Fisherman Bay Sector Light
48 31.5N, 122 55.2W, Fl W 4s (R sector), 15 ft., 5 mi., NR on pile structure, red from 172.5° to 069.5°.
Also see Fisherman Bay.

Flat Point Light
48 33.2N, 122 55.3W, Fl R 2.5s, 15 ft., 5 mi., TR on pile.

Turn Rock Light 3
48 32.1N, 122 57.9W, Fl G 4s, 18 ft., 6 mi., SG on cylindrical base, rock ledge bares at half tide.
Also see Friday Harbor.

Reid Rock Lighted Bell Buoy
48 32.9N, 122 59.4W, Fl (2+1) G 6s, 5 mi., green and red bands, rock has depth of 2.5 fathoms over it.
Also see Friday Harbor.

Shirt Tail Reef Light 1
48 35.2N, 123 01.4W, Fl G 4s, 19 ft., 5 mi., SG on skeleton tower.

Cliff Island Light 3
Fl G 6s, 15 ft., 5 mi., SG on square house.

Bird Rocks Light
48 35.9N, 123 00.9W, Fl W 4s, 15 ft., 5 mi., NB on white platform on pile structure.

Deer Harbor Pier Light
F R, 15 ft., on pile, private aid.

Pole Pass Light 2
48 36.1N, 122 59.4W, Fl R 4s, 15 ft., 4 mi., TR on skeleton tower.

Wasp Passage Light 5
Fl G 4s, 15 ft., 5 mi., SG on pyramidal structure.

Green Point Light
48 38.0N, 123 06.4W, Fl W 4s, 20 ft., 6 mi., NB on skeleton tower.

San Juan Point Light (Canada)
48 31.9N, 124 27.4W, Fl R 5s, 57 ft., 12 mi., white circular tower, red band at top, on corner of white building, horn: 1 blast every 30s.
Also see Port San Juan Lighted Whistle Buoy YK.

Sandy Point Light 1 (Saratoga Passage)
48 02.1N, 122 22.6W, Fl G 4s, 24 ft., 5 mi., SG on cassion.
Also see Saratoga Passage.

Sandy Point Light 2 (Lummi Bay)
48 47.2N, 122 42.7W, Fl R 4s, 16 ft., 5 mi., TR on pile.

Sandy Point Light 3 (Lummi Bay)
48 47.3N, 122 42.7W, Fl G 2.5s, 15 ft., 4 mi., SG on pile.
Also see Tosco Northwest Lights, Intalco Lights, *and* Atlantic Richfield Lights.

SARATOGA PASSAGE

Also see Holmes Harbor, Penn Cove, *and* Oak Harbor.

Camano Head Buoy 1 (marks submerged rocks)
48 03.0N, 122 21.3W, green can.

Sandy Point Light 1
48 02.1N, 122 22.6W, Fl G 4s,
24 ft., 5 mi., SG on caisson.

Langley Breakwater

Light A
48 02.3N, 122 24.1W, F Y, 20 ft.,
on pile breakwater, private aid.

Light B
48 02.3N, 122 24.1W, F Y, 20 ft.,
on pile breakwater, private aid.

Light C
48 02.3N, 122 24.0W, F Y, 20 ft.,
on pile breakwater, private aid.

Light D
48 02.3N, 122 24.0W, F R, 20 ft.,
on pile breakwater, private
aid.

East Point Light 3
Fl G 6s, 21 ft., 6 mi., SG on steel
tower.

Light 4
Fl R 4s, 15 ft., 5 mi., TR.

Onamac Point Light 6
Fl R 6s, 15 ft., 5 mi., TR.

Onamac Point Reef Buoy A
48 11.3N, 122 32.4W, white and
orange bands, spherical buoy,
private aid.

**Snatelum Point Buoy 1 (marks
shoal off point)**
48 13.7N, 122 37.3W, green can.
Also see Penn Cove.

Point Polnell Light
48 16.4N, 122 33.6W, Fl W 6s,
100 ft., 6 mi., NB on steel tower,
higher intensity beam toward
Onamac Point.
Also see Skagit Bay.

**Scatchet Head Lighted Gong
Buoy 1**
47 54.5N, 122 26.3W, Fl G 6s,
5 mi., green.

Scroggs Rocks Light (Canada)
48 25.6N, 123 26.3W, Fl R 4s,
24 ft., white circular tower, red
band at top.

Seabeck Marina Light
47 38.7N, 122 49.7W, Fl Y 2.5s,
4 ft., on pile, private aid.
Also see Hood Canal.

Seal Rocks Light 12
48 22.4N, 122 33.8W, Fl R 4s,
20 ft., 4 mi., TR on tower.
Also see Skagit Bay.

Seattle
See Shilshole Bay and Boat Basin,
Elliott Bay, *and* Georgetown
Reach Range.

Secret Harbor Fish Pen Lights
See Deepwater Bay.

SEMIAHMOO BAY

Light
48 59.5N, 122 47.0W, Fl W 6s,
27 ft., 12 mi., NB on skeleton
tower, visible from 024° to 294°.

Buoy 1
48 59.7N, 122 46.8W, green can.

Buoy 2
48 59.4N, 122 47.5W, red nun.

Blaine Small Boat Harbor Light 2
Fl R 2.5s, 22 ft., 6 mi., TR on
dolphin.

**International Boundary Range C
Front Light**
49 00.1N, 122 46.9W, Q G, 37 ft.,
rectangular-shaped, orange daymark on gray skeleton tower.
Also see International Boundary.

**International Boundary Range C
Rear Light**
49 00.1N, 122 45.4W, F G, 80 ft.,
rectangular-shaped, orange daymark on gray tower, visible on
rangeline only.

SEQUIM BAY

Entrance Lighted Buoy 2
48 05.1N, 123 01.7W, Fl R 4s,
5 mi., red.

Entrance Buoy 4
Red nun.

Buoy 5
48 04.6N, 123 02.6W, green can.

Buoy 7
48 04.5N, 123 02.6W, green can.

Buoy 9
Green can.

Buoy 10
Red nun.

John Wayne Marina Light 2
48 03.9N, 123 02.3W, Fl R 2.5s,
21 ft., on north breakwater,
private aid.

John Wayne Marina Light 3
48 03.8N, 123 02.3W, Fl G 2.5s,
13 ft., on south breakwater,
private aid.

Shag Rock Daybeacon
NW on spindle worded DANGER
ROCKS.

Shannon Point Light
48 30.6N, 122 41.0W, Fl W 4s,
15 ft., 6 mi., NB on dolphin,
horn: 1 blast every 30s, operates
continuously.
Also see Guemes Channel.

Sheringham Point Light (Canada)
48 22.6N, 123 55.2W, Fl G 15s,
72 ft., 14 mi., white hexagonal
tower attached to rectangular
dwelling.

SHILSHOLE BAY AND
BOAT BASIN

Approach Lighted Bell Buoy
47 40.9N, 122 25.1W, Mo (A) W,
6 mi., red and white stripes.

**Park Department Boat Ramp
Light**
47 41.2N, 122 24.2W, F G, 10 ft.,
private aid.

Boat Basin Light 2
Q R, 17 ft., 5 mi., TR on pile.

**Corps of Engineers South Lighted
Mooring Buoy**
47 40.3N, 122 25.3W, Fl Y 4s,
white can, private aid.

Entrance Range Front Light
47 40.0N, 122 24.2W, Q R, 20 ft.,
KRB on dolphin, visible 4° each
side of rangeline.

Entrance Range Rear Light
250 yards, 146° from front light,
Iso R 6s, 81 ft., KRB on skeleton
tower, visible 4° each side of
rangeline.

Entrance Buoy 1
47 40.8N, 122 24.9W, green can.

Entrance Buoy 2
47 40.7N, 122 25.0W, red nun.

NOAA Research Lighted Buoy SB
47 40.7N, 122 24.8W, Fl Y 4s, gray and yellow, 10 feet above the water's surface.

Breakwater Light 3
47 40.6N, 122 24.7W, Fl G 2.5s, 22 ft., 5 mi., SG on white house, horn: 2 blasts every 20s.

Channel Buoy 4
Red nun.

Channel Buoy 6
Red nun.

Channel Buoy 7
Green can.

Inner Light 8
47 40.3N, 122 24.5W, Fl R 4s, 15 ft., 3 mi., TR on dolphin.

Channel Buoy 10
Red nun.
Also see Lake Washington Ship Canal.

Shipmates Light
47 37.3N, 122 21.8W, Fl W 2.5s, 25 ft., on brown hexagonal structure, private aid.
Also see Elliott Bay.

Shirt Tail Reef Light 1
48 35.2N, 123 01.4W, Fl G 4s, 19 ft., 5 mi., SG on skeleton tower.
Also see San Juan Channel.

Shoal Bay Aquaculture Light (Lopez Island)
48 33.4N, 122 52.4W, Fl Y 6s, on aquaculture facility, private aid.

Sinclair Inlet
See Point Herron Light 12 *and* Port Orchard.

Sinclair Island Lighted Bell Buoy 4
48 38.3N, 122 40.1W, Fl R 2.5s, 5 mi., red.
Also see Boulder Reef Lighted Bell Buoy 2 *and* Rosario Strait.

Sisters Light 17, The
See The Sisters Light 17.

Sisters Rock Light 4
47 51.5N, 122 38.5W, Fl R 4s, 15 ft., 5 mi., TR on wooden crib.
Also see Hood Canal.

Sitcum Waterway
See Tacoma Harbor.

SKAGIT BAY

Buoy 2
48 16.3N, 122 30.3W, red nun.

Strawberry Point Light 3
48 18.0N, 122 30.2W, Fl G 4s, 17 ft., 5 mi., SG on dolphin.

Lighted Buoy 4
48 18.1N, 122 29.1W, Fl R 4s, 4 mi., red.

Buoy 6
48 19.5N, 122 30.7W, red nun.

Buoy 6A
48 19.9N, 122 31.4W, red nun.

Lighted Buoy 8
48 20.4N, 122 32.1W, Fl R 4s, 4 mi., red.

Buoy 10
48 21.1N, 122 33.0W, red nun.
Also see Swinomish Channel.

Seal Rocks Light 12
48 22.4N, 122 33.8W, Fl R 4s, 20 ft., 4 mi., TR on tower.

Hope Island Light 14
Fl R 2.5s, 23 ft., 4 mi., TR on skeleton tower.
Also see Deception Pass.

Hope Island Fish Pen Light A
48 24.4N, 122 33.6W, Fl Y 6s, 5 ft., on aquaculture facility, private aid.

Hope Island Fish Pen Light C
48 24.4N, 122 33.7W, Fl Y 6s, 5 ft., on aquaculture facility, private aid.

Skipjack Island Light
48 44.0N, 123 02.4W, Fl W 4s, 55 ft., 5 mi., NB on steel tower, obscured from 261° to 347°.
Also see Boundary Pass.

Skunk Bay Light
47 55.2N, 122 34.1W, F R, 210 ft., white octagonal tower, private aid.
Also see Admiralty Inlet.

Skyline Marina Light 1
48 29.4N, 122 40.6W, Fl G 15s, 13 ft., on pile structure, private aid.

Skyline Marina Light 2
48 29.3N, 122 40.6W, Fl R 15s, 13 ft., on dolphin, private aid.

Slip Point Light
48 15.9N, 124 15.0W, Fl W 5s, 55 ft., 17 mi., white square tower on pile structure, horn: 1 blast every 30s, operates continuously.

Smith Cove
See Elliott Bay.

Smith Island Light
48 19.1N, 122 50.6W, Fl W 15s, 97 ft., 17 mi.

Snohomish River
See Port Gardner and Snohomish River.

South Willapa Bay
See Willapa Bay.

Speiden Channel Buoy 3
48 38.1N, 123 09.7W, green can.
Also see Danger Shoal Lighted Horn Buoy.

Squalicum Creek
See Bellingham Bay.

Squaxin Island Fish Pen Light A
47 12.0N, 122 54.2W, Fl Y 6s, 4 ft., aquaculture facility, private aid.

Squaxin Island Fish Pen Light B
47 12.1N, 122 54.2W, Fl Y 6s, 4 ft., aquaculture facility, private aid.

SQUAXIN PASSAGE

Hunter Point Light 1
47 10.4N, 122 55.2W, Fl G 4s, 15 ft., 7 mi., SG on tower.

Reef Buoy 2
Red nun.

Carlyon Beach Light
47 10.9N, 122 56.2W, Q W, 15 ft., private aid.

Stanley Channel
See Willapa Bay.

Steamboat Flats Light
48 00.9N, 122 16.2W, Fl W 2.5s, 29 ft., 5 mi., NB on pile structure, radar reflector.
Also see Port Gardner.

Strait of Juan de Fuca Calibration Lighted Bell Buoy
48 14.2N, 123 21.8W, Fl Y 6s, 6 mi., yellow.

Strait of Juan de Fuca Traffic Lane Separation Lighted Buoy J
48 29.2N, 124 43.7W, Fl Y 4s, 4 mi., ycllow, racon: O (---).

Strawberry Point Light 3
48 18.0N, 122 30.2W, Fl G 4s, 17 ft., 5 mi., SG on dolphin.
Also see Skagit Bay.

Sucia Island Daybeacon 1
48 45.8N, 122 55.1W, SG on pile.
Also see Ewing Island Reef Daybeacon *on E side of Sucia Island.*

Sucia Island Daybeacon 2 (marks submerged rock)
TR on pile.

SWINOMISH CHANNEL

South Entrance
Also see Skagit Bay.

Buoy 1
48 21.7N, 122 33.4W, green can.

Lighted Buoy 2
Fl R 2.5s, 4 mi., red.

Buoy 4
48 21.7N, 122 33.1W, red nun.

Daybeacon 6 (60 ft. outside channel limit)
TR on pile.

Daybeacon 8 (60 ft. outside channel limit)
TR on pile.

Daybeacon 10 (60 ft. outside channel limit)
TR on pile.

Light 11
Fl G 4s, 10 ft., 5 mi., SG on white platform on dolphin, obscured from 072° to 255°.

Range Front Light
48 21.5N, 122 34.1W, Q W, 16 ft., KRB on skeleton tower, visible all around, higher intensity on rangeline.

Range Rear Light
1,100 yards, 252° from front light, Iso W 6s, 40 ft., KRB on skeleton tower, visible 4° each side of rangeline.

Daybeacon 11A
48 22.0N, 122 31.9W, SG on pile.

Daybeacon 11B
48 22.1N, 122 31.6W, SG on pile.

Daybeacon 11C
48 22.2N, 122 31.3W, 15 ft., SG on pile.

Light 13
48 22.3N, 122 30.6W, Q G, 15 ft., 3 mi., SG on house on concrete crib.

Light 14
Q R, 15 ft., 4 mi., TR.

Daybeacon 15
48 22.5N, 122 30.6W, SG on pile.

Light 16
48 23.0N, 122 30.4W, Fl R 4s, 15 ft., 4 mi., TR on dolphin.

La Conner Marina South Basin Light
48 23.8N, 122 29.8W, F R, 11 ft., private aid.

La Conner Marina Light
48 24.0N, 122 29.7W, F R, 8 ft., on pile structure, private aid.

La Conner Range Front Light 18
48 24.8N, 122 29.8W, Q W, 15 ft., KRB on dolphin, TR oriented up channel, visible all around, higher intensity on rangeline.

La Conner Range Rear Light
180 yards, 002° from front light, Iso W 6s, 23 ft., KRB on skeleton tower, visible 4° each side of rangeline.

Buoy 19 (marks rock)
48 25.3N, 122 30.1W, green can.

Buoy 20
Red nun.

Light 21
48 25.4N, 122 30.1W, Fl G 4s, 27 ft., 5 mi., SG on dolphin, higher intensity beam up channel.

Buoy 22
48 25.5N, 122 30.0W, red nun.

North Entrance

Light 2
48 30.6N, 122 33.4W, Fl R 4s, 18 ft., 4 mi., TR on dolphin, radar reflector.

Buoy 4
Red nun.

Light 6
48 29.9N, 122 32.9W, Fl R 6s, 15 ft., 5 mi., TR on dolphin.

Buoy 7
48 29.8N, 122 32.6W, green can.

Buoy 8
Red nun.

Buoy 12
48 29.2N, 122 32.2W, red nun.

Buoy 13
Green can.

Buoy 14
Red nun.

Buoy 17
Green can.

Light 18
Fl R 4s, 18 ft., 4 mi., TR on dolphin, radar reflector.

Buoy 20
Red nun.

Buoy 22
48 28.3N, 122 31.6W, red nun.

Buoy 23
Green can.

Light 26
Fl R 4s, 15 ft., 4 mi., TR on pile, radar reflector.

Buoy 28
Red nun.

Buoy 29
Green can.

Buoy 30
48 27.7N, 122 31.1W, red nun.

T

Tabook Point Light 18
47 44.7N, 122 48.6W, Fl R 6s, 15 ft., 5 mi., TR on pile, radar reflector.
Also see Dabob Bay.

TACOMA HARBOR

Thea Foss Waterway Light
47 15.7N, 122 26.2W, Fl W 6s, 23 ft., 11 mi., light on pile, horn on dock, horn: 2 blasts every 20s.

Commencement Bay Shoal Lighted Buoy A
47 16.4N, 122 26.0W, Fl Y 4s, yellow.

Puyallup Waterway Jetty Daybeacon 1
47 16.2N, 122 25.6W, SG on dolphin.

Sitcum Waterway Light
47 16.3N, 122 25.1W, F R, 14 ft., on pile structure, private aid.

Blair Waterway Lighted Buoy
47 16.7N, 122 25.0W, Fl Y 10s, yellow, private aid.

Tacoma Outfall Lighted Buoy
47 16.7N, 122 25.2W, Fl Y 4s, yellow, private aid.

Commencement Bay Directional Light
47 16.8N, 122 24.9W, Fl (2+1) 6s (R & G sectors), 15 ft., 4 mi., on pile, centerline bearing 124°, white visible 3.25° each side of centerline, red visible from 116.5° to 120.75°, green visible from 127.25° to 131.5°.

Blair Terminal Light B
47 15.6N, 122 23.1W, F R, 11 ft., private aid.

Blair Terminal Light A
47 15.5N, 122 22.8W, F R, 11 ft., private aid.

Pierce Barge Terminal Light
47 15.2N, 122 22.8W, F R, 11 ft., private aid.

National Guard Pier Light A
47 17.1N, 122 24.8W, F R, 7 ft., private aid.

National Guard Pier Light B
47 17.0N, 122 24.5W, F R, 7 ft., private aid.

Hylebos Waterway West Fog Signal
47 17.1N, 122 24.8W, house on dock, horn: 1 blast every 15s, private aid.

Port of Tacoma Pier No. 25 Light
47 17.1N, 122 24.6W, F R, 7 ft., private aid.

Hylebos Waterway East Fog Signal
47 17.1N, 122 24.6W, tower on dock, bell: 1 stroke every 14s, private aid.

Hylebos Waterway Lighted Buoy 1
47 17.2N, 122 24.8W, Fl G 4s, 6 mi., green.

Chinook Landing Light A
47 16.9N, 122 24.2W, Fl Y 4s, 10 ft., on pile, private aid.

Chinook Landing Light B
47 16.9N, 122 24.2W, Fl Y 4s, 10 ft., on pile, private aid.

Tyee Marina Entrance Light
47 17.7N, 122 25.1W, Q G, private aid.

Tacoma Narrows
See The Narrows.

Tala Point Junction Light
47 55.9N, 122 39.5W, Fl (2+1) R 6s, 15 ft., 5 mi., JR on dolphin.
Also see Hood Canal.

THE NARROWS

Point Defiance Ferry Dolphin Light
47 18.4N, 122 30.8W, Fl R 10s, on dolphin, private aid.

Point Defiance Light
47 19.0N, 122 32.9W, Fl W 6s, 21 ft., 11 mi., NG on pile structure, horn: 1 blast every 15s.

Gig Harbor Light
47 19.7N, 122 34.4W, Fl R 4s, 13 ft., 3 mi., hexagonal concrete building, private aid.

Point Evans Light 4
Fl R 4s, 18 ft., 4 mi., TR on pile.

Tacoma Narrows Bridge West Pier Fog Signal
Horn: low tone, 2 blasts every 30s, private aid.

Tacoma Narrows Bridge East Pier Fog Signal
Horn: high tone, 1 blast every 30s, private aid.

Gibson Point Light 6
47 13.1N, 122 36.1W, Fl R 4s, 22 ft., 6 mi., TR on dolphin, light visible from 222° to 055°.

Toliva Shoal Lighted Bell Buoy
47 12.1N, 122 36.4W, Fl (2+1) R 6s, 5 mi., red and green bands.

The Sisters Light 17
48 41.7N, 122 45.4W, Fl G 2.5s, 40 ft., 4 mi., SG on structure.
Also see Rosario Strait.

Thea Foss Waterway Light
47 15.7N, 122 26.2W, Fl W 6s, 23 ft., 11 mi., light on pile, horn on dock, horn: 2 blasts every 20s.
Also see Tacoma Harbor.

Three Tree Point Light
47 27.0N, 122 23.0W, Fl W 2s, 25 ft., 11 mi., white skeleton tower, horn: 1 blast every 15s.
Also see East Passage.

Three Tree Point Yacht Club Racing Buoy J (buoys A, I, and L in vicinity)
47 22.9N, 122 22.8W, white spar buoy, private aid.
Also see East Passage.

Tide Point Light 12
48 35.1N, 122 44.5W, Fl R 2.5s, 15 ft., 4 mi., TR on pile.
Also see Rosario Strait.

Toke Point Basin Daybeacon 4
46 42.5N, 123 58.0W, TR on pile.

Toke Point Jetty Light 3
46 42.4N, 123 58.0W, Fl G 4s, 13 ft., 6 mi., SG on piles, higher intensity beam down channel.
Also see Willapa Bay.

Toliva Shoal Lighted Bell Buoy
47 12.1N, 122 36.4W, Fl (2+1) R 6s, 5 mi., red and green bands.
Also see The Narrows.

Tolmie Beach State Park Buoy (marks fish haven)
47 07.5N, 122 46.2W, orange and white bands, private aid.
Also see Nisqually Reach.

Tom Point Light (Canada)
48 39.8N, 123 16.3W, Fl W 4s, 21 ft., white circular tower with green band at top.
Also see Haro Strait.

Tosco Northwest North and South Lights (2)
48 49.5N, 122 43.1W, F R, 16 ft., NW on dolphin, horn: 1 blast every 30s, private aids.
Also see Sandy Point Lights, Intalco Lights, and Atlantic Richfield Lights.

Totten Inlet Daybeacon 1
47 11.3N, 122 56.6W, SG on pile.

Traffic Lanes
See Strait of Juan de Fuca,
Rosario Strait, *and* Puget Sound
Traffic Lane.

Treasure Island Shoal Daybeacon 2 (Port Madison)
47 41.9N, 122 32.2W, TR on pile.

Trial Islands Light (Canada)
48 23.7N, 123 18.2W, F W, Fl G 5s,
93 ft., 15 mi., white circular
tower, FW with high-intensity
green flash every 5s, horn:
2 blasts every 60s, horn points
181° from a white rectangular
building close southeastward
of lighthouse.

Tskutsko Point Light
47 41.6N, 122 50.0W, Fl W 4s,
15 ft., 5 mi., NB on pile, radar
reflector.
Also see Hood Canal *and* Dabob
Bay.

Tulalip Bay Buoy 2
48 03.3N, 122 17.7W, red nun.

Tulalip Tribes Breakwater Light A
48 03.7N, 122 16.8W, Fl Y 2s,
13 ft., on breakwater, private aid.

Turn Point Light
48 41.3N, 123 14.2W, Fl W 2.5s,
44 ft., 8 mi., white concrete tower,
light obscured from 260.5° to
357°, horn: 2 blasts every 30s,
operates continuously.
Also see Haro Strait.

Turn Rock Light 3
48 32.1N, 122 57.9W, Fl G 4s, 18 ft.,
6 mi., SG on cylindrical base,
rock ledge bares at half tide.
Also see San Juan Channel.

Twin Rocks Daybeacon
48 26.8N, 122 54.7W, NR on iron
spindle.
Also see Richardson Daybeacon
and San Juan Channel.

Tyee Shoal Light
47 36.6N, 122 29.3W, Fl (2+1) R 6s,
15 ft., 5 mi., JR on dolphin, higher
intensity on bearing 094°, bell: 1
stroke every 15s, radar reflector.

U

Umatilla Reef Lighted Whistle Buoy 2UR
48 11.2N, 124 49.4W, Fl R 2.5s,
5 mi., red.

Undertakers Reef Daybeacon 8
48 31.3N, 122 49.6W, TR on
spindle, radar reflector.
Also see Lopez Sound.

Upright Head Ferry Landing Light
48 34.3N, 122 52.9W, F R, 15 ft.,
on black float, private aid.

V

Vancouver, Washington
See Columbia River chapter.

Vendovi Cove Light
48 36.9N, 122 36.7W, Fl Y 4s,
15 ft., steel tower, private aid.
Also see Bellingham Channel.

Vendovi Island Light 2
48 36.5N, 122 35.9W, Fl R 6s,
13 ft., 5 mi., TR on platform,
radar reflector.
Also see Padilla Bay.

Victoria Harbor Fairway Lighted Whistle Buoy VH (Canada)
48 22.5N, 123 23.5W, Mo (A) W,
red and white stripes, racon:
S (···).
Also see Victoria, British
Columbia chapter.

Village Point Light 18
Fl R 4s, 24 ft., 5 mi., TR on skele-
ton tower, higher intensity beam
towards Rosario Strait and
Boundary Bay, obscured from
180° to 264°.
Also see Rosario Strait *and*
Lummi Island.

Viti Rocks Light
48 38.0N, 122 37.4W, Fl W 2.5s,
45 ft., 5 mi., NB on steel tower.
Also see Bellingham Channel.

Viti Rocks Lighted Bell Buoy 9
48 37.8N, 122 37.1W, Q G, 3 mi.,
green.

Von Geldern Cove Light
47 16.3N, 122 45.4W, Fl Y 8s,
22 ft., on steel pile, private aid.
Also see Carr Inlet.

W

Waadah Island Light
48 23.1N, 124 36.0W, Iso W 6s (R
sector), 63 ft., white 10 mi., red
7 mi., NR on concrete tower,
red sector from 093° to 109°,
covers Duncan and Duntze
Rocks, horn: 2 blasts every 30s,
operates continuously.

Wasp Passage Light 5
Fl G 4s, 15 ft., 5 mi., SG on pyra-
midal structure.
Also see San Juan Channel.

Waterman Point Light 11
47 35.1N, 122 34.3W, Oc G 4s,
26 ft., 7 mi., SG on skeleton
tower, horn: 1 blast every 15s.
Also see Rich Passage.

Webster Point Light 33
47 38.9N, 122 16.6W, Fl G 4s,
19 ft., 6 mi., SG on white house
on pile structure, light obscured
from 121° to 199°.
Also see Lake Washington.

West Point Light
47 39.7N, 122 26.1W, Al W R 10s,
27 ft., white 19 mi., red 16 mi.,
white octagonal tower on building, lighted throughout 24 hours,
horn: 1 blast every 30s.

West Point Lighted Buoy 1
47 39.6N, 122 26.5W, Fl G 4s,
4 mi., green.

West Seattle Reef Buoy
47 33.4N, 122 24.4W, white with
orange bands, spar, private aid.
Also see East Passage.

Westhaven
See Grays Harbor.

Westport
See Grays Harbor.

Whatcom Waterway
See Bellingham Bay.

Whiffin Spit Light (Canada)
48 21.5N, 123 42.6W, Q W, 21 ft.,
6 mi., white circular tower with
green band at top, horn: 1 blast
every 30s, operated only on
request to Vancouver Coast
Guard Radio.

WILLAPA BAY

Due to frequently changing conditions, positions of many buoys are not listed.

Also see Willapa River.

Entrance

Approach Lighted Whistle Buoy W
46 41.8N, 124 10.7W, Mo (A) W, 6 mi., red and white stripes.

Leadbetter Point Buoy 1
46 38.4N, 124 07.3W, green can.

Entrance Buoy A
Yellow nun.

Entrance Buoy B
Yellow.

Entrance Buoy C
46 43.1N, 124 07.5W, yellow.

Entrance Buoy D
Yellow.

Entrance Buoy 8
Red.

Entrance Buoy 10
Red nun.

Entrance Buoy 12
46 42.8N, 124 02.6W, red nun.

Entrance Lighted Bell Buoy 13
46 42.1N, 124 01.4W, Fl G 2.5s, 4 mi., green.

Main Channel

Channel Lighted Bell Buoy 15
46 42.0N, 124 00.2W, Fl G 4s, 4 mi., green.

Channel Lighted Buoy 16
46 41.7N, 123 58.4W, Fl R 4s, 4 mi., red.

Cedar River Flats Daybeacon 2
46 42.1N, 123 57.7W, 20 ft., TR on pile structure.

Toke Point Jetty Light 3
46 42.4N, 123 58.0W, Fl G 4s, 13 ft., 6 mi., SG on piles, higher intensity beam down channel.

Toke Point Basin Daybeacon 4
46 42.5N, 123 58.0W, TR on pile.

South Willapa Bay

Light 3
46 41.3N, 123 59.7W, Fl G 6s, 15 ft., 3 mi., SG on pile.

Daybeacon 5
46 39.7N, 123 59.6W, SG on pile.

Light 7
46 36.6N, 123 58.5W, Fl G 4s, 22 ft., 5 mi., SG on pile structure, higher intensity beam up channel.

Daybeacon 8
TR on pile.

Nahcotta Channel

Light 10
46 34.3N, 123 58.7W, Fl R 4s, 22 ft., 5 mi., TR on dolphin.

Daybeacon 11
SG on pile.

Daybeacon 12
TR on pile.

Long Island Junction Light
46 32.3N, 123 58.7W, Fl (2+1) G 6s, 15 ft., 5 mi., JG on dolphin, higher intensity beam up and down channel.

Daybeacon 13
SG on pile.

Nahcotta Mooring Basin Light 2
Fl R 4s, 15 ft., 6 mi., TR on pile structure, higher intensity beam down channel.

Nahcotta Mooring Basin Light 1
46 30.1N, 124 01.6W, Q G, 15 ft., 4 mi., SG on pipe.

Stanley Channel

Daybeacon 2
46 31.2N, 123 58.6W, TR on pile.

Light 4
46 29.0N, 123 57.9W, Fl R 4s, 15 ft., 4 mi., TR on white platform on dolphin, higher intensity beam up and down channel.

Stanley Point Junction Light
Fl (2+1) R 6s, 15 ft., 5 mi., JR on pile, higher intensity beam down channel, radar reflector.

Nemah River Channel Entrance Daybeacon 1
46 34.6N, 123 56.9W, SG on dolphin.

Bay Center Channel

Due to frequently changing conditions, positions of buoys are not listed.

Light 2
46 38.6N, 123 59.4W, Fl R 2.5s, 24 ft., 4 mi., TR on dolphin.

Light 6
46 38.4N, 123 58.3W, Fl R 4s, 21 ft., 4 mi., TR on pile, higher intensity beam upstream.

Buoy 8
Red nun.

Buoy 10
Red nun.

Light 11
46 38.8N, 123 57.1W, Fl G 4s, 18 ft., 4 mi., SG on pile structure, higher intensity beam down channel.

Palix River Light 15
46 37.9N, 123 56.6W, Fl G 4s, 5 mi., SG on dolphin.

WILLAPA RIVER

Light 1
46 41.8N, 123 57.7W, Fl G 2.5s, 15 ft., 4 mi., SG on dolphin.

Range A Front Light
46 41.5N, 123 57.3W, Q W, 16 ft., KRB on dolphin, visible all around, higher intensity beam on rangeline.

Range A Rear Light
640 yards, 259° from front light, Iso W 6s, 29 ft., KRB on dolphin, visible 4° each side of rangeline.

Channel Light 7
46 41.7N, 123 56.3W, Fl G 4s, 15 ft., 5 mi., SG on pile.

Channel Light 10
46 41.8N, 123 55.1W, Fl R 6s, 15 ft., 4 mi., TR on pile.

Light 13
Fl G 4s, 28 ft., 5 mi., SG on dolphin.

Range B Front Light
46 42.6N, 123 51.3W, Q W, 18 ft., KRB on pile structure, visible all around, higher intensity on rangeline.

Range B Rear Light
1,240 yards, 074.5° from front light, Iso W 6s, 56 ft., KRB on pile structure, visible 4° each side of rangeline.

Daybeacon 15
46 42.1N, 123 54.0W, SG on pile.

Channel Light 19
46 42.2N, 123 53.3W, Fl G 6s, 15 ft., 4 mi., SG on dolphin, higher intensity beam up and down channel.

Daybeacon 22
TR on pile.

Light 24
Fl R 4s, 15 ft., 4 mi., TR on dolphin.

Daybeacon 26
46 42.4N, 123 51.6W, TR on pile, radar reflector.

Daybeacon 28
TR on pile.

Light 29
Fl G 2.5s, 15 ft., 4 mi., SG on dolphin.

Daybeacon 30
TR on pile.

Light 33
Fl G 4s, 22 ft., 5 mi., SG on dolphin, higher intensity beam up and down channel.

Light 35
Fl G 6s, 15 ft., 4 mi., SG on dolphin.

Light 39
Fl G 4s, 18 ft., 5 mi., SG on dolphin, higher intensity beam up and down channel.

Channel Daybeacon 40
TR on pile structure.

Range C Front Daybeacon
46 41.4N, 123 49.2W, KRB on pole.

Range C Rear Daybeacon
215 yards, 350.8° from front daybeacon, KRB on pole.

Channel Daybeacon 44
TR on pile structure.

Channel Light 51 (80 ft. outside channel limit)
Fl G 4s, 15 ft., 3 mi., SG on dolphin.

Channel Light 55
Fl G 4s, 16 ft., 3 mi., SG on skeleton tower.

Channel Light 56 (70 ft. outside channel limit)
Q R, 15 ft., 2 mi., TR on dolphin.

Channel Light 59
46 40.8N, 123 46.0W, Fl G 2.5s, 15 ft., 4 mi., SG on pile structure.

William Head Light (Canada)
48 20.6N, 123 31.6W, Fl (2) G, 0.5s fl. 1.0s ec., 0.5s fl. 4.0s ec., 36 ft., white tower, green band at top, whistle: 1 blast every 30s.

William Point Light
48 35.0N, 122 33.6W, Fl W 4s, 13 ft., 5 mi., NB.
Also see Padilla Bay.

Williamson Rocks Lighted Gong Buoy 4
48 26.8N, 122 42.4W, Fl R 4s, 5 mi., red.
Also see Rosario Strait.

Wing Point Reef Buoy 2
47 36.7N, 122 29.1W, red nun.

Wyckoff Shoal Buoy 1
47 14.5N, 122 42.9W, green can.
Also see Carr Inlet.

Wyckoff Shoal Buoy 3
47 14.4N, 122 43.0W, green can.
Also see Pitt Passage.

Y

Yellow Bluff Reef Obstruction Daybeacon
48 31.9N, 122 39.4W, NW on dolphin worded DANGER REEF, radar reflector.
Also see Bellingham Channel.

Z

Zero Rock Light (Canada)
48 31.4N, 123 17.4W, Fl W 4s, 28 ft., white cylindrical tower, green band on top, radar reflector.
Also see Haro Strait.

This chapter includes aids to navigation on the Columbia River as far as Vancouver and Portland. The aids to navigation are arranged geographically for the main Columbia River channel. Side channels and harbors are listed alphabetically elsewhere in this chapter.

A

Astoria West Basin North Light
46 11.4N, 123 51.3W, F R, 20 ft., private aid.
Also see Columbia River.

Astoria West Basin South Light
46 11.4N, 123 51.2W, F G, 20 ft., private aid.

B

BAKER BAY WEST CHANNEL

Entrance Jetty Light 1
46 16.1N, 124 01.8W, Fl G 4s, 15 ft., 3 mi., SG on pile, radar reflector.

Entrance Jetty Light 2
46 16.1N, 124 01.9W, Fl R 2.5s, 15 ft., 3 mi., TR on pile.

Buoy 3
Green can, position shifted with changing conditions.

Daybeacon 6
TR on pile, radar reflector.

Daybeacon 7
SG on dolphin.

Light 8
Fl R 4s, 17 ft., 4 mi., TR on pile structure.

Daybeacon 9
SG on pile.

Light 10
Fl R 4s, 15 ft., 4 mi., TR on dolphin, higher intensity beam up and down channel, radar reflector.

Light 11
46 16.8N, 124 02.4W, Fl G 4s, 20 ft., 2 mi., SG on multi-pile structure, radar reflector.

Light 12
46 16.9N, 124 02.8W, Q R, 15 ft., 4 mi., TR on dolphin.

Daybeacon 14
TR on pile, radar reflector.

Light 15
Fl G 2.5s, 7 ft., 3 mi., SG on post, radar reflector.

Daybeacon 16
TR on pile, radar reflector.

Light 17
Fl G 4s, 15 ft., 5 mi., SG on dolphin, radar reflector.

Daybeacon 18
TR on pile.

Light 20
Fl R 4s, 17 ft., 4 mi., TR on pile structure, radar reflector.

Daybeacon 21
SG on pile.

Light 22
46 17.8N, 124 02.4W, Fl R 2.5s, 15 ft., 4 mi., TR on dolphin, radar reflector.

Buoy 23
46 17.9N, 124 02.5W, green can.

Ilwaco Mooring Basin Light 2
46 18.0N, 124 02.4W, Fl R 4s, 15 ft., 5 mi., TR on pile structure, radar reflector.

Ilwaco Mooring Basin Light 3
46 18.1N, 124 02.5W, Fl G 4s, 5 mi., SG on pile.

BRADBURY SLOUGH

Pier Light B
F Y, 11 ft., on pile, private aid.

Pier Light C
F Y, 11 ft., on pile, private aid.

Pier Light D
F Y, 11 ft., on pile, private aid.

C

Cape Disappointment Light
46 16.6N, 124 03.1W, Al W R 30s, 220 ft., white 22 mi., red 18 mi., white conical tower with white band at top and bottom, black band in middle, light obscured northward of 137.5°.
Also see Columbia River.

CATHLAMET BAY NORTH CHANNEL AND PRAIRIE CHANNEL

Light 3
Fl G 6s, 15 ft., 4 mi., SG on pile structure, higher intensity beam up and down channel, radar reflector.

Buoy 4
46 12.3N, 123 42.3W, red nun.

Light 5
Fl G 4s, 18 ft., 4 mi., SG on dolphin, radar reflector.

Grassy Island Light 8
46 11.6N, 123 41.5W, Fl R 4s, 17 ft., 4 mi., TR on pile.

Lighted Buoy 10
46 10.8N, 123 40.4W, Fl R 2.5s, 4 mi., red nun, radar reflector.

Daybeacon 12
46 10.7N, 123 40.2W, TR on pile.

Svensen Island Light 12A
46 10.9N, 123 38.7W, Fl R 2.5s, 15 ft., 4 mi., TR on dolphin, higher intensity beam up and down channel.

Daybeacon 14
TR on pile structure, radar reflector.

Russian Island Light 15
46 11.9N, 123 38.2W, Fl G 4s, 15 ft., 4 mi., SG on dolphin.

Daybeacon 17
SG on pile structure, radar reflector.

Buoy 19
46 12.8N, 123 37.5W, green can.

Marsh Island Light 21
Fl G 2.5s, 15 ft., 4 mi., SG on dolphin.

Light 23
46 14.2N, 123 32.9W, Fl G 2.5s, 15 ft., 3 mi., SG on pile structure.

CATHLAMET BAY SOUTH CHANNEL

Light 2
46 12.8N, 123 45.4W, Q R, 18 ft., 6 mi., TR on pile.

Light 3 (on end of rock groin)
46 12.4N, 123 45.1W, Fl G 2.5s, 15 ft., 5 mi., SG on skeleton tower.

Light 6
46 11.8N, 123 45.1W, Fl R 6s, 12 ft., 3 mi., TR on multi-pile structure.

Buoy 7
46 10.9N, 123 44.2W, green can.

Daybeacon 8
TR on dolphin, radar reflector.

Daybeacon 10
TR on pile structure, radar reflector.

CATHLAMET CHANNEL

Also see Columbia River.

Daybeacon 2
46 12.4N, 123 24.7W, TR on pile, radar reflector.

Elochoman Buoy 1
46 12.3N, 123 23.4W, green can.

Elochoman Daybeacon 2
46 12.5N, 123 23.3W, TR on pile.

Daybeacon 6
TR on pile.

Daybeacon 7
SG on box.

Light 8
Fl R 2.5s, 15 ft., 4 mi., TR on dolphin.

Coffin Rock Light
46 02.0N, 122 52.9W, Q W, 20 ft., 5 mi., NB on house.
Also see Columbia River.

COLUMBIA RIVER

This section lists the aids to navigation in geographic order for the main Columbia River channel as far as Vancouver and Portland. Side channels and harbors are listed alphabetically elsewhere in this chapter.

In the event of flood conditions in the Columbia River, aids to navigation may be temporarily discontinued, lights may be extinguished or destroyed, and buoys may be extinguished or dragged off station. Under such conditions vessel operators should consult local authorities before attempting to navigate these waters.

Approaches

Cape Disappointment Light
46 16.6N, 124 03.1W, Al W R 30s, 220 ft., white 22 mi., red 18 mi., white conical tower with white band at top and bottom, black band in middle, light obscured northward of 137.5°.
Also see Washington chapter.

Columbia River Approach Lighted Horn Buoy CR
46 11.1N, 124 11.1W, Mo (A) W, 6 mi., Fl W 2.5s, red and white stripes, high-intensity flash tube Fl W 2.5s, racon: M (--), horn: 1 blast every 30s.
Also see Oregon chapter.

Entrance
Also see Baker Bay West Channel.

Entrance Range Front Light
46 16.6N, 124 03.0W, F R, 186 ft., KWB on skeleton structure, visible 5° each side of rangeline, lightcd throughout 24 hours.

Entrance Range Rear Light
625 yards, 045° from front light, F G, 240 ft., KWB on skeleton structure, visible 5° each side of rangeline, lighted throughout 24 hours.

Entrance Lighted Bell Buoy 1
46 13.4N, 124 11.0W, Fl G 4s, 4 mi., green.

Entrance Lighted Whistle Buoy 2
46 12.8N, 124 08.1W, Fl R 4s, 4 mi., red.

Entrance Lighted Buoy 3
46 14.3N, 124 08.7W, Fl G 4s, 5 mi., green.

Clatsop Spit Lighted Whistle Buoy 4 (100 yards outside channel limit)
46 13.6N, 124 06.8W, Fl R 2.5s, 4 mi., red.

South Jetty Bell Buoy 2SJ
46 14.0N, 124 05.8W, red.

Clatsop Spit Lighted Whistle Buoy 6 (325 yards outside channel limit)
46 14.3N, 124 05.8W, Fl R 4s, 3 mi., red.

Peacock Spit Lighted Bell Buoy 7
46 15.2N, 124 06.3W, Q G, 4 mi., green.

Clatsop Spit Lighted Bell Buoy 8
46 15.0N, 124 04.7W, Q R, 3 mi., red.

North Jetty Lighted Bell Buoy 9
46 15.6N, 124 05.1W, Fl G 4s, 3 mi., green.

Sand Island Range Front Light
46 15.9N, 123 59.6W, Q G, 19 ft., KRW on skeleton tower on pile structure, visible 4° each side of rangeline.

Sand Island Range Rear Light
1,000 yards, 080° from front light, Iso G 6s, 61 ft., KRW on skeleton tower on pile structure, visible 4° each side of rangeline.

Clatsop Spit Lighted Whistle Buoy 10
46 15.3N, 124 03.2W, Fl R 4s, 3 mi., red.

Peacock Spit Lighted Bell Buoy 11
46 15.7N, 124 02.2W, Fl G 2.5s, 3 mi., green.

Clatsop Spit Lighted Whistle Buoy 12
46 15.1N, 124 01.9W, Fl R 2.5s, 4 mi., red.

Clatsop Spit Lighted Whistle Buoy 14
46 14.9N, 124 00.6W, Q R, 3 mi., red.

Desdemona Sands
Also see North Channel, Chinook Channel, Hammond Boat Basin, *and* Skipanon Waterway.

Channel Leading Light
46 16.0N, 124 02.2W, Fl W 4s, 31 ft., 10 mi., NB on skeleton tower on pile structure, light oriented on bearing 132°, visible 15° each side of channel.

Channel Lighted Bell Buoy 20
46 14.2N, 123 59.6W, Fl R 2.5s, 4 mi., red.

Channel Lighted Bell Buoy 21
46 14.1N, 123 58.9W, Fl G 2.5s, 4 mi., green.

Channel Lighted Buoy 22 (70 yards outside channel limit)
46 13.5N, 123 58.4W, Fl R 4s, 4 mi., red.

Columbia River Entrance Dredge Lighted Buoy D
46 14.3N, 123 57.5W, Fl Y 6s, yellow, maintained from May 1 to Nov. 15.

Light
46 13.5N, 123 57.3W, Fl W 4s, 23 ft., 5 mi., NB on pile structure.

Channel Lighted Buoy 25 (250 yards outside channel limit)
46 12.8N, 123 56.8W, Fl G 4s, 4 mi., green.

Fort Stevens Wharf Light 26
46 12.4N, 123 57.1W, Oc R 4s, 35 ft., 6 mi., TR on multi-pile.

Lighted Gong Buoy 27 (285 yards outside channel limit)
46 11.9N, 123 55.3W, Fl G 2.5s, 6 mi., green.

Lighted Gong Buoy 29 (100 yards outside channel limit)
Q G, 4 mi., green.

Desdemona Lower Sands Lighted Gong Buoy 31 (90 feet outside channel limit)
46 11.6N, 123 53.0W, Fl G 6s, 5 mi., green.

Tansy Point

Range Front Light
46 11.3N, 123 55.2W, Q R, 22 ft., KRB on pile structure, on same structure as Tansy Point Leading Light, visible 2° each side of rangeline.

Leading Light
Q R, 17 ft., 5 mi., NB on pile structure, on same structure as Tansy Point Range Front Light, visible all around, higher intensity beam on 136°.

Range Rear Light
960 yards, 264° from front light, Iso R 6s, 53 ft., KRB on skeleton tower, visible 2° each side of rangeline.

Range Lighted Buoy 33
46 11.7N, 123 52.0W, Fl G 4s, 4 mi., green.

Range Buoy 35A (68 yards outside channel limit)
46 11.7N, 123 51.4W, green can.

Astoria

West Basin North Light
46 11.4N, 123 51.3W, F R, 20 ft., private aid.

West Basin South Light
46 11.4N, 123 51.2W, F G, 20 ft., private aid.

Tansy Point Range Buoy 35B (68 yards outside channel limit)
46 11.7N, 123 50.8W, green can.

Light 36
Q R, 30 ft., 6 mi., TR on dolphin.

Crossing Lighted Buoy 37
46 11.8N, 123 50.0W, Fl G 4s, 4 mi., green.

Lower Range Front Light
46 11.5N, 123 50.2W, F R, 40 ft., KRB on roof, visible 3° each side of rangeline, lighted throughout 24 hours.

Lower Range Rear Light
570 yards, 241.2° from front light, F R, 175 ft., KRB on pile structure, visible 3° each side of rangeline, lighted throughout 24 hours.

Range Lighted Buoy 39 (180 yards outside channel limit)
46 12.0N, 123 49.3W, Q G, 4 mi., green.

Range Lighted Buoy 40
46 11.9N, 123 48.8W, Q R, 4 mi., red.

Oregon Dept. of Fish and Wildlife Special Purpose Buoy
46 11.8N, 123 48.0W, Fl Y 4s, yellow.

Rock Buoy
46 11.9N, 123 47.6W, red and green bands, nun.

Range Lighted Buoy 42 (200 yards outside channel limit)
Fl R 4s, 5 mi., red.

Tongue Point Channel Lighted Buoy 43 (50 yards outside channel limit)
46 13.0N, 123 46.3W, Fl G 4s, 5 mi., green.

Tongue Point Channel Lighted Buoy 44 (100 yards outside channel limit)
Fl R 2.5s, 4 mi., red.

Tongue Point Channel Lighted Buoy 47 (30 yards outside channel limit)
46 13.7N, 123 44.2W, Q G, 4 mi., green.

Harrington Point

Range Lighted Buoy 50 (25 yards outside channel limit)
46 13.6N, 123 43.9W, Fl R 4s, 4 mi., red.

Range Front Light
46 15.4N, 123 40.6W, Q W, 20 ft., KRB on pile structure, visible 2° each side of rangeline.

Range Rear Light
1,190 yards, 054° from front light, Iso W 6s, 48 ft., KRB on skeleton tower on pile structure, visible all around, higher intensity on rangeline and upstream.

Channel Light (175 yards outside channel limit)
46 14.1N, 123 42.9W, Fl W 2.5s, 17 ft., 5 mi., NB on dolphin.

Channel Lighted Buoy 54 (75 feet outside channel limit)
46 14.6N, 123 41.9W, Fl R 4s, 4 mi., red.

Miller Sands

Range Front Light
46 15.7N, 123 38.2W, Q G, 15 ft., KRB on pile structure, visible 2° each side of rangeline.

Range Rear Light
650 yards, 070.5° from front light, Iso G 6s, 50 ft., KRB on skeleton tower, visible 2° each side of rangeline.

Channel Lighted Buoy 2 (75 yards outside channel limit)
46 15.0N, 123 40.8W, Q R, 4 mi., red.

Channel Lighted Buoy 3 (33 yards outside channel limit)
46 15.1N, 123 41.1W, Fl G 2.5s, 4 mi., green.

Dike Light 5 (83 yards outside channel limit)
46 15.4N, 123 40.1W, Fl G 4s, 15 ft., 5 mi., SG on dolphin, higher intensity beam up and down channel.

Channel Lighted Buoy 6 (50 yards outside channel limit)
46 15.3N, 123 39.9W, Fl R 4s, 4 mi., red.

Daybeacon 7
46 15.5N, 123 39.7W, SG on dolphin, on dike 23.71.

Channel Lighted Buoy 10
46 15.5N, 123 38.9W, Q R, 4 mi., red.

Dike Light 11
Fl G 6s, 19 ft., 4 mi., SG on dolphin.

Pillar Rock

Pillar Rock Lower Range Front Light
46 15.2N, 123 32.6W, Q W, 20 ft., KRB on pile structure, visible all around, higher intensity on rangeline.

Pillar Rock Lower Range Rear Light
800 yards, 096° from front light, Iso W 6s, 50 ft., KRB on skeleton tower on pile structure, visible 4° each side of rangeline.

Channel Lighted Buoy 12
46 15.5N, 123 38.3W, Fl R 6s, 6 mi., red.

Elliot Point Lighted Buoy 13
46 15.6N, 123 37.1W, Fl G 4s, 4 mi., green.

Lower Range Lighted Buoy 14
46 15.4N, 123 37.1W, Fl R 4s, 4 mi., red.

Dike Light 14A
46 15.3N, 123 35.5W, Fl R 2.5s, l12 ft., 5 mi., TR on multi-pile.

Channel Lighted Buoy 15
46 15.4N, 123 35.2W, Q G, 4 mi., green.

Light 17
46 15.5N, 123 35.2W, Iso G 6s, 25 ft., 7 mi., SG.

Upper Range Front Light
46 15.6N, 123 30.9W, Q R, 17 ft., KRB on pile structure, visible 4° each side of rangeline.

Upper Range Rear Light
1,065 yards, 083.7° from front light, Iso R 6s, 49 ft., KRB on skeleton tower on pile structure, visible 4° each side of rangeline.

Upper Range Lighted Buoy 18
46 15.4N, 123 33.8W, Fl R 4s, 4 mi., red.

Jim Crow Point Light 19
46 15.6N, 123 33.9W, Fl G 6s, 24 ft., 4 mi., SG.

Lighted Buoy 19A
46 15.5N, 123 33.6W, Fl G 2.5s, 4 mi., green.

Jim Crow Lighted Buoy 21
46 15.6N, 123 33.1W, Q G, green.

Jim Crow Lighted Buoy 22
46 15.6N, 123 32.2W, Fl R 2.5s, 4 mi., red.

Welch Island

Three Tree Point Light 23
46 16.0N, 123 31.2W, Fl G 4s, 40 ft., 6 mi., SG on white house, radar reflector.

Channel Lighted Buoy 26
Fl R 2.5s, 4 mi., red.

Rockland Light 27
46 16.3N, 123 30.3W, Fl G 2.5s, 19 ft., 5 mi., SG.

Channel Lighted Buoy 28
Fl R 4s, 4 mi., red.

Bayview Light
46 16.4N, 123 29.3W, Fl W 4s, 18 ft., 5 mi., NB on pile structure.

Channel Lighted Buoy 30
Fl R 4s, 4 mi., red.

Skamokawa Light 31
Q G, 15 ft., 4 mi., SG on dolphin.

Channel Lighted Buoy 32
46 16.0N, 123 28.0W, Q R, 4 mi., red.

Skamokawa Creek Light 33
Fl G 2.5s, 15 ft., 4 mi., SG on pile.

Skamokawa Range Front Light
46 14.1N, 123 25.4W, Q W, 17 ft., KRB on pile structure, visible all around, higher intensity beam on rangeline.

Skamokawa Range Rear Light
437 yards, 140.8° from front light, Iso W 6s, 42 ft., KRB on skeleton tower on pile structure on same structure as Puget Island Range Rear Light, visible all around, higher intensity beam on rangeline.

Price Island Light 35
Fl G 4s, 12 ft., 5 mi., SG on pile structure.

Multnomah Slough Lighted Buoy 36
Fl R 2.5s, 4 mi., red.

Steamboat Slough Lighted Buoy 37
46 14.7N, 123 25.9W, Fl G 4s, 5 mi., green.

Hunting Island Light 39
46 13.8N, 123 25.4W, Fl G 2.5s,
4 mi., SG on dolphin.

Puget Island

Range Front Light
46 13.7N, 123 25.3W, Q W, 12 ft.,
KRB on pile structure, visible 4°
each side of rangeline.

Range Rear Light
524 yards, 009° from front light,
Iso W 6s, 42 ft., KRB on skeleton
tower on pile structure, on same
structure as Skamokawa Range
Rear Light, visible all around,
higher intensity on rangeline.

Range Lighted Buoy 41
Fl G 4s, 5 mi., green.

Clifton Dike Light 42
Fl R 4s, 20 ft., 4 mi., TR on
dolphin, higher intensity beam
up and down channel.

Daybeacon 43
46 12.3N, 123 25.5W, SG on
dolphin, on dike 38.25.

Clifton Dike Light 44
46 12.0N, 123 26.1W, Fl R 6s,
20 ft., 4 mi., TR on dolphin.

Hunts Mill Point Light 44A
46 11.2N, 123 25.7W, Fl R 2.5s,
12 ft., 4 mi., TR on pipe, radar
reflector.

Bugby Hole Light 46
Q R, 15 ft., 5 mi., TR.

Light 47
46 10.8N, 123 25.5W, Q G, 15 ft.,
4 mi., SG on skeleton tower.

Light 49
Fl G 4s, 17 ft., 5 mi., SG on
dolphin.

Wauna Outfall Light
46 10.1N, 123 24.9W, Fl Y 10s,
on dolphin, private aid.

Wauna

Range Front Light
46 08.6N, 123 22.9W, Q W, KRB on
pile structure, visible all around,
higher intensity on rangeline.

Range Rear Light
673 yards, 137.5° from front light,
Iso W 6s, 56 ft., KRB on skeleton
tower, visible 4° each side of
rangeline.

Mill Water Intake Light
46 09.2N, 123 23.8W, F R, 25 ft.,
on dolphin, private aid.

Lower Light
46 09.7N, 123 24.5W, F R, 29 ft.,
on pier, private aid.

Crane Boom Light
F R, 55 ft., on crane boom, private aid.

Middle Light
F R, 11 ft., on dolphin, private
aid.

Westport Slough Buoy 56
46 08.9N, 123 23.2W, red nun.

Dike Light 57
Q G, 20 ft., 4 mi., SG on dolphin.

Driscoll Range Front Light
46 09.0N, 123 23.7W, Q W 23 ft.,
Q R 23 ft., KRB on dolphin, visible 2° each side of rangeline,
passing light visible up and
down channel.

Driscoll Range Rear Light
410 yards, 284° from front light,
Iso R 6s, 49 ft., KRB on skeleton
tower, visible 2° each side of
rangeline.

Westport

Also see Cathlamet Channel.

Dike Light 58
Fl R 4s, 15 ft., 4 mi., TR on dolphin, higher intensity beam up
and down channel.

Pancake Point Dike Light 59
46 09.0N, 123 22.4W, Fl G 6s,
15 ft., 5 mi., SG on multi-pile.

Dike Light 60
Fl R 6s, 15 ft., 4 mi., TR on pile,
higher intensity beam up and
down channel.

Range Front Light
46 08.5N, 123 21.2W, Q W, 17 ft.,
KRB on pile structure, visible all
around, higher intensity on
rangeline.

Range Rear Light
500 yards, 269.5° from front light,
Iso W 6s, 58 ft., KRB on skeleton
tower, visible 4° each side of
rangeline.

Dike Light 62
Fl R 4s, 19 ft., 4 mi., TR on dolphin, higher intensity beam up
and down channel.

Dike Light 64
Fl R 6s, 15 ft., 4 mi., TR on
dolphin.

Dike Light 66
46 08.4N, 123 18.8W, Q R, 15 ft.,
5 mi., TR on dolphin.

Turn Daybeacon 66A
TR on dolphin, radar reflector.

Cathlamet Dike Light 67
46 08.9N, 123 17.9W, Fl G 4s,
5 ft., 5 mi., SG on multi-pile.

Channel Lighted Buoy 68
46 08.7N, 123 17.0W, Fl R 2.5s,
5 mi., red.

Waterford Light 69
46 09.2N, 123 16.0W, Fl G 4s,
30 ft., 5 mi., SG on concrete pad.

Eureka

Channel Light 70
46 09.0N, 123 15.6W, Fl R 4s,
15 ft., 5 mi., TR on dolphin, radar
reflector.

Cooper Point Light 71
Q G, 23 ft., 5 mi., SG on skeleton
tower.

Channel Lighted Buoy 73
Fl G 4s, 4 mi., green.

Dike Light 76
Q R, 15 ft., 4 mi., TR on dolphin,
higher intensity beam down
channel.

Light 77
Fl G 2.5s, 13 ft., 4 mi., SG on
dolphin, higher intensity beam
up and down channel.

Dike Light 78
Fl R 4s, 17 ft., 4 mi., TR on
dolphin, higher intensity beam
down channel.

Dike Light 79
Fl G 4s, 15 ft., 4 mi., SG on pile.

Dike Light 80
46 10.1N, 123 13.1W, Fl R 6s,
13 ft., 4 mi., TR on dolphin.

Bar Dike Daybeacon
NR on pile.

Oak Point

Beaver Pier West End Light
46 10.8N, 123 11.1W, F R, private aid.

Beaver Pier East End Light
46 10.7N, 123 10.8W, F R, private aid.

Columbia River Geodetic Survey Light
46 11.1N, 123 11.2W, Fl Y 10s, 10 ft., private aid.

Light 81
46 11.2N, 123 10.9W, Fl G 4s, 14 ft., 4 mi., SG on concrete pad.

Abernathy Point Light 83
Fl G 2.5s, 20 ft., 5 mi., SG on cylinder.

Crims Island Lighted Buoy 84
Q R, 3 mi., red.

Crims Island to St. Helens
Also see Crims Island *and* Bradbury Slough.

Bunker Hill Light 85
46 11.4N, 123 08.4W, Fl G 4s, 17 ft., 5 mi., SG on tower, higher intensity beam up channel.

Crims Island Channel Lighted Buoy 86
Q R, 4 mi., red.

Stella Range Front Light
46 11.3N, 123 07.4W, F G, KRB on pile structure, visible all around, higher intensity on rangeline.

Stella Range Rear Light
257 yards, 308.5° from front light, F G, 44 ft., KRB on skeleton tower on pile structure, visible 15° each side of rangeline.

Cleaveland Light 1 (340 feet outside channel limit)
Fl G 2.5s, 12 ft., 4 mi., SG on dolphin.

Fisher Island

Cleaveland Light 3
Fl G 4s, 12 ft., 5 mi., SG on dolphin.

West Fisher Island Slough Pollution Response Buoy
46 10.4N, 123 50.1W, yellow.
[h4[Channel Lighted Buoy 5
46 09.7N, 123 04.4W, Q G, 4 mi., green.

Light 7
Fl G 4s, 13 ft., 6 mi., SG on dolphin.

Light 9
46 09.5N, 123 03.3W, Fl G 2.5s, 15 ft., 4 mi., SG on dolphin.

Channel Lighted Buoy 10
46 09.3N, 123 03.5W, Q R, 4 mi., red.

Slough Light 4
Fl R 4s, 15 ft., 4 mi., TR on dolphin.

East Fisher Island Slough Pollution Response Buoy
46 09.7N, 123 02.7W, yellow.

Longview

Walker Island Light 12
Q R, 15 ft., 4 mi., TR on pile structure.

Barrow Point Light 13
Q G, 10 ft., 4 mi., SG on dolphin.

Channel Lighted Buoy 17
46 08.2N, 123 00.6W, Fl G 2.5s, 4 mi., green.

Dock Lights (3)
46 08.2N, 123 00.1W, F R, 7 ft., on dolphins, private aids.

La Du Rock Lighted Buoy 19
Fl G 4s, 4 mi., green.

Lord Island Light 20
Fl R 4s, 25 ft., 4 mi., TR on platform, higher intensity beam up and down channel.

Mount Coffin Light 1
46 07.7N, 122 59.3W, Fl G 6s, 26 ft., 4 mi., SG on cylinder.

Range Front Light
46 07.4N, 122 58.6W, F R, 64 ft., KWR on cylinder, visible 5° each side of centerline of channel, private aid.

Range Rear Light
210 yards, 115° from front light, F R, 124 ft., white diamond daymark with red stripe on pole, visible 5° each side of centerline of channel, private aid.

Slaughters Dike Daybeacon 20A (150 ft. outside channel limit)
TR on dolphin.

Slaughters Channel Lighted Buoy 23
46 07.5N, 122 59.5W, Fl G 2.5s, 4 mi., green.

Dibblee Dike Light 22 (190 ft. outside channel limit)
46 07.1N, 122 59.2W, Fl R 6s, 15 ft., 4 mi., TR on pile structure, higher intensity beam up and down channel.

Slaughters Dike Light 26 (515 ft. outside channel limit)
46 06.6N, 122 58.6W, Fl R 2.5s, 15 ft., 4 mi., TR on dolphin, higher intensity beam up and down channel.

Lewis and Clark Bridge

Approach Buoy 1
46 06.4N, 122 57.7W, green can, private aid.

Approach Buoy 2
Red nun, private aid.

Approach Buoy 3
Green can, private aid.

Approach Buoy 4
Red nun, private aid.

Fog Signal
46 06.3N, 122 57.8W, siren on NE corner of south pier, bell on SE corner of north pier, siren: 2 blasts every 12s, bell: 1 stroke every 13s, private aids.

Longview (cont'd)

Cottonwood Island Lower Range Front Light
46 05.0N, 122 53.9W, Q W, 15 ft., KRB on pile structure, visible 4° each side of rangeline.

Cottonwood Island Lower Range Rear Light
327 yards, 115.8° from front light, Iso W 6s, 40 ft., KRB on skeleton tower, visible 4° each side of rangeline.

International Paper Dock Lights (2)
F R, 15 ft., dolphin, private aids.

Shaver Transportation Mooring Barge Light A
46 05.4N, 122 55.8W, F R, 10 ft., on mooring barge, private aid.

Shaver Transportation Mooring Barge Light B
46 05.4N, 122 55.8W, F R, 10 ft., on mooring barge, private aid.

Cottonwood Island

Dike Light 29A
46 05.5N, 122 55.0W, Fl G 6s, 17 ft., 5 mi., SG on dolphin.

Dike Light 31
Fl G 2.5s, 15 ft., 4 mi., SG on dolphin.

Dike Light 33
Fl G 4s, 12 ft., 5 mi., SG on dolphin.

Light 35
Fl G 4s, 15 ft., 5 mi., SG on pile.

Turn Lighted Buoy 36 (66 yards outside channel limit)
Q R, 4 mi., red.

Dike Light 37
Fl G 4s, 15 ft., 5 mi., SG on dolphin.

Upper Range Front Light
46 03.9N, 122 52.9W, Q W, 14 ft., KRB on skeleton tower, visible 4° each side of rangeline.

Upper Range Rear Light
337 yards, 356.1° from front light, Iso W 6s, 35 ft., KRB on skeleton tower, visible 4° each side of rangeline.

Light 39
Fl G 4s, 26 ft., 5 mi., SG on pile.

Light 41
Q G, 15 ft., 5 mi., SG on dolphin, radar reflector.

Kalama

Coffin Rock Light
46 02.0N, 122 52.9W, Q W, 20 ft., 5 mi., NB on house.

River Light 43
Fl G 2.5s, 18 ft., 5 mi., SG on dolphin.

Lower Range Front Light
46 00.6N, 122 51.0W, Q R, 28 ft., KRB on skeleton tower, visible 2° each side of rangeline.

Lower Range Rear Light
774 yards, 138° from front light, Iso R 6s, 102 ft., KRB on skeleton tower, visible 2° each side of rangeline.

Upper Range Front Light
45 58.7N, 122 50.4W, Q W, 17 ft., KRB on pile structure, visible all around, higher intensity on rangeline.

Upper Range Rear Light
750 yards, 163.4° from front light, Iso W 6s, 45 ft., KRB on skeleton tower, visible 4° each side of rangeline.

Dike Light 47A
Fl G 2.5s, 32 ft., 5 mi., SG on dolphin.

Ahle Point Light 49
45 59.9N, 122 50.7W, Fl G 4s, 26 ft., 4 mi., SG on dolphin.

Hunter Bar Light 1
45 59.5N, 122 51.2W, Fl G 2.5s, 22 ft., 4 mi., SG on dolphin.

Hunter Dike Light 52
Fl R 4s, 15 ft., 5 mi., TR on dolphin, higher intensity beam up channel.

Hunter Dike Light 54
Q R, 15 ft., 4 mi., TR on dolphin.

Martin Island

Lower Range Front Light
45 57.5N, 122 48.5W, Q W, 15 ft., KRB on dolphin, visible all around, higher intensity on rangeline.

Lower Range Rear Light
175 yards, 138° from front light, Iso W 6s, 30 ft., KRB on pile, visible 4° each side of rangeline.

Bybee Ledge Lighted Buoy 59
45 58.2N, 122 49.5W, Fl G 4s, 4 mi., green.

Bluff Lighted Buoy 60
45 57.6N, 122 48.9W, Q R, 4 mi., red.

Deer Island Lower Dike Light 62
Fl R 6s, 16 ft., 4 mi., TR on dolphin.

Dike Light 63
45 57.1N, 122 48.4W, Fl G 2.5s, 15 ft., 5 mi., SG on dolphin.

Middle Dike Light 65
Fl G 4s, 15 ft., 5 mi., SG on dolphin.

Upper Range Front Light
45 56.3N, 122 48.2W, Q W, 17 ft., KRB on pile structure, visible all around, higher intensity on rangeline.

Upper Range Rear Light
167 yards, 011.2° from front light, Iso W 6s, 35 ft., KRB on pile structure, visible 4° each side of rangeline.

Dike Daybeacon 67
SG on dolphin.

Burke Dike Light 69
45 55.9N, 122 48.1W, Fl G 2.5s, 17 ft., 5 mi., SG on dolphin, higher intensity beam downstream.

Deer Island Upper Dike Light 72
Fl R 4s, 15 ft., 4 mi., TR on dolphin, higher intensity beam up channel.

Caples Dike Light 73
Fl G 4s, 10 ft., 4 mi., SG on dolphin.

Chevron Chemical Dock Lights (2)
45 54.8N, 122 48.8W, F R, 42 ft., 5 mi., on dock, private aids.

Channel Lighted Buoy 75
45 54.5N, 122 48.4W, Q G, 4 mi., green.

Columbia City Light 76
Q R, 31 ft., 5 mi., TR on skeleton structure, higher intensity beam downstream.

St. Helens

Range Front Light
45 51.9N, 122 47.0W, Q W, 15 ft., KRB on pile structure, visible all around, higher intensity on rangeline.

Range Rear Light
660 yards, 151.5° from front light, Iso W 6s, 35 ft., KRB on skeleton tower, visible 4° each side of rangeline.

Jetty Lower Light 77
Q G, 15 ft., 5 mi., SG on dolphin.

Junction Lighted Buoy
45 52.9N, 122 47.9W, Fl (2+1) R 6s, 4 mi., red and green bands.

Jetty Light 79
45 52.2N, 122 47.1W, Fl G 4s, 22 ft., 5 mi., SG on pile structure.

Dike Light 80
45 51.8N, 122 47.4W, Q R, 15 ft., 4 mi., TR on dolphin.

Warrior Rock

Light
45 50.9N, 122 47.3W, Fl W 4s, 28 ft., 6 mi., white pyramidal structure.

Range Front Light
45 51.3N, 122 46.8W, Q W, 25 ft., KRW on skeleton tower, visible all around, higher intensity on rangeline.

Range Rear Light
167 yards, 021.5° from front light, Iso W 6s, 43 ft., KRW on skeleton tower, visible 4° each side of rangeline.

Reef Lighted Buoy 4
45 50.4N, 122 47.4W, Q R, 4 mi., red.

Duck Club Light 4A
Fl R 6s, 17 ft., 4 mi., TR on dolphin.

Duck Club Light 6
Q R, 22 ft., 5 mi., TR on dolphin, radar reflector.

Henrici

Channel Lighted Buoy 7
Q G, 3 mi., green.

Duck Club Light 8
45 49.0N, 122 47.9W, Fl R 2.5s, 17 ft., 4 mi., TR on dolphin.

Range Front Light
45 48.7N, 122 47.9W, Q W, 17 ft., KRB on pile structure, visible all around, higher intensity on rangeline.

Range Rear Light
285 yards, 328° from front light, Iso W 6s, 37 ft., KRB on skeleton tower, visible 4° each side of rangeline.

Landing Light 10
Fl R 4s, 17 ft., 4 mi., TR on dolphin.

Crossing Light 12
Fl R 2.5s, 15 ft., 5 mi., TR on dolphin.

Bachelor Point Light 13
Fl G 6s, 15 ft., 5 mi., SG on dolphin.

Bachelor Dike Light 15
Fl G 4s, 15 ft., 5 mi., SG on pile.

Fales Light 17
Q G, 22 ft., 5 mi., SG on dolphin, higher intensity beam down channel, radar reflector.

Knapp Point Light 19
45 44.7N, 122 45.3W, Fl G 4s, 21 ft., 4 mi., SG on pile structure, higher intensity beam down channel.

Willow

Lower Range Front Light
45 44.5N, 122 45.5W, Q W, 17 ft., KRB on tower on pile structure, visible all around, higher intensity on rangeline.

Lower Range Rear Light
280 yards, 013.5° from front light, Iso W 6s, 34 ft., KRB on skeleton tower, visible 4° each side of rangeline.

Dike Light 23
Fl G 2.5s, 15 ft., 4 mi., SG on dolphin.

Upper Range Front Light
45 41.0N, 122 46.7W, Q W, 15 ft., KRB on pile structure, on same structure as Morgan Upper Range Front Light, visible all around, higher intensity on rangeline and Morgan Upper Rangeline.

Upper Range Rear Light
345 yards, 193.5° from front light, Iso W 6s, 34 ft., KRB on skeleton tower, visible 2° each side of rangeline.

Dike Light 26
45 43.4N, 122 46.0W, Fl R 4s, 18 ft., 4 mi., TR on dolphin.

Reeder Point Light 28
Fl R 6s, 15 ft., 4 mi., TR on dolphin, radar reflector.

Hutchinson Dike Light 30
45 42.0N, 122 46.4W, Fl R 4s, 15 ft., 4 mi., TR on dolphin.

Morgan

Dike Light 32
Fl R 2.5s, 15 ft., 5 mi., TR on dolphin, radar reflector.

Hewlett Dike Light 33
Fl G 4s, 8 ft., 5 mi., SG on dolphin.

Upper Range Front Light
45 41.0N, 122 46.7W, Q W, 15 ft., KRB on pile structure, on same structure as Willow Upper Range Front Light, visible all around, higher intensity on rangeline and Willow Upper Rangeline.

Upper Range Rear Light
260 yards, 341.5° from front light, Iso W 6s, 35 ft., KRB on skeleton tower, visible 4° each side of rangeline.

Dike Light 36
Fl R 2.5s, 19 ft., 4 mi., TR on dolphin, radar reflector.

Dike Daybeacon 39
SG on pile.

Dike Light 40
Fl R 4s, 15 ft., 4 mi., TR on pile.

Vancouver

Lower Range Front Light
45 39.5N, 122 46.0W, Q R, 17 ft., KRB on skeleton tower, visible all around, higher intensity on rangeline.

Lower Range Rear Light
390 yards, 308° from front light, Iso R 6s, 44 ft., KRB on skeleton tower, visible 4° each side of rangeline.

Kelley Point Junction Light
45 39.2N, 122 45.8W, Fl (2+1) R 6s, 21 ft., 6 mi., JR on dolphin, radar reflector.
Also see Willamette River *for Portland.*

Channel Lighted Buoy 47 (75 feet outside channel limit)
45 38.9N, 122 44.8W, Q G, 4 mi., green.

Mathews Point East Light
F G, 34 ft., on pile, private aid.

Mathews Point West Light
F G, 34 ft., on pile, private aid.

Hayden Island Anchorage Lighted Buoy A
45 38.7N, 122 44.4W, Fl Y 6s, yellow, private aid.

Hayden Island Anchorage Lighted Buoy B
45 38.4N, 122 43.5W, Fl Y 6s, yellow, private aid.

Interstate-5 Alternate Barge Channel Buoy 2
Red nun.

Interstate-5 Alternate Barge Channel Buoy 3
45 37.1N, 122 40.4W, green can.

Interstate-5 Bridge Approach Buoy 2
Red nun.

Interstate-5 Bridge Approach Buoy 4
Red nun.

Vancouver Channel Dike Light 51
Fl G 2.5s, 24 ft., 4 mi., SG on dolphin.

Ryan Point Junction Lighted Buoy
Fl (2+1) R 6s, 4 mi., red and green bands.

North Portland Harbor

East End Range Front Light
45 36.1N, 122 38.5W, Q R, 14 ft., KRB on dike.

East End Range Rear Light
70 yards, 241° from front light, Iso R 6s, 27 ft., KRB on tripod, visible all around, higher intensity on rangeline.

Dike Light 2
45 36.2N, 122 38.1W, Fl R 4s, 38 ft., 4 mi., TR on dolphin.

Daybeacon 1
45 36.3N, 122 40.3W, SG on pile.

Vancouver Upper Bar Channel Lighted Buoy 14 (25 yards outside channel limit)
45 36.4N, 122 37.5W, Fl R 2.5s, 6 mi., red.

Portland Airport Dike Light 16
45 36.1N, 122 36.0W, Fl R 4s, 40 ft., 6 mi., TR on dolphin, higher intensity beam upstream.

Airport Bar Range Front Light
45 36.0N, 122 33.5W, F R, 34 ft., KRW on skeleton tower, F R line of light on daymark.

Airport Bar Range Rear Light
93 yards, 090.1° from front light, F G, 48 ft., KRW on skeleton tower, F G line of light on daymark.

CHINOOK CHANNEL

Also see North Channel.

Light 1
46 15.6N, 123 58.3W, Fl G 2.5s, 14 ft., 3 mi., SG on dolphin, radar reflector.

Daybeacon 2
46 15.8N, 123 57.7W, 15 ft., TR on dolphin, radar reflector.

Light 5
Fl G 4s, 15 ft., 5 mi., SG on pile structure, radar reflector.

Light 8
46 16.3N, 123 57.2W, Q R, 15 ft., 4 mi., TR on dolphin, radar reflector.

CRIMS ISLAND

Also see Columbia River.

Dike Light 2
46 10.7N, 123 07.5W, Fl R 6s, 12 ft., 4 mi., TR on dolphin.

Dike Light 6
Fl R 4s, 12 ft., 4 mi., TR on dolphin.

D

DEEP RIVER CHANNEL

Rocky Point Light 7
46 17.3N, 123 43.7W, Fl G 4s, 15 ft., 3 mi., SG on pile.

Daybeacon 8
46 17.8N, 123 43.2W, TR on dolphin.

Daybeacon 10
46 18.0N, 123 42.8W, TR on dolphin.

Daybeacon 12
46 18.1N, 123 42.6W, TR on dolphin.

Daybeacon 14
TR on dolphin, radar reflector.

Daybeacon 16
TR on dolphin, radar reflector.

E

Elochoman Buoy 1
46 12.3N, 123 23.4W, green can. *Also see* Cathlamet Channel *and* Columbia River.

Elochoman Daybeacon 2
46 12.5N, 123 23.3W, TR on pile.

H

HAMMOND BOAT BASIN

West Breakwater Daybeacon 2
TR on pipe.

East Breakwater Light 1
46 12.3N, 123 56.9W, Fl G 4s, 22 ft., 3 mi., SG on pipe.

Henrici
See Columbia River.

I

Ilwaco Mooring Basin Light 2
46 18.0N, 124 02.4W, Fl R 4s, 15 ft., 5 mi., TR on pile structure, radar reflector.
Also see Baker Bay West Channel.

Ilwaco Mooring Basin Light 3
46 18.1N, 124 02.5W, Fl G 4s, 5 mi., SG on pile.

K

Kelley Point Junction Light
45 39.2N, 122 45.8W, Fl (2+1) R 6s, 21 ft., 6 mi., JR on dolphin, radar reflector.
Also see Columbia River *and* Willamette River.

L

Lewis and Clark River
See Youngs Bay and Lewis and Clark River.

Longview
See Columbia River.

M

Mount Coffin Light 1
46 07.7N, 122 59.3W, Fl G 6s, 26 ft., 4 mi., SG on cylinder.
Also see Columbia River.

MULTNOMAH CHANNEL

Also see Willamette River.

Daybeacon 2
TR on pile.

Daybeacon 3
SG on pile.

Sauvie Island Junction Light
Fl (2+1) R 6s, 15 ft., 4 mi., JR on pile structure.

Light 6
45 50.1N, 122 48.7W, Fl R 4s, 15 ft., 4 mi., TR on dolphin, higher intensity beam up and down channel.

Multnomah Channel Pollution Response Buoy
45 37.2N, 122 48.2W, yellow.

N

NORTH CHANNEL

Sand Island Lower Dike Light 1
46 15.6N, 124 00.5W, Fl G 4s, 15 ft., 5 mi., SG on pile structure.

Sand Island Middle Dike Light 3
46 15.5N, 123 59.7W, Fl G 6s, 15 ft., 4 mi., SG on pile structure.

Sand Island Upper Dike Light 5
46 15.4N, 123 58.9W, Fl G 4s, 15 ft., 4 mi., SG on pile structure.

Chinook Dike Light 7
46 15.0N, 123 57.2W, Fl G 6s, 15 ft., 4 mi., SG on pile structure.

Daybeacon 9 (E of quarantine station)
46 16.2N, 123 49.1W, SG on pile.

Daybeacon 10
46 15.8N, 123 47.2W, TR on dolphin.

Daybeacon 12
TR on pile structure, radar reflector.

Grays Point Light 13
46 16.4N, 123 46.0W, Fl G 6s, 15 ft., 4 mi., SG on pile.

Portuguese Point Daybeacon 14A
46 16.6N, 123 45.1W, TR on dolphin.

North Portland Harbor
See Columbia River.

P

Portland
See Willamette River.

S

Sauvie Island Junction Light
Fl (2+1) R 6s, 15 ft., 4 mi., JR on pile structure.
Also see Multnomah Channel.

SKIPANON WATERWAY

West Light 4
46 11.1N, 123 54.5W, Fl R 4s, 15 ft., 5 mi., TR on dolphin.

East Light 3
Fl G 4s, 14 ft., 5 mi., SG on dolphin, radar reflector.

Range Front Light
46 10.0N, 123 54.9W, F R, 26 ft., KRB on skeleton tower, visible all around, higher intensity on rangeline.

Range Rear Light
248.5 yards, 198° from front light, F R, 39 ft., KRB on skeleton tower, visible all around, higher intensity on rangeline.

Deep Sea Pier Light
46 09.9N, 123 55.3W, F R, 16 ft., on pile, private aid.

St. Helens
See Columbia River.

V

Vancouver
See Columbia River.

W

Warrior Rock Light
45 50.9N, 122 47.3W, Fl W 4s, 28 ft., 6 mi., white pyramidal structure.
Also see Columbia River.

Westport
See Columbia River.

WILLAMETTE RIVER

Channel

Kelley Point Junction Light
45 39.2N, 122 45.8W, Fl (2+1) R 6s, 21 ft., 6 mi., JR on dolphin, radar reflector.
Also see Columbia River.

Light 2
45 39.2N, 122 46.0W, Q R, 16 ft., 4 mi., TR on dolphin.

Light 3
Fl G 4s, 15 ft., 5 mi., SG on dolphin, higher intensity beam up channel.

Light 4
Fl R 4s, 10 ft., 4 mi., TR on dolphin.

Light 6
Fl R 6s, 15 ft., 4 mi., TR on dolphin, higher intensity beam up channel.

Terminal 5 Bulk Outloader Dock Lights (2)
Fl Y 10s, 9 mi., on concrete pier, private aids.

Light 10
Fl R 2.5s, 10 ft., 4 mi., TR on dolphin, higher intensity beam up channel.

Oregon Steel Dock Lights (2)
F R, 23 ft., on dolphin, private aids.

Post Office Range Front Light
45 37.8N, 122 47.6W, Q W, 17 ft., KRB on pile structure, visible all around, higher intensity on rangeline.

Post Office Range Rear Light
235 yards, 347° from front light, Iso W 6s, 31 ft., KRB on skeleton tower, visible 4° each side of rangeline.

Ash Grove Lime Dock Lights (2)
F G, 35 ft., on pile structure, private aids.

Multnomah Channel Junction Light
45 37.2N, 122 47.7W, Fl (2+1) R 6s, 15 ft., 4 mi., JR on dolphin, higher intensity beam up and down channel.
Also see Multnomah Channel.

Burlington Northern Railroad Bridge Approach Buoy 14
45 34.6N, 122 44.9W, red nun.

Burlington Northern Railroad Bridge Approach Buoy 16
45 34.5N, 122 44.8W, red nun.

Chevron Petroleum Dock Light A
F R, 38 ft., private aid.

Chevron Petroleum Dock Light B
F R, 38 ft., private aid.

Swan Island Pier C Light
45 34.1N, 122 43.5W, Q R, 17 ft., on pile, private aid.

Swan Island Pier A Light
45 34.1N, 122 43.4W, Q R, 17 ft., on pile, light obscured from 190° to 010°.

Shaver Mooring Light
45 33.6N, 122 43.7W, Fl R 4s, 12 ft., on dolphin, private aid.

River Place Marina

Breakwater Light C
45 30.7N, 122 40.3W, F Y, floating breakwater, private aid.

Breakwater Light G
45 30.6N, 122 40.2W, F Y, floating breakwater, private aid.

Breakwater Light H
45 30.6N, 122 40.2W, F Y, floating breakwater, private aid.

Breakwater Light I
45 30.6N, 122 40.2W, F Y, floating breakwater, private aid.

Johns Landing Pier

Light 2
45 29.1N, 122 40.3W, Q R, 10 ft., on pier, private aid.

Light 1
45 29.1N, 122 40.3W, Q G, 10 ft., on pier, private aid.

Light 4
45 29.1N, 122 40.3W, Q R, 10 ft., on pier, private aid.

Light 3
45 29.1N, 122 40.3W, Q G, 10 ft., on pier, private aid.

Stevens Point Buoy 2
45 28.6N, 122 40.1W, red nun.

Stevens Point Buoy 4
45 28.6N, 122 40.0W, red nun.

Stevens Point Buoy 5
45 28.2N, 122 39.9W, green can.

Y

YOUNGS BAY AND LEWIS AND CLARK RIVER

Entrance Light 2
46 10.9N, 123 52.8W, Fl R 6s, 16 ft., 5 mi., TR on dolphin.

Channel Buoy 4
46 10.3N, 123 51.8W, red nun.

Channel Light 6
46 10.1N, 123 51.5W, Fl R 2.5s, 5 mi., TR on pile structure.

Lewis and Clark River Buoy 6
46 10.1N, 123 51.8W, red nun.

Lewis and Clark River Buoy 8
46 09.9N, 123 51.6W, red nun.

Lewis and Clark River Buoy 9
46 09.8N, 123 51.4W, green can.

Lewis and Clark River Buoy 10
46 09.7N, 123 51.4W, red nun.

Lewis and Clark River Buoy 11
46 09.7N, 123 51.3W, green can.

Oregon

Aids to navigation for the
Columbia River are listed in a
separate chapter.

A

Astoria
See Columbia River chapter.

B

Baltimore Rock Bell Buoy 2 BR
43 21.3N, 124 23.0W, red.

C

Cape Arago Light
43 20.5N, 124 22.5W, Fl (3) W 30s,
100 ft., 22 mi., white octagonal
tower attached to building,
obscured from 035° to 249°,
horn: 2 blasts every 30s, fog
signal maintained from April 15
to Oct. 15, lighted throughout
24 hours.

Cape Blanco Light
42 50.2N, 124 33.8W, Fl W 20s,
245 ft., 26 mi., white conical
tower, lighted throughout
24 hours.

Cape Kiwanda Bell Buoy 2
45 13.0N, 123 59.4W, red.

Cape Meares Light
45 29.2N, 123 58.7W, Fl W 15s,
232 ft., 17 mi., white masonry
building.

CHETCO RIVER

**Approach Lighted Whistle Buoy
CR**
42 01.7N, 124 17.0W, Mo (A) W,
6 mi., red and white stripes.

Entrance Lighted Bell Buoy 2
42 02.1N, 124 16.6W, Fl R 4s,
4 mi., red.

Entrance Range Front Light
42 02.9N, 124 16.1W, Q R, 40 ft.,
KRB on skeleton tower, visible 4°
each side of rangeline, lighted
throughout 24 hours.

Entrance Range Rear Light
277 yards, 030° from front light,
Iso R 6s, 59 ft., KRB on skeleton
tower, visible 4° each side of
rangeline, lighted throughout
24 hours.

Entrance Gong Buoy 3
42 02.4N, 124 16.4W, green,
maintained from May 1 to Oct. 1.

Entrance Light 5
42 02.6N, 124 16.3W, Fl G 4s,
23 ft., 6 mi., SG on white cylindrical concrete column, horn: 1
blast every 30s.

**Entrance Small Boat Warning
Sign**
Q Y (2), 13 ft., NW worded
ROUGH BAR in black letters,
lights flashing when seas exceed
four feet in height, lights extinguished for lesser bar conditions,
but with no guarantee that bar
is safe.

Entrance Daybeacon 9
42 02.8N, 124 16.2W, SG on pile.

Entrance Light 11
42 02.9N, 124 16.2W, Q G, 16 ft.,
2 mi., SG on pedestal structure.

Clatsop Spit
See Columbia River chapter.

Cleft of the Rock Light
44 17.5N, 124 06.5W, Al W R 10s,
110 ft., grey square tower, private
aid.

**Columbia River Approach
Lighted Horn Buoy CR**
46 11.1N, 124 11.1W, Mo (A) W,
6 mi., Fl W 2.5s, red and white
stripes, high-intensity flash tube
Fl W 2.5s, racon: M (--), horn:
1 blast every 30s.
Also see Columbia River chapter.

COOS BAY

Approach Lighted Whistle Buoy K
43 22.2N, 124 23.1W, Mo (A) W,
6 mi., red and white stripes.

Entrance Lighted Bell Buoy 1
43 21.9N, 124 21.8W, Fl G 2.5s,
4 mi., green.

Entrance Range Front Light
43 21.0N, 124 19.5W, Q R, 25 ft.,
KRB on dolphin, on same structure as Coos Bay Inside Range A
Front Light, visible 4° each side
of rangeline, lighted throughout
24 hours.

Entrance Range Rear Light
890 yards, 116° from front light,
F R, 38 ft., KRB on skeleton tower,
visible 4° each side of rangeline,
lighted throughout 24 hours.

Entrance Lighted Buoy 2
43 21.4N, 124 21.0W, Fl R 4s,
3 mi., red.

North Jetty Lighted Gong Buoy 3
43 21.7N, 124 21.3W, Fl G 4s,
3 mi., green.

North Jetty Light 3A
43 21.5N, 124 20.7W, Fl G 2.5s,
23 ft., 3 mi., SG on pedestal,
horn: 1 blast every 30s, fog signal
sounded continuously from June
1 to Sept. 15.

**Guano Rock Lighted Whistle
Buoy 4**
43 21.2N, 124 20.4W, Fl R 4s,
3 mi., red.

Leading Light
43 21.0N, 124 20.2W, Q W, 90 ft.,
4 mi., NB on skeleton tower, visible from 138° to 279° with a higher intensity beam bearing 246.5°.

Channel Lighted Bell Buoy 5
43 21.3N, 124 20.1W, Q G, 3 mi.,
green.

Channel Lighted Buoy 5A
43 21.3N, 124 19.6W, Fl G 4s,
4 mi., green.

Inside Range A Front Light
43 21.0N, 124 19.5W, Q R, 25 ft., KRB on dolphin, on same structure as Coos Bay Entrance Range Front Light, visible all around, higher intensity on rangeline.

Inside Range A Rear Light
200 yards, 203º from front light, Iso R 6s, 43 ft., KRB on pile structure, visible 15º each side of rangeline.

Channel Light 7
43 21.5N, 124 19.3W, Fl G 6s, 16 ft., 3 mi., SG on pile structure.

Inside Range B Front Light
43 22.1N, 124 18.9W, Q W, 20 ft., KRB on pile structure, visible 4º each side of rangeline.

Inside Range B Rear Light
587 feet, 023.2º from front light, Iso W 6s, 30 ft., KRB on skeleton tower on pile structure, visible 4º each side of rangeline.

Range A Front Light
43 21.7N, 124 19.2W, Q W, 19 ft., KRB on pile structure, visible 4º each side of rangeline.

Range A Rear Light
330 yards, 223.8º from front light, Iso W 6s, 37 ft., KRB on tower on pile structure, visible 4º each side of rangeline.

Channel Lighted Buoy 8
43 21.7N, 124 19.1W, Fl R 6s, 4 mi., red.

Channel Lighted Buoy 10
43 21.9N, 124 18.9W, Fl R 4s, 4 mi., red.

Channel Lighted Buoy 10A
43 22.2N, 124 18.4W, Fl R 4s, 2 mi., red.

Channel Lighted Buoy 11
43 22.6N, 124 18.1W, Fl G 4s, 4 mi., green.

Channel Lighted Buoy 12
43 23.0N, 124 17.5W, Q R, 3 mi., red.

Range B Front Light
43 23.3N, 124 17.1W, Q R, 21 ft., KRB on pile structure, visible 2º each side of rangeline.

Range B Rear Light
480 yards, 043.8º from front light, Iso R 6s, 39 ft., KRB on skeleton tower on structure, on same structure as Jarvis Lower Range A Rear Light, visible 2º each side of rangeline.

Empire Range A Front Light
43 22.5N, 124 17.8W, Q R, 19 ft., KRB on pile structure, visible 4º each side of rangeline.

Empire Range A Rear Light
283 yards, 204.8º from front light, Iso R 6s, 35 ft., KRB on skeleton tower on pile structure, visible 4º each side of rangeline.

Empire Range B Front Light
43 24.8N, 124 16.3W, Q R, 19 ft., KRB on dolphin, visible 4º each side of rangeline.

Empire Range B Rear Light
500 yards, 025º from front light, Iso R 6s, 37 ft., KRB on dolphin, visible 4º each side of rangeline.

Channel Lighted Buoy 14
43 23.5N, 124 17.1W, Fl R 6s, 4 mi., red.

Channel Lighted Buoy 15
43 24.0N, 124 17.0W, Fl G 6s, 4 mi., green.

Channel Lighted Buoy 16
Fl R 4s, 4 mi., red.

Jarvis Lower Range A Front Light
43 23.6N, 124 16.9W, Q R, 23 ft., KRB on pile structure, visible 4º each side of rangeline.

Jarvis Lower Range A Rear Light
285 yards, 188.5º from front light, Iso R 6s, 38 ft., KRB on skeleton tower pile structure, on same structure as Coos Bay Range B Rear Light, visible 4º each side of rangeline.

Sause Brothers Mooring Buoy SB
43 24.2N, 124 16.5W, white with blue bands, private aid.

Light 17
Fl G 4s, 18 ft., 3 mi., SG on dolphin.

Jarvis Lower Range B Front Light
43 25.1N, 124 16.5W, Q G, 18 ft., KRB on dolphin, visible all around, higher intensity on rangeline.

Jarvis Lower Range B Rear Light
285 yards, 009º from front light, Iso G 6s, 32 ft., KRB on tower, on same structure as Jarvis Upper Range A Rear Light, visible all around, higher intensity on rangeline.

Channel Lighted Buoy 18
43 24.8N, 124 16.6W, Q R, 3 mi., red.

Coos Bay Deflection Boom Lights A & B
43 24.9N, 124 16.6W, Fl Y 10s, on steel pile, private aids.

Jarvis Dike 6.8 Light 19
43 25.0N, 124 16.6W, Fl G 4s, 15 ft., 3 mi., SG on dolphin.

Jarvis Upper Range A Front Light
43 25.3N, 124 16.3W, Q G, 15 ft., KRB on dolphin, visible all around, higher intensity on rangeline.

Jarvis Upper Range A Rear Light
300 yards, 259º from front light, Iso G 6s, 32 ft., KRB on tower, on same structure as Jarvis Lower Range B Rear Light, visible all around, higher intensity on rangeline.

Channel Lighted Buoy 23
43 25.4N, 124 16.0W, Fl G 2.5s, 5 mi., green.

Jarvis Upper Range B Front Light
43 25.7N, 124 13.4W, Q W, 15 ft., KRB on pile structure, visible 4º each side of rangeline.

Jarvis Upper Range B Rear Light
405 yards, 079º from front light, Iso W 6s, 32 ft., KRB on tower on dolphin, visible 4º each side of rangeline.

North Bend Outfall Light
Fl Y 10s, 12 ft., on dolphin at end of submerged outfall pipe, private aid.

Douglas Fir Dock Lights
F R (4), 19 ft., dolphins and ends of dock, private aids.

Channel Light 25 (150 feet outside channel limit)
Fl G 4s, 15 ft., 3 mi., SG on dolphin.

Channel Buoy 27
Green can.

Bridge Fog Signal
43 25.6N, 124 14.1W, siren: 1 blast every 60s when draw is closed, bell: 1 stroke every 10s when draw is open, private aid.

Channel Light 28 (75 feet outside channel limit)
43 25.6N, 124 13.7W, Fl R 4s, 17 ft., 5 mi., TR on dolphin.

Channel Lighted Buoy 29
43 25.7N, 124 13.6W, Q G, 4 mi., green.

North Bend Lower Range Front Light
43 25.5N, 124 13.0W, Q G, 20 ft., KRB on dolphin, visible all around, higher intensity on rangeline.

North Bend Lower Range Rear Light
468 feet, 112.2° from front light, Iso G 6s, 25 ft., KRB on skeleton tower on pile structure, on same structure as North Bend Range Rear Light, visible all around, higher intensity on rangeline.

North Bend Range Front Light
43 25.4N, 124 12.9W, Q G, 16 ft., KRB on pile structure, visible all around, higher intensity on rangeline.

North Bend Range Rear Light
492 feet, 009° from front light, Iso G 6s, 25 ft., KRB on skeleton tower on pile structure, on same structure as North Bend Lower Range Rear Light, visible all around, higher intensity on rangeline.

Channel Light 35
.43 24.6N, 124 13.1W, Fl G 2.5s, 16 ft., 2 mi., SG on dolphin.

Channel Light 36
43 24.5N, 124 13.2W, Fl R 4s, 23 ft., 4 mi., TR on skeleton tower on pile structure.

North Bend Upper Range Front Light
43 23.6N, 124 12.9W, Q G, 16 ft., KRB on tower, visible all around, higher intensity on rangeline.

North Bend Upper Range Rear Light
233 yards, 163° from front light, Iso G 6s, 30 ft., KRB on tower on pile structure, visible all around, higher intensity on rangeline.

Ferndale Lower Range Front Light
43 24.1N, 124 12.9W, Q W, 16 ft., KRB on dolphin, visible 15° each side of rangeline.

Ferndale Lower Range Rear Light
323 yards, 013° from front light, Iso W 6s, 33 ft., KRB on dolphin, visible 15° each side of rangeline.

Channel Light 37
43 23.0N, 124 13.1W, Fl G 2.5s, 16 ft., 4 mi., SG on dolphin.

Ferndale Upper Range Front Light
43 22.4N, 124 12.4W, Q G, 11 ft., KRB on dolphin, visible all around, higher intensity on rangeline.

Ferndale Upper Range Rear Light
200.8 yards, 140.2° from front light, Iso G 6s, 34 ft., KRB on skeleton tower, visible 4° each side of rangeline.

Marshfield Range Front Light
43 22.6N, 124 12.4W, Q G, 14 ft., KRB on tower.

Marshfield Range Rear Light
619.8 feet, 024.4° from front light, Iso G 6s, 36 ft., KRB on dolphin.

Isthmus Slough Light 43
43 21.9N, 124 12.5W, Fl G 4s, 15 ft., 6 mi., SG on dolphin.

Coos River
Due to frequently changing conditions, positions of most buoys are not listed.

Marshfield Channel Range Front Light
43 22.5N, 124 10.9W, Q R, 14 ft., KRB on dolphin.

Marshfield Channel Range Rear Light
480 yards, 090° from front light, Iso W 6s, 21 ft., KRB on dolphin.

Entrance Lighted Buoy 1
43 22.5N, 124 11.2W, Fl G 4s, green.

Channel Buoy 3
43 22.6N, 124 10.4W, green can.

Channel Light 8
43 22.2N, 124 10.7W, Fl R 4s, 14 ft., 5 mi., TR on dolphin.

South Slough

Light 1
43 21.3N, 124 19.1W, Fl G 2.5s, 15 ft., 3 mi., SG on pile structure, radar reflector.

Lighted Buoy 2
43 21.3N, 124 19.2W, Fl R 2.5s, 3 mi., red.

Light 4 (20 feet outside channel limit)
43 21.2N, 124 19.1W, Fl R 4s, 15 ft., 5 mi., TR on dolphin, radar reflector.

Small Boat Warning Sign
43 20.8N, 124 19.3W, Q Y (2), NW worded ROUGH BAR, lights flashing when seas exceed four feet in height, lights extinguished for lesser sea conditions, but with no guarantee that bar is safe.

Buoy 5
43 21.1N, 124 19.1W, green can.

Buoy 6 (50 feet outside channel limit)
43 21.0N, 124 19.2W, red nun.

Light 8
43 20.9N, 124 19.2W, Fl R 2.5s, 15 ft., 3 mi., TR on pile structure.

Light 9 (50 feet outside channel limit)
Fl G 4s, 16 ft., 3 mi., SG on dolphin.

Daybeacon 10 (50 feet outside channel limit)
TR on pile.

North Slough

Channel Daybeacon 1
43 26.0N, 124 14.2W, SG on pile.

Channel Daybeacon 4
43 26.1N, 124 14.0W, 10 ft., TR on pile, private aid.

Channel Daybeacon 8
43 26.4N, 124 13.1W, 10 ft., TR on pile, private aid.

Haynes Inlet

Channel Daybeacon 1
43 26.1N, 124 13.7W, 10 ft., SG on pile, private aid.

Channel Daybeacon 4
43 26.6N, 124 12.9W, 10 ft., TR on pile, private aid.

Channel Daybeacon 5
43 26.8N, 124 12.7W, 10 ft., SG on pile, private aid.

Channel Daybeacon 7
43 26.9N, 124 12.5W, 10 ft., SG on pile, private aid.

Channel Daybeacon 8
43 26.9N, 124 12.0W, 10 ft., TR on pile, private aid.

COQUILLE RIVER

Entrance Lighted Whistle Buoy 2
43 08.1N, 124 27.8W, Fl R 4s, 5 mi., red.

Entrance Lighted Bell Buoy 4
43 07.9N, 124 27.3W, Fl R 6s, 4 mi., red.

Entrance Range Front Light
43 07.3N, 124 24.7W, Q R, 15 ft., KRB on skeleton tower, visible 4° each side of rangeline, lighted throughout 24 hours.

Entrance Range Rear Light
304 yards, 102° from front light, Iso R 6s, 30 ft., KRB on skeleton tower, visible 4° each side of rangeline, lighted throughout 24 hours.

South Jetty Light 8
43 07.4N, 124 25.8W, Fl R 4s, 30 ft., 6 mi., TR on white masonry building, horn: 1 blast every 30s, operates continuously.

Entrance Small Boat Warning Sign
43 07.3N, 124 25.1W, Q Y (2), 15 ft., NW worded ROUGH BAR, lights flashing when seas exceed four feet in height, lights extinguished for lesser bar conditions, but with no guarantee that bar is safe, maintained from May 15 to Sept. 30.

Rock Buoy 11
43 07.3N, 124 25.1W, green can, maintained from May 15 to Oct. 1.

Buoy 13
43 07.3N, 124 24.4W, green can, maintained from May 15 to Oct. 1.

Light 14
43 07.3N, 124 24.7W, Fl R 4s, 15 ft., 3 mi., TR on breakwater.

D

DEPOE BAY

Approach Lighted Whistle Buoy DB
44 48.5N, 124 05.3W, Mo (A) W, 6 mi., red and white stripes.

Entrance Lighted Bell Buoy 2
44 48.9N, 124 04.4W, Fl R 4s, 4 mi., red, replaced by bell buoy from Oct. 1 to May 1.

Fog Signal
White square house, horn: 1 blast every 30s.

Entrance Direction Light
44 48.6N, 124 03.7W, Iso W 6s (R & G sectors), 38 ft., on skeleton tower, white visible 1.25° each side of centerline of channel bearing 086°, red visible from 083.5° to 085°, green visible from 087° to 088.5°, entrance to inner harbor floodlit to assist those persons having an intimate knowledge of locality to enter the bay at night, others having limited or no knowledge of these waters should not attempt this entrance at night, especially in bad weather.

Entrance Small Boat Warning Sign
44 48.6N, 124 03.7W, Q Y (2), 25 ft., NW worded ROUGH BAR, lights flashing when seas exceed four feet in height, lights extinguished for lesser sea conditions, but with no guarantee that bar is safe, visible from 017° to 263°.

Desdemona Sands Channel
See Columbia River chapter.

F

Fort Stevens Wharf Light 26
46 12.4N, 123 57.1W, Oc R 4s, 35 ft., 6 mi., TR on multi-pile.
Also see Columbia River chapter.

G

Guano Rock Lighted Whistle Buoy 4
43 21.2N, 124 20.4W, Fl R 4s, 3 mi., red.
Also see Coos Bay.

H

Hammond Boat Basin
See Columbia River chapter.

HAYNES INLET

Also see Coos Bay.

Channel Daybeacon 1
43 26.1N, 124 13.7W, 10 ft., SG on pile, private aid.

Channel Daybeacon 4
43 26.6N, 124 12.9W, 10 ft., TR on pile, private aid.

Channel Daybeacon 5
43 26.8N, 124 12.7W, 10 ft., SG on pile, private aid.

Channel Daybeacon 7
43 26.9N, 124 12.5W, 10 ft., SG on pile, private aid.

Channel Daybeacon 8
43 26.9N, 124 12.0W, 10 ft., TR on pile, private aid.

Heceta Head Light
44 08.2N, 124 07.7W, Fl W 10s, 205 ft., 26 mi., white conical tower, lighted throughout 24 hours.

L

Lewis and Clark River
See Youngs Bay and Lewis and Clark River, Columbia River chapter.

N

NEHALEM RIVER

Approach Whistle Buoy NR
45 39.3N, 123 57.5W, red and white stripes.

Entrance Range Front Daybeacon
45 39.6N, 123 55.8W, SW with red stripe on multi-pile structure, due to seasonal changes in entrance channel, use only with local knowledge, private aid.

Entrance Range Rear Daybeacon
120 yards, 085° from front daybeacon, white diamond daymark with red stripe on tree, private aid.

NOAA Lighted Buoy 46050
44 37.3N, 124 31.7W, Fl (4) Y 20s, yellow disc-shaped buoy.

NOAA Lighted Buoy 46029
46 15.0N, 124 15.1W, Fl (4) Y 20s, yellow disk-shaped buoy.

North Portland Harbor
See Columbia River chapter.

O

Orford Reef Lighted Whistle Buoy 20R
42 45.6N, 124 38.9W, Fl R 4s, 5 mi., red.

P

Port of Gold Beach Channel Buoys
See Rogue River.

Port Orford Entrance Lighted Bell Buoy 1
42 43.3N, 124 30.6W, Fl G 4s, 4 mi., green.

Port Orford Jetty Light 3
42 44.3N, 124 29.8W, Fl G 2.5s, 4 mi., SG on skeleton tower, maintained from May 15 to Oct. 15, radar reflector.

Portland
See Willamette River, Columbia River chapter.

R

ROGUE RIVER

Approach Lighted Whistle Buoy R
42 23.6N, 124 28.6W, Mo (A) W, 6 mi., red and white stripes.

Entrance Buoy 1
42 24.8N, 124 26.7W, green can.

North Jetty Light 3
42 25.2N, 124 26.0W, Fl G 2.5s, 23 ft., 4 mi., SG on skeleton structure, horn: 1 blast every 30s, operates continuously, light and fog signal maintained from June 1 to Oct. 31.

Buoy 5
42 25.6N, 124 25.5W, green can, maintained from June 1 to Oct. 31.

Entrance Small Boat Warning Sign
42 25.6N, 124 25.5W, Q Y (2), NW worded ROUGH BAR, lights flashing when seas exceed four feet in height, lights extinguished for lesser bar conditions, but with no guarantee that bar is safe, maintained from May 1 to Sept. 30.

Port of Gold Beach Channel Buoys (12)
Red or green drums, private aids, buoys 1–6 are seasonal from May 1 to Nov. 1.

S

Salmon Harbor Entrance Light 1
43 41.2N, 124 10.8W, Fl G 4s, 15 ft., 3 mi., SG on pile structure. *Also see* Umpqua River.

Salmon Harbor Entrance Light 2
43 41.0N, 124 10.2W, Fl R 4s, 15 ft., 3 mi., TR on pile.

Scholfield Creek Channel
See Umpqua River.

SIUSLAW RIVER

Approach Lighted Whistle Buoy S
44 01.1N, 124 09.4W, Mo (A) W, 5 mi., red and white stripes with red spherical topmark.

Entrance Range Front Light
44 01.1N, 124 07.8W, F R, KRB on skeleton tower, visible 4° each side of rangeline, lighted throughout 24 hours.

Entrance Range Rear Light
370 yards, 094° from front light, F R, 65 ft., KRB on skeleton tower, visible 4° each side of rangeline, lighted throughout 24 hours.

North Jetty Light 3
44 01.1N, 124 08.8W, Fl G 2.5s, 15 ft., 3 mi., SG on skeleton tower, horn: 1 blast every 30s, light and fog signals maintained from May 20 to Oct. 1.

Small Boat Warning Sign
Q Y (2), 37 ft., NW worded ROUGH BAR, lights flashing when seas exceed four feet in height, lights extinguished for lesser sea conditions, but with no guarantee that bar is safe.

Channel Buoy 4
Red nun, position shifted with changing conditions.

Light 5
44 01.0N, 124 08.0W, Fl G 4s, 15 ft., 3 mi., SG on dolphin.

Inner Range Front Light
44 01.0N, 124 07.8W, Q W, 20 ft., KRB on pile structure, visible all around, higher intensity on rangeline.

Inner Range Rear Light
200 yards, 001° from front light, Iso W 6s, 35 ft., KRB on skeleton tower, visible 4° each side of rangeline.

Channel Buoy 6
Red nun, position shifted with changing conditions.

Channel Buoy 7
44 00.9N, 124 07.9W, green can.

Light 8
44 00.5N, 124 07.9W, Fl R 4s, 15 ft., 3 mi., TR on dolphin.

Channel Light 9 (100 feet outside channel limit)
44 00.5N, 124 07.7W, Fl G 4s, 3 mi., SG on pile, radar reflector.

Channel Buoy 11
44 00.3N, 124 07.6W, green can.

Channel Daybeacon 12
44 00.1N, 124 07.5W, TR on pile.

Range A Front Light
44 00.1N, 124 07.4W, Q W, 25 ft., KRB on pile structure, visible all around, higher intensity on rangeline.

Range A Rear Light
101 yards, 349.4° from front light, Iso W 6s, 34 ft., KRB on skeleton tower, visible 4° each side of rangeline.

Channel Daybeacon 14
43 59.4N, 124 07.3W, TR on pile.

Dike Daybeacon 16 (100 feet outside channel limit)
43 58.9N, 124 07.6W, TR on pile.

Light 18
43 58.9N, 124 07.6W, Fl R 4s, 15 ft., 4 mi., TR on pile, higher intensity beam downstream.

Dike Daybeacon 18A
43 58.9N, 124 07.6W, TR on pile.

Dike Daybeacon 20 (40 feet outside channel limit)
43 58.7N, 124 07.7W, TR on pile.

Dike Daybeacon 22 (40 feet outside channel limit)
43 58.4N, 124 07.8W, TR on pile.

Channel Light 23
43 58.2N, 124 07.2W, Fl G 4s, 18 ft., 3 mi., SG on pile.

Channel Daybeacon 25 (100 feet outside channel limit)
43 58.1N, 124 07.0W, SG on pile, radar reflector.

Channel Daybeacon 26 (100 feet outside channel limit)
43 57.9N, 124 06.3W, TR on pile, radar reflector.

Channel Daybeacon 28 (100 feet outside channel limit)
43 57.9N, 124 06.0W, TR on pile, radar reflector.

Channel Daybeacon 29
43 58.1N, 124 04.8W, SG on pile.

Skipanon Waterway
See Columbia River chapter.

Smith River Light 2
43 42.4N, 124 05.2W, Fl R 4s, 13 ft., 5 mi., TR on platform.
Also see Umpqua River.

St. Helens
See Columbia River chapter.

T

Tansy Point Channel
See Columbia River chapter.

TILLAMOOK BAY

Approach Lighted Whistle Buoy T
45 34.3N, 123 59.6W, Mo (A) W, 6 mi., red and white stripes.

Entrance Buoy 1
45 34.2N, 123 58.7W, green can.

North Jetty Light 3
45 34.2N, 123 58.0W, Fl G 2.5s, 33 ft., 5 mi., SG on skeleton tower, horn: 1 blast every 30s, light and fog signal maintained from June 1 to Oct. 1.

Entrance Range Front Light
45 34.1N, 123 56.7W, Q G, 33 ft., KRB on skeleton tower, visible all around, higher intensity on rangeline.

Entrance Range Rear Light
258 yards, 094.5° from front light, Iso G 6s, 53 ft., KRB on skeleton tower, visible 4° each side of rangeline.

Garibaldi Channel

Lighted Buoy 6
45 34.0N, 123 56.8W, Fl R 4s, 4 mi., red.

Light 10
45 33.5N, 123 56.1W, Fl R 2.5s, 16 ft., 3 mi., TR on dolphin.

Light 11
45 33.3N, 123 55.7W, Q G, 3 mi., SG on pile.

Light 12
45 33.2N, 123 55.8W, Q R, 15 ft., 3 mi., TR on dolphin.

Daybeacon 13
45 33.3N, 123 55.4W, SG on pile.

Light 14
45 33.2N, 123 55.2W, Fl R 4s, TR on dolphin.

Entrance Small Boat Warning Sign
45 34.1N, 123 56.3W, Q Y (2), NW worded ROUGH BAR, visible from 234° to 333°, lights flashing when seas exceed four feet, lights extinguished for lesser sea conditions, but with no guarantee that bar is safe.

Garibaldi Light 19
45 33.2N, 123 54.9W, Fl G 4s, 15 ft., 5 mi., SG on pile structure.

U

UMPQUA RIVER

Umpqua River Light
43 39.7N, 124 11.9W, Al (2) W R 15s, 165 ft., white 21 mi., red 20 mi., white conical tower, lighted throughout 24 hours.

Approach Lighted Whistle Buoy U
43 40.0N, 124 14.3W, Mo (A) W, 6 mi., red and white stripes.

Entrance Buoy 2
43 40.0N, 124 13.5W, red nun.

Bar Range Front Light
43 40.1N, 124 12.1W, Oc R 4s, 24 ft., KRB on skeleton tower, visible 4° each side of rangeline, lighted throughout 24 hours.

Bar Range Rear Light
876 feet, 086° from front light, Oc R 4s, 48 ft., KRB on skeleton tower, visible 4° each side of rangeline, range lights are synchronized, lighted throughout 24 hours.

South Jetty Light 2A
43 40.0N, 124 13.2W, Fl R 2.5s, 15 ft., 3 mi., TR on skeleton tower, horn: 1 blast every 15s, maintained from May 20 to Sept. 30, radar reflector.

Small Boat Warning Sign
43 40.9N, 124 11.1W, Q Y (2),
19 ft., NW worded ROUGH BAR,
lights flashing when seas exceed
four feet in height, lights extinguished for lesser sea conditions
but with no guarantee that bar
is safe.

Light 6
43 40.2N, 124 11.9W, Fl R 4s,
24 ft., 4 mi., TR on skeleton
tower, bell: 1 stroke every 20s,
higher intensity beam up and
down channel, radar reflector.

Channel Range Front Light
43 41.3N, 124 11.1W, Q W, 20 ft.,
KRB on pile structure, visible all
around, higher intensity on
rangeline.

Channel Range Rear Light
400 yards, 026.6º from front light,
Iso W 6s, 32 ft., KRB on skeleton
tower, visible 4º each side of
rangeline.

Lighted Buoy 6A
43 40.5N, 124 11.7W, Fl R 6s,
4 mi., red.

Light 8
43 41.0N, 124 11.2W, Fl R 2.5s,
22 ft., 3 mi., TR on pile structure.

Winchester Bay Harbor Entrance Daybeacon 1
43 41.0N, 124 11.1W, SG on pile.

Salmon Harbor Entrance Light 1
43 41.2N, 124 10.8W, Fl G 4s,
15 ft., 3 mi., SG on pile structure.

Salmon Harbor Entrance Light 2
43 41.0N, 124 10.2W, Fl R 4s,
15 ft., 3 mi., TR on pile.

Light 12
Fl R 4s, 22 ft., 4 mi., TR on house.

Barretts Range Front Light
43 43.9N, 124 10.0W, Q W, 18 ft.,
KRB on pile structure, visible all
around, higher intensity on
rangeline.

Barretts Range Rear Light
270 yards, 330.5º from front light,
Iso W 6s, 28 ft., KRB on skeleton
tower, visible all around, higher
intensity on rangeline.

Light 15
43 43.4N, 124 09.8W, Fl G 4s,
15 ft., 5 mi., SG on pile.

Dike Buoy 17
43 44.1N, 124 09.9W, green can.

Channel Buoy 17A (marks rocks)
43 44.7N, 124 09.3W, green can.

Light 19
43 44.9N, 124 08.9W, Fl G 4s,
15 ft., 4 mi., SG on platform.

Channel Buoy 20
43 44.9N, 124 08.4W, red nun.

Light 21
43 44.9N, 124 07.9W, Fl G 2.5s,
16 ft., 4 mi., SG on pile structure,
visible all around, higher intensity beam oriented up channel.

Channel Buoy 22
43 44.8N, 124 08.0W, red nun.

Dike Light 23
43 44.5N, 124 07.8W, Fl G 4s,
17 ft., 5 mi., SG on dolphin.

Leeds Island Range Front Light
43 43.3N, 124 07.6W, Q W, 15 ft.,
KRB on skeleton tower.

Leeds Island Range Rear Light
380 yards, 173º from front light,
Iso W 6s, 30 ft., KRB on skeleton
tower.

Dike Light 24
Fl R 2.5s, 16 ft., 3 mi., TR on
dolphin.

Channel Buoy 25
43 43.5N, 124 07.6W, green can.

Light 26
Fl R 4s, 15 ft., 3 mi., TR on
dolphin.

Channel Daybeacon 28
43 43.0N, 124 07.1W, TR on pile.

Scholfield Creek Channel Daybeacon 2
43 42.1N, 124 06.1W, TR on pile,
radar reflector.

Scholfield Creek Channel Daybeacon 3
SG on pile.

Gardiner Paper Mill Dock Light
43 44.5N, 124 07.2W, F Y, 13 ft.,
on dock, private aid.

Smith River Light 2
43 42.4N, 124 05.2W, Fl R 4s,
13 ft., 5 mi., TR on platform.

W

Warrenton
See Skipanon Waterway,
Columbia River chapter.

Westport
See Columbia River chapter.

Winchester Bay Harbor Entrance Daybeacon 1
43 41.0N, 124 11.1W, SG on pile.
Also see Umpqua River.

Y

YAQUINA BAY

Approach Lighted Whistle Buoy Y
44 35.9N, 124 06.7W, Mo (A) W,
6 mi., red and white stripes.

Yaquina Head Light
44 40.6N, 124 04.8W, Fl (2) W 20s,
162 ft., 19 mi., white conical
tower, lighted throughout
24 hours.

Entrance Range Front Light
44 37.1N, 124 03.7W, Q R, 20 ft.,
KRB on pile structure, on same
structure as Yaquina Bay Channel
Light 8, visible 2º each side of
rangeline, horn: 1 blast every 30s,
lighted throughout 24 hours.

Entrance Range Rear Light
525 yards, 060º from front light,
F R, 50 ft., KRB on skeleton tower
on pile structure, visible 2º each
side of rangeline, lighted
throughout 24 hours.

Entrance Lighted Gong Buoy 1
44 36.2N, 124 06.1W, Fl G 2.5s,
4 mi., green.

Entrance Lighted Gong Buoy 3
44 36.4N, 124 05.5W, Fl G 4s,
green, maintained from May 1
to Oct. 1.

South Jetty Light 4
44 36.5N, 124 04.9W, Fl R 2.5s,
20 ft., 5 mi., TR on skeleton tower,
horn: 1 blast every 15s, operates
continuously, light and fog signal
maintained from May 20 to Oct. 1.

Channel Lighted Buoy 7
44 37.1N, 124 03.9W, Fl G 2.5s,
5 mi., green.

Channel Light 8
Fl R 4s, 20 ft., 4 mi., TR on pile, on same structure as Yaquina Bay Entrance Range Front Light.

Inner Range Front Light
44 37.7N, 124 03.0W, Q R, 17 ft., KRB on pile structure, visible 4° each side of rangeline.

Inner Range Rear Light
133 yards, 040.8° from front light, Iso R 6s, 28 ft., KRB on skeleton tower, visible 4° each side of rangeline.

Entrance Small Boat Warning Sign
44 37.5N, 124 03.4W, Q Y (2), 25 ft., NW worded ROUGH BAR, lights flashing when seas exceed four feet in height, lights extinguished for lesser sea conditions, but with no guarantee that bar is safe.

Southbeach Marina Light 2
44 37.6N, 124 03.3W, Fl R 4s, 14 ft., 4 mi., TR on pile.

Southbeach Marina Daybeacon 3
SG on pile.

Channel Lighted Buoy 9A
44 37.6N, 124 03.2W, Fl G 2.5s, 3 mi., green.

Channel Lighted Buoy 9
44 37.7N, 124 02.9W, Fl G 4s, 5 mi., green.

Light 10
Fl R 6s, 15 ft., 5 mi., TR on dolphin.

Channel Buoy 11
44 37.5N, 124 02.4W, green can.

Boat Basin West Lighted Buoy
44 37.8N, 124 03.0W, Fl Y 4s, 4 mi., yellow.

Boat Basin East Light
Fl Y 6s, 15 ft., 5 mi., NY on pile.

Light 12 (75 feet outside channel limit)
Fl R 2.5s, 4 mi., TR on dolphin.

Channel Buoy 12A
44 37.3N, 124 02.1W, red nun.

Light 14
44 36.9N, 124 01.3W, Fl R 4s, 29 ft., 3 mi., TR on dolphin.

Yaquina River

Light 17
44 36.4N, 124 00.6W, Fl G 4s, 15 ft., 4 mi., SG on piles.

Light 19
44 35.7N, 124 00.8W, Fl G 6s,15 ft., 4 mi., SG on skeleton tower.

Light 20
Fl R 4s, 15 ft., 4 mi., TR on dolphin.

Daybeacon 21
SG on pile, radar reflector.

Light 22
44 35.1N, 124 01.5W, Fl R 4s, 15 ft., 3 mi., TR.

Light 25
Fl G 4s, 15 ft., 3 mi., SG on dolphin.

Buoy 26
Red nun.

Daybeacon 28
TR on pile, radar reflector.

Daybeacon 30
TR on skeleton tower.

Buoy 30A
Red nun.

Daybeacon 31
SG on pile, radar reflector.

Light 32
Fl R 4s, 15 ft., 5 mi., TR on dolphin.

Light 37
Fl G 4s, 15 ft., 4 mi., SG on house.

Light 38
Fl R 2.5s, 22 ft., 3 mi., TR on pile.

Light 42
44 35.2N, 123 56.7W, Fl R 4s, 20 ft., 3 mi., TR on skeleton tower.

Daybeacon 43
SG on pile.

Light 44
Fl R 4s, 4 mi., TR on wooden tower.

Channel Buoy 45
Green can.

Light 47
Fl G 4s, 23 ft., 3 mi., SG on dolphin.

Youngs Bay
See Columbia River chapter.

California

A

Alameda Boat Ramp Buoy 1
37 46.0N, 122 17.4W, green can, private aid.
Also see Alameda Naval Air Station *and* Ballena Bay.

Alameda Boat Ramp Buoy 2
Red nun, private aid.

ALAMEDA NAVAL AIR STATION

Also see Oakland Harbor, San Leandro Bay, Alameda Boat Ramp, *and* Ballena Bay.

Entrance Range Front Light
37 46.4N, 122 18.0W, Fl W 5s, 39 ft., KRW on pile, maintained by U.S. Navy.

Entrance Range Rear Light
652 yards, 094° from front light, Fl R 5s, 77 ft., KRW on pile, maintained by U.S. Navy.

Entrance Lighted Bell Buoy 1
37 46.6N, 122 20.4W, Fl G 4s, 4 mi., green.

Entrance Lighted Buoy 2
37 46.5N, 122 20.5W, Fl R 4s, 4 mi., red.

Light 3
Fl G 2.5s, 15 ft., 3 mi., SG on pile, radar reflector.

Light 4
Fl R 4s, 12 ft., 4 mi., TR on pile, radar reflector.

Light 5
Fl G 2.5s, 15 ft., 4 mi., SG on pile, radar reflector.

Light 6
Fl R 4s, 15 ft., 4 mi., TR on pile, radar reflector.

Daybeacon 8
TR on pile.

ALAMITOS BAY

East Jetty Light 2
33 44.2N, 118 07.2W, Fl R 2.5s, 25 ft., 5 mi., TR on concrete pyramid.

West Jetty Light 1
33 44.2N, 118 07.3W, Fl (2) G 6s, 16 ft., 5 mi., SG on post, bell: 1 stroke every 15s.

Channel Light 3
33 44.7N, 118 07.0W, Fl G 2.5s, 16 ft., 5 mi., SG on post.

Basin 1 Light 1
33 45.0N, 118 06.9W, F G, 20 ft., on post, private aid.

Basin 1 Light 2
33 45.0N, 118 06.9W, F R, 20 ft., on post, private aid.

Alamitos Bay Baffle Light A
33 45.1N, 118 06.8W, F W, on post, private aid.

Alamitos Bay Baffle Light B
33 45.2N, 118 06.8W, F W, on post, private aid.

61st Place Seawall Light
33 45.0N, 118 07.3W, Fl Y 4s, 15 ft., on post, private aid.

Albion River Light 1
39 13.7N, 123 46.4W, Q G, 35 ft., 5 mi., SG on tower, higher intensity beam toward entrance buoy, horn: 1 blast every 30s, operates continuously.

Albion River Lighted Whistle Buoy AR
39 13.6N, 123 47.3W, Mo (A) W, 6 mi., red and white stripes with red spherical topmark.

ALCATRAZ ISLAND

Also see San Francisco Bay.

Alcatraz Bell Buoy
37 49.7N, 122 25.7W, green and red bands.

Alcatraz Light
37 49.6N, 122 25.3W, Fl W 5s, 214 ft., 22 mi., gray octagonal tower.

South Fog Signal
White square house, horn: 1 blast every 30s, located 175 yards, 143.5° from light, structure is floodlighted.

North Fog Signal
White square house, horn: 2 blasts every 30s, structure is floodlighted.

Anacapa Island Light
34 01.1N, 119 21.6W, Fl (2) W 60s, 277 ft., 20 mi., white cylindrical tower, horn: 1 blast every 15s, operates continuously.

Anacapa Island Lighted Radar Test Buoy
33 58.8N, 119 15.5W, Fl (3) W 20s, orange and white cylinder, maintained by U.S. Navy.

ANAHEIM BAY

Entrance Lighted Bell Buoy 1 (50 feet outside channel limit)
33 43.0N, 118 06.7W, Fl G 4s, 4 mi., green.

Entrance Lighted Whistle Buoy 2 (50 feet outside channel limit)
33 43.0N, 118 06.6W, Q R, 3 mi., red.

Range Front Light
33 44.2N, 118 05.5W, Q G, 45 ft., KRW on skeleton tower, visible 4° each side of rangeline, light operates continuously.

Range Rear Light
200 yards, 036.8° from front light, Iso G 6s, 57 ft., KRW on skeleton tower, visible 4° each side of rangeline, light operates continuously.

Entrance Buoy 3 (50 feet outside channel limit)
Green can.

Entrance Buoy 4 (50 feet outside channel limit)
Red nun.

West Jetty Light 5
33 43.7N, 118 06.1W, Fl G 2.5s, 31 ft., 5 mi., SG on post, horn: 2 blasts every 20s.

East Jetty Light 6
33 43.6N, 118 06.0W, Fl R 2.5s, 27 ft., 5 mi., TR on post.

Channel Buoy 7
Green can.

Channel Buoy 8
Red nun.

Channel Daybeacon 9
33 44.1N, 118 05.7W, SG on dolphin.

Channel Light 10
33 44.1N, 118 05.6W, Fl R 4s, 15 ft., 4 mi., TR on dolphin.

Channel Light 11
33 44.0N, 118 05.5W, Fl G 2.5s, 19 ft., 4 mi., SG on pile.

Channel Buoy 13
33 44.0N, 118 05.5W, green can.

Channel Buoy 15
33 43.9N, 118 05.3W, green can.

Channel Buoy 17
33 43.9N, 118 05.3W, green can.

Angel Island
See San Francisco Bay.

Anita Rock Light
37 48.5N, 122 27.2W, Q W, 20 ft., 5 mi., NR on cylindrical structure.
Also see San Francisco Bay.

Ano Nuevo Island Lighted Whistle Buoy 8
37 05.8N, 122 20.4W, Fl R 6s, 4 mi., red.

Aquatic Park Entrance Light 1 (San Francisco)
37 48.6N, 122 25.4W, Fl G 4s, 21 ft., 3 mi., SG on post, radar reflector.
Also see San Francisco Bay.

Arena Cove Lighted Bell Buoy A
38 54.6N, 123 43.6W, Mo (A) W, 5 mi., red and white stripes with red spherical topmark.
Also see Point Arena Light.

Avalon Bay Light 1
33 20.7N, 118 19.3W, Fl G 2.5s, 21 ft., 5 mi., SG on post.
Also see Santa Catalina Island.

Avalon Bay Light 2
33 20.9N, 118 19.4W, Fl R 4s, 21 ft., 4 mi., TR on post.

Avila Beach Union Oil Pier Light B
35 10.2N, 120 44.7W, F W, 24 ft., on post, private aid.
Also see Port San Luis.

B

Balboa Island
See Newport Bay.

Ballast Point Light B
32 41.2N, 117 14.0W, Fl W 4s, 16 ft., 10 mi., NG on platform on dolphin, horn: 1 blast every 15s.
Also see San Diego Bay.

Ballena Bay Estuary Light
37 46.1N, 122 17.3W, Fl W 4s, 12 ft., NB on post, obscured from 094° to 004°, private aid.

Ballena Bay Light 1
37 45.8N, 122 17.0W, Fl G 5s, 17 ft., on dolphin, obscured from approx. 155° to 245°, private aid.
Also see Alameda Naval Air Station, Alameda Boat Ramp Buoys, *and* San Leandro Bay.

Battery Point Light
41 44.6N, 124 12.1W, Fl W 30s, 77 ft., 14 mi., white two-story structure, restored historic light, private aid.

Bay Farm Island, San Francisco Bay
See Harbor Bay Ferry *and* San Leandro Bay.

Begg Rock Lighted Whistle Buoy 4BR
33 22.0N, 119 41.8W, Fl R 4s, 4 mi., red.
Also see Pacific Missile Test Center Target Lighted Mooring Buoy.

BELMONT PIER

Also see Long Beach Harbor.

Belmont Pier East Light A
33 45.3N, 118 09.0W, Fl W 4s, 30 ft., on post, private aid.

Belmont Pier Fog Signal
33 45.3N, 118 09.0W, horn: 1 blast every 20s, private aid.

Belmont Pier West Light B
Fl W 4s, 30 ft., on post, private aid.

Belvedere Cove Lighted Buoy 1
37 52.2N, 122 27.3W, Fl G 4s, 3 mi., green.
Also see San Francisco Bay.

Benicia
See Carquinez Strait.

BERKELEY

Also see San Francisco Bay.

Marina Channel Light 2
37 50.9N, 122 21.6W, Fl R 4s, 15 ft., 4 mi., TR on pile.

Marina Channel Light 3
37 51.5N, 122 20.9W, Fl G 4s, 15 ft., 3 mi., SG on pile.

Breakwater Light 1
Q G, 15 ft., 4 mi., SG on post.

Breakwater Center Light
Q W, 12 ft., 6 mi., on post.

Breakwater Light 2
37 52.0N, 122 19.2W, Fl R 2.5s, 15 ft., 4 mi., TR on post, higher intensity beam towards Golden Gate, bell: 1 stroke every 15s, operates continuously.

North Breakwater Light 3
37 52.0N, 122 19.3W, Fl G 4s, 14 ft., 4 mi., SG on pile, radar reflector.

North Breakwater Light 4
37 52.1N, 122 19.2W, Fl R 4s, 14 ft., 4 mi., TR on pile, radar reflector.

Marina North Light
37 52.0N, 122 19.1W, Fl G 10s, 35 ft., post, private aid.

Marina South Light
Fl R 10s, 35 ft., post, horn: 1 blast every 17s, private aid.

Reef Light 1
37 52.5N, 122 20.0W, Fl G 2.5s, 13 ft., 3 mi., SG on pile.

Blossom Rock Lighted Bell Buoy BR
37 49.1N, 122 24.2W, Fl (2+1) G 6s, 4 mi., green and red bands. *Also see* San Francisco Bay.

Blunts Reef Lighted Horn Buoy 2B (ELB)
40 26.4N, 124 30.3W, Fl R 2.5s, 5 mi., red, horn: 1 blast every 30s, operates continuously.

BODEGA BAY

Also see Tomales Bay.

Bodega Head Lighted Whistle Buoy 12
38 17.1N, 123 04.2W, Fl R 6s, 4 mi., red.

Bodega Head Light
38 18.0N, 123 03.2W, Fl W 6s, 110 ft., 7 mi., NR on pile, light obscured from 047° to 205°.

Bodega Harbor

Approach Lighted Gong Buoy BA
38 17.2N, 123 02.4W, Mo (A) W, 6 mi., red and white stripes with red spherical topmark.

Entrance Light
38 18.3N, 123 03.0W, Fl W 4s, 20 ft., 6 mi., NG on skeleton tower, horn: 1 blast every 10s, operates continuously.

Channel Light 2
Q R, 15 ft., 3 mi., TR on pile.

Channel Range A Front Light 3
38 18.3N, 123 03.4W, Q G, 13 ft., KRW on pile, SG facing upstream, visible all around, higher intensity on rangeline.

Channel Range A-B Rear Light
153 yards, 269° from Range A Front Light, 193 yards, 209° from Range B Front Light, Iso G 6s, 25 ft., KRWs on frame structure, visible all around, higher intensity on rangelines.

Channel Light 4
38 18.4N, 123 03.4W, Fl R 2.5s, 15 ft., 3 mi., TR on pile.

Channel Range B Front Light 5
38 18.4N, 123 03.4W, Q G, KRW on pile, SG facing downstream, visible all around, higher intensity on rangeline.

Channel Light 6
Q R, 15 ft., 3 mi., TR on pile.

Channel Daybeacon 7
38 18.5N, 123 03.4W, SG on pile.

Channel Daybeacon 8
TR on pile.

Channel Daybeacon 9
SG on pile.

Channel Light 10
Fl R 2.5s, 15 ft., 3 mi., TR on pile.

Channel Daybeacon 11
SG on pile.

Channel Daybeacon 13
38 18.7N, 123 03.2W, SG on pile.

Channel Range C Front Light 14
Q R, 13 ft., KRW on piles, TR facing downstream, visible all around, higher intensity on rangeline.

Channel Range C Rear Light
225 yards, 179° from front light, Iso R 6s, 23 ft., KRW on pile, visible 1° each side of rangeline.

Channel Daybeacon 15
38 18.8N, 123 03.2W, SG on pile.

Channel Light 16
Fl R 4s, 15 ft., 3 mi., TR on pile.

Channel Daybeacon 17
SG on pile.

Channel Daybeacon 18
TR on pile.

Channel Daybeacon 19
SG on pile.

Channel Light 20
Fl R 2.5s, 15 ft., 3 mi., TR on pile.

Channel Daybeacon 21
SG on pile.

Channel Daybeacon 22
TR on pile.

Channel Daybeacon 23
38 19.3N, 123 03.2W, SG on pile.

Channel Light 24
38 19.3N, 123 03.1W, Fl R 4s, 15 ft., 3 mi., TR on pile.

Channel Daybeacon 25
SG on pile.

Channel Daybeacon 26
38 19.4N, 123 03.1W, TR on pile.

Channel Daybeacon 27
SG on pile.

Channel Light 28
Fl R 2.5s, 15 ft., 3 mi., TR on pile.

Channel Daybeacon 29
38 19.5N, 123 03.2W, SG on pile.

Channel Daybeacon 30
TR on pile.

Channel Daybeacon 31
38 19.6N, 123 03.2W, SG on pile.

Channel Light 32
Fl R 4s, 15 ft., 3 mi., TR on pile.

Channel Light 33
38 19.8N, 123 03.2W, Fl G 2.5s, 13 ft., 3 mi., SG on pile.

Channel Daybeacon 34
38 19.8N, 123 03.1W, TR on pile.

Spud Point Marina

Light 1
38 19.9N, 123 03.1W, Q G, 15 ft., 3 mi., SG on pile.

Light 2
Q R, 15 ft., 3 mi., TR on pile.

Buoy 3
Green can.

Buoy 4
Red nun.

Buoy 6
Red nun.

Bodega Harbor (cont'd)

Breakwater Light
38 19.9N, 123 03.4W, Fl W 4s, 9 ft., 5 mi., on pile.

Channel Daybeacon 35
SG on pile.

Channel Light 36
38 19.9N, 123 03.1W, Fl R 2.5s, 3 mi., TR on pile.

Channel Range D Front Light 37
38 20.0N, 123 03.2W, Q G, 13 ft.,
3 mi., KRW on pile, SG facing
upstream, visible all around,
higher intensity on rangeline.

Channel Range D Rear Light
275 yards, 359.5° from front light,
Iso G 6s, 23 ft., KRW on white
timber structure, visible 1° each
side of rangeline.

Channel Daybeacon 38
38 19.9N, 123 03.0W, TR on pile.

Channel Light 40
38 19.9N, 123 02.9W, Fl R 4s,
15 ft., 3 mi., TR on pile structure.

Channel Daybeacon 42
38 19.8N, 123 02.8W, TR on pile.

Channel Daybeacon 44
TR on pile.

Channel Daybeacon 46
38 19.6N, 123 02.7W, TR on pile.

Channel Daybeacon 48
38 19.6N, 123 02.6W, TR on pile.

Channel Daybeacon 50
38 19.5N, 123 02.5W, TR on pile.

Channel Daybeacon 52
38 19.4N, 123 02.5W, TR on pile.

Channel Daybeacon
38 19.4N, 123 02.4W, NB on pile.

Brisbane Marina Channel
See San Francisco Bay.

Brooklyn Basin
See Oakland Harbor.

C

Cabrillo Beach Launch Ramp
See Los Angeles Harbor.

CAMP PENDLETON

South Light
33 15.4N, 117 26.2W, Fl W 4s,
53 ft., 6 mi., white pyramidal
structure.

North Light
33 18.7N, 117 29.0W, Fl W 6s,
63 ft., 6 mi., white pyramidal
structure.

**Camp Pendleton Lighted
Calibration Buoy**
33 20.3N, 117 37.1W, Fl Y 4s,
5 mi., yellow.

Cape Mendocino Light
40 26.4N, 124 24.4W, Fl W 15s,
515 ft., 24 mi., on post.

Carlsbad Lighted Bell Buoy C
33 08.0N, 117 21.3W, Fl Y 4s,
yellow, private aid.

CARQUINEZ STRAIT

Also see San Pablo Bay *and*
Suisun Bay.

Bridge Pier Fog Signal
38 03.7N, 122 13.6W, on center
pier, horn: 1 blast every 30s, bell:
1 stroke every 10s, on N side of
center pier, private aid.

Bridge North Channel Racon
38 03.8N, 122 13.6W, N (-·),
148 ft., mid-span on north channel, bands: alternating 20s (X for
10s, S for 10s), private aid.

Bridge South Channel Racon
38 03.5N, 122 13.6W, C (-·-·),
139 ft., mid-span on south channel, bands, alternating 20s (X for
10s, S for 10s), private aid.

Bridge Pier 2 Fog Signal
38 03.9N, 122 13.6W, bell:
1 stroke every 3s, private aid.

Glen Cove Marina Entrance Light 1
38 04.0N, 122 12.8W, F G, 13 ft.,
on pile, private aid.

Glen Cove Marina Entrance Light 2
F R, 12 ft., on pile, private aid.

Light 20
38 03.2N, 122 11.7W, Fl R 4s,
16 ft., 3 mi., TR on pile.

Light 21
38 03.6N, 122 11.7W, Fl G 4s,
20 ft., 3 mi., SG on pile.

Light 22
38 02.9N, 122 11.0W, Fl R 6s,
20 ft., 4 mi., TR on pile.

Light 23
38 02.6N, 122 10.0W, Fl G 4s,
20 ft., 3 mi., SG on pile.

Lighted Buoy 25
38 02.0N, 122 09.7W, Q G, 3 mi.,
green.

Benicia Marina Light 1
38 02.5N, 122 09.5W, Fl G 5s, 5 ft.,
3 mi., SG on post, private aid.

Benicia Marina Light 2
Fl R 5s, 5 ft., 3 mi., SG on post,
private aid.

Benicia Wharf Light
38 02.4N, 122 08.3W, Fl G 4s,
12 ft., 4 mi., corner of pier.

Martinez Marina Light 1
38 01.7N, 122 08.3W, Fl G 4s, 7 ft.,
on pile, private aid.

Martinez Marina Light 2
Fl R 4s, 7 ft., on pile, private aid.

Shell Oil Wharf West End Light
38 01.9N, 122 07.9W, Oc R 2.4s,
24 ft., mooring dolphin, private
aid.

Shell Oil Wharf Fog Signal
Horn: 1 blast every 20s, private
aid.

Shell Oil Wharf East End Light
38 02.0N, 122 07.7W, Oc R 2.4s,
24 ft., mooring dolphin, private
aid.

Amoco Wharf Lights (2)
38 02.1N, 122 07.5W, F R, 26 ft.,
32 ft., on posts on dolphins, bell:
2 strokes every 15s, private aids.

**Benicia-Martinez Highway Bridge
Main Channel Fog Signal**
38 02.3N, 122 07.2W, horn: 1 blast
every 20s, private aid.

**Benicia-Martinez Highway Bridge
Racon B**
38 02.3N, 122 07.2W, B (-···),
135 ft., mid-span, center of
channel, private aid.

**Benicia-Martinez Highway Bridge
Secondary Channel Fog Signal**
38 02.6N, 122 07.5W, horn:
2 blasts every 20s, private aid.

**Benicia-Martinez Railroad Bridge
Pier 13 Fog Signal**
38 02.3N, 122 07.2W, siren:
2 blasts every 20s, private aid.

**Benicia-Martinez Railroad Bridge
Pier 17 Fog Signal**
38 02.6N, 122 07.4W, siren: 1 blast
every 20s, private aid.

Castro Rocks Lighted Buoy 2CR
37 55.9N, 122 25.3W, Fl R 4s,
3 mi., red.
Also see San Francisco Bay.

Catalina Island
See Santa Catalina Island.

Catalina Landing
See Long Beach Harbor.

CHANNEL ISLANDS HARBOR

Also see Port Hueneme.

Breakwater South Light 1
34 09.3N, 119 13.8W, Fl G 6s,
35 ft., 6 mi., SG on square platform on white column.

Breakwater North Light
Fl W 4s, 35 ft., 7 mi., NR on
square platform on white
column.

South Jetty Light 2
34 09.4N, 119 13.6W, Fl R 2.5s,
35 ft., 6 mi., rectangular concrete,
horn: 1 blast every 15s.

North Jetty Light 3
34 09.4N, 119 13.7W, Fl G 4s,
35 ft., 6 mi., SG on square platform on white column.

South Jetty Light 4
34 09.5N, 119 13.5W, Fl R 4s,
25 ft., 5 mi., TR on post, obscured
from 230° to 060°.

North Jetty Light 5
34 09.5N, 119 13.5W, Fl G 4s,
25 ft., 6 mi., SG on post.

China Point Light
32 48.2N, 118 25.5W, Fl W 5s,
112 ft., 15 mi., NR on pile, visible
from 260° to 128°, partially
obscured by hills elsewhere.
Also see San Clemente Island.

Chula Vista Channel, San Diego.
See San Diego Bay.

Cojo Anchorage Special Purpose Buoy
34 26.5N, 120 23.6W, orange and
white bands, spar, private aid.

Commercial Basin, San Diego
See San Diego Bay.

Cone Rock Light
37 51.8N, 122 28.2W, Q W, 17 ft.,
5 mi., NR on black skeleton tower.

Also see San Francisco Bay *and*
Sausalito.

Constantine Rock Buoy 1CR
35 26.2N, 120 56.7W, green can.

Corinthian Harbor
See San Francisco Bay.

Coronado Cays Channel, San Diego
See San Diego Bay.

CORTE MADERA CHANNEL

Also see San Francisco Bay.

Light 2
37 55.7N, 122 28.1W, Iso R 6s,
3 mi., TR on pile, radar reflector,
private aid.

Light 3
Fl G 2.5s, SG on pile, radar reflector, private aid.

Light 4
Fl R 2.5s, TR on pile, radar reflector, private aid.

Daybeacons 5–10
SGs and TRs on piles, radar
reflectors, private aids.

Light 11
Fl G 2.5s, 9 ft., SG on pile, radar
reflector, private aid.

Light 12
Fl R 2.5s, TR on pile, radar reflector, private aid.

Daybeacon 13
SG on pile, radar reflector,
private aid.

Daybeacon 14
TR on pile, radar reflector, private
aid.

Light 15
Fl G 2.5s, 9 ft., SG on pile, radar
reflector, private aid.

Light 16
Fl R 4s, TR on pile, radar reflector,
private aid.

Light 17
Fl G 4s, 9 ft., SG on pile, radar
reflector, private aid.

Daybeacon CM
JG on pile, radar reflector,
private aid.

Cortes Bank Lighted Bell Buoy 2CB
32 26.6N, 119 07.4W, Fl R 4s,
4 mi., rcd.

Coyote Point Yacht Harbor Light 1
37 35.3N, 122 18.8W, F G, 12 ft.,
on pile, private aid.
Also see San Francisco Bay.

Coyote Point Yacht Harbor Light 2
F R, 12 ft., on pile, private aid.

CRESCENT CITY HARBOR

Crescent City Entrance Light
41 44.2N, 124 11.5W, Fl W 5s,
55 ft., 11 mi., white cylindrical
structure, horn: 1 blast every 10s,
operates continuously.

Buoy 1
41 44.2N, 124 12.8W, green can.

Lighted Whistle Buoy 2
41 43.0N, 124 11.8W, Fl R 6s,
4 mi., red.

Lighted Whistle Buoy 4
41 43.6N, 124 11.3W, Fl R 4s,
4 mi., red.

Lighted Bell Buoy 6
41 44.2N, 124 11.3W, Fl R 2.5s,
4 mi., red.

Lighted Buoy 7
41 44.3N, 124 11.4W, Fl G 2.5s,
4 mi., green.

Inner Breakwater Light 8
41 44.6N, 124 11.3W, Fl R 4s,
30 ft., 4 mi., TR on pile.

Range Front Light
41 45.0N, 124 11.4W, Oc G 4s,
25 ft., KRW on pile, visible 4°
each side of rangeline.

Range Rear Light
79 yards, 001° from front light,
Oc G 4s, 38 ft., KRW on pile, visible 4° each side of rangeline.

D

DANA POINT

San Juan Rocks Lighted Whistle Buoy 2SJR
33 27.3N, 117 43.3W, Fl R 2.5s,
4 mi., red.

Lighted Buoy 1
33 27.1N, 117 41.9W, Fl G 2.5s,
4 mi., green.

Buoy 2
33 27.2N, 117 41.3W, red nun.

Breakwater Light 3
33 27.3N, 117 41.5W, Fl G 4s,
30 ft., 9 mi., SG on post, horn:
1 blast every 10s.

Jetty Light 4
33 27.4N, 117 41.5W, Fl R 4s,
26 ft., 6 mi., TR on post.

DANA POINT HARBOR

Daybeacon 6
33 27.4N, 117 41.7W, TR on pile,
private aid.

Daybeacon 8
33 27.4N, 117 41.8W, TR on pile,
private aid.

Daybeacon 10
33 27.5N, 117 41.9W, TR on pile,
private aid.

Daybeacon 12
33 27.5N, 117 42.0W, TR on pile,
private aid.

Daybeacon 14
33 27.5N, 117 42.2W, TR on pile,
private aid.

Del Mar Boat Basin
See Oceanside.

Drakes Bay Lighted Whistle Buoy 1
37 59.0N, 122 57.3W, Fl G 6s,
4 mi., green.
Also see Point Reyes Light.

Dumbarton Highway Bridge Fog Signal
37 30.4N, 122 07.0W, horn: 1 blast
every 20s, private aid.
Also see San Francisco Bay.

Duxbury Reef Lighted Whistle Buoy 1DR
37 51.6N, 122 41.7W, Fl G 6s,
4 mi., green.
Also see San Francisco Bay.

E

East Brother Island Light
37 57.8N, 122 26.0W, Fl W 5s,
61 ft., 17 mi., buff square tower
on dwelling, horn: 1 blast every
30s, operates continuously from
Oct. 1 to April 1.
Also see San Francisco Bay North
Channel.

East Yacht Harbor, San Francisco
See San Francisco Bay.

EL SEGUNDO

Lighted Bell Buoy 2ES
33 54.7N, 118 27.5W, Fl R 4s, red,
racon: C (-·-·), private aid.

Special Purpose Buoy A
33 54.8N, 118 26.8W, orange and
white bands, spar, private aid.

Pipeline Marker Buoy CUSA1
33 54.9N, 118 26.9W, white with
orange bands, spar, private aid.

Pipeline Marker Buoy CUSA2
33 54.9N, 118 26.9W, white with
orange bands, spar, private aid.

Pipeline Marker Buoy CUSA3
33 54.8N, 118 27.0W, white with
orange bands, spar, private aid.

Buoy 4ES
33 54.4N, 118 26.0W, red nun
worded DANGER BELOW, private
aid.

Danger Buoy South
33 54.5N, 118 25.9W, white
with orange bands and orange
diamond worded DANGER,
private aid.

Buoy 6ES
33 54.5N, 118 26.1W, red nun
worded DANGER BELOW,
private aid.

Danger Buoy North
33 54.5N, 118 26.0W, white
with orange bands and orange
diamond worded DANGER,
private aid.

Scattergood Intake Buoy 8ES
33 55.0N, 118 26.1W, red nun,
private aid.

Light ES
33 54.6N, 118 25.7W, Fl W 2.5s,
24 ft., NR on pile, private aid.

Danger Buoy East
33 54.6N, 118 25.8W, white with
orange bands and orange diamond worded DANGER SUB-
MERGED ROCKS, private aid.

Lighted Gong Buoy 10ES
33 55.2N, 118 26.6W, Q R, red,
gong: 1 stroke every 15s, private
aid.

Outfall Obstruction Buoy 12ES
33 55.1N, 118 26.9W, red nun,
private aid.

Marker Buoy C
33 55.3N, 118 26.4W, white
with orange bands and orange
diamond worded DANGER,
private aid.

Marker Buoy A
33 55.0N, 118 26.2W, white can
with orange diamond worded
DANGER SUBMERGED PIPE,
private aid.

Marker Buoy B
33 55.3N, 118 26.1W, white can
with orange diamond worded
DANGER SUBMERGED PIPE,
private aid.

EMERYVILLE MARINA

Also see San Francisco Bay.

Light 1
37 50.6N, 122 19.3W, Fl G 2s,
14 ft., SG on pile, private aid.

Light 2
Fl R 2s, 14 ft., TR on pile, private
aid.

Light 3
37 50.6N, 122 18.9W, Fl G 4s,
14 ft., SG on pile, private aid.

Light 4
Fl R 4s, 14 ft., TR on pile, private
aid.

Light 5
37 50.6N, 122 18.6W, Fl G 4s,
14 ft., SG on pile, private aid.

Light 6
Fl R 4s, 14 ft., TR on pile, private aid.

LIght 7
37 50.5N, 122 18.6W, Iso G 4s, 17 ft., SG on pile, private aid.

Light 8
37 50.5N, 122 18.6W, Iso R 4s, 17 ft., TR on pile, private aid.

ESTERO BAY

Gong Buoy 18EB
35 23.1N, 120 53.2W, red.

Lighted Whistle Buoy EB
35 24.1N, 120 56.0W, Mo (A) W, 7 mi., red and white stripes with red spherical topmark.

Pacific Gas and Electric Heading Buoy
35 23.0N, 120 52.9W, yellow nun, private aid.

Toro Creek Submarine Terminal Mooring Buoy
35 24.4N, 120 53.1W, white with blue band, private aid.

Estero Submarine Terminal Bell Buoy
35 24.9N, 120 53.4W, yellow, private aid.

Farallon Island Lighted Wave Buoy
37 30.3N, 122 52.4W, Fl (5) Y 20s, yellow worded WAVE BUOY, private aid.

Farallon Light
37 41.9N, 123 00.1W, Fl W 15s, 358 ft., 20 mi., white conical tower.
Also see San Francisco Bay.

Fishermans Wharf, San Francisco
See San Francisco Bay.

Fort Ross Bell Buoy 14
38 28.6N, 123 13.0W, red.

Four Fathom Bank Lighted Bell Buoy
37 48.7N, 122 32.4W, Fl (2+1) R 6s, 4 mi., red and green bands.
Also see San Francisco Bay.

***Gail* Platform**
See Platform *Gail*.

GAVIOTA

Tanker Mooring Buoy A
34 27.8N, 120 12.3W, white with blue band, private aid.

Tanker Mooring Buoy B
34 27.7N, 120 12.2W, white with blue band, private aid.

Tanker Mooring Buoy C
34 27.7N, 120 12.0W, white with blue band, private aid.

Tanker Mooring Buoy D
34 27.6N, 120 12.0W, white with blue band, private aid.

Tanker Mooring Buoy E
34 27.5N, 120 12.1W, white with blue band, private aid.

Tanker Mooring Buoy F
34 27.5N, 120 12.3W, white with blue band, private aid.

Gaviota Pipeline Marker Buoy A
34 28.2N, 120 12.4W, white with orange bands worded DANGER BELOW, private aid.

Gaviota Pipeline Marker Buoy B
White with orange bands worded DANGER BELOW, private aid.

Gaviota Brine Discharge Marker Buoy
White with orange bands worded DANGER BELOW, private aid.

Gaviota Wellhead Lighted Marker Buoy
34 26.6N, 120 16.3W, Fl W 4s, white with orange bands worded SUBMERGED OBJECT, private aid.

Glen Cove Marina
See Carquinez Strait.

Glorietta Bay
See San Diego Bay.

Golden Gate Bridge
See San Francisco Bay.

Guadalupe Slough
Buoys 1–6, green cans and red nuns, due to frequently changing conditions, positions of buoys are not listed.

Gull Island Light
33 56.9N, 119 49.6W, Fl W 10s, 73 ft., 16 mi., NR on post, visible from 265° to 127°, partially obscured by hills elsewhere.
Also see Santa Cruz Island.

Half Moon Bay, Southeast Reef Southern End Lighted Gong Buoy 1S
37 27.9N, 122 28.2W, Fl G 6s, 5 mi., green.

HARBOR BAY FERRY, SAN FRANCISCO BAY

Also see San Francisco Bay.

Light 1
37 44.1N, 122 16.1W, Fl G 2.5s, 14 ft., SG on pile, private aid.

Light 2
Fl R 2.5s, 14 ft., TR on pile, private aid.

Daybeacon 3
SG on pile, private aid.

Light 4
Fl R 4s, 14 ft., TR on pile, private aid.

Light 6
Fl R 4s, 14 ft., TR on pile, private aid.

Harbor Island East Basin
See San Diego Bay.

Harding Rock Lighted Buoy HR
37 50.3N, 122 26.8W, Fl (2+1) R 6s, 4 mi., red and green bands, racon: K (-··-).
Also see San Francisco Bay.

***Harvest* Light Platform**
See Platform *Harvest* Light.

Hermosa Beach Pier Fog Signal
33 51.7N, 118 24.3W, horn: 1 blast every 15s, private aid.

Hookton Channel
See Humboldt Bay.

Horseshoe Bay East Breakwater Light
37 49.9N, 122 28.5W, Fl R 3s, 25 ft., on steel pile structure, light obscured from 090° to 270°, private aid.
Also see San Francisco Bay *and* Sausalito.

HUMBOLDT BAY

Entrance Lighted Whistle Buoy HB
40 46.4N, 124 16.2W, Mo (A) W, 6 mi., red and white stripes with red spherical topmark.

Humboldt Bay Light
40 45.9N, 124 13.8W, Fl W 5s, 100 ft., 24 mi., on white column, light obscured from 208° to 020°.

Entrance Bell Buoy 2
40 46.0N, 124 14.9W, red.

Approach Range Front Light
40 45.9N, 124 13.9W, Oc W 4s, 35 ft., KRW on white house on white tower, horn: 2 blasts every 20s, operates continuously.

Approach Range Rear Light
240 yards, 105° from front light, Oc W 4s, 55 ft., KRW on pile, on same structure as Humboldt Bay Light, range lights are synchronized, visible 4° each side of rangeline.

Entrance Light 3
40 46.1N, 124 14.2W, Fl G 2.5s, 60 ft., 5 mi., SG on white cylindrical tower, NL worded NORTH.

Entrance Light 4
40 45.9N, 124 14.5W, Fl R 2.5s, 57 ft., 5 mi., TR on white cylindrical tower, NL worded SOUTH, horn: 1 blast every 10s, operates continuously.

Entrance Range Front Light
40 44.8N, 124 13.2W, Q G, 20 ft., KRW on pile, visible 5° each side of rangeline.

Entrance Range Rear Light
600 yards, 140° from front light, Oc G 4s, 38 ft., KRW on pile.

Lighted Bell Buoy 5
40 45.4N, 124 13.8W, Fl G 4s, 4 mi., green.

Light 6
40 45.4N, 124 14.0W, Fl R 4s, 30 ft., 3 mi., TR on pile.

Lighted Bell Buoy 7
40 45.4N, 124 13.5W, Fl G 4s, 4 mi., green.

Lighted Bell Buoy 8
40 45.1N, 124 13.5W, Q R, 4 mi., red.

Lighted Buoy 9
40 45.4N, 124 13.4W, Fl G 2.5s, 3 mi., green.

Lighted Buoy 10
40 45.5N, 124 13.1W, Fl R 4s, 4 mi., red.

Light 11
40 45.6N, 124 13.2W, Fl G 4s, 35 ft., 3 mi., SG on steel pile structure.

Light 12
40 45.9N, 124 12.8W, Fl R 6s, 15 ft., 4 mi., TR on pile, radar reflector.

Light 13
40 46.1N, 124 12.9W, Fl G 6s, 15 ft., 3 mi., SG on pile, radar reflector.

Light 14
40 46.1N, 124 12.6W, Fl R 2.5s, 15 ft., 3 mi., TR on pile, radar reflector.

Lighted Buoy 15
40 46.5N, 124 12.2W, Fl G 4s, 4 mi., green.

Light 16
40 46.4N, 124 12.1W, Fl R 4s, 15 ft., 4 mi., TR on pile.

Lighted Buoy 17
40 46.8N, 124 11.9W, Fl G 2.5s, 3 mi., green.

Del Norte Street Pier Light A
40 47.4N, 122 11.3W, Fl R 4s, 10 ft., on post, private aid.

Light 18
40 47.8N, 124 11.2W, Fl R 2.5s, 26 ft., 4 mi., TR on mast.

Samoa Channel Light 2
Fl R 2.5s, 15 ft., 2 mi., TR on pile, radar reflector.

Samoa Channel Light 3
Fl G 4s, 15 ft., 3 mi., SG on pile, radar reflector.

Samoa Channel Light 4
Fl R 4s, 15 ft., 3 mi., TR on pile, radar reflector.

Samoa Turning Basin Lighted Buoy A
40 49.0N, 124 10.5W, Fl Y 4s, 4 mi., yellow.

Light 19
40 48.2N, 124 10.9W, Fl G 4s, 15 ft., 3 mi., SG on pile, radar reflector.

Light 21
40 48.5N, 124 10.0W, Fl G 2.5s, 15 ft., 3 mi., SG on pile, radar reflector.

Woodley Island Marina Light
40 48.4N, 124 09.9W, Fl G 4s, 14 ft., SG on pile, private aid.

Hookton Channel

Lighted Buoy 1
40 44.9N, 124 13.3W, Fl G 4s, 4 mi., green.

Light 2
Fl R 4s, 15 ft., 3 mi., TR on pile, radar reflector.

Light 3
Fl G 2.5s, 15 ft., 2 mi., SG on pile, radar reflector.

Range Front Light 4
40 44.6N, 124 13.6W, Q R, 20 ft., 6 mi., KRW on pile, visible all around, higher intensity on rangeline.

Range Rear Light
100 yards, 326.5° from front light, Iso R 6s, 25 ft., 6 mi., KRW on pile, visible 4° each side of rangeline.

Lighted Buoy 5
40 44.5N, 124 13.4W, Fl G 4s, 4 mi., green.

Lighted Buoy 6
40 44.4N, 124 13.6W, Fl R 2.5s, 3 mi., red.

Light 7
40 44.4N, 124 13.4W, Fl G 4s, 15 ft., 3 mi., SG on pile, radar reflector.

Light 8
40 44.3N, 124 13.3W, Fl R 6s,
15 ft., 3 mi., TR on pile, radar
reflector.

**Pacific Gas and Electric Company
Dike Light**
40 44.2N, 124 13.1W, Fl W 4s,
18 ft., dolphin, private aid.

Daybeacon 9
SG on pile.

Light 10
40 44.0N, 124 13.2W, Fl R 4s,
15 ft., 3 mi., TR on pile, radar
reflector.

Lighted Buoy 12
40 43.9N, 124 13.1W, Fl R 2.5s,
3 mi., red.

Lighted Buoy 13
40 43.6N, 124 13.3W, Fl G 2.5s,
3 mi., green.

Light 14
Fl R 4s, 15 ft., 3 mi., TR on pile
structure, radar reflector.

Hunters Point, San Francisco
See San Francisco Bay.

**Huntington Beach Lighted Bell
Buoy HB**
33 38.1N, 118 00.8W, Fl Y 10s,
yellow, private aid.

Huntington Beach Pier Light A
33 39.2N, 118 00.4W, Fl W 4s,
31 ft., private aid.

**Huntington Harbor Intake
Structure Light**
33 43.0N, 118 03.8W, F W, 12 ft.,
6-foot diameter concrete tower,
private aid.

Hyperion
See El Segundo.

I

**Isthmus Cove, Santa Catalina
Island**
See Santa Catalina Island.

K

King Harbor
See Redondo Beach.

L

Lash Terminal, San Francisco
See San Francisco Bay.

Lime Point Light
37 49.5N, 122 28.7W, Fl W 5s,
15 ft., 8 mi., on post, horn:
2 blasts every 30s.
Also see San Francisco Bay.

Little River Bell Buoy LR
39 15.9N, 123 48.0W, red and
white stripes with red spherical
topmark.

LONG BEACH HARBOR

Also see Los Angeles *and*
San Pedro Channel.

Entrance Channel

**Approach Lighted Whistle Buoy
LB**
33 41.4N, 118 11.0W, Mo (A) W,
7 mi., red and white stripes,
racon: C (-·-·).

**Long Beach Breakwater East End
Light 1**
33 43.4N, 118 08.2W, Fl G 6s,
43 ft., 5 mi., SG on skeleton
tower, horn: 1 blast every 15s,
operates continuously.

Long Beach Light
33 43.4N, 118 11.2W, Fl W 5s,
50 ft., 20 mi., white rectangular
tower on building on columnar
base, horn: 1 blast every 30s,
operates continuously.

Entrance Light 2
33 43.4N, 118 10.8W, Fl R 2.5s,
41 ft., 5 mi., TR on white skeleton
tower.

Long Beach Pier A Light
33 45.2N, 118 12.0W, Fl W 30s,
147 ft., on yellow building, private aid.

Lighted Buoy 3
33 43.6N, 118 11.6W, Fl G 4s,
4 mi., green.

Light 4
33 44.0N, 118 11.7W, Fl R 4s,
30 ft., 6 mi., TR on post.

Light 6
33 44.2N, 118 12.1W, Fl R 6s,
30 ft., 6 mi., TR on post.

Light 8
33 44.3N, 118 12.3W, Fl R 2.5s,
26 ft., 5 mi., TR on post.

Pier F Light F
33 44.4N, 118 12.4W, Iso W 6s,
26 ft., 9 mi., NR on post.

Southeast Basin Entrance Light 1
33 44.4N, 118 12.3W, Q G, 14 ft.,
5 mi., SG on post.

Southeast Basin Light 3
33 44.6N, 118 12.0W, Fl G 2.5s,
14 ft., 5 mi., SG on post.

**Long Beach Midchannel Lighted
Buoy A**
33 44.4N, 118 12.4W, Mo (A) W,
6 mi., red and white stripes.

Light 9
33 44.7N, 118 13.0W, Fl G 2.5s,
26 ft., 5 mi., SG on post, higher
intensity beam up and down
channel.

Light 10
33 44.8N, 118 12.9W, Fl R 2.5s,
20 ft., 5 mi., TR on post, horn:
1 blast every 15s, higher intensity
beam up and down channel.

Fireboat Pier Light
33 44.9N, 118 13.0W, F W, on pile,
private aid.

Fireboat Pier D Light A
33 45.9N, 118 13.2W, F W, 13 ft.,
on pile, private aid.

Fireboat Pier D Light B
33 45.9N, 118 13.2W, F W, 13 ft.,
on pile, private aid.

**Long Beach Midchannel Lighted
Buoy B**
33 45.0N, 118 13.1W, Mo (A) W,
6 mi., red and white stripes.

Light 12
33 45.4N, 118 13.0W, Fl R 2.5s,
20 ft., 6 mi., TR on post.

Pier A Light
33 45.2N, 118 12.0W, Fl W 30s,
147 ft., on yellow building, private aid.

**Inner Harbor Intake Structure
South Light**
33 46.0N, 118 13.3W, Q G, 7 mi.,
on deck of pier, private aid.

Inner Harbor Intake Structure North Light
Q G, 7 mi., on deck of pier, private aid.

Outfall Buoy 13
33 45.9N, 118 13.3W, green can, private aid.

Belmont Pier

Belmont Pier East Light A
33 45.3N, 118 09.0W, Fl W 4s, 30 ft., on post, private aid.

Belmont Pier Fog Signal
33 45.3N, 118 09.0W, horn: 1 blast every 20s, private aid.

Belmont Pier West Light B
Fl W 4s, 30 ft., on post, private aid.

Downtown Marina

Jetty Light
33 45.6N, 118 10.9W, Q W, on steel post, private aid.

Breakwater Light East
33 45.5N, 118 10.9W, Fl G 4s, on post, horn: 1 blast every 20s, private aid.

Breakwater Light West
33 45.4N, 118 10.9W, Fl R 4s, on post, private aid.

Entrance Light East
33 45.5N, 118 11.0W, Q R, on steel post, private aid.

Entrance Light West
33 45.5N, 118 11.0W, Fl G 4s, on post, private aid.

Mole Light
33 45.5N, 118 11.5W, Fl W 4s, on post, private aid.

Shoreline Marina

Entrance Light East
33 45.6N, 118 11.5W, F R, on post, private aid.

Entrance Light West
33 45.6N, 118 11.6W, F G, on post, private aid.

Entrance Light
33 45.6N, 118 11.5W, Fl W 10s, 71 ft., on blue and white building, private aid.

Catalina Landing

East Light
33 45.8N, 118 12.0W, Fl W 6s, 31 ft., 6 mi., on post, private aid.

West Light
F G, 27 ft., on post, private aid.

Los Angeles River

Daybeacon A
NW on post worded SILL, private aid.

Daybeacon B
NW on post worded SILL, private aid.

Pier J

Light J
33 44.0N, 118 11.1W, Fl W 4s, 30 ft., 5 mi., NR on radar tower.

Channel Lighted Buoy 2
33 44.4N, 118 10.6W, Fl R 4s, 4 mi., red.

Mooring Buoys

Lighted Mooring Buoy CR-1
33 44.5N, 118 09.1W, Q W, white with blue band, private aid.

Lighted Mooring Buoy CR-2
33 44.4N, 118 09.4W, Q W, white with blue band, private aid.

Lighted Mooring Buoy CR-3
33 44.4N, 118 08.8W, Q W, white with blue band, private aid.

Lighted Mooring Buoy CR-4
33 44.7N, 118 09.4W, Q W, white with blue band, private aid.

Lighted Mooring Buoy CR-5
33 44.8N, 118 09.9W, Q W, white with blue band, private aid.

Lighted Mooring Buoy
33 44.8N, 118 10.0W, Fl W 5s, white with blue bands, private aid.

Lighted Mooring Buoy LB1
33 44.5N, 118 11.0W, Q W, white with blue band, private aid.

Lighted Mooring LB2
33 44.7N, 118 11.0W, Q W, white with blue band, private aid.

Lighted Mooring LB3
33 44.8N, 118 11.1W, Q W, white with blue band, private aid.

Lighted Mooring LB4
33 44.9N, 118 11.1W, Q W, white with blue band, private aid.

Lighted Mooring LB5
33 45.0N, 118 11.2W, Q W, white with blue band, private aid.

Long Point Light
33 24.4N, 118 21.9W, Fl W 5s, 71 ft., 15 mi., NR on post, obscured from 021° to 070°.
Also see Santa Catalina Island.

Los Angeles

Also see Long Beach Harbor *and* San Pedro Channel.

Los Angeles Channel

Approach Lighted Whistle Buoy LA
33 41.4N, 118 14.4W, Mo (A) W, 6 mi., red and white stripes, racon: O (---).

Los Angeles Light
33 42.5N, 118 15.1W, Fl G 15s, 73 ft., 18 mi., white cylindrical tower on concrete block, horn: 2 blasts every 30s, operates continuously.

Approach Lighted Buoy 1
33 41.9N, 118 14.7W, Fl G 2.5s, 4 mi., green.

Approach Lighted Buoy 2
33 42.0N, 118 14.5W, Fl R 4s, 4 mi., red.

Approach Lighted Buoy 4
33 42.3N, 118 14.6W, Fl R 2.5s, 4 mi., red.

Approach Lighted Buoy 5
33 42.7N, 118 15.0W, Q G, 4 mi., green.

Main Channel

Light 6
33 42.7N, 118 15.5W, Fl R 2.5s, 42 ft., 4 mi., TR on white skeleton tower on white concrete house.

Lighted Buoy 8
33 42.8N, 118 15.5W, Fl R 4s, red.

Articulated Light 9
33 42.8N, 118 15.7W, Q G, 15 ft., 4 mi., SG on mast.

Lighted Buoy 10
33 42.9N, 118 15.5W, Q R, red.

Articulated Light 11
33 43.0N, 118 16.2W, Fl G 2.5s,
8 ft., 4 mi., SG on mast.

Range Front Light
33 43.3N, 118 16.3W, F Y, 68 ft.,
KRW on post, visible all around,
higher intensity on rangeline.

Range Rear Light
160 yards, 302° from front light,
Iso Y 6s, 96 ft., KRW on building,
visible all around, higher intensity on rangeline.

Pier 400 Light N
33 43.0N, 118 15.5W, Fl W 4s,
private aid.

Light 12
33 43.3N, 118 16.1W, Fl R 2.5s,
20 ft., 5 mi., TR on post, horn:
1 blast every 15s.

Light 10
F R, 10 ft., 7 mi., red iron post
on concrete pier, private aid.

**Reservation Point Restricted
Navigation Area South Buoy**
White can with orange bands.

**Reservation Point Restricted
Navigation Area Middle Buoy**
White can with orange bands.

**Reservation Point Restricted
Navigation Area North Buoy**
33 43.8N, 118 16.0W, white can
with orange bands.

Lighted Buoy 15
33 45.2N, 118 16.4W, Q G, 3 mi.,
green.

**Los Angeles Southwest Slip
Danger Buoy**
33 45.3N, 118 16.5W, white with
orange bands and orange diamond worded DANGER SUBMERGED RAMP, private aid.

San Pedro

West Channel Buoy 1
33 42.6N, 118 16.4W, green can.

East Channel Lighted Buoy 2
Fl R 2.5s, 4 mi., red.

West Channel Lighted Buoy 3
33 42.8N, 118 16.5W, Fl G 4s,
4 mi., green.

West Channel Light 4
33 42.8N, 118 16.4W, Fl R 4s,
33 ft., 5 mi., TR on post.

Approach Range Front Light
33 42.6N, 118 17.0W, Oc Y 2s,
61 ft., on red-striped pile,
private aid.

Approach Range Rear Light
220 yards, 255° from front light,
F Y, 86 ft., on red-striped post,
private aid.

**Cabrillo Beach Launch Ramp
Light North**
33 42.8N, 118 16.9W, Fl W 4s,
11 ft., on post, private aid.

**Cabrillo Beach Launch Ramp
Light South**
33 42.8N, 118 16.9W, Fl W 4s,
15 ft., on post, private aid.

Lighted Buoy 5
33 42.8N, 118 16.7W, Fl G 4s,
4 mi., green.

No Wake Lighted Buoy
33 42.9N, 118 16.7W, Fl W 4s,
white with orange bands and
orange square worded NO WAKE,
private aid.

Los Angeles Marina Light
33 42.9N, 118 16.6W, Fl W 4s,
24 ft., on post, private aid.

Light
33 50.9N, 118 23.7W, Fl W 10s,
165 ft., on generating station,
private aid.

Terminal Island Channel

Lighted Buoy 1
33 43.3N, 118 15.8W, Fl G 4s,
green.

Lighted Buoy 3
33 43.4N, 118 15.8W, Fl G 2.5s,
green.

Lighted Buoy 4
33 43.4N, 118 15.7W, Q R, red.

Lighted Buoy 5
33 43.7N, 118 15.9W, Q G, green.

Lighted Buoy 6
33 43.7N, 118 15.5W, Fl R 4s, red.

Fish Harbor

Channel Light 1
33 43.8N, 118 15.9W, Fl G 2.5s,
25 ft., 4 mi., SG on post.

Channel Light 2
33 43.8N, 118 15.9W, Fl R 4s,
25 ft., 4 mi., TR on post.

Channel Buoy 3A
Black can, private aid.

Channel Light 4
33 44.0N, 118 16.0W, Fl R 2.5s,
15 ft., 4 mi., TR on post.

Channel Light 3
33 44.0N, 118 16.0W, Fl G 4s,
15 ft., 4 mi., SG on post.

East Basin Channel

Light 1
33 45.2N, 118 16.0W, Fl G 4s,
34 ft., 6 mi., SG on dolphin, horn:
1 blast every 30s.

Light 2
33 45.9N, 118 15.2W, Fl R 4s,
15 ft., 5 mi., TR on pile.

Buoy 4
33 46.3N, 118 14.9W, red nun.

Cerritos Channel

Lighted Buoy 1
33 45.8N, 118 15.1W, Fl G 4s,
4 mi., green.

Outer Harbor

Light A
33 42.6N, 118 15.7W, Fl W 4s,
15 ft., 4 mi., NW on steel post.

Light B
33 42.7N, 118 15.9W, Fl W 2.5s,
15 ft., 4 mi., NW on steel post.

Light C
33 42.5N, 118 16.3W, Fl W 4s,
15 ft., 4 mi., NW on steel post.

Lighted Danger Buoy 1
33 44.2N, 118 14.4W, Fl W 2.5s,
white pontoon tank, private aid.

Lighted Danger Buoy 2
33 43.9N, 118 14.3W, Fl W 2.5s,
white pontoon tank, private aid.

Lighted Danger Buoy 3
33 43.4N, 118 14.2W, Fl W 2.5s,
white pontoon tank, private aid.

Lighted Danger Buoy 4
33 43.1N, 118 14.4W, Fl W 2.5s,
white pontoon tank, private aid.

Lighted Danger Buoy 5
33 42.9N, 118 15.2W, Fl W 2.5s,
white pontoon tank, private aid.

Lighted Danger Buoy 6
33 43.1N, 118 15.6W, Fl W 2.5s,
white pontoon tank, private aid.

Lighted Danger Buoy 7
33 43.5N, 118 15.7W, Fl W 2.5s,
white pontoon tank, private aid.

Moorings

Lighted Mooring Buoy A
33 43.5N, 118 15.5W, Fl W 4s,
white with blue band, private aid.

Lighted Mooring Buoy B
33 43.5N, 118 15.3W, Fl W 4s,
white with blue band, private aid.

Lighted Mooring Buoy C
33 43.4N, 118 14.4W, Fl W 4s,
white with blue band, private aid.

Lighted Mooring Buoy D
33 43.5N, 118 14.3W, Fl W 4s,
white with blue band, private aid.

Lighted Mooring Buoy E
33 43.2N, 118 14.6W, Fl W 4s,
white with blue band, private aid.

Lighted Mooring Buoy F
33 43.3N, 118 14.5W, Fl W 4s,
white with blue band, private aid.

Lighted Mooring Buoy LA-1
33 43.9N, 118 14.0W, Fl W 4s,
white with blue band, private aid.

Lighted Mooring Buoy LA-2
33 44.0N, 118 14.1W, Fl W 4s,
white with blue band, private aid.

Lighted Mooring Buoy LA-3
33 44.1N, 118 14.1W, Fl W 4s,
white with blue band, private aid.

Lighted Mooring Buoy LA-4
33 44.2N, 118 14.2W, Fl W 4s,
white with blue band, private aid.

Lighted Mooring Buoy LA-5
33 44.3N, 118 14.2W, Fl W 4s,
white with blue band, private aid.

Los Angeles River
See Long Beach Harbor.

M

MARE ISLAND STRAIT

Also see San Pablo Bay *and*
Carquinez Strait.

Light 1
38 04.2N, 122 14.8W, Fl G 2.5s,
17 ft., 5 mi., SG on pile structure.

Light 2
Fl R 2.5s, 20 ft., 5 mi., TR on pile.

Light 3
38 04.4N, 122 14.8W, Q G, 25 ft.,
4 mi., SG on pile.

Light 4
Q R, 15 ft., 4 mi., TR on pile.

Lighted Buoy 5
38 04.8N, 122 14.9W, Fl G 2.5s,
4 mi., green.

Lighted Buoy 7
38 05.2N, 122 15.2W, Fl G 4s,
4 mi., green.

Vallejo

Yacht Club North Light
38 06.5N, 122 16.1W, F G, 5 ft.,
pile, private aid.

Yacht Club Light
F R, 5 ft., pile, private aid.

Marina North Entrance Light 1
Fl G 4s, 12 ft., pile, private aid.

Marina North Entrance Light 2
Fl R 4s, 12 ft., pile, private aid.

Marina South Entrance Light 3
Fl G 2.5s, 12 ft., pile, private aid.

Marina South Entrance Light 4
Fl R 2.5s, 12 ft., pile, private aid.

MARINA DEL REY

Also see Venice Beach Fishing
Pier Light.

Breakwater South Light 1
33 57.5N, 118 27.6W, Fl G 6s,
30 ft., 5 mi., SG on post.

Breakwater North Light 2
33 57.8N, 118 27.9W, Fl R 6s,
23 ft., 5 mi., TR on post.

Light 3
33 57.8N, 118 27.7W, Fl G 4s,
30 ft., 8 mi., SG on white building, obscured 151° to 331°, horn:
2 blasts every 20s.

Light 3A
33 58.2N, 118 27.0W, F G, 13 ft.,
SG on pile, private aid.

Light 4
33 57.6N, 118 27.6W, Fl R 4s,
45 ft., 5 mi., TR on skeleton
tower.

Pier Light
33 58.2N, 118 26.8W, Fl R 4s,
15 ft., 7 mi., NR on post.

Light 5
33 58.3N, 118 27.0W, F G, 3 ft.,
on pile, private aid.

Light 6
F R, 3 ft., on pile, private aid.

Light 7
F W, 3 ft., on pile, private aid.

Light 8
F R, 3 ft., on pile, private aid.

Light 9
F G, 3 ft., pile, private aid.

Light 10
F W, 3 ft., on pile, private aid.

Light 11
F W, 3 ft., on pile, private aid.

Light 12
F R, 3 ft., on pile, private aid.

Light 13
F G, 3 ft., on pile, private aid.

Light 14
33 58.7N, 118 26.7W, F W, on pile,
private aid.

Light 15
F W, 3 ft., on pile, private aid.

Light 16
F R, 3 ft., pile, private aid.

Light 17
F G, 3 ft., pile, private aid.

Light 18
F W, 3 ft., on pile, private aid.

Light 19
F W, 3 ft., on pile, private aid.

Light 20
F R, 3 ft., pile, private aid.

Light 21
F G, 3 ft., on pile, private aid.

Martinez
See Carquinez Strait.

MAYFIELD SLOUGH

Also see San Francisco Bay.

Daybeacon 2
37 28.1N, 122 05.8W, 25 ft., TR on pile, private aid.

Daybeacon 4
37 28.0N, 122 05.9W, 8 ft., CR on pile, private aid.

Daybeacon 6
37 27.9N, 122 05.9W, 8 ft., CR on pile, private aid.

Daybeacon 8
37 27.8N, 122 05.9W, 9 ft., CR on pile, private aid.

Daybeacons 10–24
CRs on piles, private aids.

Mendocino Bay Whistle Buoy MB
39 17.9N, 123 48.7W, red and white stripes with red spherical topmark.

Middle Point Light
38 03.3N, 121 59.5W, Fl W 4s, 20 ft., 5 mi., NR on pile.
Also see Suisun Bay.

Mile Rocks Light
37 47.6N, 122 30.6W, Fl W 5s, 49 ft., 15 mi., white caisson with orange bands, horn: 1 blast every 30s, operates continuously.
Also see San Francisco Bay.

MISSION BAY

South Jetty Light 2
32 45.4N, 117 15.5W, Fl R 2.5s, 11 ft., 5 mi., TR on column.

North Jetty Light 1
32 45.5N, 117 15.8W, Fl G 6s, 22 ft., 7 mi., SG on steel post, horn: 2 blasts every 20s.

Weir Light West End
32 45.4N, 117 15.0W, Fl W 2.5s, 19 ft., 6 mi., NW on pile, worded DANGER SUBMERGED JETTY.

Weir Light East End
32 45.4N, 117 14.9W, Fl W 2.5s, 19 ft., 6 mi., NW on pile worded DANGER SUBMERGED JETTY.

Channel Light 4
32 45.6N, 117 14.4W, Fl R 2s, 22 ft., on post, private aid.

Light 6
32 45.8N, 117 14.5W, Fl R 4s, TR on post.

MONTEREY

Bay Aquarium Research Lighted Buoy A
36 45.0N, 122 01.8W, Fl Y 4s, yellow, private aid.

Bay Aquarium Research Lighted Buoy B
36 41.4N, 122 23.3W, Fl Y 4s, yellow, private aid.

Bay Lighted Bell Buoy 4
36 37.5N, 121 53.8W, Fl R 4s, 4 mi., red.

Bay Aquarium Intake Lighted Buoy
36 37.2N, 121 54.0W, Fl W 4s, white with orange bands and orange diamond, private aid.

Bay Aquarium Lighted Buoy
36 37.3N, 121 54.0W, Fl W 6s, white with orange bands and orange diamond worded UNDERWATER OBSTRUCTION, private aid.

Harbor Light 6
36 36.5N, 121 53.4W, Oc R 4s, 20 ft., 6 mi., TR on pile, horn: 1 blast every 30s.

Monterey Harbor

Junction Buoy A
36 36.5N, 121 53.3W, red and green bands, nun, private aid.

North Channel Buoy 1
36 36.5N, 121 53.4W, green can, private aid.

North Channel Buoy 3
Green can, private aid.

North Channel Buoy 5
Green can, private aid.

Main Channel Buoy 2
36 36.4N, 121 53.4W, red nun, private aid.

Main Channel Buoy 3
Green can, private aid.

Main Channel Buoy 4
Red nun, private aid.

Main Channel Buoy 5
Green can, private aid.

Main Channel Buoy 6
Red nun, private aid.

Main Channel Buoy 7
Green can, private aid.

Fairway Buoy A
36 36.3N, 121 53.5W, white can with orange bands, private aid.

Fairway Buoy B
White can with orange bands, private aid.

Fairway Buoy C
White can with orange bands, private aid.

Fairway Buoy D
White can with orange bands, private aid.

MORRO BAY

Buoys inside the harbor are set to best mark the channel and are not charted.

West Breakwater Light
35 21.8N, 120 52.2W, Fl W 5s, 36 ft., 13 mi., white column, obscured from 176° to 207°, horn: 1 blast every 30s, operates continuously.

Approach Lighted Whistle Buoy MB
35 21.7N, 120 52.5W, Mo (A) W, 5 mi., red and white stripes.

Lighted Buoy 2
Fl R 4s, 3 mi., red.

Buoy 3
Green can.

Lighted Buoy 4
Fl R 2.5s, 3 mi., red.

Lighted Buoy 4A
Fl R 4s, 3 mi., red.

Lighted Buoy 5
Fl G 4s, 3 mi., green.

Lighted Buoy 6
Fl R 6s, 4 mi., red.

Lighted Buoy 7
Fl G 4s, 4 mi., green.

Lighted Buoy 8
Fl R 2.5s, 3 mi., red.

Buoy 10
Red nun.

Daybeacon 12
35 21.9N, 120 51.2W, TR on pile.

Daybeacon 14
35 21.7N, 120 51.2W, TR on pile.

Daybeacon 16
TR on pile.

Daybeacon 17
SG on pile.

Daybeacon 18
TR on pile.

Daybeacon 20
TR on pile.

Morro Creek Outfall Buoy A
35 23.2N, 120 52.5W, white spar with orange bands, private aid.

Morro Creek Outfall Buoy B
White spar with orange bands, private aid.

Moss Landing

Harbor Entrance Lighted Bell Buoy MLA
36 47.9N, 121 48.1W, Mo (A) W, 5 mi., red and white stripes with red spherical topmark.

Marine Optics Lighted Buoy
36 44.5N, 121 51.5W, Fl Y 2s, yellow, private aid.

Discharge Buoy 2
Red nun, private aid.

Harbor Entrance Range Front Light
36 48.6N, 121 47.7W, Q G, 15 ft., KRW on red pile, visible 5° each side of rangeline.

Harbor Entrance Range Rear Light
63 yards, 052° from front light, Iso G 6s, 25 ft., KRW on red pile.

Harbor Channel Buoy 1
Green can.

Harbor Entrance Light 3
Fl G 4s, 22 ft., 3 mi., SG on pile, radar reflector.

Harbor Entrance Light 2
36 48.3N, 121 47.4W, Oc R 4s, 22 ft., 8 mi., TR on pile, horn: 2 blasts every 30s, operates continuously, radar reflector.

Harbor Channel Light 4
Fl R 4s, 15 ft., 3 mi., TR on pile.

Harbor Channel Daybeacon 5
SG on pile.

Harbor Channel Buoy 6
Red nun.

Harbor Channel Light 8
Fl R 2.5s, 15 ft., 3 mi., TR on pile.

Harbor Channel Buoy 9
Green can.

Harbor Channel Buoy 11
Green can.

Mouse Rock Bell Buoy 3MR
35 26.3N, 120 54.5W, green.

N

Napa River
Aids to navigation for the Napa River are not included in this book.

New York Slough
See Suisun Bay.

Newport Bay

Newport Harbor Entrance Lighted Buoy NWP
33 35.1N, 117 52.6W, Mo (A) W, 5 mi., red and white stripes.

West Jetty Light 3
33 35.3N, 117 52.7W, Fl G 6s, 44 ft., 8 mi., SG on concrete building, horn: 1 blast every 30s, reduced intensity from 355° to 110°.

East Jetty Light 4
33 35.4N, 117 52.6W, Fl R 4s, 25 ft., 6 mi., TR on pile.

Channel Light 5
33 35.9N, 117 52.9W, Fl G 2.5s, 12 ft., 5 mi., SG on pile.

Channel Light 6
33 35.9N, 117 52.8W, Fl R 4s, 18 ft., 3 mi., TR on pile.

Channel Light 8
33 36.1N, 117 53.2W, Fl R 4s, 19 ft., 4 mi., TR on pile.

Channel Light 10
33 36.2N, 117 53.8W, Fl R 2.5s, 10 ft., 4 mi., TR on post.

Channel Light 11
33 36.5N, 117 54.2W, Q G, 12 ft., 5 mi., SG on pile.

Channel Light 12
33 36.7N, 117 54.5W, Fl R 2.5s, 15 ft., 4 mi., TR on post.

Anchorage Buoy A
33 36.0N, 117 54.3W, yellow, private aid, anchorage buoys maintained from May 15 to Sept. 15.

Anchorage Buoy B
33 36.5N, 117 54.3W, yellow, private aid.

Anchorage Buoy C
33 36.6N, 117 54.4W, yellow, private aid.

Anchorage Buoy D
33 36.5N, 117 54.5W, yellow, private aid.

Balboa Island North Channel Light 2
33 36.5N, 117 54.0W, Q R, 12 ft., 5 mi., TR on pile.

Ruben E. Lee Obstruction Lights
33 36.9N, 117 54.2W, F R, private aids.

NOAA Environmental Buoys

Lighted Buoy 46045
33 50.3N, 118 26.8W, Fl (4) Y 20s, yellow disc-shaped buoy.

Lighted Buoy EB 46025
33 44.8N, 119 04.1W, Fl (4) Y 20s, yellow boat-shaped buoy.

Lighted Buoy EB 46054
34 16.1N, 120 26.9W, Fl (4) Y 20s, yellow disc-shaped buoy.

Lighted Buoy 46051
34 28.8N, 120 41.7W, Fl (4) Y 20s, yellow disc-shaped buoy.

Lighted Buoy 46024
34 28.8N, 120 42.1W, Q Y, yellow disc-shaped buoy.

California

Lighted Buoy 46011 (ODAS)
34 52.7N, 120 52.4W, Fl (4) Y 20s,
yellow boat-shaped buoy.

Lighted Buoy EB 46028
35 45.3N, 121 52.0W, Fl (4) Y 20s,
yellow disc-shaped buoy.

Lighted Buoy 46049
36 44.4N, 122 26.6W, Fl (4) Y 20s,
yellow disc-shaped buoy.

Lighted Buoy 46042
36 45.0N, 122 24.5W, Fl (4) Y 20s,
yellow disc-shaped buoy.

Lighted Buoy 46012
37 23.2N, 122 43.3W, Fl (4) Y 20s,
yellow disc-shaped buoy.

Lighted Buoy 46026
37 44.7N, 122 49.3W, Fl (4) Y 20s,
yellow disc-shaped buoy.

Lighted Buoy 46059
37 59.0N, 129 59.8W, Fl (4) Y 20s,
yellow boat-shaped buoy.

Lighted Buoy EB 46013
38 13.7N, 123 17.9W, Fl (4) Y 20s,
yellow disc-shaped buoy.

Lighted Buoy EB 46014
39 13.2N, 123 58.3W, Fl (4) Y 20s,
yellow disc-shaped buoy.

Lighted Buoy EB 46030
40 25.4N, 124 31.4W, Fl (4) Y 20s,
yellow disc-shaped buoy.

Lighted Buoy EB 46006
40 48.7N, 137 39.0W, Fl (4) Y 20s,
yellow disc-shaped buoy.

Lighted Buoy EB 46027
41 51.0N, 124 23.0W, Fl (4) Y 20s,
yellow disc-shaped buoy.

**Noonday Rock Lighted Bell Buoy
NR**
37 47.7N, 123 10.7W, Fl (2+1) R 6s,
4 mi., red and green bands.

North Island
See San Diego Bay.

NOYO RIVER

**Noyo Approach Lighted Whistle
Buoy NA**
39 25.9N, 123 50.0W, Mo (A) W,
5 mi., red and white stripes with
red spherical topmark.

Entrance Lighted Bell Buoy 2
39 25.8N, 123 49.3W, Fl R 2.5s,
3 mi., red.

Entrance Buoy 3
39 25.8N, 123 49.0W, green can.

Entrance Daybeacon 4
TR on pile.

Entrance Light 5
39 25.7N, 123 48.6W, Oc G 4s,
28 ft., 4 mi., SG on pile, horn: 1
blast every 30s, located 235 ft.
inshore from light.

Range Front Light 6
39 25.6N, 123 48.4W, Q R, 15 ft.,
4 mi., KRW and TR on pile, visible all around, higher intensity
on rangeline.

Light 8
Fl R 4s, 15 ft., 4 mi., TR on pile,
radar reflector.

Light 9
Fl G 2.5s, 15 ft., 4 mi., SG on post.

Range Rear Light 10
175 yards, 104.8° from front light,
Iso R 6s, 24 ft., 5 mi., KRW and TR
on pile, visible all around, higher
intensity on rangeline.

Light 12
Fl R 4s, 5 ft., 3 mi., TR on pile.

**Oakland Bay–San Francisco
Bridge**
See San Francisco Bay.

OAKLAND HARBOR

Also see San Francisco Bay, San
Leandro Bay, Alameda Naval Air
Station, Alameda Boat Ramp
Buoys, Ballena Bay, Harbor Bay
Ferry, *and* San Leandro Marina
Channel.

**Oakland Harbor Bar Channel
Lighted Bell Buoy 1 (100 ft. outside channel limit)**
37 48.2N, 122 21.4W, Fl G 2.5s,
4 mi., green.

**Oakland Harbor Bar Channel
Lighted Buoy 2 (100 ft. outside
channel limit)**
37 48.1N, 122 21.2W, Fl R 2.5s,
4 mi., red.

Oakland Outer Harbor

Range B Front Light
37 49.0N, 122 19.5W, Q R, 25 ft.,
KRW on pile.

Range B Rear Light
In 10 feet, 335 yards, 056° from
front light, Iso R 6s, 56 ft., KRW
on pile.

Centerline Range Front Light
37 49.0N, 122 19.6W, Q Y, 25 ft.,
KWB on pile.

Centerline Range Rear Light
267 yards, 056.5° from front light,
Iso Y 6s, 42 ft., KWB on pile.

Range A Front Light
37 48.9N, 122 19.7W, Q G, 25 ft.,
KRW on white pile.

Range A Rear Light
In 10 feet, 335 yards, 059° from
front light, Iso G 6s, 35 ft., KRW
on white pile.

**Lighted Buoy 1B (100 ft. outside
channel limit)**
37 48.3N, 122 21.0W, Fl G 4s,
4 mi., green.

**Oakland Seventh Street Terminal
Light 2**
37 48.3N, 122 20.5W, Fl R 2.5s,
19 ft., private aid.

BART Obstruction Lights (2)
37 48.7N, 122 20.3W, Q W, 9 ft.,
dolphin, private aids

Lighted Buoy 3
37 48.8N, 122 20.1W, Fl G 4s,
4 mi., green.

Lighted Buoy 5
37 48.9N, 122 19.6W, Fl G 4s,
4 mi., green.

Buoy 7
37 49.0N, 122 19.3W, green can.

**Oakland Seventh Street Terminal
Light 1**
37 48.2N, 122 20.5W, Fl G 2.5s,
19 ft., on post, private aid.

Oakland Middle Harbor Lighted Buoy A
37 48.1N, 122 20.4W, Fl (2+1) G 6s, 3 mi., green and red bands.

Oakland Inner Harbor

Lighted Buoy 4 (100 ft. outside channel limit)
37 48.1N, 122 20.7W, Fl R 4s, 4 mi., red.

Light 5
37 48.0N, 122 19.9W, Fl G 4s, 30 ft., 7 mi., SG on white cylindrical tower, horn: 1 blast every 15s.

Light 6
37 47.9N, 122 19.9W, Fl R 6s, 15 ft., 4 mi., TR on pile.

Light 8
37 47.5N, 122 18.2W, Fl R 2.5s, 15 ft., 4 mi., TR on pile, radar reflector.

Coast Guard Island Pier South Light
37 46.7N, 122 14.7W, Iso Y 6s, 13 ft., 5 mi., on end of pier.

Coast Guard Island Pier North Light
37 46.8N, 122 15.1W, Iso Y 6s, 13 ft., 5 mi., on end of pier.

Brooklyn Basin

South Channel Light 1
37 47.0N, 122 15.4W, Fl G 4s, 15 ft., 4 mi., SG on pile, radar reflector.

Ninth Avenue Turning Basin Range Rear Light
257 yards, 096.4° from front light, Iso G 6s, KGW on skeleton structure, use with Brooklyn Basin South Channel Light 1 as front light, private aid.

North Channel Light 2
Fl R 2.5s, 15 ft., 3 mi., TR on pile.

North Channel Light 4
Fl R 4s, 15 ft., 3 mi., TR on pile.

North Channel Light 6
Fl R 2.5s, 15 ft., 3 mi., TR on pile.

North Channel Light 8
Fl R 4s, 15 ft., 3 mi., TR on pile.

North Channel Light 10
Fl R 6s, 15 ft., 3 mi., TR on pile.

North Channel Daybeacon 12
TR on pile.

Ocean Beach Pier Fog Signal
32 45.0N, 117 15.6W, 23 ft., horn: 1 blast every 15s, private aid.

OCEANSIDE

Due to frequently changing conditions, positions of buoys are not listed.

Approach Lighted Whistle Buoy OC
Mo (A) W, 4 mi., red and white stripes.

Breakwater Light 3
33 12.3N, 117 24.1W, Fl G 2.5s, 50 ft., 5 mi., SG on pile.

Harbor Buoy 3A
Green can.

North Jetty Danger Buoy B
White with orange band worded ROCKS.

South Jetty Light 4
33 12.4N, 117 24.0W, Fl R 6s, 26 ft., 7 mi., TR on post, horn: 2 blasts every 20s.

Junction Buoy
Green and red bands, can.

Buoy 5
Green can.

Harbor Obstruction Light A
Fl Y 5s, 35 ft., on dolphin, maintained by U.S. Army Corps of Engineers.

Harbor Construction Light B
Fl Y 5s, 35 ft., on dolphin, maintained by U.S. Army Corps of Engineers.

Light 6
33 12.4N, 117 24.0W, Q R, 26 ft., 4 mi., TR on concrete structure.

North Jetty Danger Buoy
White with orange bands and orange diamond worded SUBMERGED JETTY.

North Jetty Light
33 12.5N, 117 24.0W, Fl W 4s, 15 ft., 5 mi., NW on steel post.

Buoy 7
Green can.

Daybeacon 8
TR on pile.

Light 9
33 12.5N, 117 23.8W, Q G, 28 ft., 4 mi., SG on tower.

Del Mar Boat Basin

Buoy 1
Green can.

Buoy 2
Red nun.

Buoy 3
Green can.

Buoy 4
Red nun.

Buoy 5
Green can.

Buoy 6
Red nun.

Obstruction Light A
Fl Y 5s, 35 ft., on dolphin, maintained by U.S. Army Corps of Engineers.

Obstruction Light B
Fl Y 5s, 35 ft., on dolphin, maintained by U.S. Army Corps of Engineers.

Daybeacon 7
33 12.9N, 117 24.2W, SG on white skeleton tower.

Daybeacon 8
33 12.7N, 117 24.2W, TR on white skeleton tower.

Oil Platforms
See Platforms.

Orange County Research Buoy
33 34.8N, 118 01.7W, yellow spar, private aid.

Ormond Beach Buoy OB2
34 07.4N, 119 10.6W, red nun, private aid.
Also see Port Hueneme.

Ormond Beach Discharge Buoy
White with orange bands, triangular shaped, private aid.

Oyster Cove Marina Channel
See San Francisco Bay.

Oyster Point Marina Channel
See San Francisco Bay.

P

Pacific Gas and Electric Heading Buoy
35 23.0N, 120 52.9W, yellow nun, private aid.
Also see Estero Bay.

Pacific Missile Test Center Lighted Oceanographic Buoy
33 22.9N, 119 39.9W, Fl (5) Y 15s, yellow spherical buoy, maintained by U.S. Navy.

Pacific Missile Test Center Lighted Oceanographic Buoy
33 14.3N, 119 50.6W, Fl (5) Y 20s, yellow spherical buoy, maintained by U.S. Navy.

Pacific Missile Test Center Target Lighted Mooring Buoy
33 27.0N, 119 49.0W, F W, black with orange stripe, maintained by U.S. Navy.

Palos Verdes Point Lighted Bell Buoy 10PV
33 46.4N, 118 26.7W, Fl R 4s, 4 mi., red.

PETALUMA RIVER

Also see San Pablo Bay.

Entrance Light 1
38 02.7N, 122 25.7W, Fl G 4s, 15 ft., 3 mi., SG on pile, radar reflector.

Entrance Light 2
Fl R 2.5s, 10 ft., 3 mi., TR on pile, horn: 1 blast every 10s, operates continuously from Oct. 1 to April 1.

Entrance Channel Daybeacon 3
SG on pile.

Entrance Channel Light 4
Fl R 4s, 15 ft., 3 mi., TR on pile, radar reflector.

Entrance Channel Daybeacon 5
SG on pile.

Entrance Channel Light 6
38 04.3N, 122 25.6W, Fl R 2.5s, 15 ft., 3 mi., TR on pile.

Entrance Channel Daybeacon 7
SG on pile.

Entrance Channel Light 8
Fl R 4s, 15 ft., 3 mi., TR on pile, radar reflector.

Entrance Channel Daybeacon 9
SG on pile.

Entrance Channel Light 10
Fl R 4s, 15 ft., 3 mi., TR on pile structure.

Entrance Channel Daybeacon 11
SG on pile.

Entrance Channel Light 12
Fl R 4s, 10 ft., 3 mi., TR on pile, radar reflector.

Entrance Channel Daybeacon 13
SG on pile.

Entrance Channel Light 14
Fl R 4s, 20 ft., 4 mi., TR on white column.

Entrance Channel Daybeacon 15
SG on pile.

Entrance Channel Light 16
Fl R 4s, 10 ft., 3 mi., TR on pile, radar reflector.

Entrance Channel Daybeacon 17
SG on pile.

Entrance Channel Light 18
Fl R 6s, 10 ft., 4 mi., TR on pile, radar reflector.

Entrance Channel Daybeacon 19
SG on pile.

Entrance Channel Light 20
Fl R 4s, 15 ft., 4 mi., TR on pile structure.

Buoy 2
Red nun.

Buoy 4
38 11.9N, 122 33.8W, red nun.

Daybeacon 5
38 12.2N, 122 34.2W, SG on pile.

Piedras Blancas Light
35 39.9N, 121 17.1W, Fl W 10s, 142 ft., 25 mi., white conical tower with flat top.

Pigeon Point Light
37 10.9N, 122 23.6W, Fl W 10s, 148 ft., 24 mi., white conical tower.

PILLAR POINT HARBOR

Approach Lighted Whistle Buoy PP
37 28.3N, 122 30.9W, Mo (A) W, 5 mi., red and white stripes with red spherical topmark.

Entrance Lighted Gong Buoy 1
37 29.2N, 122 30.4W, Fl G 2.5s, 4 mi., green.

Entrance Lighted Buoy 2
37 28.4N, 122 29.0W, Fl R 4s, 4 mi., red.

Entrance Lighted Bell Buoy 3
37 28.9N, 122 29.0W, Fl G 4s, 4 mi., green.

Entrance Light
37 29.6N, 122 29.1W, Fl W 5s, 50 ft., 14 mi., white cylindrical structure, horn: 1 blast every 10s, operates continuously, high-intensity beam bearing 330°, obscured from 355° to 102°.

Light 6
Fl R 6s, 30 ft., 4 mi., TR on skeleton tower.

Inner Harbor Light 2
37 30.0N, 122 29.1W, Fl R 2.5s, 17 ft., TR on breakwater, private aid.

Inner Harbor Center Light A
37 30.0N, 122 28.9W, Fl W 3s, 17 ft., NB on breakwater, private aid.

Inner Harbor Light 1
37 30.0N, 122 28.8W, Fl G 2.5s, 17 ft., SG on breakwater, private aid.

Pilot Rock Gong Buoy 2
41 02.6N, 124 09.3W, red.

Pittsburg Marina
See Suisun Bay.

Platform *Gail* Racon
34 07.5N, 119 24.0W, G (-- -), 35 ft., private aid.

Platform *Harvest* Light
34 28.2N, 120 40.8W, Fl W 10s, 75 ft., 17 mi., racon: M (--).

Platform *Harvest* Mooring Buoy A
34 28.0N, 120 40.3W, white with blue band, private aid.

Point Arena Light
38 57.3N, 123 44.4W, Fl W 15s, 155 ft., 25 mi., white cylindrical tower, black gallery.
Also see Arena Cove.

Point Arguello Light
34 34.6N, 120 38.9W, Fl W 15s, 120 ft., 24 mi., on single post, horn: 2 blasts every 20s, located 316 yards, 270° from light tower, operates continuously.

Point Arguello Lighted Wave Measurement Buoy
34 27.8N, 120 41.8W, Fl (5) Y 20s, yellow worded WAVE BUOY, maintained by U.S. Army Corps of Engineers.

Point Arguello Lighted Wave Measurement Buoy B
34 29.7N, 120 43.6W, Fl (5) Y 20s, white with orange bands worded WAVE GAGE, maintained by U.S. Army Corps of Engineers.

Point Blunt Light
37 51.2N, 122 25.2W, Fl G 5s, 60 ft., 13 mi., white square house, horn: 1 blast every 15s.
Also see San Francisco Bay.

Point Bonita Light
37 48.9N, 122 31.8W, Oc W 4s, 124 ft., 18 mi., white tower on building, horn: 2 blasts every 30s.
Also see San Francisco Bay.

Point Buchon Lighted Whistle Buoy 2
35 14.4N, 120 54.6W, Fl R 6s, 4 mi., red.

Point Cabrillo Light
39 20.9N, 123 49.6W, Fl W 10s, 84 ft., 24 mi., white octagonal frame tower on building.

Point Conception Light
34 26.9N, 120 28.2W, Fl W 30s, 133 ft., 26 mi., white tower behind building, horn: 1 blast every 30s, operates continuously.

Point Cypress Lighted Gong Buoy 6
36 35.0N, 121 59.1W, Fl R 2.5s, 4 mi., red.

Point Delgada Lighted Whistle Buoy 20
40 00.3N, 124 04.9W, Fl R 6s, 4 mi., red.

Point Diablo Light
37 49.2N, 122 30.0W, Iso W 6s, 85 ft., 9 mi., white square house, horn: 1 blast every 15s, operates continuously.
Also see San Francisco Bay.

Point Dume Lighted Bell Buoy 12PD
33 59.6N, 118 48.3W, Fl R 4s, 4 mi., red.

Point Fermin Light
33 42.3N, 118 17.6W, Fl W 10s, 120 ft., 16 mi., pole.

Point Fermin Lighted Whistle Buoy 6PF
33 41.9N, 118 17.5W, Fl R 4s, 4 mi., red.

Point Hueneme Light
See Port Hueneme.

Point Loma Light
32 39.9N, 117 14.5W, Fl W 15s, 88 ft., 23 mi., black house on white square pyramidal skeleton tower, horn: 1 blast every 30s.
Also see San Diego Bay.

Point Montara Light
37 32.2N, 122 31.2W, Fl W 5s, 70 ft., 15 mi., white conical tower.

Point Pinole Light P
38 01.0N, 122 22.0W, Fl W 2.5s, 15 ft., 3 mi., NR on pile, radar reflector.
Also see San Pablo Bay.

Point Pinos Light
36 38.0N, 121 56.0W, Oc W 4s, 89 ft., 17 mi., white tower on dwelling.

Point Pinos Lighted Bell Buoy 2
36 38.9N, 121 56.6W, Fl R 6s, 4 mi., red.

Point Reyes Light
37 59.7N, 123 01.4W, Fl W 5s, 265 ft., 24 mi., on cylindrical structure on top of square building, horn: 1 blast every 30s, operates continuously.
Also see Drakes Bay.

Point San Luis Lighted Whistle Buoy 3
35 09.2N, 120 44.9W, Fl G 4s, 4 mi., green.
Also see Port San Luis.

Point San Pablo Terminal Light 4
37 57.9N, 122 25.7W, Iso R 5s, 12 ft., concrete dolphin, private aid.
Also see San Pablo Bay.

Point Santa Cruz Wave Measuring Lighted Buoy
36 53.4N, 122 04.3W, Fl (3) W 25s, silver spherical buoy, private aid.
Also see Santa Cruz.

Point Sur Light
36 18.4N, 121 54.1W, Fl W 15s, 250 ft., 25 mi., white tower on grey stone building.

Point Vicente Light
33 44.5N, 118 24.6W, Fl (2) W 20s, 185 ft., 24 mi., white cylindrical tower, horn: 1 blast every 30s.

PORT HUENEME

Also see Channel Islands Harbor.

Light
34 08.7N, 119 12.6W, Fl (5) W 30s, 52 ft., 20 mi., white square tower on building, light obscured from 155° to 296°, horn: 1 blast every 30s, on point 251° from light.

Ormond Beach Buoy OB2
34 07.4N, 119 10.6W, red nun, private aid.

Ormond Beach Discharge Buoy
White with orange bands, triangular shaped, private aid.

Entrance Lighted Whistle Buoy PH
34 08.3N, 119 13.0W, Mo (A) W, 4 mi., red with white stripes.

East Jetty Light 4
34 08.6N, 119 12.7W, Fl R 2.5s, 27 ft., 5 mi., TR on post.

Range Front Light
34 09.1N, 119 12.3W, Q R, 61 ft., KRW on pile, higher intensity on rangeline.

Range Rear Light
245 yards, 037° from front light, Iso R 6s, 86 ft., KRW on pile, higher intensity on rangeline.

West Jetty Light 3
34 08.6N, 119 13.0W, Fl G 2.5s, 37 ft., 6 mi., SG on post.

Channel Lighted Buoy 5
34 08.7N, 119 12.7W, Fl G 4s,
4 mi., green.

Channel Lighted Buoy 6
34 08.7N, 119 12.7W, Fl R 4s,
4 mi., red.

PORT SAN LUIS

San Luis Obispo Light
35 09.6N, 120 45.6W, Fl W 5s,
116 ft., 24 mi., on cylindrical
structure east of the old lighthouse, horn: 2 blasts every 60s,
light operates continuously.

San Luis Obispo Buoy 2
35 09.4N, 120 43.9W, red nun.

**Point San Luis Lighted Whistle
Buoy 3**
35 09.2N, 120 44.9W, Fl G 4s,
4 mi., green.

Channel Buoy 4
35 09.6N, 120 44.8W, red nun,
private aid.

Channel Buoy 5
Green can, private aid.

Channel Buoy 6
Red nun, private aid.

Channel Buoy 7
Green can, private aid.

Channel Buoy 8
Red nun, private aid.

Channel Buoy 9
Green can, Private aid.

Channel Buoy 10
Red nun, private aid.

Channel Buoy 11
Green can, private aid.

Channel Buoy 12
Red nun, private aid.

Channel Buoy 13
Green can, private aid.

Avila Beach Union Oil Pier Light B
35 10.2N, 120 44.7W, F W, 24 ft.,
on post, private aid.

Presidio Shoal Buoy 2
Red nun.
Also see San Francisco Bay.

**Punta Gorda Lighted Whistle
Buoy 24**
40 14.9N, 124 22.2W, Fl R 6s,
4 mi., red.

Pyramid Cove Anchorage Light
32 50.0N, 118 23.0W, Fl R 4s,
886 ft., 4 mi., NR on post, visible
from 307° to 040°, partially
obscured by hills elsewhere.
Also see San Clemente Island.

Pyramid Head Light
32 49.2N, 118 21.2W, Fl W 6s,
226 ft., 10 mi., NR on post, visible
from 147° to 095°, partially
obscured by hills elsewhere.
Also see San Clemente Island.

R

Raccoon Strait
See San Francisco Bay.

Reading Rocks Light
41 20.4N, 124 10.7W, Fl W 4s,
98 ft., 6 mi., NR on house, horn:
1 blast every 10s, operates continuously.

REDONDO BEACH

**Redondo Harbor Entrance
Lighted Bell Buoy RB**
33 50.3N, 118 23.8W, Mo (A) W,
3 mi., red with white stripes.

Redondo Beach West Jetty Light 3
33 50.5N, 118 23.7W, Fl G 4s,
35 ft., 4 mi., SG on column.

Redondo Beach East Jetty Light 2
33 50.5N, 118 23.6W, Fl R 4s,
20 ft., 6 mi., on post, horn: 1 blast
every 10s.

King Harbor

Midchannel Buoy A
33 50.5N, 118 23.7W, red can with
white stripes, private aid.

Channel Buoy 1
Green can, private aid.

Channel Buoy 2
Red nun, private aid.

Channel Buoy 1A
33 50.5N, 118 23.6W, green can,
private aid.

Discharge Obstruction Buoy
33 50.5N, 118 23.6W, white with
orange bands and orange diamond, private aid.

Mole C Light
F R, 17 ft., on post, private aid.

Midchannel Buoy B
33 50.6N, 118 23.8W, red can with
white stripes, private aid.

Channel Buoy 3
Green can, private aid.

Channel Buoy 4
Red nun, private aid.

Portofino Light 1
F G, on post, private aid.

Portofino Light 2
F R, on post, private aid.

Midchannel Buoy C
33 50.8N, 118 24.0W, red can with
white stripes, private aid.

Channel Buoy 5
Green can, private aid.

Channel Buoy 6
Red nun, private aid.

Light 1
F G, 17 ft., on post, private aid.

Light 2
F R, on post, private aid.

Midchannel Buoy D
33 50.9N, 118 24.0W, red can with
white stripes, private aid.

Channel Buoy 7
Green can, private aid.

Channel Buoy 8
Red nun, private aid.

Intake Obstruction Buoy
33 50.7N, 118 23.9W, white with
orange band, can, private aid.

Intake Obstruction Buoy
White with orange band, can,
private aid.

REDWOOD CREEK

Also see San Francisco Bay.

Entrance Light 2
37 33.2N, 122 11.8W, Fl R 4s,
15 ft., 4 mi., TR on pile, horn:
1 blast every 10s, operates continuously from Oct. 1 to April 1,
higher intensity beam upstream,
radar reflector.

Entrance Lighted Buoy 3
Fl G 4s, 3 mi., green, radar
reflector.

Entrance Light 4
Fl R 4s, 15 ft., 4 mi., TR on pile,
radar reflector.

Light 5
37 32.4N, 122 11.6W, Fl G 4s,
15 ft., 3 mi., SG on pile, radar
reflector.

Light 6
Fl R 4s, 15 ft., 4 mi., TR on pile,
radar reflector.

Light 8
Fl R 4s, 15 ft., 3 mi., TR on pile.

Light 7
Fl G 2.5s, 15 ft., 3 mi., SG on pile,
radar reflector.

Light 10
Fl R 4s, 15 ft., 3 mi., TR on pile.

Light 9
Fl G 4s, 3 mi., SG on pile, radar
reflector.

Daybeacon 11
SG on pile.

Light 12
Fl R 6s, 15 ft., 4 mi., TR on pile.

Light 14
Fl R 4s, 15 ft., 3 mi., TR on pile,
radar reflector.

Light 13
Fl G 2.5s, 15 ft., 3 mi., SG on pile,
radar reflector.

Light 15
Fl G 4s, 15 ft., 5 mi., SG on pile,
radar reflector.

Light 16
Fl R 6s, 15 ft., 4 mi., TR on pile,
radar reflector.

Light 18
37 30.8N, 122 12.7W, Fl R 4s,
15 ft., 4 mi., TR on pile, radar
reflector.

Light 20
Fl R 4s, 15 ft., 3 mi., TR on
column, radar reflector.

Daybeacon 21
SG on pile.

Richardson Bay
See Sausalito.

RICHMOND HARBOR CHANNEL

Also see San Francisco Bay.

Lighted Buoy 2
37 55.1N, 122 25.1W, Q R, 3 mi.,
red.

**Richmond Harbor Approach
Range Front Light**
37 54.0N, 122 23.5W, Q W, 20 ft.,
KRW on pile structure.

**Richmond Harbor Approach
Range Rear Light**
340 yards, 132° from front light,
Iso W 6s, 35 ft., KRW on pile
structure, visible all around with
higher intensity on rangeline.

Lighted Buoy 3
37 54.9N, 122 24.5W, Fl G 4s,
3 mi., green.

Light 4
Q R, 15 ft., 3 mi., TR on pile, radar
reflector.

Lighted Buoy 5
37 54.5N, 122 24.0W, Fl G 2.5s,
3 mi., green.

**Richmond Harbor Jetty
Daybeacon**
37 54.2N, 122 23.5W, NR on white
frame on pile.

Lighted Buoy 6
Fl R 4s, 3 mi., red.

Lighted Buoy 7
37 54.4N, 122 23.2W, Fl G 4s,
3 mi., green.

Light 8
Fl R 6s, 15 ft., 4 mi., TR on pile,
radar reflector.

Brickyard Cove Harbor Light 1
F G, 8 ft., pile, private aid.

Brickyard Cove Harbor Light 2
F R, 8 ft., pile, private aid.

Light 9
Fl G 4s, 10 ft., 3 mi., SG on pile,
radar reflector.

Light 10
Fl R 4s, 15 ft., 4 mi., TR on pile,
radar reflector.

Light 12
Fl R 2.5s, 25 ft., 4 mi., TR on pile,
radar reflector.

**Point Potrero Reach Range Front
Passing Light 14**
37 54.1N, 122 21.7W, Q R, 18 ft.,
3 mi., KRW on pile, radar
reflector.

**Point Potrero Reach Range Rear
Light**
343 yards, 099.3° from front light,
Iso R 6s, KRW on pile.

Buoy 16
Red nun.

Lighted Buoy 18
Fl R 2.5s, 3 mi., red.

Daybeacon 20
37 55.1N, 122 21.9W, TR on pile.

Richmond Long Wharf Fog Signal
37 55.3N, 122 24.7W, building on
wharf, siren: 2 blasts every 30s,
private aid.

**Richmond Long Wharf Inner Fog
Signal**
37 55.5N, 122 24.4W, on wharf,
bell: 1 stroke every 20s, private aid.

RICHMOND–SAN RAFAEL BRIDGE

Also see San Francisco Bay *and*
Richmond Harbor Channel.

**Richmond–San Rafael Bridge
Racon**
37 56.1N, 122 26.7W, Q (---·-),
185 ft., bands: 20s (every 30s),
private aid.

**Richmond–San Rafael Bridge
Racon**
37 56.0N, 122 25.5W, T (-), 135 ft.,
bands: 20s (every 30s), private
aid.

Richmond–San Rafael Bridge Fog Signals
Horns (2): sound simultaneously, 2 blasts every 30s, private aids.

East Channel Fog Signal
Horns (2): sound simultaneously, 1 blast every 15s, private aids.

Rincon Island Light
34 20.8N, 119 26.7W, Fl W 5s, 46 ft., on skeleton tower, horn: 1 blast every 15s, private aid.

S

Sacramento River
Aids to navigation for the Sacramento River are not included in this book.
Also see Suisun Bay.

Samoa Channel
See Humboldt Bay.

San Bruno Shoal Channel
See San Francisco Bay.

SAN CLEMENTE ISLAND

China Point Light
32 48.2N, 118 25.5W, Fl W 5s, 112 ft., 15 mi., NR on pile, visible from 260° to 128°, partially obscured by hills elsewhere.

Pyramid Head Light
32 49.2N, 118 21.2W, Fl W 6s, 226 ft., 10 mi., NR on post, visible from 147° to 095°, partially obscured by hills elsewhere.

Pyramid Cove Anchorage Light
32 50.0N, 118 23.0W, Fl R 4s, 886 ft., 4 mi., NR on post, visible from 307° to 040°, partially obscured by hills elsewhere.

Navy Anchorage South End Light
32 58.5N, 118 32.0W, Fl W 2.5s, 140 ft., 6 mi., NR on post, visible from 150° to 320°, partially obscured by hills elsewhere.

Wilson Cove

Light
33 00.2N, 118 33.2W, Fl W 4s, 125 ft., 9 mi., NR on post, visible from 155° to 317°, partially obscured by hills elsewhere.

Range Front Light
33 00.4N, 118 33.4W, F R, 27 ft., small house, maintained by U.S. Navy.

Range Rear Light
On shore, 210 yards, 198° from front light, F R, 40 ft., small house, maintained by U.S. Navy.

Fog Signal
Horn: 1 blast every 15s.

North End Light
33 01.4N, 118 33.9W, Fl W 6s, 60 ft., 7 mi., NR on post, visible from 139° to 330°, partially obscured by hills elsewhere.

North End Radar Buoy A
33 01.6N, 118 33.7W, orange and white bands, spar, maintained by U.S. Navy.

San Clemente Island Light
33 01.7N, 118 35.9W, Fl W 5s, 202 ft., 15 mi., NR on post, visible from 341° to 276°, partially obscured elsewhere.

SAN DIEGO BAY

Approaches

Point Loma Light
32 39.9N, 117 14.5W, Fl W 15s, 88 ft., 23 mi., black house on white square pyramidal skeleton tower, horn: 1 blast every 30s.

Approach Lighted Whistle Buoy SD
32 37.3N, 117 14.8W, Mo (A) W, 6 mi., red and white stripes, racon: M (--).

Approach Lighted Buoy 3
32 38.2N, 117 14.2W, Fl G 6s, 4 mi., green.

Channel Lighted Bell Buoy 5
32 39.1N, 117 13.6W, Fl G 2.5s, Fl G 2.5s, 3 mi., green.

Entrance Range Front Light
32 42.3N, 117 14.0W, Q G, 22 ft., KRW on white column, visible all around, higher intensity 4° each side of rangeline, horn: 1 blast every 10s.

Entrance Range Rear Light
500 yards, 353° from front light, Iso G 6s, 55 ft., KRW on skeleton tower, visible 4° each side of rangeline.

Channel Lighted Buoy 6
32 39.2N, 117 13.5W, Fl R 4s, 3 mi., red.

Channel Lighted Buoy 7
32 39.9N, 117 13.7W, Fl G 4s, 4 mi., green.

Zuniga Jetty Light Z
32 40.0N, 117 13.4W, Fl W 2.5s, 28 ft., 6 mi., NW on post worded DANGER SUBMERGED JETTY, horn: 1 blast every 10s, operates continuously.

Zuniga Jetty Light Y
32 40.3N, 117 13.3W, Fl W 4s, 18 ft., 5 mi., NW on post worded DANGER SUBMERGED JETTY.

Zuniga Jetty Light X
32 40.5N, 117 13.4W, Fl W 4s, 18 ft., 5 mi., NW on post worded DANGER SUBMERGED JETTY.

Zuniga Jetty Light W
32 40.7N, 117 13.4W, Fl W 4s, 18 ft., 5 mi., NW on post worded DANGER SUBMERGED JETTY.

Zuniga Jetty Light V
32 40.9N, 117 13.4W, Fl W 4s, 16 ft., 5 mi., NW on post worded DANGER SUBMERGED JETTY.

Channel Lighted Buoy 8
32 39.9N, 117 13.6W, Fl R 2.5s, 3 mi., red.

Magnetic Silencing Facility Light
32 40.3N, 117 14.1W, Fl W 5s, 18 ft., pile on platform, maintained by U.S. Navy.

Channel Lighted Buoy 9
32 40.4N, 117 13.8W, Fl G 2.5s, 3 mi., green.

Channel Lighted Buoy 10
32 40.4N, 117 13.7W, Fl R 4s, 3 mi., red.

Channel Lighted Buoy 11
32 40.9N, 117 13.9W, Fl G 4s, 3 mi., green.

Channel Lighted Buoy 12
32 40.9N, 117 13.7W, Fl R 2.5s, 3 mi., red.

Ballast Point Light B
32 41.2N, 117 14.0W, Fl W 4s,
16 ft., 10 mi., NG on platform on
dolphin, horn: 1 blast every 15s.

Ballast Point Shoal Buoy
32 41.2N, 117 14.0W, white can
with orange bands worded
SHOAL.

**Zuniga Point Degaussing Range
East Buoy**
32 41.2N, 117 13.6W, orange and
white bands, spar, maintained by
U.S. Navy.

Channel Lighted Buoy 14
32 41.7N, 117 13.9W, Q R, 3 mi.,
red.

Channel Lighted Buoy 15
32 41.7N, 117 14.0W, Fl G 2.5s,
3 mi., green.

Shelter Island Yacht Basin

Shelter Island West End Light 2
32 42.5N, 117 14.1W, Fl R 2.5s,
15 ft., 5 mi., TR on pile.

Buoy 5
32 42.5N, 117 14.2W, green can,
private aid.

Buoy 6
32 42.6N, 117 14.1W, red nun,
private aid.

Buoy 7
32 42.6N, 117 14.1W, green can,
private aid.

Buoy 9
32 42.9N, 117 13.9W, green can,
private aid.

North San Diego Bay

North Island Light 2
32 42.2N, 117 13.5W, Fl R 2.5s,
25 ft., 5 mi., TR on small house.

Channel Lighted Buoy 16
32 42.1N, 117 13.7W, Fl R 2.5s,
3 mi., red.

Channel Lighted Buoy 16A
32 42.4N, 117 13.6W, Q R, 3 mi.,
red.

Channel Lighted Buoy 17
32 42.3N, 117 13.8W, Fl G 4s,
4 mi., green.

North Island Light 4
32 42.5N, 117 13.2W, Fl R 2.5s,
23 ft., 5 mi., TR on post.

Shelter Island Light S
32 42.9N, 117 13.3W, Fl W 2.5s,
16 ft., 6 mi., NG on post.

Channel Lighted Buoy 18
32 42.3N, 117 13.0W, Fl R 4s,
3 mi., red.

Channel Lighted Buoy 19
32 42.9N, 117 13.1W, Q G, 3 mi.,
green.

Commercial Basin

Lighted Buoy 1
32 43.2N, 117 13.0W, Fl G 4s,
4 mi., green.

Shelter Cove Marina Light 1A
32 43.2N, 117 13.2W, Fl G 2.5s,
12 ft., 3 mi., SG on post,
private aid.

Shelter Cove Marina Light B
32 43.3N, 117 13.3W, Fl (2+1) R 5s,
17 ft., JR on pile, private aid.

South Channel Daybeacon 2
32 43.2N, 117 13.4W, 15 ft., TR
on pile, private aid.

South Channel Daybeacon 4
15 ft., TR on pile, private aid.

South Channel Daybeacon 6
15 ft., TR on pile, private aid.

North Channel Daybeacon 3
32 43.3N, 117 13.3W, 15 ft., SG
on pile, private aid.

North Channel Daybeacon 5
15 ft., SG on pile, private aid.

North Channel Daybeacon 7
15 ft., SG on pile, private aid.

**Naval Training Center Bait Barge
Lighted Mooring Buoys (2)**
32 44.0N, 117 12.8W, Q W, white
with blue band, barges moored
from April 1 to Sept. 15, private
aids.

North San Diego Bay (cont'd)

Harbor Island Light
32 43.5N, 117 12.8W, Fl W 4s,
56 ft., 8 mi., on top of red-roofed
building.

North Island Light N
32 42.9N, 117 12.6W, Q W, 20 ft.,
4 mi., NR on post on concrete
platform.

Channel Lighted Buoy 20
32 43.0N, 117 12.4W, Q R, 3 mi.,
red.

Channel Lighted Buoy 21
32 43.1N, 117 11.6W, Q G, 3 mi.,
green.

Lighted Mooring Buoy 19
32 43.3N, 117 11.3W, Fl W 4s,
white, maintained by U.S. Navy.

Quarantine Buoy A
32 42.7N, 117 14.0W, white and
orange bands, sphere worded
QUARANTINE AREA, private aid.

Quarantine Buoy B
32 42.7N, 117 14.1W, white and
orange bands, sphere worded
QUARANTINE AREA, private aid.

Quarantine Buoy C
32 42.7N, 117 14.1W, white and
orange bands, sphere worded
QUARANTINE AREA, private aid.

Buoy A
32 43.5N, 117 10.7W, yellow,
private aid.

Buoy B
32 43.4N, 117 10.5W, yellow,
private aid.

Buoy C
32 43.5N, 117 10.5W, yellow,
private aid.

Buoy D
32 43.5N, 117 10.4W, yellow,
private aid.

Harbor Island East Basin

Channel Buoy 1
32 43.5N, 117 11.2W, green can,
private aid.

Channel Buoy 2
32 43.5N, 117 11.1W, red nun,
private aid.

Channel Buoy 3
32 43.6N, 117 11.3W, green can,
private aid.

Channel Buoy 4
32 43.6N, 117 11.2W, red nun,
private aid.

Channel Buoy 6
32 43.6N, 117 11.3W, red nun,
private aid.

Channel Buoy 8
32 43.6N, 117 11.4W, red nun,
private aid.

Channel Buoy 10
32 43.6N, 117 11.5W, red nun, private aid.

Channel Buoy 12
32 43.6N, 117 11.6W, red nun, private aid.

North San Diego Bay (cont'd)

Pier B Fog Signal
32 43.3N, 117 10.3W, horn: 1 blast every 15s.

Safety Zone Northeast Buoy
32 43.6N, 117 10.7W, yellow can.

Safety Zone Southeast Buoy
32 43.3N, 117 10.9W, yellow can.

Safety Zone Southwest Buoy
32 43.4N, 117 11.1W, yellow can.

Safety Zone Northwest Daybeacon
32 43.6N, 117 11.1W, 12 ft., NY on post.

Channel Buoy 22A
32 42.2N, 117 10.4W, red nun.

Channel Lighted Buoy 22
32 42.5N, 117 10.7W, Fl R 4s, 3 mi., red.

Channel Lighted Buoy 23
32 42.2N, 117 10.2W, Fl G 4s, 4 mi., green.

Channel Lighted Buoy 24
32 41.9N, 117 09.9W, Fl R 4s, 3 mi., red.

Channel Lighted Buoy 26
32 41.0N, 117 08.6W, Fl R 4s, 3 mi., red.

Channel Lighted Buoy 26A
32 40.8N, 117 08.3W, Fl R 6s, 4 mi., red.

Seaport Village Speed Limit Buoy A
32 42.5N, 117 10.2W, white with orange bands, private aids.

Tenth Avenue Pier North Light
32 42.0N, 117 09.6W, F G, 10 ft., on pier, private aid.

Tenth Avenue Pier South Light
32 41.8N, 117 09.2W, F G, 10 ft., on pier, private aid.

Tenth Avenue Marine Terminal Light
32 41.7N, 117 09.2W, F G, 12 ft., on pole, private aid.

San Diego–Coronado Bay Bridge Racon T
32 41.4N, 117 09.1W, T (-), 193 ft., west span, center of channel, private aid.

San Diego–Coronado Bay Bridge Fog Signal
32 41.4N, 117 09.1W, bridge pier, horns (2): 1 blast every 10s simultaneously, private aid.

San Diego–Coronado Bay Bridge Racon C
32 41.4N, 117 09.1W, C (-·-·), 193 ft., east span, center of channel, private aid.

Glorietta Bay

Channel Lighted Buoy 1
32 41.2N, 117 09.2W, Fl G 4s, 4 mi., green.

Channel Range Front Light
32 40.6N, 117 10.1W, Q G, 11 ft., KRW on pile, visible all around.

Channel Range Rear Light
On shore, 210 feet, 232° from front light, Iso G 6s, 21 ft., KRW on post, visible all around.

Channel Buoy 2
32 41.2N, 117 09.4W, red nun.

Channel Buoy 3
32 41.0N, 117 09.5W, green.

Buoy 6
Red nun.

Channel Lighted Buoy 8
32 40.7N, 117 10.1W, Fl R 4s, red nun, private aid.

Buoy 11
Green can, private aid.

Buoy 12
Red nun, private aid.

Buoy 13
Green can, private aid.

San Diego Bay Restricted Area

Buoy A
32 40.5N, 117 10.0W, yellow can worded RESTRICTED AREA DO NOT ENTER, maintained by U.S. Navy.

Buoy B
32 40.6N, 117 09.9W, yellow can worded RESTRICTED AREA DO NOT ENTER, maintained by U.S. Navy.

Buoy C
32 40.8N, 117 09.7W, yellow can worded RESTRICTED AREA DO NOT ENTER, maintained by U.S. Navy.

Buoy D
32 40.9N, 117 09.6W, yellow can worded RESTRICTED AREA DO NOT ENTER, maintained by U.S. Navy.

Buoy E
32 40.9N, 117 09.5W, yellow can worded RESTRICTED AREA DO NOT ENTER, maintained by U.S. Navy.

Buoy F
32 40.8N, 117 09.3W, yellow can worded RESTRICTED AREA DO NOT ENTER, maintained by U.S. Navy.

Buoy G
32 40.7N, 117 09.1W, yellow can worded RESTRICTED AREA DO NOT ENTER, maintained by U.S. Navy.

Buoy H
32 40.5N, 117 08.9W, yellow can worded RESTRICTED AREA DO NOT ENTER, maintained by U.S. Navy.

Buoy I
32 40.3N, 117 08.7W, yellow can worded RESTRICTED AREA DO NOT ENTER, maintained by U.S. Navy.

Buoy J
32 40.2N, 117 08.9W, yellow can worded RESTRICTED AREA DO NOT ENTER, maintained by U.S. Navy.

Buoy K
32 40.0N, 117 09.1W, yellow can worded RESTRICTED AREA DO NOT ENTER, maintained by U.S. Navy.

Buoy L
32 39.8N, 117 08.9W, yellow can worded RESTRICTED AREA DO NOT ENTER, maintained by U.S. Navy.

Buoy M
32 39.3N, 117 08.7W, yellow can worded RESTRICTED AREA DO NOT ENTER, maintained by U.S. Navy.

Buoy N
32 39.3N, 117 08.8W, yellow can worded RESTRICTED AREA DO NOT ENTER, maintained by U.S. Navy.

Buoy O
32 39.3N, 117 08.9W, yellow can worded RESTRICTED AREA DO NOT ENTER, maintained by U.S. Navy.

North San Diego Bay (cont'd)

Channel Lighted Buoy 28
32 40.6N, 117 08.0W, Fl R 4s, 3 mi., red.

Channel Lighted Buoy 30
32 40.1N, 117 07.6W, Fl R 4s, 3 mi., red.

Channel Lighted Buoy 32
32 39.8N, 117 07.6W, Fl R 4s, 3 mi., red.

Channel Lighted Buoy 33
32 39.5N, 117 07.4W, Fl G 2.5s, 3 mi., green.

Channel Lighted Buoy 34
32 39.4N, 117 07.6W, Fl R 2.5s, 3 mi., red.

Channel Lighted Buoy 36
32 39.3N, 117 07.5W, Fl R 4s, 3 mi., red.

Sweetwater Anchorage

Lighted Buoy A
32 39.2N, 117 07.7W, Fl W 2.5s, yellow, private aid.

Lighted Buoy B
Fl W 2.5s, yellow, private aid.

Lighted Buoy C
Fl W 2.5s, yellow, private aid.

Lighted Buoy D
Fl W 2.5s, yellow, private aid.

Buoy E
Yellow, private aid.

Buoy F
Yellow, private aid.

South San Diego Bay

Channel Lighted Buoy 38
32 39.1N, 117 07.4W, Fl R 2.5s, 3 mi., red.

Channel Lighted Buoy 39
32 38.8N, 117 07.2W, Q G, 3 mi., green.

Channel Lighted Buoy 40
32 38.7N, 117 07.5W, Fl R 4s, 3 mi., red.

Channel Lighted Buoy 41
32 38.7N, 117 07.4W, Fl G 4s, 4 mi., green.

North Island Storm Drain Light A
32 41.6N, 117 09.8W, Q Y, private aid.

North Island Storm Drain Light B
32 41.8N, 117 09.9W, Q Y, private aid.

Sweetwater Channel

Light 2
32 38.8N, 117 07.2W, Fl R 4s, 11 ft., TR on pile, private aid.

Light 4
Fl R 4s, 11 ft., TR on pile, private aid.

Light 6
Fl R 4s, 11 ft., TR on pile, private aid.

Light 8
Fl R 4s, 12 ft., TR on pile, private aid.

Coronado Cays Channel

Light 1
32 38.3N, 117 07.9W, Fl G 2.5s, 8 ft., SG on pile, private aid.

Light 2
32 38.3N, 117 08.0W, Fl R 2.5s, 8 ft., TR on pile, private aid.

Daybeacon 3
SG on pile, private aid.

Daybeacon 4
TR on pile, private aid.

Daybeacon 5
SG on pile, private aid.

Daybeacon 6
TR on pile, private aid.

Light 7
32 38.0N, 117 07.9W, Q G, 8 ft., SG on plle, private aid.

Light 8
32 38.0N, 117 08.0W, Q R, 8 ft., TR on pile, private aid.

Daybeacon 9
SG on pile, private aid.

Light 10
32 37.9N, 117 07.9W, Q R, 8 ft., TR on pile, private aid.

Light 11
32 37.9N, 117 07.8W, Q G, 9 ft., SG on pile, private aid.

Light 13
32 37.8N, 117 07.8W, Q G, 9 ft., SG on pile, private aid.

Coronado Cays Pier Light C
32 37.7N, 117 07.7W, Fl W 2s, 6 ft., private aid.

Light 15
32 37.7N, 117 07.7W, Q G, 8 ft., SG on pile, private aid.

Light 16
32 37.7N, 117 07.8W, Q R, 8 ft., TR on pile, private aid.

Daybeacon 17
8 ft., SG on pile, private aid.

Daybeacon 18
8 ft., TR on pile, private aid.

Daybeacon 19
8 ft., SG on pile, private aid.

Daybeacon 20
8 ft., TR on pile, private aid.

Coronado Cays Light 21
Q G, 9 ft., SG on pile, private aid.

Coronado Cays Light 22
Q R, 8 ft., TR on pile, private aid.

Chula Vista Channel

Shoal Marker Light A
32 38.7N, 117 07.3W, Fl W 2.5s, 11 ft., white with orange bands on pile worded SHOAL, private aid.

Light 2
32 38.6N, 117 07.4W, Fl R 4s, 8 ft.,
TR on pile, private aid.

Daybeacon 3
32 38.5N, 117 07.3W, SG on pile,
private aid.

Daybeacon 4
32 38.5N, 117 07.4W, TR on pile,
private aid.

Light 5
32 38.3N, 117 07.2W, Fl G 4s, 8 ft.,
SG on pile, private aid.

Light 6
32 38.3N, 117 07.3W, Fl R 6s, 8 ft.,
TR on pile, private aid.

Light 7
32 38.2N, 117 07.1W, Fl G 2.5s,
8 ft., SG on pile, private aid.

Light 8
32 38.1N, 117 07.3W, Fl R 2.5s,
7 ft., TR on pile, private aid.

Light 9
32 38.2N, 117 07.0W, Fl G 4s, 7 ft.,
SG on pile, private aid.

Light 10
32 38.1N, 117 07.1W, Fl R 2.5s,
10 ft., TR on pile, private aid.

Light 10A
32 38.1N, 117 07.1W, Fl R 4s, 7 ft.,
TR on pile, private aid.

Light 11
32 38.2N, 117 06.9W, Fl G 2.5s,
10 ft., SG on pile, private aid.

Light 11A
32 38.2N, 117 06.8W, Q G, 7 ft.,
SG on pile, private aid.

Light 12
32 38.1N, 117 06.9W, Q R, 10 ft.,
TR on pile, private aid.

Daybeacon 13
32 38.0N, 117 06.7W, SG on pile,
private aid.

Daybeacon 14
32 38.0N, 117 06.8W, TR on pile,
private aid.

Light 15
32 37.8N, 117 06.6W, Fl G 4s, 8 ft.,
SG on pile, private aid.

Light 16
32 37.8N, 117 06.7W, Fl R 4s, 8 ft.,
TR on pile, private aid.

Daybeacon 17
32 37.7N, 117 06.5W, SG on pile,
private aid.

Daybeacon 18
32 37.6N, 117 06.6W, TR on pile,
private aid.

Light 19
32 37.5N, 117 06.4W, Fl G 2.5s,
8 ft., SG on pile, private aid.

Light 20
32 37.5N, 117 06.4W, Fl R 2.5s,
7 ft., TR on pile, private aid.

Light 21
32 37.5N, 117 06.4W, Fl G 4s, 6 ft.,
SG on pile, private aid.

Light 22
32 37.4N, 117 06.4W, Fl R 4s,
10 ft., TR on pile, private aid.

Light 22A
32 37.3N, 117 06.4W, Q R, 11 ft.,
TR on pile, private aid.

Shoal Buoy 4
32 37.4N, 117 06.3W, white can
worded SHOAL, private aid.

Chula Vista Basin North Light
32 37.6N, 117 06.2W, Fl G 4s,
19 ft., private aid.

Chula Vista Basin South Light
Fl R 4s, 18 ft., private aid.

SAN FRANCISCO BAY

Also see Sausalito, Oakland
Harbor, San Leandro Bay,
Alameda Naval Air Station,
Ballena Bay, Harbor Bay Ferry,
San Leandro Marina Channel,
Redwood Creek, Mayfield Slough,
Guadalupe Slough, Emeryville
Marina, Berkeley, Corte Madera
Channel, Richmond Harbor
Channel, San Rafael Creek, *and*
San Pablo Bay.

Traffic Lanes

South Traffic Lane Lighted Bell Buoy S
37 39.2N, 122 39.7W, Fl Y 4s,
6 mi., yellow.

West Traffic Lane Lighted Gong Buoy W
37 41.5N, 122 47.7W, Fl Y 2.5s,
5 mi., yellow.

San Francisco Northern Traffic Lane Lighted Bell Buoy N
37 48.2N, 122 47.9W, Fl Y 4s,
7 mi., yellow.

Approaches

Farallon Light
37 41.9N, 123 00.1W, Fl W 15s,
358 ft., 20 mi., white conical
tower.

Duxbury Reef Lighted Whistle Buoy 1DR
37 51.6N, 122 41.7W, Fl G 6s,
4 mi., green.

Approach Lighted Horn Buoy SF
37 45.0N, 122 41.6W, Mo (A) W,
6 mi., red and white stripes with
red spherical topmark, horn:
1 blast every 30s, operates continuously, racon: M (--), passing
light: high-intensity flash 2.5s,
operates continuously.

Mile Rocks Light
37 47.6N, 122 30.6W, Fl W 5s,
49 ft., 15 mi., white caisson with
orange bands, horn: 1 blast every
30s, operates continuously.

Point Bonita Light
37 48.9N, 122 31.8W, Oc W 4s,
124 ft., 18 mi., white tower on
building, horn: 2 blasts every 30s.

Main Ship Channel

Lighted Bell Buoy 1
37 46.2N, 122 37.9W, Iso G 6s,
5 mi., green.

Lighted Whistle Buoy 2
37 45.8N, 122 37.7W, Iso R 6s,
5 mi., red.

Lighted Buoy 3
37 46.4N, 122 37.1W, Fl G 4s,
4 mi., green.

Lighted Buoy 4
37 46.0N, 122 37.0W, Fl R 4s,
4 mi., red.

Lighted Bell Buoy 5
37 46.6N, 122 36.4W, Fl G 6s,
5 mi., green.

Lighted Buoy 6
37 46.2N, 122 36.2W, Fl R 6s,
4 mi., red.

Lighted Bell Buoy 7
37 46.9N, 122 35.4W, Fl G 2.5s,
4 mi., green.

Lighted Whistle Buoy 8
37 46.5N, 122 35.2W, Fl R 2.5s, 4 mi., red.

Point Bonita Light
37 48.9N, 122 31.8W, Oc W 4s, 124 ft., 18 mi., white tower on building, horn: 2 blasts every 30s.

Point Diablo Light
37 49.2N, 122 30.0W, Iso W 6s, 85 ft., 9 mi., white square house, horn: 1 blast every 15s, operates continuously.

Bonita Channel

Point Bonita Light
37 48.9N, 122 31.8W, Oc W 4s, 124 ft., 18 mi., white tower on building, horn: 2 blasts every 30s.

Lighted Whistle Buoy 2
37 50.0N, 122 34.1W, Fl R 6s, 4 mi., red.

Buoy 4
37 49.4N, 122 33.3W, red nun.

Lighted Bell Buoy 3
37 49.6N, 122 33.1W, Fl G 4s, 4 mi., green.

Four Fathom Bank Lighted Bell Buoy
37 48.7N, 122 32.4W, Fl (2+1) R 6s, 4 mi., red and green bands.

Golden Gate Bridge

Buoy 2
37 48.8N, 122 28.8W, red nun.

South Pier Light
Fl R 15s, 50 ft., horns (2): sound simultaneously 1 blast every 20s, private aid.

Racon G
G (--·), 229 ft., mid-span, center of channel, private aid.

Midchannel Fog Signal
Diaphone: 2 blasts every 40s, private aid.

Lime Point Light
37 49.5N, 122 28.7W, Fl W 5s, 15 ft., 8 mi., on post, horn: 2 blasts every 30s.

Marin Peninsula
Also see Sausalito.

Horseshoe Bay East Breakwater Light
37 49.9N, 122 28.5W, Fl R 3s, 25 ft., on steel pile structure, light obscured from 090° to 270°, private aid.

Yellow Bluff Light
37 50.2N, 122 28.3W, Fl W 6s, 75 ft., 9 mi., NR on single pile.

San Francisco Waterfront

Presidio Shoal Buoy 2
Red nun.

Anita Rock Light
37 48.5N, 122 27.2W, Q W, 20 ft., 5 mi., NR on cylindrical structure.

San Francisco Submarine Outfall Light
37 48.4N, 122 26.9W, Fl R 4s, 10 ft., on pile, private aid.

West Yacht Harbor Lighted Buoy 1
37 48.5N, 122 26.3W, Fl G 4s, green can, private aid.

West Yacht Harbor Light 2
37 48.5N, 122 26.4W, Q R, 21 ft., on pile, private aid.

West Yacht Harbor Lighted Buoy 3
37 48.4N, 112 26.4W, Fl G 4s, green can, private aid.

East Yacht Harbor Light 2
37 48.5N, 122 25.8W, Iso R 6s, 13 ft., on post, private aid.

Aquatic Park Entrance Light 1
37 48.6N, 122 25.4W, Fl G 4s, 21 ft., 3 mi., SG on post, radar reflector.

Fishermans Wharf Breakwater Light A
37 48.7N, 122 25.4W, Fl Y 2.5s, 21 ft., 5 mi., NR on post, radar reflector.

Fishermans Wharf Breakwater Light B
37 48.7N, 122 25.3W, Fl Y 2.5s, 21 ft., 5 mi., NR on post, radar reflector.

Fishermans Wharf Entrance Light 2
37 48.7N, 122 25.2W, Fl R 2.5s, 21 ft., 3 mi., TR on post, radar reflector.

Pier 45 East Light
37 48.7N, 122 25.3W, F R, 22 ft., brown pyramidal structure, private aid.

Pier 45 West Lights (2)
F R, 28 ft. and 19 ft., gray building, lights mounted vertically, private aids.

Pier 39

Breakwater Light 4
Fl R 4s, 14 ft., TR on breakwater, private aid.

Breakwater Light A
37 48.7N, 122 24.6W, Fl W 4s, 14 ft., on breakwater, private aid.

Breakwater Light B
Fl W 2.5s, 14 ft., on breakwater, private aid.

Breakwater Center Light C
Q W, 14 ft., NB on breakwater, private aid.

Breakwater Light D
Fl W 4s, 14 ft., on breakwater, private aid.

Breakwater Light E
Fl W 2.5s, 14 ft., on breakwater, private aid.

Breakwater Light F
Fl W 6s, 14 ft., on breakwater, private aid.

Marina Light 1
37 48.5N, 122 24.5W, Fl G 4s, 23 ft., SG on pile, private aid.

Marina Light 2
37 48.5N, 122 24.5W, Fl R 2.5s, 14 ft., TR on post, private aid.

Pier 27-29 West Light
37 48.5N, 122 24.1W, Iso W 2s, 16 ft., gray building, private aid.

Pier 27-29 East Light
Iso R 2s, 16 ft., private aid.

Pier 17 Light
F W, 29 ft., gray building, private aid.

Pier 1 North Light
F R, 26 ft., gray building, private aid.

Pier 1 South Light
F W, 26 ft., gray building, private aid.

South Beach Harbor

North Entrance Light 2
Fl R 2s, 18 ft., TR on breakwater, private aid.

North Entrance Light 1
37 46.9N, 122 23.1W, Fl G 2.5s, 14 ft., SG on breakwater, private aid.

Breakwater Light A
37 46.7N, 122 23.1W, Fl W 2.5s, 14 ft., NW on breakwater, private aid.

Breakwater Light B
Fl W 2.5s, 14 ft., NW on breakwater, private aid.

South Entrance Light 1
37 46.7N, 122 23.1W, Fl G 2.5s, 18 ft., SG on breakwater, private aid.

South Entrance Light 2
Fl R 4s, 14 ft., TR on breakwater, private aid.

San Francisco Bay

Alcatraz Bell Buoy
37 49.7N, 122 25.7W, green and red bands.

Alcatraz Light
37 49.6N, 122 25.3W, Fl W 5s, 214 ft., 22 mi., gray octagonal tower.

Alcatraz South Fog Signal
White square house, horn: 1 blast every 30s, located 175 yards, 143.5° from light, structure is floodlighted.

Alcatraz North Fog Signal
White square house, horn: 2 blasts every 30s, structure is floodlighted.

Blossom Rock Lighted Bell Buoy BR
37 49.1N, 122 24.2W, Fl (2+1) G 6s, 4 mi., green and red bands.

Harding Rock Lighted Buoy HR
37 50.3N, 122 26.8W, Fl (2+1) R 6s, 4 mi., red and green bands, racon: K (-·-).

Point Blunt Light, Angel Island
37 51.2N, 122 25.2W, Fl G 5s, 60 ft., 13 mi., white square house, horn: 1 blast every 15s.

Raccoon Strait

Lighted Buoy 1
37 50.6N, 122 27.2W, Fl G 4s, 4 mi., green.

Lighted Buoy 2
37 51.2N, 122 26.6W, Fl R 4s, 3 mi., red.

Lighted Buoy 3
37 51.7N, 122 27.4W, Fl G 4s, 3 mi., green.

Light 4
37 51.7N, 122 26.8W, Iso R 6s, 80 ft., 7 mi., TR on white square house.

Belvedere Cove Lighted Buoy 1
37 52.2N, 122 27.3W, Fl G 4s, 3 mi., green.

Corinthian Harbor Light 1
37 52.3N, 122 27.4W, F G, 9 ft., on pile, private aid.

Corinthian Harbor Light 2
F R, 9 ft., on pile, private aid.

Light 5
37 52.8N, 122 26.3W, Fl G 4s, 20 ft., 3 mi., SG on pile.

San Francisco–Oakland Bay Bridge West Crossing
Aids to navigation on bridge maintained by California Department of Transportation.

Pier A Fog Signal
30 ft., horn: 1 blast every 30s.

Pier B Fog Signal
30 ft., horn: 2 blasts every 30s.

Racon N
37 47.5N, 122 22.7W, N (-·), 184 ft., A-B span, center of channel, private aid.

Pier B North Buoy
37 47.8N, 122 22.9W, green and red bands, can.

Pier C East Side Fog Signal
30 ft., bell: 1 stroke every 30s.

Pier C West Side Fog Signal
30 ft., bell: 2 strokes every 30s.

Pier D Fog Signal
30 ft., horn: 3 blasts every 30s.

Racon B
37 48.0N, 122 22.6W, B (-···), 219 ft., C-D span, center of channel, private aid.

Pier D North Buoy
37 48.1N, 122 22.6W, red and green bands, nun.

Pier D South Buoy
37 48.0N, 122 22.4W, red and green bands, nun.

Pier E Fog Signal
30 ft., horn: 2 blasts every 30s.

Racon Y
37 48.9N, 122 21.4W, Y (-·--), 184 ft., D-E span, center of channel, private aid.

Yerba Buena and Treasure Islands

Yerba Buena Island Light
37 48.4N, 122 21.7W, Oc W 4s, 95 ft., 14 mi., white octagonal tower, horn: 1 blast every 30s.

Yerba Buena Island Wharf Light
37 48.4N, 122 21.7W, F R, 18 ft., 6 mi., on post.

Treasure Island East Channel Lighted Buoy 3
37 48.7N, 122 21.1W, Fl G 2.5s, 3 mi., green.

Treasure Island North End Light 6
37 50.0N, 122 22.3W, Fl R 2.5s, 30 ft., 10 mi., TR on pile.

San Francisco–Oakland Bay Bridge East Crossing
Aids to navigation on bridge maintained by California Department of Transportation.

Pier G Fog Signal
30 ft., horn: 1 blast every 20s.

Pier H Fog Signal
30 ft., horn: 2 blasts every 20s.

Pier I Fog Signal
30 ft., bell: 3 strokes every 20s.

San Francisco Bay South Channel

Lighted Buoy 1
37 46.1N, 122 21.8W, Fl G 4s, 4 mi., green.

Anchorage 9 Lighted Buoy A
37 44.8N, 122 19.4W, Fl Y 4s, 4 mi., yellow.

Hunters Point

Lash Terminal Lighted Buoy 2
37 45.5N, 122 22.1W, Fl R 2.5s,
3 mi., red.

Lash Terminal Approach Lighted Buoy 3
37 44.7N, 122 22.2W, Fl G 4s,
4 mi., green.

Lash Terminal Lighted Buoy 5
37 44.4N, 122 21.6W, Fl G 4s,
4 mi., green.

Pier 94 North End Light
37 44.7N, 122 22.4W, Iso R 4s,
11 ft., on post, private aid.

North Channel Range Front Light
37 44.6N, 122 22.7W, F Y, 52 ft.,
KRW on post, private aid.

North Channel Range Rear Light
244 yards, 203° from front light,
F Y, 68 ft., KRW on post, private
aid.

South Channel Range Front Light
37 44.5N, 122 22.3W, Iso Y, 52 ft.,
KRW on post, private aid.

South Channel Range Rear Light
635 yards, 293° from front light,
Oc Y, 68 ft., KRW on post, private
aid.

Pier 96 Lighter Basin Entrance Light 2
Iso R 4s, 15 ft., TR on wharf,
private aid.

Pier 96 Lighter Basin Entrance Light 1
Iso G 4s, 15 ft., SG on dolphin,
private aid.

San Bruno Shoal Channel

Light 1
37 41.7N, 122 20.4W, Fl G 4s,
15 ft., 4 mi., SG on pile, horn:
1 blast every 30s, operates continuously from Oct. 1 to April 1,
radar reflector.

Lighted Buoy 2
37 41.7N, 122 20.5W, Fl R 4s,
3 mi., red.

Light 3
37 40.2N, 122 19.6W, Fl G 2.5s,
10 ft., 3 mi., SG on pile.

Light 4
37 40.1N, 122 19.7W, Fl R 2.5s,
15 ft., 4 mi., TR on pile.

Light 5
37 38.6N, 122 18.8W, Fl G 4s,
15 ft., 3 mi., SG on pile, horn:
1 blast every 10s, operates continuously from Oct. 1 to April 1.

Light 6
37 38.6N, 122 18.9W, Fl R 4s,
15 ft., 4 mi., TR on pile.

San Francisco Bay South Channel (cont'd)

Light 8
Fl R 4s, 15 ft., 4 mi., TR on pile.

Daybeacon 8A
TR on pile.

San Mateo–Hayward Bridge Fog Signal
Horns: 2 blasts every 30s, private
aid.

San Mateo–Hayward Bridge Racon
37 35.1N, 122 15.1W, M (--),
133 ft., mid-span, center of
channel, private aid.

Buoy 10
37 35.0N, 122 15.2W, red nun.

Buoy 11
37 35.0N, 122 14.9W, green can.

Tower Light
37 34.9N, 122 15.1W, Fl W 2.5s,
12 ft., transmission tower,
private aid.

Light 12
Fl R 4s, 15 ft., 4 mi., TR on pile,
higher intensity beam down
channel toward San
Mateo–Hayward Bridge, radar
reflector.

Light 14
37 30.8N, 122 08.1W, Fl R 4s,
15 ft., 4 mi., TR on pile, higher
intensity beam down channel,
radar reflector.

Dumbarton Highway Bridge Fog Signal
37 30.4N, 122 07.0W, horn: 1 blast
every 20s, private aid.

Light 16
Fl R 4s, 15 ft., 3 mi., TR on pile,
radar reflector.

Light 17
Fl G 4s, 15 ft., 3 mi., SG on pile,
radar reflector.

Light 18
Fl R 4s, 15 ft., 3 mi., TR on pile,
radar reflector.

Daybeacon 20
TR on pile.

Brisbane Marina

Light 1
37 40.3N, 122 22.2W, Fl G 4s,
13 ft., SG on pile, private aid.

Light 2
Fl R 2.5s, 13 ft., TR on pile, private aid.

Daybeacon 3
13 ft., SG on pile, private aid.

Daybeacon 4
13 ft., TR on pile, private aid.

Light 5
Fl G 2.5s, 13 ft., SG on pile, private aid.

Light 6
37 40.2N, 122 22.7W, Fl R 2.5s,
13 ft., TR on pile, private aid.

Daybeacon 7
13 ft., SG on pile, private aid.

Light 8
37 40.3N, 122 22.7W, Fl R 4s,
13 ft., TR on pile, private aid.

Light 9
Fl G 4s, 13 ft., SG on pile, private
aid.

Oyster Cove Marina

Light 1
37 40.2N, 122 22.7W, Fl G 4s, 6 ft.,
SG on pile, radar reflector, private aid.

Light 2
Fl R 4s, 6 ft., TR on pile, radar
reflector, private aid.

Daybeacons 3–10
SGs and TRs on piles, radar
reflectors, private aids.

Light 11
Fl G 2.5s, 6 ft., SG on pile, radar
reflector, private aid.

Light 12
Fl R 2.5s, 6 ft., TR on pile, radar
reflector, private aid.

Light 13
Fl G 4s, 6 ft., SG on pile, radar
reflector, private aid.

Light 14
Q R, 13 ft., TR on pile, higher intensity beam up channel, radar reflector, private aid.

Light 16
Fl R 4s, 6 ft., TR on pile, radar reflector, private aid.

Oyster Point Marina

Light 1
37 39.8N, 122 22.2W, Fl G 4s, 17 ft., pile structure, private aid.

Light 2
Fl R 4s, 17 ft., pile structure, private aid.

Light 8
37 39.9N, 122 22.4W, Q R, 13 ft., TR on pile, private aid.

Light 9
Q G, 13 ft., SG on pile, private aid.

Light A
Fl W 4s, 13 ft., NR on pile, private aid.

Light 10
Fl R 2.5s, 13 ft., TR on pile, private aid.

San Francisco Airport and San Mateo

Airport Daybeacon 1
37 37.9N, 122 22.7W, SG on pile.

Coyote Point Yacht Harbor Light 1
37 35.3N, 122 18.8W, F G, 12 ft., on pile, private aid.

Coyote Point Yacht Harbor Light 2
F R, 12 ft., on pile, private aid.

San Francisco Bay North Channel

Blossom Rock Lighted Bell Buoy BR
37 49.1N, 122 24.2W, Fl (2+1) G 6s, 4 mi., green and red bands.

Lighted Buoy 1
37 49.9N, 122 24.5W, Fl G 6s, green.

Lighted Buoy 2
37 50.0N, 122 23.8W, Fl R 6s, 4 mi., red.

Treasure Island North End Light 6
37 50.0N, 122 22.3W, Fl R 2.5s, 30 ft., 10 mi., TR on pile.

Lighted Buoy 3
37 51.0N, 122 25.0W, Q G, green.

Lighted Horn Buoy 4
37 50.8N, 122 23.8W, Fl R 4s, 4 mi., red, horn: 1 blast every 10s, operates continuously.

Point Blunt Light, Angel Island
37 51.2N, 122 25.2W, Fl G 5s, 60 ft., 13 mi., white square house, horn: 1 blast every 15s.

Light 5
37 51.7N, 122 25.1W, Fl G 2.5s, 30 ft., 3 mi., SG on pile.

Lighted Buoy A
37 51.8N, 122 24.5W, Mo (A) W, 5 mi., red and white stripes with red spherical topmark.

Southampton Shoal Light
37 52.9N, 122 24.0W, Iso R 6s, 32 ft., 6 mi., white cylindrical tower, bell: 1 stroke every 10s, operates continuously.

Lighted Bell Buoy 6
37 51.7N, 122 23.8W, Fl R 4s, 4 mi., red.

Lighted Buoy 8
37 52.8N, 122 24.9W, Fl R 2.5s, 4 mi., red.
Also see Southampton Shoal Channel, San Francisco Bay.

Raccoon Strait Light 5
37 52.8N, 122 26.3W, Fl G 4s, 20 ft., 3 mi., SG on pile.
Also see Raccoon Strait, San Francisco Bay.

National Marine Fisheries Service Light South
37 53.4N, 122 26.7W, Fl W 2.5s, 8 ft., NR on pile, maintained by National Marine Fisheries Service.

National Marine Fisheries Service Light North
Fl W 2.5s, 8 ft., NR on pile, maintained by National Marine Fisheries Service.

Light 9
37 53.7N, 122 27.0W, Fl G 4s, 25 ft., 4 mi., SG on pile, higher intensity beam up channel.

Lighted Buoy B
37 54.1N, 122 26.7W, Mo (A) W, 6 mi., red and white stripes with red spherical topmark.

Lighted Bell Buoy 10
37 54.0N, 122 26.2W, Fl R 4s, 4 mi., red.

Lighted Buoy 12
37 54.8N, 122 26.7W, Fl R 4s, 4 mi., red.

Lighted Buoy C
37 54.8N, 122 27.0W, Mo (A) W, 5 mi., red and white stripes with red spherical topmark.

Lighted Buoy 14
37 55.8N, 122 26.6W, Fl R 4s, 3 mi., red.

Richmond–San Rafael Bridge Racon
37 56.1N, 122 26.7W, Q (--·-), 185 ft., bands: 20s (every 30s), private aid.

Richmond–San Rafael Bridge Racon
37 56.0N, 122 25.5W, T (-), 135 ft., bands: 20s (every 30s), private aid.

Richmond–San Rafael Bridge Fog Signals
horns (2): sound simultaneously, 2 blasts every 30s, private aid.

Buoy 15
37 56.2N, 122 26.8W, green can.

Lighted Buoy 16
37 57.3N, 122 26.5W, Q R, 3 mi., red.

Lighted Bell Buoy 18
37 57.6N, 122 26.4W, Fl R 2.5s, 3 mi., red.

Light 17
37 57.4N, 122 27.4W, Fl G 4s, 15 ft., 6 mi., SG on pile, high-intensity beams on 215°, 333°, and 113°, radar reflector.

East Brother Island Light
37 57.8N, 122 26.0W, Fl W 5s, 61 ft., 17 mi., buff square tower on dwelling, horn: 1 blast every 30s, operates continuously from Oct. 1 to April 1.
Also see San Pablo Bay *for continuation of channel.*

Southampton Shoal Channel

Also see Richmond Harbor Channel.

Southampton Shoal Light
37 52.9N, 122 24.0W, Iso R 6s, 32 ft., 6 mi., white cylindrical tower, bell: 1 stroke every 10s, operates continuously.

Lighted Buoy 1
37 54.0N, 122 25.3W, Fl G 4s, 3 mi., green.

Lighted Buoy 2
Fl R 2.5s, 3 mi., red.

Lighted Buoy 4
37 55.0N, 122 25.3W, Fl R 4s, 3 mi., red.

Lighted Buoy 5
37 55.3N, 122 25.6W, Fl G 2.5s, 3 mi., green.

Outfall Lighted Buoy WCA 1
37 54.7N, 122 25.2W, Fl W 4s, white with orange bands, radon: K (-··-), private aid.

Outfall Lighted Buoy WCA 2
37 54.7N, 122 24.9W, Fl W 4s, white with orange bands, private aid.

Richmond–San Rafael Bridge East Channel.

Also see Richmond Harbor Channel.

Lighted Buoy 1
37 55.8N, 122 25.7W, Fl G 4s, 3 mi., green.

Castro Rocks Lighted Buoy 2CR
37 55.9N, 122 25.3W, Fl R 4s, 3 mi., red.

Fog Signal
Horns (2): sound simultaneously, 1 blast every 15s, private aids.

Buoy 6
37 56.2N, 122 25.6W, red nun.

Molate Point Wharf South End Light
37 56.7N, 122 25.6W, Oc R 4s, 32 ft., 8 mi., tower, horn: 1 blast every 15s, maintained by U.S. Navy.

Molate Point Wharf North End Light
Iso R 6s, 30 ft., 8 mi., tower, maintained by U.S. Navy.
Also see San Pablo Bay *for continuation of channel.*

San Joaquin River
Aids to navigation for the San Joaquin River are not included in this book.
Also see Suisun Bay.

San Juan Rocks Lighted Whistle Buoy 2SJR
33 27.3N, 117 43.3W, Fl R 2.5s, 4 mi., red.
Also see Dana Point.

SAN LEANDRO BAY

Tidal Canal Daybeacon 1
SG on pile.

Airport Daybeacon 3
SG on pile.

Airport Daybeacon 4
TR on pile.

Airport Daybeacon 5
SG on pile.

Airport Daybeacon 6
TR on pile.

SAN LEANDRO MARINA CHANNEL

Also see San Francisco Bay.

Directional Light
37 41.7N, 122 11.5W, F W (R&G sectors), white 13 mi., red 10 mi., green 10 mi., on pile, white from 046.5° to 047°, red from 045.5° to 046.5°, green from 047° to 048°.

Light 1
Fl G 4s, 14 ft., 5 mi., SG on pile, horn: 1 blast every 30s, operated continuously from Oct. 1 to April 1.

Light 2
Fl R 4s, 15 ft., 4 mi., TR on pile.

Daybeacons 3–11
TRs and SGs on piles.

Light 14
Fl R 2.5s, 4 mi., TR on pile.

Daybeacon 15
SG on pile.

Light 6
Fl R 2.5s, 15 ft., 3 mi., TR on pile, radar reflector.

Light 10
Fl R 4s, 15 ft., 3 mi., TR on pile, radar reflector.

Light 12
37 41.5N, 122 11.8W, Fl R 6s, 15 ft., 3 mi., TR on pile, radar reflector.

San Luis Obispo Light
35 09.6N, 120 45.6W, Fl W 5s, 116 ft., 24 mi., on cylindrical structure east of the old lighthouse, horn: 2 blasts every 60s, light operates continuously.

San Luis Obispo Buoy 2
35 09.4N, 120 43.9W, red nun.
Also see Port San Luis.

San Mateo, San Francisco Bay
See Coyote Point *and* San Francisco Bay.

San Mateo–Hayward Bridge
See San Francisco Bay.

San Mateo Point Light
33 23.3N, 117 35.8W, Fl W 4s, 63 ft., 10 mi., NR on post.

SAN NICOLAS ISLAND

South Side Light
33 13.0N, 119 28.2W, Fl W 6s, 50 ft., 6 mi., NR on post, visible from 262° to 100°, partially obscured by hills elsewhere.

East End Lighted Bell Buoy 3
33 13.4N, 119 23.9W, Fl G 4s, 4 mi., green.

East End Light
33 13.8N, 119 26.1W, Fl W 2.5s, 55 ft., 6 mi., NR on post, visible from 145° to 005°, partially obscured by hills elsewhere.

North Side Light
33 15.5N, 119 28.0W, Fl W 6s, 33 ft., 10 mi., NR on post, visible from 121° to 308°, partially obscured by hills elsewhere.

San Onofre

Unit 1 Intake Buoy
33 21.8N, 117 33.7W, red nun worded SUBMERGED SUCTION TOWER, private aid.

Unit 1 Discharge Buoy
White nun with orange bands worded SUBMERGED SUCTION TOWER, private aid.

Unit 2 Intake Buoy
Red nun worded SUBMERGED SUCTION TOWER, private aid.

Unit 3 Intake Buoy
Red nun worded SUBMERGED SUCTION TOWER, private aid.

San Pablo Bay

Also see San Francisco Bay, San Rafael Creek, Petaluma River, Mare Island Strait, Vallejo, Carquinez Strait, *and* Suisun Bay.

Point San Pablo Terminal Light 4
37 57.9N, 122 25.7W, Iso R 5s, 12 ft., concrete dolphin, private aid.

Lighted Buoy 2
37 58.1N, 122 25.8W, Fl R 4s, 3 mi., red.

Light 4
Fl R 6s, 15 ft., 4 mi., TR on pile, radar reflector.

Channel Light 5
Fl G 2.5s, 15 ft., 4 mi., SG on pile structure, radar reflector.

Channel Lighted Buoy E
38 00.6N, 122 24.2W, Mo (A) W, 6 mi., red and white stripes with red spherical topmark.

Point Pinole Light P
38 01.0N, 122 22.0W, Fl W 2.5s, 15 ft., 3 mi., NR on pile, radar reflector.

Channel Light 7
Fl G 4s, 10 ft., 3 mi., SG on pile structure, radar reflector.

Channel Lighted Buoy 8
38 01.8N, 122 22.3W, Fl R 4s, 3 mi., red.

Channel Light 9
Fl G 6s, 16 ft., 4 mi., SG on pile, radar reflector.

Channel Lighted Buoy 10
38 02.4N, 122 21.0W, Fl R 6s, 4 mi., red.

Channel Light 11
Q G, 15 ft., 3 mi., SG on pile, radar reflector.

Channel Light 12
Fl R 2.5s, 15 ft., 3 mi., TR on pile structure, radar reflector.

Channel Light 13
Fl G 4s, 15 ft., 3 mi., SG on pile structure, radar reflector.

Channel Light 14
Fl R 4s, 15 ft., 3 mi., TR on pile structure, radar reflector.

Channel Light 15
Fl G 2.5s, 15 ft., 4 mi., SG on pile structure, horn: 1 blast every 10s, operates continuously from Oct. 1 to April 1, radar reflector.

Sequoia Oil Wharf West Light
38 03.2N, 122 16.5W, F W, 31 ft., on wharf, private aid.

Sequoia Oil Wharf Fog Signal
Horn: 1 blast every 20s, private aid.

Sequoia Oil Wharf East Light
F W, 31 ft., private aid.

Oleum Wharf West Lights (4)
38 03.4N, 122 15.8W, F R, 12 ft., bell: 1 stroke every 5s, private aids.

Oleum Wharf East Lights (4)
F R, 12 ft., horn: 1 blast every 18s, private aids.

Light 17
38 04.1N, 122 15.2W, Fl G 6s, 30 ft., 6 mi., SG on post.

San Pedro Channel

Traffic Lane Lighted Buoy S
33 37.7N, 118 08.9W, Fl Y 4s, 4 mi., yellow.

San Pedro Precautionary Area Lighted Buoy A
33 42.0N, 118 09.8W, Fl Y 4s, 6 mi., yellow.

San Pedro Precautionary Area Lighted Buoy B
33 42.0N, 118 12.1W, Fl Y 6s, 6 mi., yellow.

Traffic Lane Lighted Buoy W
33 39.2N, 118 17.5W, Fl Y 6s, 4 mi., yellow.

Traffic Lane Lighted Buoy SP
33 39.3N, 118 26.2W, Mo (A) W, 4 mi., red and white stripes.

San Pedro Harbor, Los Angeles
See Los Angeles Harbor.

San Rafael Creek

Also see San Rafael Outfall Light *and* San Francisco Bay.

Range Front Light
37 58.3N, 122 29.8W, Q R, 15 ft., KRW on pile, visible all around, higher intensity on rangeline.

Range Rear Light
360 yards, 293° from front light, Oc R 4s, 25 ft., KRW on pile, visible 1° each side of rangeline.

Light 1
Fl G 2.5s, 20 ft., 4 mi., SG on pile.

Light 3
37 57.8N, 122 28.6W, Fl G 4s, 20 ft., 3 mi., SG on pile.

Light 5
Fl G 6s, 20 ft., 5 mi., SG on pile.

Light 6
Fl R 4s, 10 ft., 4 mi., TR on pile, radar reflector.

Light 7
Fl G 2.5s, 10 ft., 4 mi., SG on pile, radar reflector.

San Rafael Outfall Light
37 56.9N, 122 27.7W, Fl Y 4s, 13 ft., NW on pile worded OUTFALL, private aid.
Also see San Rafael Creek *and* San Francisco Bay.

San Simeon Lighted Bell Buoy 1
35 37.7N, 121 11.3W, Fl G 6s, 4 mi., green.

Santa Ana Lighted Bell Buoy 4SA
33 35.2N, 117 57.3W, Fl R 4s, 4 mi., red.

Santa Barbara

Santa Barbara Island follows this section.

Santa Barbara Light
34 23.8N, 119 43.4W, Fl W 10s, 142 ft., 25 mi., white tower, light obscured from 090° to 275°.

Santa Barbara Sewer Outfall Buoy
White with orange bands and orange circle worded PIPELINE, NO ANCHORING, private aid.

Santa Barbara Harbor
Buoys inside the harbor are set to best mark the channel and are not charted.

Breakwater Light
34 24.3N, 119 41.3W, Fl W 2.5s, 35 ft., 9 mi., NG on white column.

Lighted Bell Buoy SB
34 24.1N, 119 40.8W, Mo (A) W, 5 mi., red and white stripes.

Lighted Buoy 3
34 24.3N, 119 41.0W, Fl G 2.5s, 4 mi., green.

Light 4
34 24.5N, 119 41.1W, Fl R 6s, 25 ft., 7 mi., on post, horn: 2 blasts every 20s.

Breakwater Extension Light
34 24.5N, 119 41.3W, Fl W 4s, 20 ft., 6 mi., on post.

Buoy 5
Green can.

Lighted Buoy 5A
Fl G 4s, 3 mi., green.

Buoy 6
Red nun.

Buoy 6A
Red nun.

Buoy 7
Green can.

Buoy 8
Red nun.

Light 12
34 24.4N, 119 41.5W, Q R, 15 ft., 5 mi., TR on post.

Santa Barbara Island Light
33 29.2N, 119 01.8W, Fl W 6s, 195 ft., 10 mi., NR on post, visible from 089° to 353°, partially obscured by hills elsewhere.

Santa Catalina Island

Long Point Light
33 24.4N, 118 21.9W, Fl W 5s, 71 ft., 15 mi., NR on post, obscured from 021° to 070°.

Avalon Bay Light 1
33 20.7N, 118 19.3W, Fl G 2.5s, 21 ft., 5 mi., SG on post.

Avalon Bay Light 2
33 20.9N, 118 19.4W, Fl R 4s, 21 ft., 4 mi., TR on post.

Pebbly Beach Quarry Lighted Mooring Buoy PB-2
32 19.2N, 118 18.0W, Q W, white with blue band, private aid.

Pebbly Beach Quarry Lighted Mooring Buoy PB-4
Q W, white with blue band, private aid.

Pebbly Beach Quarry Lighted Mooring Buoy PB-6
Q W, white with blue band, private aid.

Abalone Point Bait Barge Lighted Mooring Buoy
33 20.6N, 118 18.9W, Fl W, white with blue band, private aid.

East End Light
33 18.1N, 118 19.0W, Fl W 10s, 212 ft., 16 mi., NR on post, visible from 253° to 068°, partially obscured by hills elsewhere.

Catalina Harbor Light
33 25.4N, 118 30.8W, Fl W 4s, 400 ft., 7 mi., on post, obscured from 104° to 288°, higher intensity beam on bearing 030°.

West End Light
33 28.7N, 118 36.3W, Fl W 6s, 76 ft., 10 mi., NR on post, visible from 336° to 266°, partially obscured by hills elsewhere.

Ship Rock Light
33 27.8N, 118 29.4W, Fl W 4s, 75 ft., 6 mi., on steel box, radar reflector.

Isthmus Cove

Harbor Reefs Light
33 26.9N, 118 29.4W, Fl W 2.5s, 21 ft., 5 mi., NW on post.

North Entrance Lighted Buoy 1
33 26.9N, 118 29.6W, Fl G 4s, green.

Northwest Entrance Buoy 2
33 27.7N, 118 30.4W, red nun.

Santa Cruz

Buoys inside the harbor are set to best mark the channel and are not charted.

Santa Cruz Light
36 57.1N, 122 01.6W, Fl W 5s, 60 ft., 17 mi., white lantern house on square brick tower attached to brick building, obscured from 085° to 220°.

Point Santa Cruz Wave Measuring Lighted Buoy
36 53.4N, 122 04.3W, Fl (3) W 25s, silver spherical buoy, private aid.

Lighted Whistle Buoy SC
36 56.3N, 122 00.6W, Mo (A) W, 5 mi., red and white stripes.

West Breakwater Light
36 57.6N, 122 00.1W, Oc G 4s, 36 ft., 6 mi., white cylindrical structure, horn: 1 blast every 30s.

Harbor Buoy 1
Green can, maintained from May 1 to Nov. 1.

Harbor Lighted Buoy 2
Fl R 4s, 3 mi., red, maintained from May 1 to Nov. 1.

Harbor Buoy 3
Green can, maintained from May 1 to Nov. 1.

Harbor Buoy 4
Red nun, maintained from May 1 to Nov. 1.

Municipal Wharf Fog Signal
36 57.5N, 122 00.9W, horn: 1 blast every 15s, maintained from April 1 to Nov. 1, private aid.

SANTA CRUZ ISLAND

Gull Island Light
33 56.9N, 119 49.6W, Fl W 10s, 73 ft., 16 mi., NR on post, visible from 265° to 127°, partially obscured by hills elsewhere.

Meteorological Lighted Buoy
33 58.3N, 119 38.5W, Fl (4) W 1s, yellow, maintained by U.S. Navy.

Oceanographic Lighted Buoy 2
33 24.0N, 119 39.0W, Fl (3) W 20s, yellow, maintained by U.S. Navy.

Oceanographic Lighted Buoy 4
33 58.3N, 119 06.7W, Fl (4) Y 1s, yellow, maintained by U.S. Navy.

Oceanographic Lighted Buoy 5
34 05.3N, 119 06.8W, Fl (3) W 20s, yellow, maintained by U.S. Navy.

SANTA MONICA

Entrance Lighted Bell Buoy 1
34 00.2N, 118 30.2W, Fl G 4s, 4 mi., green.

Pier Fog Signal
34 00.5N, 118 29.8W, horn: 1 blast every 20s, private aid.

Breakwater South End Danger Buoy
34 00.3N, 118 30.0W, white with orange bands and orange diamond worded JETTY, private aid.

Breakwater North End Danger Buoy
34 00.6N, 118 30.3W, white with orange bands and orange diamond worded JETTY, private aid.

East Cable Area Buoy
34 01.4N, 118 32.3W, orange and white bands, spar worded SUBMARINE CABLE, private aid.

West Cable Area Buoy
Orange and white bands, spar worded SUBMARINE CABLE, private aid.

Santa Rosa Island, South Point Light
33 53.8N, 120 07.1W, Fl W 6s, 530 ft., 8 mi., small white house, visible from 272° to 115°, partially obscured by hills elsewhere.

Saunders Reef Lighted Gong Buoy 16
38 50.7N, 123 40.1W, Fl R 6s, 4 mi., red.

SAUSALITO

Also see San Francisco Bay.

Marin Peninsula

Lime Point Light
37 49.5N, 122 28.7W, Fl W 5s, 15 ft., 8 mi., on post, horn: 2 blasts every 30s.

Horseshoe Bay East Breakwater Light
37 49.9N, 122 28.5W, Fl R 3s, 25 ft., on steel pile structure, light obscured from 090° to 270°, private aid.

Yellow Bluff Light
37 50.2N, 122 28.3W, Fl W 6s, 75 ft., 9 mi., NR on single pile.

Sausalito Channel and Richardson Bay

Cone Rock Light
37 51.8N, 122 28.2W, Q W, 17 ft., 5 mi., NR on black skeleton tower.

Light 2
Fl R 4s, 14 ft., 4 mi., TR on pile.

Light 4
Fl R 6s, 15 ft., 3 mi., TR on pile, radar reflector.

Sausalito Cruising Club Light
37 51.7N, 122 29.2W, Oc W 3s, red and white striped conical tower on building, private aid.

Light 6
37 51.9N, 122 29.2W, Fl R 4s, 15 ft., 4 mi., TR on pile, radar reflector.

Kappas Marina Channel
Daybeacons 8 through 20, TRs and SGs on piles, private aids.

SCRIPPS INSTITUTE RESEARCH BUOYS

Lighted Buoy
34 05.4N, 119 19.8W, Fl Y 4s, yellow sphere, private aid.

Lighted Buoy
34 07.2N, 119 51.0W, Fl Y 4s, yellow sphere, private aid.

Lighted Buoy
34 09.5N, 120 27.0W, Fl Y 4s yellow sphere, private aid.

Lighted Buoy
34 15.0N, 119 31.8W, Fl Y 4s, yellow sphere, private aid.

Lighted Buoy
34 22.0N, 119 51.0W, Fl Y 4s, yellow sphere, private aid.

Lighted Buoy
34 24.0N, 120 27.0W, Fl Y 4s, yellow sphere, private aid.

Shelter Cove Entrance Bell Buoy 1
40 00.6N, 124 03.6W, green.

Shelter Cove Marina, San Diego
See San Diego Bay.

Shoreline Marina
See Long Beach Harbor.

South Beach Harbor, San Francisco
See San Francisco Bay.

South Point Light, Santa Rosa Island
33 53.8N, 120 07.1W, Fl W 6s, 530 ft., 8 mi., small white house, visible from 272° to 115°, partially obscured by hills elsewhere.

Southampton Shoal Channel
See San Francisco Bay.

Southampton Shoal Light
37 52.9N, 122 24.0W, Iso R 6s, 32 ft., 6 mi., white cylindrical tower, bell: 1 stroke every 10s, operates continuously.
Also see San Francisco Bay North Channel.

Southeast Reef Southern End Lighted Gong Buoy 1S (Half Moon Bay)
37 27.9N, 122 28.2W, Fl G 6s, 5 mi., green.

Souza Rock Lighted Gong Buoy 14SR
35 07.8N, 120 44.4W, Fl (2+1) R 6s, 4 mi., red and green bands.

Spud Point Marina
See Bodega Bay.

St. George Reef Lighted Horn Buoy 2SG
41 50.2N, 124 23.2W, Q R, 15 ft., 5 mi., red, horn: 1 blast every 30s, operates continuously.

Suisun Bay

Also see Carquinez Strait.

Channel Buoy 2
38 02.2N, 122 07.3W, red nun.

Channel Buoy 3
38 02.3N, 122 07.4W, green can.

Channel Buoy 4
38 02.3N, 122 07.2W, red nun.

Channel Buoy 5
38 02.4N, 122 07.2W, green can.

North Channel

Light 2
38 02.9N, 122 06.7W, Fl R 2.5s, 15 ft., 5 mi., TR on pile, radar reflector.

Light 4
Fl R 6s, 15 ft., 4 mi., TR on pile, radar reflector.

Light 6
Fl R 4s, 15 ft., 3 mi., TR on pile, radar reflector.

Suisun Slough Entrance Light 9
Fl G 4s, 15 ft., 3 mi., SG on pile, radar reflector.

Suisun Slough Entrance Light 10
38 07.1N, 122 03.7W, Fl R 4s, 15 ft., 3 mi., TR on pile, radar reflector.

Suisun Bay Channel (cont'd)

Lighted Buoy 6
38 02.5N, 122 06.7W, Fl R 4s, 3 mi., red.

Lighted Buoy 7
38 02.9N, 122 06.0W, Fl G 4s, 3 mi., green.

Avon Wharf West Lights (3)
38 02.5N, 122 05.7W, F R, 16 ft., on wharf, horn: 1 blast every 10s, private aids.

Avon Wharf East Light
F W, 21 ft., on wharf, horn: 2 blasts every 25s, 65 yards, 083° from light, private aid.

Point Edith Crossing South Range Front Light
38 02.9N, 122 05.4W, Q W, 24 ft., KRW on pile, radar reflector.

Point Edith Crossing South Range Rear Light
439 yards, 236.7° from front light, rangeline is 25 feet south of channel centerline, Iso W 6s, 32 ft., KRW on pile, radar reflector.

Channel Lighted Buoy 9
38 03.2N, 122 04.9W, Fl G 2.5s, 3 mi., green.

Seal Islands Channel

Light 2
38 03.2N, 122 04.3W, Fl R 6s, 20 ft., 4 mi., TR on pile.

Daybeacons 3–6
SGs and TRs on piles.

Daybeacon 9
38 03.5N, 122 02.3W, SG on pile.

Suisun Bay Channel (cont'd)

Lighted Buoy 10
38 03.5N, 122 04.3W, Fl R 2.5s, 3 mi., red.

Point Edith Crossing Range Front Light
38 03.9N, 122 03.5W, Q W, 18 ft., KRW on pile, visible all around, higher intensity on rangeline.

Point Edith Crossing Range Rear Light
333 yards, 056° from front light, Iso W 6s, 30 ft., KRW on pile, visible all around, higher intensity on rangeline.

Light 11
Fl G 4s, 16 ft., 3 mi., SG on pile, radar reflector.

Lighted Buoy 12
38 03.8N, 122 03.7W, Fl R 4s, 3 mi., red.

Lighted Buoy 13
Q G, 3 mi., green.

Lighted Buoy 14
38 03.9N, 122 03.2W, Q R, 3 mi., red.

Lighted Buoy 15
38 04.0N, 122 02.6W, Fl G 4s, 3 mi., green.

Light 16
Fl R 4s, 15 ft., 3 mi., TR on pile, radar reflector.

Lighted Buoy 16A
38 03.8N, 122 01.9W, Fl R 6s, red.

Roe Island Channel Range Front Light
38 04.0N, 122 02.8W, Q W, 19 ft., KRW on pile structure, visible 4° each side of rangeline.

Roe Island Channel Range Rear Light
515 yards, 284° from front light, Iso W 6s, 31 ft., KRW on pile structure, visible 4° each side of rangeline.

Pier 2 West End Light
38 03.5N, 122 01.6W, F R, 25 ft., 8 mi., on post, horn: 2 blasts every 20s, maintained by U.S. Navy.

Lighted Buoy 17
38 03.7N, 122 01.2W, Fl G 2.5s, 3 mi., green.

Lighted Buoy 19
38 03.6N, 122 00.1W, Q G, 3 mi., green.

Pier 4 East End Light
F R, 25 ft., 8 mi., on post, horn: 1 blast every 15s, maintained by U.S. Navy.

Middle Point Light
38 03.3N, 121 59.5W, Fl W 4s, 20 ft., 5 mi., NR on pile.

Lighted Buoy 20
Fl R 4s, 3 mi., red.

Restricted Area Buoy A
38 03.4N, 121 59.3W, yellow nun.

Lighted Buoy 21
38 03.6N, 121 59.0W, Fl G 4s, 3 mi., green.

Lighted Buoy 22
38 03.5N, 121 58.8W, Q R, 3 mi., red.

Lighted Buoy 23
38 03.5N, 121 57.8W, Fl G 2.5s,
3 mi., green.

Lighted Buoy 24
38 03.4N, 121 57.8W, Fl R 2.5s,
3 mi., red.

Light 24A
38 03.3N, 121 57.3W, Fl R 4s,
15 ft., 3 mi., TR on pile, radar
reflector.

Harris Yacht Harbor Light 1
38 02.9N, 121 57.4W, Fl G 6s,
10 ft., SG on post, private aid.

Light 26
38 03.1N, 121 57.0W, Fl R 4s,
16 ft., 4 mi., TR on pile structure.

Light 27
Fl G 4s, 20 ft., 4 mi., SG on white
pile, radar reflector.

Light 28
38 02.6N, 121 55.1W, Fl R 2.5s,
20 ft., 4 mi., TR on pile structure,
higher intensity beam up and
down channel.

Lighted Buoy 30
38 02.7N, 121 53.4W, Q R, 4 mi.,
red.

Light 31
Fl G 6s, 15 ft., 4 mi., SG on pile,
radar reflector.

Light 33
Fl G 2.5s, 15 ft., 4 mi., SG on pile,
higher intensity beam toward
Sacramento Ship Channel, radar
reflector.

Light 34
38 03.5N, 121 52.0W, Fl R 2.5s,
16 ft., 2 mi., TR on pile, radar
reflector.

New York Slough

Lighted Buoy NY
38 02.7N, 121 53.1W, Fl (2+1) G 6s,
3 mi., green and red bands.

Light 2
38 02.6N, 121 53.2W, Fl R 4s,
20 ft., 4 mi., TR on pile structure,
higher intensity beams up and
down reach.

Light 3
38 02.3N, 121 52.8W, Fl G 4s,
20 ft., 3 mi., SG on pile.

Light 5
38 02.0N, 121 52.1W, Fl G 2.5s,
20 ft., 4 mi., SG on pile.

Light 7
Fl G 4s, 15 ft., 4 mi., SG on pile.

Light 8
38 01.8N, 121 51.2W, Fl R 2.5s,
20 ft., 4 mi., TR on pile.

Light 10
38 01.6N, 121 50.8W, Fl R 4s,
15 ft., 3 mi., TR on post.

Light 11
38 01.7N, 121 50.6W, Fl G 2.5s,
18 ft., 4 mi., SG on pile.

**Delta Diablo Outfall Lighted Buoy
DD**
38 01.6N, 121 50.4W, Fl W 4s, 8 ft.,
white with orange bands, private
aid.

Lighted Buoy 13
38 01.7N, 121 50.0W, Q G, 3 mi.,
green, radar reflector.

Pittsburg Marina

West Basin Light 1
38 02.4N, 121 53.2W, Fl G 2.5s,
5 ft., SG on pile, private aid.

West Basin Light 2
Fl R 2.5s, 5 ft., TR on pile, private
aid.

Light 1
38 02.2N, 121 52.9W, Fl G 4s,
11 ft., on breakwater, private aid.

Light 2
Fl R 4s, 11 ft., on breakwater,
private aid.

Light 4
Fl R 4s, 11 ft., on breakwater,
private aid.

Sweetwater Channel, San Diego
See San Diego Bay.

T

TOMALES BAY

Also see Bodega Bay.

Tomales Point Lighted Bell Buoy 2
38 15.1N, 123 00.2W, Fl R 6s,
4 mi., red.

Outside Bar Gong Buoy TB
38 14.6N, 122 59.3W, red and
white stripes with red spherical
topmark.

Inside Bar Buoy 1
Green can.

Buoy 3
Green can.

Lawsons Landing Daybeacon 1
SG on pile, private aid.

Lawsons Landing Daybeacon 3
SG on pile, private aid.

Lawsons Landing Daybeacon 5
SG on pile, private aid.

Lawsons Landing Daybeacon 7
SG on pile, private aid.

Daybeacon 5
8 ft., SG on pile.

Hog Island Daybeacon
8 ft., JG on pile.

Daybeacon 7
8 ft., SG on pile.

Daybeacon 10
8 ft., TR on pile.

**Toro Creek Submarine Terminal
Mooring Buoy**
35 24.4N, 120 53.1W, white with
blue band, private aid.
Also see Estero Bay.

**Treasure Island East Channel
Lighted Buoy 3**
37 48.7N, 122 21.1W, Fl G 2.5s,
3 mi., green.
Also see San Francisco Bay.

Treasure Island North End Light 6
37 50.0N, 122 22.3W, Fl R 2.5s,
30 ft., 10 mi., TR on pile.

Trinidad Harbor Bell Buoy 4
41 03.0N, 124 08.6W, red.

Trinidad Head Light
41 03.1N, 124 09.1W, Oc W 4s,
196 ft., 14 mi., white square
tower, horn: 1 blast every 30s,
light obscured northward of 140°.

**Trinidad Head Lighted Whistle
Buoy 26**
41 03.1N, 124 10.4W, Fl R 6s,
4 mi., red.

Turtle Rocks Bell Buoy 28
41 08.2N, 124 11.8W, red.

U

U.S. Navy Lighted Oceanographic Buoy
34 06.3N, 119 09.5W, Fl W 4s, orange, U.S. Navy Maintained.

USC Lighted Research Buoy
33 33.9N, 118 08.3W, Fl Y 4s, 5 mi., yellow, private aid.

V

VALLEJO

Also see Mare Island Strait.

Yacht Club North Light
38 06.5N, 122 16.1W, F G, 5 ft., pile, private aid.

Yacht Club Light
F R, 5 ft., pile, private aid.

Marina North Entrance Light 1
Fl G 4s, 12 ft., pile, private aid.

Marina North Entrance Light 2
Fl R 4s, 12 ft., pile, private aid.

Marina South Entrance Light 3
Fl G 2.5s, 12 ft., pile, private aid.

Marina South Entrance Light 4
Fl R 2.5s, 12 ft., pile, private aid.

Venice Beach Fishing Pier Fog Signal
33 58.6N, 118 28.2W, horn: 1 blast every 10s, private aid.

Venice Beach Fishing Pier Light
33 58.6N, 118 28.2W, Fl W 6s, 33 ft., on pile, private aid.
Also see Marina del Rey.

VENTURA HARBOR

Buoys inside the harbor are set to best mark the channel and are not charted.

Ventura Entrance Lighted Whistle Buoy 2V
34 14.4N, 119 16.7W, Fl R 2.5s, 4 mi., red.

Breakwater South Light 3
Fl G 2.5s, 26 ft., 5 mi., SG on post.

Channel Buoy 4
Red nun.

South Jetty Light 6
34 14.8N, 119 16.2W, Fl R 4s, 26 ft., 6 mi., TR on pole, horn: 1 blast every 10s.

North Jetty Light 7
Fl G 4s, 26 ft., 5 mi., SG on pole.

Channel Buoy 8
Red nun.

Channel Buoy 9
Black can.

Channel Buoy 10
Red nun.

Channel Buoy 11
Green can, private aid.

Channel Buoy 12
Red nun, private aid.

Channel Buoy P
Red and green bands, can, private aid.

Channel Buoy 13P
Green can, private aid.

Channel Buoy 14P
Red nun, private aid.

Ventura Texaco Pipeline Marker Buoy
34 15.8N, 119 18.0W, yellow nun, private aid.

W

West Yacht Harbor, San Francisco
See San Francisco Bay.

Westdahl Rock Lighted Bell Buoy 1
35 08.8N, 120 47.1W, Fl G 6s, 4 mi., green.

Wilson Cove, San Clemente Island
See San Clemente Island.

Woodley Island Marina Light
See Humboldt Bay.

Y

Yellow Bluff Light
37 50.2N, 122 28.3W, Fl W 6s, 75 ft., 9 mi., NR on single pile.
Also see San Francisco Bay *and* Sausalito.

Yerba Buena Island Light
37 48.4N, 122 21.7W, Oc W 4s, 95 ft., 14 mi., white octagonal tower, horn: 1 blast every 30s.
Also see San Francisco Bay.

Yerba Buena Island Wharf Light
37 48.4N, 122 21.7W, F R, 18 ft., 6 mi., on post.

Z

Zuniga Jetty
See San Diego Bay.

Hawaii

A

ALA WAI BOAT HARBOR

Also see Kewalo Basin *and* Honolulu Harbor.

Entrance Lighted Buoy 1
21 16.6N, 157 50.8W, Fl G 2.5s, 5 mi., green.

Entrance Lighted Buoy 2
21 16.6N, 157 50.8W, Fl R 2.5s, 5 mi., red.

Channel Range Front Light
21 17.3N, 157 50.6W, F Y, 30 ft., KRW on post, lighted throughout 24 hours, private aid.

Channel Range Rear Light
90 yards, 013.5° from front light, Q Y, 48 ft., KRW on post, lighted throughout 24 hours, private aid.

Channel Daybeacons 3–8
SGs and TRs on piles, private aids.

B

BARBERS POINT

Anchorage Area Charlie Lighted Buoy A
21 16.5N, 158 04.0W, Fl Y 4s, yellow, private aid.

Anchorage Area Charlie Lighted Buoy B
21 16.5N, 158 04.5W, Fl Y 2s, yellow, private aid.

Anchorage Area Charlie Buoy C
21 16.8N, 158 04.5W, yellow spar, private aid.

Anchorage Area Charlie Buoy D
21 16.8N, 158 04.0W, yellow spar, private aid.

Anchorage Area Bravo Tanker Terminal Lighted Buoy A
21 16.2N, 158 05.3W, Q Y, yellow, three lighted fluorescent orange fuel lines extend 840 feet from the buoy, private aid.

Light
21 17.8N, 158 06.4W, Fl W 7.5s, 85 ft., 24 mi., white cylindrical concrete tower, obscured from 147.7° to shore, lighted throughout 24 hours.

Radiobeacon
21 17.8N, 158 06.4W, BP (-··· ·--·), 5 mi., 310 kHz.

Harbor Entrance Channel Lighted Buoy 2
21 18.9N, 158 07.7W, Fl R 2.5s, 4 mi., red, racon: B (-···).

Harbor Entrance Channel Range Front Light
21 19.7N, 158 06.8W, F G, 50 ft., KRW on post, visible 4° each side of rangeline.

Harbor Entrance Channel Range Rear Light
125 yards, 045° from front light, F G, 75 ft., KRW on post, visible 4° each side of rangeline.

Harbor Entrance Channel Light 4 (75 feet outside channel limit)
21 19.1N, 158 07.5W, Fl R 4s, 15 ft., 3 mi., TR on pile.

Harbor Entrance Channel Light 5
21 19.2N, 158 07.5W, Fl G 2.5s, 3 mi., SG on dolphin.

Harbor Entrance Channel Light 6
21 19.3N, 158 07.3W, Fl R 6s, 15 ft., 4 mi., TR on post.

Harbor Entrance Channel Daybeacon 7
21 19.4N, 158 07.3W, 15 ft., SG on pile.

C

Cape Kumukahi Light
19 31.0N, 154 48.6W, Fl W 6s, 156 ft., 24 mi., white pyramidal skeleton tower, lighted throughout 24 hours, obscured from 015° to 120°, operates during periods of darkness only.

Coconut Point Directional Light
19 43.6N, 155 05.2W, F G, 38 ft., 10 mi., white concrete tower, visible 4° each side of 197°. *Also see* Hilo Harbor.

D

Diamond Head Light
21 15.3N, 157 48.6W, Oc (2) W 10s (R sector), 147 ft., white 17 mi., red 14 mi., white concrete tower, obscured from 110° to 272°, red from 099° to 110°, lighted throughout 24 hours.

Diamond Head Reef Lighted Buoy 2
21 14.8N, 157 48.9W, Q R, 4 mi., red.

F

FORACS III Lighted Buoy
21 22.2N, 158 08.6W, Q Y, white with orange bands, maintained by U.S. Navy.

H

HALEIWA HARBOR

Range Front Light
21 35.7N, 158 06.2W, F G, 24 ft., KRW on post, visible 4° each side of rangeline.

Range Rear Light
305 yards, 129° from front light, F G, 46 ft., KRW on post, visible 4° each side of rangeline.

Entrance Lighted Buoy 2
21 36.2N, 158 06.8W, Fl R 2.5s,
4 mi., red.

Buoy 3
Green can.

Buoy 4
Red nun.

Light 6
21 35.8N, 158 06.4W, Fl R 4s,
20 ft., 4 mi., TR on post.

Light 7
21 35.7N, 158 06.3W, Fl G 6s,
20 ft., 4 mi., SG on post.

Hana Bay Daybeacon
20 45.4N, 155 59.0W, two white
diamond daymarks with red
vertical stripe, private aid.
Also see Kauiki Head Light.

Hanamanioa Point Light
20 35.0N, 156 24.7W, Fl W 4s,
73 ft., 8 mi., NB on post,
obscured from 124° to 290°.

HANAPEPE BAY

Lighted Buoy 1
21 53.5N, 159 35.4W, Fl G 2.5s,
4 mi., green.

Breakwater Light 2
21 53.8N, 159 35.5W, Q R, 32 ft.,
5 mi., TR on spindle.

Lighted Buoy 3
Fl G 4s, 4 mi., green.

Buoy 5
Green can.

**Port Allen Small Boat Harbor
Breakwater Light 1**
21 54.1N, 159 35.4W, Fl G 4s, 9 ft.,
SG on spindle, private aid.

Hawea Point Light
21 00.2N, 156 40.0W, Fl W 6s,
75 ft., 9 mi., NB on post.

**Heeia Kea Small Boat Harbor
Daybeacon 1**
21 26.8N, 157 48.4W, 13 ft., SG
on pile.
Also see Kaneohe Bay.

**Heeia Kea Small Boat Harbor
Light 2**
21 26.9N, 157 48.5W, Iso R 6s,
15 ft., 4 mi., TR on pile.

HICKAM HARBOR

Channel Buoy 1
21 18.2N, 157 57.2W, green can.

Channel Light 2
21 18.2N, 157 57.1W, Fl R 4s,
16 ft., 4 mi., TR on pile.

Channel Daybeacon 3
15 ft., SG on pile.

Channel Daybeacon 4
15 ft., TR on pile.

Channel Buoy 5
Green can.

Channel Light 6
Fl R 2.5s, 16 ft., 4 mi., TR on
concrete pile.

HILO HARBOR

Entrance Lighted Buoy 1
19 44.5N, 155 04.8W, Fl G 2.5s,
5 mi., green.

Breakwater Light
19 44.5N, 155 04.5W, Fl W 2.5s,
39 ft., 6 mi., NB on white post.

Coconut Point Directional Light
19 43.6N, 155 05.2W, F G, 38 ft.,
10 mi., white concrete tower, visible 4° each side of 197°.

Lighted Buoy 3
Q G, 4 mi., green.

Range Front Light
19 43.9N, 155 03.2W, F G, 75 ft.,
KRW on post, visible 4° each side
of rangeline, lighted throughout
24 hours.

Range Rear Light
470 yards, 097.5° from front light,
F G, 124 ft., KRW on square pyramidal skeleton tower, visible 4°
each side of rangeline, lighted
throughout 24 hours.

Lighted Buoy 4
Fl R 4s, 4 mi., red.

Lighted Buoy 5
Fl G 2.5s, 4 mi., green.

Buoy 6
Red nun.

Lighted Buoy 7
Fl G 4s, 4 mi., green.

Reeds Bay Rock Daybeacon A
NW on pile worded ROCK,
private aid.

Reeds Bay Rock Daybeacon B
NW on pile worded ROCK,
private aid.

Lighted Buoy 9
Fl G 2.5s, 4 mi., green.

Buoy 10
Red nun.

Waiakea Light
19 43.5N, 155 04.2W, Q W, 47 ft.,
6 mi., NB on white steel tower.

**Wailoa Basin Channel
Daybeacon 1**
19 43.5N, 155 04.2W, S G on pile.

Wailoa Basin Channel Buoy 2
19 43.5N, 155 04.3W, red nun.

HONOKOHAU HARBOR

Approach Lighted Buoy 1
19 40.1N, 156 01.9W, Fl G 2.5s,
3 mi., green.

**Entrance Channel Directional
Light**
19 40.2N, 156 01.9W, Iso W 6s
(R&G sectors), 27 ft., NB on pile,
white 2° each side of centerline
of channel (bearing 064°), red
when right of white beam
(062°–057°), green when left of
white beam (066°–071°), when
entering from seaward.

Entrance Channel Light 3
19 40.2N, 156 01.6W, Fl G 4s,
25 ft., 4 mi., SG on spindle.

Channel Light 4
Fl R 4s, 25 ft., 4 mi., TR on post.

Channel Daybeacon 5
32 ft., SG on pile.

HONOLULU HARBOR

Also see Ala Wai Boat Harbor, Kewalo Basin, Kalihi Channel, Keehi Lagoon, Hickam Harbor, *and* Pearl Harbor.

Entrance Light
21 17.7N, 157 52.1W, Fl G 7.5s, 95 ft., 20 mi., on white post, visible from 305° to 089°.

Entrance Lighted Buoy H
21 16.8N, 157 52.8W, Mo (A) W, 6 mi., Fl W 2.5s, 8 mi., red and white stripes with red spherical topmark, high-intensity flash-tube Fl W 2.5s, racon: O (---).

Channel Lighted Buoy 1
21 17.5N, 157 52.4W, Fl G 4s, 5 mi., green.

Entrance Channel Range Front Light
21 18.3N, 157 51.9W, F R, 45 ft., KRW on concrete structure, visible 4° each side of rangeline, lighted throughout 24 hours.

Entrance Channel Range Rear Light
164 yards, 028° from front light, F R, 60 ft., KRW on single pile mast, visible 4° each side of rangeline, lighted throughout 24 hours.

Channel Lighted Buoy 2
Fl R 4s, 5 mi., red.

Channel Buoy 3
Green can.

Channel Buoy 4
21 17.6N, 157 52.2W, red nun.

Channel Lighted Buoy 5
Fl G 2.5s, 3 mi., green.

Channel Lighted Buoy 6 (marks shoal)
21 17.7N, 157 52.2W, Fl R 2.5s, 3 mi., red.

Channel Light 7
21 18.1N, 157 52.1W, Iso G 6s, 15 ft., 5 mi., collision tolerant pile structure.

Buoy 8
21 18.3N, 157 51.9W, red nun.

Buoy 10
21 18.5N, 157 51.9W, red nun.

Kapalama Basin Buoy 2
21 19.0N, 157 52.8W, red nun.

K

Ka Lae Light
18 54.7N, 155 40.9W, Fl W 6s, 60 ft., 8 mi., NB on white concrete post.

Kaamola Point Light
21 03.0N, 156 50.9W, Fl W 4s, 23 ft., 5 mi., NB on spindle.
Also see Kamalo Bay Reef Lighted Buoy 2.

Kaena Point Light
21 34.3N, 158 15.8W, Fl W 10s, 931 ft., 25 mi., on top of building, lighted throughout 24 hours.

Kaena Point Passing Light
21 34.5N, 158 16.7W, Fl W 2.5s, 71 ft., 7 mi., NR on pile.

Kahala Point Light
22 08.8N, 159 17.7W, Fl W 4s, 42 ft., 11 mi., NB on spindle.

Kahoolawe Island Southwest Point Light
20 30.1N, 156 40.0W, Fl W 6s, 120 ft., 7 mi., on white skeleton tower, obscured over Kealaikahiki Point north of 123°.

KAHULUI HARBOR

Entrance Range Front Light
20 53.4N, 156 28.3W, F R, 49 ft., KRW on post, visible 4° each side of rangeline, lighted throughout 24 hours.

Entrance Range Rear Light
470 yards, 177° from front light, F R, 91 ft., KRW on post, visible 4° each side of rangeline, lighted throughout 24 hours.

Entrance Breakwater Light 3
20 54.0N, 156 28.3W, Fl G 2.5s, 36 ft., 5 mi., SG on post.

Entrance Breakwater Light 4
20 54.0N, 156 28.4W, Fl R 2.5s, 36 ft., 5 mi., TR on post.

Buoy 5
Green can.

Buoy 6
Red nun.

Lighted Buoy 8
Fl R 6s, 4 mi., red.

Buoy 10
Red nun.

Lighted Buoy 12
Fl R 4s, 3 mi., red.

Kahului Boat Ramp Range Front Daybeacon
20 53.7N, 156 28.7W, 6 ft., KRW on post, private aid.

Kahului Boat Ramp Range Rear Daybeacon
20 53.7N, 156 28.7W, 12 ft., KRW on post, private aid.

Kahului Boat Ramp Buoy 1
20 53.9N, 156 28.7W, green can, private aid.

Kahului Boat Ramp Buoys 2–11
Red nuns and green cans, private aids.

Kailua Bay Entrance Directional Light
19 38.3N, 155 59.8W, Oc W 4s (R&G sectors), 31 ft., NB on post, white 3° each side of channel centerline (bearing 023°), green when left of channel (026°–060°), red when right of channel (310°–020°), when entering from seaward.

Kailua Light
19 38.5N, 156 00.0W, Iso W 6s (R sector), 32 ft., white 13 mi., red 10 mi., white pyramidal concrete tower, red from 110° to 120°, obscured from 120° to 263°.

Kaiser Boat Channel Daybeacon 1
21 16.6N, 157 50.4W, SG on pile, private aid.

Kaiser Boat Channel Daybeacons 2–4
TRs and SGs on piles, private aids.

Kalanipuao Rock Buoy 2
21 52.6N, 159 31.3W, red nun.
Also see Puolo Point Light.

KALIHI CHANNEL

Entrance Lighted Buoy 1
21 17.4N, 157 53.9W, Fl G 2.5s,
5 mi., green.

Range Front Light
21 18.5N, 157 53.7W, Q G, 36 ft.,
KRW on skeleton tower, visible
4° each side of rangeline.

Range Rear Light
677 yards, 007° from front light,
Iso G 6s, 65 ft., KRW on skeleton
tower, visible 4° each side of
rangeline.

Lighted Buoy 3
Oc G 4s, 4 mi., green.

Lighted Buoy 4
Oc R 4s, 4 mi., red.

Lighted Buoy 5
21 18.0N, 157 53.8W, Fl G 2.5s,
4 mi., green.

Lighted Buoy 6
21 17.9N, 157 53.8W, Fl R 2.5s,
red.

Light 7
Fl G 4s, 15 ft., 4 mi., SG on
dolphin.

Light 8
Q R, 15 ft., 4 mi., TR on dolphin.

Light 10
Fl R 2.5s, 15 ft., 4 mi., TR on
dolphin.

Light 11
Fl G 2.5s, 15 ft., 4 mi., SG on
dolphin.

Light 12
Fl R 4s, 15 ft., 4 mi., TR on
dolphin.

Light 13
Fl G 2.5s, 15 ft., 4 mi., SG on
dolphin.

Light 14
Fl R 2.5s, 15 ft., 4 mi., TR on
dolphin.

Light 15
Fl G 4s, 15 ft., 4 mi., SG on
dolphin.

**Kamalo Bay Reef Lighted Buoy 2
(marks entrance to Kamalo Bay)**
21 01.9N, 156 52.6W, Fl R 4s,
4 mi., red.
Also see Kaamola Point Light.

KANEOHE BAY

Also see Heeia Kea Small Boat
Harbor, Sampan Channel, *and*
Kaneohe Bay Utility Channel.

**Entrance Channel Approach
Lighted Buoy K**
21 31.1N, 157 48.2W, Mo (A) W,
6 mi., red and white stripes with
red spherical topmark.

Channel Lighted Buoy 2
21 30.9N, 157 48.6W, Fl R 4s,
4 mi., red.

Channel Buoy 3
21 30.6N, 157 48.9W, green can.

Channel Buoy 4
Red nun.

Channel Daybeacon 5
13 ft., SG on multi-pile structure.

Channel Daybeacon 6
13 ft., TR on multi-pile structure.

**Entrance and Kualoa Point Range
Front Light**
21 29.7N, 157 49.9W, Q R, 22 ft.,
KRW on multi-pile structure, visible all around with higher intensity beam on rangeline.

Entrance Range Rear Light
550 yards, 227° from front light,
Iso R 6s, 42 ft., KRW on multi-pile
structure, obscured from 272°
to 182°.

Kualoa Point Range Rear Light
240 yards, 349.5° from front light,
Oc R 4s, 38 ft., KRW on multi-pile
structure, obscured from 140°
to 196°.

Channel Buoy 7
Green can.

Channel Daybeacon 7A
13 ft., SG on pile.

Channel Daybeacon 8
13 ft., TR on pile.

Channel Daybeacon 9
13 ft., SG on pile.

Channel Light 10
21 28.4N, 157 49.5W, Fl R 4s,
15 ft., 4 mi., TR on pile.

Channel Daybeacon 11
13 ft., SG on pile.

Channel Lighted Buoy 11A
21 27.9N, 157 49.4W, Q G, green.

Channel Light 12
Fl R 2.5s, 15 ft., 4 mi., TR on pile.

Channel Lighted Buoy 12A
21 27.4N, 157 48.7W, Fl R 4s,
4 mi., red.

Channel Light 13
Fl G 4s, 15 ft., 5 mi., SG on pile.

Channel Danger Light
21 26.9N, 157 47.6W, Q W, 15 ft.,
4 mi., NW on pile worded
DANGER SUBMERGED REEF.

Channel Light 16
Fl R 4s, 15 ft., 4 mi., TR on pile.

Channel Daybeacon 17
13 ft., SG on pile.

Channel Light 19
Q G, 15 ft., 4 mi., SG on pile.

Channel Buoy 20
Red nun.

Yacht Club Race Buoy A
21 26.0N, 157 46.1W, yellow
sphere, private aid.

Yacht Club Race Buoy B
21 26.5N, 157 47.0W, yellow
sphere, private aid.

Yacht Club Race Buoy C
21 25.7N, 157 47.3W, yellow
sphere, private aid.

Yacht Club Race Buoy D
21 25.4N, 157 47.0W, yellow
sphere, private aid.

Yacht Club Race Buoy E
21 25.2N, 157 46.9W, yellow
sphere, private aid.

KANEOHE BAY
UTILITY CHANNEL

Buoy 2 (marks shoal area)
21 27.1N, 157 47.0W, red nun.

Daybeacon 3
15 ft., SG on pile.

Light 4
21 27.0N, 157 46.9W, Fl R 2.5s, 15 ft., 2 mi., TR on pile.

Buoy 5
Green can.

Kaneohe Bay Warning Lighted Buoy
21 26.4N, 157 46.8W, Fl W 2.5s, 5 mi., white with orange bands and orange diamond worded JET BLAST, marks south boundary of prohibited area.

Makani Kai Range Front Light
21 25.1N, 157 47.4W, F R, 17 ft., KWR on pile, private aid.

Makani Kai Range Rear Light
22 yards, 254° from front light, F R, 24 ft., KWR on pile, private aid.

Kauhola Point Light
20 14.8N, 155 46.3W, Fl W 6s, 116 ft., 24 mi., white cylindrical concrete tower, obscured from 306° to 101°, lighted throughout 24 hours.

Kauiki Head Light
20 45.4N, 155 58.7W, Fl W 2.5s, 85 ft., 6 mi., white pyramidal concrete tower.
Also see Hana Bay Daybeacon.

KAUMALAPAU HARBOR

Light
20 47.0N, 156 59.5W, Fl W 4s, 68 ft., 5 mi., NB on post, obscured from 180° to 000°.

Entrance Lighted Buoy 1
20 47.1N, 156 59.5W, Fl G 2.5s, 4 mi., green.

Buoy 2
Red nun.

Buoy 4
Red nun.

NASA/NOAA Research Lighted Buoy
20 49.1N, 157 11.8W, Fl Y 4s, yellow cylindrical buoy with pipe mast, unlighted orange 2 ft. diameter cylindrical marker attached to main buoy by 300 ft. of submerged line, 150 ft. below the surface.

KAUNAKAKAI HARBOR

Lighted Buoy 2
21 04.6N, 157 01.9W, Fl R 4s, 4 mi., red.

Entrance Range Front Light
21 05.3N, 157 01.5W, F R, 27 ft., KRW on skeleton tower on house, visible 4° each side of rangeline.

Entrance Range Rear Light
200 yards, 034° from front light, F R, 41 ft., KRW on skeleton tower, visible 4° each side of rangeline.

Lighted Buoy 3
Fl G 4s, 4 mi., green.

Buoy 4
Red nun.

Buoy 5
Green can.

Kaunakakai Small Boat Harbor Buoy 2
21 04.8N, 157 01.7W, red nun, private aid.

Kaunakakai Small Boat Harbor Buoys 3–8
Green cans and red nuns, private aids.

Daybeacon REEF
5 ft., NW on pile worded REEF, private aid.

KAWAIHAE

Light
20 02.5N, 155 49.9W, Fl W 6s, 59 ft., 9 mi., white pyramidal concrete tower.

Entrance Lighted Buoy 1
Fl G 2.5s, 4 mi., green.

Entrance Lighted Buoy 2
20 02.4N, 155 50.4W, Fl R 4s, 4 mi., red.

Channel Range Front Light
20 02.1N, 155 49.6W, F G, 70 ft., KRW on post, higher intensity on rangeline, lighted throughout 24 hours.

Channel Range Rear Light
247 yards, 120° from front light, F G, 93 ft., KRW on pile, higher intensity on rangeline, lighted throughout 24 hours.

Channel Buoy 3
Green can.

Channel Buoy 4
Red nun.

South Breakwater Light 6
20 02.2N, 155 50.0W, Fl R 2.5s, 20 ft., 4 mi., TR on post.

Kawaihae Small Boat Basin Light 1
20 02.3N, 155 49.9W, Fl G 4s, 20 ft., 3 mi., SG on pile.

South Breakwater Light 8
20 02.1N, 155 50.0W, Fl R 2.5s, 20 ft., 4 mi., TR on pile, obscured from 320° to 176°.

Keahole Point Light
19 43.7N, 156 03.6W, Fl W 6s (R sector) 43 ft., white 12 mi., red 9 mi., white pyramidal concrete tower, red from 185° to 343°, covers rocks off Makolea and Kaiwi Points.

KEAUHOU BAY

Light
19 33.7N, 155 57.7W, Fl W 4s, 35 ft., 8 mi., on post.

Entrance Directional Light
F W R G, 25 ft., on post on same structure as Keauhou Bay Light, white 1° each side of channel centerline (bearing 069°), red when right of white beam (068°–064°), green when left of white beam (070°–074°), when entering from seaward.

Range Front Daybeacon
6 ft., KRW on post.

Range Rear Daybeacon
30 ft., KRW on post, on same structure as Keauhou Bay Light.

KEEHI LAGOON

Barge Channel Range Front Light
21 19.8N, 157 53.9W, F G, 16 ft., KRG on post, lighted throughout 24 hours, private aid.

Barge Channel Range Rear Light
200 yards, 334° from front light,
F G, 22 ft., KRG on post, lighted
throughout 24 hours, private aid.

Barge Channel Buoy 2
Red nun, private aid.

Pipeline Marker Buoy A
21 19.5N, 157 53.7W, white
sphere with orange diamond
worded PIPELINE, private aid.

Pipeline Marker Buoy B
21 19.5N, 157 53.8W, white
sphere with orange diamond
worded PIPELINE, private aid.

Pipeline Marker Buoy C
21 19.6N, 157 53.9W, white
sphere with orange diamond
worded PIPELINE, private aid.

KEWALO BASIN

Also see Ala Wai Boat Harbor *and*
Honolulu Harbor.

Entrance Range Front Light
21 17.6N, 157 51.4W, Q G, 63 ft.,
KRW on post, visible 4° each side
of rangeline.

Entrance Range Rear Light
77 yards, 034.7° from front light,
Oc G 4s, 75 ft., KRW on skeleton
tower, visible 4° each side of
rangeline.

Lighted Buoy 1
21 17.3N, 157 51.7W, Fl G 2.5s,
5 mi., green.

Lighted Buoy 2
21 17.3N, 157 51.7W, Fl R 4s,
5 mi., red.

Buoy 4
Red nun.

Buoy 6
Red nun.

Kihei Boat Ramp Daybeacon 1
20 42.5N, 156 26.8W, 6 mi., SG on
pile, private aid.

Kihei Boat Ramp Daybeacons 2–5
6 ft., TRs and SGs on piles, private aids.

KIKIAOLA BOAT HARBOR

Range Front Light
21 57.6N, 159 41.6W, F R, 16 ft.,
steel pole on concrete base,
located west of harbor, private
aid.

Range Rear Light
71 yards, 351.1° from front light,
Q R, 28 ft., steel pole on concrete
base, located west of harbor,
private aid.

Light 1
Q G, 16 ft., yellow pole on concrete base, located on western
harbor entrance, private aid.

Light 2
Q R, 16 ft., yellow pole on concrete base, located on eastern
harbor entrance, private aid.

Kilauea Point Light
22 13.9N, 159 24.1W, Fl W 10s,
174 ft., 25 mi., white concrete
post, obscured from 295° to 065°,
lighted throughout 24 hours.

Kokole Light
21 58.7N, 159 45.4W, Fl W 6s,
58 ft., 6 mi., NB on three-legged
tower, obscured from 163°
to 283°.

Kualoa Point Range
See Kaneohe Bay.

KUAPA ENTRANCE CHANNEL

Buoy 1
Green can, private aid.

Buoy 2
21 16.7N, 157 42.7W, red nun,
private aid.

Buoys 3 and 4
Green can and red nun, private
aids.

Kukii Point Light
21 57.4N, 159 20.8W, Fl W 2.5s
(R sector), 47 ft., white 6 mi., red
5 mi., white pyramidal concrete
tower, red from 256° to 296°.
Also see Nawiliwili Harbor.

Kukuihaele Light
20 07.7N, 155 33.3W, Iso W 6s,
154 ft., 8 mi., white concrete
tower.

L

Laau Point Light
21 06.0N, 157 18.3W, Fl W 2.5s,
151 ft., 7 mi., NB on splndle,
obscured from 189° to 286°.

LAHAINA

Light
20 52.3N, 156 40.7W, Fl R 7.5s,
44 ft., 12 mi., on white pyramidal
concrete tower, obscured from
142° to 333°.

Floating Fish Pier
20 52.5N, 156 41.8W, Q W, 10 ft.,
50 ft. X 50 ft. floating platform,
private aid.

Entrance Lighted Buoy L
20 52.1N, 156 41.0W, Mo (A) W,
6 mi., red and white stripes with
red spherical topmark.

**Lahaina Boat Basin Range Front
Light**
20 52.3N, 156 40.7W, F G, 16 ft.,
KRW on pile, visible 4° each side
of rangeline.

**Lahaina Boat Basin Range Rear
Light**
50 yards, 044.4° from front light,
F G, 22 ft., KRW on post, visible
4° each side of rangeline.

Lahaina Boat Basin Buoy 1
20 52.3N, 156 40.8W, green can,
private aid.

Lahaina Boat Basin Buoys 2–6
Red nuns and green cans,
private aids.

**Laupahoehoe Harbor Breakwater
Light 2**
19 59.5N, 155 14.4W, Fl R 4s,
27 ft., 3 mi., TR on pile.

Laupahoehoe Point Light
19 59.6, 155 14.2W, Fl W 2.5s,
39 ft., 7 mi., NB on post.

Lehua Rock Light
22 01.1N, 160 05.9W, Fl W 4s,
704 ft., 7 mi., on post, obscured
from 344° to 045°.

MAALAEA BASIN

Range Front Light
20 47.5N, 156 30.6W, F R, 23 ft.,
KRW on post, visible 4° each side
of rangeline.

Range Rear Light
82 yards, 339° from front light,
F R, 30 ft., KRW on post, visible 4°
each side of rangeline.

Channel Buoy 1
20 47.4N, 156 30.6W, green can,
private aid.

Channel Buoy 2
Red nun, private aid.

Maalaea East Basin Buoy 4
Red nun, private aid.

Maalaea East Basin Buoy 6
Red nun, private aid.

Daybeacon J
JR on post, private aid.

**Maalaea West Basin Daybeacon
2W**
TR on pole, private aid.

Acoustic Range Lighted Buoy
20 44.7N, 156 37.2W, Q Y, yellow,
maintained by U.S. Navy, racon:
O (---).

Mahukona Light
20 10.8N, 155 54.1W, Fl W 4s,
64 ft., 6 mi., white pyramidal
concrete tower.

Makahuena Point Light
21 52.1N, 159 26.6W, Fl W 2.5s,
80 ft., 11 mi., NB on post,
obscured from 110° to 237.5°.

Makai Channel Daybeacon 3
21 19.1N, 157 40.0W, SG on pile,
private aid.
Also see Makapuu Point Light.

Makai Channel Daybeacons 4–7
TRs and SGs on piles or dolphins,
private aids.

Makani Kai Range
See Kaneohe Bay Utility Channel.

Makapuu Point Light
21 18.6N, 157 38.9W, Oc W 10s,
420 ft., 19 mi., white cylindrical
concrete tower, obscured west of
011°, and may be obscured westward of 154° by points northward
of light, lighted throughout
24 hours.

MALA CHANNEL

Directional Light
20 53.2N, 156 41.2W, F RWG,
25 ft., on post, white 1° each side
of channel centerline (bearing
140.4°), red when right of white
beam (139.4°–137.9°), green
when left of white beam
(141.4°–142.9°), when entering
from seaward, private aid.

Daybeacons 1–6
10 ft., SGs and TRs on piles,
private aids.

Danger Daybeacon
10 ft., NW on pile worded
DANGER ROCKS, private aid.

MANELE BAY

Lighted Buoy 2
20 44.3N, 156 52.8W, Fl R 4s,
4 mi., red.

Breakwater Light
20 44.5N, 156 53.2W, Fl W 4s, 20 ft.,
6 mi., on post on white house.

Manele Small Boat Harbor Buoy 1
20 44.5N, 156 53.2W, green can,
private aid.

**Manele Small Boat Harbor Buoys
2–8**
Red nuns and green cans,
private aids.

Maunalua Bay Light 1
21 16.3N, 157 42.9W, Fl G 4s,
15 ft., 4 mi., SG on multi-pile
structure.

Maunalua Bay Daybeacons 1A–21
SGs and TRs on piles,
private aids.

McGregor Point Light
20 46.6N, 156 31.4W, Iso G 6s,
72 ft., 10 mi., on white tower,
obscured from 082° to 221°.

**Merry Point Light, Pearl Harbor
Southeast Loch**
21 20.9N, 157 56.4W, F G, 30 ft.,
7 mi., NB on post, lighted
throughout 24 hours.
Also see Pearl Harbor.

**Milolii Beach Range Front
Daybeacon**
22 08.7N, 159 43.4W, KRW on
post, maintained from June 1
to Sept. 8, private aid.

**Milolii Beach Range Rear
Daybeacon**
33 yards, 168.2° from front daybeacon, KRW on post, maintained from June 1 to Sept. 8,
private aid.

Milolii Point Light
19 11.2N, 155 54.5W, Fl W 4s,
44 ft., 7 mi., NB on post.

Molokai Island Light
21 12.6N, 156 58.1W, Fl W 10s,
213 ft., 25 mi., on white tower,
lighted throughout 24 hours.

Molokini Island Light
20 37.7N, 156 29.7W, Fl W 2.5s,
182 ft., 7 mi., NR on pile.

Nakalele Point Light
21 01.7N, 156 35.4W, Fl W 2.5s,
142 ft., 6 mi., NB on pile,
obscured from 301° to 106°.

Napoopoo Light
19 28.7N, 155 56.2W, Fl W 6s,
27 ft., 7 mi., white pyramidal
concrete tower, obscured in
Kealakekua Bay when bearing
is less than 291°.

**NASA/NOAA Research Lighted
Buoy**
20 49.1N, 157 11.8W, Fl Y 4s,
yellow cylindrical buoy with
pipe mast, unlighted orange
2 ft.-diameter cylindrical marker
attached to main buoy by 300 ft.
of submerged line, 150 ft. below
the surface.
Also see Kaumalapau Harbor.

NAWILIWILI HARBOR

Nawiliwili Harbor Light
21 57.3N, 159 20.2W, Fl W 15s, 112 ft., 24 mi., buff-colored cylindrical concrete tower, obscured from 065° to 115°, lighted throughout 24 hours.

Kukii Point Light
21 57.4N, 159 20.8W, Fl W 2.5s (R sector), 47 ft., white 6 mi., red 5 mi., white pyramidal concrete tower, red from 256° to 296°.

Range Front Light
21 57.4N, 159 21.1W, Q R, 45 ft., KRW on post, visible 4° each side of rangeline.

Range Rear Light
181 yards, 289.4° from front light, F R, 68 ft., KRW on tank, visible 4° each side of rangeline.

Breakwater Light
21 57.2N, 159 20.9W, Q W, 21 ft., 6 mi., NB on post.

Entrance Buoy 1 (marks submerged end of breakwater)
21 57.2N, 159 20.9W, green can.

Buoy 2
Red nun.

Buoy 4
Red nun.

Lighted Buoy 5
Fl G 2.5s, 3 mi., green.

Buoy 7
Green can.

Small Boat Harbor Light 1
21 57.0N, 159 21.4W, Fl G 6s, 18 ft., 4 mi., SG on pile, obscured from 244° to 021°.

Small Boat Harbor Light 2
21 56.9N, 159 21.5W, Fl R 4s, 18 ft., 4 mi., TR on pile.

Small Boat Harbor Daybeacons 3–15
10 ft., SGs on piles, private aids.

Ninini Point Lighted Buoy 2 (marks shoal off Ninini Point)
21 57.1N, 159 20.2W, Fl R 4s, 4 mi., red.

NOAA OFFSHORE DATA LIGHTED BUOYS

NOAA Data Lighted Buoy 51004
17 27.3N, 152 29.4W, Fl (4) Y 20s, yellow boat-shaped weather buoy.

NOAA Data Lighted Buoy 51002
17 09.9N, 157 49.1W, Fl (4) Y 20s, yellow boat-shaped weather buoy.

NOAA Data Lighted Buoy 51003
19 09.5N, 160 49.2W, Fl (4) Y 20s, yellow boat-shaped weather buoy.

NOAA Data Lighted Buoy EB 51001
23 26.0N, 162 18.0W, Fl (4) Y 20s, yellow boat-shaped weather buoy.

Nohili Point Light
22 03.7N, 159 46.9W, Fl W 4s, 120 ft., 8 mi., NB on spindle, obscured from 230° to 330°.

Nualolo Beach Range Front Daybeacon
22 09.5N, 159 42.0W, KRW on post, maintained from June 1 to Sept. 8, private aid.

Nualolo Beach Range Rear Daybeacon
33 yards, 149° from front daybeacon, KRW on post, maintained from June 1 to Sept. 8, private aid.

P

Palaoa Point Light
20 43.9N, 156 57.8W, Fl W 6s (R sector), 91 ft., white 7 mi., red 5 mi., on white skeleton tower, red from 260° to 280°, covers rocks off of Puupehe Point.

Paukaa Point Light
19 45.7N, 155 05.4W, Fl G 6s, 145 ft., 9 mi., white pyramidal concrete tower, obscured from 350° to 190°.

Pauwela Point Light
20 56.7N, 156 19.3W, Fl W 15s, 170 ft., 24 mi., white pyramidal skeleton tower, lighted throughout 24 hours.

PEARL HARBOR

Main Channel

Entrance Lighted Buoy 1
21 17.9N, 157 57.4W, Fl G 4s, 5 mi., green.

Entrance Lighted Buoy 2
Fl R 2.5s, 5 mi., red.

Entrance Range Front Light
21 19.6N, 157 58.2W, Q R, 51 ft., F R, 48 ft., KRW on skeleton tower, quick flashing red light visible 4° either side of centerline over fixed line of red light on daymark.

Entrance Range Rear Light
750 yards, 333.6° from front light, Iso G 6s, 97 ft., F G, 94 ft., KRW on skeleton tower, isophase flashing green light visible 4° on either side of centerline over fixed line of green light on daymark.

Buoy 3
Green can.

Buoy 4
Red nun.

Light 5
21 18.7N, 157 57.8W, Fl G 2.5s, 15 ft., 4 mi., SG on pile.

Light 6
Fl R 4s, 15 ft., 4 mi., TR on pile.

Light 7
Fl G 4s, 16 ft., 4 mi., SG on dolphin, radar reflector.

A Docks Basin Daybeacon 2
TR on pile.

Light 9
Fl G 4s, 15 ft., 4 mi., SG on pile.

Lighted Buoy 11
21 20.2N, 157 58.3W, Fl G 2.5s, 4 mi., green.

Light 13
21 20.3N, 157 58.1W, Oc G 4s, 15 ft., 4 mi., SG on post.

Light 15
Fl G 4s, 15 ft., 4 mi., SG on multi-pile structure.

Light 16
Q R, 15 ft., 3 mi., TR on multi-pile structure.

Light 17
Q G, 15 ft., 4 mi., SG on pile.

Light 18
Fl R 2.5s, 15 ft., 3 mi., TR on pile.

Light 19
Fl G 6s, 15 ft., 4 mi., SG on multi-pile structure.

Light 20
Fl R 4s, 15 ft., 3 mi., TR on pile.

Light 21
Q G, 16 ft., 3 mi., SG on multi-pile structure.

Light 23
Fl G 2.5s, 15 ft., 3 mi., SG on pile.

Buoy 26
21 22.4N, 157 56.7W, red nun.

Lighted Buoy 27
Fl G 2.5s, 3 mi., green.

Lighted Buoy 29
21 22.4N, 157 57.3W, Fl G 6s, 4 mi., green.

Light 33
Fl G 4s, 15 ft., 4 mi., SG on multi-pile structure.

Light 35
Fl G 2.5s, 15 ft., 3 mi., SG on multi-pile structure.

Lighted Buoy 36
Fl R 4s, 3 mi., red.

Pearl Harbor West Loch

Entrance Range Front Light
21 20.9N, 157 58.8W, F G, 32 ft., KRW on skeleton tower, visible 4° each side of rangeline, operates during periods of darkness only.

Entrance Range Rear Light
300 yards, 323° from front light, F G, 47 ft., KRW on skeleton tower, visible 4° each side of rangeline, operates during periods of darkness only.

Daybeacon 1
21 20.3N, 157 58.5W, SG on pile.

Light 3
Q G, 15 ft., 3 mi., SG on pile.

Light 5
Fl G 2.5s, 15 ft., 3 mi., SG on pile.

Lighted Buoy 6
Q R, 3 mi., red.

Lighted Buoy 7
Q G, 3 mi., green.

Lighted Buoy 8
21 21.4N, 157 59.6W, Fl R 2.5s, 3 mi., red.

Light 9
Fl G 2.5s, 15 ft., 3 mi., SG on multi-pile structure.

Light 10
Fl R 4s, 15 ft., 3 mi., TR on multi-pile structure.

Daybeacon 11
13 ft., SG on pile.

Pearl Harbor East Loch

Daybeacon 2
21 22.3N, 157 56.3W, TR on pile.

Light 4
Fl R 4s, 15 ft., 3 mi., TR on pile.

Danger Daybeacon
21 22.9N, 157 57.4W, 4 ft., NW on structure, private aid.

Pearl Harbor Southeast Loch, Merry Point Light
21 20.9N, 157 56.4W, F G, 30 ft., 7 mi., NB on post, lighted throughout 24 hours.

Pepeekeo Point Light
19 50.8N, 155 04.9W, Oc W 4s, 147 ft., 13 mi., white pyramidal skeleton tower.

Pohakuloa Point Light
20 55.7N, 156 59.3W, Fl W 6s (R sector). 30 ft., white 8 mi., red 6 mi., NB on pile, red from 268.5° to 276.5°.

Pohoiki Bay Breakwater Light 2
19 27.3N, 154 50.4W, Fl R 4s, 11 ft., 5 mi., TR on spindle.

Pokai Bay Breakwater Light 2
21 26.6N, 158 11.5W, Fl R 4s, 30 ft., TR on pile, private aid.

Port Allen Small Boat Harbor Breakwater Light 1
21 54.1N, 159 35.4W, Fl G 4s, 9 ft., SG on spindle, private aid.
Also see Hanapepe Bay.

Puako Small Boat Harbor Buoys 1–9
Green spars and cans, and red spars and nuns, private aids.

Puako Small Boat Harbor Light
19 58.4N, 155 49.9W, Oc G 5.5s, 30 ft., on power pole, flood light for launching ramp also on power pole, private aid.
Also see Kawaihae.

Puolo Point Light
21 53.6N, 159 36.3W, Fl W 4s (R sector), 28 ft., white 5 mi., red 4 mi., NB on post, red from 261° to 282°, covers Kalanipuao Rock.
Also see Kalanipuao Rock Buoy 2.

Pyramid Rock Light
21 27.7N, 157 45.8W, Oc W 4s, 101 ft., 10 mi., white square concrete house with black diagonal stripes.

SAMPAN CHANNEL

Also see Kaneohe Bay.

Entrance Lighted Buoy 2
21 28.1N, 157 46.6W, Fl R 2.5s, 4 mi., red.

Range Front Light
21 26.1N, 157 48.3W, Q R, 38 ft., KRW on post, visible 4° each side of rangeline.

Range Rear Light
475 yards, 217.2° from front light, F R, 80 ft., KRW on pyramidal skeleton tower, visible 4° each side of rangeline.

Daybeacon 4
13 ft., TR on pile.

Light 5
Fl G 2.5s, 16 ft., 4 mi., SG on pile.

Daybeacon 7
15 ft., SG on pile.

Daybeacon 8
15 ft., TR on pile.

Daybeacon 9
15 ft., SG on multi-pile structure.

Buoy 10
21 26.9N, 157 47.6W, red nun.

W

Waiakea Light
19 43.5N, 155 04.2W, Q W, 47 ft., 6 mi., NB on white steel tower. *Also see* Hilo Harbor.

WAIANAE HARBOR

Breakwater Light 1
21 26.9N, 158 11.8W, Fl G 4s, 20 ft., 6 mi., SG on pile.

Range Front Light
21 26.9N, 158 11.7W, Q R, 20 ft., KRW on post.

Range Rear Light
78 yards, 003° from front light, Iso R 6s, 27 ft., KRW on post.

Waihee Reef Lighted Buoy 2
20 55.7N, 156 28.5W, Fl R 4s, 4 mi., red.

WAIKAEA

Light 1
22 04.4N, 159 18.6W, Fl G 4s, 12 ft., SG on pile, private aid.

Light 2
Fl R 4s, 12 ft., TR on pile, private aid.

Light 3
Fl G 2.5s, 12 ft., SG on pile, private aid.

Light 4
Fl R 2.5s, 12 ft., TR on pile, private aid.

Light 5
Fl G 6s, 12 ft., SG on pile, private aid.

Light 6
Fl R 6s, 12 ft., TR on pile, private aid.

Wailoa Basin Channel Daybeacon 1
19 43.5N, 155 04.2W, S G on pile. *Also see* Hilo Harbor.

Wailoa Basin Channel Buoy 2
19 43.5N, 155 04.3W, red nun.

WEST BEACH MARINA

Light 1
21 19.2N, 158 07.1W, Fl G 4s, 20 ft., SG on pile, private aid.

Light 2
Q R, 20 ft., TR on pile, private aid.

Daybeacons 3–12
5 ft., SGs and TRs on piles, private aids.

Light 13
Fl G 6s, 20 ft., SG on pile, private aid.

Daybeacons 14–18
5 ft., TRs on piles, private aids.

Mexico

Major revisions have been made recently to the government aids to navigation listings for Mexico. Mariners should review *Notice to Mariners* carefully for further changes, and should expect to see similar revisions made to listings in other Central American countries.

The lights of Mexico are characterized by the number of flashes, etc.; the periods are subject to fluctuations and irregularities.

Some latitude/longitude positions are only reported in whole minutes in the government light lists (rather than to the nearest tenth of a minute). These positions should be assumed to be less accurate than those reported with greater precision.

Abreojos, Punta
  See Punta Abreojos.

Acamama
  16 32.0N, 98 51.5W, Fl (3) W 12s, 48 ft., 10 mi., white cylindrical concrete tower.

Acapulco, Bahía de
  See Bahía de Acapulco.

Agiabampo
  26 17.0N, 109 17.0W, Fl (2) W 10s, 43 ft., 10 mi., truncated pyramidal aluminum tower.

Agua Brava
  22 06.0N, 105 38.6W, Fl (2) W 10s, 36 ft., 11 mi., truncated pyramidal aluminum tower, red and white checkered base.

Agujas, Punta
  See Punta Agujas.

Altamura, Isla
  See Isla Altamura.

Altata, Puerto de
  See Puerto de Altata.

Ángel, Puerto
  See Puerto Ángel.

Ángel de la Guarda, Isla
  See Isla Ángel de la Guarda.

Arboleda, Punta
  See Punta Arboleda.

Arena, Punta
  See Punta Arena.

Arista, Puerto
  See Puerto Arista.

Arroyo Conejo
  24 04.5N, 111 00.0W, Fl (2) W 10s, 56 ft., 11 mi., truncated pyramidal metal tower.

Asadero, El
  See El Asadero.

Ayutla, Morro
  See Morro Ayutla.

Azufre, Punta
  See Punta Azufre.

Bahía de Acapulco

Yerbabuena
  16 49.0N, 99 54.0W, Fl (2) W 10s, 43 ft., 10 mi., truncated pyramidal aluminum tower.

Punta Grifo
  16 49.8N, 99 53.8W, Fl (3) W 12s, 115 ft., 10 mi., white truncated pyramidal concrete tower.

Tourist Wharf (E end)
  16 50.8N, 99 55.8W, Iso R 2s, 20 ft., 7 mi., red cylindrical metal tower, hut.

Commercial Wharf (W end)
  16 50.8N, 99 55.9W, Iso G 2s, 20 ft., 7 mi., green cylindrical metal tower, hut.

Las Dos Piedras (White Rocks, off N point of St. Lucia Bay, W rock)
  16 50.3N, 99 54.6W, Fl (2) W 10s, 16 ft., 7 mi., red cylindrical concrete tower, hut.

Bahía de Ballenas
  26 43.5N, 113 32.9W, Fl W 6s, 30 ft., 11 mi., truncated pyramidal aluminum tower.

Bahía Concepción
  26 44.7N, 111 52.5W, Fl W 6s, 92 ft., 11 mi., white and red striped skeleton tower.

Bahía Lobos (N mouth of bay)
  27 25.0N, 110 34.0W, Fl (2) R 10s, 36 ft., 9 mi., truncated pyramidal metal tower.
  Also see Isla Lobos.

Bahía Lobos (E side of bay)
  27 22.0N, 110 27.0W, Fl (3) W 12s, 33 ft., 11 mi., truncated pyramidal metal tower.

Bahía Magdalena

Man of War Cove (on mole)
  24 38.4N, 112 08.9W, Fl (2) W 10s, 56 ft., 8 mi., truncated pyramidal aluminum tower.

Puerto de San Carlos, Muelle Fical
  24 47.3N, 112 07.4W, Iso W 2s, 66 ft., 8 mi., square metal tower.

Isla Mangrove, Range Front Light
  24 32.5N, 111 49.3W, Fl W 3s, 72 ft., 8 mi., white metal tower.

Isla Mangrove, Range Rear Light
  About 594 meters, 087° from front light, 24 32.5N, 111 48.9W, Iso W 2s, 89 ft., 8 mi., white metal tower.

Marcy Channel Range Front Light
  24 27.8N, 111 48.7W, Fl W 3s, 39 ft., 8 mi., white tower.

Marcy Channel Range Rear Light
  907 meters, 154° from front light, 24 26.4N, 111 48.5W, Iso W 2s, 56 ft., 8 mi., white truncated pyramidal metal tower.

Bahía Pichilingue (S mole)
  24 16.0N, 110 20.0W, Iso R 2s, 32 ft., 6 mi., cylindrical concrete tower.

Bahía Pichilingue (N mole)
24 16.5N, 110 20.0W, Iso R 2s, 32 ft., 6 mi., cylindrical concrete tower.

Bahía San Carlos
27 56.0N, 111 04.0W, Fl R 5s, 66 ft., 8 mi., truncated pyramidal metal tower.
Also see Punta San Guillermo.

Bahía de San Francisquito
28 26.1N, 112 54.1W, Fl W 6s, 46 ft., 11 mi., concrete tower.

Bahía de Santa María
30 44N, 114 42W, Fl (2) W 10s, 66 ft., 10 mi., white cylindrical concrete tower.

Bahía la Ventana (S of Punta Gorda)
24 06.8N, 109 59.8W, Fl W 6s, 69 ft., 11 mi., white truncated pyramidal tower.

Bahía de Yavaros, Isla de las Viejas
26 42.0N, 109 32.1W, Fl W 6s, 112 ft., 20 mi., white cylindrical concrete tower, black bands, visible 306°–077°.
Also see Puerto Yavaros.

Baja, Punta
See Punta Baja.

Bajos de la Lobera
26 40.0N, 109 30.0W, Fl G 5s, 36 ft., 8 mi., truncated pyramidal metal tower.
Also see Puerto Yavaros.

Ballena, Isla
See Isla Ballena.

Balleto Anchorage
See Islas Marías.

Banda, Punta
See Punta Banda.

Barra San Juan
15 08.3N, 92 50.3W, Fl (4) W 16s, 46 ft., 8 mi., cylindrical concrete tower.

Blanca, Punta
See Punta Blanca.

Boca del Cocoraquito (N side)
27 06.0N, 110 05.0W, Fl (4) W 16s, 46 ft., 11 mi., truncated pyramidal metal tower.

Boca del Cocoraquito (S side)
26 59.4N, 109 56.5W, Fl (3) W 12s, 49 ft., 11 mi., truncated pyramidal metal tower.

Boca de Comichin
21 46.0N, 105 31.0W, Fl W 6s, 26 ft., 6 mi., cylindrical concrete tower.

Boca de Macepule
25 21.5N, 108 45.0W, Fl (3) W 12s, 56 ft., 12 mi., white truncated pyramidal tower.

Boca de Pabellon
25 48N, 112 07W, Fl (2) W 10s, 45 ft., 10 mi., white concrete tower, red bands.

BOCA DE SANTO DOMINGO

Light
25 38N, 112 06W, Fl (3) W 12s, 42 ft., 9 mi., white concrete tower, red bands.

Muelle Naval (W side)
25 38N, 112 06W, Iso R 2s, 25 ft., 5 mi., white concrete tower.

Muelle Naval (E side)
25 35N, 112 06W, Iso R 2s, 25 ft., 5 mi., white concrete tower.

Boca de Soledad
25 17.3N, 112 07.2W, Fl (4) W 16s, 30 ft., 8 mi., white metal framework tower, red bands.

Boca del Tule
23 14.2N, 109 26.3W, Fl (3) W 12s, 102 ft., 11 mi., red truncated pyramidal metal tower.

Bonanza, La
See La Bonanza.

Borrascosa, Punta
See Punta Borrascosa.

Boundary Aviation Light (U.S./Mexico border)
32 30N, 117 01W, Fl W, occasional.

Brujas, Punta
See Punta Brujas.

Bufadero Bluff
18 03.6N, 102 44.9W, Fl (4) W 16s, 138 ft., 13 mi., white stone tower.

C

Cabeza Ballena
22 54.2N, 109 50.6W, Fl (3) W 12s, 131 ft., 10 mi., white cylindrical concrete tower.

Cabeza de Caballo
28 58N, 113 29W, Fl R 6s, 33 ft., 8 mi., metal tower.

Cabeza Negra
18 35.5N, 103 42.5W, Fl W 6s, 262 ft., 8 mi., truncated pyramidal metal tower.

Cabo Colonet
30 57.7N, 116 19.8W, Fl W 6s, 230 ft., 14 mi., truncated pyramidal aluminum framework tower.

Cabo Corrientes (on slope of wooded mountain)
20 24.0N, 105 42.8W, Fl W 6s, 305 ft., 25 mi., white truncated pyramidal octagonal tower, house with red cupola.

Cabo Falso Light
22 52.7N, 109 57.6W, Fl W 6s, 623 ft., 35 mi., red hexagonal tower, visible 270°–130°, racon: F (··-·) 20 mi.
Also see Cabo San Lucas.

Cabo Haro (approach to Guaymas, S extremity, E part of cape)
27 50.4N, 110 53.3W, Fl (3) W 20s, 351 ft., 34 mi., white square concrete tower, visible 216°–113°.
Also see Guaymas.

Cabo Lobos
29 54.0N, 112 45.0W, Fl (3) W 12s, 39 ft., 9 mi., white truncated pyramidal metal tower.

Cabo San Lázaro
24 47.7N, 112 18.5W, Fl W 6s, 230 ft., 10 mi., white square tower, dwelling, visible 319°–202°, racon: Y (-·--), 20 mi.

CABO SAN LUCAS

Cabo Falso Light
22 52.7N, 109 57.6W, Fl W 6s, 623 ft., 35 mi., red hexagonal tower, visible 270°–130°, racon: F (··-·) 20 mi.

North Breakwater
22 52.9N, 109 54.3W, Fl R 5s,
52 ft., 7 mi., truncated pyramidal
metal tower.

South Breakwater
22 52.8N, 109 54.3W, Fl G 5s,
52 ft., 7 mi., truncated pyramidal
metal tower.

Cabo San Lucas Range Front Light
22 52.8N, 109 54.7W, Fl W 3s, 85 ft.,
17 mi., tower on roof of hotel.

Cabo San Lucas Range Rear Light
About 290 meters, 268° from
front light, 22 52.8N, 109 54.9W,
Iso W 2s, 125 ft., 17 mi., truncated
pyramidal metal tower.

Cabo Tepoca
30 16.3N, 112 51.1W, Fl (3) W 12s,
128 ft., 20 mi., white cylindrical
concrete tower, red bands.

Cabo Vingenes
27 31.3N, 112 21.0W, Fl (4) W 16s,
52 ft., 10 mi., red and white concrete tower.

Cabras, Punta
See Punta Cabras.

Caleta Santa María, La Cia Minera Copas Mole
27 24.5N, 112 19.0W, Iso W 2s (3),
dolphins.

Calvario, El
See El Calvario.

Campos, Punta
See Punta Campos.

Cape de Las Golondriuas Range Front Light
27 55.9N, 110 53.2W, Fl W 3s,
295 ft., 14 mi., truncated pyramidal metal tower, red pentagon
daymark, white center.
Also see Guaymas.

Cape de Las Golondriuas Range Rear Light
About 500 meters, 316° from
front light, 27 56.1N, 110 53.4W,
Iso W 2s, 328 ft., 14 mi., truncated
pyramidal metal tower, red pentagon daymark, white center.

Carmen, Isla del
See Isla del Carmen.

Careyes Range Front Light
19 25.0N, 105 02.0W, Fl W 3s,
75 ft., 9 mi., white cylindrical
tower, red bands.
Also see Punta Farrallón.

Careyes Range Rear Light
19 25.0N, 105 02.0W, Iso W 2s,
180 ft., 9 mi., white cylindrical
tower, red bands.

Carrizal, Morro
See Morro Carrizal.

Cedros, Isla
See Isla Cedros.

Cerralvo, Isla
See Isla Cerralvo *and* Piedras
Gordas.

Cerro Hermoso
15 57.0N, 97 32.0W, Fl R 6s, 36 ft.,
10 mi., truncated pyramidal
metal tower.

Cerro Partido (entrance to Topolobampo Harbor)
25 32.0N, 109 06.2W, Fl W 7s,
312 ft., 35 mi., white cylindrical
concrete tower.
Also see Topolobampo.

Chacala
21 10.8N, 105 15.0W, Fl (3) W 12s,
98 ft., 11 mi., truncated pyramidal aluminum tower, red and
white checkered, concrete base.

Chalacatepec, Punta
See Punta Chalacatepec.

Chichi, La
See La Chichi.

Chivato, Punta
See Punta Chivato.

Chivos, Isla
See Mazatlán.

Cholla, Punta
See Punta Cholla.

Clarion, Isla
See Isla Clarion.

Cocoraquito, Boca del
See Boca del Cocoraquito.

Colonet, Cabo
See Cabo Colonet.

Comichin, Boca de
See Boca de Comichin.

Concepción, Bahía
See Bahía Concepción.

Corbetena, Roca
See Roca Corbetena.

Coronados, Isla
See Isla Coronados.

Coronados, Islas Los
See Islas Los Coronados.

Corralero, El
See El Corralero.

Corrientes, Cabo
See Cabo Corrientes.

Coyote, Punta
See Punta Coyote.

Creston, Isla
See Isla Creston *and* Mazatlán.

Danzante, Isla
See Isla Danzante.

Don Lorenzo
24 09.2N, 110 20.4W, Fl (2) W 10s,
13 ft., 9 mi., white mast on hulk,
marks wreck *Don Lorenzo*.
Also see La Paz Harbor.

El Asadero
21 40.8N, 105 22.1W, Fl (2) W 10s,
125 ft., 12 mi., aluminum structure.

El Calvario
17 23.0N, 101 09.0W, Fl W 6s,
492 ft., 14 mi., truncated pyramidal aluminum tower.

El Corralero
16 12.5N, 98 12.1W, Fl W 6s, 66 ft.,
10 mi., truncated pyramidal
metal tower.

El Explorado
See San Lorenzo Sur.

El Recodo
See Punta Maldonado.

El Sombrerito Point
See Muleje.

Ensenada, Puerto de
See Puerto de Ensenada.

Entrada, Punta
See Punta Entrada.

Escondido, Puerto
See Puerto Escondido.

Espolon del Diablo
See Islas Marías.

ESTERO DE SAN JOSÉ (LAGUNA DE GUERRERO NEGRO)

Approach Buoy
28 09N, 114 11W, Fl W 2s, red and white striped buoy, radar reflector, bell.

Range No. 1 Front Light
28 06N, 114 07W, F Y, red triangular daymark, point down, S side of channel is marked by range of black and white banded towers showing F Bu G lights.

Range No. 1 Rear Light
495 meters, 124.1° from front light, F Y, red triangular daymark, point up, N side of channel is marked by range of beacons with black triangular daymarks showing F W lights. When dredging, temporary F W range lights are shown to northward of above. Lights are moved as channel over bar changes.

Range No. 2 Front Light
28 04N, 114 08W, F G, wooden post, dark-colored rectangular daymark.

Range No. 2 Rear Light
305 meters, 187° from front light, Q W, wooden post, dark-colored diamond daymark.

Range No. 3 Front Light
28 02N, 114 07W, F G, black beacon, rectangular daymark.

Range No. 3 Rear Light
393 meters, 164.1° from front light, Q W, black beacon, diamond daymark.

Estrella, Punta
See Punta Estrella.

Eugenia, Punta
See Punta Eugenia.

Explorado, El
See San Lorenzo Sur.

F

Falso, Cabo
See Cabo Falso Light.

Farrallón, Punta
See Punta Farrallón.

Frailes, Los
See Los Frailes.

G

Galera, Punta
See Punta Galera.

Garrobo, Punta
See Punta Garrobo.

Gemelo del Este, Islote
See Islote Gemelo del Este.

Gorda, Punta
See Punta Gorda.

Graham, Punta
See Punta Graham.

Grande, Isla
See Isla Grande.

Grifo, Punta
See Punta Grifo *and* Bahía de Acapulco.

Guadalupe, Isla
See Isla Guadalupe.

Guatemala/Mexico Border Light Front
14 31.8N, 92 13.3W, Fl W 4s, 49 ft.

Guatemala/Mexico Border Light Rear
14 31.9N, 92 13.2W, Fl W 4s, 95 ft.

GUAYMAS

Cabo Haro (approach to Guaymas, S extremity, E part of cape)
27 50.4N, 110 53.3W, Fl (3) W 20s, 351 ft., 34 mi., white square concrete tower, visible 216°–113°.

Isla Pajaros (SW extremity)
27 53.2N, 110 51.0W, Fl R 5s, 82 ft., 8 mi., white truncated pyramidal hexagonal concrete tower, visible 281°–212°.

Punta Baja
27 54.0N, 110 51.6W, Fl W 5s, 33 ft., 8 mi., white truncated pyramidal concrete tower.

Range Front Light (on W side of Isla Morrito)
27 54.7N, 110 51.5W, Fl W 3s, 33 ft., 11 mi., red pentagon daymark, white center, on concrete structure.

Range Rear Light (on Isla Tio Ramon)
About 1.38 miles, 355° from front light, 27 56.1N, 110 51.6W, Iso W 2s, 56 ft., 9 mi., red pentagon daymark, white center, on concrete structure.

Muelle de la Ardilla (W end, head)
27 54.9N, 110 52.6W, Iso R 2s, 26 ft., 10 mi., cylindrical tower.

Muelle de la Ardilla (E end)
27 54.9N, 110 52.6W, Iso G 2s, 26 ft., 10 mi., cylindrical tower.

Cape de Las Golondriuas Range Front Light
27 55.9N, 110 53.2W, Fl W 3s, 295 ft., 14 mi., truncated pyramidal metal tower, red pentagon daymark, white center.

Cape de Las Golondriuas Range Rear Light
About 500 meters, 316° from front light, 27 56.1N, 110 53.4W, Iso W 2s, 328 ft., 14 mi., truncated pyramidal metal tower, red pentagon daymark, white center.

Guerrero Negro, Laguna de
See Estero de San José.

H

Hadas Marina, Las
See Las Hadas Marina.

Haro, Cabo
See Cabo Haro *and* Guaymas.

Huanacaxtle
20 44.0N, 105 24.0W, Fl G 6s, 30 ft., 6 mi., red truncated pyramidal aluminum tower.

Huatulco
15 44N, 96 08W, Fl (3) W 18s, 197 ft., 15 mi., white octagonal concrete tower, black stripes.

I

Inocentes, Los
See Los Inocentes.

Ipala, Punta
See Punta Ipala.

Isla Altamura
24 48.0N, 108 06.4W, Fl (3) W 12s, 36 ft., 11 mi., white truncated pyramidal metal tower.

Isla Ángel de la Guarda (N side of island)
29 34N, 113 33W, Fl W 6s, 79 ft., 11 mi., aluminum tower.

Isla Ángel de la Guarda (point)
29 00N, 113 09W, Fl (2) W 10s, 89 ft., 11 mi., metal tower.

Isla Ballena (SW end)
24 28.7N, 110 24.1W, Fl W 6s, 39 ft., 11 mi., truncated pyramidal metal tower.

Isla del Carmen
25 49.6N, 111 14.3W, Fl (2) W 10s, 39 ft., 11 mi., truncated pyramidal metal tower.

Isla Cedros

Northeast Point
28 21.8N, 115 11.6W, Fl (4) W 16s, 36 ft., 10 mi., white pyramidal masonry tower.

Breakwater
28 22N, 115 12W, Fl R 5s, 35 ft., 5 mi., metal tower.

Pier
28 22N, 115 12W, Fl G 5s, 35 ft., 5 mi., metal tower.

Punta del Morro Redondo
28 02.6N, 115 11.1W, Fl W 6s, 72 ft., 10 mi., metal pyramidal tower.

Isla Cerralvo (S point)
24 08.2N, 109 47.5W, Fl (4) W 16s, 69 ft., 11 mi., truncated pyramidal metal tower.
Also see Piedras Gordas.

Isla Chivos
See Mazatlán.

Isla Clarion
18 20.8N, 114 44.2W, Fl W 6s, 115 ft., 11 mi., truncated pyramidal metal tower.

Isla Coronados
26 06.3N, 111 16.3W, Fl (3) W 12s, 121 ft., 11 mi., truncated pyramidal metal tower.

Isla Creston (summit)
23 10.6N, 106 25.7W, Fl W 7s, 515 ft., 33 mi., white square masonry tower, visible 310°–140°, F R on radio mast at Mazatlán appears to vessels to S to be of same height as this light, racon: C (-·-·) 20 mi.
Also see Mazatlán.

Isla Danzante

East
25 48.3N, 111 15.7W, Fl W 6s, 43 ft., 11 mi., white truncated pyramidal tower.

South
25 45.7N, 111 15.0W, Fl (2) W 10s, 30 ft., 11 mi., truncated pyramidal metal tower.

North
25 49.0N, 111 16.1W, Fl (4) W 16s, 43 ft., 11 mi., truncated pyramidal metal tower.

Isla Grande (Piedra Ahogada)
17 40.7N, 101 40.0W, Fl W 6s, 39 ft., 14 mi., white truncated pyramidal aluminum tower.

Isla Guadalupe

Isla Guadalupe Light
28 59N, 118 19W, Fl (4) W 16s, 157 ft., 10 mi., metal pyramidal tower.

North Side
29 09N, 118 16W, Fl (2) W 10s, 45 ft., 9 mi., metal pyramidal tower.

South Side
28 53N, 118 17W, Fl (3) W 12s, 124 ft., 10 mi., metal pyramidal tower.

Isla Isabela
21 50.0N, 105 52.8W, Fl (4) W 16s, 180 ft., 11 mi., truncated pyramidal aluminum tower, red and white checkered concrete base.

Isla Las Ánimas
25 06.4N, 110 31.5W, Fl (3) W 12s, 161 ft., 11 mi., truncated pyramidal metal tower.

Isla Las Galeras (N)
25 44.2N, 111 03.0W, Fl W 6s, 56 ft., 11 mi., truncated pyramidal metal tower.

Isla Lobos (NW point)
27 19.5N, 110 34.0W, Fl W 6s, 82 ft., 14 mi., white truncated pyramidal metal tower, racon: K (-·-) 20 mi.
Also see Bahía Lobos.

Islas Los Coronados (cove on NE end of island)
32 24.8N, 117 14.7W, Fl (2) W 10s, 246 ft., 10 mi., white octagonal concrete tower, visible 169°–341°, racon: C (-·-·) 20 mi.

Islas Los Coronados (on S end of Island)
32 24N, 117 14W, Fl (3) W 12s, 157 ft., 10 mi., white concrete tower, visible 263°–155°, North Coronado Island obscures the light 135°–139°, and Middle Coronado Island obscures it 148°–151°.

Isla de Los Pelicanos
21 03.0N, 105 17.0W, Fl (2) W 10s, 108 ft., 10 mi., cylindrical concrete tower.

Isla Mangrove, Range Front Light
24 32.5N, 111 49.3W, Fl W 3s, 72 ft., 8 mi., white metal tower.
Also see Bahía Magdalena.

Isla Mangrove, Range Rear Light
About 594 meters, 087° from front light, 24 32.5N, 111 48.9W, Iso W 2s, 89 ft., 8 mi., white metal tower.

Islas Marías

Isla San Juanito
21 45.5N, 106 40.6W, Fl W 6s, 171 ft., 14 mi., white truncated pyramidal metal tower.

Isla María Madre, Balleto Point
21 37.0N, 106 32.2W, Fl (2) W 10s,
203 ft., 15 mi., white cylindrical
concrete tower, visible 165°–314°.

Espolon del Diablo
21 36.0N, 106 37.0W, Fl (3) W 12s,
33 ft., 13 mi., truncated pyramidal metal tower.

Balleto Anchorage North (head of molc)
21 38.5N, 106 33.3W, Iso R 2s,
39 ft., 10 mi., red iron column.

Balleto Anchorage South (head of mole)
21 38.5N, 106 33.3W, Iso R 2s,
39 ft., 10 mi., red iron column.

Isla María Cleofas
21 17.3N, 106 13.9W, Fl (4) W 16s,
492 ft., 14 mi., white truncated
pyramidal metal tower.

Isla Marieta
20 41.0N, 105 36.6W, Fl (2) W 10s,
75 ft., 11 mi., red truncated pyramidal metal tower.

Isla Marieta, La Redonda
20 41.0N, 105 36.6W, Fl (3) W 12s,
282 ft., 11 mi., red truncated
pyramidal metal tower.

Isla Miramar
30 06.3N, 114 36.8W, Fl (2) W 10s,
66 ft., 10 mi., concrete tower, red
and white bands.

Isla Monserrat
25 38.5N, 111 03.0W, Fl (4) W 16s,
66 ft., 11 mi., truncated pyramidal metal tower.

Isla Montague
31 41.0N, 114 42.0W, Fl (2) W 10s,
46 ft., 10 mi., truncated pyramidal metal tower.

Isla Natividad (SE side)
27 52.4N, 115 10.6W, Fl (2) W 10s,
364 ft., 20 mi., cylindrical masonry tower, dwelling, obscured
122°–137°.

Isla Pajaros (SW extremity)
27 53.2N, 110 51.0W, Fl R 5s,
82 ft., 8 mi., white truncated
pyramidal hexagonal concrete
tower, visible 281°–212°.
Also see Guaymas.

Isla Partida (on islet to N)
24 35.5N, 110 23.8W, Fl (2) W 10s,
131 ft., 12 mi., truncated pyramidal metal tower.

Isla Patos
29 16.4N, 112 27.0W, Fl (2) W 10s,
233 ft., 14 mi., white cylindrical
concrete tower.

Isla Pelicano
28 49.0N, 111 59.2W, Fl W 6s,
39 ft., 11 mi., truncated pyramidal metal tower.

Islas Revillagigedo
See Isla Socorro *and* Isla Clarion.

Islas San Benito (NW side of island)
28 18.9N, 115 35.7W, Fl (3) W 20s,
426 ft., 30 mi., white cylindrical
concrete tower, racon: B (-···),
30 mi.

Islas San Benito (S side of W island)
28 18N, 115 35W, Fl W 6s, 118 ft.,
9 mi., white cylindrical masonry
tower.

Isla San Diego
25 12.0N, 110 42.2W, Fl (3) W 12s,
66 ft., 11 mi., truncated pyramidal metal tower.

Isla San Esteban
28 42.8N, 112 32.2W, Fl W 6s,
56 ft., 11 mi., white truncated
pyramidal metal tower.

Isla San Ildefonso
26 37.9N, 111 26.5W, Fl (4) W 16s,
56 ft., 11 mi., truncated pyramidal aluminum tower.

Isla San Jerónimo
29 48N, 115 48W, Fl (2) W 10s,
154 ft., 11 mi., white hexagonal
masonry tower.

Isla San Jorge
31 01.0N, 113 15.3W, Fl (4) W 16s,
273 ft., 11 mi., cylindrical concrete tower.

Isla de San José (on Punta Colorado)
25 01.4N, 110 35.7W, Fl (2) W 10s,
141 ft., 10 mi., truncated pyramidal metal tower.

Isla San Juanito
21 45.5N, 106 40.6W, Fl W 6s,
171 ft., 14 mi., white truncated
pyramidal metal tower.
Also see Islas Marías.

Isla San Lorenzo
28 35.2N, 112 46.0W, Fl (3) W 12s,
46 ft., 11 mi., concrete tower.

Isla San Marcos
27 12.1N, 112 06.2W, Fl (3) W 12s,
26 ft., 11 mi., truncated pyramidal metal tower.

Isla de San Martín
30 29N, 116 07W, Fl (2) W 10s,
164 ft., 10 mi., metal pyramidal
tower.

Isla San Pedro Martir
28 23.0N, 112 20.0W, Fl (4) W 16s,
279 ft., 11 mi., white truncated
pyramidal metal tower.

Isla San Pedro Nolasco
27 57.7N, 111 22.1W, Fl (3) W 12s,
62 ft., 11 mi., truncated pyramidal aluminum tower.

Isla San Roque
27 08.8N, 114 22.5W, Fl (2) W 10s,
92 ft., 10 mi., red truncated pyramidal metal tower.

Isla Santa Catalina
25 35.5N, 110 47.1W, Fl (3) W 12s,
220 ft., 11 mi., white truncated
pyramidal metal tower.

Isla Santa Cruz
25 15.7N, 110 44.2W, Fl (2) W 10s,
39 ft., 11 mi., truncated pyramidal tower.

Isla Socorro
18 42.7N, 110 57.0W, Fl (3) W 12s,
59 ft., 14 mi., truncated pyramidal metal tower.

Isla de Soto (W side)
23 12.5N, 106 24.3W, Fl G 3s, 22 ft.,
6 mi., green concrete column.
Also see Mazatlán.

Isla Tiburón
See Punta Willard.

Islas de Todos Santos (NW end of N island)
31 48.5N, 116 48.7W, Fl W 7s,
161 ft., 22 mi., truncated conical
tower, red and white bands,
racon: X (-··-), 20 mi.

Islas de Todos Santos (on S end of S island)
31 48N, 116 48W, Fl (3) W 12s, 112 ft., 10 mi., white concrete tower, visible 194°–115°.

Isla Tortugas (N side of island)
27 27.3N, 111 53.9W, Fl (3) W 12s, 105 ft., 11 mi., truncated pyramidal metal tower.

Isla Tortugas (S side of island)
27 26.7N, 111 52.9W, Fl (4) W 16s, 79 ft., 11 mi., truncated pyramidal aluminum tower.

Isla Turner
28 43.4N, 112 19.5W, Fl (2) W 10s, 256 ft., 11 mi., white cylindrical concrete tower.

Isla de las Viejas
See Bahía de Yavaros.

Isla Willard
29 49N, 114 25W, Fl (3) W 12s, 82 ft., 10 mi., metal tower.
Also see Punta Willard.

Islote Gemelo del Este
28 58N, 113 28W, Fl (2) W 10s, 30 ft., 11 mi., metal tower, red bands.

Islote de la Reina (Seal Rock)
24 26.3N, 109 57.5W, Fl W 6s, 46 ft., 11 mi., white cylindrical metal tower.

Izuca, Punta
See Puerto Ángel.

K

Kelp, Punta
See Punta Kelp.

L

La Bonanza
24 27.5N, 110 18.0W, Fl W 6s, 39 ft., 11 mi., truncated pyramidal metal tower.

La Chichi

La Chichi Light
16 11.0N, 94 27.8W, Fl (2) W 10s, 49 ft., 12 mi., cylindrical concrete tower.

Muelle Fiscal
16 10.4N, 95 12.0W, Fl R 5s, 19 ft., 7 mi., cylindrical concrete tower.

Puente Fiscal
16 10.4N, 95 12.0W, Fl G 5s, 19 ft., 7 mi., cylindrical concrete tower.

La Lobera
27 16.0N, 112 06.9W, Fl R 6s, 56 ft., 7 mi., truncated pyramidal metal tower.

La Paz Harbor

First Range Front Light
24 12.5N, 110 18.0W, Fl W 3s, 49 ft., 10 mi., white square stone tower.

First Range Rear Light
About 164 meters, 147° from front light, 24 12.5N, 110 18.0W, Iso W 2s, 62 ft., 10 mi., white square concrete tower.

Second Range Front Light
24 10.6N, 110 18.2W, Fl W 3s, 59 ft., 10 mi., white square stone tower.

Second Range Rear Light
About 914 meters, 181° from front light, 24 10.4N, 110 18.2W, Iso W 2s, 62 ft., 10 mi., white square stone tower.

Third Range Front Light
24 11.3N, 110 18.1W, Fl W 3s, 105 ft., 11 mi., white square stone tower.

Third Range Rear Light
About 183 meters, 027° from front, 24 11.4N, 110 18.1W, Iso W 2s, 125 ft., 17 mi., white square stone tower, seaward face white.

T-Wharf (E head)
24 09.7N, 110 19.2W, Iso G 2s, 26 ft., 6 mi., white truncated conical masonry tower, green bands.

T-Wharf (W head)
24 09.7N, 110 19.2W, Iso R 2s, 28 ft., 6 mi., white truncated cylindrical masonry tower, red bands.

Don Lorenzo
24 09.2N, 110 20.4W, Fl (2) W 10s, 13 ft., 9 mi., white mast on hulk, marks wreck *Don Lorenzo*.

La Redonda
20 41.0N, 105 36.6W, Fl (3) W 12s, 282 ft., 11 mi., red truncated pyramidal metal tower.
Also see Isla Marieta.

La Reforma
25 08.0N, 108 14.0W, Fl (2) W 10s, 46 ft., 12 mi., truncated pyramidal aluminum tower.

La Roqueta (N point of island)
16 49.1N, 99 54.9W, Fl W 2s, 75 ft., 7 mi., white cylindrical concrete tower, black bands.

La Roqueta (center)
16 48.9N, 99 54.7W, Fl W 10s, 377 ft., 25 mi., white concrete tower, visible 220°–137°, racon: Q (---·-) 20 mi.

La Soledad (Gulf of California)
30 49.0N, 113 07.0W, Fl (3) W 12s, 49 ft., 11 mi., truncated pyramidal aluminum tower.

La Soledad (Gulf of Tehuantepec)
16 04.1N, 94 09.3W, Fl W 6s, 49 ft., 12 mi., white concrete tower, red diagonal bands.

La Solitaria (Piedras Negras)
17 35.5N, 101 33.5W, Fl (2) W 10s, 62 ft., 14 mi., white truncated pyramidal aluminum tower.

La Tonina, Punta
See Punta La Tonina.

Laguna de Guerrero Negro
See Estero de San José.

Las Ánimas, Isla
See Isla Las Ánimas.

Las Dos Piedras (White Rocks, off N point of St. Lucia Bay, W rock)
16 50.3N, 99 54.6W, Fl (2) W 10s, 16 ft., 7 mi., red cylindrical concrete tower, hut.
Also see Bahía de Acapulco.

Las Galeras, Isla
See Isla Las Galeras.

Las Golondriuas Range
See Guaymas.

Las Guásimas
27 49.0N, 110 36.5W, Fl (2) W 10s, 33 ft., 9 mi., truncated pyramidal metal tower.

Las Hadas Marina (N breakwater)
19 05.9N, 104 20.8W, Fl R 5s,
23 ft., 5 mi., cylindrical concrete
tower.

Las Hadas Marina (S breakwater)
19 05.9N, 104 20.7W, Fl G 5s,
23 ft., 5 mi., cylindrical concrete
tower.

Las Loberas
24 50.2N, 110 34.6W, Fl (3) W 12s,
36 ft., 11 mi., truncated pyramidal metal tower.

LÁZARO CÁRDENAS

Lázaro Cárdenas Light
17 55.3N, 102 10.1W, Fl W 7s,
131 ft., 18 mi., white concrete
tower, blue bands.

**Canal Industrial Range Front
Light**
17 56.7N, 102 10.3W, Fl W 3s,
33 ft., 9 mi., gray truncated pyramidal metal tower.

Canal Industrial Range Rear Light
17 56.7N, 102 10.3W, Iso W 2s,
43 ft., 9 mi., gray truncated pyramidal metal tower.

East Breakwater
17 55.6N, 102 09.8W, Fl R 5s, 30 ft.,
5 mi., white truncated pyramidal
metal tower, blue bands.

West Breakwater
17 55.3N, 102 09.8W, Fl G 5s, 30 ft.,
5 mi., white truncated pyramidal
metal tower, blue bands.

East Side
17 56.1N, 102 10.6W, Fl R 6s,
26 ft., 4 mi., red truncated pyramidal metal tower.

West Side
17 55.8N, 102 10.6W, Fl G 6s,
20 ft., 4 mi., green cylindrical
metal post.

Range Front Light
17 56.3N, 102 11.2W, Fl W 3s,
49 ft., 9 mi., truncated pyramidal
metal tower.

Range Rear Light
About 310 meters, 302° from
front light, 17 56.4N, 102 11.3W,
Iso W 2s, 66 ft., 9 mi., truncated
pyramidal metal tower.

North Mole
17 56.4N, 102 10.8W, Iso R 2s,
26 ft., 4 mi., cylindrical tower.

South Mole
17 56.0N, 102 10.9W, Iso R 2s,
26 ft., 4 mi., cylindrical tower.

Lesna, Punta
See Punta Lesna.

Libertad, Puerto
See Puerto Libertad.

Lobos, Bahía
See Bahía Lobos.

Lobos, Cabo
See Cabo Lobos.

Lobos, Isla
See Isla Lobos.

Lobos, Punta
See Punta Lobos.

Lobos, Roca
See Roca Lobos.

Lopez, Puerto
See Puerto Lopez.

Lorenz, Punta
See Punta Lorenz.

Loreto, Port
See Port Loreto.

Los Frailes (SE rock)
19 04.6N, 104 23.5W, Fl (2) W 10s,
36 ft., 11 mi., cylindrical fiberglass tower.

Los Inocentes
23 46.0N, 110 40.7W, Fl (4) W 16s,
43 ft., 14 mi., white cylindrical
concrete tower, red bands.

Los Pelicanos, Isla de
See Isla de Los Pelicanos.

M

Macepule, Boca de
See Boca de Macepule.

Madero, Puerto
See Puerto Madero.

Magdalena, Bahía
See Bahía Magdalena.

Maldonado, Punta
See Punta Maldonado.

Man of War Cove (on mole)
24 38.4N, 112 08.9W, Fl (2) W 10s,
56 ft., 8 mi., truncated pyramidal
aluminum tower.
Also see Bahía Magdalena.

Mangrove, Isla
See Isla Mangrove.

MANZANILLO

Also see San Pedrito.

Head of Breakwater
19 03.7N, 104 18.9W, Fl R 5s,
52 ft., 7 mi., cylindrical concrete
tower.

North Breakwater
19 03.7N, 104 18.3W, Fl G 5s,
39 ft., 7 mi., cylindrical concrete
column.

South Breakwater
19 03.6N, 104 18.3W, Fl R 5s,
33 ft., 7 mi., cylindrical concrete
tower.

Marcy Channel Range Front Light
24 27.8N, 111 48.7W, Fl W 3s,
39 ft., 8 mi., white tower.
Also see Bahía Magdalena.

Marcy Channel Range Rear Light
907 meters, 154° from front light,
24 26.4N, 111 48.5W, Iso W 2s,
56 ft., 8 mi., white truncated
pyramidal metal tower.

Marguis, Punta
See Punta Marguis.

Marías, Islas
See Islas Marías.

Marieta, Isla
See Isla Marieta.

MAZATLÁN

Isla Creston (summit)
23 10.6N, 106 25.7W, Fl W 7s,
515 ft., 33 mi., white square
masonry tower, visible 310°–140°,
F R on radio mast at Mazatlán
appears to vessels to S to be of
same height as this light, racon:
C (-·-·) 20 mi.

Piedra Negra
23 10.0N, 106 25.1W, Fl (2) W 10s,
26 ft., 14 mi., white square concrete column, concrete base.

Isla Chivos (E breakwater)
23 10.7N, 106 25.1W, Fl R 5s, 52 ft., 13 mi., red concrete column.

West Breakwater
23 10.8N, 106 25.2W, Fl G 5s, 52 ft., 13 mi., green concrete column.

North Breakwater
23 11.1N, 106 25.1W, Fl Y 3s, 10 ft., 5 mi., white cylindrical metal column.

Playa Sur
23 11.3N, 106 25.0W, Fl G 3s, 20 ft., 9 mi., port, green, topmark.

Tourist Mole
23 11.3N, 106 25.0W, Fl G 3s, 30 ft., 9 mi., green cylindrical metal column.

Harbor Channel Range Front Light
23 12.6N, 106 24.4W, Fl W 3s, 52 ft., 17 mi., orange truncated pyramidal metal tower.

Harbor Channel Range Rear Light
1,450 meters, 018.5° from front light, 23 13.4N, 106 24.2W, Iso W 2s, 157 ft., 17 mi., orange truncated pyramidal metal tower.

Piedra Blanca
23 11.6N, 106 24.7W, Fl R 3s, 30 ft., 9 mi., red truncated pyramidal concrete tower.

Harbor Canal Range Front Light
23 12.7N, 106 23.8W, Fl W 3s, 55 ft., 17 mi., metal tower.

Harbor Canal Range Rear Light
Iso W 2s, 61 ft., 17 mi., metal tower.

Harbor Entrance Channel Range Front Light
23 12.8N, 106 24.1W, Fl W 3s, 56 ft., 17 mi., orange truncated pyramidal metal tower.

Harbor Entrance Channel Range Rear Light
500 meters, 023° from front light, 23 13.1N, 106 24.0W, Iso W 2s, 69 ft., 17 mi., orange truncated pyramidal metal tower.

Isla de Soto (W side)
23 12.5N, 106 24.3W, Fl G 3s, 22 ft., 6 mi., green concrete column.

Miramar, Isla
See Isla Miramar.

Mita, Punta de
See Punta de Mita.

Monserrat, Isla
See Isla Monserrat.

Montague, Isla
See Isla Montague.

Morro Ayutla
15 52.5N, 95 46.8W, Fl (4) W 16s, 138 ft., 21 mi., white cylindrical concrete tower, dwelling.

Morro Carrizal
19 05.1N, 104 26.4W, Fl (2) W 10s, 89 ft., 11 mi., truncated pyramidal metal tower.

Morro Carrizal, Nearby Aviation Light
19 09N, 104 33W, Al W G 10s, 15 mi.

Morro Papanoa
17 16.1N, 101 03.2W, Fl (2) W 10s, 427 ft., 14 mi., aluminum truncated pyramidal tower.

Morro Redondo, Punta del
See Punta del Morro Redondo *and* Isla Cedros.

Morro de Salinas
16 09.7N, 95 12.2W, Fl W 5s, 272 ft., 23 mi., white octagonal concrete tower, dwelling, visible 265°–048°.
Also see Salina Cruz.

Morro de Santo Domingo
28 15.4N, 114 07.3W, Fl (4) W 16s, 125 ft., 10 mi., white cylindrical concrete tower.

Muleje (on El Sombrerito Point)
26 53.9N, 111 58.1W, Fl (4) W 16s, 138 ft., 10 mi., square concrete tower, white house, visible 181°–273°.

N

Natividad, Isla
See Isla Natividad.

Negra, Cabeza
See Cabeza Negra.

Negra, Punta
See Punta Negra.

Negra, Roca
See Roca Negra.

Nexpa
16 35.7N, 99 04.5W, Fl W 6s, 39 ft., 10 mi., truncated pyramidal aluminum tower.

O

Ostiones, Punta de los
See Punta de los Ostiones.

P

Pabellon, Boca de
See Boca de Pabellon.

Pajaros, Isla
See Isla Pajaros *and* Guaymas.

Papanoa, Morro
See Morro Papanoa.

Paredon
16 02.7N, 93 52.5W, Fl (2) W 10s, 30 ft., 11 mi., cylindrical concrete tower.

Partida, Isla
See Isla Partida.

Patos, Isla
See Isla Patos.

Pelicano, Isla
See Isla Pelicano.

Pelicanos, Isla de Los
See Isla de Los Pelicanos.

PEÑASCO, PUERTO
See Puerto Peñasco.

Pequeña, Punta
See Punta Pequeña.

Perihuete
25 11.5N, 108 23.6W, Fl (4) W 16s, 75 ft., 13 mi., white truncated pyramidal metal tower.

Piaxtla, Punta
See Punta Piaxtla.

Pichilingue, Bahía
See Bahía Pichilingue.

Piedra Ahogada
See Isla Grande.

Piedras Ahogadade (on rock)
16 47.8N, 99 50.7W, Fl (2) W 10s, 16 ft., 9 mi., white aluminum tower.

Piedras Ahogadade, Nearby Aviation Light
16 46N, 99 46W, Al W G.

Piedra Blanca
27 14.2N, 112 07.7W, Fl (2) W 10s, 52 ft., 11 mi., truncated pyramidal metal tower.

Piedras Gordas (on SW point of Isla Cerralvo)
24 09.2N, 109 50.8W, Fl (2) W 10s, 69 ft., 11 mi., truncated pyramidal metal tower.
Also see Isla Cerralvo.

Piedra Negra
23 10.0N, 106 25.1W, Fl (2) W 10s, 26 ft., 14 mi., white square concrete column, concrete base.
Also see Mazatlán.

Piedras Negras
See La Solitaria.

Port Loreto (E of Loreto)
26 00.6N, 111 20.8W, Fl (2) W 10s, 39 ft., 11 mi., truncated pyramidal aluminum tower.

Prieta, Punta
See Punta Prieta.

Puertecitos
30 26N, 114 37W, Fl (4) W 16s, 49 ft., 10 mi., metal tower.

Puerto de Altata
24 37.0N, 107 55.0W, Fl W 6s, 46 ft., 12 mi., truncated pyramidal aluminum tower.

PUERTO ÁNGEL

Puerto Ángel Light (on Punta Izuca)
15 38.6N, 96 31.2W, Fl W 5s, 184 ft., 24 mi., white octagonal concrete tower, dwelling, visible 266°/094°.

Range Front Light
15 39.5N, 96 31.2W, Fl W 3s, 26 ft., 8 mi., truncated pyramidal metal tower.

Range Rear Light
15 39.5N, 96 31.2W, Iso W 2s, 33 ft., 8 mi., truncated pyramidal metal tower.

Wharf
15 39.5N, 96 31.3W, Iso G 2s, 15 ft., 7 mi., truncated pyramidal concrete tower.

Wharf
15 39.5N, 96 31.3W, Iso G 2s, 15 ft., 7 mi., truncated pyramidal concrete tower.

Puerto Arista
15 56.5N, 93 49.8W, Fl (2) W 10s, 79 ft., 17 mi., white cylindrical concrete tower, visible 288°–122°, dwelling.

PUERTO DE ENSENADA

Head of West Breakwater
31 50.4N, 116 37.7W, Fl G 5s, 49 ft., 7 mi., truncated pyramidal tower.

Head of East Breakwater
31 50.4N, 116 37.5W, Fl R 5s, 33 ft., 7 mi., truncated pyramidal aluminum tower.

No. 2
31 51N, 116 38W, Fl R 5s, 33 ft., metal tower.

Puerto Escondido
15 51.0N, 97 04.5W, Fl (2) W 10s, 131 ft., 20 mi., white octagonal concrete tower.

Puerto Libertad
29 54.0N, 112 45.5W, L Fl W 10s, 43 ft., 11 mi., white cylindrical metal tower.

Puerto Lopez
25 12.0N, 112 08.8W, Fl W 6s, 43 ft., 10 mi., white cylindrical concrete tower, red bands.

PUERTO MADERO

Puerto Madero Light
14 42.7N, 92 25.0W, Fl W 5s, 79 ft., 23 mi., white cylindrical concrete tower, red bands.

West Breakwater
14 42.0N, 92 24.7W, Fl G 5s, 33 ft., 8 mi., truncated pyramidal metal tower.

East Breakwater
14 41.7N, 92 24.6W, Fl R 5s, 33 ft., 8 mi., truncated pyramidal metal tower.

Entrance Range Front Light
14 42.6N, 92 23.9W, Fl W 3s, 69 ft., 14 mi., white cylindrical concrete tower.

Entrance Range Rear Light
250 meters, 044° from front light, 14 42.7N, 92 23.8W, Iso W 2s, 79 ft., 15 mi., white cylindrical concrete tower.

Muelle de Pesca, No. 1
14 44.3N, 92 25.1W, Iso R 2s, 15 ft., 9 mi., red tubular tower.

Muelle de Pesca Range Front Light
14 42.2N, 92 23.5W, Fl W 3s, 49 ft., 13 mi., truncated pyramidal metal tower.

Muelle de Pesca Range Rear Light
250 meters, 099° from front light, 14 42.1N, 92 23.3W, Iso W 2s, 66 ft., 13 mi., truncated pyramidal metal tower.

Muelle Fiscal, No. 1
14 42.7N, 92 24.3W, Iso G 2s, 15 ft., 9 mi., green tubular tower.

Muelle Fiscal Range Front Light
14 43.3N, 92 24.2W, Fl W 3s, 52 ft., 13 mi., truncated pyramidal metal tower.

Muelle Fiscal Range Rear Light
270 meters, 006° from front light, 14 43.5N, 92 24.2W, Iso W 2s, 62 ft., 13 mi., truncated pyramidal metal tower.

El Gancho Range Front Light
14 33.0N, 92 15.0W, Fl W 3s, 69 ft., 14 mi., white cylindrical concrete tower.

El Gancho Range Rear Light
30 meters, 270° from front light, 14 33.0N, 92 15.0W, Iso W 2s, 79 ft., 15 mi., white cylindrical concrete tower.

Puerto Peñasco

Puerto Peñasco Light
31 17.1N, 113 34.7W, Fl W 8s,
318 ft., 28 mi., white octagonal
concrete tower.

Range Front Light
31 18.2N, 113 32.6W, Fl W 3s,
33 ft., 8 mi., truncated pyramidal
metal tower.

Range Rear Light
About 146 meters, 116° from
front light, 31 18.2N, 113 32.6W,
Iso W 2s, 66 ft., 11 mi., truncated
pyramidal metal tower.

Range Front Light
31 18.0N, 113 33.0W, Fl W 3s,
69 ft., 11 mi., truncated pyramidal metal tower, red stripes.

Range Rear Light
31 18.0N, 113 33.0W, Iso W 2s,
98 ft., 11 mi., truncated pyramidal metal tower red stripes.

East Breakwater
31 18.4N, 113 32.9W, Fl G 5s,
33 ft., 8 mi., metal tower.

West Breakwater
31 18.3N, 113 33.1W, Fl R 5s,
33 ft., 8 mi., metal tower.

Puerto de San Carlos, Muelle Fical
24 47.3N, 112 07.4W, Iso W 2s,
66 ft., 8 mi., square metal tower.
Also see Bahía Magdalena.

Puerto Vallarta

Range Front Light
20 39.5N, 105 14.5W, Fl W 3s,
43 ft., 9 mi., white truncated pyramidal metal tower, red bands.

Range Rear Light
140 meters, 053° from front light,
20 39.5N, 105 14.4W, Iso W 2s,
56 ft., 9 mi., white truncated pyramidal metal tower, red bands.

Inner Breakwater (N head)
20 39.3N, 105 15.3W, Fl G 5s,
36 ft., 7 mi., green cylindrical
concrete tower.

Inner Breakwater (S Head)
20 39.2N, 105 14.7W, Fl R 5s,
43 ft., 7 mi., red truncated pyramidal metal tower.

Range Front Light
20 39.4N, 105 15.2W, Fl W 3s,
20 ft., 5 mi., white cylindrical
metal structure, red bands.

Range Rear Light
270° from front light, 20 39.4N,
105 15.2W, Iso W 2s, 20 ft., 5 mi.,
white cylindrical metal structure,
red bands.

Puerto Vicente (N breakwater)
17 16.8N, 101 03.0W, Fl R 5s,
35 ft., 13 mi., white truncated
pyramidal metal tower.

Puerto Vicente (S breakwater)
17 16.8N, 101 03.1W, Fl G 5s,
36 ft., 13 mi., white truncated
pyramidal metal tower.

Puerto Yavaros

Bahía de Yavaros, Isla de las Viejas
26 42.0N, 109 32.1W, Fl W 6s,
112 ft., 20 mi., white cylindrical
concrete tower, black bands,
visible 306°–077°.

Range Front Light
26 40.4N, 109 29.8W, Fl W 3s,
33 ft., 11 mi., white truncated
pyramidal metal tower.

Range Rear Light
0.5 mile, 000° from front light,
26 40.4N, 109 29.8W, Iso W 2s,
46 ft., 11 mi., white truncated
pyramidal metal tower.

Bajos de la Lobera
26 40.0N, 109 30.0W, Fl G 5s,
36 ft., 8 mi., truncated pyramidal
metal tower.

No. 3
26 41.8N, 109 30.4W, Fl W 3s,
26 ft., 11 mi., white truncated
pyramidal metal tower.

Punta Abreojos
26 45.0N, 113 34.2W, Fl (3) W 12s,
82 ft., 11 mi., truncated pyramidal concrete tower.

Punta Agujas
26 52.0N, 111 52.0W, Fl (2) W 10s,
56 ft., 11 mi., truncated pyramidal metal tower.

Punta Arboleda
26 50.0N, 109 50.9W, Fl (2) W 10s,
49 ft., 11 mi., white truncated
pyramidal metal tower.

Punta Arena, Sur
23 33.3N, 102 28.3W, Fl (4) W 16s,
66 ft., 15 mi., white truncated
conical concrete tower, black
bands, masonry house, visible
150°–324°.

Punta Arena de la Ventana
24 03.2N, 109 49.6W, Fl (3) W 12s,
49 ft., 11 mi., white cylindrical
concrete tower.

Punta Arenas
28 57.3N, 113 32.5W, Fl (4) W 16s,
43 ft., 11 mi., white cylindrical
concrete tower, red bands.

Punta Azufre
30 23.8N, 115 59.2W, Fl (3) W 12s,
42 ft., 9 mi., metal pyramidal
tower.

Punta Baja
29 57N, 115 49W, Fl (4) W 16s,
38 ft., 10 mi., metal pyramidal
tower.

Punta Baja
28 28.2N, 111 42.6W, Fl (3) W 12s,
39 ft., 11 mi., white truncated
pyramidal metal tower.

Punta Banda
31 45N, 116 45W, Fl (2) W 10s,
49 ft., 10 mi., white masonry
tower.

Punta Blanca
29 06N, 114 42W, Fl (2) W 10s,
81 ft., 10 mi., metal pyramidal
tower.

Punta Borrascosa
31 30.0N, 114 03.1W, Fl (2) W 10s,
43 ft., 11 mi., white cylindrical
concrete tower, red bands.

Punta Brujas
16 48.5N, 99 52.8W, Fl (2) W 10s,
131 ft., 20 mi., white truncated
pyramidal metal tower, red band,
visible 320°–094°.

Punta Cabras
31 20.0N, 116 28.0W, Fl W, 11 mi.

Punta Campos
19 01.3N, 104 20.0W, Fl W 5s,
358 ft., 26 mi., white octagonal
concrete tower, dwelling.

Punta Chalacatepec
19 41.0N, 105 16.0W, Fl (3) W 12s, 39 ft., cylindrical concrete structure.

Punta Chivato
27 05.5N, 111 58.3W, Fl (4) W 16s, 59 ft., 11 mi., truncated pyramidal metal tower.

Punta Cholla
26 00.0N, 111 10.7W, Fl W 6s, 39 ft., 11 mi., truncated pyramidal metal tower.

Punta Colorado
See Isla de San José.

Punta Coyote
24 21.0N, 110 23.0W, Fl (3) W 12s, 38 ft., 11 mi., metal tower.

Punta Coyote
25 48.5N, 111 18.3W, Fl W 6s, 26 ft., 11 mi., truncated pyramidal metal tower.

Punta Entrada
30 22N, 115 59W, Fl W 6s, 38 ft., 10 mi., metal pyramidal tower.

Punta Estrella
30 55.0N, 114 43.0W, Fl (3) W 12s, 89 ft., 10 mi., white cylindrical concrete tower.

Punta Eugenia
27 50.8N, 115 04.7W, Fl (3) W 12s, 46 ft., 10 mi., white pyramidal masonry tower, obscured by Isla Natividad 090°–113°.

Punta Farrallón
19 22.5N, 105 01.5W, Fl (2) W 10s, 203 ft., 23 mi., white cylindrical concrete tower.

Punta Galera
15 56.9N, 97 42.0W, Fl (3) W 12s, 105 ft., 12 mi., truncated pyramidal metal tower.

Punta Garrobo
17 37.0N, 101 33.0W, Fl (3) W 12s, 377 ft., 18 mi., square concrete tower, white house, visible 270°–132°.

Punta Gorda
17 32.0N, 101 27.0W, Fl (4) W 16s, 394 ft., 14 mi., truncated pyramidal aluminum tower.

Punta Graham
19 10.6N, 104 41.5W, Fl (3) W 12s, 656 ft., 21 mi., square concrete tower, visible 289°–135°.

Punta Grifo
16 49.8N, 99 53.8W, Fl (3) W 12s, 115 ft., 10 mi., white truncated pyramidal concrete tower. *Also see* Bahía de Acapulco.

Punta Ipala
20 13.5N, 105 35.5W, Fl (4) W 16s, 315 ft., 11 mi., white truncated pyramidal metal tower.

Punta Izuca
See Puerto Ángel.

Punta Kelp
27 40.0N, 114 54.0W, Fl (4) W 16s, 105 ft., 10 mi., truncated pyramidal metal framework tower.

Punta La Tonina
24 30.2N, 107 40.6W, Fl (2) W 10s, 49 ft., 12 mi., metal tower.

Punta Lesna
28 12.2N, 111 23.0W, Fl (2) W 10s, 154 ft., 11 mi., truncated pyramidal metal tower.

Punta Lobos
26 04.1N, 111 05.6W, Fl (4) W 16s, 33 ft., 14 mi., cylindrical concrete tower.

Punta Lorenz
16 49.3N, 99 55.2W, Fl W 3s, 118 ft., 10 mi., white cylindrical concrete tower, red bands, visible 021°–141°.

Punta Maldonado (on El Recodo)
16 19.8N, 98 35.0W, Fl (2) W 10s, 130 ft., 15 mi., square white concrete tower.

Punta Marguis
23 57.5N, 110 52.3W, Fl W 6s, 39 ft., truncated pyramidal metal tower.

Punta de Mita
20 45.7N, 105 33.0W, Fl (3) W 12s, 69 ft., 11 mi., red truncated pyramidal metal tower.

PUNTA MORRO

Punta Morro Light
31 52N, 116 40W, Fl W 6s, 39 ft., 10 mi., white concrete tower.

East Breakwater
31 52.0N, 116 40.0W, Fl G 5s, 36 ft., cylindrical metal tower.

West Breakwater
31 52.0N, 116 40.0W, Fl R 5s, 33 ft., cylindrical metal tower.

Punta del Morro Redondo
28 02.6N, 115 11.1W, Fl W 6s, 72 ft., 10 mi., metal pyramidal tower. *Also see* Isla Cedros.

Punta Negra
28 49N, 114 24W, Fl (3) W 12s, 52 ft., 10 mi., white cylindrical concrete tower.

Punta de los Ostiones
25 02N, 110 43W, Fl W 6s, 39 ft., 11 mi., aluminum colored metal tower.

Punta Pequeña
26 14.2N, 112 29.3W, Fl W 6s, 50 ft., 8 mi., white metal framework tower, red bands.

Punta Piaxtla
23 38.8N, 106 49.1W, Fl (3) W 12s, 98 ft., 14 mi., white cylindrical concrete tower, red bands.

Punta Pinto
25 34.2N, 109 04.5W, Fl R 3s, 26 ft., 8 mi., white cylindrical concrete tower. *Also see* Topolobampo.

Punta Prieta
24 13.2N, 110 18.7W, Fl (3) W 12s, 98 ft., 15 mi., white square masonry tower, on roof of dwelling, visible 290°–148°.

Punta Redonda
24 31.0N, 112 00.7W, Fl (2) W 10s, 62 ft., 8 mi., white truncated pyramidal tower, visible 330°–242°.

Punta Riscion
25 07.2N, 108 20.5W, Fl W 6s, 46 ft., 12 mi., white truncated pyramidal metal tower.

Punta San Guillermo, Puerto San Carlos
27 56.0N, 111 03.7W, Fl G 5s, 56 ft., 8 mi., truncated pyramidal aluminum tower. *Also see* Bahía San Carlos.

Punta San José
31 28N, 116 36W, Fl (4) W 16s, 115 ft., 10 mi., white concrete tower.

Punta San Miguel
31 54N, 116 45W, Fl (2) W 10s,
190 ft., 10 mi., concrete tower.

Punta San Telmo
18 19.6N, 103 29.5W, Fl (2) W 10s,
230 ft., 14 mi., white square concrete tower, dwelling, visible
279°–149°.

Punta Santa Agueda
27 19.0N, 112 15.1W, Fl (4) W R
16s, 49 ft., 10 mi., metal tower,
R 110°–155°, W elsewhere.

Punta Santa Inés
27 03.8N, 111 57.8W, Fl W 6s,
52 ft., 11 mi., truncated pyramidal aluminum tower.
Also see Santa Inés Islands.

Punta Santa Teresa
26 41.0N, 111 34.0W, Fl (3) W 12s,
52 ft., 11 mi., truncated pyramidal metal tower.

Punta Sargento (N of point)
31 37N, 114 47W, Fl W 6s, 39 ft.,
10 mi., truncated pyramidal
metal tower.

PUNTA SAUZAL

El Sauzal Range Front Light
31 54N, 116 42W, Fl W 3s, 64 ft.,
9 mi., truncated pyramidal metal
tower.

Range Rear Light
31 54N, 116 42W, Iso W 2s, 74 ft.,
9 mi., metal tower.

Punta Sauzal Light
31 54.0N, 116 42.0W, Fl G 5s,
38 ft., 7 mi.

East Breakwater
31 53.5N, 116 42.5W, Fl R 5s,
32 ft., 7 mi., truncated pyramidal
aluminum framework tower.

No. 2
31 53.4N, 116 42.6W, Fl R 5s,
32 ft., 7 mi., truncated pyramidal
metal framework tower.

West Breakwater
31 53.4N, 116 42.6W, Fl G 5s,
38 ft., 7 mi., white metal framework structure.

Punta Tosca
24 18.6N, 111 43.0W, Fl W 6s,
266 ft., 10 mi., white square concrete tower, dwelling, visible
191°–118°.

Punta Willard
29 51N, 114 25W, Fl W 6s, 46 ft.,
9 mi., aluminum colored metal
tower.
Also see Isla Willard.

**Punta Willard (on W extremity of
Isla Tiburón)**
28 53.3N, 112 35.8W, Fl (3) W 12s,
46 ft., 11 mi., truncated pyramidal metal tower.

Punta Zicatela
15 49.0N, 97 03.0W, Fl (2) W 10s,
36 ft., 10 mi., truncated pyramidal metal tower.

R

Redonda, La
See La Redonda.

Redonda, Punta
See Punta Redonda.

Reina, Islote de la
See Islote de la Reina.

Revillagigedo, Islas
See Isla Socorro *and* Isla Clarion.

Rio Balvarre
22 48.0N, 106 02.4W, Fl (3) W 12s,
26 ft., 14 mi., truncated pyramidal metal tower.

Rio de la Concepción
30 33.2N, 113 00.0W, Fl (2) W 10s,
85 ft., 18 mi., white truncated
pyramidal concrete tower, red
bands.

Rio San Ignacio
29 29.7N, 112 25.0W, Fl W 6s,
52 ft., 11 mi., white truncated
pyramidal metal tower.

Rio San Lorenzo
24 16N, 107 27W, Fl (4) R 16s,
58 ft., 14 mi., white metal tower.

Rio Yaqui
27 40.3N, 110 35.3W, Fl (4) W 16s,
56 ft., 11 mi., truncated pyramidal metal tower.

Riscion, Punta
See Punta Riscion.

Roca Atano
27 39.2N, 114 52.5W, Fl W 6s,
72 ft., 10 mi., metal pyramidal
tower.

Roca Consgracion
31 06.4N, 114 28.5W, Fl W 6s,
38 ft., 10 mi., white cylindrical
concrete tower, red bands.

Roca Corbetena
20 43.7N, 105 51.0W, Fl (4) W 16s,
56 ft., 15 mi., red aluminum
tower, truncated pyramidal base.

Roca Lobos
24 17.8N, 110 20.9W, Fl W 6s,
43 ft., 11 mi., white metal tower.

Roca Negra
19 46.0N, 105 21.5W, Fl (2) W 10s,
102 ft., 11 mi., white truncated
pyramidal metal tower.

Roqueta, La
See La Roqueta.

S

SALINA CRUZ

Morro de Salinas
16 09.7N, 95 12.2W, Fl W 5s,
272 ft., 23 mi., white octagonal
concrete tower, dwelling, visible
265°–048°.

Head of West Breakwater
16 09.6N, 95 11.9W, Fl G 5s, 23 ft.,
9 mi., truncated pyramidal tower.

Head of East Breakwater
16 09.7N, 95 11.7W, Fl R 5s, 23 ft.,
9 mi., truncated pyramidal concrete tower.

Range Front Light
16 10.4N, 95 12.0W, Fl W 3s, 23 ft.,
9 mi., truncated pyramidal metal
tower.

Range Rear Light
280 meters, 346.5° from front
light, 16 10.6N, 95 12.0W, Iso W
2s, 220 ft., 7 mi., truncated pyramidal metal tower.

San Bartolome (landing)
27 40N, 114 50W, Fl W 6s, 51 ft.,
10 mi., white concrete tower, red
bands.

San Benito, Islas
See Islas San Benito.

SAN BLAS

San Blas Light (Vigia Hill)
21 32.1N, 105 18.5W, Fl (2) W 10s,
144 ft., 22 mi., white cylindrical
concrete tower, red bands.

Range Front Light
21 32.0N, 105 19.0W, Fl W 3s,
46 ft., 11 mi., truncated pyramidal metal tower, red and white
checkered, concrete base.

Range Rear Light
21 32.0N, 105 19.0W, Iso W 2s,
62 ft., 11 mi., truncated pyramidal metal tower, red and white
checkered, concrete base.

East Jetty
21 32.0N, 105 19.0W, Fl R 5s, 46 ft.,
6 mi., red truncated pyramidal
aluminum tower, concrete base.

West Jetty
21 32.0N, 105 19.0W, Fl G 5s,
43 ft., 6 mi., green truncated
pyramidal aluminum tower,
concrete base.

San Carlos
25 35.0N, 109 03.0W, Fl R 3s,
33 ft., 8 mi., white cylindrical
concrete tower.
Also see Topolobampo.

San Carlos, Bahía
See Bahía San Carlos *and* Punta
San Guillermo.

San Carlos, Puerto de
See Puerto de San Carlos.

**San Carlos (near Punta San
Guillermo)**
See Punta San Guillermo.

San Diego, Isla
See Isla San Diego.

San Dionisio Del Mar
16 16N, 94 46W, Fl (4) W 16s,
55 ft., 14 mi., white cylindrical
concrete tower.

San Esteban, Isla
See Isla San Esteban.

San Evaristo
24 53.8N, 110 43.3W, Fl (3) W 12s,
72 ft., 11 mi., truncated pyramidal metal tower.

SAN FELIPE

San Felipe Light
31 03.0N, 114 49.0W, Fl W 5s,
114 ft., 18 mi., white cylindrical
concrete tower, aeromarine light.

North Mole
31 01N, 114 49W, Iso W 2s, 49 ft.,
6 mi., white cylindrical concrete
tower.

South Mole
31 01N, 114 49W, Iso W 2s, 49 ft.,
6 mi., white cylindrical concrete
tower.

North Breakwater
31 01N, 114 49W, Fl R 5s, 38 ft.,
7 mi., aluminum-colored tower.

South Breakwater
31 01N, 114 49W, Fl G 5s, 38 ft.,
7 mi., aluminum-colored tower.

Range Front Light
31 01N, 114 49W, Fl W 3s, 69 ft.,
6 mi., aluminum-colored tower.

Range Rear Light
31 01N, 114 49W, Iso W 2s, 62 ft.,
6 mi., aluminum-colored tower.

San Francisco
16 12.8N, 94 48.5W, Fl (3) W 12s,
56 ft., 14 mi., red cylindrical concrete tower, yellow bands.

San Francisquito, Bahía de
See Bahía de San Francisquito.

San Guillermo, Punta
See Punta San Guillermo.

San Hipólito
26 58.5N, 113 59.3W, Fl (4) W 16s,
46 ft., 10 mi., white concrete
tower, red stripes.

San Ignacio Farallon
25 26.2N, 109 24.1W, Fl (2) W 10s,
394 ft., 14 mi., white truncated
pyramidal metal tower.

San Ildefonso, Isla
See Isla San Ildefonso.

San Jerónimo, Isla
See Isla San Jerónimo.

San Jorge, Isla
See Isla San Jorge.

San José
29 17.0N, 114 51.8W, Fl W 6s,
79 ft., 10 mi., white cylindrical
concrete tower.

San José, Estero de
See Estero de San José.

San José, Isla de
See Isla de San José.

San José, Punta
See Punta San José.

San José del Cabo
23 03.8N, 109 39.9W, Fl (2) W 10s,
118 ft., 15 mi., white concrete
tower, red bands, masonry
house.

San Juan de la Costa
24 23.7N, 110 41.4W, Fl (2) W 10s,
341 ft., 11 mi., truncated pyramidal metal tower.

San Juanito, Isla
See Isla San Juanito *and* Islas
Marías.

San Lázaro, Cabo
See Cabo San Lázaro.

San Lorenzo, Isla
See Isla San Lorenzo.

San Lorenzo Norte
24 22.7N, 110 18.6W, Fl (4) R 16s,
26 ft., 6 mi., cylindrical metal
tower.

San Lorenzo Sur ("El Explorado")
24 21.8N, 110 18.0W, Fl (2) W 10s,
33 ft., 11 mi., white cylindrical
concrete tower, red bands.

San Lucas, Cabo
See Cabo San Lucas *and* Cabo
Falso Light.

San Marcial Rock
25 29.8N, 111 01.5W, Fl W 6s,
56 ft., 11 mi., truncated pyramidal metal tower.

San Marcos, Isla
See Isla San Marcos.

San Martín, Isla de
See Isla de San Martín.

San Miguel, Punta
See Punta San Miguel.

San Pedrito Entrance Range Front Light
19 03.8N, 104 17.4W, Fl W 3s, 46 ft., 16 mi., truncated pyramidal mctal towcr.
Also see Manzanillo.

San Pedrito Entrance Range Rear Light
About 400 meters, 077° from front light, 19 03.9N, 104 17.1W, Iso W 2s, 75 ft., 16 mi., truncated pyramidal metal tower.

San Pedro Martir, Isla
See Isla San Pedro Martir.

San Pedro Nolasco, Isla
See Isla San Pedro Nolasco.

San Roque, Isla
See Isla San Roque.

San Telmo, Punta
See Punta San Telmo.

Santa Agueda, Punta
See Punta Santa Agueda.

Santa Barbara
26 41.0N, 109 41.0W, Fl (3) W 12s, 43 ft., 11 mi., truncated pyramidal metal tower.

Santa Catalina, Isla
See Isla Santa Catalina.

Santa Clara
31 41.0N, 114 30.0W, Fl W 6s, 135 ft., 19 mi., white cylindrical concrete tower, red bands.

Santa Cruz
15 33.4N, 93 18.5W, Fl (3) W 12s, 52 ft., 11 mi., red cylindrical concrete tower, yellow bands.

Santa Cruz, Isla
See Isla Santa Cruz.

Santa Inés Islands (N)
27 02.6N, 111 55.2W, Fl (2) W 10s, 52 ft., 11 mi., truncated pyramidal metal tower.
Also see Punta Santa Inés.

Santa Inés Islands (S)
27 01.6N, 111 55.6W, Fl (3) W 12s, 52 ft., 11 mi., truncated pyramidal metal tower.

Santa María, Bahía de
See Bahía de Santa María.

SANTA ROSALIA

N Head of Outer Breakwater
27 19.8N, 112 16.3W, F R, 36 ft., 7 mi., white cylindrical concrctc tower.

Head of S Mole
27 19.7N, 112 16.4W, F G, 36 ft., 7 mi., white cylindrical concrete tower.

NE of Outer Breakwater
27 19.8N, 112 16.3W, Iso W 2s, 56 ft., 13 mi., white cylindrical concrete tower.

Outer Breakwater (middle)
27 20.0N, 112 16.3W, Fl W 3s, 39 ft., 11 mi., white cylindrical concrete tower.

Santa Teresa, Punta
See Punta Santa Teresa.

Santo Domingo
27 10.6N, 110 18.0W, Fl (2) W 10s, 30 ft., 11 mi., truncated pyramidal metal tower.

Santo Domingo, Boca de
See Boca de Santo Domingo.

Santo Domingo, Morro de
See Morro de Santo Domingo.

Sargento, Punta
See Punta Sargento.

Sauzal, Punta
See Punta Sauzal.

Seal Rock
See Islote de la Reina.

Socorro, Isla
See Isla Socorro.

Soledad, La
See La Soledad.

Soledad, Boca de
See Boca de Soledad.

Solitaria, La
See La Solitaria.

T

Tapachula (Aviation Light)
14 55N, 92 16W, Al Fl W G 5s, 197 ft., private light.

Teacapan
22 32.0N, 105 45.5W, Fl W 6s, 52 ft., 14 mi., white truncated pyramidal metal tower.

Tepoca, Cabo
See Cabo Tepoca.

Tiburón, Isla
See Punta Willard.

Tijuana
32 31.8N, 117 06.9W, Fl (3) W 6s, 105 ft., 20 mi., white cylindrical concrete tower.
Also see Boundary Aviation Light.

Todos Santos
23 26.9N, 110 14.6W, Fl W 6s, 43 ft., 14 mi., white cylindrical concrete tower, black bands.

Todos Santos, Islas de
See Islas de Todos Santos.

TOPOLOBAMPO

Las Ánimas Range Front Light
25 35.0N, 109 07.0W, Fl W 3s, 98 ft., 20 mi., white truncate pyramidal metal tower.

Las Ánimas Range Rear Light
051° from front light, 25 35.0N, 109 07.0W, Iso W 2s, 328 ft., 20 mi., truncated pyramidal metal tower.

Punta Copas Range Front Light
25 32.6N, 109 06.9W, Fl W 3s, 43 ft., 12 mi., white truncated pyramidal metal tower.

Punta Copas Range Rear Light
420 meters, 232.5° from front light, 25 32.6N, 109 06.9W, Iso W 2s, 52 ft., 20 mi., white truncated pyramidal metal tower.

Punta Prieta Range Front Light
25 33.0N, 109 05.0W, Fl W 3s, 20 ft., 9 mi., white cylindrical concrete tower.

Punta Prieta Range Rear Light
1.5 miles, 093° from front light, 25 33N, 109 05W, Iso W 2s, 49 ft., 12 mi., white pyramidal concrete tower.

Cerro Partido (entrance to Topolobampo Harbor)
25 32.0N, 109 06.2W, Fl W 7s, 312 ft., 35 mi., white cylindrical concrete tower.

Punta Pinto
25 34.2N, 109 04.5W, Fl R 3s,
26 ft., 8 mi., white cylindrical
concrete tower.

San Carlos
25 35.0N, 109 03.0W, Fl R 3s,
33 ft., 8 mi., white cylindrical
concrete tower.

Tortugas, Isla
See Isla Tortugas.

Tosca, Punta
See Punta Tosca.

Tule, Boca del
See Boca del Tule.

Turner, Isla
See Isla Turner.

U

U.S./Mexico Border
See Boundary Aviation Light.

V

Vallarta, Puerto
See Puerto Vallarta.

Ventana, Bahía la
See Bahía la Ventana.

Vicente, Puerto
See Puerto Vicente.

Viejas, Isla de las
See Bahía de Yavaros.

Vingenes, Cabo
See Cabo Vingenes.

W

White Rocks
See Bahía de Acapulco.

Willard, Punta and Isla
See Punta Willard *or* Isla Willard.

Y

Yameta
24 47.0N, 108 05.0W, Fl (4) W 16s,
43 ft., 14 mi., white cylindrical
concrete tower, red bands.

Yavaros, Puerto
See Puerto Yavaros.

Yelapa
20 30.5N, 105 25.5W, Fl (3) W 12s,
279 ft., 11 mi., white truncated
pyramidal metal structure.

Yerbabuena
16 49.0N, 99 54.0W, Fl (2) W 10s,
43 ft., 10 mi., truncated pyramidal aluminum tower.
Also see Bahía de Acapulco.

Z

Zicatela, Punta
See Punta Zicatela.

Guatemala

Note: Many navigational lights in Panama, Costa Rica, Nicaragua, El Salvador, and Guatemala have been reported as irregular or unreliable.

Some latitude/longitude positions are only reported in whole minutes in the government light lists (rather than to the nearest tenth of a minute). These positions should be assumed to be less accurate than those reported with greater precision.

C

Champerico (near head of pier)
14 18N, 91 56W, Iso W 4s, 68 ft., 13 mi., tower on concrete tank.

M

Mexico/Guatemala Border
See Guatemala/Mexico Border, Mexico chapter.

O

Ocos
14 31.8N, 92 13.3W, Fl W 4s.

Ocos
14 31.9N, 92 13.1W, Fl W 4s.

P

PUERTO QUETZAL

Entrance Range Front Light
13 55.3N, 90 48.1W, Q W, 43 ft., white and red rectangular daymark.

Entrance Range Rear Light
About 200 meters, 295° from front light, 13 55.4N, 90 48.2W, Oc W 4s, 59 ft., 12 mi., red and white daymark.

Light No. 1, S Breakwater
13 55.0N, 90 47.7W, Q G, 39 ft., 4 mi.

Light No. 2, N Breakwater
13 55.2N, 90 47.6W, Q R, 43 ft., 4 mi.

Light No. 6
13 55.3N, 90 47.9W, Q R, 43 ft., 4 mi.

Aviation Light
13 55.6N, 90 48.7W, Aero Fl (2) W 5s, 96 ft.

Q

Quetzal, Puerto
See Puerto Quetzal.

S

San Jose
13 55.2N, 90 49.7W, Iso W 20s, 92 ft., 15 mi., white skeleton tower, red bands, white tank, aero radiobeacon 6 mi. ENE.

San Jose (end of wharf)
13 55.0N, 90 49.7W, F R, 49 ft., 3 mi.

Note: Many navigational lights in Panama, Costa Rica, Nicaragua, El Salvador, and Guatemala have been reported as irregular or unreliable.

Some latitude/longitude positions are only reported in whole minutes in the government light lists (rather than to the nearest tenth of a minute). These positions should be assumed to be less accurate than those reported with greater precision.

A

Acajutla
13 35N, 89 50W, Iso W 12s, 75 ft., 8 mi., white metal framework tower, reported extinguished (April 1985).

Acajutla, Head of National Pier
13 34.5N, 89 50.2W, F R, 85 ft., 7 mi.

Amapala, Punta
See Punta Amapala.

C

Chiquirin, Punta
See Punta Chiquirin.

I

Isla del Tigre
13 16.6N, 87 38.5W, Iso R 2s.

Isla Zacatillo (Isla Punta Zacate, W side of island)
13 18.6N, 87 46.2W, Fl W 10s, 60 ft., 5 mi., aluminum tower, concrete base.

L

La Union, Cutuco Pier (on center of E end of shed)
13 20.0N, 87 49.2W, F R, 36 ft., 3 mi., metal tower, F R 5m to the north, F G 5m to the south.

P

Punta Amapala
13 09.3N, 87 54.0W, Fl W 15s, 90 ft., 12 mi., aluminum square framework tower, reported extinguished (March 1986).

Punta Chiquirin (S extremity)
13 17.4N, 87 46.8W, Fl W 5s, 68 ft., 10 mi., aluminum painted steel tower, concrete base.

Punta Remedios
13 32N, 89 48W, L Fl W 20s, 82 ft., 14 mi., white steel skeleton tower, reported difficult to distinguish from shore lights (March 1982).

Punta Zacate, Isla
See Isla Zacatillo.

R

Remedios, Punta
See Punta Remedios.

T

Tigre, Isla del
See Isla del Tigre.

U

Union, La
See La Union.

Z

Zacatillo, Isla
See Isla Zacatillo.

Honduras

S

SAN LORENZO

No. 1
13 12.5N, 87 35.0W, Fl G 3s,
articulated light.

No. 2
13 12.4N, 87 34.8W, Fl R 3s,
articulated light.

No. 5
13 14.3N, 87 34.7W, Fl G 5s,
articulated light.

No. 6
13 14.2N, 87 34.6W, Fl R 5s,
articulated light.

No. 11
13 16.9N, 87 32.8W, Fl G 5s,
articulated light.

No. 12
13 16.8N, 87 32.7W, Fl R 5s,
articulated light.

No. 16
13 18.4N, 87 29.3W, Fl R 3s,
articulated light.

No. 17
13 18.6N, 87 29.5W, Fl G 3s,
articulated light.

No. 21
13 20.3N, 87 28.8W, Fl G 3s,
articulated light.

No. 25
13 21.7N, 87 27.7W, Fl G 7s,
articulated light.

No. 28
13 21.7N, 87 26.2W, Fl R 3s,
articulated light.

No. 29
13 21.9N, 87 26.3W, Fl G 3s,
articulated light.

No. 33
13 22.9N, 87 25.8W, Fl G 5s,
articulated light.

Nicaragua

Note: Many navigational lights in Panama, Costa Rica, Nicaragua, El Salvador, and Guatemala have been reported as irregular or unreliable.

Some latitude/longitude positions are only reported in whole minutes in the government light lists (rather than to the nearest tenth of a minute). These positions should be assumed to be less accurate than those reported with greater precision.

C

Corinto, Puerto
See Puerto Corinto.

D

Dona Paula Range
See Puerto Corinto.

M

Morro Cardon (N point of Isla El Cardon)
12 28.5N, 87 11.4W, L Fl W 10s, 87 ft., 10 mi., white round concrete tower, red lantern.
Also see Puerto Corinto.

P

PUERTO CORINTO

Morro Cardon (N point of Isla El Cardon)
12 28.5N, 87 11.4W, L Fl W 10s, 87 ft., 10 mi., white round concrete tower, red lantern.

Entrance Range Front Light, No. 1
12 29.1N, 87 10.8W, F R, beacon.

Entrance Range Rear Light, No. 2
720 meters, 076.7° from front light, Fl R 10s, beacon.

Dona Paula Range Front Light, No. 3 (on Castanones Peninsula)
12 27.9N, 87 10.3W, F G, beacon.

Dona Paula Range Rear Light, No. 4
810 meters, 122.4° from front light, Fl G 4s, beacon.

Isla En Cantada Range Front Light, No. 5
12 28.8N, 87 09.2W, F R, beacon.

Isla En Cantada Range Rear Light, No. 6
250 meters, 074.5° from front light, Fl R 10s, beacon.

Puerto Somoza
12 11N, 86 46W, Fl W 10s.

PUERTO SONDINO

Range Front Light
12 10.2N, 86 46.9W, F G, 10 mi., black and white checkered tower.

Range Rear Light
245 meters, 080° from front light, Oc G 9s, 10 mi., black and white checkered tower.

S

SAN JUAN DEL SUR

San Juan del Sur Light (S side of entrance)
11 15N, 85 53W, Fl W 6s, 100 ft., 16 mi., white circular wooden tower, red lantern.

Head of Bay Range Front Light (N of town)
11 15N, 85 53W, Fl R 6s, 33 ft., 5 mi., house, green roof.

Head of Bay Range Rear Light
213 meters, 067° from front, F R, 53 ft., 5 mi., white water tower.

Somoza, Puerto
See Puerto Somoza.

Sondino, Puerto
See Puerto Sondino.

Costa Rica

Note: Many navigational lights in Panama, Costa Rica, Nicaragua, El Salvador, and Guatemala have been reported as irregular or unreliable.

Some latitude/longitude positions are only reported in whole minutes in the government light lists (rather than to the nearest tenth of a minute). These positions should be assumed to be less accurate than those reported with greater precision.

B

Banco, Punta
See Punta Banco.

C

Cabo Matapalo
8 22.8N, 83 17.8W, Fl W 10s.

Cajoo Blanco, Isla
See Isla Cajoo Blanco.

Caldera, Puerto
See Puerto Caldera.

Cano, Isla del
See Isla del Cano.

Curapacha Point (W of entrance to Golfito)
8 38N, 83 13W, Fl W 4s, 300 ft., 12 mi., yellow steel framework structure.

G

GOLFITO HARBOR

Also see Curapacha Point.

Beacon H (S side of entrance, 926 meters S of Voladero Pt.)
8 37N, 83 12W, Fl R 3s, 30 ft., steel tower with reflectors radar reflector.

Beacon A (N side of entrance of Voladero Pt.)
8 38N, 83 11W, Q G, 75 fl. per minute, 15 ft., steel tower with reflectors.

Entrance Range Beacon Front
8 38.4N, 83 10.3W, F R, white diamond-shaped daymark, black stripe.

Entrance Range Beacon Rear
About 6 meters, 047° from front beacon, F R, white diamond-shaped daymark, black stripe.

Golfo de Nicoya (on dock N of small customs office at bend of mole)
9 58.2N, 84 49.9W, Oc (4) R 10s, 51 ft., 12 mi., aluminum-colored iron tower.

H

Herradura, Isla
See Isla Herradura.

I

Isla Cajoo Blanco
9 32.4N, 85 06.7W, Fl (2) W 18s, 20 mi.

Isla del Cano (W end)
8 43N, 83 54W, Fl W 4s, 207 ft., 12 mi., steel skeleton tower, red lantern, visible 311°–247°, reported extinguished (Jan. 1982).

Isla Herradura
9 38N, 84 41W, Fl W 10s, 325 ft., 15 mi., skeleton steel tower, reported FW (Jan. 1994).

Islas Negritos (E end)
9 49.3N, 84 49.6W, Fl (4) W 20s, 156 ft., 15 mi., skeleton steel tower, reported extinguished (Jan. 1994).

M

Matapalo, Cabo
See Cabo Matapalo.

N

Negritos, Islas
See Islas Negritos.

Nicoya, Golfo de
See Golfo de Nicoya.

P

Puerto Caldera
9 54.7N, 84 43.5W, Fl R 3s.

Punta Banco
8 22.0N, 83 08.6W, Fl (2) W 15s.

Punta Quepos
9 24N, 84 10W, Fl W 3s, 511 ft., 8 mi., steel framework tower, visible 295°–192°.

Q

Quepos, Punta
See Punta Quepos.

Note: Many navigational lights in Panama, Costa Rica, Nicaragua, El Salvador, and Guatemala have been reported as irregular or unreliable.

Some latitude/longitude positions are only reported in whole minutes in the government light lists (rather than to the nearest tenth of a minute). These positions should be assumed to be less accurate than those reported with greater precision.

Aquadulce, Puerto
See Puerto Aquadulce.

Armuelles, Puerto
See Puerto Armuelles.

Aviation Light
See Northwards Aviation Light.

Batatilla, Isla
See Isla Batatilla.

Bona, Isla
See Isla Bona.

Brujas, Punta
See Punta Brujas.

Burica, Isla
See Isla Burica.

C

Canal de Afuera, Isla
See Isla Canal de Afuera.

Cebaco, Isla de
See Isla de Cebaco.

Cerro Cedro Aviation Light
9 00N, 79 33W, Fl R 2s, 500 ft., occasional.
Also see Gulf of Panama.

Chepillo, Isla
See Isla Chepillo.

Cocalito, Punta
See Punta Cocalito.

Contreras, Islas
See Islas Contreras.

Corozal Aviation Light
8 59N, 79 34W, Al Fl W G 6.6s, 379 ft., steel tower, occasional, F R on tank 90 meters NW.
Also see Gulf of Panama.

Dulce, Puerto
See Puerto Dulce.

E

Ensillada, Isla
See Isla Ensillada.

F

Flamenco Island (SW side)
8 54.4N, 79 31.2W, Oc (2) W R 5s, 154 ft., 19 mi., white square concrete pedestal, white 267°–003°, red 003°–054°, storm signals shown from radio tower 3.4 mi. NNW, racon: N (-·).
Also see Gulf of Panama.

Frailes del Sur
7 20.3N, 80 08.7W, Fl R 4s, 59 ft., 12 mi., white pyramidal concrete tower.

Galera, Isla
See Isla Galera.

Garachine, Punta
See Punta Garachine.

GULF OF PANAMA

Punta Mala
7 28.2N, 80 00.0W, L Fl W 20s, 138 ft., 15 mi., white framework tower, reported Fl W 10s (1995), racon: M (--).

Isla Bona (on Los Farallones, off S side of island)
8 33.8N, 79 35.2W, L Fl W 13s, 157 ft., 15 mi., white skeleton steel tower, reported extinguished (Aug. 1986).

Breakwater (head)
8 51.7N, 79 40.2W, Fl (2) W 10s, 28 ft., 7 mi., white tower, 3 Q W lights mark jetty heads inside harbor.

Valladolid Rock
8 43N, 79 36W, Fl (2) W 30s, 75 ft., 11 mi., white tower.

Vacamonte Range Front Light
8 52.0N, 79 40.2W, F W, 58 ft., 13 mi., white triangle on tower.

Vacamonte Range Rear Light
150 meters, 321° from front light, F W, 71 ft., 13 mi., white triangle on tower.

Perique Rock
8 45N, 79 35W, L Fl W 15s, 75 ft., 9 mi., white tower.

Terapa Islet
8 46N, 79 32W, Fl W 5s, 46 ft., 9 mi., white skeleton steel tower.

Isla Taboguilla (small island on E side)
8 48N, 79 31W, L Fl W R 7s, 184 ft., 14 mi., white skeleton steel tower, white 180°–000°, red 000°–040°, aero radiobeacon 2.8 mi. SW (on Taboga Island), reported extinguished (Aug. 1986).

Isla Taboguilla (N side of island)
8 49N, 79 31W, L Fl W 20s, 65 ft., 7 mi., white tower, reported at reduced intensity (Aug. 1986).

Flamenco Island (SW side)
8 54.4N, 79 31.2W, Oc (2) W R 5s, 154 ft., 19 mi., white square concrete pedestal, white 267°–003°, red 003°–054°, storm signals shown from radio tower 3.4 mi. NNW, racon: N (-·).

Howard Aviation Light
8 55N, 79 35W, Al Fl W G 5s, 300 ft., occasional.

West Bank of Canal (opposite Balboa) Range Front Light
8 58N, 79 35W, F G, 65 ft., 14 mi., concrete tower, visible on range-linc only, canal markcd by lights and range lights.

West Bank of Canal Range Rear Light
4.1 km, 322° from front light, Oc G 5s, 200 ft., 20 mi., concrete tower.

Corozal Aviation Light
8 59N, 79 34W, Al Fl W G 6.6s, 379 ft., steel tower, occasional, F R on tank 90 meters NW.

Cerro Cedro Aviation Light
9 00N, 79 33W, Fl R 2s, 500 ft., occasional.

Tocumen Aviation Light
9 05N, 79 23W, Al Fl W G 10s, 200 ft., tower, occasional.

Isla Chepillo (summit)
8 57N, 79 08W, Fl W 8s, 194 ft., 5 mi., white iron framework tower.

Isla Pacheca
8 40N, 79 03W, Fl W 7s, 39 ft., 7 mi., white steel skeleton tower.

San Miguel (on Isla del Rey)
8 27.4N, 78 56.5W, Fl W 5s, 85 ft., 6 mi., concrete pedestal, visible 086°–180°.

Isla San Jose (SW extremity)
8 13N, 79 08W, L Fl W 6s, 210 ft., 14 mi., white pyramidal skeleton steel tower, white rectangular daymarks, visible 291°–148°.

Morro Pelado
8 38.0N, 78 42.2W, Fl W 5s, 154 ft., 6 mi., concrete pedestal.

Punta Brujas
8 35.2N, 78 32.7W, Fl W 4s, 115 ft., 6 mi., concrete pedestal, visible 345°–215°.

Isla Batatilla
8 19N, 78 23W, Fl W 5s, 36 ft., 5 mi., white skeleton steel tower.

La Palma (on W side of Punta Virago)
8 25N, 78 10W, Fl W 5s, 6 ft., 4 mi., white cement block pyramid, visible 047°–222°.

Isla Patinito (summit)
8 15.5N, 78 18.7W, Fl W 3s, 564 ft., 4 mi., white cement block pyramid, visible 338.6°–227.4°.

Isla Galera
8 11.7N, 78 46.6W, Fl W 15s, 98 ft., 12 mi., white framework tower on 4 legs, visible 301°–151°.

Punta Garachine
8 05N, 78 25W, Fl W 4s, 56 ft., 5 mi., white skeleton steel tower.

Punta Pina
7 34N, 78 12W, Fl W 5s, 223 ft., 5 mi., white metal skeleton tower.

H

Howard Aviation Light
8 55N, 79 35W, Al Fl W G 5s, 300 ft., occasional.
Also see Gulf of Panama.

I

Iguana, Isla
See Isla Iguana.

Isla Batatilla
8 19N, 78 23W, Fl W 5s, 36 ft., 5 mi., white skeleton steel tower.
Also see Gulf of Panama.

Isla Bona (on Los Farallones, off S side of island)
8 33.8N, 79 35.2W, L Fl W 13s, 157 ft., 15 mi., white skeleton steel tower, reported extinguished (Aug. 1986).
Also see Gulf of Panama.

Isla Burica
8 01.1N, 82 52.8W, Fl W 10s, 137 ft., 13 mi., fiberglass tower, racon: B (-··), 20 mi.

Isla Canal de Afuera (S side)
7 41N, 81 38W, L Fl W 6s, 86 ft., 5 mi., white square framework tower.

Isla de Cebaco (on W point of island)
7 29N, 81 16W, Fl W 3s, 348 ft., 5 mi., white square framework tower.

Isla Chepillo (summit)
8 57N, 79 08W, Fl W 8s, 194 ft., 5 mi., white iron framework tower.
Also see Gulf of Panama.

Islas Contreras (Isla Uva)
7 47.9N, 81 46.1W, Fl W 19s, 288 ft., 8 mi., white framework tower.

Isla del Rey
See San Miguel.

Isla Ensillada
8 09.1N, 82 09.8W, Fl W 5s, 167 ft., 5 mi., white framework tower.

Isla Galera
8 11.7N, 78 46.6W, Fl W 15s, 98 ft., 12 mi., white framework tower on 4 legs, visible 301°–151°.
Also see Gulf of Panama.

Isla Iguana
7 37.7N, 79 59.8W, Fl W 13s, 83 ft., 8 mi., white framework tower, obscured 090°-184.8°.

Isla Jicarita (SE extremity)
7 12.4N, 81 48.1W, 2 Fl W (vert.) 15s, 328 ft., 19 mi., white steel framework tower, visible 270°–118°, reported extinguished (Jan. 1994).

Isla Ladrones
7 52N, 82 26W, L Fl W 9s, 213 ft., 16 mi., white metal framework tower.

Isla Montuosa
7 28.3N, 82 14.5W, L Fl W 8s, 98 ft., 11 mi., white metal framework tower, reported L Fl W 10s (March 1994).

Isla Pacheca
8 40N, 79 03W, Fl W 7s, 39 ft., 7 mi., white steel skeleton tower.
Also see Gulf of Panama.

Isla Parida
8 06.0N, 82 22.0W, L Fl W 8s, 125 ft., 7 mi., white metal framework tower.

Isla Patinito (summit)
8 15.5N, 78 18.7W, Fl W 3s, 564 ft., 4 mi., white cement block pyramid, visible 338.6°–227.4°.
Also see Gulf of Panama.

Isla San Jose (SW extremity)
8 13N, 79 08W, L Fl W 6s, 210 ft.,
14 mi., white pyramidal skeleton
steel tower, white rectangular
daymarks, visible 291°–148°.
Also see Gulf of Panama.

Islas Secas
7 57N, 82 01W, L Fl W 9s, 167 ft.,
7 mi., white metal framework
tower.

Isla Taboguilla (small island on E side)
8 48N, 79 31W, L Fl W R 7s,
184 ft., 14 mi., white skeleton
steel tower, white 180°–000°, red
000°–040°, aero radiobeacon
2.8 miles SW (on Taboga Island),
reported extinguished (Aug.
1986).
Also see Gulf of Panama.

Isla Taboguilla (N side of island)
8 49N, 79 31W, L Fl W 20s, 65 ft.,
7 mi., white tower, reported at
reduced intensity (Aug. 1986).

Isla Uva
See Islas Contreras.

Isla Villa
7 56.1N, 80 18.1W, Fl W 18s,
112 ft., 8 mi., white framework
tower.

Jicarita, Isla
See Isla Jicarita.

La Palma (on W side of Punta Virago)
8 25N, 78 10W, Fl W 5s, 6 ft.,
4 mi., white cement block pyramid, visible 047°–222°.
Also see Gulf of Panama.

Ladrones, Isla
See Isla Ladrones.

Mala, Punta
See Punta Mala.

Mariato, Punta
See Punta Mariato.

Montuosa, Isla
See Isla Montuosa.

Morro Pelado
8 38.0N, 78 42.2W, Fl W 5s, 154 ft.,
6 mi., concrete pedestal.
Also see Gulf of Panama.

Morro de Puercos
7 15N, 80 26W, Fl W 7.5s, 269 ft.,
19 mi., white metal framework
tower, visible 245°–072°, reported
extinguished (1990).

N

Northwards Aviation Light
7 40.4N, 80 25.9W, F R, obstruction with W and R lights close by.

P

Pacheca, Isla
See Isla Pacheca.

Palma, La
See La Palma.

Panama Canal Approaches
See Gulf of Panama.

Parida, Isla
See Isla Parida.

Patinito, Isla
See Isla Patinito.

Perique Rock
8 45N, 79 35W, L Fl W 15s, 75 ft.,
9 mi., white tower.
Also see Gulf of Panama.

PETROTERMINAL DE PANAMA

Berth 1
8 12.0N, 82 53.0W, Q R.

Berth 2
8 12.0N, 82 53.0W, Q R.

Berth 3
8 12.0N, 82 53.0W, Q W.

Pina, Punta
See Punta Pina.

Puerto Aquadulce, No. 13
8 12.3N, 80 28.2W, Fl W, 3 ft.,
2 mi., black beacon.

Puerto Aquadulce, No. 14
8 12.3N, 80 28.2W, Fl R, 3 ft.,
2 mi., starboard, red.

Puerto Armuelles (head of pier)
8 16N, 82 52W, Oc R 2s, F R
(vert.), 68 ft., 9 mi., aero
radiobeacon 27 mi. ENE, Oc R on
radio towers 0.45 mi. and 0.5 mi.
NW, F R on radio towers 0.46 mi.
and 0.83 mi. NNW.

Puerto Dulce
8 17.3N, 82 52.2W, Fl R, red and
white framework tower.

Punta Brujas
8 35.2N, 78 32.7W, Fl W 4s, 115 ft.,
6 mi., concrete pedestal, visible
345°–215°.
Also see Gulf of Panama.

Punta Cocalito
7 17.7N, 77 58.3W, Fl W 10s,
121 ft., 18 mi., white metal framework tower.

Punta Garachine
8 05N, 78 25W, Fl W 4s, 56 ft.,
5 mi., white skeleton steel tower.
Also see Gulf of Panama.

Punta Mala
7 28.2N, 80 00.0W, L Fl W 20s,
138 ft., 15 mi., white framework
tower, reported Fl W 10s (1995),
racon: M (--).
Also see Gulf of Panama.

Punta Mariato
7 12.6N, 80 53.2W, L Fl W 25s,
178 ft., 15 mi., white framework
tower, reported Fl W 30s (1993).

Punta Pina
7 34N, 78 12W, Fl W 5s, 223 ft.,
5 mi., white metal skeleton tower.
Also see Gulf of Panama.

R

Rey, Isla del
See San Miguel.

S

San Jose, Isla
See Isla San Jose.

San Miguel (on Isla del Rey)
8 27.4N, 78 56.5W, Fl W 5s, 85 ft.,
6 mi., concrete pedestal, visible
086°–180°.
Also see Gulf of Panama.

Secas, Islas
See Islas Secas.

T

Taboguilla, Isla
See Isla Taboguilla.

Terapa Islet
8 46N, 79 32W, Fl W 5s, 46 ft.,
9 mi., white skeleton steel tower.
Also see Gulf of Panama.

Tocumen Aviation Light
9 05N, 79 23W, Al Fl W G 10s,
200 ft., tower, occasional.
Also see Gulf of Panama.

U

Uva, Isla
See Islas Contreras.

V

Vacamonte Range Front Light
8 52.0N, 79 40.2W, F W, 58 ft.,
13 mi., white triangle on tower.

Vacamonte Range Rear Light
150 meters, 321° from front light,
F W, 71 ft., 13 mi., white triangle
on tower.
Also see Gulf of Panama.

Valladolid Rock
8 43N, 79 36W, Fl (2) W 30s, 75 ft.,
11 mi., white tower.
Also see Gulf of Panama.

Villa, Isla
See Isla Villa.

Characteristics of Lights

1. **F—Fixed:** A light showing continuously and steadily.

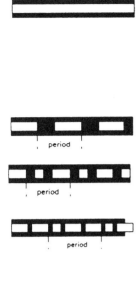

2. **Occulting:** A light in which the total duration of light in a period is longer than the total duration of darkness, and the intervals of darkness (eclipses) are usually of equal duration.

    2.1 Oc—Single-occulting: An occulting light in which an eclipse is regularly repeated.

    2.2 Oc (2)—Group-occulting: An occulting light in which a specific number of eclipses is regularly repeated as a group.

    2.3 Oc (2+1)—Composite group-occulting: A light similar to a group-occulting light, except that successive groups in a period have different numbers of eclipses.

3. **Iso—Isophase:** A light in which all durations of light and darkness are equal. (Formerly called *equal interval light.*)

4. **Flashing:** A light in which the total duration of light in a period is shorter than the total duration of darkness, and the appearances of light (flashes) are usually of equal duration.

    4.1 Fl—Single-flashing: A light in which a flash is regularly repeated up to 30 times per minute.

    4.2 Fl (2)—Group-flashing: A light in which a specific number of flashes is regularly repeated as a group.

    4.3 Fl (2+1)—Composite group-flashing: A light similar to a group flashing light except that the groups have varying numbers of flashes.

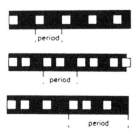

5. **Quick:** A light that produces 60 flashes per minute. (Formerly called *quick flashing light*.)

> 5.1 Q—Continuous quick: A quick light in which a flash is regularly repeated.

> 5.2 IQ—Interrupted quick: A quick light in which the sequence of flashes is interrupted by regularly repeated eclipses of constant and long duration.

6. **Mo (A)—Morse code:** A light in which appearances of light of two clearly different durations (dots and dashes) are grouped to represent a character or characters in the Morse code.

7. **FFl—Fixed and flashing:** A light in which a fixed light is combined with a flashing light of higher luminous intensity.

8. **Al RW—Alternating:** A light showing different colors alternately.

Dayboard Abbreviations

CG Diamond-shaped green dayboard bearing small green diamond-shaped reflectors at each corner.

CR Diamond-shaped red dayboard bearing small red diamond-shaped reflectors at each corner.

JG Dayboard bearing horizontal bands of green and red, green band topmost, with a green reflective border.

JG-I Square dayboard bearing horizontal bands of green and red, green band topmost, with a green reflective border and a yellow reflective horizontal strip.

JG-SY Square dayboard bearing horizontal bands of green and red, green band topmost, with a green reflective border and a yellow reflective square.

JG-TY Square dayboard bearing horizontal bands of green and red, green band topmost, with a green reflective border and a yellow reflective triangle.

JR Dayboard bearing horizontal bands of red and green, red band topmost, with a red reflective border.

JR-I Dayboard bearing horizontal bands of red and green, red band topmost, with a red reflective border and a yellow horizontal strip.

JR-SY Dayboard bearing horizontal bands of red and green, red band topmost, with a red reflective border and a yellow reflective square.

JR-TY Dayboard bearing horizontal bands of red and green, red band topmost, with a red reflective border and a yellow reflective triangle.

KBG Rectangular black dayboard bearing a central green stripe.

KBG-I	Rectangular black dayboard bearing a central green stripe and a yellow reflective horizontal strip.
KBR	Rectangular black dayboard bearing a central red stripe.
KBR-I	Rectangular black dayboard bearing a central red stripe and a yellow reflective horizontal strip.
KBW	Rectangular black dayboard bearing a central white stripe.
KBW-I	Rectangular black dayboard bearing a central white stripe and a yellow reflective horizontal strip.
KGB	Rectangular green dayboard bearing a central black stripe.
KGB-I	Rectangular green dayboard bearing a central black stripe and a yellow reflective horizontal strip.
KGR	Rectangular green dayboard bearing a central red stripe.
KGR-I	Rectangular green dayboard bearing a central red stripe and a yellow reflective horizontal strip.
KGW	Rectangular green dayboard bearing a central white stripe.
KGW-I	Rectangular green dayboard bearing a central white stripe and a yellow reflective horizontal strip.
KRB	Rectangular red dayboard bearing a central black stripe.
KRB-I	Rectangular red dayboard bearing a central black stripe and a yellow reflective horizontal strip.
KRG	Rectangular red dayboard bearing a central green stripe.

KRG-I	Rectangular red dayboard bearing a central green stripe and a yellow reflective horizontal strip.
KRW	Rectangular red dayboard bearing a central white stripe.
KRW-I	Rectangular red dayboard bearing a central white stripe and a yellow reflective horizontal strip.
KWB	Rectangular white dayboard bearing a central black stripe.
KWB-I	Rectangular white dayboard bearing a central black stripe and a yellow reflective horizontal strip.
KWG	Rectangular white dayboard bearing a central green stripe.
KWG-I	Rectangular white dayboard bearing a central green stripe and a yellow reflective horizontal strip.
KWR	Rectangular white dayboard bearing a central red stripe.
KWR-I	Rectangular white dayboard bearing a central red stripe and a yellow reflective horizontal strip.
MR	Octagonal dayboard bearing stripes of white and red, with a white reflective border.
MR-I	Octagonal dayboard bearing stripes of white and red, with a white reflective border and a yellow horizontal strip.
NB	Diamond-shaped dayboard divided into four diamond-shaped colored sectors with the sectors at the sides white and the sectors at the top and bottom black, with a white reflective border.

NG	Diamond-shaped dayboard divided into four diamond-shaped colored sectors with the sectors at the sides white and the sectors at the top and bottom green, with a white reflective border.
NR	Diamond-shaped dayboard divided into four diamond-shaped colored sectors with the sectors at the sides white and the sectors at the top and bottom red, with a white reflective border.
NW	Diamond-shaped white dayboard with an orange reflective border and black letters describing the information or regulatory nature of the mark.
ND	Rectangular white mileage marker with an orange reflective border and black letters indicating the location.
NY	Diamond-shaped yellow dayboard with a yellow reflective border.
SG	Square green dayboard with a green reflective border.
SG-I	Square green dayboard with a green reflective border and a yellow reflective horizontal strip.
SG-SY	Square green dayboard with a green reflective border and a yellow reflective square.
SG-TY	Square green dayboard with a green reflective border and a yellow reflective triangle.
TR	Triangular red dayboard with a red reflective border.
TR-I	Triangular red dayboard with a red reflective border and a yellow reflective horizontal strip.
TR-SY	Triangular red dayboard with a red reflective border and a yellow reflective square.
TR-TY	Triangular red dayboard with a red reflective border and a yellow reflective triangle.

Geographic Range Table

The following table gives the approximate geographic range of visibility for an object which may be seen by an observer at sea level.

Determine the range for the height of eye of the observer; then add the range for the height of the object being observed.

Example:

Height of object = 65 feet	range = 9.4 NM
Height of observer = 35 feet	range = 6.9 NM
Computed geographic visibility	16.3 NM

Height in Feet	Distance in Nautical Miles (NM)	Height in Feet	Distance in Nautical Miles (NM)
1	1.2	50	8.3
2	1.7	55	8.7
3	2.0	60	9.1
4	2.3	65	9.4
5	2.6	70	9.8
6	2.9	75	10.1
7	3.1	80	10.5
8	3.3	85	10.8
9	3.5	90	11.1
10	3.7	95	11.4
15	4.5	100	11.7
20	5.2	110	12.3
25	5.9	120	12.8
30	6.4	130	13.3
35	6.9	140	13.8
40	7.4	150	14.3
45	7.8	200	16.5

Luminous Range Diagram

The nominal range given in this book is the maximum distance a given light can be seen when the meteorological visibility is 10 nautical miles. If the existing visibility is less than 10 miles, the range at which the light can be seen will be reduced below its nominal range. And if the visibility is greater than

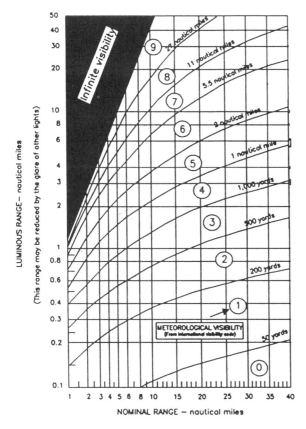

METEOROLOGICAL VISIBILITY		
(From International Visibility code)		
Code	Metric	Nautical (approximate)
0	Less than 50 meters	Less than 50 yards
1	50–200 meters	50–200 yards
2	200–500 meters	200–500 yards
3	500–1,000 meters	500–1,000 yards
4	1–2 kilometers	1,000–2,000 yards
5	2–4 kilometers	1–2 nautical miles
6	4–10 kilometers	2–5.5 nautical miles
7	10–20 kilometers	5.5–11 nautical miles
8	20–50 kilometers	11–27 nautical miles
9	Greater than 50 km	Greater than 27 nm

10 miles, the light can be seen at greater distances. The distance at which a light may be expected to be seen in the prevailing visibility is called its *luminous range.*

This diagram enables the mariner to determine the approximate luminous range of a light when the nominal range and the prevailing meteorological visibility are known. The diagram is entered from the bottom border using the nominal range listed in this book. Move horizontally to the left border to ascertain the luminous range at the intersection of the nominal range with the appropriate visibility curve (or, more often, a point between two curves).

Caution: Users of this diagram must remember that
1. the ranges obtained are approximate;
2. the transparency of the atmosphere may vary between the observer and the light;
3. glare from background lighting will considerably reduce the range at which lights are sighted;
4. the rolling motion of the mariner and/or of a lighted aid to navigation may reduce the distance at which lights can be detected and identified.

adrift: Afloat and unattached in any way to the shore or seabed.

aid to navigation: Any device external to a vessel or aircraft specifically intended to assist navigators in determining their position or safe course, or to warn them of dangers or obstructions to navigation.

alternating light: A rhythmic light showing light of alternating colors.

arc of visibility: The portion of the horizon over which a lighted aid to navigation is visible from seaward.

articulated beacon: A beaconlike buoyant structure, tethered directly to the seabed and having no watch circle. Called articulated light or articulated daybeacon, as appropriate.

assigned position: The latitude and longitude for an aid to navigation.

beacon: A lighted or unlighted fixed aid to navigation attached directly to the earth's surface. (Both lights and daybeacons are beacons.)

bearing: The horizontal direction of a line of sight between two objects on the surface of the earth.

bell: A sound signal producing bell tones by means of a hammer actuated by electricity or, on buoys, by sea motion.

bifurcation: The point where a channel divides, or conversely, where two tributaries meet.

characteristic: The audible, visual, or electronic signal displayed by an aid to navigation to assist in its identification. Characteristic refers to lights, sound signals, racons, radiobeacons, and daybeacons.

commissioned: The active state of a previously discontinued aid to navigation that is back in operation.

composite group-flashing light: A group-flashing light in which the flashes are combined in successive groups of different numbers of flashes. *Also see* Appendix A.

composite group-occulting light: A light similar to a group-occulting light except that the successive groups in a period have different numbers of eclipses. Also see Appendix A.

conventional direction of buoyage: The general direction taken by the mariner when approaching a harbor, river, estuary, or other waterway from seaward, or proceeding upstream or in the direction of the main stream of the flood tide or in the direction indicated in appropriate nautical documents (normally, following a clockwise direction around landmasses).

daybeacon: An unlighted fixed structure that is equipped with a dayboard for daytime identification.

dayboard: The daytime identifier of an aid to navigation presenting one of several standard shapes (square, triangle, rectangle, diamond, or octagon) and one or more standard colors (red, green, white, orange, yellow, or black). *Also see* Appendix B.

daymark: The daytime identifier of an aid to navigation. *Also see* Appendix B.

diaphone: A sound signal that produces sound by means of a slotted piston moved back and forth by compressed air. A two-tone diaphone produces two sequential tones with the second tone of lower pitch.

directional light: A light illuminating a sector or very narrow angle and intended to mark a direction to be followed.

discontinued: The withdrawn state of a previously authorized aid to navigation that has been removed from operation (permanently or temporarily).

discrepancy: Failure of an aid to navigation to maintain its position or function as prescribed in the government light lists.

discrepancy buoy: An easily transportable buoy used to temporarily replace an aid to navigation not watching properly.

dolphin: A minor aid-to-navigation structure consisting of a number of piles driven into the seabed or riverbed in a circular pattern and drawn together with wire rope.

eclipse: An interval of darkness between appearances of a light. *Also see* Appendix A.

emergency light: A light of reduced intensity displayed by certain aids to navigation when the main light is extinguished. Note: In general, emergency lights are not listed in this book.

establish: To place an authorized aid to navigation in operation for the first time.

extinguished: The state of a lighted aid to navigation that fails to show a light characteristic.

fixed light: A light showing continuously and steadily, as opposed to a rhythmic light. (Do not confuse with fixed as used to differentiate from floating.) *Also see* Appendix A.

flash: A relatively brief appearance of a light, in comparison with the longest interval of darkness in the same character. *Also see* Appendix A.

flash tube: An electronically controlled high-intensity discharge lamp with a very brief flash duration.

flashing light: A light in which the total duration of light in each period is clearly shorter than the total duration of darkness and in which the flashes of light are all of equal duration. (Commonly used for a single-flashing light that exhibits only single flashes repeated at regular intervals. *Also see* Appendix A.

floating aid to navigation: A buoy secured in its assigned position by a mooring.

fog detector: An electronic device used to automatically determine conditions of visibility that warrant the activation of a sound signal or additional light signals.

fog signal: *See* **sound signal.**

geographic range: The greatest distance the curvature of the earth permits an object of a given height to be seen from a particular height of eye without regard to the object's luminous intensity or to visibility conditions. *Also see* Appendix C.

Global Positioning System (GPS): A satellite-based radionavigation system with continuous worldwide coverage, providing navigation, position, and timing information to air, marine, and land users.

gong: A wave-actuated sound signal on buoys that uses a group of saucer-shaped bells to produce different tones.

group-flashing light: A light in which a specific number of flashes is regularly repeated as a group. *Also see* Appendix A.

group-occulting light: An occulting light in which a specific number of eclipses is regularly repeated as a group. *Also see* Appendix A.

horn: A sound signal that uses electricity or compressed air to vibrate a disc diaphragm.

inoperative: The state of a sound signal or electronic aid to navigation that is out of service due to a malfunction.

interrupted quick light: A quick flashing light in which the rapid alternations are interrupted at regular intervals by eclipses of long duration. *Also see* Appendix A.

isolated danger mark: A mark erected on, or moored above or very near, an isolated danger surrounded by navigable water.

isophase light: A rhythmic light in which all durations of light and darkness are equal. (Formerly called equal interval light.) *Also see* Appendix A.

junction: The point where a channel divides or where a side channel departs from the main stream.

large navigational buoy (LNB): A 40-foot-diameter, automated disc-shaped buoy used to replace lightships. Most LNBs are used in conjunction with major traffic separation schemes. All LNBs are equipped with emergency lights.

lateral system: A system of aids to navigation in which characteristics of buoys and beacons indicate the sides of the channel or route relative to a conventional direction of buoyage (usually upstream).

light: The signal emitted by a lighted aid to navigation. The illuminating apparatus used to emit the light signal. A lighted aid to navigation on a fixed structure.

light sector: The arc over which a light is visible, described in degrees true, as observed from seaward toward the light. May be used to define the distinctive color difference of two adjoining sectors, or an obscured sector.

lighted ice buoy (LIB): A lighted buoy without a sound signal, and designed to withstand the forces of shifting and flowing ice. Used to replace a conventional buoy when that aid to navigation is endangered by ice.

lighthouse: A lighted beacon of major importance.

Local Notice to Mariners: A written document issued by each U.S. Coast Guard district to disseminate important information affecting aids to navigation, dredging, marine construction, special marine activities, and bridge construction on the waterways within that district.

loran: An acronym for LOng RAnge Navigation. An electronic aid to navigation consisting of shore-based radio transmitters. The loran system enables users equipped with a loran receiver to determine their position quickly and accurately, day or night, in practically any weather.

luminous range: The greatest distance a light can be expected to be seen given its nominal range and the prevailing meteorological visibility. *Also see* Appendix D.

mark: A visual aid to navigation. The term includes floating marks (buoys) and fixed marks (beacons). (Often called navigation mark.)

meteorological visibility: The greatest distance at which a black object of suitable dimension could be seen and recognized against the horizon sky by day, or, in the case of night observations, could be seen and recognized if the general illumination were raised to the normal daylight level. *Also see* Appendix D.

mileage number: A number assigned to aids to navigation that gives the distance in sailing miles along the river from a reference point to the aid. The number is used principally in the Mississippi River system.

nominal range: The maximum distance a light can be seen in clear weather (meteorological visibility of 10 nautical miles). Listed for all lighted aids to navigation except range lights, directional lights, and private aids to navigation. *Also see* Appendix C.

occulting light: A light in which the total duration of light in each period is clearly longer than the total duration of darkness, and in which the intervals of darkness (eclipses) are all of equal duration. (The term is commonly used for single-occulting light, a light that exhibits only single occultations repeated at regular intervals.)

Ocean Data Acquisition System (ODAS): A network of certain very large buoys in deep water and the collection therefrom of oceanographic and meteorological information. All ODAS buoys are yellow and display a yellow light.

off station: The whereabouts of a floating aid to navigation that is not on its assigned position.

offshore tower: A monitored light station built on an exposed marine site to replace a lightship.

passing light: A low-intensity light that may be mounted on the structure of another light to enable the mariner to keep the aid to navigation in sight when passing out of its beam during transit.

period: The interval of time between the commencement of two identical successive cycles of the characteristic of a light or sound signal.

pile: A long, heavy timber driven into the seabed or riverbed to serve as a support for an aid to navigation.

port hand mark: A buoy or beacon that is left to the port hand when the mariner is proceeding in the conventional direction of buoyage.

preferred channel mark: A lateral mark indicating a channel junction or bifurcation, or a wreck or other obstruction that may be passed on either side after the mariner has consulted a chart.

primary aid to navigation: An aid to navigation established for the purpose of making landfalls and coastwise passages from headland to headland.

quick light: A light exhibiting very rapid regular alternations of light and darkness, normally 60 flashes per minute. (Formerly called quick flashing light.)

racon: A radar beacon that produces a coded response, or radar paint, when triggered by a radar signal.

radar: An electronic system designed to transmit radio signals and receive reflected images of those signals from a targeted objected in order to determine the bearing and distance to that target.

radar reflector: A special fixture fitted to or incorporated into the design of certain aids to navigation to enhance their ability to reflect radar energy.

radiobeacon: Electronic apparatus that transmits a radio signal for use in providing the mariner a line of position. This book does not list radiobeacons (except in the Bahamas) unless they correspond to light structures.

range: A line formed by connecting two charted points.

range lights: Two lights associated to form a range that often, but not necessarily, indicates a channel centerline. The front range light is the lower of the two, and nearer to the mariner using the range.

rebuilt: The restored state of a fixed aid to navigation, previously destroyed.

regulatory mark: A white and orange aid to navigation with no lateral significance. Used to convey a special meaning to the mariner, such as danger, restricted operations, or an exclusion area.

relighted: The state of an extinguished aid to navigation that has been returned to its advertised light characteristics.

replaced: The state of an aid to navigation previously off station, adrift, or missing, that has been restored by another aid to navigation of the same type and characteristics.

replaced temporarily: The state of an aid to navigation previously off station, adrift, or missing, that has been restored by another aid to navigation of a different type and/or different characteristics.

reset: The state of a floating aid to navigation previously off station, adrift, or missing, that has been returned to its assigned position (station).

rhythmic light: A light showing intermittently and regularly.

sector: *See* **light sector.**

setting a buoy: The act of placing a buoy on an assigned position in the water.

siren: A sound signal that uses electricity or compressed air to actuate either a disc- or cup-shaped rotor.

skeleton tower: A tower, usually of steel, constructed of heavy corner members and various horizontal and diagonal bracing members.

sound signal: A device that transmits sound, intended to provide information to mariners during periods of restricted visibility and foul weather.

starboard hand mark: A buoy or beacon that is left to the starboard hand when the mariner is proceeding in the conventional direction of buoyage.

station buoy: An unlighted buoy set near a large navigation buoy or another important buoy as a reference point should the primary aid to navigation be moved from its assigned position.

topmark: One or more relatively small objects of characteristic shape and color placed on an aid to identify its purpose.

traffic separation scheme: The design that uses buoys to establish shipping corridors by separating incoming from outgoing vessels. Improperly called sea lanes.

watching properly: The functioning of an aid to navigation on its assigned position that exhibits the advertised characteristics in all respects.

whistle: A wave-actuated sound signal on buoys that produces sound by emitting compressed air through a circumferential slot into a cylindrical bell chamber.

winter light: A light that is maintained during those winter months when the regular light is extinguished. It is of lower candlepower than the regular light but usually of the same characteristic.

winter marker: An unlighted buoy without sound signal, used to replace a conventional buoy when that aid to navigation is endangered by ice. Note: This book does not list winter markers.

withdrawn: The discontinued state of a floating aid to navigation during severe ice conditions or for the winter season.